The Shadow World

The Shadow World
Inside the Global Arms Trade

ANDREW FEINSTEIN

Research: Paul Holden and Barnaby Pace

HAMISH HAMILTON
an imprint of
PENGUIN BOOKS

HAMISH HAMILTON

Published by the Penguin Group
Penguin Books Ltd, 80 Strand, London WC2R ORL, England
Penguin Group (USA) Inc., 375 Hudson Street, New York, New York 10014, USA
Penguin Group (Canada), 90 Eglinton Avenue East, Suite 700, Toronto, Ontario, Canada M4P 2Y3
(a division of Pearson Penguin Canada Inc.)
Penguin Ireland, 25 St Stephen's Green, Dublin 2, Ireland (a division of Penguin Books Ltd)
Penguin Group (Australia), 250 Camberwell Road, Camberwell, Victoria 3124, Australia
(a division of Pearson Australia Group Pty Ltd)
Penguin Books India Pvt Ltd, 11 Community Centre, Panchsheel Park, New Delhi – 110 017, India
Penguin Group (NZ), 67 Apollo Drive, Rosedale, Auckland 0632, New Zealand
(a division of Pearson New Zealand Ltd)
Penguin Books (South Africa) (Pty) Ltd, 24 Sturdee Avenue, Rosebank, Johannesburg 2196, South Africa

Penguin Books Ltd, Registered Offices: 80 Strand, London WC2R ORL, England

www.penguin.com

First published 2011
1

Copyright © Andrew Feinstein, 2011

The moral right of the author has been asserted

Set in Bembo 11.25/14.5pt
Typeset by Jouve (UK), Milton Keynes
Printed in Great Britain by Clays Ltd, St Ives plc

A CIP catalogue record for this book is available from the British Library

HARDBACK ISBN: 978-0-241-14441-1
TRADE PAPERBACK ISBN: 978-0-241-14524-1

www.greenpenguin.co.uk

To the memory of my mother
Erika Feinstein
1929–2009

To the memory of
Erison Durdaj
27 November 2000–4 April 2008
(and all who died at Gerdec)

And in honour of the 'closet patriots', the whistle-blowers,
who dare speak truth to power

'Show me who makes a profit from war, and I'll show you
how to stop the war'

Henry Ford

'Once a gun runner, always a gun runner.'

Efraim Diveroli

Contents

List of Figures   ix

Illustration Credits   x

Dramatis Personae   xi

Prologue   xvii

Introduction   xxii

SECTION I: THE SECOND-OLDEST PROFESSION

1. *Sins of Commission*   3

2. *The Nazi Connection*   19

SECTION II: NICE WORK IF YOU CAN GET IT

3. *The Saudi Connection*   35

4. *In Defence of Humanity*   56

5. *The Ultimate Deal or the Ultimate Crime?*   74

6. *Diamonds and Arms*   98

7. *Buckling to Bandar*   127

8. *And Justice for None?*   154

SECTION III: BUSINESS AS USUAL

9. *Things Fall Apart – with Help from BAE*   175

10. *After the Wall: Capitalism BAE-Style*   197

11. *The Ultimate Cop-Out*   225

SECTION IV: THE ARMS SUPERPOWER

12. *Legal Bribery*   237

13. *In the Name of Uncle Sam*   262

14. *Taking the Mickey, the Toilet Seat and the Hammer . . .*
   in a Galaxy Far, Far Away   273

15. *Illegal Bribery*   305

16. *Beyond Utopia, Hope?*   330

17. *America's Shop Window*   373

18. *Making a Killing: Iraq and Afghanistan*   395

SECTION V: THE KILLING FIELDS

19. *Cry, the Beloved Continent*   435

SECTION VI: END GAME

20. *Bringing Peace to the World*   501

21. *Future Imperfect*   523

Acknowledgements   532

Notes and References   537

Index   643

Figures

1. Payment chain for the Al Yamamah deal   37

2. False end-user certificate used by Leonid Minin to
   transport weapons through the Ivory Coast to Liberia   113

3. BAE's web of payments in Tanzania   195

4. BAE's Eastern European network   207

5. Randy Cunningham's bribe menu   327

6. Comparative job creation figures for defence and other
   sectors in the US   366

7. US Department of Defense budget and spending
   on the wars in Iraq and Afghanistan   412

8. Share price movement in BAE, Lockheed Martin
   and Northrop Grumman   415

Illustration Credits

Dramatis Personae

Basil Zaharoff
Godfather of BAE

Marcel Dassault
French defence industry pioneer

Gerhard Mertins
Founder of Merex

Prince Bandar
Al Yamamah beneficiary

Richard Evans
Former BAE chairman

Wafic Said
Al Yamamah intermediary

Prince Turki Bin Nasser
Al Yamamah beneficiary

Joseph der Hovsepian
Merex arms dealer

Leonid Minin
Arms dealer

Charles Taylor
Dictator and arms agent

Viktor Bout
'The Merchant of Death'

Monzer Al-Kassar
Arms dealer

Robert Wardle
Former SFO Director

Helen Garlick
Former SFO investigator

Richard Alderman
Current SFO Director

Thabo Mbeki and Jacob Zuma
South African Presidents

The Brothers Shaik
SA arms deal protagonists

John Bredenkamp
Arms dealer

Andrew Chenge
*Former Tanzanian
Attorney General*

Count Alfons
Mensdorff-Pouilly
Arms agent

John Murtha
'The King of Pork'

Charlie Wilson
'The King of Blowback'

Chuck Spinney
Pentagon insider and critic

Yoshio Kodama
aka 'The Monster'

Adnan Khashoggi
Arms agent

Darleen Druyun
Convicted official

Randy Cunningham
Corrupt former Congressman

Efraim Diveroli
Gun runner

Erison Durdaj
Arms trade victim

Amir Ardebili
Iranian arms procurer

Manucher Ghorbanifar
Iranian arms dealer

Dale Stoffel
US arms adventurer

J.-C. Mitterrand
Angolagate beneficiary

Arcadi Gaydamak
Arms dealer

Pierre Falcone
Arms dealer

Prologue

The Prince alighted from his gleaming silver-blue jet, his mind firmly on the task at hand: to persuade his close friend to go to war.

Prince Bandar bin Sultan bin Abdul Aziz Al-Saud, Saudi Arabia's ambassador to Washington, was in Crawford, Texas, in August 2002 to visit the President of the United States, his close friend George W. Bush. At the President's ranch the two men, comfortable in one another's company, chatted for an hour. The President was in determined mood. Bandar's exhortation that he should not back off, that he should complete what his father had failed to do, that he should destroy the regime of Saddam Hussein once and for all, gratified the President. Satisfied by their mutual reinforcement, the dapper enigmatic Prince and the cowboy President took lunch with their wives and seven of Bandar's eight children.

A few weeks later, President Bush met the British Prime Minister, Tony Blair, at Camp David. The two leaders declared they had sufficient evidence that Iraq was developing weapons of mass destruction to justify their acting against Saddam, with or without the support of the United Nations.

Prince Bandar's role in Washington and London was unique: diplomat, peacemaker, bagman for covert CIA operations and arms dealer *extraordinaire*. He constructed a special relationship between Washington, Riyadh and London, and made himself very, very wealthy in the process.

The £75m Airbus, painted in the colours of the Prince's beloved Dallas Cowboys, was a gift from the British arms company BAE Systems. It was a token of gratitude for the Prince's role, as son of the country's Defence Minister, in the biggest arms deal the world has seen. The Al Yamamah – 'the dove' – deal signed between the United Kingdom and Saudi Arabia in 1985 was worth over £40bn. It was also arguably the most corrupt transaction in trading history. Over £1bn was paid into accounts controlled by Bandar. The Airbus – maintained and operated by BAE at least until 2007 – was a little extra, presented to Bandar on his birthday in 1988.

A significant portion of the more than £1bn was paid into personal and Saudi embassy accounts at the venerable Riggs Bank opposite the White House on Pennsylvania Avenue, Washington DC. The bank of choice for Presidents, ambassadors and embassies had close ties to the CIA, with several bank officers holding full agency security clearance. Jonathan Bush, uncle of the President, was a senior executive of the bank at the time. But Riggs and the White House were stunned by the revelation that from 1999 money had inadvertently flowed from the account of Prince Bandar's wife to two of the fifteen Saudis among the 9/11 hijackers.

On the night of 4 August 2000, police barged into Room 341 of a tawdry hotel in Cinisello Balsamo, a nondescript working-class town in northern Italy, just outside Milan. There they found a pale, fleshy 53-year-old man lying amidst a jumble of bedclothes and underwear, a pornographic film flickering on the wall in the background. He was surrounded by four prostitutes: Russian, Albanian, Kenyan and Italian. Cocaine littered the floor, together with half a million dollars' worth of diamonds.

Leonid Minin, a Ukrainian-born Israeli and part owner of the Europa hotel, used his two-room suite as a bedroom, office and den of debauchery. A cursory search unearthed hundreds of pages of documents in English, Russian, German, Dutch and French. They revealed Minin's role in an extraordinary network of defence companies, arms dealers, banks, front companies, drug runners, bent politicians, intelligence agents, government officials, ex-Nazis and militant Islamists.

Among the documents was correspondence detailing the sale of millions of dollars of weapons to the Liberian government in exchange for diamond and timber concessions. Investigators used the flight logs and end-user certificates they found to reconstruct numerous deliveries of weapons and matériel into West Africa and other conflict zones. A number of these deliveries were made using Leonid Minin's personal British Aircraft Corporation 1-11 jet, which still bore the insignia of the Seattle Sonics basketball team, which had previously owned the plane.

Manufactured by a company in the BAE group, Minin's jet was more basic than Prince Bandar's opulent gift, but its journeys were no less significant in their impact.

The horror descended on Freetown at 3 a.m. on 6 January 1999.

Rebel elements of the army joined forces with troops of the Revolutionary United Front (RUF) to invade the capital of Sierra Leone in an orgy of killing and destruction. They called it 'Operation No Living Thing'.

This most horrific civil war on a continent of civil wars had begun in March 1991 as a spill-over from Liberia, which itself had been wracked by internecine violence since an invasion on Christmas Eve 1989 by a small group of armed men led by a former government junior minister, Charles Ghankay Taylor, with purported links to the CIA. He extended his war into neighbouring Sierra Leone to exploit that country's massive diamond wealth through the RUF and its psychopath leader, Foday Sankoh, a dismissed army corporal and sometime photographer.

Throughout its eleven-year campaign the RUF killed and mutilated the very civilians it claimed to champion in an orgy of bewildering cruelty, while looting the country's rich diamond reserves and trading them profitably with outsiders through Charles Taylor and his network that included Leonid Minin.

After Sankoh was captured in late 1998, his deputy commander, Sam Bockarie (aka 'Mosquito'), declared that to free his imprisoned leader he was going to kill everyone in the country 'to the last chicken'. In the first few days of 1999, the rebels infiltrated Freetown by joining civilians flocking into the city from the violence-ravaged surrounding towns. Their weapons were wrapped in dirty bundles. Another small group had fought its way to Mount Aureol overlooking the east end of Freetown. A rugged bush road winds from the top of the hill down to Savage Square, the heart of the east end. All they needed was extra weaponry.

On 22 December 1998, Leonid Minin had personally ferried guns and other equipment in his BAC 1-11 from Niamey in Niger to Monrovia, Liberia, where they were offloaded onto vehicles of President Charles Taylor's armed forces and ferried to the outskirts of Freetown. With the safe arrival of the illegal arms, the order to attack was given.

In the early hours of 6 January, under cover of near-total darkness, the rebels made for Pademba Road Prison. They blasted open the gates and freed and armed the detainees. Foday Sankoh, however, had been removed from the prison two weeks before.

What followed was a two-day apocalyptic horror. Thousands of armed teenage soldiers, almost all of them wearing thick bandages on the side of the head where incisions had been made to pack crack cocaine under their skin, swarmed the city. Insane and delirious, they attacked the homes of civilians, killing those who refused to give them money, who were insufficiently welcoming, who looked well fed, or whose face they simply disliked. Thousands of innocent people were gunned down in their houses, rounded up and massacred on the streets, thrown from the upper floors of buildings, used as human shields and burned alive in cars and houses. They had their limbs hacked off with machetes, eyes gouged out with knives, hands and jaws smashed with hammers and bodies burned with boiling water. Women and girls were systematically sexually abused and children and young people abducted by the hundreds.

A group of rebels raided a World Food Programme warehouse looking for sustenance, but instead discovered hundreds of brand-new machetes intended for the cultivation of food. The machetes were used to crudely and methodically cut off the hands of hundreds of people – adults, children, even tiny babies. Because they had heard that an aid agency was sewing up severed hands, they took the hands with them.

At night during the blackout rebels chanting, 'We want peace! We have come for peace!' locked up whole families in their houses and set them ablaze so there would be light in the area. Fire was everywhere. Torches – raffia mats rolled and soaked in kerosene – ignited home after home; flames ravished the hills; family after family was burned alive.

Next to a roadblock a female soldier checked the virginity of her captives, prodding with her fingers after the girls were stripped naked and pinned to the ground. Then she made her suggestions to the senior officers of her unit. And in the city, on the grounds of the State House where the rebels ran a command post, hundreds of young women were rounded up, to be raped in the offices or on the walkways. Everywhere, hoping to be undesired, the youthful tried to look haggard, and with mixtures of water, soil and ash the light-skinned tried to make themselves dark.

Distinct units existed for committing particular acts: the Burn House Unit, Cut Hands Commando and Blood Shed Squad. Each had a trademark approach to their task: the Kill Man No Blood Unit who beat people to death without shedding blood or the Born Naked Squad who stripped their victims before killing them.

In less than two weeks almost 100,000 people were driven from their homes. Tens of thousands were left maimed and bloodied. Six thousand civilians were murdered.[1]

The arms trade did not cause this barbarism, but it facilitated and fuelled it.

At the time, Sierra Leone was the world's least developed country. Most of its people lived on less than seventy cents a day and life expectancy was thirty-seven. Charles Taylor, Leonid Minin and their associates, who included the Al Qaeda network, made tens of millions of dollars out of the gun-running and diamond-trading operations associated with the brutal civil war.

Introduction

In our twenty-first-century world the lethal combination of techno-logical advances, terrorism, global crime, state-sponsored violence and socio-economic inequality has raised instability and insecurity to alarming levels. At the same time, the engine that has driven this escalation, the global arms trade, grows ever more sophisticated, complex and toxic in its effects.

It might therefore be thought essential that the world's democratic nations should address this trade collectively and urgently. If it must exist, then surely it should be coherently regulated, legitimately financed, effectively policed and transparent in its workings, and meet people's need for safety and security?

Instead the trade in weapons is a parallel world of money, corruption, deceit and death. It operates according to its own rules, largely unscrutinized, bringing enormous benefits to the chosen few, and suffering and immiseration to millions. The trade corrodes our democracies, weakens already fragile states and often undermines the very national security it purports to strengthen.*

Global military expenditure is estimated to have totalled $1.6tn in 2010, $235 for every person on the planet. This is an increase of 53 per cent since 2000 and accounts for 2.6 per cent of global gross domestic product.[1] Today, the United States spends almost a trillion dollars a year on national security with a defence budget of over $703bn.[2] The trade in conventional arms, both big and small, is worth about $60bn a year.[3] †

* This book will deal primarily with the trade in conventional weapons, large and small, which, unlike weapons of mass destruction, are legitimate tools of government. This includes military vehicles, aircraft, ships, submarines, helicopters, missiles and bombs as well as small arms and ammunition. I will only refer to nuclear weapons as they intersect with the functioning of the arms industry and the trade in the goods it produces, which I refer to as 'the arms trade'.
† This figure varies considerably from year to year. The trade in small arms is worth about $4bn a year and has an impact far beyond this monetary value because small

The US, Russia, the UK, France, Germany, Sweden, Holland, Italy, Israel and China are regularly identified as the largest producers and traders of weapons and matériel.*

Almost always shrouded in secrecy, arms deals are often concluded between governments who then turn to manufacturers, many of which are now privately owned, to fulfil them. In some instances, governments enter into contracts directly with commercial suppliers. And companies do business with each other or third parties, some of whom are not even legal entities. These include non-state actors – from armed militias to insurgent groups and informal clusters of 'terrorists' – and pariah states. The sale and supply of weapons often involves murky middlemen or agents, also referred to as arms brokers or dealers.†

Many arms deals contain elements of all these arrangements stretching across a continuum of legality and ethics from the official, or formal trade, to what I will refer to as the shadow world, also known as the grey and black markets. The grey market alludes to deals conducted through legal channels, but undertaken covertly. They are often utilized by governments to have an illicit impact on foreign policy. Black market deals are illegal in conception and execution. Both black and grey deals frequently contravene arms embargoes, national and multilateral laws, agreements and regulations. In practice, the boundaries between the three markets are fuzzy. With bribery and corruption *de rigueur* there are very few arms transactions that are entirely above board.‡

---

and light weapons are easy to use and maintain and are abundantly available. (R. Stohl and S. Grillot, 'The International Arms Trade' (Cambridge: Polity Press, 2009).)

* 'Matériel' refers to the equipment, apparatus and supplies of a military force.

† Dealers are generally defined as middlemen who buy the weapons and sell them on for profit, while brokers do not own the weapons but broker their sale either for cash or for commodities such as diamonds, oil or timber.

‡ It should be noted that clearly not all arms sales are illegal and that illegality is often determined by particular national and international legal standards applicable at the time of specific transactions. On occasion, the legal framework governing a particular deal might be unclear due to issues of jurisdiction or changing legal standards during the course of the deal. Hence, the use of terms such as 'bribery', 'corruption', 'commissions', etc. must be understood in their context and are not necessarily allegations of law breaking in all cases. Similarly and quite obviously, not everyone involved, directly or indirectly, in the arms trade is engaging in criminal activity, or protecting or condoning such activity.

The arms trade operates on collusion between world leaders, intelligence operatives, corporations at the cutting edge of technological development, financiers and bankers, transporters, shady middlemen, money launderers and common criminals.

This unholy alliance attempts to avoid responsibility for the gruesome consequences of their actions with the oft-quoted mantra: 'Guns don't kill people, people kill people.'[4] But even technologically advanced forms of warfare, such as the use of unmanned drone aircraft to eliminate enemies, cannot minimize the sheer brutality of the trade and the destruction it causes.*

Supplying conflicts from world wars to the Cold War to the War on Terror, from small insurgencies to large-scale revolutions, arms dealers, weapons manufacturers and even governments have fuelled and perpetuated tensions in pursuit of profit, on occasion selling to all sides in the same conflict.

In addition to the primary moral issue of the destruction caused by their products, there is the related concern of the 'opportunity cost' of the arms business. For while a weapons capability is clearly required in our unstable and aggressive world, the scale of defence spending in countries both under threat and peaceable results in the massive diversion of resources from crucial social and development needs, which in itself feeds instability.

A stark example of this cost could be seen in the early years of South Africa's democracy. With the encouragement of international arms companies and foreign states, the government spent around £6bn on arms and weapons it didn't require at a time when its President claimed the country could not afford to provide the antiretroviral drugs needed to keep alive the almost 6 million of its citizens living with HIV and Aids. Three hundred million dollars in commissions were paid to middlemen, agents, senior politicians, officials and the African National Congress (ANC – South Africa's ruling party) itself. In the following five years more than 355,000

---

* This 'sanitized' combat is criticized because it hasn't significantly reduced the killing of innocents. It also raises the moral issue of whether a controller sitting sometimes hundreds of miles from a conflict zone might not kill more readily and uncontrollably at such a physical and psychological remove. Against this is set the contention, heard most loudly in the wake of the atomic explosions in Hiroshima and Nagasaki, that targeted killing can minimize later violence and death.

South Africans died avoidable deaths because they had no access to the life-saving medication,[5] while the weapons remain largely under-used.

The corrupt and secretive way the industry operates undermines accountable democracy in both buying and selling countries. The arms trade accounts for over 40 per cent of corruption in all world trade.[6] The combination of the sheer magnitude of the contracts, the very small number of people who make the purchasing decisions and the cloak of national security lends itself to bribery and corruption on a massive scale. Some states are active participants in this illegality, while many more are content to countenance the behaviour. Almost all governments make weapons procurement decisions with huge financial implications that are neither cost-effective nor in the best interests of their countries. And the goods purchased often cost far more than initially quoted, are not able to perform as promised, and are produced or delivered years behind schedule.

There is clearly some need to maintain national security and commercial confidentiality. However, the all-encompassing secrecy that often characterizes arms deals hides corruption, conflicts of interest, poor decision-making and inappropriate national security choices. As a consequence, this trade, which should be among the most highly controlled and regulated, is one of the least scrutinized and accountable areas of government and private activity. Subsequent attempts to cover up malfeasance lead to additional illegal activity and the weakening of government. For instance, in the South African arms deal Parliament was undermined, anti-corruption bodies were disbanded and prosecuting authorities were weakened in order to protect politicians all the way up to the President.

It is hardly surprising that the agenda of weapons manufacturers and their supporters is at the centre of the governance process. For there is a continuous 'revolving door' through which people move between government, the military and the arms industry. The companies not only make significant financial contributions to politicians and their parties but also provide employment opportunities to former state employees, retired officers and defeated politicians. Nowhere is this more apparent than in the United States of America.

The pervasive, largely unchallenged common interests of defence manufacturers, the Pentagon, intelligence agencies, and members of Congress and the executive suggest that the US is effectively a national security state. This ensures that irrelevant weapons programmes which do little to make the country more secure continue to harvest billions of dollars in every budgetary cycle. For instance, during these straitened economic times the United States will ultimately spend over $380bn on a fighter jet that is of little use in current conflicts and has been described by a former Pentagon aerospace designer as 'a total piece of crap'.[7] The real security and economic interests of ordinary American taxpayers are sacrificed on the altar of this legalized bribery.

The 'revolving door' of people and money perpetuates what C. Wright Mills described as the 'military metaphysic', a militaristic definition of reality justifying 'a permanent war economy'.[8] This, despite the warning of the former General, Dwight D. Eisenhower, in his farewell address as President of the United States:

> [with] the conjunction of an immense military establishment and a large arms industry . . . in the councils of government we must guard against the acquisition of unwarranted influence by the military-industrial complex. The potential for the disastrous rise of misplaced power exists and will persist. We must never let the weight of this combination endanger our liberties or democratic processes.[9]

Within a year of George W. Bush assuming the presidency, over thirty arms industry executives, consultants and lobbyists occupied senior positions in his administration. Half a dozen senior executives from Lockheed Martin alone were given crucial appointments in the Bush government during 2001. By the end of that year the Pentagon had awarded the company one of the biggest military contracts in US history.[10]

Dick Cheney had served George W. Bush's father as Secretary of Defense before becoming CEO of Halliburton. During his tenure as Vice President under Bush junior, Cheney's former company garnered over $6bn in contracts from the Department of Defense.[11] Its oil-related contracts in Iraq trebled that number.[12] Cheney still held stock in the company and left office a very wealthy man.[13] Too little has changed under the Obama administration.

But it is not just the contracts. It is also the pernicious influence that this complex has on all aspects of governance, including economic and foreign policy and decisions to go to war. This unease is intensified because a large part of what it does is not open to scrutiny by law makers, the judiciary, the media or civil society watchdogs.

The arms industry and its powerful political friends have forged a parallel political universe that largely insulates itself against the influence or judgement of others by invoking national security. This is the shadow world.

The United Kingdom is hostage to a similar collusion between the main arms companies, especially the large and powerful BAE Systems,* and the executive branch of government, which acts as salesperson-in-chief for the industry. This relationship intensified during the Premiership of Margaret Thatcher, and Tony Blair's New Labour happily followed suit. Over the past decade BAE has been investigated for bribery in at least five separate arms deals.

In France, where parts of the industry are still in state hands, arms companies receive similarly enthusiastic levels of support from governments of every stripe. But the country's media and opinion-formers, with rare exceptions, appear mostly unconcerned by the dubious practices of their defence industry. That said, one or two investigating prosecutors have been more intrepid than their British counterparts in seeking legal recourse in cases of grand corruption. German, Swedish and Italian companies also receive massive assistance from their governments. Prosecutors in Germany do investigate arms companies but seldom with any publicly embarrassing consequences. In Italy and Sweden, where Saab has partnered BAE in many of the deals under scrutiny, investigations are rare.

The relationship between the defence industry and government is even more symbiotic in less democratic countries. The role of the weapons business is a crucial component of the People's Liberation Army's vast and growing commercial empire, which has become a defining feature of China's autocratic command capitalism. While weapons have always been a tool of foreign policy, China's use of cheap arms sales to expand its influence has reached unprecedented levels.[14] Those who operate the levers of power of the Russian state – the so-called *siloviki* around Vladimir Putin – exercise complete control over the country's arms business, which is an important source of patronage.[15]

China and Russia sell weapons to many of the world's despots, including Sudan, Syria, Burma, Iran, North Korea and Zimbabwe.[†] Their small

* Until 1999, the company was known as British Aerospace, and thereafter as BAE Systems. Throughout I refer to the company in its various manifestations as BAE.
† The latter two countries are predominantly supplied by China.

arms proliferate in conflict zones from Darfur to Mullaitivu. The Chinese were willing suppliers of weapons to Hosni Mubarak's Egypt, along with Russia, France, the UK and the United States.[16] The NATO powers, in their attacks on Libya's Muammar Gaddafi, have had to destroy not only Russian weapons, but also those sold to the dictator by France, Germany, Italy and the UK.[17]

Such blowback – the unintended and unexpected negative consequences of weapons sales – is commonplace in the arms trade, often undermining the security of the selling country. Perhaps the most obvious example is the US arming of the *mujahideen* in Afghanistan. Armed and trained to drive the Soviet Union out of the country, the same trained fighters, with the same weapons, formed the core of the Taliban and the adumbral Al Qaeda network that today constitute America's greatest enemy.

Blowback is also a commonplace when weapons, often surplus stock from the Cold War, the Balkans conflicts or the battlefields of Iraq and Afghanistan, are resold by 'merchants of death' such as Leonid Minin and Viktor Bout. Mostly small and light arms, these weapons have fuelled and prolonged conflicts in Africa, the Middle East, Latin America and South Asia.

When these numerous cases of blowback are blamed on the weapons manufacturers and their defenders in government, they retort that these unfortunate incidents are outweighed by the industry's economic contribution, particularly the number of jobs it creates. In reality the record is mixed.

The positive economic impact of the arms business is often overstated by the powerful PR machines, think-tanks and lobbyists that the industry funds. Not only are the numbers of job opportunities vastly exaggerated but it is overlooked that these jobs usually require significant subsidy from the public purse that could be used to create far more numerous and less morally tainted jobs in other sectors.

There is little doubt that the defence industry has contributed to significant progress in technological development.[18] But it is arguable that with the same or even fewer resources, other sectors might have similar impact.

The arms industry's economic contribution is also undermined by the frequency with which its main players around the world – Lockheed Martin, BAE, Boeing, Northrop Grumman, and those closely linked to it such as KBR, Halliburton and Blackwater – are implicated in grand corruption, inefficiency and wastage of public resources. They are very seldom forced to pay any significant price for their malfeasance and are always allowed to continue bidding for massive government contracts.

While there is a plethora of national, regional, multilateral and even some international regulation of the arms trade, the reality is that the symbiotic and secretive relationship between the industry, middlemen and their governments has meant that, in practice, this regulation is seldom fully enforced and is sometimes completely ignored. Since the modern inception of UN arms embargoes, there have been 502 investigated, documented and publicized allegations of violations of such embargoes, but to the best of our knowledge, there is only one instance where this has led to legal accountability of any sort, and this one case resulted in an acquittal.[19]

The arms business has a huge impact on the lives of most of the world's people, not only by fuelling and perpetuating conflict but also because of its profound impact on government, not least of which is the nature and extent of the wars we find ourselves fighting. Its victims include the taxpayers of the countries whose companies produce the weapons, the often more impoverished people of the purchasing countries and, of course, those who suffer at the deadly receiving end of the weapons themselves.

The arms trade – an intricate web of networks between the formal and shadow worlds, between government, commerce and criminality – often makes us poorer, not richer, less not more safe, and governed not in our own interests but for the benefit of a small, self-serving elite, seemingly above the law, protected by the secrecy of national security and accountable to no one.

The Shadow World is a journey of discovery into this powerful, but secretive world.

It begins with an arms company founded by a group of senior former Nazi officers in the aftermath of Germany's defeat that developed into one of the most nefarious networks of arms dealers the world has known. And it ends with the ill-conceived wars in Iraq and Afghanistan that have been a goldmine for US and allied defence manufacturers, as well as for the shadow world.

Along the way, the book traces the growing wealth of Saudi Arabia and its increasing influence on the global weapons trade, and especially its role in the development of the British defence behemoth BAE via the world's largest arms contract, the infamous Al Yamamah deal. It looks at how BAE and its US counterpart, Lockheed Martin, consolidated their relationships with governments and intelligence agencies in order to win weapons deals in their home countries, while also using these contacts and dubious agents to bribe their way into spectacularly lucrative contracts abroad.

It tracks the rise of rogue dealers like the Lebanese-Armenian Joe der Hovsepian, and the merging of the state, criminal activity and gun running which reached its apogee with the diamonds-for-weapons transactions overseen by the former Merex agent and Liberian President, Charles Taylor. It surveys the devastation of swathes of the African continent, enmired in seemingly endless civil wars and ethnic conflicts, fuelled by the rapaciousness of the arms trade. And it examines the role of the very wealthiest nations of the world, from Israel to Sweden, in facilitating this trade.

Finally, *The Shadow World* reveals the current status and whereabouts of the main characters and companies chronicled, before highlighting emerging trends in the arms trade, as well as the prospects for improved regulation, enforcement and accountability.

At our journey's end, I hope that you might ask whether we, the bankrollers, should not know more, far more, of this shadow world that affects the lives of us all. Whether we shouldn't demand greater transparency and accountability from politicians, the military, intelligence agencies, investigators and prosecutors, manufacturers and dealers, who people this parallel universe. Whether we shouldn't emerge from the shadows that blight our world.

SECTION I
The Second-Oldest Profession

1. Sins of Commission

'Here I am, a profiteer in mutilation and murder' is the proud self-description of Andrew Undershaft, the munitions manufacturer who bestrides George Bernard Shaw's *Major Barbara*. Unlike the often one-dimensional Lords of War and Merchants of Death who have littered literature, television and film in the more than hundred years since Shaw wrote his play, Undershaft embodies the complexities and contradictions of the manufacture of and trade in weapons.

He suggests there are only two things necessary to salvation: 'money and gunpowder'. Of government, 'that foolish gaggle shop', he says:

> you will do what pays us. You will make war when it suits us, and keep peace when it doesn't. You will find out that trade requires certain measures when we have decided on those measures. When I want anything to keep my dividends up, you will discover that my want is a national need. When other people want something to keep my dividends down, you will call out the police and military. And in return you shall have the support and applause of my newspapers, and the delight of imagining that you are a great statesman.[1]

The true faith of Shaw's 'Armorer' lies in selling 'arms to all men who offer an honest price for them, without respect of persons or principles . . . tak[ing] an order from a good man as cheerfully as from a bad one'. But, interjects a foppish man-about-town with designs on Undershaft's daughter, 'the cannon business may be necessary and all that: we can't get on without cannons; but it isn't right you know.'[2]

Shaw's inspiration for Andrew Undershaft was Basil Zaharoff, godfather of the modern BAE, together with the Swedish and German armaments magnates, the Alfreds Nobel and Krupp. Known variously as 'the super-salesman of death', 'the mystery man of Europe', 'the Monte Cristo of our time', Zaharoff was the world's first flamboyant, larger-than-life arms dealer, providing the template for those who followed him.

As Anthony Sampson, the renowned author of *The Arms Bazaar*, notes:

Zaharoff was a figure of historical importance; for he was not merely a master of salesmanship and bribery, but an operator who understood the connections between arms and diplomacy, between arms and intelligence, and who could serve both as salesman and spy. He represented all the mixed loyalties of the burgeoning arms business: 'I sold armaments to anyone who would buy them. I was a Russian when in Russia, a Greek in Greece, a Frenchman in Paris.'[3]

Everything about Zaharoff's cosmopolitan life, including his date and place of birth and his original name, are shrouded in mystery and intrigue, largely of his own making and in no small measure to facilitate his business interests.[4] A Greek of humble origins, probably born between 1849 and 1851, Zaharoff initially worked as a tout for local brothels. He was also a member of the *Tulumbadschi*, the Constantinople firemen-gang who would only put out fires for a bribe, and frequently started blazes in order to solicit the money. He soon travelled the world, under the identity of Prince Gortzacoff, the son of a Russian officer.

Arriving in Cyprus almost penniless, Zaharoff moved into arms dealing, first selling hunting guns and then cheap military equipment. He claims to have sailed the coast of Africa in a ship loaded with war materials which he sold to the chiefs of two warring West African tribes. He later said: 'I made my first hundreds gun-running for savages. I made wars so that I could sell arms to both sides. I must have sold more arms than anyone else in the world.'[5]

Back in Athens in 1874, an influential political journalist, who would later become Prime Minister of Greece, arranged Zaharoff's first job in the trade which became his métier.[6] During his early years with the Swedish weapons-maker Nordenfelt, Zaharoff rapidly increased his knowledge of weaponry, persuading the company to sell its new submarine not only to Greece but also to his homeland's bitter rival, Turkey: 'He considered it an unpatriotic act and somewhat immoral to sell submarines to the mortal enemies of [Greece], namely the Turkish navy, but he always had the strength to overcome such reservations.'[7]

It was during these early arms-trading days that the singular activities of his later life began: the dissemination of military propaganda to the press and the art of the bribe, leading one observer to comment:

Even a veteran armaments salesmen would hesitate before trying to sneak a five-digit check to a defence minister in the presence of the Parliamentary Control Commission. But hesitation was not for Zaharoff. He would not have been too timid to put bags of gold pieces on the Minister's desk, even in the presence of the district attorney dedicated to suppressing corruption.[8]

Nordenfelt's competitors – which included the large British manufacturers Vickers and Armstrong, the German giant Krupps and the Schneider–Creusot company of France – adopted the view that the cheapest offer had the best prospect of acceptance. Zaharoff applied the opposite method: 'He offered his guns for twice the competition's price, and slipped the politicians deciding the sales three times more in bribes than his competitors would dare to offer.'[9]

He was always happy to stoke conflict to ensure the prosperity of his business. It has been suggested that one of the key reasons peace was not restored in the Balkans from the late nineteenth century until after the First World War was because 'A few thousand gold francs paid to the editor of a normally peace-loving newspaper, a few hundred leva to a border guard who had never before fired a shot – and a new incident was created. The parliaments approved new armaments credits; the ministerial offices allocated – for still higher percentages of still higher priced bids – new orders for weapons.'[10]

Zaharoff was also accused of chasing, if not helping incite, wars between Bolivia and Paraguay and Spain and America, among others.[11] He sold weapons to both sides in the Boer War and the Russo-Japanese conflict, clashing with an opposition MP, Lloyd George, who took issue with the practice.[12]

He expended enormous energy and money ingratiating himself to the courts and chancelleries of the world.[13] Stories proliferated in European capitals of Zaharoff's corruption and deviousness. Even a historian for Vickers, who had bought Nordenfelt in part to secure Zaharoff's services, concluded: 'There is evidence that on two or three occasions in Serbia in 1898, in Russia later, and probably in Turkey, Zaharoff paid secrecy commissions, or bribes.'[14]

The reasons for the bribes were those that apply today: as the commission increased, officials might well favour bigger orders, beyond the capacity or needs of their country, to ensure that their share would be greater. A story was told of a salesman who paid a succession of commissions to officials on a contract with a European government for a cruiser, until one official made such an exorbitant demand that the Englishman exclaimed: 'How can I build the cruiser?' The official replied: 'What does that matter, so long as you get paid and we get paid?'[15]

In the lead-up to the First World War Zaharoff seemed to be everywhere, involved in everything that could increase profits. He stayed one step ahead of his competitors not only through straightforward corruption, but also through his mastery of influence and information.[16] There were very real fears, especially among some British politicians, that the arms companies in general and Zaharoff in particular were setting their own foreign policy and having undue influence over government.[17] When, on 28 July 1914, the war so badly desired by the industry was declared, Zaharoff was perfectly positioned to take maximum advantage. At the time he was arming both sides, as he probably did up to 1915.[18] In fact, for the thirty years leading up to the war, the British arms industry did as much to support the enemy's military as anyone else. Armstrong-Whitworth built thirty-six naval ships for the Royal Navy, but over 100 for foreign fleets, twenty-six of which went to the eventual enemy.[19]

Nevertheless, Zaharoff grew close to the former arms industry critic, Lloyd George, during his time as Minister for Munitions and then later as Prime Minister. The arms dealer even acted as a spy king, working directly for Lloyd George.[20] Of course, Zaharoff used his espionage activities as further justification for arms sales to all and sundry, arguing that 'the nation which sells [arms] to other nations understands best the real military and naval positions inside those countries to which it sells'.[21]

The First World War ran its course, taking the lives of millions and causing unimaginable destruction, but for Zaharoff 'it brought high honours and made him a multimillionaire'.[22] He was knighted by the King of England, received the highest orders of merit and was appointed adviser to the British Prime Minister for peace negotiations.[23] In reality, whenever peace sentiment was making headway among any of the war-weary allies in the later years of the conflict, the arms salesman declared himself in favour of carrying on the war 'to the bitter end'.[24]

In his later years in Monte Carlo, the one-time 'super-salesman of death' was primarily interested in destroying evidence of his past activities. And when, on 27 November 1936 he died at the age of eighty-seven in a wheelchair on the balcony of his Hôtel de Paris, he could afford a final wry, cynical smile: he had enjoyed his millions derived from wars, which gave him his titles, degrees and every possible luxury. But he took most of his secrets to the grave with him, leaving behind a template for the archetypal arms dealer: an aura of mystery, flamboyance and high living; friendships in the corridors of power; the habitual use of bribery and corruption; engagement in deception and covert intelligence activities; manipulation of public policy and opinion through ownership of, or influence in the media; involvement in financial services so crucial both to trading activities and to laundering of the resultant profits; the charm, ability and bloody-mindedness to sell anything to anybody. In short, a life spent operating in the opaque interstices between the legal and illegal, while buying respectability through gifts, endowments and the company of the rich and powerful.

The First World War led to a broad backlash against the arms-makers.[25] Zaharoff's close associate Lloyd George recalled that, at the war's conclusion, when the Allies gathered in Paris to sign the peace treaty 'there was not one there who did not agree that if you wanted to preserve peace in the world you must eliminate the idea of profit of great and powerful interests in the manufacture of armaments'.[26]

The discovery that Zaharoff's Vickers had armed Britain's enemies heightened the antipathy. But the most influential critic of the arms companies was the United States' President Woodrow Wilson, fired with his zeal for the League of Nations. It was he who inspired the historic paragraph of the Covenant of the League which agreed 'that the manufacture by private enterprise of munitions and implements of war is open to grave objections'.[27] This led to the establishment of a commission to reduce arms. Its 1921 report was a devastating indictment of arms companies, accusing them of 'fomenting war scares, bribing government officials, disseminating false reports concerning the military programmes of countries and organizing international armaments rings to accentuate the arms race by playing one country off against another'.[28]

Despite this trenchant, far-reaching criticism, in practice little was done. The arms industry was in an unparalleled slump and Vickers and its rival, Armstrong, were in such bad shape that the British government forced them into a merger, creating Vickers-Armstrong.[29]

Between the world wars, all the large arms companies, including Vickers-Armstrong, agitated against the prospect of a permanent peace. At the Geneva disarmament conference in 1927 an ebullient arms lobbyist, William G. Shearer – employed by three big American shipbuilding companies at huge cost – was instrumental in sabotaging any moves towards international agreements on disarmament by stoking fears and spreading propaganda to encourage the building of warships. Shearer's lobbying, however, had an unintended consequence, leading to an unprecedented crusade against the arms companies: soon after the Geneva conference, he filed a suit against the three companies that had employed him for $258,000 in unpaid lobbying fees, thus making public not only the exorbitant cost of his employment but also the arms companies' opposition to disarmament.[30]

While over the previous decade the American public had been largely apathetic towards arms control, the Shearer revelations coincided with a growing wave of pacifism and an underlying distrust of big corporations made more intense by the Great Crash of 1929. The indiscretions of a single salesman became the passionate concern of a nation. At the end of 1933, pacifists won the support of a Progressive Republican junior Senator from North Dakota, Gerald P. Nye, who embraced the campaign against the arms trade with rhetorical fervour: 'Was ever a more insane racket conceived in depraved minds or tolerated by an enlightened people?'[31]

In April 1934, the Senate established a committee with Nye as chairman. The press acclaimed the campaign. In the spring of that year *Fortune* magazine published a vituperative article entitled 'Arms and the Men', which calculated that in the First World War it had cost $25,000 to kill a soldier, 'of which a great part went into the pocket of the armament maker'.[32] A polemical book, *The Merchants of Death*, became a bestseller and the *Chicago Daily News* described how 200 firms were earning 'cold cash profits on smashed brains or smothered legs'.[33]

Later that year, Nye's committee delivered a stunning report. It uncovered correspondence between the president of the Electric Boat company and his counterpart at Vickers, revealing the general amorality of the weapons business in their disdain for any kind of control over the arms trade, their dislike of attempts to promote peace, and their willingness to use bribes.[34] The committee asked Clarence Webster of the Curtiss-

Wright aircraft company to explain what was meant by a commission: 'In fact it would be bribery, would it not?' He replied: 'It would. It is rather a harsh word, but it would, strictly speaking.'

Nye's committee vividly revealed the arms industry's 'constant tendency towards bribery, and the playing off of one country against another to sell arms'. It also exposed the extent to which arms salesmen were supported by their governments: 'It makes one wonder,' commented the Senator, 'whether the army or the navy are just organisations of salesmen for private industry, paid for by the American government.'[35] A witness suggested that 'the Vickers crowd are the dirtiest, they have almost an entire embassy in number working for them and use women of doubtful character freely'.[36]

The Nye Committee's findings, while fairly widely criticized, at least led to the creation of a national Munitions Control Board. This didn't give government the power to stop arms deals in peacetime but gave some hope of an international agreement on the issue.

In the UK the findings of the Nye committee, combined with popular pressure, led the Labour Party to demand 'the prohibition of the private manufacture of arms' in 1934. During the parliamentary debate, Clement Attlee, the future Prime Minister, compared the trade in arms to prostitution and slavery. After a ballot in Britain in which over 90 per cent of respondents felt 'the manufacture and sale of armaments for private profit [should] be prohibited by international agreement', the government was forced to set up a Royal Commission on the issue.[37] It provided a wide-ranging, if muted, critique of the British arms trade but did include a fiery intervention from Lloyd George: 'I think the less you leave to private manufacture, the less is the incentive to promoting agitation for war.'[38] By this time, the ageing Zaharoff clearly had little influence over his old wartime friend.

Vickers' spokesmen at the Commission made clear the company's modus operandi:

Mr. Yapp [Vickers]: . . . We pay our agents a percentage of commission.
Dame Rachel Crowdy: A percentage?
Yapp: Yes, but as to what part of that goes into his own pocket or what he does with it we have no control. . . .
Crowdy: Therefore any entertainment has to come out of his commission, really.

Sir Charles Craven [Vickers]: Yes.
Crowdy: And any 'palm-greasing' has to come out of his commission?
Craven: Certainly.[39]

By the time the Committee reported, the state of British arms companies and of public opinion had started to shift in response to the aggressive behaviour of Nazi Germany, where Krupp had come to terms with Hitler and handed over his factories to the making of weapons. Britain's massive rearmament in response was the saviour of its arms companies. The direct and menacing threat to the country, the accompanying war propaganda and the canonizing of the military put an end to criticism of arms manufacturers.

The companies received heavy state support to revitalize shipyards and factories and, thanks to strict government control over their profits, were insulated from accusations of war profiteering. The export of arms became less relevant and more strictly controlled. The Air Ministry had some acrimonious disputes with Vickers and other companies over late and inadequate deliveries and had to look to Lockheed in America to provide enough bombers. But the celebrated Spitfire, mythologized after the Battle of Britain, massively enhanced the image of Vickers and obliterated the memories of the late Basil Zaharoff. This was the high point of the company's national role and public image.[40]

The Second World War signalled the creation of the military-industrial complex in Britain and elsewhere. This militarized economy, born out of an imperial system and expanding to vast proportions during the war, largely remained in place into the Cold War.

For a decade after the war, the arms trade was virtually an Anglo-American monopoly.[41] Britain's industry was kept buoyant by the decline of Empire, for as countries gained their independence they sought arms to enhance their status and security. From 1945 to 1955, Britain sold arms worth over $2bn to private traders and $1.7bn to foreign governments, excluding warships.[42] The formation of NATO and the flow of American aid to Europe provided extra opportunities for sales. The Americans, whose concerns were more diplomatic than commercial, bought equipment from Britain for the Continent. The two countries worked closely together, and by obeying unwritten understandings about areas of influence they avoided any drastic competition in arms sales.[43]

It is surprising, with the reaction to the First World War in mind, that there was not more public concern about the rush of arms sales in the aftermath of the most destructive war in the history of mankind. Certainly the problems of disarmament were discussed as never before, but it was nuclear disarmament which understandably dominated the arguments and conferences. Compared to the new danger of a nuclear holocaust, the problem of the export of conventional arms seemed relatively harmless, and inevitable as a by-product of the growing Cold War.

As the Cold War extended and British influence diminished, so the Americans moved into traditional British areas in response to Soviet threats and the Soviet Union's growing arms industry. By the early sixties, the United States was by far the biggest exporter of arms, forcing Britain to compete more desperately for her markets abroad.

Vickers-Armstrong's attempts to remain the biggest arms company were futile. The battleship, which had been the jewel in Vickers' crown for fifty years, was much less important after the war and the manufacture of jet aircraft was becoming too complex and expensive for a single British firm.[44]

Even in Europe Britain was being challenged by the re-emergence of France as a major manufacturer of arms and particularly aircraft. The French arms industry was championed by Marcel Dassault. The son of a Jewish doctor, Marcel was brought up in Paris at the end of the nineteenth century and developed an early passion for flight. He set up his own company to make planes during the First World War. After the fall of France in 1940 he was interned with other French aircraft designers. He refused to work for the Nazis in return for his freedom and in 1944 was transported to Buchenwald, where he still refused to cooperate and was sentenced to death, to be saved only by the arrival of the Allied armies. He emerged a frail-looking man of fifty-two, partly deaf, with weak eyesight, but still burning with ambition to build aircraft. After the war he changed his name from Bloch to Dassault (his brother's pseudonym during the Resistance), formed a close political alliance with De Gaulle, was elected a Deputy of the French Parliament for seven years from 1951, and built an organization more compact and impressive than its Anglo-Saxon equivalents.[45] His most glorious creation was the Mirage jet, famed for its Delta wing and rocket booster. It became one of the most successful of all French exports and a major factor in French foreign policy. With his immense wealth, dominance of the French arms industry, political connections and newspapers, Dassault became a one-man military-industrial complex.

However, neither the French nor the British could effectively compete in the long term with growing American exports. To address this the British government actively encouraged the rationalization of the industry, with Rolls-Royce, Hawker Siddeley Aviation and the British Aircraft Corporation (BAC) emerging as the main consolidated players.[46] BAC was formed on 1 July 1960 as a result of the merger of Vickers-Armstrong's aircraft division and three other smaller companies. It was 40 per cent owned by Vickers-Armstrong. Its only real success was a smallish civil airliner, the BAC 1-11, later Leonid Minin's plane of choice. The government, fearing the company's failure but unwilling to bail it out, eventually nationalized BAC in 1977 and merged it with Hawker-Siddeley and Scottish Aviation. The new group was named British Aerospace.[47]

In 1979, an election in the UK brought Margaret Thatcher to power. Her fundamentalist free market ideology was underpinned by a deep commitment to widespread privatization of the public sector. BAE's short-lived nationalization came to an end in early 1981 when it was made a public limited company. In February the government sold just over 51 per cent of its shares, shedding its remaining holding in 1985, although it retained a Golden Share giving it the power to veto foreign control.[48]

In 1987, BAE bought Royal Ordinance, a collection of nationalized arms factories producing ammunition, small arms, tanks, artillery and explosives. Four years later the small-arms manufacturer Heckler and Koch was also purchased.[49] British Aerospace became BAE Systems in 1999 after it merged with Marconi Electronic Systems. The name change was clearly intended to alter the company's image of a purely British entity, given that it sells more to the US Department of Defense than to the UK's Ministry of Defence.[50]

The 'new' BAE's early survival was dependent not on the Pentagon, but primarily on a desert kingdom of dubious reputation. Saudi Arabia came into being as a modern state in 1925 after a 24-year-long campaign by Abdul Aziz, also known as Ibn Saud, in which he subdued and drew together the various tribes of Arabia. The Saudi state is to this day an absolute monarchy, with the kingship and many of the most important

ministries still in the hands of the children of King Abdul Aziz.[51] The
country's wealth and status are determined by the vast oilfields in the east
and the two holiest cities of Islam, Mecca and Medina, in the west. The
combination of gargantuan oil wealth and strict, fundamentalist religion
has produced one of the world's great enigmas.

Saudi Arabia holds approximately one fifth of all the world's proven oil
reserves,[52] and has long been the world's largest oil exporter, although
Russia may have recently overtaken it.[53] The black gold – which accounts
for 80 per cent of Saudi budget revenues, 90 per cent of its export earnings
and 45 per cent of its GDP[54] – was first discovered in 1938 after King Abdul
Aziz's English adviser, Jack Philby, persuaded the King to allow prospecting. Philby, who was the father of Kim, the notorious Briton unmasked as
a Soviet spy, was dismissed by the British government as a bit player and
was taken on by Standard Oil of California. He secured a prospecting concession for his new employers, which cost $175,000 in gold up front and
loans of $600,000. The agreement was good for sixty years and covered
360,000 square miles and was surely the steal of the century. For a generation after its discovery, the Saudi oil business was effectively controlled
by ARAMCO (The Arabian American Oil Company), a consortium of
Saudi and American oil companies.[55]

The country's oil riches have enabled it to forge a symbiotic relationship
with the West, in which oil flows plentifully in return for an unwritten
guarantee of protection, and a seemingly insatiable appetite for arms deals.
The US and the UK, who are party to laws and agreements obliging them
to consider human rights before agreeing to arms exports, are blind to the
kingdom's autocratic, oppressive and misogynistic rule when it comes to
selling weapons. Human rights abuses are frequent. The practice of any religion other than Islam is illegal and political parties are outlawed. Amnesty
International described the situation in 2009:

> Thousands of people continued to be detained without trial. Human
> rights activists and peaceful critics of the government were detained or
> remained in prison, including prisoners of conscience. Freedom of expres-
> sion, religion, association and assembly remained tightly restricted. Women
> continued to face severe discrimination in law and practice. Migrant workers
> suffered exploitation and abuse with little possibility of redress. The admin-
> istration of justice remained shrouded in secrecy and was summary in

nature. Torture and other ill-treatment of detainees were widespread and systematic, and carried out with impunity. Flogging was used widely as a punishment. The death penalty continued to be used extensively and in a discriminatory manner against migrant workers from developing countries, women and poor people. At least 102 people were executed.[56]

Geoffrey Edwards, a rugged Yorkshire businessman with a commanding voice, big chin and leonine head, who had travelled to Saudi Arabia in 1960 looking for civil construction projects, saw the potential for arms contracts. He contacted UK companies and became an agent for a consortium of BAC, AEI and Airwork. Edwards lived in Jeddah, developing a close relationship with Prince Sultan, the Minister of Defence and Aviation from 1962, King Faisal's half-brother and father of Prince Bandar. Edwards shrewdly employed Prince Sultan's brother, Prince Abdul Rahman, as an agent, offering him half the commission he was receiving from AEI. The Englishman also consulted Gaith Pharaon, an influential Saudi financier whose father was the King's physician. Edwards later said that he paid Pharaon £80,000.[57]

At the time, the Saudis coveted the latest-generation jet fighter aircraft. However, Edwards was not alone in bidding for Saudi Air Force contracts. There was stiff competition from Dassault and the American companies Lockheed and Northrop. Initially, a prospective deal was of little interest to the Foreign Office, who regarded Saudi Arabia as the Americans' preserve. But when a Labour government came to power in 1964 faced with a financial crisis, the right-wing Edwards saw an opportunity. He gained access to the then Aviation Minister and persuaded him of the enormous economic benefits of the deal. The minister dispatched his Parliamentary Secretary, John Stonehouse, to support the negotiations. Stonehouse later remarked:

> Most people in Government frowned upon Geoffrey Edwards as an arms salesman grasping after his fat commissions. I did not. In an area such as Arabia much of the commission would any way have to be spent in bribes and, anyhow what was the point of adopting a 'holier-than-thou' attitude when Britain's factories sorely needed that business and our balance of payments need the foreign currency.[58]

Edwards was aware that Prince Sultan wanted British Lightning aircraft. He heard that the Prince was frustrated with the Americans and was keen to shift away from dependence on them. The Saudi royal may well have dropped these encouraging hints as a ploy to increase the competition and gain better terms from the Americans. The situation was complex as the British and Americans were still wary of trespassing on each other's turf. By September of 1965 the British seemed to have lost out to the US. However, because the Americans were not keen on Saudi Arabia acquiring the Lockheed Starfighter, which was so advanced that it would upset the balance of power in the region, particularly in relation to Israel, high-level diplomacy between London and Washington resulted in a joint offer being made to the Saudis. In December 1965, the Saudis accepted the joint offer, which from the British side comprised forty-two BAC Lightning Fighters and an AEI radar system, with Airwork providing training. It was announced as Britain's biggest ever export deal.

While negotiations were taking place between London and Washington the companies and their agents made mischief. Every company had its own group of agents, some of whom clandestinely represented more than one of the bidders. Each accused the others of bribery. Kim Roosevelt, the Northrop agent, had been in charge of the CIA coup to overthrow Mossaddegh and restore the Shah to power in Iran, and was not averse to using his deep intelligence contacts, telling Northrop executives: 'my friends in the CIA are keeping an eye on things'.[59] Prince Mohammed, another Northrop agent, kept the King informed of the bribes Lockheed were paying. Adnan Khashoggi, then a young, virtually unknown arms dealer who would later emerge as the Basil Zaharoff of his era, was hired by Lockheed. He developed close links with Prince Sultan and was used extensively as a deniable conduit for bribes.[60]

At least £7.8m was paid in commissions on the British contracts with the knowledge of three separate UK government entities: the Export Credit Guarantee Department, the Treasury and the tax authorities.[61] Geoffrey Edwards, who was instrumental in securing the Lightning contract for BAC, charged 1.5 per cent commission, worth over £2m, a staggering sum at the time.[62] He nonchalantly suggested that 'the payments were normal practice, legal and out in the open. They were for business services rendered.'[63] To cover these massive commissions, BAC inflated the price of each Lightning jet by £50,000, listing the cost as 'Agency Fees'. The commissions went not only to Gaith Pharaon but also to five Saudi princes.[64]

After the deal Edwards sued AEI, which was refusing to pay him commission on its contract, instead rewarding a shady agent who was later murdered in Paris. Edwards was himself sued by three agents, including Prince Abdul Rahman, who insisted that the Yorkshireman owed them money on the deal.[65] Edwards retired to the island of Jersey, working briefly as an agent for Lockheed before setting up his own company dealing with the Middle East. It later transpired that the original British contract and the commissions paid to Edwards were dwarfed by the contracts with Lockheed and Northrop and the colossal commissions paid to Khashoggi.

John Stonehouse, who had been so important in pushing the deal through, had clearly been exposed to the dark side by his Saudi experience. After rising in government service, he soon began speculating in private ventures, which led him into considerable debt. He disappeared off a beach in Miami in 1974, was discovered living under an assumed name in Australia and in 1976 was convicted of fraud and forgery and sentenced to seven years in jail.[66]

The deal was hardly a triumph for the Saudis. The Lightning aircraft were more suited to the coastal defence of Britain than the vast deserts of Arabia.[67] After numerous technical problems with the jets as they were being delivered, a Lightning crashed on a demonstration flight over Riyadh in September 1966. However, the biggest problem the Saudis had to contend with was the inadequacies of Airwork, the providers of the training and maintenance contracts. The company's commitments proved beyond its resources. The Ministry of Defence was compelled to become more deeply involved. Ex-RAF pilots were recruited to fly the planes, becoming, in effect, sponsored mercenaries to the Saudis; and eventually the British government had to set up its own organization in Riyadh, jointly with the Saudis, to supervise the programme. What began as an apparently simple commercial sale ended up, like many future arms deals, as a major government commitment.[68]

Despite the dissatisfaction and renewed competition with US companies, a new deal was signed between the Saudis and the UK in 1973 for the purchase of ten Strikemaster fighter jets and maintenance, worth

£253m.[69] At least £30m in commissions was paid in this government-to-government deal.[70] The British government was directly involved in passing on the payments, as the Ministry of Defence signed the contract with Riyadh and with BAC as the lead supplier. The officially controlled profit margin of the company was a fiction used to finance the commissions which flowed into anonymous Swiss bank accounts.[71]

Willie Morris, the British ambassador to Saudi Arabia between 1968 and 1972, wrote that 'The Saud family regard Saudi Arabia as a family business. . . . The sheer effrontery is breathtaking of a prince who will keep on talking about rights and wrongs, when you know (and he probably knows you know) that his cut may be 20% of the contract price.'[72] The world of Saudi arms sales, he said, was 'crooked. The question of corruption is obviously crucial . . . the "system" is at best an infernal nuisance, and it is potentially explosive – a time bomb under the regime. . . . It is a jungle inhabited by beasts of prey in which one must move with caution and uncertainty.' He added that Prince Sultan 'has, of course, a corrupt interest in all contracts . . .'[73]

On assuming office in 1977, the new British Foreign Secretary, David Owen, was made aware of the tactics of bribing the kingdom's royal family, being told in a dispatch: 'To secure a contract, a company must secure the support not merely of a senior prince, often through an established agent through whom very substantial commissions have to be paid; but also of many ministers and officials down the line.'[74]

To legalize this practice, in May 1977 the Cooper Directive was issued. Named for its author Frank Cooper, Permanent Secretary at the MoD, this secret policy gave the senior bureaucrat the power to authorize commissions on government-to-government contracts and withhold information of their payment from the minister. The commissions would be regarded as acceptable as long as the UK firm involved confirmed that they were legitimate to the winning of the contract. The directive instructed officials to avoid 'over-extensive inquiries' of the companies.[75] In 1994 the Cooper Directive was rewritten in more obscure terms: 'Officials would no longer visibly "authorise" commission payments, or correspond about them. Instead, they were to merely "consider" and "advise".' According to the response to a Freedom of Information request this policy is still in place today.[76]

And so with the sweep of a bureaucratic hand and with the blessing of his political master, the Prime Minister, who had informally told fellow ministers that the UK could not hold to the same high standard as the US on corruption, Britain had irrevocably decided that it would break the law in arms deals with the kingdom of Saudi Arabia for evermore.[77]

This only enhanced the relationship. Appropriately, when King Faisal died in March 1975 it was the Secretary of State for Defence who was sent to represent the British government at his funeral. In 1976, Prince Sultan, still Minister of Defence and Aviation, made his first visit to London. The UK was by then interested in selling Jaguar aircraft to the kingdom.[78] The Saudis had been steadily buying from the US. However, in 1976 Congress blocked the transfer of Maverick missiles to the kingdom and the liberal Jimmy Carter was elected President. During this time of uncertainty the Saudis wanted to strike rapid deals with its other arms providers.

In September 1977, BAC signed a follow-on contract to continue the 'Saudization' of the kingdom's Air Force up to 1982. The contract was thought to be worth £500m.[79] Commissions of £60m were paid with the certain knowledge of the UK government. The head of the government's Defence Sales Organisation (DSO) described the size of the commissions as what was 'commonly charged', though 'the sums involved are very large, and in future, as defence projects become more ambitious, the agency fees demanded will, unless some restraint is applied, become enormous'.[80]

The commissions, totalling 15 per cent of the contract value, were paid for by charging the Saudis 'admissible costs' of 10 per cent of the contract value, while the other 5 per cent was taken from BAC's inflated profit margin.[81]

Throughout the 1970s, not just Britain but also the US and France continued to benefit from the munificence of Saudi arms spending. The total value of Britain's 1967, 1973 and 1977/78 deals with Saudi Arabia was approximately £4.5bn in today's money, with at least £500m paid in commissions.[82]

However, the real bonanza was still to come.

2. The Nazi Connection

Where large British and American firms became the pinnacle of the formal trade in arms, a small German company run by an affable, rotund former Nazi represented the murkiest depths of the shadow world, the borderland between the legal and illegal trade in weapons.

Merex had its genesis in early June 1945, just over a month after Adolf Hitler had committed suicide, as two men sat on a verandah in Wiesbaden in western Germany. One, General Reinhard Gehlen, was a German prisoner of war, who had turned himself over to the Allies a month previously. The other was John R. Boker Jr, an American officer in military intelligence whose task it was to interrogate senior German operatives captured by the Allies. Together they discussed an arrangement that would have deep ramifications for both Germany and the world's future: to secure the survivors of Nazi Germany's wartime intelligence in service of the West.[1]

For Gehlen, and the wide network of operatives he directed, the Second World War had been but a prefiguring of the great global conflict to come. In May 1942, Gehlen was appointed as the Chief of the Fremde Heere Ost (Foreign Armies East), the intelligence branch of the German General Staff on the Eastern Front.[2] His experience there was eye-opening; a committed Nazi, Gehlen was nevertheless forced to admit that Germany's chances of winning the war were slim. Directly appraised of the methods and might of the Soviets, Gehlen confided in his Fremde Heere Ost colleague Lt Col. Gerhard Wessel that the end of the conflict would bring into sharp relief what the exigencies of war had hidden: that the next decades would witness a severing of the world in two, the West on one side and the East on the other. More importantly, the East–West conflict would spare none, demanding allegiances without option: 'It would be essential to ally with one side or other; no neutral position was possible,' Wessel recalled in a later statement given to US authorities.[3] Caught between two global forces, Gehlen and Wessel chose the West.

Coming to this realization, Gehlen and his organization made plans. Large dossiers of German intelligence on Soviet activities, which included surveillance photos of Russian industrial complexes and detailed intelligence on the capacity of the Soviet air force, were consolidated and hidden, often in makeshift holes beneath the floorboards of foresters' cottages. When the time came Gehlen and his colleagues would present themselves to the Allies, offering up their cache in return for lenient treatment.

It was a deal that John R. Boker Jr felt was good value. Convinced of the quality of German intelligence, Boker oversaw the reconstitution of the hidden files and scoured POW camps to reunite Gehlen with his former colleagues. Fearful that US authorities with a less sympathetic approach to Nazi officers would scupper his plans, Boker did what he could to hide his activities and protect Gehlen's organization.[4] In August, Gehlen and a number of high-ranking colleagues were transported under Boker's watch to Washington in the private plane of a US General and from there to the Pentagon.

After initially being placed in solitary confinement,[5] within a year, having impressed US Intelligence, who trained him intensively, Gehlen was returned to Germany to head a massive US-backed German spy-ring to monitor Russian activities. Over the next decade, the US poured an estimated $200m into the ring, known colloquially as Gehlen Org.

In 1955, now staffed by thousands of undercover agents, Gehlen Org was formally handed over to the German government and integrated into the newly created West German intelligence agency, the Bundesnachrichtendienst (BND).[6] Gehlen, the star of German Intelligence, would head the BND until his retirement in 1968. For his part, John R. Boker, who would become a world-renowned stamp-collector in his private life, was given belated recognition for his foresight when he was inducted into the 'Hall of Fame of Military Intelligence Service' in 1990.

Gehlen's soft landing following the war was matched by other prominent Nazis, many of whom formed a post-war nexus of contacts that frequently fed into the activities of Gehlen Org and the BND. In what was probably not an uncommon discovery, a BND employee was found to have been a prominent member of an SS unit responsible for the liquidation of 24,000 civilians in Russia, mostly Jews.[7] Befitting these sordid origins, this network traded in the depraved: torture training, mercenary services and, most notably, arms dealing.

Gerhard Mertins was one such character who emerged from the rubble of the war unscathed and would make hay from his contacts within the

Gehlen group. Mertins had excelled during the war, rising to the rank of Major in the Wehrmacht. In 1944, he was awarded the Knight's Cross – one of only 7,000 German soldiers to receive the honour – for acts of bravery during the unsuccessful attempts to repel the Allies' D-Day invasion.[8]

Despite appearing a happy, easy-going man, always ready to help, Mertins was also shrewd and 'cheated everybody', according to a close associate.[9] Soon after the war he took up a position at Volkswagen, a company with an impeccable Nazi pedigree. Little is known of his activities until the early 1950s, although it is almost certain that he kept curious company. According to US Army Intelligence documents, Mertins was the leader of the Bremen branch of the Green Devils, a group of Second World War parachutists agitating for a rearmed Germany.[10] The branch included a number of suspected war criminals as well as General Kurt Student, the man responsible for masterminding the German invasions of Holland, Belgium and Luxembourg.

Closely connected to neo-Nazis of all stripes and unrepentant about his right-wing views, Mertins was more than comfortable with the considerable neo-Nazi sentiment evident in Germany after the war. For instance, he invited Otto Ernst Remer, founder of the Socialist Reich Party (SRP) in 1950, to address members of his veterans' group in Bremen. The SRP's platform was almost indistinguishable from Hitler's and included denial of the Holocaust. Despite disagreeing with some of Remer's points on rearmament,[11] Mertins was 'considered to be an important SRP sympathizer' who US Intelligence believed 'will aid the party financially'.[12]

Mertins's connections to the world of veterans and ex-Nazis was to stand him in good stead when he decided to leave the employ of Volkswagen. In September 1952, he travelled to Egypt to participate in a bizarre project that was to provide an entrée to the world of arms dealing.

In 1948, the Egyptian army had been humiliated in a war with the newly created state of Israel. The response of the then Egyptian ruler, King Farouk, was to hire a number of ex-military Germans to assist in training his troops, allegedly with the tacit support of both the CIA and Gehlen Org. When Mertins arrived in Egypt in September 1951 he became a top aide to one of the group's leaders, the former Wehrmacht General Wilhelm Fahrmbacher, like Mertins a recipient of the Knight's Cross.[13]

When the young General Gamal Abdel Nasser led a coup against King Farouk in July 1952, he turned to the Germans who had been training his

erstwhile enemy's forces to create his own intelligence and security network in order to consolidate power. Seamlessly shifting their allegiance
from King Farouk, the German detachment set about their new task, still
with the backing of the CIA and Gehlen Org. The training was led by
Otto Skorzeny, a notorious ex-Nazi who had been part of an elite unit
that helped Mussolini escape from Allied jails during the war. Skorzeny
himself escaped from a US prison camp in 1948 – possibly with a wink
from US intelligence services – and joined the like-minded Spanish dictator, General Francisco Franco. Skorzeny set himself up as an agent for
various Spanish arms companies, most notably ALFA. Mertins was in
contact with him in 1954 to discuss a potential arms deal that Skorzeny
was negotiating with Nasser.

While it is unlikely that Mertins was 'at the right hand' of King Farouk,
as he boasted in a rare 1968 interview,[14] he was certainly less ideologically
disposed towards Nasser, especially when the Egyptian Prime Minister
moved towards the Soviets for support. Mertins left his Egyptian posting
but remained active in the Middle East during the mid-1950s. He trained
parachute regiments in Syria and worked as a sales agent for a number of
German firms throughout the region. His most notorious employer was a
company run by one Herbert Quandt, for whom Mertins sold Mercedes-
Benz vehicles in the Middle East, most notably 500 'wine-red' cars to the
officer corps of Saudi Arabia.[15] Quandt, who had served in the same parachute regiment as Mertins, also had impeccable Nazi credentials: his
mother, Magda, had married Joseph Goebbels, Hitler's Minister of Propaganda, and committed suicide in the presence of Hitler in the Führer's
bunker as the war came to an end.[16]

As a result of his activities in the region, Mertins was considered a
potentially useful intelligence asset. He was approached by US Army
Intelligence during the mid-1950s and immediately put on the payroll.
His job was to provide his new friends with information about the Middle
East gleaned from his work as a salesman.[17] It was the first time, but certainly not the last, that Mertins made money from his relationship with
intelligence services.

Mertins returned to Germany in the late 1950s, and attempted unsuccessfully to rejoin the German army. However, his disappointment was soon
forgotten in the excitement of a lucrative offer: Reinhard Gehlen asked

Mertins to act as the middleman for German arms sales to the Third World. Gehlen would assist Mertins with intelligence about potential clients and help him to arrange the necessary papers – end-user certificates and export licences which are essential to any arms deal.[18]

Germany at the time was hoping to remilitarize. The thinking was that in addition to using arms to peddle influence, selling its old surplus stock would raise much-needed money for new arms purchases. For this purpose, in 1963 Mertins established a new company, Merex, which was jointly based in Bonn and Vevey in Switzerland.[19] He suggested that the name had been intended as a contraction of Mercedes-Export, despite the fact that it was 'not connected with the car company'.[20] Humility might have prevented him admitting that it could as easily be a syncopation of Mertins-Export.

The company boss soon forged a crucial new contact to add to his large intelligence network. In 1965, Merex was hired as the German sales agent for Interarms, the International Armament Corporation run by the infamous Sam Cummings, who was sometimes referred to as the 'new Zaharoff' and delighted in pointing out that his house in Monte Carlo was close to the former Zaharoff home.[21] Cummings had served as a Lieutenant with US Army Secret Services during the Second World War, after which he was recruited as an undercover agent for the CIA with responsibility to buy up surplus German weapons on the black market.[22] He had formed Interarms in 1953 at the tender age of twenty-six and proceeded to make a fortune with help from the CIA. In 1954, he undertook his first major CIA-sponsored mission, to supply arms to a right-wing coup in Guatemala. Three years later Interarms supplied weapons to the forces of Fidel Castro in Cuba – a transaction sanctioned by the CIA.[23] It was believed that by supplying Castro with arms, the US may have been able to keep the bearded revolutionary onside: a spectacular, if not uncommon, case of misplaced strategic thinking and blowback.

Together, Mertins and Cummings were a formidable arms-dealing force. In 1965 they worked together to sell seventy-four US-made F-86 fighter planes to Venezuela, fifty-four of which were surplus German stock and a further twenty procured from active Luftwaffe service.[24] It was a hugely profitable deal. The planes from German surplus stock were bought at a price of $46,400 each and sold to the Venezuelan air force for $141,000 per plane, netting a total profit of $6.926m, which Cummings claimed was transferred in its entirety to Mertins.[25] The deal was riven with corruption.[26]

The following year, Merex sealed a series of controversial deals that would almost spell an end to Mertins's nascent career as an arms dealer. Zaharoff-like, he sold fighter planes to both sides in South Asia, one of the world's less stable regions at the time. The first involved the sale of ninety F-86 aircraft to Pakistan, once again raised from surplus German stock. At the time Pakistan was a no-sale zone, embargoed by NATO because of its simmering conflict with India. The required subterfuge was undertaken with the help of the Shah of Iran, who allowed the planes to be delivered to Tehran by Luftwaffe officers and then flown to Pakistan by Iranian pilots dressed up as Pakistani officers.[27]

Mertins sold the weapons to Pakistan even though Merex had a standing order with India. In August 1965, India had placed an order with the company for twenty-eight Seahawk MK 100s and 101s, old sub-sonic jets that had been used by the Luftwaffe and were now considered surplus. When the India–Pakistan war erupted that year both countries were embargoed. But in June 1966 Mertins was given the go-ahead by German authorities to sell the planes to a company in Italy. He leased a ship, the *Billetal*, to transport his cargo. It set sail from the tiny German port of Nordenham, and once in the Mediterranean passed straight through Italian territorial waters, and wound its way down the Suez Canal and landed in India.[28] Purchased for a reported $625,000 by Merex, the jets were sold for $875,000, raising a profit of around DM 5m.[29]

At precisely the same time that the *Billetal* was carrying cargo for Merex to India, its sister ship, the *Werretal*, was on its way to Pakistan, traversing much the same route in order to deliver Cobra anti-tank rockets sold to Pakistan by Merex.[30] The *Werretal* made a second delivery on the same trip, docking in Iran, where the ship disgorged its cargo of missiles, cannons, machine guns and other matériel. An Iranian end-user certificate, signed by the country's envoy to Germany, gave the deal legitimacy. But, as with the Pakistan deal, the cargo was instead rerouted to Saudi Arabia – a country with whom Germany had severed diplomatic ties a year previously.[31] This time the cargo was valued at DM 12.58m.[32]

Mertins's duplicitous adventures were leaked to the media. An intensive campaign in Swiss newspapers persuaded Mertins that he was no longer welcome in the country.[33] The news was also met with outrage in the US, as the planes sold to Pakistan were ex-US stock given to Germany after the war. As often happens in such deals, the providing country retains the right to veto any deal to sell the weaponry on. Selling to Pakistan during a period of conflict was a violation of US and international law. Congressional hearings were held under the chairmanship of Senator Stuart Symington. Mertins was not called, but instead met Symington privately. But Sam Cummings was forced to appear before the assembled politicians, where he confirmed Symington's astonishing finding that 'our own intelligence services knew exactly at that time that these F-86s were meant for Pakistan'.[34]

As Congress was holding hearings into the Pakistan deal, the FBI was investigating whether Merex should be registered as an agent of the West German government. After considerable paperwork had been collected indicating that Merex was in constant contact with the US Departments of State and Defense, Army Intelligence intervened to ensure that the company was not registered as an agent, lest it lose its secrecy and anonymity: 'The Army has opposed registration of Merex or Mertins (as a former agent) on any basis which could jeopardize [their] continued use.'[35]

With US Army Intelligence in his corner, Mertins decided to establish an American branch. Merex Corporation was set up in a home in Bethesda, Maryland, just north of Washington DC. In an interview granted as the hearings into his South Asian activities were taking place, Mertins indicated his closeness to the US establishment, by referring openly to Henry J. Kuss – the man who approved or rejected the sale of surplus weapons gifted by the US – by his first name.[36] Unfazed by possibly negative press, Mertins distributed Merex memorial calendars, replete with stirring pictures of heavily armed soldiers entering combat, reflecting the experiences of both the 'new' and the 'old' Germany.[37]

The opening of the US branch was the final nail in the coffin of the brief but profitable relationship between Mertins and Sam Cummings, which had begun to sour after the Pakistan deal became public. Previously, Interarms had acted as Mertins's agent in the US, but this was no longer necessary. They relinquished their agency commitments to each other and engaged in some less than flattering portrayals to the press. Mertins was often quoted belittling Cummings's legendary self-aggrandizement: 'I know him. He's Cassius Clay – the greatest! I've heard it all. He's a *scrap dealer!* He keeps files the way he learned as a corporal. Merex is not on the level of scrap!'[38] Ironically, when Mertins lost his sympathetic contacts with the German establishment, Cummings was the one to take advantage, signing a joint agency deal with Mertins's replacement, a company led by a former Nazi Lieutenant General, Gerhard Engel, who had served as Hitler's adjutant.[39]

Mertins installed a close friend, Gerard Bausch, as the CEO and president of the company, although Merex Corp remained entirely owned by the European business. Bausch, who had initially run the company from his basement, came with his own very useful connections. Much like Mertins he had carved a useful niche for himself in the operations of German Intelligence. In 1962, on Reinhard Gehlen's instructions, he was named station chief in Mertins's old stomping ground, Cairo. He was briefly arrested in 1965, suspected of involvement in a plot with Wolfgang Lotz, a joint German–Israeli agent, who was discovered forwarding information to Mossad from Egyptian generals unhappy with Nasser, while also sending letter bombs to German scientists who were working with the Egyptian ruler. Bausch was eventually freed after three trips to Egypt by Hans-Heinrich Worgitzky, the Vice-President of German Intelligence.[40]

Even with Bausch's connections, Mertins's relationship with German Intelligence cooled after the Pakistan deal, for which he eventually faced criminal charges. It hardly helped that at around the same time Mertins also completed the sale of 6 million rounds of ammunition to the Nigerian government, soon after West Germany had officially stopped supplying the country after a military takeover.[41] Nigeria was increasingly moving towards the Soviets, who would supply arms without fuss,[42] so Mertins was providing ammunition to a Soviet-linked state in defiance of his own government.

With his German government links in a fragile state, Mertins began to pursue other avenues and continents in search of new sales. In some cases he was helped by connections to US Intelligence. In 1972, for example, just over a decade after leaving Egypt because of political differences, Mertins was called in by General Sadiq, a trusted lieutenant of the new Egyptian leader, Anwar Sadat. The Egyptians were frustrated by the slow pace with which Soviet supplies had been delivered. At a meeting with Mertins in Egypt, General Sadiq asked the weapons dealer to sound out US officials as to whether they would be willing to step into the breach if the Soviets were expelled. Also on the table was a potential deal for bridging equipment supplied by Merex.[43]

But it was in South America where Mertins was able to secure most of his new deals, using, once again, his enduring Nazi connections. In Peru Mertins appointed Commercial Agricola as Merex's local representative in the country.[44] The company was run by Fritz Schwend, who, during the Second World War, had been part of Operation Bernhard, a madcap scheme to undermine the British economy by flooding the UK market with masses of counterfeit pounds.[45] Schwend had, like many Nazis, escaped post-war justice and settled in Peru. He and Mertins were assisted by Otto Skorzeny. Skorzeny struck up a close relationship with Peruvian Intelligence, which led to a request for M14 tanks.[46]

Mertins's South American network included other, even more extreme, Nazis, such as Hans Rudel and Klaus Barbie.[47] A fanatical right-winger, Rudel frequently travelled to Germany in the early 1950s to speak at the behest of the Freikorps, of which he was 'patron'.[48] The Freikorps was 'the most flagrantly nationalistic right-wing organization in Western Germany since the Nazi Party . . . adher[ing] closely to the policies of the Nazi regime, even to advocating return to a dictatorship'.[49]

But the most notorious of Mertins's South American cabal was Klaus Barbie, nicknamed the 'Butcher of Lyon', and a close friend of Fritz Schwend. Barbie personally oversaw the torture and killing of 4,000 residents of occupied Lyons during the war, including a group of Jewish orphans he had ferried to concentration camps. After the war Barbie worked for US Intelligence before settling in Bolivia. In fact, the US aided his move to South America after French authorities had discovered his whereabouts. Barbie's depraved skills proved useful to Bolivia's military dictators. During the reign of Hugo Panzer, Barbie was hired to set up internment camps for political opponents, where torture and executions were common. Usefully for Mertins, Barbie also became the dictatorship's official weapons-purchasing agent. In February 1968, Schwend wrote to Mertins to inform him that Barbie's company, Transmaritima, was looking to buy used ships for the Bolivian navy. Although it is unclear whether the deal took place, Mertins certainly intended to help; the request to speak to Barbie was forwarded to Merex's 'Naval Department'.[50]

Mertins's deepest and most profitable connection in South America was with Chile. Merex first entered the Chilean market in 1971 when

Gerard Bausch travelled to the country to sell $800,000 of bridles and sad-
dles to the Chilean cavalry, as well as 20,000 rounds of ammunition.[51]*
Their point-man was an influential and ambitious General, Augusto Pinochet, who took power in an infamous coup two years later, supported
by the US and in which the democratically elected President, Salvador
Allende, was either murdered or compelled to commit suicide. Mertins
was delighted that the country was in the hands of a virulently anti-
communist strongman and frequently travelled to Chile, where he
witnessed Pinochet's propensity for violence and torture. During these
visits Mertins often stayed at Colonia Dignidad, a German community
camp based in the southern Andes. He was so impressed with the colony
that he formed the Circle of Friends in Germany to raise funds for it.[52]

    Colonia Dignidad was no ordinary community. It was formed in 1961
by yet another ex-Nazi, Paul Schäfer, a German priest who had fled his
home country after being accused of child molestation. The camp was
heavily fortified, watched over by guard towers and protected by barbed
wire, as much to keep residents in as visitors out. The community mixed
bizarre social values – autarky and a German agrarian lifestyle from the
1930s – with the fervour of a self-styled militia. When Colonia Dignidad
was eventually closed down at gunpoint after Pinochet's overthrow, a
massive weapons cache was discovered which included private handguns,
grenade launchers and a buried tank. A secret warren of tunnels had been
constructed under the colony, featuring torture rooms allegedly designed
by Michael Townley, a CIA operative who worked closely with the
Chilean Secret Police (DINA).[53] DINA, which maintained regular radio
contact with Colonia Dignidad, used the rooms to torture political
opponents, often 'to the strains of Wagner and Mozart'.[54] The well-
stocked facility was also alleged to be a laboratory for the development
and testing of biological weapons, which may have been used on those
tortured. When the colony was finally raided, it was clear that Schäfer
also engaged in the ritual molestation of young boys forced to stay at
Colonia Dignidad, a charge on which he was found guilty *in absentia* by
Chilean courts in 2004.[55]

---

* The deal signalled the end of the Bausch–Mertins relationship, as Bausch felt
Mertins did not give him a fair share of the commission on the sale, a common complaint throughout Mertins's career.

During the late 1960s and early 1970s, Mertins also pursued deals in East Asia. US Senate hearings in 1978 heard that the company provided price lists to a notorious South Korean businessman, Tongsun Park, who was accused of inappropriately buying influence in the US Congress in the 1970s.[56] In 2005, Park was alleged to have been involved in the Iraq Oil-for-Food scandal. Two years later he was sentenced to five years in prison for his role in attempting to bribe UN officials at the behest of Saddam Hussein.[57] In 1972, Mertins entered into a long-lasting relationship with the Chinese military parastatal NORINCO, a relationship that also involved Saddam.

With deals stretching from South America to Asia, the late 1960s and early 1970s were the 'salad days' of Merex and Gerhard Mertins.[58]

The good times didn't last. Mertins's cachet stemmed from his Intelligence connections in Germany and then the US. In the early 1970s, he worked as an agent for the Field Activities Command (USAFAC), an Army-run espionage unit whose brief was to collect human intelligence – what people are doing, and why – from around the world. Mertins frequently upset his handlers, often selling to countries that were considered, at the very least, anti-American. His relationship with US Intelligence ended in 1972 during the Vietnam War, after he had barged his way into US military headquarters in Saigon, announced he was with American Intelligence and demanded to see the officer in charge.[59] His bombast and indiscretion had gone too far. Mertins was dismissed as a USAFAC operative. Refusing to accept his dismissal, Mertins took the unprecedented step of taking USAFAC to court. The proceedings were declared classified, but because of the scare with Mertins it was decided to disband the unit altogether.

Mertins's star was also waning in Germany. The media, still outraged at his involvement in sales to Pakistan, intensified their coverage of the arms dealer after the District Attorney decided to prosecute Merex for breaking German export laws and falsifying documents. Also accused with Mertins were his business partners, Gunter Laurisch, a former Nazi parachutist who had served under Mertins, Karl von Brackel, a Luftwaffe member, and Heinz Hambrusch, an Austrian gun-maker who also served as a Merex sales agent. The legal proceedings marked a slump in the company's profitability until the early 1980s. Indeed, after the trial concluded,

'Mertins [was] a broken man, [claiming] he only contravened a few laws because his government had told him to.' The once brash arms dealer appeared 'tired and tousled'.[60]

His defence team claimed that his dealings in Pakistan were at the explicit behest of the German government. Mertins explained his relationship to the German Intelligence network, BND, and the judge found little to discredit his evidence, especially after a BND operative testified that the government was almost always aware of what Mertins had done in Pakistan,[61] as part of a project codenamed Uranus.[62] At the end of 1975, Mertins was eventually cleared of any technical wrongdoing in the Pakistan deals, even though he had provided weapons to both sides of the conflict in contravention of the law. But Mertins was nothing if not combative: feeling that his name had been ruined by the trial, he took the German government to court, requesting financial relief. He did so partly out of pride but primarily out of financial necessity. By 1977, Mertins was so strapped for cash that his estate in the Rhine was seized.[63] Merex financial statements from the time read like a disaster story: by 1980, the company had costs of DM 8.2m, but only DM 1m in holdings and a paltry DM 500,000 in turnover.[64] This second trial provided some relief for Mertins, who received DM 5m in compensation, although he had requested DM 12m.

The latter part of the 1970s was a fight for survival for Mertins, who became even less discriminating in his selection of customers. He was an example of blowback writ large, working for both sides in the Cold War battle of ideologies. By the early 1980s, he had, remarkably, again ingratiated himself with US Intelligence structures, this time working with the CIA. He befriended James Atwood, an American with strong CIA links who was regarded as an oddball small-arms dealer. Atwood was a minor celebrity in neo-Nazi circles as a result of his book *The Daggers and Edged Swords of Hitler's Germany*. By the mid-1980s, Atwood and Mertins shared office space in the US and worked together on a deal, in September 1986, that supplied weapons to the Nicaraguan Contras as part of the Iran–Contra affair.

Iran–Contra was the highly controversial and illegal arrangement whereby the Americans sold weapons to Iran – then run by the Islamic regime of Ayatollah Khomeini and subject to a US arms embargo – and used the proceeds to fund right-wing Nicaraguan rebels who were fighting to overthrow the left-wing Sandinista government. It was a disastrous operation undertaken by Colonel Oliver North and conceived at the highest levels of the Reagan administration. Vice President George H. W. Bush played a leading role, along with his Saudi Arabian friend, Prince Bandar, the Israelis, and a host of unscrupulous arms dealers, in the debacle that ultimately armed the same Iran that is today regarded as the US and Israel's most implacable foe.

Merex's role in Iran–Contra was to sort out one of the many potentially embarrassing foul-ups in the affair. Oliver North's front company, Enterprise, had purchased $2.2m of illicit arms from Monzer Al-Kassar, a prominent and controversial arms dealer known as the Prince of Marbella, using money raised from selling arms to Iran. While the weapons were en route from communist Poland, where they had been purchased, to Portugal, US authorities lifted the arms embargo on the Nicaraguan Contras, leaving Enterprise with a huge cache of overpriced weapons. To save face, Mertins and Atwood interceded on behalf of Enterprise and convinced the CIA to purchase the weapons. Helmut Mertins, the son of Gerhard, was duly sent to Portugal to clean up the mess. He contracted another ship and oversaw the transfer of the weapons to a CIA depot in the US from where they were reportedly transferred on to the Contras.[65]

At much the same time as Mertins was working with the CIA to assist the Contras, he was also developing a relationship with China. As noted earlier, Merex had had contact with the Chinese military parastatal NORINCO as early as 1972, providing it with invaluable access to Western arms and intelligence networks.[66] As a consequence, Mertins was on good terms with the head of NORINCO, Zhao Fei. Chinese authorities coveted a powerful and accurate 120mm cannon produced by the huge German conglomerate Rheinmetall. Mertins acquired the plans of the cannon and provided them to NORINCO.[67] Such are the morals of the arms dealer: developed and nurtured by German Intelligence as the arms dealer of choice for shadowy transactions, Mertins was willing, only a decade later, to undermine the military capacity of his fatherland so as to support communist China.

Mertins's correspondence with Zhao Fei made clear that Merex had engaged in arms deals with China that flew in the face of US policy, despite his connections to American Intelligence. The correspondence also revealed that Saddam Hussein was a potential Merex customer only two years before the Iran–Contra scandal, in the middle of the Iran–Iraq War.

In one throwaway line in a letter from Mertins to Fei, the German reported that 'we have contacted Saddam Hussein and pointed out again the quality of Chinese military production'.[68]

Mertins's relationship with Zhao Fei had become public as a result of another questionable transaction. In 1982, the US company Fairchild Weston retained the services of Merex to help sell its products in China. One item in particular caught the attention of the Chinese: a long-range spy camera known as the LORAP. NORINCO decided to buy two of the cameras at a price of $20m. The US Department of Defense was concerned that the cameras would greatly enhance Chinese intelligence capacity. They suggested that 'due to technology involved, advance in intelligence-gathering capability and resultant threat to US allies, we would recommend denial'.[69] Reagan administration officials disagreed. The Pentagon was overruled and the NORINCO deal given the green light. Mertins was nevertheless angry, believing that he had been sold short on his commission on the deal. Fairchild Weston objected, claiming that Mertins had been more of a hindrance than a help in the transaction. Mertins sued the company, with the German's claims overturned on appeal. The arms dealer would never see any money from the project.

His double-dealing, constant deception and lack of loyalty not only to a country or ideology, but even to his closest partners, were proving the undoing of Gerhard Mertins. But Merex would continue to prosper in the depths of the shadow world.

SECTION II
Nice Work If You Can Get It

3. The Saudi Connection

The Prime Minister curtsied so low she was almost squatting. Margaret Thatcher, the Iron Lady of whom Prince Bandar once said: 'that woman was a hell of a man', did not take kindly to subservience. But on arriving in Saudi Arabia, where women are not allowed to drive let alone participate in politics, she was more than happy to supplicate before the Saudi royal family. After all, they were about to save the newly privatized BAE from financial collapse, with the biggest arms deal of all time.

Signed in 1985, the Al Yamamah deal netted British companies, predominantly BAE, over £43bn for the supply and support of 96 Panavia Tornado ground attack aircraft, 24 Air Defence Variants (ADVs), 50 BAE Hawk and 50 Pilatus PC-9 aircraft, specialized naval vessels, missiles, shells, support services and various infrastructure works. In return the Saudis would supply 400,000 barrels of oil per day.[1] In later years, the quantities of matériel and oil would both increase.*

Britain was awarded the deal not because of the superiority of its products but because the US Congress, under pressure from the powerful Israel lobby, would not agree to the sale of the F-15 fighter jets that the Saudis wanted. But France almost trumped the British. Throughout 1984 and 1985 it appeared France's Mirage 2000 fighter had won out against the UK's bid on the grounds of cost and earlier delivery. Michael Heseltine, the British Defence Minister, was dispatched to Riyadh to push the UK's case. However, France's more amenable foreign policy approach in the Middle East had swayed King Fahd, who gave Heseltine a rough reception.[2] The French jet had already been successfully sold to Greece, India and Abu Dhabi and had the great advantage of being 25–30 per cent

---

* The deal was a government-to-government agreement between the UK and Saudi Arabia, but it was BAE, along with its subcontractors Rolls-Royce, Plessey, Ferranti, GEC and Dowty, who would supply the arms and BP and Shell were the recipients of the oil.

cheaper than the Tornado.[3] President Mitterrand had lobbied Crown Prince Abdullah in a meeting in February 1985 and by March the French deal was said to be near completion.[4] It was thought at the time that the Saudis still hoped to convince the Americans to sell them F-15s and were using progress on the French deal to pressure the US.[5] But April came and it was clear that the F-15s would not be sold.[6]

Where Heseltine failed to charm, Thatcher succeeded. The Prime Minister interrupted a holiday in Salzburg in Austria to hold talks with Prince Bandar.[7] The charismatic, dashing Saudi operator presented Mrs Thatcher with a letter from King Fahd containing a formal request for the Tornado purchase. Thatcher's immediate response was 'You have a deal.' Bandar claims the conversation lasted no more than twenty-five minutes, the easiest arms deal he ever clinched.[8] Exactly what was offered to secure the deal is still hotly debated.

The first Al Yamamah contract was formally signed in Lancaster House on 25 September 1985, for 132 military aircraft. Michael Heseltine and Prince Sultan, the Saudi Defence Minister, were the signatories. The French expressed shock at losing out, telling the *Observer* with typical Gallic understatement that it was 'unexpected, incomprehensible and catastrophic', and asserting that 'this brutal change [was] of a political nature'.[9] They may have been referring to the suspicion of bribes, or that the US administration, not able to supply their own F-15s, pushed the Saudis towards their loyal ally. A British 'aviation official' opined that 'the American Jewish lobby has done us a favour'.[10]

Industry experts suggest that the Tornado might have been the better strategic option for the Saudis, as it is both an interceptor and strike fighter, whereas the Mirage lacked the same strike capability.[11] However, the equipment offered was far from state of the art. So bad were the reliability issues with British aircraft in previous deals, especially, as we've seen, Lightning jets unsuited to the desert environment, that engineers working at the Dhahran airbase were known to joke that the only Tornado they could keep in the air was the one mounted on a plinth outside the main gate.[12]

Under the terms of the contract, BP and Shell processed and sold the oil that was used as payment for the aircraft. The proceeds were deposited, less a fee, into a Ministry of Defence account at the Bank of England, from which BAE would be paid. The deal was to prove the company's lifeline for decades to come.*

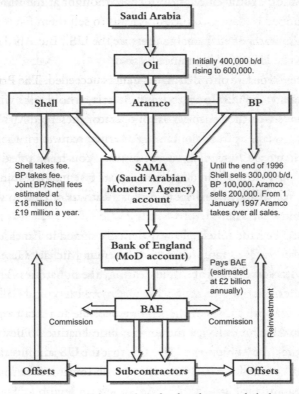

Figure 1: Payment chain for the Al Yamamah deal

In July 1988, a second phase of Al Yamamah was announced. Al Yamamah-2 was estimated to be worth up to £10bn.[13] It included 48 Tornadoes, along with the weapons and spares required, 60 Hawk jets, 88 Westland helicopters – mainly Black Hawks – 6 Sandown class minesweepers, a few BAE 125 and 146 aircraft for communications, the construction of an airbase – though this was later dropped – and facilities

* British civil servants from the Defence Export Services Organisation (Deso), paid out of the Saudi funds, were to administer the deal. Even up to 2008, over 100 civil servants and a similar number of military personnel were paid £41.8m in that financial year by this foreign government. (CAAT, information from Freedom of Information request dated 15 July 2009, quoted at http://www.caat.org.uk/campaigns/controlBAE/.)

for the minesweepers, as well as training for the Air Force and Navy. The deal was signed on 3 July 1988 by Prince Sultan and the UK's Defence Secretary, George Younger. Margaret Thatcher was again involved in the negotiations.[14]

The continuation of Al Yamamah was a clear indication of Saudi frustration with the US attitude to arms exports to the country. In the years between the two phases of the deal, the Saudis had several large arms purchases blocked by the US Congress. Had Congress not refused them, BAE would not have won the contracts. As one Saudi official put it: 'We would prefer buying weapons from the USA. American technology is generally superior. But we are not going to pay billions of dollars to be insulted. We are not masochists.'[15] In May 1986, Congress had overwhelmingly opposed the sale of missiles to Saudi Arabia. With more than a two-thirds majority against the sale, the pro-Saudi President Reagan was unable to use his veto. The vote reflected both the power of the Israel lobby and scepticism over Saudi support for the US following an American air strike on Libya, with some US politicians fearing Saudi Arabia might divert weapons to 'terrorists'.[16]

Payments for both phases of the deal were affected by a fall in the price of oil by 1989 which meant that the 400,000 barrels a day would be insufficient to pay for the equipment. The falling oil price also precipitated a budget crisis in Saudi Arabia. Unwilling to borrow substantially from abroad, the Saudis' profligate arms spending was under threat. Some of the equipment bought under the first phase of Al Yamamah was intended to be sold on to Iraq but the end of the Iran–Iraq War in 1988 left the Saudis without a buyer.[17] However, their insatiable desire for weapons, and the accompanying bribes, motivated the Saudis to make a cash payment of £1.3bn and increase the flow of oil by an additional 100,000 barrels a day.[18]

The use of oil as the medium of exchange for the Al Yamamah contracts made bribes easier to hide, allowed Saudi Arabia to bypass OPEC's restrictive quota guidelines and enabled the Saudi Ministry of Defence to continue to purchase weapons with no scrutiny.[19] Tony Edwards, the head of Deso from 1998 to 2002, admitted that 'for the Saudis the use of oil meant that the contract was effectively an off-balance-sheet transaction: it did not go through the Saudi treasury'.[20] Chas Freeman, a former US ambassador in Riyadh, described the mechanism whereby the oil companies paid the proceeds from the sale of the Al Yamamah oil into a bank account administered by the UK MoD, with BAE the custodian, as 'a general slush fund for the Saudi Ministry of Defence. They could debit anything they wanted against this account and BAE would do the procurement. And it was not subject to public scrutiny in either country. It was off budget and because it was out of sight, it was peculiarly susceptible to corruption.'[21]

The Iraqi invasion of Kuwait in August 1990, accompanied by a huge American airlift to protect Saudi Arabia from Saddam's aggression, changed the political dynamic towards the Arab nation in the US. In no small part due to Prince Bandar's tireless diplomatic efforts and legendarily generous schmoozing, the desert kingdom was once again seen as a crucial guardian of Western interests in the region.* This shift made it easier for the US to supply its Saudi ally directly rather than have the UK do it for them. The perceived superior quality of US equipment, battle-tested in the Middle East environment, contrasted with the poor reliability of BAE's Tornado jets.[22] In fact, the US was forced to fly extra sorties to cover for the Tornadoes incapacitated by sand and a radar fault which required the manual tracking of targets using stopwatches.[23] Dick Cheney, then US Defense Secretary, promised Saudi Arabia a wealth of new military equipment previously disallowed by Congress, on the basis that 'the situation in the Gulf region has changed dramatically'.[24]

However, in September 1990 Prince Bandar made clear that 'we have no intention of scaling down our British purchases. If anything, we might be looking for more co-operation with our friends in Europe, including Britain, and for more equipment to equip our armed forces.'[25] This reduced Saudi dependency on US supplies in what remained a volatile political environment. In 1991, Bandar announced that the kingdom would conclude deals for the equipment still outstanding from the Al Yamamah-2 deal. Despite the evidence to the contrary, Bandar praised the British equipment for its performance during the First Gulf War, saying: 'We are very pleased with the performance of the Tornado in the Gulf War. When we first ordered the fighter in 1985 we needed strike capability and it proved itself during the conflict. We are also grateful for the support shown to our country by Mrs Thatcher and for the continued support from

* Of course, schmoozing aside, the US–Saudi relationship was fundamentally founded on the Saudis' access to one third of the Middle East's oil reserves.

Mr Major.'[26] The Al Yamamah deal in its entirety would eventually be worth over £43bn to BAE.[27]

While the second part of the deal included an offset component, investment was limited and the jobs created never rose above the hundreds.[28] One of the stranger spin-offs of the deal was the appearance of the England football team in the kingdom in November 1988, to play a friendly international. They were flown on a Concorde jet chartered by BAE and 'topped up with the company's officials, customers and clients'. The Football Association's chief executive, Graham Kelly, announced that 'The FA are more than happy to assist the government to fulfil its obligation to Saudi Arabia.'[29]

On the British side, BAE's Richard (Dick) Evans was almost as crucial as Margaret Thatcher. The bluff, pugnacious, Blackpool-born salesman was prepared to go to any lengths to win the Al Yamamah contract, including 'swallowing sheep's eyeballs as if they were canapés' to ingratiate himself to the Saudis.[30] Evans had started work at the Ministry of Transport in 1960, before moving on to the Ministry of Technology. He soon entered the revolving door between government and the private sector when he joined the defence electronics company Ferranti, in 1967, as a government contracts officer. Two years later he joined BAC, one of the companies merged to create BAE, rising to become commercial director for the Warton Division of BAE in 1978. In 1983, Evans was appointed deputy managing director for BAE Warton.

Evans's career was made when he was posted to Saudi Arabia as head of operations, making him the point-man when it came to negotiating the Al Yamamah deal. His vast network of contacts in the kingdom was the stuff of legend. The success of the deal led to his appointment as chief executive of BAE in 1990, and he became chairman in 1998. During his reign, a City analyst commented that 'BAE is run by a "mafia", that Dick is the head and that they are a law unto themselves'.[31] A former employee suggested that 'he is a very affable guy and is very well liked . . . but there's a ruthless side – you need to count your fingers after you have shaken hands with him'.[32]

But the real star of the Al Yamamah show was Prince Bandar bin Sultan. As his name implies, Bandar is the son of Prince Sultan, the Saudi Defence Minister, Crown Prince and heir-apparent to the throne if his health holds. Bandar was born in March 1949 to a sixteen-year-old servant named Khizaran. Sometimes described as a family slave, Bandar has referred to his mother as a concubine.[33] Though under sharia law all sons are born equal, Bandar has always seen himself as an outsider, the illegitimate child among his thirty-two half-brothers and half-sisters. As a young boy he had very little contact with his father, living instead with his mother and aunt. Fortunately for the young Bandar his grandmother, Princess Hussa, the influential favourite wife of King Abdul Aziz, took a shine to him, brought him to live with her and persuaded Prince Sultan to recognize his illegitimate son.[34] So when Bandar was aged eleven he and his mother moved into the palace with his grandmother,[35] a development he described as 'a practical decision, but it completely altered my life'.[36] Prior to his arrival at the palace his was a relatively simple childhood spent playing barefoot in Riyadh's dirt streets, making his own toys in a house that was only partially electrified.[37] This has led the flamboyant and now very wealthy royal to describe himself as the 'peasant prince'.[38]

Bandar attended school at the Institute of Riyadh, rather than following many family members to Eton, in what might have been a reflection of his lower status.* In his semi-authorized, sometimes hagiographic biography of Bandar, the writer William Simpson quotes a school friend, now General, Mifgai, saying of Bandar: 'he had a superb academic record. He was also a very popular student . . . charming, outgoing, and was fun to be around. He was a mature, placid, and well-balanced young man. He was slow to anger and never lost his temper, choosing instead to ignore someone and walk away.'[39]

A combination of being around military men from when his father was made Defence Minister in 1962, the mood of patriotism sweeping the Saudi royal family during their intervention on behalf of the royalists in the Yemeni civil war and a desire to impress his father motivated Bandar to pursue the prestigious career of a fighter pilot. He said of his choice: 'When you're flying an airplane, it doesn't matter who you are. An airplane doesn't know if you're Prince Bandar or no. Either you know what you're doing or you don't. If you know, you live; if you don't, you kill yourself.'[40]

Bandar faked his age on the application to gain entrance to the Royal Air Force College at Cranwell in England.[41] Prince Sultan bought his son

---

* Interestingly three of Bandar's sons have been sent to Eton.

a white Mercedes for his English sojourn, which Bandar promptly crashed. He replaced it with an Aston Martin, which he would drive to London at the weekend and if stopped would show a Saudi driving licence and claim diplomatic immunity. Bandar's training sergeant recounts that 'he had a drawer for parking tickets picked up in London, which were never paid, and he had a set of CD plates [*Corps Diplomatique*] which he used to stick on the car for weekends'.[42]

There were differing opinions of the Prince's flying prowess. On the one hand he flew solo for the first time after only nine hours' training, but a fellow pilot and friend John Waterfall bluntly opined that 'he was pretty shit at Cranwell'.[43] In one incident, Bandar joined the airfield circuit in the wrong direction, flying against the flow of the other air traffic. His flying instructor, Tony Yule, reported: 'Sultan flies with spirit and enthusiasm. He has had a problem in the circuit, but was coping quite well by the end of the course.'[44]

After graduating from Cranwell in 1969 Bandar joined the Royal Saudi Air Force as a Second Lieutenant stationed at Dhahran, where he was trained by American instructors under the Peace Hawk training programme.[45] He was complemented for his charisma and leadership as a company commander. Unlike other royalty in the military, Bandar preferred to use his rank of Captain or Major, rather than being addressed as 'Prince'. He only started using his title again when he became ambassador to the US.[46] Despite this supposed humility, Bandar maintained his status by insisting that all his fellow pilots stand when he entered a room.[47] In 1970, he trained in the US, spending time in Texas, South Carolina and Arizona for training on the F-102 and the F-5A/B fighter aircraft that were being brought into the Saudi Air Force.[48]

On his first day in America, while changing planes in Dallas, Bandar encountered a rowdy group of American football players from the Dallas Cowboys. Though the players were attracting a lot of attention in the airport terminal, what really caught Bandar's eye were the 'magnificent' cheerleaders. From that day on Bandar was an avid Cowboys fan, a fixture at their home matches as a guest of the owner, before he bought himself a $500,000-a-year private box. He is so well known to the team's players that they refer to him simply as 'the prince'. In turn, Bandar describes himself as 'their number one international cheerleader'.[49]

In 1972, stationed again in Saudi Arabia as an F-5 pilot, Bandar married

Princess Haifa bint Faisal bin Abdul Aziz Al-Saud. Princess Haifa is one of the daughters of the then ruler, King Faisal. The following year, with the outbreak of the Yom Kippur War, Bandar was part of a group of pilots ordered to attack Israeli oil and refinery installations near the Jordanian border. Expectations were that as many as nine out of ten pilots could be killed on the mission. Bandar recalls: 'We had got as far as the end of the runway preparing to launch; it was the real attack when we received [an] eleventh-hour reprieve.' Henry Kissinger had negotiated a ceasefire that may well have saved Bandar's life.[50] The Prince and his wife returned to the US in 1974 so that the pilot could undergo training on the new F-5E aircraft. Over the next few years he trained pilots on the new jet in Saudi Arabia.

Prince Bandar's success as a pilot, a trainer and a commander of pilots clearly pleased him. A biographer observed that 'it really appealed to [his] ego and self-satisfaction' to know that he could fly a hundred feet above the ground, roll the aircraft 360 degrees and not kill himself.[51] In 1977, his passion for stunt flying almost proved his undoing as his landing gear failed at an air show in Abha, south-west Saudi Arabia. Rather than eject as he had been trained to do, the Prince attempted to land the plane on its belly. He hit the runway hard, seriously injuring his back, a lifelong problem that would eventually end his flying career.

In April 1978, Bandar, then twenty-nine and still focused on his Air Force career, was travelling back to Saudi Arabia from California when he stopped overnight in Washington DC. Crossing the lobby of the fashionable Madison Hotel, a favourite haunt of wealthy Saudis only five minutes' walk from the White House, he ran into his brother-in-law, Prince Turki al-Faisal.[52] Once Bandar had explained that he was homeward bound from an Air Force mission, Turki responded: 'you know, you came to me from heaven. I need you.' At the time, Turki was leading the lobbying effort to persuade the US to sell sixty F-15 fighter jets to the kingdom. Bandar was taken upstairs to a room full of American advisers and PR experts, who bombarded the young Air Force Major with questions about Saudi Arabia's military need for the F-15. He responded that the fighter was essential to protect oil infrastructure and the holy sites of Mecca and Medina, as well as to counter the threat from Marxist South Yemen. He adroitly dodged questions about the fighter being a threat to Israel, avoiding any mention of the deployment of jets at the Tabuk base within reach of the Jewish state.

Bandar so impressed Turki and the American advisers that he was asked to stay on. The following day he was taken to see Senators John Glenn and Barry Goldwater, two key members of the Senate Armed Forces Committee and former pilots, who were favourable to the sale of the jets. He then met with Senators Frank Church and Jacob Javits, who were opposed to the sale. Bandar found traipsing from one office to another answering mostly hostile questions 'boring work' and wanted to go home to his wife.[53] However, Turki called Crown Prince Fahd, asking for Bandar to stay on. Fahd agreed and when Turki passed on the royal order, Bandar simply didn't believe him and responded: 'No, thank you. I've stayed two days to help you as a friend and colleague.' He headed to Paris to join his wife but the next day received a phone call from Crown Prince Fahd, ordering him to 'report to the White House' to help win the vote on the F-15 sale.[54] Bandar had only been to the White House as a tourist in 1973 while stationed in Alabama. On this occasion, 'I went to the White House, and Hamilton Jordan [Chief of Staff] took me in to see President Carter. Suddenly, there I was sitting in the Chief of Staff's office, and they take me to the Oval Office. I left really in a daze.'[55]

Bandar was needed because legislation passed in 1974 required the support of Congress for all arms sales over $25m, with thirty days' advance notice. While the administration's priority lay in securing the country's oil supply through as close an alliance as possible with Saudi Arabia, the powerful pro-Israel lobby led by the American Israel Public Affairs Committee (AIPAC) was highly active in lobbying against arms sales to hostile, or potentially hostile, Arab nations. AIPAC literature described the F-15 as 'the most advanced air-superiority fighter in the world', claiming the aircraft would enable the Saudis to 'strike deep into Israel'.[56] The Carter administration had inherited President Ford's secret 1976 commitment to sell Saudi Arabia the F-15s to replace the ageing British Lightning interceptors and renewed the pledge during a visit by Crown Prince Fahd to Washington in May 1977.

The original informal deal was to sell sixty F-15s to Saudi Arabia, balanced by the sale of seventy-five F-16s to Israel and fifty F-5s to Egypt. Congress was only notified of the deal on 18 April 1978, setting the thirty-day clock ticking as Bandar was ordered to lead the lobbying effort. The Saudis had employed a selection of experienced US political advisers, including Frederick Dutton, who had been President Kennedy's Special

Assistant for Intergovernmental Affairs and Assistant Secretary of State for Congressional Affairs; John West, a former Governor of South Carolina and Carter's ambassador to Riyadh; and David Long, a State Department Middle East specialist and professor of International Affairs.[57] Dutton would remain a close companion and political adviser to Bandar for the next twenty-seven years, earning the nickname 'Fred of Arabia' among the Washington Press Corps. Dutton's wife, Nancy, undertook legal work for the Saudi foreign ministry in Washington at the time and was still working as the Saudi embassy's legal adviser in late 2007.[58]

Bandar quickly learned the Washington lobbying game. His ambition was to adopt the tactics of the hugely successful AIPAC, to create a rival Arab lobby.[59] The difficulty of Bandar's task was made clear by a study carried out by Carter's staff indicating that AIPAC could count on 65–75 votes in the Senate whenever needed. Bandar – whom John West, the ambassador to Riyadh, described as 'the best thing that happened to the F-15 fight'[60] – set about building a constituency for the sale. The Saudis decided to communicate personally with as many AIPAC-supporting Senators as possible and contacted McDonnell Douglas (since merged with Boeing), which made the F-15, and many other contractors, subcontractors and labour unions to lobby Congress in favour of the sale. Bandar was the PR pointman to the media, members of Congress and influence peddlers.

As part of the lobbying effort Bandar visited the former Republican Governor Ronald Reagan, then plotting his presidential bid. He had no idea who Reagan was, which highly amused Carter. They hoped Reagan might support the sale, persuading fellow Republicans on the basis of Saudi Arabia's strong anti-communist credentials. Bandar contacted Thomas Jones, the chairman of the F-5's maker, Northrop Grumman, and a close friend of Reagan's, and was soon invited to see the Governor in California. As Bandar tells it:

> I sat down with Governor Reagan, and we chatted a little bit. Then I explained why we needed the aircraft. He said to me at the end of it, 'Prince, let me ask you this question. Does this country consider itself a friend of America?' I said, 'Yes, since King Abdulaziz, my grandfather, and President Roosevelt met. Until now, we are very close friends.' Then Reagan asked a second question. 'Are you anticommunist?' I said, 'Mr. Governor, we are the only country in the world that not only does not have relationships

with communists, but when a communist comes in an airplane in transit, we don't allow him to get out of the airplane at our airport.'[61]

Bandar says he was expecting a long discussion about the sale but 'That was it. Two things were important. Are you friends of ours? Are you anticommunist? When I said yes to both, he said, "I will support it."' Bandar then asked Reagan to voice his support to a reporter from the *Los Angeles Times* whom Dutton had tipped off. According to Bandar, the reporter asked: 'Do you support the sale of the F-15s to Saudi Arabia that President Carter is proposing?' Reagan responded: 'Oh yes, we support our friends and they should have the F-15s. But I disagree with him [Carter] on everything else.'[62]

While campaigning, Bandar also met Senator Russell Long, the powerful Chairman of the Finance Committee and son of the notoriously corrupt Senator and Governor of Louisiana, Huey Long. Bandar was surprised when Long asked to have the meeting with no aides present. As soon as they were alone the Senator said: 'You want my vote, don't you?' 'Yes,' responded Bandar. 'It will cost you ten million,' said Long, putting an arm around Bandar and easing him into a chair. 'Did I shock you?' asked the Senator, before explaining that the money wasn't for himself but for a bank in Louisiana that was a major backer of his re-election campaign. In order to be certified to transact abroad the bank required a $10m foreign deposit. Bandar agreed to ask the Saudi government. It is unknown whether the transfer was made. Long voted in favour of the F-15 sale and was re-elected but died in 2003 without confirming the story.[63]

The vote was won 55–44 by the Saudis, with the sale authorized on 15 May. John West praised Bandar for his 'boundless energy' and 'utter politeness and courtesy' in his dealings with members of Congress. He told Crown Prince Fahd that 'Prince Bandar evinced such enviable maturity as to rank him among prominent international statesmen and diplomats.'[64] While Bandar certainly galvanized the Saudi intervention, it would have been largely irrelevant without President Carter's personal lobbying effort, along with many members of his Cabinet.

After the F-15 campaign Bandar returned to Saudi Arabia and his duties in the Air Force. He maintained his friendship with John West, with whom he would often discuss US politics and the Middle East peace process.

In autumn 1978, Carter and Crown Prince Fahd used Bandar to ferry messages between Washington and Riyadh. In the first instance they concerned the relationship between Saudi Arabia and Anwar Sadat, the Egyptian President ostracized in the Arab world after his Camp David peace deal with the Israelis. The offer was rejected by Fahd, who responded: 'We will sort out our problems with Egypt directly, not with you.'[65] But Bandar had been initiated into the craft of secret diplomacy and had developed a closer relationship with his uncle, the Saudi heir. Before long Fahd, who was the *de facto* ruler, made Bandar his personal ambassador to Washington.

The Prince returned to the US as an Air Force officer in 1979, initially to Maxwell Air Force Training School in Alabama. But John West and David Long arranged a special programme for Bandar at Johns Hopkins University in Washington.[66] A memorandum from May 1979 showed that Long was acting 'with the encouragement' of the White House Chief of Staff, Hamilton Jordan, and the Secretary of State, Cyrus Vance.[67] The special programme allowed Bandar to commute twice a month from Alabama to undertake one-to-one tutorials with professors who were paid extra for the sessions. He took courses in international economics and politics, leading to a masters degree in International Public Policy with a thesis on the domestic origins of US foreign policy, on which he almost certainly received help from Fred Dutton.[68]

President Carter's re-election campaign in 1979 commenced amid spiralling global oil prices. With Bandar's help, Carter drafted a letter to Fahd requesting Saudi Arabia to put more oil on the market.[69] Fahd responded: 'Tell my friend, the president of the United States of America, when they need our help, they will not be disappointed.'[70] He promised to do 'anything in his power externally or internally to ensure your re-election', since this was 'essential if there was ever to be a just and lasting peace in the Middle East'.[71] This assistance, which saw Saudi oil trading $4–5 a day below other suppliers, cost the kingdom $30m to $40m a day. In gratitude, Carter invited Bandar to the White House in early December 1979, where they discussed Middle East politics and the US–Saudi relationship.

With Carter's earlier request for Saudi–Egyptian rapprochement still in mind, Bandar took it upon himself to meet the then Egyptian Vice-President, Hosni Mubarak, in Washington DC in November 1979. Bandar

had neither the permission of the Saudi government nor prior authorization from Fahd, although the Crown Prince approved the continuation of
the initiative after the meeting.[72] Bandar's idea was for Carter to ask Fahd
to write a conciliatory letter to Sadat, which would be delivered in person
in Washington when the Egyptian President was meeting with Israel's
Menachem Begin and Carter. Fahd initially hesitated but then wrote the
letter just in time, allowing Bandar to walk into the meeting between
Carter and Sadat and present it. Bandar had, however, altered Fahd's letter to make it more conciliatory. He defended his actions audaciously,
claiming: 'I knew what Fahd wanted to say, and needed to say, so I translated it that way.'[73] Bandar's high-risk creative diplomacy failed in this
instance, as Egyptian–Saudi reconciliation remained elusive. But it revealed
a great deal about the intermediary.

In 1980, Saudi Arabia's dependence on the US increased further when
the kingdom's woeful human rights record and unequal, sometimes violent, treatment of women was highlighted by the broadcast of *Death of a
Princess* in the UK. The film dramatized the story of a young princess from
a fictitious Middle Eastern Islamic nation and her lover who had been publicly executed for adultery. It was widely believed to be based on the tragic
story of Princess Misha'al bint Fahd al Saud, grandniece of King Khalid.
Princess Misha'al had been shot dead, kneeling on the ground of a Jeddah
car park in 1977 and her Lebanese boyfriend, Khalid Mulhalal, beheaded.
The Saudi royal family attempted to cover up the deaths, claiming the
Princess had died in a 'swimming pool accident'.[74] The airing of the drama
incensed the Saudis, casting an icy chill on UK–Saudi relations and leaving
the Saudis few alternatives to the US for their defence needs.

The Saudis were keen to purchase aerial refuelling tankers from the
Americans to extend the capabilities of their F-15 fighters. However, the
effort was stymied by an AIPAC-organized letter signed by seventy Senators. The outbreak of the Iran–Iraq War in 1980 changed the situation. In
response to Saudi concern that the conflict could spread towards their
country, and with Bandar again acting as intermediary, the ambassador,
John West, asked Prince Sultan if the Saudis 'wanted equipment such as
AWACS and an anti-aircraft Hawk missile battery'.[75] The exchange initiated an epic battle that would dominate the early days of the Reagan era.

AWACS was the most sophisticated control, command and surveillance
system yet developed. No non-NATO country had access to it, not even

Israel. The system is essentially a military aircraft based on a Boeing 707 jet with a distinctive radome over its fuselage. Bandar arranged for the top Saudi brass to be taken up in the aircraft, convinced that once they experienced it, there would be no talking them out of it. 'Like selling them a new car.'[76] The Carter administration, though not yet willing to sell the AWACS system, did send four manned AWACS to Saudi Arabia as a show of commitment to Saudi security. A potential diplomatic storm about whether Saudi Arabia requested the aircraft or the US offered them was averted by Bandar, who suggested that the press releases in Arabic and English provide different versions of the story. The gesture so pleased Fahd that he was willing to approve 'just about everything' the Pentagon requested in Saudi Arabia – pre-positioning of war matériel, joint military planning and access to Saudi bases for the AWACS. Apparently both Fahd and Prince Abdullah, at the time commander of the National Guard, travelled to Mecca to offer special prayers for Carter's re-election.[77]

Their prayers were in vain as Ronald Reagan swept to power in the 1980 election. As the only Saudi royal to have met Reagan, Bandar was chosen to make first contact with the new President. When the Secretary of State, Alexander Haig Jr, visited Saudi Arabia in April 1981 to drum up support for the anti-communist crusade, he was told that the Saudis' key concerns were the Palestinian issue and the acquisition of the AWACS system. While discussing the problem of getting the sale past Congress, Haig suggested that 'maybe Prince Bandar could come back and help with Congress'. Fahd agreed.[78] Bandar was now officially the chief Saudi lobbyist with a royal mandate.

The Reagan administration believed that the AWACS sale 'was important to strengthen ties with this relatively moderate Arab country, not only because its oil exports were essential to our economy, but because, like Israel, it wanted to resist Soviet expansionism in the region'.[79] But Israel clearly felt that the arms sale threatened it, not only because the AWACS system would enable the Saudis to track Israeli military movements, but also because Reagan intended to include upgrades to the F-15 that would enhance the fighter, making it capable of strike missions against Israel. This ensured that Congressional debate on the sale was dragged out for nine months.[80] The outcome was always going to be close. Fred Dutton, Bandar's adviser, came up with the crude slogan for the campaign, 'Reagan or Begin'. It proved apposite as the Israeli Prime Minister, Menachem

Begin, made life difficult for the Israel lobby. First he ordered the bombing of the Osirak nuclear reactor in Iraq without informing the Reagan administration beforehand. And then, after being asked by the new President not to lobby on the AWACS deal when he visited the US during debate on the issue, he proceeded to do just that outside the White House gates.

Bandar was again the point-man on the deal, still only thirty-two and not even an accredited diplomat. *Newsweek* described how he had 'dazzled senators with his grave wit and charm'. The Prince had taken up regular squash matches with General David Jones, the Chairman of the Joint Chiefs of Staff, and took to mimicking aerial dogfights with John Glenn, a Democratic Senator and former pilot and astronaut, as if they were 'old pilot buddies'.[81] He became closely acquainted with James Baker III, Reagan's Chief of Staff who would one day be President George H. W. Bush's Secretary of State, and at one point was involved in negotiating between King Khalid and President Reagan about the type of compromises that might secure the sale.[82] A compromise was eventually struck to sell the AWACS on the condition that there would be sharing of information with the US, and various safeguards were included to prevent third parties from accessing the system. The deal, together with other initiatives to extend its military influence in the region, would culminate in the US using the kingdom as a launching pad for the First Gulf War.

Soon after the successful AWACS sale Bandar was named Defence Attaché to the Saudi embassy in Washington DC. While the job was usually the kiss of death for a military career, Bandar took the assignment to be a test of his abilities on the part of King Khalid.[83] He undertook his new role just as Israel began its massive invasion of Lebanon, hoping to drive out the PLO and eliminate Yasser Arafat. A week after the invasion King Khalid died, to be succeeded by Bandar's uncle and mentor, King Fahd, in June 1982. Bandar claims that, at the time, he was at the centre of negotiations to allow the PLO to evacuate Lebanon, though neither Reagan nor his two Secretaries of State give the Saudi more than a passing mention in their recollection of the events. Whatever his role in this instance, it was hardly a surprise when on 24 October 1983 Prince Bandar was made the Saudi ambassador to the United States.

As the new emissary was presenting his credentials, President Reagan cut him short. 'You know something? You came a long way. When I first met you, you were a young major in your air force. And now, you are an ambassador of your country to the United States of America.' Bandar responded: 'Well, Mr. President, you didn't do too shabbily yourself. When I first met you, you were an unemployed governor, and now you're president of the greatest country in the world.'[84]

Bandar had such regular access to the Reagan White House that, at one point, the Israeli ambassador to Washington complained.[85] The Saudi would prove to be of great value to the Reagan administration, believing that by assisting the administration internationally and domestically he could act as a counterweight to the powerful Israel lobby.

An opportunity soon arose to demonstrate his worth in the Iran–Contra scandal. As mentioned, in 1984, despite Congressional rulings forbidding the US government from providing material support to the right-wing Nicaraguan Contras, President Reagan and his National Security Planning Group were committed to aiding the rebels in order to prevent the spread of communism in Central America. Reagan directed his National Security Advisor, Robert McFarlane, to 'keep the Contras together body and soul'. In essence, the proceeds of illegal weapons sales to Iran through Israel – which broke US law and undermined America's own campaign to cut off arms sales to the Khomeini regime – were used to fund the Contras.

This complex arrangement took time to implement. In the interim, after Congress withdrew funding from the Contras, McFarlane asked Prince Bandar to make up the shortfall. After meeting with McFarlane and the Defense Secretary, Caspar Weinberger, Bandar ensured that the Contras received $1m a month from mid-1984. At a breakfast meeting with Reagan in early 1985 King Fahd offered to double the remittances. Over time, the Saudis gave $32m to the Contras.[86] The routing of this money was linked to the AWACS sale in that a fund was created from the sale, from which the Contras' monthly money was diverted.[87]

Bandar would say later: 'I didn't give a damn about the Contras – I didn't even know where Nicaragua was.'[88] This support was the Saudi way of investing in America, the ultimate aim being a Saudi–American alignment to compete with Israel's relationship with the US.[89] The strategy was further oiled by the Saudis' legendary schmoozing. King Fahd, as confirmation of his support for the American cause, lavished Arabian horses and diamonds worth $2m on the President and First Lady. Bandar was inventive in ensuring that the gifts became the personal property of the first couple rather than, as protocol demanded, being accepted and registered on behalf of the American people. Bandar, who was particularly close to Nancy, helped the family in countless ways. When Nancy asked him to employ Michael Deaver, the powerful Deputy Chief of Staff to the President who was leaving the White House broke, with legal problems and drinking heavily, Bandar hired him as a consultant for $50,000 a month, even though he had absolutely no contact with him throughout the year that he was on the payroll.[90]

Given Saudi willingness to provide covert assistance on Iran–Contra, Caspar Weinberger attempted to hide their involvement when the scandal was investigated by Congress.[91] On 31 July 1987, Weinberger was questioned about a conversation he had with the CIA's Director, William Casey, at their weekly breakfast meeting, in which it was mentioned, and memo'd, that Prince Bandar had earmarked $25m for the Contras in $5m increments. Weinberger suffered severe memory loss throughout the hearings, claiming he couldn't remember saying it. General John (Jack) Vessey, Chairman of the Joint Chiefs of Staff at the time, contradicted the Secretary, confirming that Weinberger had ensured $25m for the Contras. In addition, Vessey revealed in a 1992 interview with counsel in the investigation that Bandar had twice told him about his contribution. One of the conversations took place in a White House meeting on 25 May 1984 about the AWACS sale at which Robert McFarlane was present.[92] It transpired that Weinberger kept diary entries of a number of these conversations and had noted at least sixty-four contacts with Bandar, including sixteen meetings at the Pentagon.[93]

The Secretary of Defense was indicted for perjury and obstruction of justice but given a presidential pardon by George H. W. Bush in 1992. Bandar also denied involvement, claiming in a 21 October 1986 press release that 'Saudi Arabia is not and has not been involved either directly or indirectly in any military or other support activity of any kind for or in connection with any group or groups concerned with Nicaragua.' When his lies were revealed Bandar defended the actions, claiming that they 'broke no US law per se'.[94] This was yet another lie, as Congress had explicitly prohibited soliciting donations for the Contras from other countries. Casey had effectively used the Saudis as proxies to do what Congress had banned. Though the evidence led to senior officials including Weinberger and the notorious Colonel Oliver North, Casey was careful to protect himself by never discussing the matter with the Saudis. Bandar also avoided a banking paper trail by flying to Switzerland to have his own bank transfer money into Cayman Island accounts, en route to the Contras.[95] The Prince, who had diplomatic immunity, refused throughout to cooperate with investigators. Revealing his cavalier attitude to the truth, Bandar voiced his disappointment at the exposure of the Saudi role to McFarlane: 'I don't care what the truth is: if you're going to tell some story, let's tell it together. If it's a lie, then let's lie together.'[96]

The Saudis also funded Jonas Savimbi's brutal UNITA forces in Angola, who, with the substantial backing of the nearby apartheid regime, were trying to overthrow the communist MPLA government. A Palestinian-American businessman, Sam Bamieh, testified before the US House Subcommittee on African Affairs that he had met Fahd in 1981 and was told by the then Crown Prince that if they received the AWACS the Saudis would be willing to fund 'anti-communist movements around the world'.[97] Bamieh testified that Bandar was put in charge of making it happen. He and Bandar, therefore, met in February 1984 in Cannes, France, to discuss setting up a shell company to funnel money to the Angolan rebels and to Afghanistan. Bandar told Bamieh that, as they were meeting, Casey and Fahd were discussing the same issue aboard the royal yacht. Bamieh claimed the Saudis had provided over $50m, through Morocco, to fund the Angolan rebels.

Bandar's next covert mission allegedly came at the request of William Wilson, the US ambassador to the Vatican and a close friend of Reagan. According to one account, Bandar was asked to provide and deliver $2m to the Italian Christian Democratic Party to help prevent the feared victory of the communists in the 1985 elections.[98] The Saudi 'donation' was packed in a suitcase with which Bandar then supposedly flew to Rome in a private Airbus. He personally took it in a Saudi diplomatic car to the Vatican Bank, where a priest came to the bottom of the stairs to take delivery of the suitcase, without a question being asked. The Vatican distributed the money to the Christian Democrats, who ultimately triumphed at the polls by 4 per cent of the vote.[99] The veracity of this account is difficult to discern as it has only been told to four people, three at the *Washington Post* and William Simpson. The ambassador, Wilson, denied all knowledge of the events, saying that if it happened 'it sure took place without my knowledge'.[100] Simpson claims the plan was cooked up by Reagan, Fahd and Thatcher, and Bandar's involvement was so that 'it was done with a deniability factor, because you would never see American fingerprints – or the British – on it. The money didn't come from them. They didn't authorize it through Congress or Parliament. Everybody could say, "I had nothing to do with that; it's nothing to do with me", but yet that's the way things got done . . . This was a classic example of how strategic cooperation took place between Reagan, Fahd and Thatcher in many, many ways.'[101]

Had Bandar become a bagman for the Pope? If there is any truth to the story it would render deeply hypocritical Bandar's court statement in 1993 when he sued the *Guardian* newspaper for libel, after the paper claimed in error that he had secretly made donations to the Conservative Party. Bandar told the court that the mere idea that he should seek to influence an election in another country caused him extreme 'embarrassment and distress'.[102]

On 8 March 1985, a massive car bomb exploded outside a mosque near the apartment of Sheikh Mohammed Hussein Fadlallah, the spiritual leader of the newly formed Hezbollah. It killed eight people and injured at least 200 more. Many of the victims were worshippers leaving the mosque. Fadlallah was unharmed. The acclaimed *Washington Post* reporter Bob Woodward claims that William Casey and Prince Bandar had conspired to carry out the attempted assassination, hiring a former British commando, who was paid $3m by Bandar.[103] The Saudi strenuously denied the accusation, which Woodward repeated in a 2001 *Frontline* programme. The reporter claims that during 'a stroll in the garden' at Bandar's residence in McLean, Virginia, he and William Casey agreed that the Saudis would 'put up the money to hire some professionals to go and try to car-bomb Sheikh Fadlallah'. Casey said the operation would be 'off the books' so that not even Reagan would know about it.[104] Supposedly, exposure of the abortive operation cost Bandar the job he wanted in Riyadh at the time, as National Security Adviser.[105] Bandar steadfastly maintained that allegations of Saudi involvement in the attempt on Fadlallah's life were completely without foundation and he stated explicitly that he played no role in the endeavour.[106]

The Saudis spent several billion dollars on arms and economic assistance for the war in Afghanistan against the Soviets, and worked with the CIA to fund Afghan madrassas in the 1980s.[107] Prince Bandar claims that he also played an essential role in convincing President Gorbachev to withdraw

from Afghanistan. On a visit to Moscow in 1988 Gorbachev told the Prince
that the Russians knew the Saudis had been providing $200m every year to
the *mujahideen*. Bandar responded: 'You are absolutely wrong, Mr. President. We are paying five hundred million, not two hundred million, and
we're willing to pay a billion if you don't get out of Afghanistan.'[108] Bandar
suggests that Gorbachev almost immediately agreed to leave Afghanistan
by the following March. Whatever the truth of the content of the discussions, Bandar came away with a remarkable souvenir, a photo of Gorbachev
and Reagan with the words 'Trust But Verify' written on it, a favourite
phrase of Reagan's. Gorbachev gave Bandar one of only fifty copies of the
photo in existence. The next time Bandar saw Reagan the Saudi asked:
'Why do you think he gave it to me, Mr. President?' 'What did he tell
you?' asked Reagan. 'He said, "I want you to know I'm a friend of your
friend, too."' Reagan then wrote on the photograph: 'Prince Bandar,
Trust But Verify'. When Bandar next met Gorbachev a few years later he
too wrote on the picture in Russian: '*Doverey no Proverey*'. Bandar kept this
photo on prominent display in his office for many years.[109]

Prince Bandar has the ability to charm the powerful and his country's
money with which to buy friendship and influence. He is comfortable
and inventive at circumventing laws and restrictions and has on occasions
appeared to be loose with the truth. This made him the ideal person to
negotiate the world's ultimate arms deal.

As Bandar has said, Mrs Thatcher was very accommodating of the
Saudis' weapons needs. While the US option was not open to them and
the French had done themselves a disservice by purchasing more Iranian
oil, another factor that influenced the Saudi decision to buy British was
the most base of all: money. The deal is probably the most corrupt transaction in arms-trading history, with Bandar, Thatcher's son and many
others implicated in receiving payments on an epic scale.

As Bandar recalled to Nihad Ghadry, a former adviser to the Saudi
royal family: 'I told her [Mrs Thatcher] that this deal is between us directly, between the two countries. It should go no further. Whatever is
related to us is our concern and no one else's . . . I also told her that we are
a royal family and around us are a lot of people and a lot of responsibilities. My conversation with Mrs. Thatcher ended with her understanding
what I meant.'[110]

4. In Defence of Humanity

The fall of the Berlin Wall in 1989 led to a major change in the way arms dealers did business around the world. Rather than reflecting 'an end to history' and thus conflict, as the US model of market-led democracy was embraced globally, the post-Cold War world was wracked by ever more complex armed conflicts. The collapse of the support that had sustained many of the world's less stable regimes on the basis of their affiliation to the US or the Soviets prefigured a massive outbreak in conflict between ethnic, intra-state and non-state actors. Disparate groups emerged within countries or without any national affiliation in the case of religious extremism, seeking power or to cause maximum disruption for a diversity of reasons – the promise of ethnic utopia, economic advantage or religious expression. For the smaller arms dealers operating in the shadows, these new clients were fertile ground.

Merex for one was quickly able to move into these new markets, taking advantage of the explosion of civil wars and ethnic conflicts across a number of continents. The company expanded its reach exponentially, running a raft of notorious sales agents, including the likes of the Liberian brothers Charles and Bob Taylor. It profited from some of the most notorious conflicts of the next decade and a half, including the civil wars in Yugoslavia and Liberia/Sierra Leone and the US invasion of Iraq. In so doing, Merex was connected into a vast, international network of arms dealers, revolutionaries, despots, charlatans, warmongers, religious extremists, torturers, sanctions busters, money launderers, shady intelligence operatives and opportunistic entrepreneurs, all of them operating wherever there was enough chaos to turn a profit. This anarchic labyrinth was the shadow world in the new global reality.

In 1990, Merex restructured to deal with legal and financial difficulties and to prepare for a profitable existence in the new world. In a significant move, Joe der Hovsepian was brought in as a partner. A self-proclaimed 'citizen of the globe',[1] der Hovsepian is of Armenian and Lebanese origin with strong links to Germany, Italy, Switzerland and France.

I met him in Amman, Jordan, in May 2010. His office, on Mecca Street, all glass and dark wood, is decorated with posters of guns and other weaponry. Der Hovsepian is an imposing man. His craggy face reflects his cosmopolitan origins: Teutonic and Middle Eastern features, a trim Germanic moustache below a bulbous red nose. The large black Stetson and cowboy boots make him appear even taller than he is.

Garrulous, charming, sometimes brusque, der Hovsepian described his early career: the son of a Legionnaire father and a Lebanese mother, he had travelled the globe, always in military circles. Following his father's military instincts, he joined the Lebanese army, where he trained as a fighter pilot, including at bases in the US. His own adventurous spirit, and marital ties to one of Lebanon's pre-eminent families, saw the young Joe quickly attain the rank of Colonel – an appellation by which he was to become known in arms-dealing circles.

By 1978 der Hovsepian had left the Lebanese armed forces and opened a rifle and sports shooting store in Bonn – the home town of the former Nazi and Merex founder, Gerhard Mertins. And by the early eighties, he had started to work with Mertins as an arms dealer.[2] Der Hovsepian was initially vague about the work he and Merex undertook for much of the 1980s, but it was clear that he was often in the loop about what Mertins was up to – not least because the two lived on the same property. Mertins had used his considerable windfall from his trial against the German intelligence agency, the BND, to purchase a massive chicken farm and estate in Thomasberg, a district of Königswinter across the Rhine from Bonn. Der Hovsepian suggested that Mertins had used his substantial government connections to increase the value of his property by persuading the German Department of Foreign Affairs, for whom his niece's husband worked, to build an office complex on a plot next to his.

As Mertins was often cash-strapped during the 1980s, he sometimes paid those who undertook work for him with small slices of land from the Thomasberg estate. Der Hovsepian was one such recipient, living on the property along with Mertins and a hodgepodge of contacts that the German had developed. Der Hovsepian now claims that Mertins swindled him out of nearly $3m: instead of paying der Hovsepian for services rendered, Mertins offered him a prime piece of the Thomasberg estate for redevelopment. When developed, it was assumed, its value would sky-rocket. There was only one problem that Mertins kept to himself:

planning regulations specifically forbade any building on der Hovsepian's newly acquired land. This was one of a litany of instances in which der Hovsepian claims Mertins cheated him out of money.

When der Hovsepian became a partner in Merex in 1990, the company was floundering. Financial reports from the time suggest a rapid increase in costs amid falling income, a downswing in fortunes that almost eradicated the gains of its halcyon days.[3] For salvation Mertins turned to a long-time partner, Saudi Arabia. The Saudis were looking to purchase Leopard tanks (known as Leos) from Germany. Mertins, with his government connections, was willing to undertake the deal, for which Saudi Arabia agreed to pay him DM 16m to DM 17m, enough to stave off bankruptcy. The Thomasberg property was raised as collateral against the cash advance. This unusual arrangement was negotiated by Mertins's friend Prince Turki al-Faisal, brother of the Minister of Foreign Affairs, brother-in-law of Prince Bandar, son of the late King Faisal and, at the time of the deal, director of the Al Mukhabarat, the Saudi intelligence agency. The contracts were, therefore, signed in the name of Turki's assistant, Ahmed Badeeb, and Gerhard Mertins.

Mertins's key government contact on the deal was a controversial Bavarian politician and former Defence Minister, Franz Josef Strauss. Embroiled in the Lockheed bribery scandals in the early 1960s, among others (see Chapter 12), Strauss was described by Joe as 'very corrupt', perhaps explaining his willingness to engage with Mertins and Merex. However, the Bavarian leader died unexpectedly while out hunting in 1988. So Mertins was unable to deliver the Leos for which he had already been paid. Refusing to return the money and unable to supply the tanks, Mertins had only one option – to close down the company and reopen a new incarnation.

The restructuring of Merex was also motivated by Mertins's advanced age – he would die in 1993. So the new company, named Deutsche Merex, was structured to reflect Mertins's declining role. After some horse-trading, in 1992 the new company's ownership was split equally between der Hovsepian and Mertins's sons Helmut and Joerg Thomas (known as 'JT'). One per cent of the company remained in the hands of the US Merex Corp, which, at the time, was still headed by Gerhard Mertins.[4]

Other parts of the Merex network mutated into bizarre forms. One, Merex AG, was cannibalized into a company running a hotel and sports centre in Gut Buschhof, a suburb of Königswinter, suggesting that some members of the Mertins clan may have been seeking a line of work less stressful than arms dealing.[5] Soon after Gut Buschhof was formed, and after Mertins's death in 1993, Thomasberg Hotel und Sportanlagen was established to run the centre.[6] Officially, the director of the company was Ahmed Badeeb, Prince Turki's assistant.

Deeply embedded in Saudi Arabian intelligence services, Badeeb had a relatively unremarkable career until the Soviet invasion of Afghanistan in the 1980s. As a biology teacher working under the Saudi Ministry of Education, Badeeb's most famous pupil was Osama bin Laden. Badeeb befriended his student, whose family was from the same area of Yemen as his own.[7] He rose through the ranks of the Saudi civil service and was, by his mid-thirties, Chief of Staff to Prince Turki al-Faisal. The assassination of Prince Turki's father, King Faisal – by his half-brother's son – didn't affect Turki's upward trajectory, which culminated in his appointment as head of the Al Mukhabarat, a post he held for the next two decades.[8] He was the ambassador to the United Kingdom from 2003 to 2005 before briefly being made Saudi ambassador to the US to replace Prince Bandar, a post he held from July 2005 to December 2006.[9]

Badeeb, in his role as right-hand man to one of the most powerful intelligence figures in the desert kingdom, was often sent to mediate with important intelligence allies, arranging arms deals and cash drop-offs. In one deal Badeeb travelled to Pakistan, where he met with the military ruler, President Zia. Sent by Prince Turki with a considerable amount of cash, Badeeb informed his Pakistani hosts that Saudi Arabia was willing to fund the purchase of a range of high-precision rockets from Chinese suppliers. His handlers, scarcely believing the offer, pried open Badeeb's suitcase to confirm the generous bounty, while he was speaking with President Zia.[10] Badeeb was also active in Afghanistan, shepherding the relationship between his homeland and the *mujahideen* fighters. It is assumed that Badeeb took ownership of the Thomasberg estate in lieu of the money owed to the Saudis for Mertins's failed Leo contract.

While it may have seemed strange to retain the Merex name, given the company's difficulties, in some ways Deutsche Merex had cachet. According to der Hovsepian, the German and neo-Nazi connections won over Arab customers, some of whom believed that 'if Hitler had finished off the Jews they wouldn't have all the problems they have today [with

Israel]'.[11] Der Hovsepian didn't shrink from capitalizing on this tortured logic, greeting Arab clients with a nonchalant 'Walaikum Salaam, wie gehts dir?' This may be the gimmick he alludes to when suggesting that 'to be successful [in arms dealing] you need a good gimmick, good quality equipment and you must not cheat a client'.[12] As important, and part of the reason so many dealers are gregarious, larger-than-life characters, is an ability to foster close relationships with those in power, something der Hovsepian has done with aplomb in Saudi Arabia, where the new Merex secured its first major deal.

In August 1990, Saddam Hussein, fresh from his bruising decade-long conflict with Iran, launched an invasion of Kuwait. The Saudis were deeply worried, especially at the prospective use of biological and chemical weapons by Saddam. Merex was approached to arrange the purchase of a million gas masks. For such a massive deal der Hovsepian required discreet assistance, so he recalled the Mertins brothers from the US. After patching together multiple suppliers, der Hovsepian was able to secure the consignment, personally flying the gas masks into Saudi Arabia. It was a lucrative contract, by der Hovsepian's own account worth $126m. As further reward for his rapid delivery, the arms dealer was awarded an official citation by the Saudi government.

Der Hovsepian was nevertheless scathing about the 'special' costs of doing business with the Saudis. Using a glass on his desk, he described the process to me: 'They are very greedy. You always have to pay bribes. If they want to buy this glass you tell them it's five dollars. They will beat you down to one dollar, then they will say, "OK I will give you $3, but you give me $2 back!"' Der Hovsepian claims that on his Saudi deals he has to give more than half of the contract price back in bribes. The local Saudi embassy military attaché always signs the receipts. 'Money is paid to them in Germany and the kick-back is transferred to the local military attaché and he transfers it to the princes.' He concluded: 'Not a piece of equipment would go from the US to Saudi without Bandar getting a commission.'[13]

Merex and der Hovsepian were prominent players in the Balkans as Yugoslavia collapsed in the wake of the Cold War. In June 1991, the country began to unravel as Slovenia declared its independence from the union, followed shortly by Croatia and Macedonia. It was the first act in a brutal four-year war of startling complexity, seared into the memory by the ethnic cleansing of Bosnian Muslims by the Serbs.

With arms embargoes quickly imposed on the region, each side had to scramble for whatever arms they could find – a veritable feast for daring arms dealers. Croatia, seeing the likelihood of war, started to equip itself as early as January 1991. An Italian, Lorenzo Mazzega, was ideally placed to help Croatia restock. At the time he was based in the Croatian city of Zara, where he had established useful links to the Croatian leadership.[14] Mazzega's reputation preceded him, at least as far as Franco Giorgi, an Italian born in 1943 who had travelled to Libya in 1975 to work – as what, he would not explain. In 1979, Libyan authorities decided he was a security risk who was spying for Israel. Following an eight-month incarceration he 'turned', now providing intelligence for Libyan authorities on figures in Italy and elsewhere. By 1990, he had returned to Italy, to his wife who ran a store in Venice, where Giorgi met a number of his contacts.[15] He had heard, via a business acquaintance, that Mazzega was able to trade weapons freely throughout Eastern Europe through his company Venimpex. After being introduced through a mutual acquaintance in Venice, Giorgi travelled to Zara to discuss business.[16] His objective: to sell arms and supplies to Croatia on behalf of Merex. Mazzega would later recall that Giorgi claimed that he 'represented Merex in Italy, Croatia and Eastern European countries . . . He also showed me a Merex catalogue. He was in Zara because Merex produced police equipment – binoculars, bullet-proof jackets, radios and so on.'[17] As a result of their meeting Merex did indeed secure a deal in Croatia, the order emanating from a company in Zara for which Mazzega was acting as a consultant. Giorgi duly approached der Hovsepian with the details of the deal. Der Hovsepian, despite initial scepticism, agreed to participate.

What the Croatian authorities needed – and fast – was ammunition – roughly a million dollars' worth. Der Hovsepian turned to a long-time acquaintance, Eli Wazan, to help him secure the supplies. Wazan was a successful arms dealer in his own right, having acted as an equipment purchaser for Christian militias in Lebanon during the early 1980s. In the mid-1980s, after developing useful connections with Israeli intelligence, Wazan went into business for himself, dealing in weapons in East Beirut. He also rose to the position of Honorary Consul in Lebanon, which conferred useful diplomatic privileges. One of Wazan's best suppliers was the

South African parastatal Armscor, which was established by the apartheid government following the imposition of a mandatory UN arms embargo on the country – an embargo that also outlawed any Armscor sales abroad. Fed huge sums of money, Armscor turned into an industrial behemoth, churning out supplies needed by the apartheid government to undertake its reign of terror internally and throughout sub-Saharan Africa. To solicit its foreign sales, which were needed to subsidize domestic production, Armscor often relied on a web of dubious middlemen and agents. Wazan was one of their favourites, having worked with the company since 1983. By 1990, he had been appointed an 'exclusive agent' for Armscor.[18]

To secure the ammunition for Croatia, der Hovsepian and Wazan would need to break the UN arms embargo against South Africa. Fearful that German authorities would be alerted to the deal if it was done through Merex, der Hovsepian decided to conduct it through his sister company, Intersystems Beirut, even though he had met with Giorgi to discuss the deal in Germany – in itself an illegal act. Der Hovsepian and Wazan had to mislead South African officials too. At the time, a South African Cabinet injunction prevented Armscor from selling to any former Yugoslavian country.[19] Sales to Lebanon, however, were not barred. So Wazan lied that the Armscor stock would be delivered to the Lebanese Christian militia, landing and unloading in Beirut.[20] In reality the weapons freighted aboard the ship *Anke* were destined for Croatia, where they arrived in March 1991 to the immense relief of Croatian authorities.[21] While the equipment cost just over $1m, Franco Giorgi was given a $200,000 commission for his role as middleman.

It was considerable effort for a relatively small deal. But it convinced Croatian authorities that Giorgi and der Hovsepian could be trusted. In 1992, just over a year after hostilities had broken out in the region and the UN had instituted a mandatory arms embargo against all the participants,[22] Croatia went looking for more weapons. This time it was a much larger consignment, including missiles, valued at $26.1m.[23] The deal was again initiated by Lorenzo Mazzega, who contacted Franco Giorgi on behalf of the Croatian authorities. Leaping at the opportunity, Giorgi travelled to Croatia to discuss the deal with an assortment of Croatian generals and the Minister of Finance, Jozo Martinovic.[24] The former director of the Croatian state bank Privredna, Martinovic is alleged to have

been heavily involved in many negotiations for arms deliveries in violation of the UN embargo.[25]

Giorgi turned once more to der Hovsepian, who made use of the same
network of contacts he had used to secure the first Croatian shipment.
Armscor was contacted and the deal agreed. An American shipping agent,
Michael Steenberg, was drafted in to take care of transport.[26] The weapons were delivered aboard the *Sky Bird* in mid-1992 – with two UN arms
embargoes being violated by a single deal. In order to avoid detection, the
shipping manifests were altered. Repeating their previous ruse, it was
claimed that the shipment was intended for the Lebanese Christian militia.[27] Umag, a port city in Croatia, was the real destination, with an
end-user certificate provided by the Finance Minister, Martinovic.[28] He
also provided der Hovsepian with a promissory note agreeing to pay the
dealer a $5m down-payment, followed by five monthly payments through
Privredna of $4.35m dollars each.[29] As the shipments started arriving,
der Hovsepian received a steady flow of money. But payment was soon
stopped by the Croatian authorities after der Hovsepian had received
roughly $12m, with a further $14m outstanding.[30]

Why the Croatians stopped paying is still something of a mystery.
According to der Hovsepian they complained about the quality of the
material he delivered, claiming it was old, secondhand and unusable. Der
Hovsepian was flabbergasted: the equipment was five years old, but had
never been used, and performed perfectly under testing which he undertook personally. Franco Giorgi recalled that the Croatians insisted the
equipment had been 'dismissed [sic] by the Lebanese army'[31] – when, in
fact, the weapons had been entirely sourced from Armscor in South
Africa. And while Armscor was certainly a shadowy operator, it maintained a reputation for solidly built weapons. More likely is that der
Hovsepian was being played. Once the weapons had been delivered, the
dealer had no means of ensuring the continued flow of money. According
to Franco Giorgi, der Hovsepian received a strange delegation in Germany from Croatia, comprised of a woman and two men accompanied
by Lorenzo Mazzega. 'They tried to obtain a bribe from Hovsepian in
exchange of a positive report about the weapons he had supplied [sic].
Hovsepian refused and sent them away briskly.'[32] Either der Hovsepian
was being conned by the cash-strapped Croatians or he was being set up

to pay a commission to well-connected Croatian officials. Either way, der Hovsepian received no further income from the deal.

Things got even worse for the arms dealer. While the deal was underway another Merex export agent, Gerhard Doerfel, had made contact with the Croatian government. An engineer by trade, Doerfel was also a close confidant of Gerhard Mertins. He had come to the attention of Croatian authorities as a result of his links to the German company Gesiecke & Devrient, which they wanted to print the country's new currency.[33] Lorenzo Mazzega, the fixer for so much of Croatia's business, frequently acted as Doerfel's chaperone, and befriended him. Mazzega recalled that he had often travelled to Mertins's Thomasberg estate to meet with Mertins and Doerfel, sometimes seeing der Hovsepian driving past in his car. This overlap of business interests was fatal for der Hovsepian, who had tried to keep the Croatian transaction secret from Mertins. Doerfel found out about the deal from the Croatian authorities and immediately informed Mertins. He was incandescent, as much out of professional jealousy as fear of attracting the unwanted attention of German authorities. Mertins decided to get even. He rifled through der Hovsepian's papers that were filed on the Thomasberg estate, and gave the whole incriminating pile to the German authorities.[34] Mertins had snitched on his partner.

German law enforcers opened an investigation, often liaising with Italian police officials who had begun to examine the activities of Franco Giorgi and Lorenzo Mazzega throughout the former Yugoslavia. It seems highly unlikely that Mertins decided to betray der Hovsepian for moral reasons. More likely, he was motivated by possible financial gain. For after Croatian authorities had rejected der Hovsepian's cargo, Martinovic decided to try and settle the matter. Through Mazzega, he made contact with Mertins and proposed that if the German could convince der Hovsepian to stop badgering Croatia for the balance of the money, der Hovsepian would receive a one-off payment of just over $1m in full and final settlement. Mertins suggested that he could persuade der Hovsepian to accept the proposal, even though he had no intention of discussing it with his partner. In August 1992, in a bar at Munich airport, Lorenzo Mazzega placed in Mertins's hands a briefcase containing over $1m in cash.[35] True to character, Mertins never gave the money to der Hovsepian, believing that his partner would be too busy dealing with the attentions of German prosecutors to discover Mertins's subterfuge.

As a result of Mertins's disclosures der Hovsepian was forced to flee Germany to avoid prosecution, only returning years later, when it was clear that the investigation had come to a standstill.[36] Mertins was a million dollars richer but his deceit marked the end of their relationship and, as a result, the end of Deutsche Merex GmBH as a going concern. Der Hovsepian remained on close terms with Mertins's sons, both of whom displayed a canny awareness of their father's conniving business practices. After Gerhard died der Hovsepian received a congenial letter from J. T. Mertins confessing that der Hovsepian was 'only about twelfth on a list of people Gerhard Mertins had cheated'.[37]

Der Hovsepian's enforced exile from Germany didn't mark the end of the ill-fated Croatian deal. In 1998, he took the bizarre decision to pursue the matter in the Swiss courts, demanding that the remainder of the money be paid to him by the Croatian state.[38] Finally in March 2001, after the matter had been appealed by der Hovsepian, the Swiss Supreme Court rejected his claim for the outstanding monies. The court found that while the promissory note was unambiguous and the violation of sanctions was not a reason to cancel the contract – Switzerland was not, at the time of the transaction, a part of the UN – the deal offended conceptions of Swiss public order, and therefore universal public order, because the transfers to Yugoslavia were unethical.[39] When I asked der Hovsepian about the court's decision his mood darkened. He barked an obscenity and pounded the table in fury. How, he wondered, could any arms deal be considered unethical, when he undertook his dealings for a moral purpose? 'I'm in this business for the defence of humanity,' he explained. 'You have to prepare for war to make peace.' In an ironic twist of fate, der Hovsepian may have unintentionally done his bit for peace and humanity: the decision of the Swiss court has become a much discussed topic among legal experts, raising hopes that other shady deals could be blocked by Switzerland's legal obligation to maintain universal public order.

Merex's involvement in the former Yugoslavia did not end with the Croatian fiasco. Like most weapons dealers, the company had connections to a group of individuals who were supplying weapons to the arch-enemies of der Hovsepian's Croatian clients. In particular, Nicholas Oman, listed in a 2005 German investigation as a foreign representative of Merex during the early 1990s, was highly active in the region. Little is known of

Oman's background, except that he was born in 1943 in Podkoren in Slovenia.[40] From at least the 1960s onwards he made Australia his home. Under interrogation by Italian officials investigating his activities in the Balkans, Oman claimed to be a commercial pilot who had graduated from the NASA pilot school in the 1960s and a committed democrat with strong emotional ties to Slovenia.[41] Australian authorities paint a far less rosy portrait. The Canberra branch of Interpol confirmed that Oman had frequent run-ins with the law. In 1966, he was found guilty of 'assault with a weapon'. A year later he was found in possession of a 'restricted substance'. 1973 saw him charged with unlawful assault. And in the mid-1980s he was acquitted on charges of 'theft by deception', 'fraudulent use of a number plate' and 'armed robbery'.[42]

Oman travelled to Italy in 1989 to meet an infamous Italian, Licio Gelli, on three occasions.[43] Gelli had gained notoriety in the early 1980s when he was accused of – but not prosecuted for – being involved in a massive banking scandal, in which over \$1bn had inexplicably gone missing from the giant Banco Ambrosiano. Gelli had been appointed as the 'Venerable Master' of a Masonic lodge known as Propaganda Duo, or P2,[44] a sprawling network of far right-wing figures in Italian industry, the media and politics, many of whom would go on to have a major impact on Italian political life.[45] In 1987, Gelli was found guilty of financing right-wing terrorist organizations in Italy. He had fled to Switzerland by the time of his conviction and only returned when he had negotiated an extradition agreement that ring-fenced his political crimes.[46]

Nicholas Oman claims to have met the insalubrious Gelli as part of an effort to raise investments into the small Pacific state of Tonga on behalf of its government.[47] He believed that Gelli might be interested in such investment, as the government of Tonga offered diplomatic recognition, and thus immunity, to major investors.[48] Oman's meeting with Gelli in 1989 belied his claim to be simply a commercial pilot. A former aide to Oman, Jornej Cepin, admitted under interrogation that Oman had told him in explaining his considerable wealth that he had 'worked with Iran at the time of the Iran–Iraq War, and that he had been paid these sums in recognition of this. This enabled him to develop his arms business. The amount was \$35m.'[49] Cepin believed this account, citing Oman's travel to Iran in 1990 as additional evidence.

In 1991, Oman moved back from Australia to his homeland in Slovenia.

He set himself up in an ostentatious castle in Bled from where he conducted most of his business. His aim, he claimed, was to assist Slovenia move towards independence and out of the clutches of communism.[50] The lord of the castle was a distinctive figure, often described as resembling a stick insect due to his thin, lanky frame. Slovenian police once described him uncharitably as '185cm tall, average height, wedged face, dark brown (greying hair), dark brown eyes, middle nose, askew head, oval ear'.[51]

From his lofty castle this ungainly character set about establishing a profitable network of devious accomplices. He found a ready partner in the kleptocratic government of Liberia. Oman was soon involved in the trading of diamonds from that impoverished country to various parts of Europe. In 1992, the Liberian ambassador Taylor Nill – later a confidant of the brutal dictator Charles Taylor, another Merex agent – flew to meet Oman in Liberia. A few days later it was announced that Oman had been appointed the Slovenian Honorary Consul to Liberia, conferring on him both a diplomatic passport and diplomatic immunity.[52]

The diplomatic title was in return for helping Liberian elites move diamonds and buy arms, despite a UN arms embargo imposed on the country in 1992. Cepin recalled that Oman frequently travelled to Liberia on 'business' and that he employed a South African diamond expert on a retainer to help him smuggle the goods. Lorenzo Mazzega, whom Oman referred to during cross-examination as his 'pleasant Italian friend',[53] recalled that in the mid-1990s Oman had travelled to the Liberian capital for ten days. 'As war had broken out in Liberia, shortly after Oman had gone there, I remember asking him, somewhat ironically, if he had gone to Liberia to trigger a war. He told me at the time that he had gone there specifically to conclude a contract for the supply of arms.'[54] The Liberian Truth and Reconciliation Commission found Oman guilty of a number of economic crimes, including 'illegal arms dealing', 'aiding and abetting European Community actors [i.e. arms suppliers]' and 'smuggling and other customs violations'.[55]

With his base in Slovenia and diplomatic immunity Oman was in a unique position to supply weapons to most sides of the Yugoslav conflict. Slovenia, which had once been part of Yugoslavia, declared independence from the union in June 1991 on the same day as Croatia. The declaration precipitated a ten-day war between remnants of the Yugoslav army, which was simultaneously mobilizing against Croatia, and Slovenian forces. The Yugoslavs made little headway and soon declared a ceasefire with Slovenia, which was granted independence and, buffered geographically from Serbia by Croatia, witnessed little further conflict. This relative tranquillity and its location made it the perfect terminus for arms deals. Nicholas Oman was quick to take advantage, using his connections at the very top of the Slovenian political and military establishment.

He hosted elaborate and gaudy diplomatic functions at his castle, during which he befriended the Slovenian Ministers of Defence and the Interior. He also developed 'collegial relations' with the Slovenian President, Milan Kukan.[56] Initially Oman helped Kukan's government acquire lines of credit and foreign exchange, a role he fulfilled with aplomb.[57] Soon the government approached him to help acquire arms in the build-up to independence. Oman contacted a friend in Greece, Konstantin Dafermas, whose company, Scorpion, quickly arranged to forward a considerable stock of arms via Oman to the Slovenian leadership.[58]

The brevity of the Slovenian fighting caused Oman to start providing supplies to others in the Yugoslav conflict. At first he focused on supplying arms to Croatia. An invoice dated 28 October 1991, just after the declaration of the UN arms embargo, and written on the letterhead of Oman's company, Orbal Marketing Services, was addressed to the 'Ministry of Defence, Republic of Croatia, for the delivery of "blowpipe portable anti-aircraft missile systems"'. The equipment was of NATO stock built in the UK in 1980.[59] In total Oman invoiced a fee of $15.6m for 400 MK40 missiles and eighty launchers.[60]

By 1992, Oman was involved in delivering arms to both Croatia and Bosnia. The Bosnian Serbs at the time were resisting Croatian aims to expand its borders into parts of Bosnia-Herzegovina. On 8 January 1992, according to a Slovenian investigation, a ship named *Hel*, sailing under the Antiguan flag, docked at the port of Koper in Slovenia. Its manifest stated that it was carrying agricultural equipment destined for Croatia. But when its forty-six freight containers were unloaded and searched, 13,000 AK-47 rifles with 13 million rounds of ammunition, 10,000 Makarov pistols with 5 million rounds, 14 mortars and 2,000 winter military uniforms were discovered. They had been supplied by Oman's Orbal Marketing with Scorpion reselling them to all sides in the conflict.[61] The total cost of the cache was $8.9m.[62]

Oman also developed relationships in Russia, where he had contact with former Soviet generals looking to dispose of the country's massive Cold War arsenal. A visitor of Oman's, Fulvio Leonardi, recalls dropping in on the Slovenian at his castle in Bled, where he was invited to join his host and VIP guests in a restaurant Oman owned. To Leonardi's surprise he had been asked to a meeting of major weapons traffickers. Among the guests were the ex-president of Russia's Sukhoi Corporation, an important weapons manufacturer, and a former General named Kuzin. The General was particularly forthcoming after a few bottles of *rakija*, bragging that he had been appointed by corrupt officers to arrange for the sale of old Red Army stock, including but not limited to tanks and heavy-weapons systems. 'Kuzin,' Leonardi confirmed, 'made no mystery about introducing himself as an arms trafficker at a very high level.'[63]

It is because of these Russian contacts that in 1994 Oman was approached by the Bosnian Serb leader, Radovan Karadzic, to discuss a special need. Karadzic, currently on trial for war crimes including the Srebrenica genocide, wanted to acquire something that would fundamentally alter the conduct of the Balkans conflict: a weapon of mass destruction.[64] Karadzic believed that Oman could use his connections in the Russian military to deliver a so-called 'vakuum' or elipton bomb. The device, roughly suitcase size with a kiloton payload powered by nuclear material – either red mercury or osmium – was known to be immensely powerful.[65] Vladimir Zhirinovsky, the ultra-nationalist Russian leader famous for his racist and anti-Semitic diatribes, had incessantly bragged about this Russian 'secret weapon' on his visits to Serbia.[66] The Russian, who during a trip to the United States famously warned Americans that the country needed to do more for the 'preservation of the white race' in the face of potential Hispanic and black domination, and was banned from Australia and Japan, was not only a major presence in Serbia but also friendly with Nicholas Oman, whose castle he had once stayed at.[67] This relationship lent credence to Oman's claim that he could source the bomb for the Bosnian Serb leader, who agreed to pay $60m for it. Ten per cent of the payment – $6m – was paid in cash as a deposit, transported to Oman in Slovenia by his friend and fellow fixer, Lorenzo Mazzega, in the back of his Saab.[68] As collateral for the balance Oman was allowed to take out a mortgage on one of Bosnia's oil refineries.

Oman was unable to deliver the armed bomb to Karadzic's satisfaction.

The Slovenian seemed able to get his hands on nuclear material, as a 1996 raid on a safety deposit box of his revealed 30 grams of osmium.[69] But Franco Giorgi recalled that Oman had offered him a kilogram of osmium for resale.[70] This suggests that Oman may have had no intention of providing the bomb and had been misleading Karadzic the whole time, in the hope of swindling the alleged war criminal out of a cool $6m. The *New York Times* had a different take, suggesting that Oman had handed over a makeshift bomb in a suitcase to Karadzic but that its red mercury content, encased in red jelly-like tubes, was inactive.[71]

The bottom line is that Karadzic was left without the weapon and $6m out of pocket. Determined to get the money back, the enraged Bosnian enlisted the help of Branislav Lainovic, one of his former militia commanders and now a businessman known by the nickname 'Dughi'.[72] Lainovic contacted Franco Giorgi, whom he saw as an 'arms dealer and mafiosi' who could intimidate Oman into relenting.[73] Oman meanwhile, yet to hear of Karadzic's displeasure, had brazenly sent two couriers – one of whom was Mazzega – to Sarajevo to collect the remainder of the money. Instead of receiving the outstanding $54m, they were held hostage by Lainovic, who took their passports and agreed to release them only if the money was forthcoming from Oman. To Lainovic's anger, a US bombardment of the area where the two were held allowed Mazzega and his colleague to escape.[74]

Undeterred, 'Dughi' paid a visit to Oman in Slovenia with the intention of retrieving the money and assassinating the double-dealing broker. The wily Oman, however, talked Lainovic into accepting a bribe of $1.2m in return for which he would let Oman live and inform his superiors that the Slovenian could not be found. For Lainovic it proved a fatal decision. Soon after his bosses discovered the deceit, 'Dughi' was found murdered.[75] On hearing of his accomplice's demise, Oman fled his castle and settled in Australia. His five-year reign as one of Yugoslavia's most successful and least scrupulous arms dealers was over.

For both der Hovsepian and Oman, Yugoslavia was an unmitigated disaster. But while Oman was forced to flee into obscurity, der Hovsepian moved back into his comfort zone: the Middle East. In September 1993, he began to supply arms to a group deeply at odds with Merex's previous customers: left-leaning militias in South Yemen.[76] Der Hovsepian was involved in the deal as a result of his close relationships in Saudi Arabia, in particular with Prince Anwar Bin Fawaz Bin Nawaf Al-Shalaan. According to the report of a South African Commission of Inquiry into the deal, 'the Prince's trust of Hovsepian, his business associate, was profound and complete – even to the point of his according Hovsepian some implicit mandate to wheel and deal, provided it was in the Prince's ultimate interest, and that his honour was not impugned'.[77]

Prince Al-Shalaan is a typical member of the Saudi royal family, with fingers in a considerable array of entrepreneurial pies. He had a particular interest in the South Yemeni commodity market, a potentially lucrative and largely untapped opportunity. He was informed, however, that in order to gain access he would have to secure arms for the South Yemenis, many of whom formed a secessionist movement that baulked at the unification of the country in 1990.[78] For this he turned to his trusted confidant, der Hovsepian, whom the Commission of Inquiry described, with a degree of understatement, as in possession of a 'sophisticated appreciation of the international arms business'.[79]

To secure arms for the Prince, der Hovsepian used the same network he had utilized in Croatia. Through Eli Wazan he purchased the cargo – a collection of rifles and ammunition – from Armscor and shipped them through Michael Steenberg aboard the *Vinland Saga* to Yemen. When Armscor was forced to explain the transfer of weapons – it was still encumbered by the arms embargo – it pointed out that the stated end-user was, as with the previous deals, the Lebanese Christian militia. Armscor claimed it was not responsible for onward transfer. According to der Hovsepian Armscor knew that Lebanon was the end-user, especially as the Prince himself, with no connection to Lebanon, had travelled to South Africa to inspect the weapons. And der Hovsepian was always clear where the weapons were going, regardless of the end-user certificate.[80] How much der Hovsepian made from the deal is unclear. The purchase price was $350,175. However, the Prince paid an initial $510,000 and a further $902,455 when it was agreed to parlay the first agreement into a second deal. Of this, Wazan received a total of $484,780 between September 1993 and 1994, giving some indication of the size of commission payments in the industry.[81]

The clause in the contract with Armscor for a second tranche of equipment related to G3 rifles, AK-47s and ammunition. The now familiar network was again utilized for this shipment, which set sail aboard the *Arktis Pioneer*.[82] With such a well-rehearsed channel in place trouble was not anticipated. But der Hovsepian and his friends didn't count on the fickleness of their clients or the deceptive nature of relationships between arms dealers. Eli Wazan, who had been almost entirely excluded from the second deal, was brought back in when it was realized he was needed to provide a fraudulent end-user certificate. He produced a crude forgery at great cost that was easily spotted. But what really scuppered the deal was the purchasers' indecision.

When the cargo finally reached Yemen, it was roundly rejected. Officially, the Yemenis claimed to be unimpressed by the quality of the goods. Der Hovsepian knew better. In fact, by the time the equipment arrived the Yemenis had decided they no longer needed it – far more pressing within their limited resources was the acquisition of a naval vessel. As a result the *Arktis Pioneer* was turned back,[83] arriving in a South Africa where the ANC's Nelson Mandela had just been elected the country's first democratic President. The local press got wind of the shipment and broke the story at the end of 1994, suggesting the ANC was aware of the deal and intended for some of the arms to go to their erstwhile allies in Palestine. As a result the ship was impounded and a public Commission of Inquiry instituted. The inquiry resulted in a warts-and-all retelling of der Hovsepian's Croatian and Yemen deals with Armscor. For many involved it was a disaster: Steenberg feared further legal action and caved in while the Armscor official, Vermaak, felt obliged to resign his position.

When I initially contacted der Hovsepian requesting an interview, I mentioned that he had not given any public statement about the Commission of Inquiry and suggested he might want to tell his side of the story. He responded nonchalantly: 'my caravan drives through in spite of the barking dogs'. Of far greater concern to him was the bottom line. With the *Arktis Pioneer* impounded he was staring at the loss of significant cargo and capital. Der Hovsepian thus employed a South African lawyer to pursue its release, which was finally secured in 1998. The ship made its way back to Yemen four years late, arriving with its cargo which by then had been massively devalued. Der Hovsepian recalled that his Yemeni buyers 'beat the price down' and, as a result, he 'lost a hell of a lot of money'.[84]

After his experiences in Croatia and Yemen, der Hovsepian claims to have learned a number of useful lessons. The first is that he would only deal with government-to-government contracts. The second, that he would now refuse to supply goods on spec – all money had to be paid up front. But while he didn't say as much in our interview, he could have added a third: to keep a low profile. Besides his ill-advised court case against Croatia in 2001 he has been unmentioned in the press for over a decade. When I first contacted him his immediate response was 'But what's in it for me? I have never got anything for nothing in my life, nor do I give anything for nothing.'

Der Hovsepian's long silence has only reinforced an image of fear around him. Both Steenberg and the Armscor official, Vermaak, professed to have been terrified of the man.[85] When I asked der Hovsepian about this he chuckled to himself. 'Of course they were scared of me,' he explained. 'I put a gun to their head and told them I would kill them. But what they didn't know is that I'm a pacifist. I only trade this stuff, I don't use it.'[86]

5.   The Ultimate Deal or the Ultimate Crime?

Riggs Bank of Washington DC was not only the capital's oldest and largest financial institution but also its most august.[1] It financed the Mexican–American War in 1847, the purchase of Alaska from the Russians in 1868 and the completion of the Capitol.[2] It was banker to twenty-two Presidents, including Lincoln, Roosevelt, Eisenhower and Nixon,[3] and most of the world's Washington-based embassies.[4] Riggs was so much a part of the American establishment that its majestic colonnaded headquarters, which neighbour the White House, were featured on the ten-dollar note for decades.[5]

Among its most valued customers was the long-time Saudi ambassador to the US, and the Bush family's confidant, Prince Bandar bin Sultan. George W. Bush's uncle was an executive at the bank during this time.[6]

Despite the bank's stellar reputation, it came to light that in 2000, about two weeks after a fellow Saudi, Omar al-Bayoumi, opened bank accounts for two of the 9/11 hijackers, al-Bayoumi's wife began to receive monthly payments that amounted to tens of thousands of dollars from an account at Riggs Bank held by Princess Haifa bint Faisal, the wife of Prince Bandar.[7]

When these transactions were discovered, the FBI began investigating the bank for possible connections with money laundering and the financing of terrorism.[8] Although the FBI and later the 9/11 Commission ultimately stated that the money was not intentionally being diverted to fund terrorists,[9] investigators were surprised to discover how lax the safeguards at Riggs Bank were,[10] especially as the bank was known to have close links to the CIA.[11]

In addition to revealing accounts for the Liberian dictator and one-time Merex arms dealer Charles Taylor, the Chilean military ruler Augusto Pinochet and assorted other despots, several Saudi accounts were discovered to contain financial improprieties, including a lack of the required background checks and a consistent failure to alert regulators to large transactions, in violation of federal banking laws.[12]

Many of these transactions involved Prince Bandar personally, often transferring over \$1m at a time. For instance, he transferred a total of \$17,478,870.87 to the architect/builder of his palace in Riyadh.[13] The source of much of the money in Bandar's account was the British arms company BAE, which had transferred in excess of £1bn into the Washington bank, over a period of a decade and a half, through the Bank of England account jointly controlled by BAE and Deso, the UK arms export promotion agency.[14] The money was at least in part the Prince's commission for his involvement in the world's biggest ever arms deal.[15]

Police estimate that commissions of more than £6bn were paid on the Al Yamamah deal, primarily through a British Virgin Islands-based company, Poseidon Trading Investments Ltd, the Bank of England account and sub-contractor payments.[16] In addition to the more than £1bn that went into Prince Bandar's accounts,[17] Mark Thatcher, the son of the British Prime Minister at the time, is reported to have received about £12m as an agent on the deal, an allegation he denies.[18]

Corruption has been rife in Saudi Arabia since the discovery of oil, with three main methods employed. The most common is where the supplier makes payments to his agent in the kingdom. The agent could be a Saudi or foreign citizen with good contacts in the country's hierarchy, and he simply passes money from the source to his mentor or key decision-maker within the royal family. There are also barter agreements, where military hardware is exchanged for oil. How this works is that a delivery of say 400,000 barrels is transferred to the military supplier's agent. However, a delivery of 440,000 barrels is recorded in the Saudi accounts. The extra 40,000 barrels is diverted and sold by the Saudi dealer and his associates for their own profit.[19] The barter system is also open to abuse, especially where an oil fund is created to be used against expenditure by the parties. And finally, there is the trusted and simple mechanism of overcharging for various aspects of a contract.

All three methods were employed on Al Yamamah, with members of the Saudi royal family and Saudi agents netting millions, sometimes billions, of pounds. As Lord Gilmour, a former Defence Minister, told

BBC's *Newsnight* in an interview: 'You either got the business and bribed, or you didn't bribe and didn't get the business. You either went along with how the Saudis behaved, or what they wanted, or you let the US and France have all the business. It's not something you emblazon or are particularly proud of. It just happens to be the terms of trade.'[20]

The suspicion of bribery in the Al Yamamah deal started while its final details were still being negotiated. An Arabic language newsletter, *Sourakia*, raised concerns in its October 1985 issue, soon after the deal was announced. The *Guardian* picked this up and ran a front page story headlined 'Bribes of £600m in jets deal'.[21] The day before, the Labour Party's defence spokesman, Denzil Davies, had called on the government to confirm or deny reports that it was to pay secret commissions of between £300m and £600m to secure the deal. The MoD 'refused to comment, although officials said negotiations were still going on'.[22] At the time, the *Guardian* cited Arab sources who alleged that the commission would be shared between two or three leading members of the royal family, two relatives by marriage of King Fahd and a business agent. Whitehall advice to ministers was not even to attempt a denial but rather: 'We suggest MoD should simply refuse all comment.'[23]

For years, whenever questioned, the Conservative government denied that Al Yamamah involved any commissions. Roger Freeman, the Defence Procurement Minister, stated in the House of Commons in October 1994: 'The transaction between Her Majesty's government and Saudi Arabia was on a government-to-government basis in which no commissions were paid and no agents or any middlemen were involved.' He added that 'Details of the contracts are confidential between the British and Saudi governments.'[24]

However, these lies were soon exposed when that same year executives from an Al Yamamah subcontractor, Thorn EMI, better known as a music label, disclosed that they had paid £40m in commissions on their contract for bomb fuses on the deal. The commissions, totalling 26 per cent of the contract price, were split between their Saudi agent and the Bermuda account of a Preston-based agency run by a former BAE employee.[25] Once ranks had been broken, further corruption among subcontractors soon came to light. Rolls-Royce, which manufactured the engine for the Tornado and Hawk jets, admitted to paying £23m as an 8 per cent commission to a Panama-registered entity, Aerospace Engineering Design Corporation (AEDC). The company was controlled by members of the Ibrahim family, the favoured in-laws of King Fahd. The Ibrahims claimed that Rolls-Royce had committed to a commission of 15 per cent on the £600m engine deal. AEDC issued a writ on 12 December 1997 demanding the unpaid sum and plunging the Rolls-Royce and BAE boards into ill-disguised panic. As the embarrassment grew Rolls-Royce and AEDC hired heavyweight legal teams to hastily negotiate an out-of-court settlement.[26]

Vosper Thorneycroft was also said to have paid substantial commissions on its Al Yamamah contract. The MP George Galloway told the Commons under parliamentary privilege:

> Another part of the deal was concluded in 1988, when the regime agreed to buy minesweepers from Vosper Thorneycroft. Vosper used as its agent a Saudi named Fahd al-Athel, who, like the right hon. Member for South Thanet [Jonathan Aitken], worked for Prince Mohammed. Vosper made huge payments to al-Athel's company, which were laundered with the knowledge of Vosper through a front company in Saudi Arabia and were divided 20 per cent to al-Athel, 40 per cent to Prince Mohammed and 40 per cent to unnamed others, some of them known to be prominent figures in British life.[27]

Colonel Thomas Dooley, an executive of Sikorsky, the helicopter manufacturer, testified in a United States court that, while trying to sell Black Hawk helicopters to the Saudi regime, he experienced a 'competition for bribes'. He explained that Prince Bandar told him explicitly 'what bribes needed to be paid for the deal, through which middleman they must be routed and how he would distribute the money to other members of the royal family'.[28]

The British government's discomfort intensified during a 1997 High Court libel case in which the MP named by Galloway, the former Defence Procurement Minister Jonathan Aitken, sued the *Guardian* and Granada TV. David Trigger, a former executive at BMARC, a company where Aitken was a director, testified that he had negotiated a deal between BAE and Royal Ordnance for armaments to equip the Tornado fighter jets. When asked about the commission rate on the deal Trigger replied: 'No, I cannot tell you that.' When asked if it was a secret, Trigger responded: 'Yes, it is. The Al Yamamah contract is a very complicated one that has an involvement with the Government, British Aerospace and other people, and it would be very difficult to put a figure on commission. Commission was obviously paid but my understanding is that all my work connected with that contract is governed by the Official Secrets Act.'[29] Trigger also admitted that he negotiated a 15 per cent commission agreement with Sheikh Fahad al-Athel, Mr Aitken's business friend, for future contracts.[30] Saudi Arabian law allowed agents only 5 per cent. After giving evidence Trigger walked to the back of the court and presented a memento to Aitken from his briefcase. As journalists present recorded: 'The former Cabinet minister turned on his usual puckered grin, and affected a friendly interest. Inside, his gut must have been knotting in disbelief.'[31]

Years later, after being jailed for perjury, Aitken would contradict his government's constant denials: 'Living in the real world there were always going to be some parts of the contract – training, spares and construction, for example – for which agents would receive commission. Sales commission is what makes the world of commerce go round. The big picture is that Saudi Arabia is a crucial ally for intelligence and is a stabilising influence in a volatile region.'[32] The former Defence Secretary Michael Heseltine agreed: 'If this is the way the Saudis want arrangements for their procurement programme, an international company would have had no choice but to go along with that. It's massively important to us and the stability of the Middle East that we have those defence interests in Saudi.'[33]

But it took intrepid work from a pair of *Guardian* journalists, with the help of a number of whistle-blowers, to reveal the full extent of the corruption perpetrated by the main contractor, BAE, in the Al Yamamah deal.[34]

David Leigh is an unassuming man. His bespectacled, donnish appearance is that of an unambitious academic. His craggy features, however, hint at a more stressful and interesting life. A *Guardian* veteran of over twenty years, David is one of the world's leading investigative reporters. He was famously responsible for bringing down Jonathan Aitken after the minister had sued the *Guardian* for reporting a trip to Paris, where he stayed at the Ritz Hotel at the expense of Said Ayas, 'man of business' to King Fahd's son, Prince Mohammed. Aitken, after denying he had made the trip and claiming that he would 'cut out the cancer of bent and twisted journalism in our country with the simple sword of truth and the trusty shield of British fair play',[35] was found guilty of lying to the court once Leigh produced receipts the minister had signed at the Ritz. Aitken ultimately served seven months of an eighteen-month prison sentence, and Leigh's reputation was made.

Leigh, together with his meticulous colleague Rob Evans, had written a few articles about the British government and the arms trade, including US complaints about alleged BAE skullduggery in bidding for contracts in Eastern Europe. During their trawl through government archives, they came upon the Stokes Report, a 1965 document that led to the setting up of the Defence Sales Organisation (DSO, renamed the Defence Export Services Organisation (Deso) in 1985). The report's author, the industrialist Donald Stokes, remarked that 'a great many arms sales were made not because anyone wanted the arms, but because of the commission involved en route',[36] and that 'it was often necessary to offer bribes to make sales'.[37] He also reported that 'good commercial agents . . . are better placed than an official to dispense the less orthodox inducements'.[38] These comments, and the corrupt UK–Saudi arms deals that followed the Stokes report, piqued the journalists' interest. They began to dig deeper into BAE's more recent business practices.

The journalists' investigations took them to a dark council flat in Liverpool, home to Eddie Cunningham, a disgruntled ex-employee of a company called Robert Lee International (RLI), which was contracted by BAE in 1986 to make the arrangements for Saudi pilots to travel to the UK in relation to the Al Yamamah deal. RLI was requested to provide 'hospitality' for the pilots and Cunningham was their minder. He was more than willing to spill the beans on BAE.

Cunningham described the 'hospitality' the pilots enjoyed as amounting to millions of pounds spent providing cars, yachts, pleasure trips and a constant stream of women. He related how the Saudi Royal Air Force pilots 'would ask me to get women for them . . . they would have two or three women a night and then they'd want to go have a meal somewhere at three in the morning, come back again and start again . . . it used to wear me out'.[39] Cunningham was told by senior BAE executives that the entertainment was paid for with Saudi money and was allowed for in the Al Yamamah contract: 'I was told that this was necessary otherwise you could say goodbye to this contract and they'd look elsewhere.'[40]

Cunningham recounted how, a few years before in 1996, he had alerted a BAE security officer to the fact that there was fraud taking place in the administration of these 'hospitality' funds. The officer's report documented:

> blackmail by an ex-prostitute over sex and bondage with Saudis, tax evasion and VAT fraud valued at over a million pounds. It also made reference to a house, paid for by BAE but registered in the name of a Saudi prince, which was actually occupied by a BAE executive and his mistress, who was employed at RLI. The director of RLI claims it was a gift from the Saudi prince.[41]

The nature and extent of this fraud were confirmed by Sylvia St John, the mistress of the BAE executive Tony Winship, a debonair, silver-haired former RAF wing commander, who was officially BAE's Saudi 'customer relations officer' and in charge of the 'hospitality' funds. St John personally acquired two houses worth £300,000, one in south-west London and another in Northern Ireland. The money went through the books as payments to the Saudi Prince Turki, though it seems it passed straight to Ms St John. According to a signed statement by the manager of RLI, John Sharp, 'BAe authorised and approved the expenditure.' The London house is held in the name of Prince Turki, the Northern Ireland house in the name of Ms St John, who claims that she holds the title deeds to the London house as well and lived there with Winship.[42] Sharp claimed that Prince Turki wanted St John to have the houses as a gift, adding that the fund under Winship's control would be used to pay the council tax and utility bills of the Northern Ireland house, while receipts ranging from building renovation to 'a pair of antique brass firedogs' were also charged to BAE. Ms St John, although employed at RLI, described herself as a 'customer families officer, Saudi Arabian support department, British Aerospace (Military Aircraft) Ltd'. She justified the gifts on the basis that she had visited in hospital and comforted a sister of Prince Turki's who was dying of cancer, and had, therefore, 'earned the money'.[43]

The *Guardian* also unearthed an £80,000 yacht, the *Faye Samantha*, that had been bought using the funds, and was owned by Tony Winship and moored at Lymington in Hampshire, near his home.[44]

Cunningham described how, shortly after raising his concerns about the fraud, he was fired. He was furious, took issue with BAE and was ultimately awarded £20,000 in a settlement. Not satisfied, in 2001 he approached the UK's Serious Fraud Office (SFO) with evidence of unsupported invoices for amounts up to £250,000 a month billed to BAE by RLI and 'excessive expenses, hospitality and some evidence of assets being used for private purposes'.[45]

The SFO raised the case with the Ministry of Defence as the overseer of the government-to-government deal. But the SFO's concern that government money was being misused was rejected by Sir Kevin Tebbit, the Permanent Secretary at the MoD: 'I have no wish to set damaging hares running, but given the sensitive issues raised in your letter, I have conducted a discreet initial exploration of the allegations' implications for the department.'[46] This inquiry seems to have amounted to the acceptance of personal assurances from BAE's chairman, Dick Evans, that there was no need for an investigation. Cunningham was angry, claiming: 'it's an unhealthy relationship between MoD and BAE. I found the attitude of the MoD was "don't upset these people, they're bringing money into this country, look at this money . . . we can condone these little things".'[47]

The MoD issued a statement in which it reiterated that Tebbit's actions were in the context of 'the Government's robust anti-fraud policy'. The statement went on to say that the SFO acknowledged that proper action was taken and that it was grateful for Sir Kevin's help.[48]

Cunningham further claimed to Leigh and Evans that the expenditure on the pilots was just the tip of the iceberg. Saudi royals were the beneficiaries of far greater munificence, diverted from a massive slush fund operated by BAE through RLI and another company, Traveller's World Ltd, run by Peter Gardiner.

After seeing their articles in the *Guardian*, Gardiner made contact with the journalists. Confronted with Cunningham's information he was desperate to be a witness rather than a suspect and he too turned whistle-blower. He told the journalists how his small travel agency had been transformed into a conduit for millions of BAE's pounds spent secretly on Saudi royals. He had boxes and boxes of documents to back up his claims. The two reporters spent weeks with Gardiner going through piles of invoices, linking events, locations and people. At the same time, they encouraged Cunningham to use the Data Protection Act to access further information.

Based on the information in Gardiner's boxes and the replies to Cunningham's data protection requests they were able to piece together the mechanics of the massive slush fund: 'The Principal Beneficiary' of the fund, unimaginatively codenamed PB, was Prince Turki Bin Nasser.

Married to King Abdullah's niece, Prince Sultan's daughter, Princess Nura, Turki was head of the Saudi Royal Air Force and a key Saudi politician for arms purchases until 2000. He was paid £17m in benefits and cash, mainly through large payments into his Bank of America account in Los Angeles.[49] The benefits included luxury holidays, shopping sprees and, of course, women.

While the Saudi rulers demand that their subjects adhere strictly to a rigid Wahhabism, their own behaviour could not be further removed from their faith. Anouska Bolton-Lee, a vivacious actress-model and former girlfriend of Leonardo Di Caprio, revealed how for two years she was Prince Turki's mistress. She was introduced to the Prince by Tony Winship. Between 2001 and 2003, Mr Winship 'took care' of the £13,000-a-year rent on Ms Bolton-Lee's Holland Park flat and paid for her to attend a two-year drama course in London. On several occasions Winship handed her cash in white envelopes to pay for bills and the cost of driving lessons. She received around £4,000 in this way and said of the cash: 'I thought this was all the prince's money.' In addition to the money from Winship there were also times when Prince Turki would give Anouska wads of cash himself: £12,000 for a sheepskin coat, for instance, and £3,000 for a Fendi handbag. She believed that 'the prince had paid for my flat and drama school and driving lessons, but now it seems that wasn't true and that it was BAE. I find that very sad.'[50]

While romancing glamorous women at BAE's expense, the Prince ensured that his family did not want. They received gifts from the company, most often cars, including a $30,000 Mercedes for his daughter, a peacock blue Rolls-Royce for his wife and a £175,000 Aston Martin Le Mans for himself. The cars were regularly transported between Saudi Arabia and Los Angeles on privately chartered aircraft. In 1995, a cargo plane was hired for almost $300,000 to carry cars and Prince Turki's shopping home to Saudi Arabia.[51] They were treated to luxurious annual holidays at the most expensive hotels in the world, where they were accompanied by a thirty-five-strong entourage of servants, drivers and bodyguards.

In August 2001, the Turki family flew in two private airliners – an Airbus and their pink Boeing business jet – for a holiday in Cancún, Mexico. BAE picked up the £41,000 tab at the Cancún Ritz-Carlton. The defence company paid £99,000 for Nura's son, the thirty-year-old Prince Faisal, to ski at an exclusive Colorado resort and another £56,000 to charter him a plane. He arrived in Colorado fresh from spending £21,000 at the Four Seasons in Milan. That summer his mother cost BAE £56,000 at the Intercontinental hotel in Athens and a further £36,000 on a limousine service during her stay. Hiring a yacht cost another £13,000. She then moved on to Italy, where at the Grand Hotel des Bains, near Rimini, BAE handed over a further £26,000, plus £28,000 for limousines and £14,000 for bodyguards. The Princess and her family proceeded to the south of France, where they ran through £99,000 at the Majestic in Cannes. But the summer's climax was to fly across the Atlantic to settle friends and guests in at the Beverly Hills Hilton, within walking distance of the famously expensive shopping of Rodeo Drive. The cost to BAE: £101,000.[52]

After the Cancún trip with her husband, Princess Nura headed back east in leisurely fashion. Her stay at the Plaza – 'Crown Jewel of Manhattan's Fifth Avenue' – is alleged to have cost BAE no less than £195,000. Her transit via Paris's Hôtel Le Bristol took another £102,000 and a brief autumn stopover in Egypt, at the Cairo Marriott, added a final £35,000 to BAE's recorded bill for Princess Nura for 2001. Throughout the family's itinerant summer the company also paid more than £400,000 for squads of twenty-four-hour bodyguards at their residential mansion in Beverly Hills.[53]

BAE also secretly paid nearly £250,000 out of the slush fund for a honeymoon for the daughter of Prince Bandar, Princess Reema bint Bandar, who had married Prince Turki's son, the ski-loving, jet-setting Prince Faisal. After a trip to the Great Barrier Reef in Australia in a private jet, Prince Faisal, who like his new father-in-law is a fan of the Dallas Cowboys, was keen to watch an important game. The whole of a private club sixty miles away was hired in the middle of the night so that Bandar's daughter and her husband could watch the match live. The three-hour stay cost £6,000.[54]

By the time the slush fund was shut down in 2002 the bills sometimes exceeded a million pounds a month and averaged around £7m per year. Peter Gardiner explained that all the individual items were paid for by his company, which would then bill BAE for the lump sum at the end of the month, under the accounting title of 'Accommodation, services and support for overseas visitors'. All monies were reimbursed by BAE, and every item was authorized by the company.[55] Those who had knowledge of the payments included the former chief operating officer, Steven Mogford,

Tony Winship and his close friend Dick Evans, the chairman.[56] The UK's Ministry of Defence was unwittingly complicit in the affair, as the ministry paid BAE for the fraudulent invoices and then endorsed them for repayment by the Saudi government.[57]

As a consequence of the *Guardian* revelations, at dawn on 3 November 2004 eighty police and investigators from the SFO and the Economic Crimes Unit of the City of London Police raided a warehouse in Hertfordshire, north of London. They uncovered 386 boxes of slush fund accounts which revealed the names of all the Saudi officials who received benefits from BAE as part of the fund, including a number of Saudi military attachés at the London embassy who were given luxury homes by BAE, as well as Prince Turki's family.[58]

The raids resulted in the arrests of Tony Winship and John Sharp.[59] In addition to the payments and benefits to the Saudis, Winship was also accused of giving lavish gifts to an official of the MoD, Deso and the Ministry of Defence Saudi Armed Forces Project.[60]

None of these individuals were convicted, and where arrested were released without charge.

David Leigh and Rob Evans thought they had unearthed a massive story but were puzzled as to BAE's relative silence. 'The reason why BAE never said anything to us – we thought we were clever. We had exposed this slush fund. They were obviously sitting there, thinking, "Well, thank goodness they don't know the real story."'[61]

After exposing the massive slush fund the reporters were contacted by a former BAE agent who had fallen out with the company. David Leigh met him outside the UK, where he revealed the existence of a labyrinthine network of companies through which he was paid and which he, in turn, used to pay key decision-makers. The whistle-blower handed over bank records, 'which were the key to revealing an entire global money laundering system, an enormous worldwide network of secret cash payments amounting to literally billions of dollars that had gone on for years with the connivance of the British government'.[62]

At the centre of the system lay two companies, Poseidon Trading Investments Ltd and Red Diamond Trading Ltd in the obscure British Virgin Islands (BVI). This Caribbean idyll, sighted by Christopher Columbus in 1493 on his second voyage to the Americas, is an archipelago of sixty islands. He named them Saint Ursula and her 11,000 Virgins, later shortened to the Virgin Islands. There is nothing innocent about the British Virgin Islands, which are home to over 820,000 offshore companies, 41 per cent of the world's total in 2000.[63] It is, therefore, unsurprising that when BAE set about establishing a maze of companies to conceal its slush fund and massive illicit payments to agents and Saudi royals, it should choose the BVI.

The *Guardian* reporters wrote up their story as soon as David Leigh returned home. The news desk initially planned to print it on page seven of the next day's edition, believing it was only of interest to arms trade or offshore financing anoraks. Leigh and Evans, who realized the enormity of what they had uncovered, took their information to the SFO and collaborated with journalists in the UK and around the world in the hope of revealing the full extent of BAE's criminal conduct. The SFO, which was now compelled to investigate the allegations, ordered Lloyds Bank and others to turn over their records relating to BAE. These proved a treasure trove.

They established that Red Diamond had been set up in the BVI in February 1998[64] and used accounts in London, Switzerland and New York with Lloyds Bank, UBS and Chase Manhattan. Red Diamond payments were made to agents in South America, Tanzania, Romania, South Africa, Qatar, Chile and the Czech Republic, as well as the UK. BAE used an online Lloyds banking service which automatically transferred cash through Red Diamond and on to the final destination.[65] BAE has never mentioned the existence of Red Diamond in its published company accounts and has never explained why it was set up.

Red Diamond though was only one part of the elaborate global network that BAE had set up to hide bribery and corruption. Already in 1995 BAe had around 700 agency agreements, in addition to those linked to its subsidiaries Royal Ordnance and Heckler and Koch. The company had at least 300 agents, to whom it was paying out nearly £50m a year. There were so many agency agreements that it found it 'impossible to remember them all'.[66] A company called Novelmight was created to 'provide services to other group companies through a branch in Switzerland'. Its original registered address was BAE's Farnborough base,[67] but in 1999 Novelmight's UK registration was terminated and shifted to the BVI.[68] The operation was actually run out of HQ Marketing Services, which was initially headed by Hugh Dickinson, also the BAE liaison with MI6, and his long-serving deputy, Julia Aldridge.[69] Documents indicate that a board-level committee met to approve each agency agreement.[70]

To further conceal illegal activity, contracts would sometimes be signed outside UK jurisdiction. One source recalled having to fly to Switzerland in the 1980s to sign secret deals on arms contracts to India.[71] When secret payments were organized, a single copy of an agency agreement was made and BAE representatives would fly to Geneva to deposit the document. The signings would sometimes take place at Lombard Odier, a Swiss private bank well known for sheltering funds for the notoriously corrupt late President Marcos of the Philippines. The bank would keep the single copy and only allow it to be viewed in the presence of both parties to the contract.[72] In 1997, the custodial relationship was shifted to Swiss lawyers Rene Merkt and Cyril Abecassis, who also set up offshore companies for arms agents.[73]

When bribery of foreign public officials became entirely illegal in the UK after the OECD Anti-Bribery Convention was incorporated into British law in early 2002, BAE, with the help of the Swiss branch of its bankers, Lloyds TSB, discreetly rented a high-security office in Geneva on the sixth floor of a block at 48 Route des Acacias. CCTV cameras, an encrypted fax and a phone system were installed and a trusted UK specialist was flown in to sweep for bugs. One night, shortly before the OECD Anti-Bribery Convention was signed, BAE loaded its filing cabinets and safes containing its contracts and agent agreements into a nondescript van and then had it driven by trusted staff to Geneva, beyond the prying eyes of British authorities.[74] Thereafter, if documents needed signing or renewing, key BAE personnel flew to Geneva and unlocked the office at Route des Acacias. On some occasions an agent would sign a contract in London for straightforward, honest payments and possibly a reasonable rate of commission. But then a second parallel contract would be signed in Switzerland, offering much higher and more corrupting sums.[75]

Specifically for Al Yamamah, BAE had set up Poseidon Trading Investments Ltd, incorporated in the BVI on 25 June 1999. Over £1bn moved through Poseidon accounts to Saudi agents using Lloyds bank.[76]

An agent who has spent his career concealing and laundering commissions paid on weapons transactions told David Leigh and Rob Evans, with a hint of awe in his voice: 'I've worked for a lot of aircraft companies, but BAE is the only one with such an institutionalised system.'[77] Although at the time the system wasn't illegal, a big multinational company setting up a secretive shadow finance system to pay agents and middlemen certainly gives rise to suspicion. The SFO would later conclude that 'The whole system is maintained in such conditions of secrecy that there is a legitimate suspicion concerning the real purpose of the payments.'[78]

A billion pounds was directed through companies in the BVI, which was then moved into Swiss bank accounts thought to be linked to agents and to Prince Sultan, Prince Bandar's father and the Defence Minister who signed the deal. Some of these commissions were offset by massive overcharging, up to 32 per cent in the case of the Tornado jets.[79] As mentioned, total corruption in the deal, utilizing all three of the usual methods, amounted to over £6bn.[80]

Prince Bandar's accounts had meanwhile been credited with more than £100m a year, paid quarterly into Riggs Bank and authorized by Deso, ultimately totalling in excess of £1bn. Part of these funds had been used for 'the gift' of the brand-new widebody Airbus 340 jet. The fuel, maintenance and crew of the aircraft were paid for from the same source at least until 2007.[81]

While significant amounts of Prince Bandar and Prince Sultan's money went directly to their accounts, some payments on the deal were thought to be made through facilitators, primarily Wafic Said and Mohammad Safadi.

Said, a suave Syrian anglophile, is thought to be one of the richest people in the United Kingdom. With a fortune estimated at £1bn, he was placed 40th in the *Sunday Times* Rich List of 2009.[82] Always dressed in beautifully tailored Parisian suits, he owns palatial homes around the world.[83] His country mansion in Oxfordshire is valued at £35m.[84] Said is thought to have kept a Boeing 737 jet, a stable of racehorses,[85] and art works by Monet, Modigliani,[86] Picasso and Matisse, among others.[87]

Born in Syria in 1939, Said was the son of an eye surgeon who served as the country's Minister of Education. Wafic began his career in investment banking in 1963 with UBS in Geneva, where he met his British wife, Rosemary, a businessman's daughter.[88] The couple moved to London in the late 1960s to help Wafic's brother run a restaurant in the city's fashionable Kensington High Street. One evening two young fun-loving Saudi princes, Bandar and Khalid, ate at the restaurant. Said introduced himself and over several weeks the group became friends.[89] Wafic and Rosemary relocated to Saudi Arabia in 1969, where he worked briefly for the Saudi government and then started to prosper in the construction business.

In 1969, Said linked up with Akram Ojjeh, a Saudi arms dealer and financier. Ojjeh's son Mansour would become a friend of Mark Thatcher while involved in their mutual passion, motor racing. In 1973, through Ojjeh, Said became president of TAG Construction in Paris, where he brokered building deals for defence-related projects. He was also the agent for Raytheon, the US company best known for the production of missiles and bombs, and was involved in the sale of Hawk missiles to Saudi Arabia.[90] Said and Ojjeh set up Sifcorp in 1980, an investment and finance company supposedly based in Bermuda but controlled in Luxembourg by the Said Trust.[91]

Wafic displayed his considerable charm to befriend the rich and powerful in Saudi Arabia, specifically renewing his acquaintance with the two princes he'd met in the restaurant, and their father, Prince Sultan. He would later become a financial and personal adviser to the princes, managing their properties and making investments on their behalf. He gained Saudi citizenship in 1981 by royal decree, the same year his eldest child, Karim, drowned in the swimming pool at the home of Prince Sultan at the age of ten.[92]

His involvement in the Al Yamamah contract was originally kept secret. He now openly admits his role as an adviser on the deal but denies taking commissions. He told the *Daily Telegraph* in 2001:

> This is a deal which brought a huge boost to British industry: you are talking about thousands of jobs. But for some reason, which I cannot understand, the press want to portray this as a shady, mysterious deal. Due to my extensive contacts in Saudi Arabia, I played a very small role: the big role was played by Lady Thatcher.
>
> Quite honestly, I thought I was doing this country a favour. I have never even sold a penknife. I was not paid a penny [for advising British Aerospace] but I benefited because the project led to construction in Saudi Arabia that involved my companies.
>
> But it [the Al Yamamah deal] has led me to being portrayed as an arms dealer: as if I had a catalogue of weapons. Even now I get letters from people inquiring whether I can help them sell second-hand tanks or ammunition.[93]

On another occasion he opined: 'if I am an arms dealer then the chairman of British Aerospace is an arms dealer, and the Prime Minister is an arms dealer'.[94] However he chooses to describe his role, there is little doubt that Said was a facilitator of benefit to the Saudis on the Al Yamamah deal.

It is also alleged that Said was the source of the reported multimillion-pound payment to Mark Thatcher, in order to gain access to Number 10.[95] He dismisses the claim, defending his political idol: 'It's such an injustice to Lady Thatcher and her son to suggest this.'[96] Adnan Khashoggi, a notorious arms dealer (see Chapter 13), claimed that 'Wafic was using Mark's intelligence. His value to Wafic was his name, of course, and whenever Wafic needed a question answered Mark would go directly to his mother for the answer.'[97] Khashoggi later recanted, saying: 'I deny having any knowledge of . . . Mr. Thatcher's involvement in (the) transaction.'[98]

Mark Thatcher has repeatedly denied the allegation that he received £12m in relation to the deal.[99] The figure is derived from transcripts of conversations between Saudi princes and agents recorded by Saudi Intelligence while monitoring rival bids by the British, French and Americans for the deal. The transcripts were leaked by Mohammed Khiweli, the Saudi First Secretary to the United Nations, who defected in May 1994 and was granted asylum by the United States.[100]

Howard Teicher, a Middle East expert on Ronald Reagan's National Security Council in the 1980s, claimed:

> I read of Mark Thatcher's involvement in this arms deal in dispatches from our embassy in Saudi Arabia, from intelligence reports that were gleaned in Saudi Arabia and Europe and in diplomatic dispatches from other European capitals. I considered these dispatches totally reliable, totally accurate . . . I did not think that people would loosely accuse the son of the Prime Minister of being involved in such a transaction unless they were certain it was the case, and the fact that I saw his name appear in a number of different sourced documents convinced me of the authenticity of at least the basic involvement on Mark Thatcher's part. He was clearly playing some kind of role to help facilitate the completion of a transaction between the two governments.[101]

Teicher reaffirmed his view years later: 'He was playing an active role in the arms transaction and it was unambiguous that he was involved in a business capacity.'[102] Teicher's view was based on Khiweli's transcripts, which confirmed that the Saudis paid Mark to utilize his 'excellent connections with the government . . . regarding the military equipment'.[103]

Thatcher's closest associates confirmed his role: 'I know for a fact that on one occasion Wafic rang Mark, who then arranged for him to fly by helicopter to Chequers to see Margaret,' said Rodney Tyler, a friend of the Thatchers.[104] BAE executives at the time also confirmed Mark's involvement and the alleged £12m commission he received.[105] 'Mark was useful to ensure his mother was onside', according to a former BAE consultant and friend of Said.[106] A British MP was sent a document anonymously that claimed: 'The additional financial benefits to Mark T. and his friend Wafiq Said [sic] and other middlemen, all non-tax paying residents of the UK and to the Conservative Party are absolutely enormous, according to the BAE executive.'[107]

The authors of a book on Mark Thatcher claim that his mother was informed of Mark benefiting from the deal. Given that he was arranging meetings for her with Said and Prince Bandar, she could hardly be unaware of his involvement. And, according to Wafic Said's former aviation director, Mark's dealings with Said were 'at Mrs. Thatcher's insistence'.[108] A former defence industry executive, Gerald James, alleges Mark also benefited from Al Yamamah-2.[109]

Mark's benefiting from a deal in which his mother played a crucial role would come as no surprise to those who have followed his career. His personal fortune has been estimated at £60m,[110] and his mother's assistance has not been unhelpful in its accumulation. Mark, who inherited his father's baronetcy in 2003, pocketed payments in relation to a £300m contract to construct a university in Oman which his mother had clinched for a British construction company in 1981. When asked about it in Parliament, Margaret Thatcher denied any wrongdoing, claiming she was just 'batting for Britain'.[111] It is also alleged he used a handwritten note from his mother to secure a valuable deal in Abu Dhabi.[112]

The nadir of his career, however, came when he was arrested at his home in the up-market Cape Town suburb of Constantia on 25 August 2004 for his role in an attempted coup d'état in Equatorial Guinea. Thatcher was accused of providing funding and logistical support for the abortive coup planned by a British mercenary, Simon Mann, a close personal friend. After his mother's intervention secured a plea bargain in terms of South Africa's anti-mercenary laws, Thatcher pleaded guilty to negligence in investing in an aircraft 'without taking proper investigations into what it would be used for', claiming that he thought it would be used as an air ambulance in Africa.[113] He received a fine of R3m ($450,000) and a four-year suspended sentence, and was deported. Simon Mann recently reaffirmed that Thatcher was deeply involved in the coup, providing $350,000 and 'was not just an investor, he came completely on board and became a part of the management team'.[114]

After the Al Yamamah deal was concluded, Mark Thatcher purchased a luxurious Belgravia flat through a Panamanian company, Formigol, which was registered to Wafic Said's business address.[115] Said would often take Mark shooting or golfing on Prince Bandar's Oxfordshire estate. Alex Sanson, a former managing director of BAE's Dynamics Division during the Al Yamamah deal, who told the *Observer* that Said played a pivotal role in the transaction, commented that 'He [Mark Thatcher] was very close to Wafic Said and Prince Bandar. A number of people were aware that he was involved. He is bad news. He was a user of people to make connections. That was his technique and with the image of his mother at the time it was a useful asset.'[116] Such were the benefits of Al Yamamah to Thatcher *fils* that some refer to the deal as 'who's ya mama'.[117]

Wafic Said, although in virtual retirement, is still listed as a director of two Panamanian companies, Mitrasur Corporation, formed in 1975, and Al Mulk Holdings SA. Mitrasur's directors include Nabil Naaman, who is also the chief executive officer of a Libyan tourism development company, Magna.[118] Said is reported to be a backer of Magna, which is chaired by Charles Powell, Margaret Thatcher's former adviser and an adviser to BAE. Charles Powell's brother, Jonathan, was Chief of Staff to Tony Blair at 10 Downing Street.[119] Said is also a former director of AHI plc, formerly known as Aitken Hume Holdings plc, Jonathan Aitken's bank. He is still a director of the Said Foundation, which 'works for a brighter future for disadvantaged children and young people in the Middle East'.[120] Jonathan Aitken is also a director.[121]

The Said Business School was established in 1996 at Oxford University, and its new building finished in 2001 after a £20m donation from Wafic Said.[122] In 2008, he gave another £25m to the business school. Among the school's trustees is Charles Powell.[123] It was alleged that Downing Street intervened to speed up a planning application for the school.[124] Said's involvement has prompted numerous protests from students, academics[125]

and local activists.[126] A few years ago I gave a lecture to the Desmond
Tutu African Leadership Institute at the school. Unaware of its links to
Wafic, I made a joke about the irony of giving a lecture on ethics in a
school that shares the name of an alleged arms agent. After the lecture my
host politely informed me that it was the same Wafic Said who had
endowed the school.

Wafic Said was a founding patron of the Centre for Lebanese Studies,
as was Said Ayas, Prince Mohammed's 'man of business', who was linked
to Jonathan Aitken.[127] The holder of a number of titles,[128] Said has been
the ambassador and head of the delegation of St Vincent and the Gren-
adines to UNESCO since 1996.[129] In his decorations and ennoblement
he is continuing the tradition of Sir Basil Zaharoff – ingratiating himself
with the establishment and being well rewarded for it. This is reflected in
Said's intimate involvement in British politics. During the Thatcher and
Major years of Tory government in the UK, Said donated at least
£350,000 to the Conservative Party.[130] In 2004 and 2005 his family gave
about £550,000 to the party through auctions.[131] He or his family are
thought to have donated tens of thousands of pounds to the Conservative
Party in 2005, despite new laws preventing foreign nationals donating to
British political parties.[132]

While New Labour was in power Said ensured he was close to the party's 'Prince of Darkness', Peter Mandelson. Mandelson met Said in Syria
weeks before resigning as Secretary of State for Northern Ireland, claiming that he had not registered the trip with the Foreign Office as required
because it was personal.[133] Nevertheless, Mandelson met the Syrian President, Bashar al-Assad, for two hours on the visit. A Said company, First
Saudi Investment Co., was part of an Arab consortium trying to secure
lucrative contracts in Syria at the time.[134] Mandelson and Charles Powell,
the BAE adviser and brother of Tony Blair's Chief of Staff, are not only
friends of Said, but are also themselves friends. It is relationships such as
these that have enabled Wafic Said to remain close to political power of
whatever stripe for over three decades.

The second major facilitator in the Al Yamamah deal, Mohammad Safadi,
is, like Wafic Said, prodigiously well connected but is also a politician in
his own right. The Lebanese billionaire businessman and politician, whose
Swiss bank accounts were used as conduits for Al Yamamah commissions,
has been close to the Saudis and BAE for decades. He is thought to have

represented Prince Turki bin Nasser's interests in the deal and acted as a business manager for the Prince. A potential witness in the SFO's case told David Leigh and Rob Evans that 'I was asked by them [the SFO] about Mr Safadi's role. I told them that his UK firm, Jones Consultants, had paid bills for Prince Turki bin Nasser, head of the Saudi air force.'[135]

Safadi was born in Tripoli in 1944 and graduated from the American University of Beirut with a degree in Business Management. He worked in the family business, the well-known Safadi Brothers merchants, until moving to Beirut in 1969 at the time of the Gaddafi coup. In Beirut he started an investment business in housing, aviation, tourism, computing and banking.[136] When civil war broke out in Lebanon in 1975, Safadi moved to Riyadh, where he built residential compounds for companies such as BAE and began to act on behalf of relatives of Prince Sultan.

In 1995 he returned to Lebanon, setting up the Safadi Group in the country and entered politics, rising to the position of Minister for Public Works in 2005.[137] He was made the Economy and Trade Minister in the new Unity government formed in November 2009 and led by Saad Hariri in coalition with Hezbollah.[138] While being in charge of one of the most crucial political portfolios for government contracts, he continued to control the Safadi group of companies. His interests include a property company, Stow Securities, with assets of £200m, and property firms with stakes in office blocks in London worth £120m.[139] Stow is largely composed of anonymous offshore entities in Jersey and Gibraltar. One listed investor is General Ahmed Ibrahim Behery, a former senior commander in the Saudi Air Force.[140] The company has also invested in TAG Aviation, a private jet company operating partly out of Farnborough airport, BAE's headquarters. Safadi is a director on the TAG Aviation Holding Board along with Mansour and Abdulaziz Ojjeh,[141] while his UK firm, Jones Consultants, and Saudi Arabian company, Allied Maintenance, have both received contracts from BAE.[142]

Safadi's close relationship with BAE is further reflected in his making available a luxury penthouse flat at Roseberry Court, Mayfair, to Sir Dick Evans through one of his offshore companies. It adjoins the flat previously made available to Evans by a company belonging to Wafic Said.[143] Safadi was also an investor in British Mediterranean Airways, an entity set up in 1994 to fly predominantly to the Middle East.[144] Wafic Said invested in the company, which had Charles Powell on the board.[145] With links like these it is unsurprising that he played a crucial role in the routing of payments on Al Yamamah.

It should be noted that the use of foreign bank accounts to funnel payments in this way was not strictly illegal until the introduction of anti-bribery and anti-money laundering legislation in the UK in 2002.

Like Wafic Said, most of those involved in Al Yamamah have claimed their roles were negligible or non-existent. This was not an option open to Prince Bandar. Instead he argued that the money which accumulated in the Bank of England Deso account from the 2 per cent commission taken on oil sales was used by BAE and Deso to purchase weapons on behalf of the Saudis that the US would not sell directly to them. Sources close to Prince Bandar have said: 'if the Saudis wanted to buy ten Super Puma helicopters, and the Ministry of Defence budget is X amount, the Ministry of Finance will say this is what you've been allocated this year. It means that you have to defer this purchase until next year.' A deferral, it is argued, would give AIPAC in the US time to mobilize against the arms sale. The source continues:

> What Al Yamamah did, because it is oil for services, is to say: Okay. Al Yamamah picks up the tab; Saudi Arabia will sign with the French or who-ever and Britain pays them on their behalf. So suddenly now the Saudis have an operational weapons system complete with its support that doesn't reflect on Al Yamamah as a project. Therefore, if Saudi Arabia wants some services from the Americans, or some weapons systems that they have to buy now, otherwise Congress will object to it later, and they can't get it from their current defense budget, then they simply tell Al Yamamah, 'You divert that money.'[146]

There is some evidence to support Bandar's contention. For instance, a State Department cable from 2004 states that a Saudi deal to buy twelve Cougar helicopters for $600m and forty-four Bell 412 helicopters for $400m would be financed through Al Yamamah. BAE would pay the French firm Eurocopter and Canadian firm Bell on behalf of the Saudis after receiving funds from oil sales through the Al Yamamah deal. The State Department raised questions about the steep price of the helicopters, noting, however, that the department was 'not aware of any financial inducements, incentives, commissions, offsets, or investments associated with either transaction'.[147]

The cable went on to say: 'Inquiry with local sources into the general subject of financial inducements drew raised eyebrows, smirks and comments like, "You can buy a large chateau with a lot of acreage in southern France at that price." We can only speculate that commissions will be included in the Cougar purchase, although post is not aware of in what amounts and for whom.'[148] It was also mentioned that 'the driving force behind the acquisition of combat search and rescue aircraft for the RSAF has been Maj Gen Prince Turki bin Nasser bin Abd Al-Aziz Al Saud, RSAF director of operations. . . . Turki bin Nasser apparently has hit upon a means to purchase helicopters he badly wants but cannot afford: Oil, employing the Al Yamamah vehicle for payment (needless to say, BAE is outraged over the encroachment).'[149]

The use of Al Yamamah money to buy arms for Saudi Arabia was a defence repeated by Louis Freeh, Prince Bandar's lawyer and a former Director of the FBI (1993–2001), despite the fact that it would undermine the oversight role of the US Congress in relation to arms exports and frustrate any attempt at accountable budgeting.

Even if one accepts this rather dubious defence, it still does not answer any of the questions about the personal use of vast amounts of the money, despite Prince Bandar denying any wrongdoing. Asked specifically about the $17m from the accounts spent on a palace for Prince Bandar, Louis Freeh offered the following explanation on PBS:

> **Narrator:** According to these Suspicious Activity Reports, there were transactions that appear to be personal, for example, payments to an architect in Saudi Arabia for work on a new palace for Prince Bandar totaling $17m.
>
> **Dennis Lormel:** That's something you don't see in the normal course of business, an individual moving $17m from an account, a business account, to what appears to be personal.
>
> **Louis Freeh:** The $17m for his 'residence' – quote, unquote – was not his residence. It's a government-owned property in the kingdom of Saudi Arabia which they make available to senior members of the royal family to live.

He went on:

LF: Allegations that my client received $2 billion in bribes, received for free as a bribe an Airbus 340, those allegations are totally false.

Lowell Bergman: In U.S. government documents, the al Yamamah contract is described as off the books of the regular budget of the Saudi Ministry of Defense. Is that correct?

LF: It's an off-balance barter deal, oil for planes.

LB: But it was a pile of money, if you will, large amounts of money that didn't go through the regular budgetary process of the government of Saudi Arabia.

LF: That's correct.

Narrator: Freeh has an explanation for the $2 billion that was sent to Washington.

LF: Look at it this way, Lowell. This was a treaty that was set up to ensure maximum flexibility for the purchase of arms. If the Ministry of Defense and Aviation wanted to purchase U.S. arms, U.S. arms could be purchased through BAE and the U.K. ministry in a way that did not deal with the objection of the U.S. Congress to the selling of American equipment to the Saudis.

LB: So proceeds from the oil could be used under this contract to purchase arms from other countries, including the United States?

LF: Of course.

Narrator: Following this interview, FRONTLINE asked Louis Freeh for a specific example of an arms deal with the U.S. paid for from the $2 billion. He did not provide one. Freeh had responded to our questions about that Airbus 340.

LB: Can't you even see that as an indication there's something funny going on here?

LF: No. Absolutely not. Absolutely not. The plane was assigned to him. It was owned by the Royal Saudi Air Force, operated by them principally for my client because he travelled the most, and was never a gift or a bribe to my client.

LB: Do you know of any other military aircraft that's painted in the colours of the Dallas Cowboys?

LF: Don't know of any.

LB: Sound like a private plane?

LF: No, it doesn't sound like a private plane.

LB: But when is something a government expenditure and when is something a personal expenditure when it's a prince like Bandar in the Saudi government?

LF: Let's look at it from their perspective. If his majesty, the king of Saudi Arabia, and the Minister of Defense and Aviation –

LB: Who's his father.

LF: Who's his father, and the minister of oil and the minister of finance – if they all agree and are aware of what's being expended by whom, how they disbursed it or how they distributed it, including dividing what was personal or not personal, is really none of the business of the United States.[150]

That a former Director of the FBI would defend these actions is surprising. But it reflects the nature of the relationship between the American political elite and the Saudi royal family, whose attitude to corruption was best encapsulated by Prince Bandar himself:

Prince Bandar: You know what? I would be offended if I thought we had a monopoly on corruption.

Narrator: Prince Bandar would not give us an interview today, but he did in 2001 when FRONTLINE asked him about corruption and the Saudi Royal Family.

PB: But the way I answer the corruption charges is this. In the last 30 years, we have made, we have implemented a development program that was approximately, close to $400 billion worth. You could not have done all of that for less than, let's say, $350 billion. Now, if you tell me that building this whole country and spending $350 billion out of $400 billion, that we had misused or got corrupted with $50 billion, I'll tell you, 'Yes.' But I'll take that any time.

But more important, who are you to tell me this? I mean, I see every time all the scandals here, or in England, or in Europe. What I'm trying to tell you is, so what? We did not invent corruption. This happened since – since Adam and Eve. I mean, Adam and Eve were in heaven and they had hanky-panky and they had to go down to earth. So I mean this is – this is human nature. But we are not as bad as you think![151]

6.   Diamonds and Arms

The 'pacifist' der Hovsepian and Nicholas Oman were but two of many members of the Merex network who were actively involved in arms trafficking in Africa, the conflict-ridden Mecca for the trade. The network was well-connected in the less stable regions of the continent, counting among its agents the notorious Liberian warlord-President Charles Taylor and his brother Bob, an employee of Barclays Bank.[1]

With his considerable connections, Taylor was able to manoeuvre himself into power in the small West African state that had been formed by 'free slaves' given leeway by the US to return to their 'homeland' from 1821. His battle to achieve and maintain power turned an already impoverished nation into a brutalized killing field. Its horrors were spread into its resource-rich neighbour Sierra Leone, unleashing a whirlwind of human brutality: amputations, mass killings, beheadings and ritualized murder – all made possible by a network of arms dealers, diamond smugglers and timber merchants who populated the shadow world. Most were thuggish criminals moving in the crevices of international legal jurisdiction. Some were more organized, such as the network of arms dealers linked to Merex and the web of Al Qaeda diamond dealers that used Liberia to turn streams of foreign currency into the most mobile asset in the world.

Taylor's background gave little hint of his later endeavours. Born in 1948 just outside the Liberian capital of Monrovia, he was the third of fifteen children in an American-Liberian household.[2] His father had a stable job as a schoolteacher and as a result the Taylor family were able to live a solid middle-class lifestyle. Charles initially followed in his father's footsteps, starting his training as a teacher. However, in 1972 he relocated to the US – the promised land of Liberia's elite – to study economics at Bentley College, ten miles from Boston.[3] During his five years at Bentley, Taylor gained a reputation among his US classmates as a feisty leader, impressing himself upon local political circles.[4]

Taylor's education guaranteed him a place at the banquet table of the Liberian elite, undoubtedly aided by his political sympathies. During a demonstration in New York in 1979 he made public his distaste for the then President of Liberia, William Tolbert. The following year he travelled to Liberia, where he actively supported the military overthrow of Tolbert by Samuel Kanyon Doe, who would rule Liberia by diktat for the next decade. Later Taylor would have a hand in Doe's overthrow. But in 1980 Taylor was a loyalist and was given a senior position in Doe's government overseeing all public acquisition.[5] His star waned shortly afterwards when he was accused of using his government post for rampant embezzlement, siphoning off $900,000 into his personal accounts.[6] These accusations forced him to flee the country in the early 1980s under threat of prosecution. He re-established himself in his old stamping ground of Massachusetts, where he was a wanted man after Liberia requested his extradition. He was arrested in 1984 and held in the Plymouth County Correctional Facility.

Jail could not hold Taylor for long. The following year he escaped from Plymouth County in circumstances that remain mysterious. One account has it that Taylor banded together with four other inmates to saw through their cell bars and escape using knotted bed sheets, with Taylor paying $50,000 to be part of the plan.[7] However, the ease with which he escaped and was able to quickly move abroad has belied the idea of a simple jailbreak. Assistance may have been forthcoming from more official quarters. According to Taylor's own account he did not escape but was rather 'released' with the help of US intelligence agencies.[8] He recalled that he was led out of his cell in the maximum security section of the prison and walked into the minimum security section, where he was allowed to climb out using roped bed clothes. Outside he found a car ready to take him around the US.[9] The CIA has denied any complicity in the escape,[10] but the agency's denial is undermined by two facts. Only a few days after his escape Taylor's Liberian ally Thomas Quiwonkpa, who had allegedly received limited US backing, attempted to overthrow the President, Samuel Doe.[11] And secondly, Taylor was able to travel unhindered from Plymouth County to Washington, then Atlanta and finally Mexico, despite using his own passport.[12]

He swiftly returned to Africa with the intention of overthrowing Samuel Doe and seizing power in Liberia. He was received sympathetically in a number of countries, including Burkina Faso, where he joined forces with various Liberian exiles, most notably Prince Johnson, a would-be warlord who had been part of Quiwonkpa's failed attempt to overthrow Doe. They formed the National Patriotic Front of Liberia (NPFL), a group that would oversee the country's brutal misery for fifteen years. With military training and ambitions the Liberian exiles caught the attention of the Burkinabe presidential hopeful, Blaise Compaore, who asked for help in overthrowing the President of Burkina Faso, Thomas Sankara. The support of President Houphouët-Boigny of the Ivory Coast added impetus to the plan. On 15 October 1987 Sankara was killed by a Burkinabe squad that included a number of Liberian operatives, one of whom was Prince Johnson.[13] Many suggest that Taylor had an active role in the murder.[14] As a consequence, when he was preparing to invade Liberia two years later, Taylor could rely on Burkina Faso and the Ivory Coast for support, initially diplomatically and later as a channel through which arms and supplies could be delivered.

This support provided Taylor and the NPFL with considerable diplomatic cachet. But what they needed was a benefactor who could provide more than diplomatic cover. They found this in the figure of Libya's maverick dictator, Muammar Gaddafi. In 1987, Taylor travelled to Libya, where he and his Liberian partners were inducted into Gaddafi's World Revolutionary Headquarters,[15] a training camp for those groups Gaddafi wished to see achieve their national ambitions, as well as his own megalomaniacal vision.[16] As an oil-rich state often involved in military intrigue, Libya was able to provide Taylor and the NPFL with what they really needed: military training, weapons, ammunition and millions of dollars.

At the same time Gaddafi was overseeing the creation of the Revolutionary United Front (RUF), a sadistic group who were preparing to take over Liberia's diamond-rich neighbour, Sierra Leone, by force.[17] Taylor befriended the RUF leader, Foday Sankoh.[18] It was to be a fateful friendship. Between 1990 and 2005 the RUF and NPFL would symbiotically feed off each other's resources to take control of their respective countries, in one of the world's most bountiful diamond-producing regions.

On Christmas Eve 1989, Charles Taylor and the NPFL made their move. Their aim was simple: progress through the countryside, gather supporters and overthrow the existing dictator while taking control of the capital, Monrovia. His swift march through Liberia was aided by the cheering support of locals, some of whom believed he would remove the genuinely unpopular Doe and install a form of responsible government.

A number of the so-called 'country people' were driven by their antipathy towards Americo-Liberians, while others were fuelled by the temptation of looting. Taylor later recalled that as the NPFL advanced into Liberia 'we didn't even have to act. People came to us and said: "Give me a gun. How can I kill the man who killed my mother?"'[19] By June 1990, the NPFL had reached the capital and victory seemed assured.[20] Samuel Doe, whose presidency had been inaugurated with the murder of the former President Tolbert, was to suffer a similar fate. A splinter group of the NPFL led by Prince Johnson instead of Taylor, stormed into Doe's office. Over the course of a number of excruciating hours Doe was viciously tortured. As his ears were cut off amidst blood-curdling screams an insouciant Johnson sipped on celebratory Budweisers, demanding to know the dictator's banking details.[21] The grisly video of the murder was quickly reproduced and sold in huge numbers throughout West Africa.[22]

Just as Taylor believed that his blitzkrieg assault on Liberia had succeeded, his advance was blocked by interference from other West African states. A number of them, Nigeria in particular, worried about the impact of Taylor's accession on the balance of power in the region: with Taylor backed by Burkina Faso and the Ivory Coast, Nigeria's role in regional politics would be considerably weakened. Therefore, to prevent Taylor and the NPFL seizing power, a nominally independent force was put together by the Economic Community of West African States (ECOWAS). Most of the troops were provided by Nigeria. When the regional body's monitoring group, ECOMOG, was deployed, Taylor's forces were already in Monrovia but had been unable to take the presidential palace. ECOMOG immediately reclaimed some of the territory Taylor's forces had gained. It was a setback that Taylor would turn into a long-lasting grudge.

By the end of 1990, the warring parties had reached a stalemate. Monrovia was under the control of ECOMOG troops, a number of whose officers pursued criminal and business interests in the capital – which provided a powerful motivation for continuing the war. Prince Johnson's NPFL splinter group had set itself up in a corner of Monrovia, failing to make any meaningful impact, while Charles Taylor, by virtue of his political nous and constant access to radio production facilities and the international news media, established himself as the pre-eminent leader of the NPFL. He formalized the area under his control, naming it Greater Liberia, and operated a virtual second state from this base.[23]

His control over Greater Liberia gave Taylor the perfect opportunity to consolidate his power and earn considerable amounts of money. He ensured that one of the biggest employers in the area, the Firestone Tyre company, returned to operation. By 1992 Firestone was turning a good profit and paying Taylor's NPFL $2m a year for 'protection'.[24] It was later alleged that a number of the warlord's most notorious operations were launched from the properties of Firestone.[25] Taylor also oversaw the re-emergence of the Liberian timber sector, whose 'taxes' further boosted his 'second state'. Besides demanding that foreign businessmen build roads and other necessities, Taylor also took a cut of every business deal. It was estimated that he extorted between $75m and $100m every year in this way, with his loot secreted in personal accounts throughout Africa.[26] It was a system that Taylor would perfect when he was eventually elected President in 1997.

Taylor's relationship with the Revolutionary United Front (RUF) in Sierra Leone further fattened his bank accounts and aided his military effort. The RUF was the spitting image of the NPFL. It was constituted by a small handful of Sierra Leonean exiles and had been officially estab-lished at Muammar Gaddafi's World Revolutionary Headquarters. In 1991, the RUF invaded Sierra Leone assisted by the NPFL.[27] Ostensibly it sought to take political power, symbolized by the overrunning of Free-town, the seat of government. But of greater importance was control over large swathes of the countryside that offered glittering wealth in the form of diamonds. The RUF 'remained a bandit organization solely driven by the survivalist needs of its predominantly uneducated and alien-ated commanders'.[28]

As a well-armed group of bandits and thugs the RUF was as brutal as the NPFL, using child soldiers to fight many of its wars. Local citizens were forced into compliance and servitude in an orgy of amputations and rapes. Slave labour was also used to translate the diamonds into the real currency in the region – weapons. Local citizens were forced to walk from the diamond fields to the porous border of Liberia and Sierra Leone, where diamonds were given to the NPFL and crates of weapons handed over in return. Without rest and under the constant threat of beatings if they stumbled, most of the human mules used by the RUF died within a couple of months.[29] For Liberia it meant a massive increase in diamond exports, even though diamond production in the country was minimal.

In Sierra Leone official diamond exports fell from 2 million carats per year in the 1960s to a risible 9,000 carats in 1999.[30] Liberia was suddenly exporting 6 million carats annually by the early 2000s, even though it could only produce 200,000 carats from its own diamond fields.[31]

To maintain both his military challenge for power in Liberia and his support for the RUF, Taylor needed a range of interconnected services from the early 1990s: arms dealing, diamond smuggling and money laundering. Each was complicated by international approbation, especially weapons dealing, which was criminalized by a UN arms embargo in November 1992 that prohibited the sale of arms to any side in the Liberian conflict.[32] To secure these services Taylor used the interconnected web of Merex agents, becoming an agent himself in the process.

Nicholas Oman, the Australian-Slovenian arms dealer who had been a part of the Merex network in the Balkans, was involved in Liberia from 1992. He allied himself with Charles Taylor and supplied him with weapons. This relationship revealed itself in a number of related ways. While Nicholas Oman was stripped of his diplomatic relationship with Liberia in 1996, just prior to Charles Taylor's election to the position of President, his son, Mark Oman, was appointed the official representative of Liberia in Australia soon after, a position he held until Taylor's fall from power.[33] Mark also continued to run his father's company, Orbal Marketing, in Liberia,[34] and even announced a fire sale of diamonds in violation of international embargoes in 2003,[35] suggesting that the Oman family remained in close contact with Taylor and the NPFL.

Nicholas Oman worked closely with the relatively unknown Taylor Nill, who (falsely) presented himself as an ambassador for the US in Liberia. Nill would later emerge as an important player in International Business Consult (IBC), along with other shareholders such as the RUF's Ibrahim Bah and Charles Taylor himself.[36] IBC was the vehicle Taylor used to secure a substantial amount of arms using the extended Merex network. This was confirmed by Roger D'Onofrio. Holding joint US–Italian citizenship, D'Onofrio was frequently fingered as a CIA agent who had retired from active service in the early 1990s.[37] He both affirmed and denied his CIA connections, flip-flopping as the situation required. After his 'retirement' from the CIA, D'Onofrio settled in Naples and busied himself in the affairs of Italy's criminal and Mafiosi elites, where he met a man who would become his close confidant, the Catania lawyer Michele Papa.[38]

Papa had made a name for himself in Italy through the 1970s and 1980s for his role as a go-between for Italian business and Libya. From the 1970s, Libya had bought significant stakes in Italian enterprises, at one time holding 13 per cent of the shares in Italy's mega-corporation, FIAT.[39] In the 1980s, Italy was the second-largest importer of Libyan oil, just behind America.[40] As a result of this economic activity Libya needed Italian intermediaries and Michele Papa rose to become one of the most influential of these, a position cemented by his heading the Sicilian–Libyan friendship organization and overseeing the building of the first mosque in Italy.[41] His role was not without controversy, as the French daily *Le Monde* reported:

> He periodically organizes Italian–Libyan friendship fetes with gigantic portraits of [Gaddafi] and President Sandro Pertini, thus stirring up protests from the presidency of the Republic [of Italy]. He has also enabled Libyans to obtain indirect control of two local television stations in Sicily. In his newspaper, *Sicilia Oggi*, he extols the achievements of the Libyan Revolution and sings the praises of its leader.[42]

Papa's links to Libya embroiled him in the so-called 'Billygate' scandal in the US in the late 1970s, which was named after the bumbling brother of President Jimmy Carter. From the early 1970s, Libya had been stifled by its acrimonious relationship with the US administration, reflected in the halting of weapons and aircraft purchases worth $300m.[43] What Libya needed was a friendly ear in proximity to the White House. Billy Carter's was available for purchase. In January 1978, Papa invited the President's brother to visit Libya. Over the next twelve months Carter made a number of visits in the company of Papa, even forming his own version of Papa's association, the Libya–Arab–Georgia Friendship Society.[44] So aggressive was Billy in his promotion of Libya that he was forced to register as a foreign agent with the CIA.[45] When news broke that he had received a loan of $220,000 from his new friends, all hell broke loose in Washington. Although Jimmy Carter was eventually cleared of ever being susceptible to the sales pitch of his brother, 'Billygate' overshadowed his presidency just as his campaign for re-election against Ronald Reagan was beginning.

In 1992, Papa and D'Onofrio set their sights on Africa. Through IBC they aimed to engage in the import and export of various products.[46] Papa suggested that they operate from Liberia, a country with close links to Libya. 'Liberia has always been a great country for offshore finance deals,' D'Onofrio enthused to Italian interrogators.[47] D'Onofrio put the plan in motion by travelling to Foya in Liberia, a province controlled by Charles Taylor which borders Sierra Leone and Guinea. There he met with Taylor and the Libyan-trained RUF leader Ibrahim Bah.[48] For Taylor, IBC was the perfect company through whom to acquire arms and sell his diamonds. 'Taylor and I spoke at length with Bah, and we decided that IBC would be used to get arms for them,' D'Onofrio recalled.[49] IBC would pay for the arms in smuggled Sierra Leonean diamonds, carried into Liberia by the RUF's slave labour. To convince the warlord of their bona fides, Papa and D'Onofrio transferred 50 per cent of IBC's shares to Charles Taylor and his associates, ensuring that half of any profits made would be recycled back into the accounts of Taylor and co.[50] In 1993 alone the company made a profit of $3m.[51]

None of the parties to the IBC agreement knew how to organize money transfers in a way that would obscure the origins of their ill-gotten gains. Nor did many arms dealers trust Taylor and Bah to make good on their promise to supply diamonds. One man provided the solution. Dennis Anthony Moorby, himself a Merex agent,[52] was the chief executive officer of Swift International Services based in Canada, which had signed a number of working agreements with IBC in the early 1990s.[53] According to a joint investigation by Italian and Canadian police services, Moorby was deeply connected with Mafia families in the United States, including the infamous Gotti family and the Gambino clan.[54] Moorby appointed one Francesco Elmo as legal officer for Swift International Services.[55] Elmo was a well-connected Italian arms dealer who, when apprehended, provided detailed evidence to Italian authorities that helped unravel the activities of the like of Nicholas Oman, Franco Giorgi, Joe der Hovsepian, Gerhard Mertins, as well as D'Onofrio and Moorby.

Through an intricate system of credit lines based on pre-war German bonds and valuable minerals held in banks in the US and elsewhere, Swift assisted IBC to effectively launder Liberia's diamonds, providing a clean pile of money with which to buy arms. The effectiveness of the system was illustrated in 1993 when an order was placed with clean money for a range of ammunition and guns to be supplied to IBC by a Swiss contact with the Bulgarian arms manufacturers Kintex. The arms were delivered to Liberia disguised as an innocuous load of oranges and olives.[56]

Kintex was linked by Western officials to major drug and weapons trafficking from at least 1985 onwards. In the early 1990s, it was reportedly Bulgaria's single largest foreign exchange earner. In the late 1980s, BNL, a bank used by the US to channel funds to Saddam Hussein, gave two unsecured loans to Kintex to buy equipment on behalf of Iraq – one for $30m and another for $11m. The first was used to purchase computer equipment which later turned up at an Iraqi complex known as Al Hatteen, where Iraqis were allegedly working on high explosives as part of its nuclear weapons experiments. The $11m was used to purchase electronic equipment, material and machinery on behalf of the Iraqi defence ministry.[57]

By the mid-1990s, matters in Liberia had reached a stalemate. ECOMOG forces had pushed Charles Taylor further back into the countryside. At one time it seemed that he might even be dislodged from the country entirely. But Taylor frequently regrouped, pushing ECOMOG back in turn and threatening the fragile peace that held in Monrovia. Taylor's relationship with Nigeria began to improve after the departure of President Babangida in 1993. By late 1996 it was clear that Nigeria would allow Taylor a crack at the presidency via an election. In August 1997, seven years after he had first invaded the country, Charles Taylor was elected President. The NPFL won nearly 75 per cent of the vote in a campaign that was marked by their supporters' chants of 'He killed my pa, he killed my ma, but I'll vote for him.'[58] That a brutal warlord could win so overwhelmingly in a generally free and fair election may seem incomprehensible. But for many in Liberia granting Taylor power seemed the only way to end one of Africa's most brutal conflicts.[59]

Hopes of peace were quickly dashed as Taylor faced continuing insurgencies against his rule, especially from 1999 onwards. He also continued his support of RUF rebels in Sierra Leone, reaping the benefits of their mutual kleptocracy. As President, Taylor stepped up the systems he had developed to perfection in Greater Liberia, earning considerable income from timber production and mineral extraction. His needs during the civil war were replicated in the post-election period: arms, diamond smuggling and money laundering. Unfortunately for Taylor much of the network he had used prior to 1997 had dissipated by the time he won power. While Nicholas Oman was forced to flee the Balkans to escape the clutches of Radovan Karadzic, others had been apprehended. By 1996, the Italian police had stitched together a sprawling patchwork of international criminality as part of an investigation known as 'Cheque to Cheque'. Arrest warrants were issued for key players in the extended Merex network, including Oman, Moorby, Roger D'Onofrio and Swift International's Rudolf Meroni. While none were ever prosecuted, the arrests, temporarily at least, disrupted their activities.

Fortunately for Taylor there were others equally nefarious, delighted to step into the breach. A retired Israeli Defence Force Colonel, Yair Klein, provided matériel and training to Liberia's Anti-Terrorism Unit and, in violation of the UN arms embargo, to the RUF as part of a diamonds-for-arms operation involving two other Israelis, Dov Katz and Dan Gertler. In January 1999, Klein was arrested in Sierra Leone on charges of smuggling arms to the RUF.[60]

In September 1998, Taylor had a fateful meeting with an insalubrious Ukrainian-Israeli, Leonid Minin.[61] Born Leonid Bluvstein in Odessa, Ukraine, in 1947, Minin followed the route of many Jewish Russian émigrés and settled in Israel, arriving via Austria. Around 1975 he moved once more, eventually receiving permanent residence while living in the town of Norvenich, close to Bonn and Cologne in West Germany.[62]

During the 1970s and 1980s, Minin had dabbled unsuccessfully in a variety of business activities. By the early 1990s, he appeared on the radars of investigative authorities in Italy and beyond. In 1992, Russian police investigated him for involvement in smuggling art works and antiques.[63] Two years later a former model, Kristina Calcaterra, was caught at the border between France and Switzerland carrying a small bag of cocaine. According to Calcaterra the cocaine belonged to Minin, who had asked her to deliver it to him in Switzerland. In March 1997, he was arrested by police in Nice as he attempted to board his personal jet. He was carrying a small bag of cocaine, for which he received an eight-month prison sentence. This arrest alerted authorities in Monaco, where Minin had a number of businesses. In June 1997, he was informed by letter that he was no longer welcome in Europe's glitziest principality. His German visa was also repealed and his name entered on the Schengen Index as 'a person not to be admitted' to this group of European states.[64]

His drug misdemeanours seem minor in contrast to his involvement in mafia activities in the Ukraine. The collapse of the Soviet Union provided a once-in-a-lifetime opportunity for smart, tough criminals. The temporary collapse of the state, corruption among senior politicians and the rapid privatization of primary resources allowed mafia groups to seize control of highly valuable assets. The oil and gas industry was immediately lucrative because of the voracious export market.[65] By the early 1990s, it was reported that 67 per cent of all oil exports from Russia were controlled by organized crime, whose tentacles stretched to the highest corridors of power.[66] Odessa on the Black Sea was the gateway for much of the East's oil and gas exports. In the early 1990s, the Odessa *Neftemafija* (oil mafia) took control of the town's exporting facilities.[67] Minin was 'one of the most important' members of the entire *Neftemafija* network. His companies, Limad and Galaxy, had a major foothold in the area, controlling large parts of the export trade. They were given a contract to build a refinery that would boost Odessa's ability to refine Russia's crude oil prior to export.[68] In addition to making a fortune in the oil business, the broader mafia network under Minin's control was also allegedly 'involved in international arms and drug trafficking, money laundering, extortions and other offences'.[69]

While international police services struggled for hard evidence to turn these allegations into a prosecution, Belgian police believed they had gathered enough information to implicate Minin in a murder. In December 1994, a Russian entrepreneur, Vladimir Missiourine, was shot dead by three men in the Brussels suburb of Uccle. Belgian police traced a series of phone calls from Missiourine's business to Minin's Galaxy group. Missiourine, who was also suspected of links to Russian organized crime, had developed a business relationship with Minin before they fell out. Police uncovered an invoice sent by Missiourine to Minin's Galaxy Energy, demanding a commission payment of $117,240. It had been sent to Minin's company only four days before Missiourine was found murdered.[70] However, as with most of the investigations into Minin, little hard evidence was presented that could definitively link the Ukrainian to the murder. He was free to carry on his business unhindered.

Given the company he kept and the activities he engaged in, it is hardly surprising that in the second half of the 1990s rumours abounded that elements of the Russian mafia had ordered a hit on Minin.[71] As a consequence he was keen to expand his empire beyond Europe. In 1998, he had a chance encounter that would lead him to Liberia. Minin was in Ibiza exploring the potential for entering the real estate business, where he met a Russian estate agent, Vadim Semov. Semov introduced Minin to a close Spanish friend, Fernando Robleda. After lengthy conversations it became clear that Robleda could offer Minin an escape to Africa via his company Exotic Tropic Timber Enterprises (ETTE) in Liberia.[72]

Robleda had formed ETTE as a logging company in February 1997.[73] To make serious profits the logging company required a licence, or concession, from the government. In May, ETTE was granted a concession to harvest the sizeable Cavalla Reforestation and Research Plantation in Liberia.[74] Unfortunately for Robleda the concession had been granted by the opponents of Charles Taylor two months before he was elected President. Robleda's concessions were 'unilaterally' revoked by the Liberian Forest Development Agency in November 1997.[75] He had a logging company but no access to logs. It was a devastating blow for ETTE, especially as Robleda had already spent nearly half a million dollars in advanced taxes to the previous administration and on machinery.[76]

Robleda hoped that the arrival of new investors would not only inject capital into the company but also help to regain its Cavalla plantation concession. In September 1998, Minin travelled with Robleda to Liberia, where they met Charles Taylor. What happened at the meeting is contested: Robleda, when later interrogated by Italian police, recalled that he had travelled with Minin to Liberia but was not privy to any meetings between Taylor and Minin. Instead he claimed that Minin met Taylor a number of times over the course of the week. What they discussed remained secret, although Robleda says Minin continually remarked that he was 'in debt' to Taylor, suggesting some sort of deal had been struck.[77] By contrast, Minin claimed that Robleda had attended the meetings and convinced him to pay 'advance taxes', effectively a bribe, directly to Taylor. The President then demanded a commitment to further commission payments in the future.[78] Minin's testimony was a clear acknowledgement that, coerced or not, he had agreed to play the corrupt game Taylor demanded of new entrants into Liberia.

Following the meetings events moved swiftly. An ETTE board meeting was held on 10 December at the Hotel Africa in Monrovia, the chosen meeting place of nearly every schemer, businessman and arms dealer in

Liberia, even after it had been reduced to a shell during the civil war. At the meeting ETTE was reconstituted and its shareholding restructured. Minin now controlled 34 per cent while Robleda and his friend Semov held the rest. Confirming his seniority Minin was appointed chairman of the board of ETTE, Semov president and Robleda treasurer.[79] Barely four days later, ETTE was granted the concession to harvest the Cavalla plantation. The agreement noted that ETTE was looking to acquire additional concessions, which the government indicated it would grant.[80]

It was a remarkable turnaround for the company, indicating the impact that Minin had on Taylor. In addition to cash payments Minin made clear to the bellicose President that he could also provide him with weapons. Within a week of the company receiving its concession Minin helped Taylor move a considerable stock of arms. It is assumed that the cache had been sourced by Minin in the Ukraine before being transported on two trips to Monrovia in December 1998. On the second trip the plane was loaded with 68 tons of ammunition and weapons which had cost roughly $1.5m.[81] The weapons were quickly ferried across the border to be used in the brutal attack known as 'Operation No Living Thing' in early January.

In less than two weeks 6,000 innocent people were murdered and tens of thousands injured, most maimed for life. Over 500 buildings were destroyed by fire and ransacking, leaving a shell of a city.[82] 'There was a millenarian quality to the terror, random, ecstatic and finally comprehensive.'[83]

Minin's successful gun-run, while brutal in consequence, was considerably smaller in scale than those that would follow. Over the next year and a half he conducted at least two further deals with Liberia and possibly another one which remains shrouded in mystery. The first involved another shipment of 68 tons of assorted arms: 715 boxes of weapons and cartridges, 408 boxes of cartridge powder, a smattering of anti-tank missiles, and RPG launchers and ammunition.[84] The weapons had come from the Ukrainian state-owned company Ukrspetsexport. An end-user certificate dated 10 February 1999 indicates that the weapons were to be sold to a Gibraltar-based company, Chartered Engineering and Technical Services, and delivered to the Ministry of Defence in Burkina Faso aboard a giant Ukrainian Antonov 124. It was signed by Lieutenant-Colonel Gilbert Diendere, the head of the Presidential Guard of Burkina Faso.[85] Some of the weapons remained in Ouagadougou while the rest were trucked to the town of Bobo Dioulasso. From 17 to 30 March, Minin used his jet to transport the weapons from the two depots in Burkina Faso to Liberia.[86] Pictures later presented in court showed the weapons crates hastily buckled into plush leather seats.[87]

Whether Minin began arranging a second arms transaction in 1999 is still unclear, a situation that has suited Minin's erstwhile business partner, Erkki Tammivuori. Tammivuori, a Finnish national, has a history of links to political power. His father, Olavi, was a prominent Finnish business-man who made his name developing opportunities for Finnish entre-preneurs in Turkey, becoming Finland's Honorary Consul to Istanbul towards the end of the 1980s.[88] Son Erkki also married into Finnish polit-ical royalty when he wed the daughter of Ahti Karjalainen, twice Prime Minister. Tammivuori followed in his father's footsteps by establishing a number of business interests in Turkey. It was on the letterhead of one of these companies, MET AS, that Tammivuori corresponded frequently with Leonid Minin through 1999 and 2000.

Minin suggests he first met Tammivuori through one of his pilots, who was also Finnish, at a New Year celebration in Switzerland at the turn of the millennium.[89] The written record suggests earlier contact. On 20 March 1999, Tammivuori faxed Minin asking whether he could source Ukrainian boats, including hovercraft, for the Turkish navy.[90] Over the next year Tammivuori and Minin attempted a number of transactions in Liberia, facilitated not only by Minin's contact with Charles Taylor but also the rapport that was established between Tammivuori and Taylor's son, 'Chucky' or 'Junior'.[91] In June 1999, Tammivuori formalized his role as a 'consultant' to Minin's companies[92] as they explored opportunities in helping to privatize Liberian port and airport facilities.[93] A fax sent to Minin by Tammivuori on 19 September 1999 confirmed that Tammivuori would buy 'ten items of package [sic]' that could be displayed to potential customers in Amsterdam. Italian prosecutors believed that the 'ten items of package' were most likely blood diamonds exported from Liberia and Sierra Leone.[94]

It was through Chucky Taylor, with Minin's assistance, that Tammi-vuori is alleged to have organized his own weapons deal in Liberia. On 23 March 1999, Tammivuori wrote to Minin on a fax headed '"Konkurs" missiles procurement' describing the opportunity as a 'special one'. It detailed a potential transaction in which '"Konkurs" missiles would be procured (only missiles, no launchers), with a configuration [of] "TANDEM WARHEAD FOR REACTIVE ARMOUR".'[95] Tammivuori estimated that the 'buyer' would need eighty missiles, a hundred if the price was right. Intriguingly the Finn claimed that the transaction could be 'done with End-User or without Certificate', which suggested he would be happy to have the deal go ahead without any of the paperwork necessary for it to be legal.[96] Later that year, Tammivuori wrote once again to Minin informing him that he had started to work on a 'special package for JUNIOR' and that he would be happy to deliver it 'provided [Junior] can afford it'. Tammivuori asked Minin to open 'a line of communication with JUNIOR in case I need it' and confirmed that 'the package consists of 20–30 items in addition to the 100 units you know about'.[97] When interviewed, Tammivuori claimed that the deal did not involve Liberia but another potential buyer, whom he wasn't prepared to name.[98] However, one of Taylor's right-hand men, Sanjivan Ruprah, showed UN investigators lists of all weapons that had been transported into Liberia in a shipment in May 2000, which included a range of missile types and a handful of Konkurs missile launchers.[99]

Minin's final successful deal took place in mid-2000. This time the arms were to be delivered via the Ivory Coast, rather than Burkina Faso. On 14 July 2000, a giant Antonov-124 took off from the Ukrainian airport of Gostomel. Its cargo was a massive 113 tons, including '10,500 AK-47 assault rifles, 120 sniper rifles, 100 grenade-launchers, night-vision goggles and 8 million rounds of ammunition'.[100] The weapons had, once again, been sourced from the Ukraine, this time from the state-run Spetsehnoexport. After a brief stopover the plane touched down in the Ivory Coast on 15 July. It was allowed to land on the basis of an end-user certificate signed by an Ivory Coast official, a signature procured on the understanding that, once the plane had landed, Liberia would give half the cargo to the Ivory Coast government. The cargo was transported from the Ivory Coast to Liberia using smaller aircraft under the direction of Taylor's lieutenant, Sanjivan Ruprah.

Remarkably, 113 tons of matériel wasn't enough for Liberia and the Ivory Coast. The July 2000 deal with Minin included a second consignment of weapons, which were standing ready to be delivered once the first shipment had been made. This was never to happen.

Présidence de la République

Le Président

N°22 /PR

République de Côte d'Ivoire
Union – Discipline – Travail

Abidjan, le 26 Mai 2000

CERTIFICAT D'ACHAT

Nous, son Excellence Général de Brigade, Robert GUEI, Ministre de la Défense de la République de Côte d'Ivoire autorisons la Compagnie AVIA TREND représentée par Monsieur CHERNY VALERY de conclure le contrat d'achat des articles ci-dessous désignés :

N° D'ORDRE	LIBELLES	QUANTITES
1 a	Ammunition 76 2x39 mm Ball	5 000 000
1 b	Grenade Launcher M93 30 mm	50
2	30 mm Bombs for M93 Launcher	10 000
3	Thermal Image Binoculars	20
4	Thermal Image Weapon Sights	20
5	RPG-26 Launcher or M80 launcher	50
6	Grenade for RPG – 26 or M80	5000
7	PG-OG7 Grenades	1000
8	Ammunition 9X19 mm Parabellum	1 000 000
9	AGS-17 Grenade Launcher	50
10	Grenades for AGS-17	1000
11	Night VisionMonocular	50
12	GP –Kastyor Launcher	80
13	45 Pistol or CZ 99 9mm Para Pistol	2000
14	RPG-7	200
C1)	Sniper Gun 12,7 mm	50
2	Ammunition ="cal 12.7	5000
3	Sniper Gun cal 7.9 mm	50
4	Ammunition cal7,92 mm	5000
5	Sniper cal 7,62X51 (308)	70
6	Ammunition cal 7,62X51 mm	50 000
7	AK-47 Assault Rifle	10 500
	End of list-Total 21 items (Twenty-one)	
8	PK/ms	200
9	Ammunition PK/Ms	2 000 000
10	Pallard	2 000
11	40 mm Grenade for Pallard	10 000
12	60 mm	50
13	Rounds for 60 mm	1000

Nous Ministre de la Défense de la République de Côte d'Ivoire certifions que ces présents articles sont exclusivement pour utilisation et emploi sur le territoire ivoirien et non pour exportation dans un pays tiers.

Vu pour la légalisation de la signature
apposée ci-dessus de St Ma la Général
Robert GUEI, Ministre de la défense, Président de
la République de Côte d'Ivoire

N° 012/2000

Abidjan le 02 Juin 2000

L'Ambassadeur

Président de la République

Général Robert GUEI

Figure 2: False end-user certificate used by Leonid Minin to transport weapons through the Ivory Coast to Liberia

Early the following month, while celebrating his recent sales to Liberia, Leonid Minin was unceremoniously arrested.[101] 'We raided the Hotel Europa, surprising Minin, who was in bed, nude, with four prostitutes who were also nude. And they were in the process of passing a drug vial around,' the Police Chief of Cinisello Balsamo recounted.[102] Supposedly a disgruntled prostitute whom Minin had failed to pay provided a random tip-off to the police.[103] As the room was searched police realized the flabby, stoned man they had arrested was more than just a low-life with a drug problem. Diamonds worth $500,000 were discovered, which Minin could not prove came from a legitimate source, along with a bag holding $35,000 in Hungarian, American, Italian and Mauritian currency. But the real goldmine was Minin's briefcase of documents: nearly 1,500 papers in numerous languages painting a vivid portrait of his life as one of Liberia's chief arms dealers.[104]

Although he had been followed by Italian police since the early 1990s, Minin was not at first recognized for the gangster he was. It was only a few days later, after the documents had been translated, that Minin's real identity became clear. Charges were filed against him for drug offences, a prelude to indictment for illegal arms dealing. Minin would be out of action for a considerable period of time. Charles Taylor was down one arms dealer.

Minin's arrest was not the only impediment to his operations in Liberia. His involvement in ETTE was also running into trouble. Under interrogation Minin claimed that Fernando Robleda had been cheating him of money, embezzling large amounts and leaving a 'hole' of $300,000 in the accounts of the business.[105] Robleda claimed that, as soon as Minin had got involved, he had sent a bunch of Ukrainian 'thugs' to take control of the company. Over time the Spaniard was frozen out and feared for his life to the extent that he fled Liberia.[106] By September 1999, Robleda had found an alternative partner in the form of a company called Forum Liberia, which had been created earlier that year.[107] Minin agreed to relinquish his hold on ETTE if he was bought out by the new partner. Forum Liberia agreed to pay him $5m, disguised as an agreement to purchase plant and machinery. It would have been a smart profit of over $4m on the $900,000 Minin had originally invested. Robleda believed this would be enough to get Minin to leave the business. Instead, the Ukrainian pocketed an upfront payment of $1.5m and, according to Robleda, refused to hand back the forestry concessions or relinquish his shares. It was easy for Minin to hold on in this way as Forum's agreement with him had specifically eschewed talk of transferring ownership as they were keen to hide their involvement in the Liberian logging industry because an embargo on Liberian wood products was in place. Months after Minin had been arrested Robleda was still writing to him frantically to convince him to withdraw from ETTE, which would allow Robleda to continue working with Forum Liberia.

Unfortunately for Robleda, in May 2006 the Spanish holding company of Forum Liberia, known as Forum Filatelico,[108] was discovered to be a massive scam.[109] Forum Liberia, needless to say, was finished.

Minin's personal, legal and commercial difficulties, together with his extensive drug use, had made him erratic and unreliable for years before his eventual arrest. Mimicking his boss's behaviour, one of Minin's pilots was too drunk to fly a load for the Liberians. Charles Taylor was furious. His son, Chucky, knew of a Russian who registered some of his planes under the Liberian flag and claimed to be able to deliver anything to anywhere. He contacted Viktor Bout, who quickly arranged a pilot to assist the Taylors.[110]

Bout, known by a number of aliases, including Boutov, But, Budd and Bouta, was the most notorious arms dealer of the late 1990s and early 2000s. Born in 1963 in the small town of Dushanbee in the USSR,[111] Bout was highly proficient at languages, enrolling at the Soviet Union's Military Institute of Foreign Languages after his basic military training, reaching the rank of Lieutenant.[112] The institute, where he held senior rank, was closely connected to Russia's infamous GRU, the country's largest foreign intelligence service. Bout's father-in-law was a senior member of the KGB, perhaps even serving as one-time Deputy Chairman of the feared security service.[113]

Fluent in six languages and capable of flying a variety of aeroplanes, Bout decided in 1991 to pursue a career in the freighting business, a popular endeavour in the chaotic times following the fall of the Berlin Wall.[114] Acquiring planes was easy. Surplus military matériel was freely sold by army officials keen to make a quick buck, so Bout was able to purchase three massive transport aircraft for a mere $120,000.[115] Bout chroniclers Douglas Farah and Stephen Braun suspect that the Russian may have got the planes so cheap, along with an extensive and detailed list of ex-Soviet weapons clients, as a result of support from the KGB.[116] Russian military officials often declared planes unusable and sold them for scrap, despite the fact that they were fully operational, enabling Bout to rapidly grow his fleet to fifty planes.[117]

By 1992, Bout had entered the feral world of arms dealing. His first client was the newly installed Northern Alliance government of Afghanistan, who had previously fought a devastating war against nascent Taliban fighters. Bout travelled frequently to the treacherous country, where he came to know Ahmed Shah Massoud, a notable local politician, both war-lord and poet, dubbed the 'Lion of Panjshir'. Massoud and the gregarious Russian adventurer bonded over lavish dinners and a mutual affinity for hunting, which was often conducted from one of Massoud's helicopters with sniper rifles. The relationship secured Bout a number of profitable arms deals in which he ferried Russian weapons to Massoud.[118]

Bout's dealings with the Northern Alliance caused him considerable problems. On a routine flight in 1995, one of Bout's air freighters carrying ammunition to Kabul was intercepted and forced to land by an old MiG fighter jet belonging to the Taliban. Its occupants, all Bout employ-ees, were taken hostage and the onboard matériel seized. In August 1996, the captured pilots supposedly overpowered their captors and fled. The escape was probably staged to secure the pilots' freedom without dimin-ishing the fearsome reputation of their captors, who had become clients of the Russian. Ever the salesman, while negotiating with the Taliban about his captured jet and crew, Bout persuaded them of his skills as an arms dealer. Over the next few years he delivered massive quantities of weapons to the Taliban from his base in Sharjah in the United Arab Emir-ates, netting an estimated $50m.[119] He also helped the Taliban set up its own transport network by selling the organization a fleet of cargo planes in 1998.[120] In the wake of 9/11 Bout's relationship with the Taliban would make him an international pariah.

However, before his business dealings with the Taliban, Bout had already broken arms sanctions in Bosnia. He supplied weapons to Muslim Bos-nians who were facing the depredations of Serbian nationalists. The deals were funded by the Third World Relief Agency, a charity with links to Islamic extremists, including Osama bin Laden. Between 1992 and 1995, the agency handled over $400m.[121] In September 1992, some of this money was used to hire an Ilyushin 76 to deliver a substantial cache of arms from Khartoum in Sudan to Maribor, an airport in Slovenia close to Bosnia.[122] Bout owned the plane and was probably involved in the procurement of the weapons as well. So at the time at least three individuals linked to the Merex network – Bout, der Hovsepian and Nicholas Oman – were sup-plying arms to various participants in the Balkans conflict.

The fighting-ridden and resource-rich continent of Africa was a mag-net for Viktor Bout, as it was and remains for most arms dealers. He transported a contingent of French UN peacekeepers to Rwanda in a belated and futile attempt to prevent the Rwandan genocide. His first major African client was the Angolan government, which was fighting a decades-long conflict with the one-time US and apartheid South African ally UNITA. Bout developed a close working relationship with the Angolan military, in particular the country's air force. He supplied them with a wide range of matériel, creating a company in Belgium for the specific purpose. Between 1994 and 1998, Bout concluded contracts to the value of $325m with the Angolan air force.[123] However, in 1998 the Angolan government discovered that Bout had been supplying its mortal enemy, UNITA, with a range of weapons from Bulgarian arms manufacturers. Bout made thirty-seven delivery flights to UNITA, paid for with blood diamonds. The cargo included millions of rounds of ammunition, rocket launchers, cannons, anti-aircraft guns, mortar bombs and anti-tank rockets.[124] When the Angolan government discovered his duplicity Bout's contracts were cancelled. This was one of the few times a client had taken umbrage at Bout supplying both sides in a conflict.

The Russian had been introduced to Liberia and its lax aircraft registration rules, which he used extensively, by Sanjivan Ruprah, Taylor's lieutenant. A Kenyan national, Ruprah held mining interests in Kenya and was associated with a company, Branch Energy, which had diamond-mining rights in Sierra Leone.[125] Initially Ruprah had introduced the Sierra Leonean government, the RUF's opponents, to Executive Outcomes,[126] a mercenary group constituted by former apartheid special forces and other assorted rogues.[127] Executive Outcomes were highly effective after their entry into the war in 1995, forcing back the RUF's advances and regaining control of a number of valuable diamond fields.[128] Such were the fickle politics of the region that two years later Ruprah was working for Charles Taylor in sponsoring the RUF's seizure of Sierra Leone. By November 1999, Ruprah had so integrated himself into the Taylor inner circle that he was appointed 'Global Civil Aviation agent worldwide for the Liberian Civil Aviation Register'.[129] In effect he was the boss of Liberia's aeroplane registry, which Bout had already been using to conceal his arms-trading activities with considerable success. By 2000, Ruprah was directly involved with Bout in setting up front companies in Abidjan to effect arms deals. He had become Bout's 'business partner'.

By this time Bout was undertaking major deliveries for Taylor. He used a baffling array of front companies to do so, registering airline agencies such as San Air, Centrafrican Airlines and MoldTransavia in different countries around the world.[130] In the case of Centrafrican, Bout used a corrupt official in the Central African Republic to get the plane registered without the government's knowledge. In July and August 2000, one of Bout's planes made four deliveries to Liberia from Europe. The Ilyushin-76 was first registered in Liberia in 1996 in the name of another of his companies, Air Cess. It was later deregistered in Liberia and re-registered in Swaziland until a survey by that country's aviation authorities discovered major irregularities in the paperwork. It was again registered in the Central African Republic operating under the Centrafrican Airlines banner. Its call sign, painted onto the tail, had been fraudulently wrangled from a corrupt official without his government's knowledge.[131] In addition, the plane had dual registration, sometimes flying under the flag of Congo (Brazzaville). And when it was not making deliveries it was parked at Bout's main business hub in Sharjah.[132] When the shipment was about to be delivered it was transferred into the name of Abidjan Freight, a front company owned by Ruprah, before embarking on its journey on the multiregistered aircraft.[133]

This incredibly convoluted system was used to conceal not only the standard fare of rockets and ammunition, but also entire advanced weapons systems, which significantly enhanced the military potency of his clients. According to the UN: 'The cargo included attack-capable helicopters, spare rotors, anti-tank and anti-aircraft systems, armoured vehicles, machine guns and almost a million rounds of ammunition.'[134] Bout continued his arms deliveries into Liberia throughout the remainder of 2000 and into early 2001. Acting much like a legal defence contractor, he even provided after-sales support in the form of helicopter spares and rotor blades.

Many of the weapons provided by Bout and Minin were sourced in the Ukraine. After the collapse of the Soviet Union, the Ukraine was left with one of the largest surpluses of weapons. As the country spiralled into economic crisis army officers in cahoots with the shadow dealers plundered these stocks. A parliamentary commission constituted to investigate allegations of illicit arms trading reached the sensational conclusion that Ukraine's military stocks were worth $89bn in 1992 and that, in the course of the following six years, arms, equipment and military property worth $32bn were stolen, much of it resold. So explosive were the findings that the investigation was suddenly closed down, seventeen volumes of its work vanished and its members were cowed into silence. The MP who headed the inquiry, a former Deputy Defence Minister, Lieutenant General Oleksandr Ignatenko, was hauled before a court martial and stripped of his rank.[135] Bout's past military and political connections probably secured him access to this weapons trove, while Minin's route was more likely through his organized-crime contacts.

But by late 2001 Bout faced increasing international obstacles to his deliveries to Liberia. Inspectors for the UN repeatedly named him and Ruprah in its investigations into the Liberia and Sierra Leone conflicts, recommending Bout be placed on international travel ban lists. But it was 9/11 that really upset the Russian's plans. After the attacks, the US identified Bout as playing a role in arming the Taliban and he became one of the primary targets of the War on Terror. Making matters worse, Belgium issued a warrant for his arrest in 2002, claiming he had illegally hidden money flows of over $300m from tax authorities.[136] Ruprah was arrested in Belgium in the same year, but later freed.[137] Bout had to move fast. He uprooted himself from Africa and relocated to Russia, where he was protected by the state, which denied his presence in the country, despite regular sightings. While Bout had escaped justice, at least temporarily, Charles Taylor was now without the services of two of his favourite Eastern European arms dealers.

Taylor and the RUF turned to another, more infamous source, for weapons: Al Qaeda. Islamist operatives had been exploring diamond deals in Liberia and Sierra Leone since 1998, when the US sought to curtail the organization's revenue streams following the bombings of US embassies in Kenya and Tanzania. In June of that year US investigators froze about $240m of Al Qaeda's assets,[138] a large portion of which was gold deposits held at the US Federal Reserve.[139] Diamonds seemed a perfect source of income that was difficult to trace: small, valuable, highly mobile and difficult to detect. The traditional Islamic system of *hawala*, an informal network of money lenders that involves no paperwork and which exists throughout the Arab world, further aided Al Qaeda's dual quest for monetary mobility and secrecy.[140]

Three months after the US seized the organization's assets, a senior Al

Qaeda operative, Abdullah Ahmed Abdullah, travelled to Liberia.[141] Abdullah is suspected by US authorities of being the mastermind behind the US embassy attacks and was described by the FBI as a 'top Bin Laden advisor'[142] and the organization's treasurer in Afghanistan and Pakistan.[143] He was one of the original twenty-two members, and remains on the list of the FBI's 'Most Wanted Terrorists'.[144] Abdullah had met the RUF's General Ibrahim Bah in Libya, where Bah was being trained after working with the *mujahideen* in Afghanistan.[145] Once in Liberia, Abdullah was introduced to the RUF leader, Sam 'Mosquito' Bockarie, to whom he handed over $100,000 in return for a small package of diamonds. He then met Charles Taylor and travelled to Foya aboard a Liberian helicopter, the same diamond centre to which Roger D'Onofrio had been taken years earlier.[146]

The RUF and Taylor expected Al Qaeda to follow up this initial meeting with a delivery of weapons. In March 1999, two Al Qaeda operatives, Ahmed Khalfan Ghailani and Fazul Abdullah Mohammed, went on a diamond-buying spree across the Central African Republic, the Democratic Republic of Congo and Angola before arriving in Liberia to see Taylor. To their immense embarrassment they hadn't brought weapons for the Liberian leader. The relationship between Taylor and Al Qaeda faltered, at least for the moment.[147] In December 2000, a few months after Minin's arrest, the two Al Qaeda operatives returned to the country. At the Hotel Boulevard in Monrovia they met Ali Darwish and Samih Ossaily, who worked for a Lebanese diamond dealer, Aziz Nassour, who had operated widely in Africa and acted as 'bagman' for Zaire's kleptocratic dictator, Mobutu Sese Seko.[148] The four crossed into Sierra Leone and met the RUF for at least three days. Ossaily was there to negotiate on Nassour's behalf and to take photographic evidence that the RUF could deliver diamonds. He was convinced of the RUF's bona fides and entered into an agreement with the rebels, who agreed to sell huge quantities of diamonds to Nassour in return for weapons.[149]

By March 2001, the arrangement was operating at full steam. Ghailani and Mohammed returned to Liberia, from where they conducted diamond trades with the RUF for at least the next nine months. At first they lived at the Hotel Boulevard, which was both Sam 'Mosquito' Bockarie's home-away-from-home and Samih Ossaily's base. Mohammed was dispatched to the countryside to oversee the relationship with the RUF, while Ghailani remained in Monrovia. He was later moved to a safe house which had been leased by Aziz Nassour. Business was going so well that Nassour himself travelled to Liberia in July 2001 to implore Taylor to pull strings to double diamond production in Sierra Leone, a request accompanied by a $250,000 'donation' to the President. Nassour had already made $1m in 'donations' to Taylor over the course of their relationship.[150]

Nassour also took personal responsibility to source the arms promised to Liberia in return for the diamonds. His first attempt was vigorous but unsuccessful. In December 2000, he approached Shimon Yelenik, a former Israeli army officer who was linked to the supply of weapons to Colombian paramilitaries[151] and had worked as head of security for Mobutu Sese Seko, Nassour's one-time employer.[152] From his base in Panama Yelenik approached a Guatemalan arms firm which was represented by another Israeli, Ori Zoller, who had once served with the Israeli special forces. Zoller contacted the head of the Nicaraguan armed forces and received a list of available weapons and their pricing. Nassour then instructed his henchmen, Darwish and Ossaily, to brief the RUF. However, the deal did not go through. Ossaily claims to have had a sudden change of heart about his involvement and decided to tell all to the Belgian authorities while in Antwerp, the diamond centre of the world, to which he frequently travelled.[153] No action was taken at the time by the Belgian authorities, but it halted the arms deal.

Nassour's second attempt took place in May and July 2002. He paid for two shipments of weapons and ammunition which had been sourced from Bulgaria via a middleman in Paris, and passed through Nice before finally reaching Harper in Liberia. The first shipment was a massive 30 tons, and the second 15 tons of ammunition. Once it was offloaded in Liberia the ammunition was moved onto trucks and transported to Lofa County to be used against the biggest threat to Taylor's presidency, the massed forces of Liberians United for Reconciliation and Democracy (LURD).[154]

Prior to Nassour's second, successful arms deal, the entire operation was uncovered in a remarkable investigation by Doug Farah, the West Africa correspondent for the *Washington Post*. Using a senior source who was deeply embedded in the Liberian and Sierra Leonean networks, Farah unravelled the imbroglio and provided the information to American authorities.[155] While US authorities, and the CIA in particular, were irked by a journalist stepping on their traditional turf, other countries took notice of the information. On 12 April 2002, Samih Ossaily was arrested in Belgium on suspicion of dealing in blood diamonds and was sentenced to three years in jail. At the same trial Nassour was found guilty *in absentia*, although his whereabouts remain unknown to this day.

Another source of weapons for Taylor during this time was Gus Kouwen-hoven, a Dutch national, who like Leonid Minin mixed interests in logging with arms dealing. Heavy-set with a barrel-like chest and scruffy black hair, Kouwenhoven has a penchant for gold jewellery and distinct-ive gold-rimmed glasses that darken in bright light.

Born in Rotterdam,[156] he made a name for himself as something of an international entrepreneur. In the early 1970s, after completing his mili-tary service, he went into business supplying tax-free cars for NATO personnel and later importing and exporting rice from South Asia. Through the 1970s he moved in the diplomatic set, was often spotted at high-profile parties, and frequented bars and clubs in downtown Amster-dam, where one bartender recalls him as 'a flashy guy with the gift of the gab, fast cars and fast women'.[157] Always a fixer – he was allegedly caught stealing petrol while in the military – his career as an international man about town was ended in Los Angeles when he was caught in an FBI sting trying to sell a stolen Rembrandt.[158] He was released after just seventeen days but was deported from the US.

Kouwenhoven disappeared for a while, was in Sierra Leone in the late 1970s and surfaced in Liberia in the early 1980s. He quickly settled into the country, then run by President Samuel Doe, and married a Liberian woman, who bore him a number of children.[159] His initial business in the country was the provision of luxury goods, in particular luxury cars. But his major investment was in Hotel Africa, a run-down 300-room hotel in the centre of Monrovia. He turned it around, opening a disco, the Barcadi Club, a restaurant, a pool and a casino.[160] It became, in Kouwenhoven's own words, the 'oasis of Monrovia'.[161] It was a major hub, the spot where the great and the good, both local and foreign, met to make deals and be seen. A former guard recalled that 'every day there would be a parade of senators and ministers'.[162] And it secured Kouwenhoven's place at the heart of the Liberian elite.

In 1999, Kouwenhoven branched out from his life as a flashy hotelier, utilizing his now extensive government connections. In July 1999, the

Oriental Timber Company (OTC) received a major concession for Liberian timber: roughly 1.6 million hectares, or 42 per cent of all of the country's productive forests.[163] OTC was majority-owned by the Hong Kong-based firm Global Star Holdings, itself a part of an Indonesian group of companies called Djan Djajanti. Kouwenhoven retained 30 per cent of the shares and was made the managing director of OTC and a sister company with considerable concessions, the Royal Timber Company.[164] He was responsible for the day-to-day management of the companies and oversaw much of the $110m OTC invested in Charles Taylor's Liberia. Operating largely from the port of Buchanan, OTC became a mini-government. It repaired a 108-mile stretch of road from Buchanan to inner Liberia, refurbished the port[165] and even ran a private militia of security guards totalling nearly 2,500 armed soldiers.[166]

OTC was close to Taylor's heart. He publicly referred to the company as his 'pepper bush', something of immense personal value.[167] His concern for OTC's well-being was because he received considerable money from its operations. In return for the concessions Kouwenhoven frequently made large payments to Taylor, which the Dutchman would later justify as 'public relations' expenses.[168] It is unclear exactly how much Kouwenhoven transferred to Taylor but they were substantial amounts over and above an initial $5m payment in 'advance taxes'.[169] In an interview Kouwenhoven once admitted that he paid roughly 50 per cent of all his royalties from OTC to Taylor to fund his warmongering administration.[170] It is likely that Taylor received not only ad-hoc payments, but was also made a shareholder in the company.[171]

OTC was important for reasons besides earning Taylor a decent income. In particular, the company's refurbishment and control of Buchanan and its transport nodes gave Taylor another route to transfer arms into the country. Where Minin and Bout used air transport, OTC and Kouwenhoven relied on ships. According to a number of witnesses Kouwenhoven oversaw the importation of large quantities of weapons aboard a ship owned by OTC, the *Antarctic Mariner*, which was often used for logging exports.[172] Witnesses recall that the ship docked a number of times between July 2001 and May 2002, and again between September 2002 and May 2003, disgorging huge quantities of weapons upon landing. Once unloaded, the AK-47s, RPGs and ammunition were transported by truck and jeep to Taylor's presidential compound to be distributed among NPFL troops.[173]

Many of the shipments were organized via Abidjan Freight, a dummy company established by Sanjivan Ruprah. UN investigations revealed that Abidjan Freight was a useful cover for both Viktor Bout and Kouwenhoven, both of whom used the company to 'conceal the exact routing and final destination of an aircraft delivering military goods to Monrovia'.[174] Despite these attempts to hide their actions, OTC and Kouwenhoven were soon in the spotlight. Investigations by the UN and Global Witness began reporting on Kouwenhoven's timber enterprises and his links to arms trafficking as early as December 2000. Soon after, much like Bout and Minin, he was placed on the official UN travel ban and had his assets frozen. But Kouwenhoven frequently broke the terms of his ban and was often seen visiting neighbouring countries. One trip to Holland was a journey too far and he was eventually arrested in his home town of Rotterdam.

By mid-2003 it was clear that Charles Taylor's time was running out. Despite his control over large pockets of Liberia's resources he was slowly losing ground to his opponents. One group, LURD, backed by Guinea,[175] had been slowly advancing on Taylor's territory since they first launched an anti-NPFL rebellion in 1999. Another group, known as the Movement for Democracy in Liberia (MODEL), had initiated its own rebellion with Ivorian support in 2003.[176] Their blitzkrieg through Liberia devastated Taylor's once iron grip on the country, only one third of which – Monrovia and its surrounds – he still controlled. The actions of the UN and international forces in disrupting the flow of arms to Taylor from the likes of Minin, Bout, Kouwenhoven and Nassour played a key role in weakening Taylor's position.

In March 2003, the Special Court for Sierra Leone – a joint UN and Sierra Leone investigative tribunal – filed a sealed indictment against Taylor. By June 2003, its contents had been made public: Charles Taylor was to be arrested and face eleven charges of war crimes and crimes against humanity.[177] If caught and found guilty he would spend the rest of his life in jail. It was not just his control over Liberia that was under threat, it was his liberty too.

Under these suffocating pressures Taylor initiated peace talks with his opponents. Over the course of an excruciating month a deal was hammered out. Once ratified in August 2003, the agreement stipulated that Liberia would be ruled by a transitional government until elections could take place in 2005. All parties agreed to the creation of a Truth and Reconciliation Commission, which would examine Liberia's brutal past and grant amnesty to political criminals in return for disclosure of information.[178] Under the terms of the agreement Charles Taylor would retain his liberty despite the indictments filed by the Special Court for Sierra Leone. In return for his promise to resign peacefully Taylor was granted political asylum in Nigeria by President Olusegun Obasanjo. He appeared on television to announce his resignation and his imminent relocation. Chillingly, he vowed: 'God willing, I will return.'[179]

Taylor's new home was in the illustrious Calabar area of Nigeria. Located in the south of the country, Calabar is a picture of tropical bliss, with the sea on one side and lush tropical forests on the other. Taylor and his entourage moved into a grand colonial mansion fronted by slim white columns on the prestigious Diamond Hill, virtually next door to the Old Residency, the mansion from which successive British Governors ruled Nigeria. And within a stone's throw of the lodge where President Obasanjo resided when he was in the area.[180]

Taylor's Calabar bolt-hole was supposed to be under lock and key. His mansion was located in a government zone and Nigerian security patrolled the perimeter of his property. Liberians, however, were convinced that he continued to influence their country's politics. He certainly had the resources to do so. Of an estimated $685m earned during his presidency, Taylor had spent $70m to $80m on military operations every year, leaving between $150m and $200m at his disposal in exile.[181] He also had ongoing investments in Liberia from which money was couriered to him in Nigeria by loyalists still operating in the Liberian government.[182] He used his vast wealth to continually interfere with Liberia's fragile transition. The Special Court for Sierra Leone claims that nearly half of the eighteen political parties which contested the 2005 elections were funded by Taylor, leading the UN Secretary General, Kofi Annan, to report to the UN Security Council that Taylor's 'former military commanders and business associates, as well as members of his political party, maintain regular contact with him and are planning to undermine the peace process'.[183]

Taylor's continuing presence in Nigeria caused considerable consternation in international circles. The US, in particular, pushed hard for him to be returned to Liberia and face charges in Sierra Leone, a demand that was consistently rebuffed by Nigeria. In 2006, however, the newly installed

President of Liberia, Ellen Johnson-Sirleaf, officially requested that Taylor be extradited from Nigeria to Liberia. Obasanjo, the Nigerian President who was rumoured to have benefited from Taylor's generosity, reluctantly agreed and announced at the end of March 2006 that 'the government of Liberia is free to take former President Taylor into its custody'.[184]

Taylor didn't wait for the Liberians to act. In flowing white robes he fled his Calabar compound in a Jeep Cruiser displaying diplomatic plates, in which he had stashed money in a variety of currencies. He headed for Cameroon but was captured at the border town of Gamborou, nearly 600 miles from Calabar.[185] Taylor has remained adamant that he had no desire to escape but was merely undertaking a trip to Chad about which he had informed Nigerian authorities.[186] Regardless, he was arrested at the border and flown directly to Monrovia. From there he was taken aboard a helicopter to Freetown, where he was held in captivity.

During his violent six-year kleptocracy 60,000–80,000 Liberians were killed and countless more were brutalized, most traumatically the child soldiers who were forced to kill their parents and ordinary victims alike.[187] Charles Taylor was undoubtedly the most brutal and venal of all the Merex operatives but the network was one in which he felt serenely comfortable.

7. Buckling to Bandar

Helen Garlick is a statuesque woman in her fifties. Her attractive, soft-featured face is framed by striking white hair. In appearance and voice she is British landed gentry. But her upper-class charm belies a steely determination. She is a crusading barrister of over thirty years' experience, a renowned corruption and fraud investigator who assisted the Nigerian government's investigation of theft on a grand scale by its former Head of State, General Sani Abacha, and the Italian authorities' inquiry into allegations of fraud by the Prime Minister, Silvio Berlusconi. At the UK's Serious Fraud Office (SFO) she served as Head of Policy before becoming the first head of its Overseas Corruption Unit, in which capacity she led the investigation into the Al Yamamah deal, which began in July 2004.

The SFO first got wind of possible corruption in the deal when Edward Cunningham, the Saudis' pleasure valet, brought evidence of fraud in the management of the BAE slush fund to the office in 2001. The MoD, through its Permanent Secretary, Sir Kevin Tebbit, rejected the concerns, based on assurances from BAE's Richard Evans that there was nothing untoward. Nevertheless, the SFO and the Economic Crimes Unit of the City of London Police began to investigate the slush fund, interviewing Peter Gardiner and others, and culminating in the dramatic raid in Hertfordshire in late 2004.

When David Leigh and Rob Evans of the *Guardian* came to see the SFO with revelations of BAE's system of covert payments to agents around the world, Garlick's team sprang into action. They issued a blizzard of requests for Mutual Legal Assistance from foreign jurisdictions and requisitioned BAE's bank records, which helped them build an ever-growing picture of the payments and the mind-boggling web of financial complexity with which they were concealed. They achieved a major breakthrough in early 2006 with the arrest of the BAE agent Barry George, a Briton married to a Romanian, who had secretly received £7m to fix a remarkable deal in which two surplus British frigates were transferred to Romania in 2003. The ships

had cost the British taxpayer about £250m to build only fourteen years earlier. But the Ministry of Defence handed them over to BAE for a scrap value
of £100,000 each. The company received £116m from Romania to refurbish
the ships, plus a lucrative further contract to maintain them.[1] With the knowledge of how George had been paid his fee, and particularly useful information
from the Swiss authorities, by September 2006 the SFO had learned about
Red Diamond and Poseidon, the key companies used to divert the commissions, and the trail of money to Prince Bandar and other Saudis.[2]

From the early days of the investigation, the government's attitude was
one of ambivalence. This followed a pattern that had been established as
early as 1985 when a question was asked in Parliament about possible
commission payments related to the Al Yamamah deal. The government
deflected the matter by referring it to the National Audit Office (NAO),
which undertook an investigation from 1989 to 1992. This report has
never been released, making it the first and, so far, only NAO report
to remain secret.[3] Attempts to access the report under Freedom of Information requests have been rebuffed on grounds of sensitive international
relations, parliamentary privilege and commercial interests. An MoD
spokesperson said the report was not released to avoid breaking a confidentiality agreement with the Saudis: 'The report remains sensitive.
Disclosure would harm both international relations and the UK's commercial interests.'[4] A briefing note prepared for John Major for Prime
Minister's Questions in Parliament confirmed that: 'The NAO has been
monitoring MoD's involvement in Al Yamamah to ensure that proper
accounting arrangements are followed. In particular, MoD has introduced
special accounting arrangements for Al Yamamah, for example, to ensure
that Saudi confidentiality is preserved. If the normal rules had been followed, Saudi transactions would appear each year in the department's
published appropriation accounts, laid before parliament; and we need to
avoid this.'[5] When the SFO and Ministry of Defence Police attempted to
obtain the NAO report in 2003 and 2006 they were told that the report
had been suppressed due to fears that it could upset the Saudis. The SFO
even considered raiding the watchdog in order to obtain it.[6]

The government's Chief Auditor at the time, Sir John Bourne, was not
only criticized for undermining the integrity of the independent watchdog body but was also accused of conflicts of interest as he had worked at
the Ministry of Defence on the Al Yamamah project as Under-Secretary

for Defence Procurement from 1985.[7] The continued suppression of Bourne's NAO report suggests that successive British governments were prepared to ensure the truth about Al Yamamah was not revealed.

During the SFO's investigation, the government's senior legal adviser, who has a seat at the Cabinet table, the Attorney General, Peter Goldsmith, met Robert Wardle, the diminutive and seemingly nervous Director of the SFO, and the head of the Ministry of Defence Fraud Squad, on a number of occasions to discuss developments in the case. He would be crucial in determining the investigation's ultimate fate.

Virtually from its inception BAE launched a calculated campaign to shut down the investigation. It employed the prestigious law firm of Allen & Overy, which in turn hired a lawyer who knew the Attorney General personally. He used this relationship to call Lord Goldsmith at home about the case. Goldsmith claims that he rejected these 'private and confidential' approaches.[8]

BAE's chairman, Dick Evans, wrote an unsolicited letter to Sir Gus O'Donnell, the Cabinet Secretary, who in turn raised the possibility of consulting with government departments to establish whether there was a public interest argument for discontinuing the nascent investigation.[9] The company's legal director, Michael Lester, wrote to the Attorney General in November 2005 suggesting that 'recent developments in this investigation raise in our view serious public interest issues which we consider should be brought to your personal attention having regard to the prosecutorial discretion conferred upon you'.[10] He confirmed that he had discussed the issue with Sir Kevin Tebbit, Permanent Secretary at the MoD. Appended to the letter was a four-page memorandum, arguing that the public interest dictated that the investigation be discontinued on the basis that the company had on 27 July 2005 voluntarily released 'a written analysis of the accounting treatment of the [redacted] prepared by Price Waterhouse Coopers and Allen & Overy, the Company's accounting and legal advisers respectively. The conclusion reached in this analysis was that the costs were effectively borne by the Saudi customer in accordance with the terms of contract with the customer.' The memorandum continued: 'Allen & Overy have written to the SFO on a number of occasions questioning whether the SFO has a legal basis for continuing the investigation given that the investigation has revealed no evidence of criminal conduct and the conclusion reached in the analysis provided to the SFO on

27th July 2005.'[11] Essentially BAE was saying: we've looked at ourselves and haven't seen anything criminal so why should anyone else investigate us?

The company refused to identify its agents, despite repeated requests from the SFO, and then complained that the SFO had obtained:

> the name of consultants engaged by the Company and the amounts paid to them, notwithstanding written assurances of confidentiality given by the then Inland Revenue to the Company and a conversation between the Permanent Secretary of the Ministry of Defence (Sir Kevin Tebbit) and the then head of the Inland Revenue (Sir Nicolas Montagu) at which the highly confidential nature of the information to be provided by the Company to the Inland Revenue was explained.[12]

The memorandum referred to Tony Blair's recent visit to Saudi Arabia, his planned future visit 'to cement the relationship between the two countries' and his efforts, together with the MoD, to secure 'the next tranche of work under the Al Yamamah programme'.[13] BAE continued:

> Disclosure to the SFO of the information relating to Al Yamamah requested in the section 2 notice [effectively a subpoena] would be regarded by the Saudi Arabia government as a serious breach of confidentiality by the Company and the UK government. The Company believes that if this information is provided there is little prospect of it remaining confidential with the consequent jeopardy to the next tranche of the Al Yamamah programme relating to the sustainment of Tornado aircraft and the sale of Typhoon aircraft being agreed between the UK and Saudi Arabian governments.[14]

In a nutshell the company believed that providing the information for a criminal investigation 'will be seriously contrary to the public interest in that:

> i) it would adversely and seriously affect relations between the UK and Saudi Arabia governments at a time when the UK government and the Prime Minister in particular, is seeking to nurture the relationship between the two countries in pursuit of the UK's strategic objectives in the Middle East: and
>
> ii) it would almost inevitably prevent the UK securing its largest export contract in the last decade of some [redacted] with the consequent adverse

consequences for the UK economy in general and employment, both in the UK and Continental Europe, in particular.[15]

This despite the fact that the OECD Anti-Bribery Convention, to which the UK was a founding signatory, specifically rejects international relations consequences or commercial considerations as a reason for failing to take action against bribery and corruption.[16]

The memo concluded: 'The Company does not believe that it has committed any offence in connection with its [redacted, but last letter is 'n'] relation to the Al Yamamah programme, notwithstanding the SFO's assertion that it has reason to suspect that an offence has been committed. The SFO has not given any indication of the grounds for its suspicion.'[17]

The strategy of this well-connected, some would say protected, company was to claim that it had done nothing wrong despite overwhelming evidence of corruption, drop the names of powerful politicians and repeat endlessly that any investigation would annoy the Saudis and cause the loss of future contracts.

Illustrating BAE's desire for secrecy and its sense of the way things work politically, it wrote a 'STRICTLY PRIVATE & CONFIDEN-TIAL' letter to Lord Goldsmith. The Legal Secretary to the Attorney General suggested that 'It is not appropriate for representations to be made to the Law Officers on such a private and confidential basis. The proper recipient of such representations is the Serious Fraud Office and I have therefore forwarded your letter and the memorandum to the Director of the SFO.'[18] BAE responded: 'my letter dated 7 November to the Attorney General was marked strictly private and confidential in accordance with good practice. I would however be happy to re-submit this memorandum with the legend removed.' BAE continued: 'representations made in my letter related essentially to public interest issues affecting this country's international relations. In these circumstances, I concluded that it would be appropriate if these representations were made at ministerial level. It is my understanding that the Attorney General is the minister responsible for the Serious Fraud Office and I accordingly wrote to him.'[19]

According to sources close to the investigation, Robert Wardle, Helen Garlick and case controller Matthew Cowie were incensed that the company, which was after all under investigation for criminal wrongdoing, was making representations to the Attorney General. And in the process refusing to respond to what is, in effect, a subpoena for information, referred to as the '5th notice'. They wrote a letter to BAE's lawyers that, in typically British fashion, was courteous, curt and devastating:

> I refer to your fax received at 3pm yesterday. . . .
>
> You are asking the SFO to give full and proper consideration to the contents of a memorandum, apparently prepared by the company and not by yourselves, addressed not to the SFO but to the Attorney General and sent to the Attorney without providing the SFO with a copy, or even giving us notice that this approach had been made.
>
> The return date in relation to hard copy documents under the 5th notice was yesterday. The notice is dated 14th October and was sent to you on that date. The memorandum was dated 7th November, a bare week before compliance was required and would appear to amount to a fundamental objection to compliance with the 5th notice. It also raises the same claim of public interest as a ground to discontinue the entire SFO investigation. However, as I set out in my last letter dated yesterday, your firm had never sought to raise any such concerns or objections in the previous detailed correspondence that had passed between us.
>
> I have no reason to believe that the terms of the 5th notice raise any issues that could amount to a reasonable excuse for the company to refuse to comply.
>
> . . . Further, no explanation is given for the assertion that compliance by the company with a compulsory statutory requirement is capable of being regarded as a breach of confidentiality on the part of the company, or why the pursuance by the SFO of its independent statutory powers of investigation could properly be regarded as a breach of a duty of confidentiality by the United Kingdom government. . . .
>
> On th[e] basis [of Article 5 of the OECD Anti-Bribery Convention] I can confidently discount the public interest considerations raised in the memorandum based on economic considerations as irrelevant. . . .
>
> We have no duty to consult with other Government departments on operational matters; however we will receive and consider any representations that are properly brought to us from any quarter. Strictly speaking the SFO need not take representations concerning public interest until it has completed its investigation, however in matters as serious as these, we

would not stand in the way of direct information being made available to the SFO at this stage. BAE has had a month to make such information known to the SFO and it has failed to do so.[20]

The SFO team and the Attorney General met on 2 December and agreed to carry out a Shawcross exercise.[21] This enables the SFO to canvass the views of government ministers in order to assess any relevant considerations in continuing the case. In this instance the exercise included consultations with the Prime Minister's office, the Foreign and Commonwealth Office (FCO), the MoD, DTI, the Home Office and the Treasury.[22] The Cabinet Secretary passed on a note to the SFO from the Prime Minister, the Foreign Secretary and the Defence Secretary which identified concerns about the investigation's impact on the 'commercial importance of the Al Yamamah programme'. The note also raised the possibility that counter-terrorism cooperation might be endangered by the investigation, though Wardle said he 'was not convinced that the danger referred to was imminent'.[23]

The letter asking for responses to the Shawcross exercise reiterated that matters excluded by Article 5 of the OECD convention would not be considered in the public interest test. The Cabinet Secretary's note made clear that this was ignored: 'It is, of course, for the Attorney General and the prosecuting authorities to decide whether there should be a prosecution, and also to decide how Article 5 bears on the current circumstances. We have, however, assumed that it may be possible for considerations of the kind mentioned in Article 5 at least to be taken into account for the purpose of taking an early view on the viability of any investigation.'[24]

And sure enough the note spoke about the 'importance of the relationship with Saudi Arabia and that the Al Yamamah air defence programme, including the upgrade programme for Tornado aircraft, was a cornerstone of that relationship'.[25] It referred specifically to the purchase by the Saudis of the next generation of attack aircraft, the (Eurofighter) Typhoon, and to the importance of Saudi Arabia in the fight against Islamic terrorism and the potential damage to British security interests should the investigation continue. The note described Saudi Arabia as a key country in the Middle East because of its advocacy of moderate foreign policy, concluding that Saudi stability was of vital strategic interest to the United Kingdom and to the West generally.[26]

While the exercise was underway the SFO investigating team continued their efforts to access BAE documents on their agents. On 7 December 2005, Matthew Cowie and Helen Garlick phoned Michael Lester, BAE's legal head, and made the obvious point that 'a formal consultation on the public interest was being undertaken but we do not see how public interest considerations would prevent the company providing us with the documents now'. Lester and BAE were playing for time. 'Mr Lester said that there was and it concerned the duty of confidentiality and that they would wish to make further representations.' Cowie and Garlick replied that 'at this stage, bearing in mind that BAE was the suspect company, it was best if they set it out in writing and without wishing to be offensive BAE was a suspect in a criminal investigation and the amount of weight that can be given to a suspect's representations as to the public interest in continuing an investigation are [sic] likely to be much less than those of a Government Department.'[27] Nevertheless, the SFO extended the time allowed for BAE to give up the documents identifying its agents.

The next day BAE sent a second memorandum to the SFO, reinforcing that Al Yamamah was a government-to-government contract. The company argued that 'First, the provision of defence equipment by one state to another is key to a much broader political and strategic relationship. It is symbolic of mutual trust between the two countries. Second, Saudi Arabia has a culture which is markedly different from that of western nations with, in particular, a higher degree of respect of privacy.'[28] BAE repeated that providing the information would amount to a breach of confidentiality and that the 'highly confidential nature' of the information was underlined by the fact that the documentation was also classified by the UK MoD. It continued: 'It is important to understand that, in the context of a sensitive and strategic inter-governmental relationship, an understanding between governments that certain matters will be kept confidential must be respected, whether or not that understanding is based on a strict legal obligation.' There is then a portion redacted before the memo goes on to say: 'The sanctions that can be imposed for perceived breaches are political and economic. It would be a mistake to proceed simply on the basis that unless a strict legally enforceable duty of confidentiality exists, the Saudi Arabian government would not perceive disclosure of information, which it understands to be confidential, as a breach of confidentiality.'[29]

BAE's contention was that if another country has colluded in the breaking of British law, but likes to keep things private, Britain should simply overlook the crimes. Besides the obvious implications for the British justice system and the international rule of law, there is also the hard reality, always avoided by Saudi sycophants, that the Saudi royal family also wants to keep the extent of its own corruption and debauchery hidden from the Saudi people.

The company goes on to remind the SFO that its political friends in government will soon be in Saudi Arabia, drumming up more business for Britain:

> Arrangements have been made for the Secretary of State for Defence to visit Saudi Arabia on 19 December. During the course of this visit, it is intended that the Secretary of State for Defence will attend meetings with the King and Saudi Defence Secretary with a view to signing a Memorandum of Understanding for the sale of 72 Typhoons pursuant to an extension of the Al Yamamah programme. The Saudi Arabia government has already complained to the UK government about the SFO investigation announced in November 2004.[30]

Matthew Cowie argued passionately in reaction to BAE's arguments, stating in a memo he circulated to his superiors:

> The SFO must investigate crime. It has a reasonable belief that crime has been committed. It must investigate all reasonable lines of enquiry and do so in the light of our domestic and international obligations. Those international instruments envisage an independent role for law enforcement outside of economic or political considerations. To have any meaningful effect they must have application, regardless of the seriousness of the consequences stated. There are always likely to be economic and political consequences of any major enquiry into defence contracts. That is why such considerations must ultimately be irrelevant to the independent conduct of such enquiries.
>
> Have they [the Cabinet] given full consideration to the public interest in the rule of law, the independence of the SFO and MDP and the role of central government, all of which could suffer reputational damage if it emerged that an investigation by the SFO had been cut short, [REDACTION – half sentence][31]

This was the approach taken by the SFO when it met BAE, the Attorney General and Detective Superintendent Robert Allen of the Ministry of Defence Police, on 11 January 2006. In a somewhat frosty encounter, Helen Garlick and Robert Wardle made clear that they were conscious of the competing arguments but reaffirmed the importance of tackling overseas corruption and the government's obligations to do so in terms of the OECD convention. They also pointed to the reputational damage to the SFO and the UK if the case were dropped, a view reinforced by the gruff Detective Superintendent Allen. The SFO made clear that it viewed efforts to prevent prosecution as an attempt to avoid the anti-bribery law. Robert Wardle felt that the balance of public interest was in continuing the case and in enforcing the notices on BAE to divulge documents. Following the meeting the Attorney General came round to allowing the investigation to continue,[32] which it did unhindered for a few months.[33]

But in April and May 2006 the pressure on the investigators began to mount again. The Attorney General determined that in terms of UK anti-bribery legislation it was crucial whether any of the payments were authorized by the Saudi government. In other words, ask those being bribed whether the bribes were authorized. The OECD had previously pressed the UK to fix this loophole in its very weak legislation. By stating that proof was required that there was no authorization to receive a bribe, the Attorney General was effectively destroying what there was of the UK's pitiful anti-bribery law.[34] Lord Goldsmith continued to push this issue in September and October 2006, deeply frustrating Garlick and Cowie, who were puzzling over how this evidence of authorization, or the lack of it, could be found.[35]

On 29 September 2006, the Cabinet Office made further representations to the SFO, raising the issue of counter-terror cooperation and strongly reiterating the financial impact of losing the Typhoon contract.[36] The next day the Attorney General passed the letter on to Robert Wardle, who still believed that Goldsmith was in favour of continuing the case.

After an impassioned internal meeting on 30 September at which the Cabinet Office's response to the Shawcross exercise was discussed, Helen Garlick made clear that complaints about the investigation breaching confidentiality were not going to stop it.[37] Garlick then made the point that the investigation had not yet caused commercial harm and that even if it did it would still be the SFO's duty to keep investigating corruption.[38]

She repeated the multiple concerns and threats raised – disruption to oil supplies, loss of contracts, undermining Middle East peace initiatives and retraction of intelligence assistance – and warned her colleagues that the Saudis and BAE, as the accused parties, would say anything to stop the investigation. She expressed surprise that these real concerns weren't raised a year earlier and questioned whether the Saudi threats were credible. Defiantly, she concluded by saying that the information requested was now long overdue.[39] Her exasperation and determination were clear to everyone in the meeting.

In November 2006, Jack Straw, a senior minister in the New Labour firmament and the Leader of the House of Commons at the time, requested a meeting with the Attorney General to discuss the BAE case. A former Home Secretary and future Justice Secretary, Straw is known as a strong BAE supporter as his Blackburn constituency is home to many company workers.[40] In the same month the British ambassador to Saudi Arabia, Sherard Cowper-Coles, met Robert Wardle, members of the SFO case team, the Director General of the Attorney General's office, and officials from the Cabinet and Foreign Offices. This was the first of three meetings between the Attorney General's office and the ambassador in two months, Lord Goldsmith attending the final meeting on 12 December.[41] Clearly a great deal of scheming in the ranks of the New Labour great and good was underway.

Towards the end of 2006, the public BAE and Saudi campaign to have the investigation closed down intensified. In December, the SFO even contemplated approaching BAE and negotiating a plea bargain in which the company and certain executives would plead guilty.[42] Dick Evans would admit guilt on the relatively minor slush fund charges, in exchange for which the more embarrassing counts relating to the gargantuan payments handled by Prince Bandar, Safadi and Said would be dropped.[43] But there was insufficient support for this approach inside the SFO, despite the mounting pressure.

In November, the *Sunday Times* had reported that the Saudis were threatening to cut off diplomatic ties unless Downing Street blocked the investigation.[44] A few days later the *Daily Mail* printed a headline claiming that 50,000 British jobs were at stake.[45] At the end of the month, BAE stated publicly that the Eurofighter deal had stalled, the *Financial Times* quoting the CEO, Mike Turner, as saying: 'We don't want to interfere with the judicial process . . . but we do want to see a resolution. It is damaging for our business.'[46] On 30 November, Michael Jack, a Tory MP for Fylde, where a large BAE factory is based, said in the House of Commons that the SFO investigation was 'gumming up' the negotiations. He claimed: 'As the Leader of the House will know from aerospace workers in his constituency, that is now causing a great deal of concern, as it appears that the current inquiry is impacting on important negotiations.' The Leader of the House praised Jack, saying: 'I applaud the way in which he has represented the interests of the British aerospace industry . . . I will pass his remarks to my right honourable and noble friend the attorney-general.'[47]

In December, the *Daily Telegraph* reported that the Saudis had given Britain ten days to halt the SFO investigation or lose the prospective Al Salam contract.[48] The *Sunday Times* chimed in that local MPs were planning to lobby Tony Blair.[49] The National Defence Industries Council, chaired by Rolls-Royce's chief executive, Sir John Rose, announced that it would write to the Trade and Industry Secretary, Alistair Darling.[50]

This PR campaign was masterminded by Timothy Bell, who had been a consultant to Margaret Thatcher during Al Yamamah and also advised her on how to deal with the controversy over allegations of Mark Thatcher's receiving contracts in Oman after his mother's visit.[51] After the fall of the Conservative government, Bell worked for, among others, the Malaysian offshoot of GEC, which was part of the Pergau Dam controversy, in which British aid for the building of a dam was linked to £1.3bn in arms contracts to Malaysia.[52] When interviewed about Al Yamamah he commented:

> 'The suspicion is that if you have a deal like that, with that much money floating around in cash. Of course there's suspicion and of course people are entitled to be suspicious, but there is a difference between suspicion and fact. As far as I'm concerned, if the British government and the Saudi government reached a sovereign agreement over an arms contract that resulted in a tremendous number of jobs in Britain, a great deal of wealth creation in Britain, and enabled Saudi Arabians to defend themselves, I think that's a jolly good contract.'[53]

He described the SFO investigation as 'all tosh', suggesting that there was no *prima facie* evidence.[54]

Bell's deluded perspective was matched by the jobs figures bandied about in the PR campaign, which claimed that anywhere up to 100,000 jobs were at risk due to the SFO investigation.[55] The figures were entirely fictional. The MoD's estimate, quoted in the Shawcross exercise, put the figure between 10,000 and 15,000 British jobs at BAE and subcontractors, as well as 2,000 expatriate jobs in Saudi Arabia sustained by the Al Yamamah deal.[56] York University put the figure at only 5,000 British jobs.[57] But the inflated figures ensured a willing audience when MPs and trade unionists were briefed to complain to Downing Street about the jobs threat of the investigation.[58]

The Al Salam deal was crucial to these jobs figures and the commercial argument against the investigation. Meaning 'peace' in Arabic – arms dealers not being strong on irony – Al Salam is the successor deal to Al Yamamah, consisting of the sale of seventy-two Eurofighter Typhoon jets for more than £4.43bn. The exact terms of the contract are secret and the actual value of the deal is likely to be much higher, as the £4.43bn only reflects the price of the planes but not the training, supply services and spare parts. Some estimates suggest the deal is potentially worth as much as £40bn.[59] The deal was laid down on 21 December 2005, and finalized and signed in September 2007.[60] It is, like Al Yamamah, a government-to-government transaction with BAE acting as the prime contractor. It will be paid for in cash from the Saudi defence ministry coffers rather than oil. The first twenty-four aircraft are to be built at BAE's site in Warton, Lancashire, and the remaining forty-eight in Saudi Arabia[61] by a consortium that also includes EADS in Germany and Spain and Alenia Aerospazio in Italy.[62]

The Eurofighter was originally designed for dogfights with Soviet aircraft over Europe, and as its relevance has plummeted, its cost has spiralled upwards. The UK portion of the project will cost at least £20bn,[63] £13bn more than initially projected.[64] This equates to £350 for every person in the UK and £1.1m for every job estimated to have been sustained by the project. The project took thirty years and came into service ten years later than predicted.[65] It is both a drain on UK finances and designed for a situation that no longer exists. As the flamboyant former Defence Minister Alan Clark said with characteristic candour, the Eurofighter is 'essentially flawed and out of date . . . we must find a less extravagant way of paying people to make buckets with holes in them'.[66] The UK is desperate to sell the Eurofighter because the country is tied into buying a set number of the aircraft and would face substantial penalties if it cancelled orders; and the UK currently has a budget shortfall of approximately £36bn for its arms procurement programme.[67]

The Al Salam and Al Yamamah deals have almost single-handedly sustained the UK arms trade. Military exports to Saudi Arabia accounted for 62 per cent of all Britain's military exports from 1997 to 1999. In 1987–91 it was 73 per cent.[68] As Mike Turner, CEO of BAE at the time, said shortly before a visit to Riyadh by Tony Blair in 2005: 'The objective is to get the Typhoon into Saudi Arabia. We've had 43 billion pounds from Al Yamamah over the last 20 years and there could be another 40 billion pounds.'[69]

Despite this dependency the Al Salam deal was criticized as being inconsistent with Britain's human rights obligations and the UK and EU's code of conduct on arms exports. A study concluded that 'the evidence suggests that a deal of this scale with Saudi Arabia would see the UK government fundamentally undermining a series of key criteria within the EU Code. This raises important questions about the government's real commitment to the consistent implementation of the Code of Conduct that it has signed up to.'[70]

With New Labour's brief embrace of an ethical foreign policy long abandoned, government was committed to safeguarding the Al Salam deal. To this end, the Foreign Secretary, Margaret Beckett, instructed senior diplomats to dissuade Robert Wardle from continuing with the investigation: 'Wardle was told he was pissing the Saudis off big-time, and that this involved security, terrorism, the whole future of the Middle East.'[71]

The Saudis communicated regularly with the UK government about the investigation, primarily through Deso and the UK ambassador to Saudi Arabia, Cowper-Coles. In September 2006, in a letter to Peter Ricketts, the Permanent Secretary at the Foreign and Commonwealth Office, the ambassador said:

> I recall that, in the margins of the meetings, and possibly on one or two other occasions (e.g. during The Prince of Wales's visit in March this year), I had brief oral exchanges with [a senior representative of the Saudi Arabian Government – assumed to be Bandar] on the SFO enquiry. . . . I remember [the Saudi representative] giving the impression that he had information of his own about the SFO enquiry (for example, he once volunteered that he understood that the enquiry could be discontinued if it

was not in the public interest – although he used a curious phrase which I can't now recall). I remember telling him more than once that senior officials in London were well aware of just how serious the enquiry could be, and that we were working to persuade the legal authorities of this. But I always made clear that the enquiry was not in our hands, and that there could be no guarantees. I remember being worried that [the senior representative of the Saudi government] was more optimistic about the SFO enquiry than seemed justified on the facts available to me. I confess that I did ask myself at least once whether I should have done more to disabuse him. But he always gave the impression he had his own information, and really just wanted to use me to convey to London how concerned he was.[72]

Prince Bandar operated deviously and brilliantly in trying to end the investigation. Allegedly, it was Bandar who made the threats about withdrawing intelligence cooperation, meeting Blair and Jonathan Powell, his Chief of Staff, in July 2006. 'Bandar went into No 10 and said: "Get it stopped." [Words omitted.] Bandar suggested to Powell he knew the SFO were looking at the Swiss accounts . . . if they didn't stop it, the Typhoon contract was going to be stopped and intelligence and diplomatic relations would be pulled.'[73] He also allegedly met Blair in London in December 2006 to convey the threat to withdraw intelligence cooperation.[74] And the month before he ostentatiously visited Paris to discuss buying Rafale jets to exert commercial pressure on the UK government, even though the Saudis had no intention of purchasing the French jets.[75]

On 8 December, Tony Blair sent Robert Wardle an extraordinary personal minute, directed through the Attorney General, about the 'real and immediate risk of a collapse in UK/Saudi security, intelligence and diplomatic cooperation' and 'the critical difficulty presented to the negotiations over the Typhoon contract'.[76] The attachment to Blair's minute on the national security considerations deals primarily with the issue of terrorism in Saudi Arabia, including the British role in securing the oil supply, but at no point mentions a threat of imminent terrorist attacks in the UK, although the document is heavily redacted.[77] The second attachment concentrates on Saudi Arabia's role in Middle East foreign policy and its support for the Israel/Palestine peace process, but again no threat to the UK is mentioned.[78] In an astonishing indictment of Blair's scaremongering, MI6, in later discussions with the OECD, refused to say that it 'agreed with [this security] assessment'.[79]

A few days later, Lord Goldsmith told Blair that halting the investigation over Saudi claims to withdraw cooperation 'would send a bad message about the credibility of the law in this area, and look like giving in to threats'.[80] The Prime Minister responded that 'he felt higher considerations were at stake. Proceeding with the case would lead to the end of Saudi–UK cooperation. . . . While the Prime Minister understood that halting the investigation was not a step to be taken lightly, he was clear that in this case there was a supervening national interest at stake, and that the British people would regard these as higher interests.'[81]

On 13 December 2006, Robert Wardle and Helen Garlick were summoned to see the Attorney General. In a tense and emotional meeting the investigators were told that there was not enough evidence to continue and that the strength of the public interest case compelled them to close down the investigation. Wardle angrily denied that there was insufficient evidence and tried to buy time to take advice from their barrister, Timothy Langdale QC. Garlick, fuming at the capitulation of the Attorney General, was asked her view specifically in the context of the threat to British lives. Isolated, she felt unable to argue against the others on the issue of national security:

> AG asked for my views. I said that the SFO had never sought to place the interests of our investigation above those of national and international security. It seemed to me that the AG and RW were in the same position. We were qualified to make judgements on the law and the evidence. On questions of security, we had to take the advice of others. The SFO had only heard first hand from HM ambassador, we assumed that the AG had better advice, including advice from the Security Services. At the meeting at the FCO attended by JJ we had been told that 'British lives on British streets' were at risk, also that [redaction]. If this caused another 7/7 how could we say that our investigation, which at this stage might or might not result in a successful prosecution, was more important?[82]

They discussed the implications of dropping the case, including the likelihood that the US and the Swiss would take on different elements of it, which could prove embarrassing for the UK government. The Attorney General asked Wardle and Garlick to inquire into the Swiss and US positions. Throughout the meeting Goldsmith suggested that while he wished to test the SFO's case and would support it if it was viable, he was unhappy at the implications of dropping it at this point.[83] He claimed that:

> Having considered the various views conveyed as to the public interest, including those of the ambassador, the Director of the SFO independently concluded that it would not be in the public interest to continue with the investigation because of the risk to national and international security. He conveyed this view to the Attorney General on 13 December 2006 and, having considered the matter further overnight, confirmed his decision to the AGO on 14 December 2006.[84]

Some close to the investigation contend that Wardle had no choice. He was intimidated by Goldsmith, who could be arrogant, cold and disrespectful to people. A reliable source claims that at one point the investigators were told that 'the Cabinet Office had met and decided the fate of the investigation, and then this was quickly changed to "no, it's the AG's Office".' If correct, this makes clear that the executive were instructing the prosecutors what to do.

The same source suggests that 'Goldsmith knew exactly what he was doing the whole time – his political master's bidding. He was never sincere about wanting it to go ahead. It was always all about how to close it down.' This view is supported by at least one other source close to the investigation. Goldsmith was desperate to show the investigation to be flawed, so that national security would not have to be invoked. But the SFO refused to allow him to trash what was a strong, well-marshalled case.[85]

The following morning a meeting was held between the Attorney General, the Solicitor General, the heads of the security and intelligence agencies and the Cabinet Office Permanent Secretary for Intelligence to discuss the possible consequences if the Saudis withdrew cooperation with the UK. The Attorney General claimed that 'None of those consulted disagreed with the overall assessment that the Saudi threats were real. The Chief of the Secret Intelligence Service's view was that the Saudis might withdraw their co-operation if the SFO investigation continued, and that they could decide to do so at any time.'[86] He also came to the conclusion that a prosecution against BAE would not be possible given the need 'to obtain evidence to refute the proposition that the payments made by BAE were approved by or on behalf of the Saudi principal(s)'.[87]

At 5.21 p.m. on 14 December the Attorney General announced that the investigation into the Al Yamamah arms deal would be stopped.[88] Conveniently, in terms of the news cycle, the announcement was made the night before a report into the death of Princess Diana was due out and Tony Blair became the first serving Prime Minister to be interviewed by police in a criminal case – the loans-for-peerages inquiry in which his most important fundraiser, personal aide and friend had been arrested.

After the announcement BAE shares, which had been depressed by the investigation, rose significantly.[89] Robert Wardle, whose application for the renewal of his contract as Director of the SFO had been sitting on the Attorney General's desk, was 'rewarded' with a one-year extension.

The *Guardian* said of Tony Blair at the time: 'For a prime minister who once taunted his predecessor as someone "knee deep in dishonour" over an arms deal and who promised that he would be "purer than pure" in office, yesterday was a shabby, shaming day, among the most inglorious he has spent in office.'[90]

Even John Scarlett – rewarded for his role in producing the sexed-up dossier used to justify the invasion of Iraq by being made head of the British intelligence agency MI6 – publicly questioned the national security justification for the decision.[91]

Tony Blair, who never downplayed his role in ending the investigation,[92] had caved in to the pressure of a corrupt, undemocratic ally, in the process sullying the reputation and standing of the United Kingdom around the world.

Embarrassingly for the government, the Organisation for Economic Co-operation and Development (OECD) instituted an inquiry into whether the British government contravened the organization's Anti-Bribery Convention. In March 2007, the OECD sent inspectors to establish why the investigation had been dropped and also why the UK had yet to bring a single prosecution since incorporating the OECD's anti-bribery treaty into UK law.[93] In response the British government attempted, from behind the scenes, to have the head of the OECD's Anti-Bribery Commission removed from his position.[94] It failed. Lord David Chidgey was moved in the House of Lords to remark that 'Britain has become a laughing stock within the OECD' and suggested that 'something must be done to restore faith in the British justice system urgently'.[95]

The news that the brother of Tony Blair's Chief of Staff, Jonathan Powell, was hired as a lobbyist by BAE to press their case for the termination of the Al Yamamah investigation, and that he might have chatted to his brother about it, only deepened the growing sense of a decision made by desperate politicians, motivated by more than national security.[96] Charles Powell said he had discussed the investigation with 'senior government officials' and that it was 'perfectly possible' these included his brother. A Downing Street spokesman insisted that Jonathan Powell did not discuss the case with his brother. 'The fact that they are brothers is therefore totally irrelevant', and added that Jonathan Powell was not involved in the decision whether to prosecute. But Charles, in trying to recall whether he had discussed the matter with his brother, said: 'It's perfectly possible. If you were told that, then you can print it. I mean I honestly can't remember . . . We discussed all sorts of things.' He added that the contents of discussions with members of his family were 'sacrosanct'.[97]

Blair's contention that 'the British people would regard these [intelligence concerns] as higher interests' was not a view unanimously endorsed. The Campaign Against the Arms Trade (CAAT) and the Corner House, a social justice NGO, wrote to the government immediately after the announcement, arguing that closing the investigation was unlawful and demanding that it be reopened. This was followed in January 2007 by a letter to Tony Blair from 140 NGOs from thirty-seven countries protesting at the decision and reiterating the grievous effect of corruption on democracy, sustainable development, human rights and poverty.[98]

Even elements in the business community spoke out against the decision. Hermes, the UK's biggest pension fund, wrote to the Prime Minister that the decision had threatened the UK's reputation as a leading financial centre and would have a high long-term cost for business and markets.[99] F&C Asset Management, with more than £100bn under management, felt that the decision was bad for business, stating in a letter to the government:

> We believe that, for long-term investors, bribery and corruption distort and destabilise markets, expose companies to legal liabilities, disadvantage non-corrupt companies and reduce transparency for investors seeking

investment opportunities. . . . There is a danger that the government's recent action will be perceived as undermining the consistent application of the UK's national legislation governing corrupt practices, precisely at a time when wider take-up of the OECD convention is beginning to take root.[100]

In November 2007, CAAT and the Corner House were granted permission to bring a full judicial review in the High Court. The NGOs argued that the decision to discontinue the investigation was based on considerations of potential damage to the UK's relations with Saudi Arabia, in particular damage to UK/Saudi security, intelligence and diplomatic cooperation, thus contravening Article 5 of the convention. They argued further that the UK effectively colluded with Saudi Arabia to breach the Saudis' international legal obligations to cooperate and share information on terrorist activities. They also believed that government ministers, including the Prime Minister, gave the SFO tainted advice insofar as it took into account the risk of the UK not being able to sell the Typhoon and other commercial, economic and diplomatic matters, despite being told by the Attorney General that the convention forbids such considerations. They suggested that neither the Director nor government ministers assessed or took into account the harm to the UK's national security of discontinuing the investigation.

Most grievously they argued that government ministers expressed a view on what decision the Director of the Serious Fraud Office should take. Despite the rules on public interest consultations forbidding ministers from giving an opinion on whether a prosecution should proceed or not, Tony Blair made clear that the public interest would best be served by halting the investigation. And finally they contended that it is unlawful for an independent prosecutor to permit threats or blackmail to influence his decision to discontinue a criminal investigation or prosecution. To do so is to surrender the rule of law.

In April 2008, the High Court ruled decisively in CAAT's and the Corner House's favour. The judges' verdict was damning of the British government, describing its 'abject surrender to the threat' which was 'an attempt by a foreign government to pervert the course of justice in the UK'.[101] The High Court agreed that the Shawcross exercise had been tainted by representations that should not have been taken into account and also noted that the SFO had correctly stood up to attempts to shut down the investigation. Importantly, the government did not dispute in court the NGOs' contention that Bandar went into Number 10 and threatened to halt both the Typhoon deal and intelligence and diplomatic cooperation if the investigation was not stopped.[102] The court also took exception to the force with which the Prime Minister intervened, concluding:

> He [the Director of the SFO] submitted too readily [to the threat] because he, like the executive, concentrated on the effects which were feared should the threat be carried out and not on how the threat might be resisted.
>
> No-one, whether within this country or outside is entitled to interfere with the course of our justice. It is the failure of Government and the defendant to bear that essential principle in mind that justifies the intervention of this court. . . . We intervene in fulfilment of our responsibility to protect the independence of the Director and of our criminal justice system from threat. On 11 December 2006, the Prime Minister said that this was the clearest case for intervention in the public interest he had seen. We agree.[103]

In effect the court had determined that the investigation was stopped because Prince Bandar had threatened that if it was not, the withdrawal of Saudi intelligence would lead to 'blood on the streets of London'.[104] The judgment stated that 'had such a threat been made by one who was subject to the criminal law of this country, he would risk being charged with an attempt to pervert the course of justice'.[105]

The judgment was widely praised. Susan Hawley of the Corner House proclaimed it 'a great day for British justice', while CAAT said it 'brings Britain a step closer to the day when BAE is no longer calling the shots'.[106] The renowned philosopher A. C. Grayling wrote that the judgment:

> strikes at the heart of the dilemma of our time: the way our democracy and its institutions are being subjected to manipulation, cover-up and dishonesty of purpose, to the extent that they can even be bought by outsiders. One might even say that [Lord Justice] Moses has brought tablets of law from the mountain top; down below, the worshippers at the golden calf of expediency are preparing to smash them, in part to cover their own backs in an ignominious matter in which the honour and integrity of British law

has been sold for a large mess of pottage; thereby not just covering the country in ignominy, but seeking to undermine the justice system itself.[107]

Even the right-wing *Daily Mail* agreed that the UK should stop grovelling to the Saudis, on the grounds of not giving in to threats from foreigners.[108] The *New York Times* editorialized that:

> British Prime Minister Tony Blair seems determined to use his final weeks in office to show how far he has strayed from the pledges of clean government that helped sweep him to power a decade ago. . . . Mr. Blair said last week that the probe would have led nowhere except to the 'complete wreckage' of a vital strategic relationship. That glib dismissal ignores the crucial point: bribery is never justified, smart or legal.'[109]

A key aspect of the judgment was that the government and the SFO had not considered how the Saudi threat might be dealt with other than merely submitting to the pressure. They never considered how unlikely it was that Saudi Arabia, a key target of Al Qaeda, would withdraw intelligence-sharing when they are more dependent on the UK and the US than the UK is on them. If the Saudis had carried out their threat they would have seriously damaged their relationship with the US and undermined their position in George W. Bush's War on Terror. As likely as Bandar's threatened 'blood on the streets' is that terrorist groups would decide to attack the UK specifically for engaging in a massive arms deal with their enemy, the Saudis.

It is of course quite likely that the threats were never real, but simply a tool with which to end the potentially embarrassing investigation: utilized by the Saudis who did not want their corrupt behaviour exposed, and seized upon by the British to hide government complicity in what was, after all, a government-to-government transaction. It also served to protect BAE and its future commercial prospects. David Howarth MP suggested as much, claiming that moves to end the investigation were motivated by machinations to protect BAE,[110] the company which the late Foreign Secretary, Robin Cook, described as 'having the key to the garden door of Number 10 [Downing Street]. . . . I never knew No 10 to come up with any decision that would be incommoding to BAE.'[111] A senior source close to the investigation concurred: 'BAE are the ultimate establishment, part of government really.'

★

In the aftermath of the damaging High Court judgment, BAE attempted to take the moral high ground by releasing a report it had commissioned from a former Chief Justice, Lord Woolf, on the company's ethical practices. Though BAE referred to the Woolf report as an independent review, the news that it had paid him £6,000 per day for nine months raised questions of its independence, as did the stricture that he could not consider any of the company's historical actions but could only look forward.[112] When asked by *The Economist* about the extortionate sum of money he was paid to run a PR event, Woolf replied: 'Have I been influenced by the amount of money? I don't deserve to be approached on that basis.'[113]

I reluctantly agreed to give evidence to the Woolf Commission and used the opportunity to criticize Lord Woolf for accepting so limited a brief. I told him that to do so meant he could not understand the true nature and instincts of the company. In informal conversation I suggested that BAE's morality and ethics could never be enhanced unless it came clean about its corrupting history. He replied that the law made it difficult to do so. So a former Chief Justice of the United Kingdom was suggesting that a company that had broken the law should just move on, forgetting about its past involvement in criminal acts. And he was helping them do so.

The entire report contained little mention of BAE's use of dodgy agents, the payment of enormous bribes, the corrupting of governments around the world, or even the company's infiltration of spies into the Campaign Against the Arms Trade.[114] The report made some sensible, if obvious, recommendations such as not making facilitation payments, acknowledging the need for updated anti-corruption law in the UK and using a due diligence process in dealing with advisers.[115] However, the Woolf Report was never meant to solve or even really address BAE's problems. As David Leigh commented on the whole initiative: 'Woolf commands [a] fact-free zone with aplomb.'[116] The £1.7m spent on the Woolf report was a wasted expense on what was a whitewashing PR exercise.[117]

The amnesiac approach to the past undermined what was supposed to be a new dawn at BAE. The statement by the chairman, Dick Olver, at the company's 2008 AGM, that BAE would not just be the most ethical of arms companies but would reflect the gold standard for ethics of any company in any industry bordered on the delusional.[118] I can't imagine

Dick Olver, or any defence industry executive, grappling with the fundamental problem of whether it is even possible to be an ethical arms
company.

Part of the PR reinvention of the company was to claim that a new
management team under Dick Olver had moved on from the days of
Dick Evans and Mike Turner, who were credited with the establishment of the system of slush funds and covert financial transactions. But
then it transpired that Dick Evans, who had built his career in BAE on
his relationships in Saudi Arabia and had run operations in Saudi during Al Yamamah, was retained as a consultant by Olver's BAE after
his ignominious retirement. Dick Olver was forced to reveal that Evans
earned almost £1.5m from BAE after stepping down in 2004. His role?
Specifically to advise the company on its relationships with Saudi
Arabia.[119] His contract was only ended after massive public fallout in
early 2010.[120]

BAE had attempted to reinvent itself as an ethical arms company
before, and would continue to do so. In 2006, Deborah Allen, director of
corporate responsibility, told the BBC that BAE was doing 'Everything
from looking at making a fighter jet more fuel-efficient and looking at
the materials that munitions are made of and what their impact on the
environment would be.'[121] The company had plans to manufacture 'green'
lead-free bullets so that once in the environment they 'do not cause any
additional harm'.[122] Additional that is to the harm they've caused to the
injured or dead target. BAE also spoke about making a quieter bomb so
that the users' exposure to fumes would be reduced. And the company
was reported to be making landmines which would turn into manure
over time. As Allen put it, they would 'regenerate the environment that
they had initially destroyed'.[123] She continued: 'It is very ironic and very
contradictory, but I do think, surely, if all the weapons were made in this
manner it would be a good thing.' This green initiative led only to much
mirth at the absurd notion of the ethical arms company making weapons
and ammunition that would be more caring. The plan to make green bullets was scrapped two years later after BAE discovered that tipping bullets
with tungsten instead of lead resulted in higher production costs, making
the venture unprofitable.[124]

The company also launched a mass advertising drive using a BAE
slogan laid over a Union Flag. The adverts were placed in publications,

including the left-leaning *Guardian* and *New Statesman* – in one issue of the latter alongside a critical article I had written on the company – and on many London taxis and buses. The wrapped-in-the-flag series of adverts continues, spawning a minor industry in satirical spoofs.

Amid this PR onslaught Dick Olver spoke out against the SFO investigation, claiming it was 'doomed to failure' and suggesting that it should be abandoned.[125] A year after the High Court judgment the SFO had come under new leadership. Richard Alderman, a career civil servant who had previously been head of tax investigations at the Inland Revenue, was perceived as a safe choice by the Attorney General, Lady Scotland, 'a tax settlements guy, who likes files', according to one insider. A candidate from outside government with a strong track record of combating bribery and corruption would have strengthened the SFO's independence and reputation, rather than its choice reinforcing the perception of a tired government that had lost its moral compass.[126]

Alderman aimed to raise public awareness of fraud and focus on cases with clear victims. He insisted that investigations would still take priority but soon after withdrew an application to the Attorney General for consent to prosecute a high-profile overseas corruption case relating to the activities of London-based firms in Bosnia. His arrival coincided with the mass exodus of a third of the SFO's senior management, many of whom felt the new direction was a mistake and would lead to even fewer convictions.[127]

With Alderman's arrival, the High Court decision was appealed to the Law Lords, the antiquated bastion of the British establishment. The government changed tack before the Lords, denying that Bandar had tried to stop the investigation. Jonathan Sumption, the government's QC, claimed that there was 'no basis' for saying that Bandar had acted out of his own interest to seek an end to the investigation. He said the suggestion had been based on an article in a Sunday newspaper but had never been admitted by the government. He did not say who had made the threat to ministers but contended it was 'perfectly clear' it had come from the highest level of the Saudi state 'from several channels over a period of time'.[128] Documents revealed by the government in the Lords intended to show that they had resisted the Saudi representations by repeatedly stating that the SFO and Attorney General were independent and that they had no power over the prosecution.

The Lords rapidly found for the SFO and the government. One of the five judges expressed regret in having to acquiesce to the dropping of the investigation. Lady Hale found it 'extremely distasteful that an independent public official should feel himself obliged to give way to threats of any sort'. She maintained that the threats and risks were matters that the director was entitled to take into account, but unlike the other four Law Lords she did not 'accept that this was the only decision he could have made'. She added: 'I would wish that the world were a better place where honest and conscientious public servants were not put in impossible situations such as this.'[129]

The Law Lords also ruled that it was not for the UK courts to determine whether the SFO Director's decision was compatible or not with Article 5 of the OECD Anti-Bribery Convention, but for the OECD's Working Group on Bribery to do so, as the dispute mechanism provided for in the convention. They were also swayed by the SFO Director's admission that he would have taken the same decision irrespective of the convention. This is a startling admission that the UK had failed to incorporate Article 5 of the Anti-Bribery Convention into its domestic legislation, that the government and the SFO were not prepared to follow it, and that the article's provisions are unenforceable in the UK. As Corner House pointed out: 'This means that, regardless of whether or not it was unlawful for the SFO to halt its BAE–Saudi investigation, the UK is in breach of its international law obligations.'[130]

The decision was widely condemned. The *Guardian*, which helped spark the SFO investigation, responded to the Law Lords:

'Whether or not patriotism is the last refuge of the scoundrel, national security can be the last refuge of the tyrant.' Lord Walker issued that shrewd warning before going on to side with the government in a landmark case concerning the legality of heavy-handed terrorism laws. While well aware of the scope for abuse, the courts are always reticent about second-guessing the executive on national security; ministers, after all, have special responsibilities and privileged information here. Yesterday, the law lords unanimously displayed the traditional deference. They ruled that it had been lawful to axe a police probe into BAE Systems – a move made, officially, out of concern for public safety.[131]

Sue Hawley opined: 'It is a very disappointing and very conservative judgment . . . If the courts are not prepared to hold the government to account, who will do that job? As Moses and Sullivan's judgment most powerfully put it: "The rule of law is nothing if it fails to constrain overweening power".'[132] Lawrence Cockcroft, the UK chairman of Transparency International (TI), lamented that 'The hope that our courts might rescue the credibility of the government's duty to fight corruption has evaporated.'[133]

As Robert Wardle admitted, the SFO had submitted to blackmail, and the Law Lords made prosecuting major arms companies with powerful friends virtually impossible.[134] Blackmail and threatening a government into dropping inconvenient investigations was now permissible.

On 1 April 2009, Helen Garlick said her farewell to friends and colleagues at the SFO. The venue was the basement of the Bung Hole Cellars on High Holborn in central London. The bunker-like subterranean gloom suited the occasion perfectly. Courageous people of integrity and principle, like Helen, were no longer wanted. As she said her dignified and heartfelt goodbyes, people wept openly, as much for the colleagues they were losing as the dark future facing the fight against corruption in the UK.[135]

8.   And Justice for None?

By the late 2000s some of the extended Merex network's nefarious activities – selling arms to most sides in Yugoslavia, gun running in Liberia and Sierra Leone, and dealing diamonds with Al Qaeda – had been exposed by the UN and NGOs such as Global Witness and Amnesty International. Viktor Bout, known as *the* merchant of death, was used as the basis for a Hollywood blockbuster, *Lord of War*, starring Nicolas Cage. The term 'blood diamonds' seeped into the popular consciousness, propelled by the Hollywood fictionalization of the horrors of Sierra Leone, featuring a scowling, heavily accented Leonardo Di Caprio. Though many activities remained unexamined – the history of Joe der Hovsepian and the evil machinations of Nicholas Oman, for example – the once secret netherworld of arms dealers and swindlers had been exposed to the public gaze.

And yet not a single member of the network had faced a successful prosecution for arms dealing. Some had been arrested and even found guilty on other charges, but none had yet faced the judicial consequences of their arms trafficking which wreaked such havoc and caused such suffering around the world.

The reasons for this are both legal and political. A number of the few prosecutions initiated against network members foundered on the treacherous rocks of jurisdiction, itself a function of a very weak international regulatory and legal framework. Because arms brokers operate from many locations around the world, transfer money, weapons and other commodities across multiple jurisdictions through intricate channels, and are seldom physically present when the arms are delivered, it is easy for courts to rule that the offences fall outside their ambit. Despite the European Union, for instance, adopting a strong common position on arms trafficking, the lack of integrated legal mechanisms to prosecute dealers across jurisdictions has left these purveyors of death largely untouched.

An equally difficult issue is the collection and nature of evidence from conflict zones. A court in Holland, for example, rejected 'conflicting' evidence gathered from informants in war zones without accounting for the complex context of the investigation or how local conceptions and descriptions of events could be misunderstood by Western eyes.[1]

These difficult legal issues are often buttressed by a distinct lack of political will to prosecute arms dealers on the part of many countries. The early history of Merex illustrates how dealers are often protected from prosecution by their links to state intelligence agencies or other quasi-state actors. In extreme cases dealers are integral components of organized crime networks that include political actors, while others are or have been useful to powerful politicians or officials, who explicitly or tacitly condone their actions. Their apprehension and prosecution could result in severe embarrassment and politico-legal difficulties for their abettors. With friends in high places some arms dealers have been able to evade arrest and prosecution throughout their illicit careers and beyond.

Viktor Bout's evasion of justice for many years is an exemplar of how these issues have combined to bedevil the prosecution of arms dealers.

In February 2002, Belgian authorities issued an Interpol 'red notice'* that they were seeking the arrest of Bout on charges of money laundering and arms dealing. In theory, if he was in a member state, local police authorities were obliged to arrest him and hand him over to Belgium. Soon after the 9/11 attacks Bout's African colleague, Sanjivan Ruprah, had been in contact with US intelligence officials, starting a long-running correspondence. Ruprah was even flown into the US at one stage for a debriefing, bypassing the passport and immigration checks that would have identified him on the UN travel ban list. He promised to provide his US contact, 'Brad', with a wide range of intelligence.[2] This included the movements of the Taliban and Al Qaeda in Afghanistan, which he and Bout had insight into as a consequence of supplying arms to these groups.[3] With this new knowledge and their extensive network, Bout and Ruprah would be useful 'dirty' contacts in the War on Terror.

Whether US Intelligence ever did an official deal for information with Bout and Ruprah is unclear but it is suspected that US Intelligence

* A red notice is an Interpol declaration to seek the provisional arrest of a wanted person with a view to extradition based on an arrest warrant or court decision. It can be compared against other colour codes, such as a green notice, which provides warning or criminal intelligence about a potential criminal who may repeat the crime, or a black notice, which seeks information about unidentified bodies.

interventions prevented Bout's arrest for many years. So deep were these suspicions that the Belgian authorities attempted to keep their arrest warrant secret from leaky US intelligence networks.[4] Belgian and European authorities joined forces with British Intelligence under the aegis of a new taskforce known as Operation Bloodstone to monitor Bout's frequent travels in violation of his travel ban. In late February 2002, firm intelligence identified that Bout would be flying aboard one of his planes from Moldova to Athens. A plan was hatched to arrest him when he landed in Athens and bring him to justice in Belgium.[5]

Soon after Bout's flight took off, British field agents sent an encrypted message to London informing them that 'the asset' was in the air. Minutes later the plane changed direction, abandoning its flight plan. It disappeared into mountainous territory out of reach of local radars. The plane re-emerged ninety minutes later and landed in Athens. When police boarded the aircraft it was empty except for the pilots. Twenty-four hours later Bout was spotted 3,000 miles away in the Democratic Republic of Congo. Bout's crew had been informed of the plan to arrest him in Athens and had arranged to drop him off safely elsewhere. For a European investigator all signs pointed towards US complicity: 'There were only two intelligence services that could have decrypted the British transmission in so short a time,' he explained. 'The Russians and the Americans. And we know for sure it was not the Russians.'[6]

Shortly after Bout's narrow escape he moved back into the safety of his 'home territories' in Russia. Russian officials were reluctant to see Bout prosecuted as he had close contacts within the Russian establishment through whom he had been able to source surplus matériel for years. In 2002, in response to a request to reveal his whereabouts, Russian authorities declared that Bout was definitely not in Russia.[7] As they were issuing this definitive denial Bout was giving a two-hour interview in the Moscow studios of one of the country's largest radio stations. Shortly afterwards Russian authorities released a second clarifying statement. It was a thinly veiled message, in classic Orwellian doublespeak, that Bout was now untouchable. With this Russian protection – known locally as *krisha* – Bout was able to resume operations, albeit with a higher degree of caution. As a consequence, as recently as 2006, Bout was sending weapons to Islamist militants in Somalia and Hezbollah in Lebanon.[8] During this period he was also providing air-freighting services for the US in Iraq and Afghanistan.[9]

By 2007, Bout's notoriety had caught the attention of the US Drug Enforcement Administration (DEA). Tasked with fighting the country's 'war on drugs' the DEA had its remit enhanced after 9/11 to pursue aggressive sting operations against those who were engaged in a range of activities that supported 'terrorists', of which drug trafficking might be only a small part. Its vast infrastructure – the DEA has more foreign bureaus than the CIA – is especially useful in pursuing the complex multinational crimes from which arms dealers profit. So it proved with a sting that was undertaken in 2006 against the semi-retired arms dealer Monzer Al-Kassar.

Al-Kassar got his start in the trade when the government of Yemen asked him to buy rifles and pistols from Poland, where, in the 1980s, he served as commercial attaché for the Yemenis. He assisted the Polish military with illegal arms transactions until 2002.[10] Besides his involvement in Iran–Contra (see Chapter 2), he supplied weapons to his friend Abu Abbas, the leader of the hijackers of the *Achille Lauro* cruise ship in 1985 who murdered a disabled American passenger, Leon Klinghoffer. And he violated the UN arms embargoes in Croatia, Bosnia and Somalia. He may have been involved in procuring components of a Chinese anti-ship missile for Iran, according to records cited by the *Washington Post*. A report in the Library of Congress charges that he delivered explosives to a group headed by a known terrorist in Brazil and that he had earlier sold arms to Iranian militias in Cyprus.[11]

He was well connected to the highest echelons of the Syrian state, which his father had served as a diplomat. But most crucially he was accused of supporting the Sunni insurgency in Iraq.[12]

The DEA used a turned former member of the Black September group (a Palestinian paramilitary group with whom he had worked previously) to build a relationship with Al-Kassar, claiming to have a client who needed arms. The client was represented by two Guatemalan DEA informers posing as FARC (Revolutionary Armed Forces of Colombia) representatives. FARC had long been listed as a terrorist organization by the US. This meant that any attempt to supply them with arms was, in legal terms, participation in a conspiracy to kill US nationals.[13] Over a series of recorded discussions and meetings with Al-Kassar, the agents agreed a deal for the supply of nearly 12,000 weapons, including thousands of machine guns, rocket-propelled grenades and surface-to-air missiles.[14] They persuaded the arms dealer to travel to Madrid to meet 'a senior

FARC leader', where he was arrested by Spanish police under instructions from the Americans. His intelligence links in Spain and other countries, who used him for information, as they so often do arms dealers, failed to protect him. In June 2008, Al-Kassar was flown in shackles from Spain to the US, where he faced trial.[15]

As Viktor Bout had previously air-dropped weapons into the Colombian jungle for FARC in 1998 and 1999, it made sense to use a similar ruse in an attempt to lure the Russian from the safety of his *krisha*. A DEA agent, Michael Braun, felt it was possible to use a similar scam twice, based on a psychological insight he had gained from years pursuing the world's 'potpourri of scum: The more arrogant they are, the better off you are. Guys like that say to themselves, "There's no way in hell they'll do that a second time."'[16]

After months of intensive planning based on analyses of Bout's past behaviour, the sting began in earnest in November 2007. The first step was to contact somebody close to Bout, in this case Andrew Smulian, a mysterious British national in his mid-forties who had previously worked as a military pilot.[17] According to one of the DEA's key informants, code-named CS-1 (Confidential Source 1), Smulian was still working closely with Bout and could act as a means of access. CS-1 had previously worked with Smulian and had interacted with Bout. In the mid-1990s, Bout had approached CS-1 and Smulian to fly from Bulgaria and air-drop crates of supplies over Chechnya.[18] They refused as 'while never explicitly told what was inside the crates, CS-1 understood that they contained arms shipments'.[19] CS-1, whose identity remains hidden, had maintained intermittent contact with Bout thereafter, on one occasion sharing a plane for a flight to Dubai from Africa.[20]

In November 2007, under the direction of the DEA, CS-1 emailed Andrew Smulian claiming to have a business opportunity for Bout. Smulian replied that the Russian was interested and had suggested that Smulian meet up with CS-1 to discuss the deal. In a December email Smulian confirmed that he 'spoke to Boris, and anything is possible with farming equipment [assumed to be a euphemism for arms] . . . I don't think he can move stuff around, but it may be that he can get his hands on items which you require.'[21] Smulian advised CS-1 of the need for extreme caution, confirming that 'Our man has been made persona non-g[rata] – for the world through the UN. The supporting action through the US,

Europe, and Switzerland. All assets cash and kind frozen, total value is around 6bn USD, and of course no ability to journey anywhere other than home territories. . . . we should not make any use of any form of contact, and all existing and past comms are electronically interrogated and copied.'[22]

Smulian, CS-1 and two men masquerading as his colleagues, CS-2 and CS-3, met in person for the first time in January 2008 in Curaçao, a balmy island off the coast of Venezuela. CS-2 and CS-3 posed as representatives of FARC, a ruse that Smulian bought without question. The fake representatives gave Smulian a list of the weapons FARC wanted to buy. In addition to the usual machine guns, it also included surface-to-air missiles. If Smulian agreed to obtain these the deal would take on grave consequences, as the sale of surface-to-air missiles to any party not contracting directly with the US is illegal under US law.[23] To further cement the deal, and as a gesture of their goodwill, the DEA agents gave Smulian $5,000 in cash to defray the costs of his travel.

With the shopping list agreed, a further series of meetings was scheduled to discuss the terms of the trade. At one of these meetings, in Copenhagen in January, Smulian confirmed that they would soon have a meeting with Bout, spelling out the Russian's name for CS-2 and affirming that he was known as 'the merchant of death'. Smulian confirmed that '100 pieces' were immediately available, presumably referring to the missiles. He also passed on an offer from Bout to launder FARC's money for the transaction, suggesting a fee of 40 per cent of the total funds laundered.[24]

At a meeting in Romania a few days later Bout attempted to increase the size of the deal. After he had spoken on the phone to CS-2 about potential meeting spots, Bout asked to speak to his business partner. Smulian replaced the phone in a state of excitement, confirming that 100 Igla missiles were definitely available and then offering 'special helicopters that can wipe out their helicopters', training in the use of the helicopters and more modern rocket launchers capable of firing three missiles simultaneously.[25] The weapons were to be supplied by an arms manufacturer in Bulgaria and would be air-dropped, buoyed by 200 parachutes, into Colombia during a fly-over from Nicaragua to Guyana. If FARC did not want their money laundered, Bout suggested he could pick up the cash directly from them as he always had an empty plane near their territory.[26]

It would be a further agonizing month before Bout was finally drawn out of hiding. The fake representatives insisted that they would only do the deal if they were able to meet Bout in person. A planned rendezvous in Bucharest, Romania, fell through: Bout's contact in the country was about to organize a visa for him when a documentary appeared on Romanian TV identifying Bout's connections there. The contact warned that Romania was now too hot for a Bout visit. But finally an arrangement to meet was confirmed. The DEA agents, in contact with Bout via his newly created Yahoo email address, informed him that they would be travelling to Thailand for business at the end of February.[27] Bout, who seemed eager to move the deal forward, called CS-2 directly, despite his fears over surveillance, and agreed to meet the agents in Bangkok. After months of painstaking work the DEA had finally smoked the merchant of death out of his protective *krisha*. In late February they hurriedly submitted an arrest warrant to the New York courts and headed to Thailand to set up their operation.

Bout arrived in Bangkok on 6 March 2008 and checked into the five-star Sofitel Hotel in the city's central business district just before noon. DEA agents who had been monitoring the site since 5 a.m. watched as Bout made his way to reception and booked a conference room on the twenty-seventh floor of the building for 3 p.m. After freshening up, the Russian met with CS-2 and CS-3 at a bar in the hotel. Over drinks: 'Bout stated, in sum and substance, that the fight against the United States was also his fight and that he intended to supply the FARC with the arms to shoot down American-made helicopters.'[28] Turning on the salesman's patter he sang the praises of an 'ultra light' two-seater fighter plane that could be equipped with grenade launchers and missiles, and was perfect for downing helicopters. They moved upstairs to the conference room. To clinch the deal Bout summarized that for 'fifteen million' he would supply '700 to 800 surface-to-air missiles, 5,000 AK-47 firearms, millions of rounds of ammunition, various Russian spare parts for rifles, anti-personnel land mines and C-4 explosives, night-vision equipment, ultra-light airplanes and unmanned aerial vehicles'.[29] Producing pamphlets detailing their specs, Bout also recommended that FARC buy two cargo planes, an Antonov and an Ilyushin, in order to transport their own weapons in future.

As the sales pitch ended swarms of Thai police and DEA agents invaded the conference room. Bout offered no resistance. As he was handcuffed, he muttered: 'The game is over.'[30] He was unceremoniously marched through the lobby, which was packed with DEA agents congratulating each other and CS-2 and CS-3. The next day Andrew Smulian was picked up by officers in New York and taken to the District Court, where his arrest was confirmed.[31] Smulian reportedly agreed to a plea bargain with US officials in return for a reduced sentence and witness protection and has revealed all about Bout's role in the operation.[32]

With a key informant and so much explicit evidence the US authorities should have had little problem successfully prosecuting Bout. The speedy trial and conviction of Monzer Al-Kassar would have encouraged them. As with Al-Kassar, it was crucial to arrange for Viktor Bout to be extradited quickly to face justice in the US courts. The first extradition request was filed in April 2008, just as Thai authorities decided not to prosecute Bout. An extradition requires not only that the offence is punishable by both the host and the extraditing country, but also that the offence is not being prosecuted by the host country. Attached to the US extradition request were a series of 'incriminating' documents seized from Bout at the time of his arrest, including articles about FARC, a map of South America and his own handwritten notes of the meeting.[33]

In August 2009, the Thai courts finally pronounced judgment, ruling against extradition. Central to the case was whether the alleged crimes constituted an overtly criminal, rather than political, act. The extradition treaty between the US and Thailand states that extradition cannot occur if 'the extradition is requested for political purposes' or the crime was 'an exclusively military offence or a political offence'.[34] The Thai judges determined that providing support to FARC had to be considered a political act, rather than a merely criminal endeavour. Their view was informed by the fact that the Thai government does not identify FARC as a terrorist organization and the court could not act according to the dictates of foreign policy rather than the law.[35] The judgment may have been informed by more than narrow legalistic concerns. *Realpolitik* could have played its role as well. For, as the trial unfolded, considerable pressure was brought to bear on the Thai authorities, with Russian efforts countervailing American demands.

In Russia, Bout's extradition was strongly opposed. Key political players lined up to defend Bout, portraying the charges against him as a sordid US political plot. 'Just because the cold war is over doesn't mean the competition between military-industrial interests has ended,' said Sergei Markov, a pro-Kremlin deputy of the Russian State Duma. 'It's not about ideology, but it is about competing interests. Russia extends official support to Bout because he's a citizen, and because the Russian public doesn't see him as any kind of criminal. They expect him to be supported.'[36] Bout played to the gallery, frequently linking his incarceration to unpopular aspects of US policy, on one occasion expressing the fear that extradition would lead to his internment at Guantanamo Bay.[37] One particularly vocal, high-profile supporter was Vladimir Zhirinovsky, the ultra-nationalist who had made use of the Merex network's Nicholas Oman in an attempt to secure nuclear weapons, and who had a working relationship with Bout. Zhirinovsky, as Deputy Chairman of the Duma, had sent a number of telegrams to the Thai Prime Minister, requesting Bout's release and suggesting a meeting in Moscow to discuss the issue.[38] The Duma too issued a statement damning Bout's continued arrest. Rumours were rife that Russia was offering Thailand considerable inducements to release Bout, including cheap oil and even cheaper military equipment.[39]

In February 2009, roughly six months prior to the decision of the Thai courts, a number of Representatives from the US Congress wrote an open letter to the newly installed Secretary of State, Hillary Clinton, and the Attorney General, Eric Holder. The letter pleaded that 'this international arms dealer's extradition [should] remain a top priority for your Departments and the United States government'.[40] Two months after the judgment President Barack Obama used a trip to Asia to canvass for Bout's swift extradition, while the US Deputy Attorney General, David Ogden, commented that Bout facing charges in the US was 'still a matter of great importance to the United States'.[41]

This political horse trading raises questions both about the judgment and the pressures brought to bear on the judges. At one point in the court proceedings the Thai judge complained that he was in a 'tough position [as] bilateral ties with Russia and the United States could be at stake'.[42] For Doug Farah, the judgment was a recognition that the judge 'feared the Russians more than the Americans' rather than an objective application of legal principles.[43] The American Congressman Ed Royce was even more forthright in his view of the judgment: 'While the Thai Foreign Ministry has stated that the extradition request meets the conditions of the Thai–American extradition treaty, the Russian government has been pushing hard for Bout's release. Politics seems to have trumped the law. Something is rotten in Bangkok.'[44]

The soundness of the judgment was further questioned because of a number of additional statements that went beyond the court's core mandate of examining the extradition request. One such example was that the court did not find the charges against Bout believable. 'The accused was charged with selling [a] large quantity of war weapons and fighter aircraft [of which] the price is too high to believe it can be illegally traded. It is in doubt where to find an illegal source of [such] large quantity,' stated the judge, displaying a remarkable ignorance of the illicit arms trade.[45]

While the Thai Public Prosecutor's Office immediately gave notice to appeal the decision to reject extradition, the response of US authorities suggested that they had little confidence in its likely success. Instead, the US issued a second arrest warrant on different charges in March 2010. This gave them the option of lodging another extradition request if the appeal found in Bout's favour.[46] Reflecting the difficulties of prosecuting arms dealing, the newly formulated charges focused on Bout's and his alleged colleague Richard Chichakli's violation of a US presidential order freezing the assets of both in the US. This injunction on their assets had been passed in response to UN sanctions placed on Bout. The new charges claimed that Bout had used a newly formed company, Samar Airlines, to purchase two aeroplanes – a Boeing 727 and a Boeing 737 – from a Florida-based company at a cost of just over $17m. In addition, Samar had used a Florida company to provide the crew to fly the planes from the US to Tajikistan. According to US prosecutors, while Bout's name did not appear on Samar's registration documents, he was the 'real' owner of the company.[47]

On 20 August 2010, the Appeals Court in Thailand overturned the earlier decision, saying FARC was a proscribed terrorist organization and that Thailand was obliged to extradite Bout in accordance with treaties with the US.[48] Bout's lawyer immediately announced his intention to lodge a petition with the Thai government to block the extradition. 'The defence believes Bout will not be safe in the US and he will not receive a fair trial,' the lawyer said. The Russian Foreign Minister, Sergey Lavrov, fulminated that Russia 'regret[s] this unlawful, political decision', which he argued was made 'under very strong external pressure'. He repeated, as he has on many occasions, that Russia continued to work for Bout's return to his home country.[49]

Bout responded defiantly, shouting: 'We will go to court in America, and we will win.'[50] However, there was a final legal twist in the tale. As a US government aircraft sat on the tarmac at Bangkok airport, waiting to transport Bout to the US, the Thai Attorney General warned that the Russian could not be moved. The sticking point was the secondary charges that the US filed against Bout, as insurance against losing the primary case. The Attorney General insisted that all legal proceedings against Bout had to be completed before he could be extradited. But the terms of his extradition stipulated that if he was still in Thailand three months after the court order, he had to be set free.

Bout's lawyers tried every legal gambit imaginable to prolong his stay in Thailand. But as 20 November loomed, with the Russian media trumpeting Bout's imminent freedom,[51] the Thai Cabinet acted. Four days shy of the deadline, the Cabinet approved the extradition, and within hours of the decision Bout was removed from his prison cell, placed in a bullet-proof vest and escorted to a chartered plane by police commandos in balaclavas and combat gear. He was handed over to DEA agents and ushered aboard the plane to begin his journey to New York and American justice.

Bout's wife, Alla, rushed to the prison with his lawyer but did not get to see him. 'The operation was secret,' she told the *Russia Today* television channel. 'The cabinet ordered the extradition of Viktor Bout, even though the prime minister of Thailand had said that while court proceedings are ongoing, he wouldn't be extradited . . . he was shipped to the United States as if he was just a thing, without his documents and without the Russian embassy being informed. The operation was so quick because it is illegal under Thai law. I plan to appeal.' The Russian foreign ministry concurred, describing the 'illegal extradition, a result of the unprecedented political pressure by the United States'.[52]

While the Department of Justice certainly pulled out all the stops to have Bout extradited, in the years since the Russian was arrested questions have been raised about the US's real desire to prosecute and Bout's levels of political protection. I was told by two separate sources in different US government departments that, especially during 2008 under the Bush administration, there were profound differences within the Department of Justice and between the department and the Pentagon about the initial ensnaring of Bout and the efforts to extradite him. Supposedly, the Pentagon and the intelligence agencies feared Bout would reveal the extent of his historical involvement with them, while the DEA and others in the Department of Justice believed that Bout's arms trading constituted a real threat to US homeland security.[53] As the *Washington Post* commented in response to the successful extradition decision: 'Oh, the stories this Russian could tell.'[54]

On 17 March 2005, the Dutch arms dealer Gus Kouwenhoven was dramatically arrested in Holland while waiting for a ride at the Rotterdam train station. Kouwenhoven had long piqued the interest of organizations examining the morass of human misery in Liberia and Sierra Leone. As early as 2000 he was named by UN investigative reports as 'responsible for the logistical aspects of many of the arms deals' undertaken by Charles Taylor.[55] Further investigations painted a picture of a man in the 'inner circle' of Charles Taylor's regime who had used monies raised from his logging interests to financially support the rule of the NPFL.[56] It was also reported that Kouwenhoven had helped ship weapons into the country from China via the Liberian port of Buchanan, a believable claim as his company, the Oriental Timber Corporation (OTC), owned at least two ships and effectively managed the port.[57]

Revelations by NGOs and the UN led to an investigation by Dutch authorities in which they travelled to Liberia to interview witnesses, before filing a range of serious charges against Kouwenhoven. The indictment accused the controversial Dutchman of war crimes in contravention of the Geneva Convention. These included making use of OTC's security personnel to fight a number of skirmishes from 2000 to the end of 2002. In one such incident, Kouwenhoven was accused of being party to a vicious assault on the town of Gueckedou in Guinea. It was claimed that during the attack shots were 'randomly' fired into the town without distinction between civilians and soldiers. A house packed with prisoners of war was set alight and another building filled with locals who had surrendered was destroyed with grenades. One or more babies died after being hurled against a wall and at least three people were beheaded after they had given themselves up.[58] Kouwenhoven was considered an active participant in the conflict, either by directly ordering, or allowing Charles

Taylor to order, troops employed by OTC into battle, selling and supplying arms for the attacks, putting a helicopter at the disposal of Taylor and
his inner circle, and providing material support in the form of money and
cigarettes or marijuana to Taylor's troops and accomplices.[59]

In addition to the three war crimes charges, Kouwenhoven was also
accused of two further counts of arms dealing. It was claimed that he
was materially involved in supplying arms, other equipment and military
technology in defiance of UN sanctions and Holland's own Economic
Offences Act. While the arms-dealing offences would most likely be punished with a decade or so behind bars, the war crimes charges could attract
a sentence close to life imprisonment. The prosecutors' ultimate objective
was, therefore, to prove Kouwenhoven guilty of war crimes.

In March 2006, the three judges of The Hague's Criminal Division
ruled that while it was clear that the awful atrocities had occurred, there
was insufficiently clear evidence to convict Kouwenhoven. 'The evidence
does not convince the court that the defendant was actually involved in,
nor had the knowledge of the facts charged inasmuch as many different
and even contradictory statements were recorded and written documents
have not been able to give sufficient evidence to prove that involvement.'[60]

The judges were, however, convinced both about the nature of the
relationship between the Dutchman and the dictator and Kouwenhoven's
arms dealing on Taylor's behalf. Under oath Kouwenhoven admitted that
he was in charge of the day-to-day running of the logging company and
that he frequently made payments to Taylor and his entourage on behalf
of OTC, above and beyond the $5m in 'advance taxes' that the company
paid to the NPFL.[61] He also admitted to providing a blue and white OTC
helicopter for Taylor's use so that he could move swiftly around the local
area. The judges believed that the relationship between Kouwenhoven,
Taylor and OTC went beyond the ad hoc. Documents strongly suggested
that Charles Taylor was, in fact, a beneficial owner of the company. By this
account, Kouwenhoven was Charles Taylor's business partner.[62]

The Dutchman admitted that OTC was responsible for the everyday
running of the Buchanan port and that the port's staff complement was
made up almost entirely of OTC employees. The testimony of the more
than fifty witnesses confirmed that one or more ships belonging to OTC
had frequently docked in Buchanan, most notably the *Antarctic Mariner*.
This was confirmed by travel logs and bills of landing. On at least one

occasion, if not more often, the ships were carrying massive crates of weapons, mostly AK-47s and RPGs. Once unloaded, they were transported past Charles Taylor's 'White Flower' residence for inspection. Some were retained for use by OTC security guards, many of whom testified about the shipments. One guard recalled that little was done to hide the contents of the crates once shipped: 'Every time the *Antarctic Mariner* arrived, there were weapons on board. The weapons were packed in crates and containers. I have seen that it was written down on the crates that they carried weapons. For instance "AK47 rifle" was written on the crate.'[63]

Given that Kouwenhoven was the single and most important point of contact between Charles Taylor and OTC, the judges were satisfied that he was directly involved in the arms deals. 'There is no doubt that the defendant has continuously and from the start, played an important role in this structural weapons importation. Therefore, the court considers proven that the defendant, together with one or more persons, has supplied weapons to Charles Taylor [and] Liberia.'[64] On 7 June 2006, Kouwenhoven was sentenced to eight years in prison for his illegal arms dealing.

Immediately after the judgment, both the Dutch Prosecutor's Office and Kouwenhoven launched appeals. The prosecutor felt that the charges of war crimes had been unfairly dismissed, while Kouwenhoven's lawyers raised a number of objections to the findings on the arms-dealing charges. Central to Kouwenhoven's appeal was the claim that the evidence presented against him was unreliable. The majority of this evidence was, of necessity, in the form of witness statements, which the defence team complained were inconsistent on key facts. During the appeal proceedings, Kouwenhoven's lawyers painstakingly walked the court through these inaccuracies, aided by the use of PowerPoint slides.

To the shock of everyone who had followed Kouwenhoven's career, the Dutch Appeal Court agreed with his defence in its judgment delivered in March 2008. After lambasting the conduct of the investigation and especially the use of confidential informants, the judge fairly eviscerated the witness testimonies, describing them as self-contradictory. In some instances, the judge claimed, witnesses had made statements that simply could not be true. The 'most striking' example of this provided by the court was the naming of the *Antarctic Mariner*:

Witnesses stated emphatically that they saw the Antarctic Mariner deliver its first shipment of arms in early October or December 1999 (and that the defendant was seen on board the vessel around this time in the port of Buchanan), whereas it was established that the vessel did not start to sail under this name until May 2000, after it had been acquired by OTC, and therefore can never have been in the port of Buchanan in 1999 bearing this name; and the Court of Appeal has no indications that the vessel at the time was present in that port under its previous name of 'Sinela.'[65]

This example of inconsistencies identified by the Appeal Court, as well as others, was less than convincing in proving that entire swathes of witness testimonies were unreliable. Larissa van den Herik, Associate Professor of Law at Leiden University, commented on this example:

It may well be that the ship that would later be called Antarctic Mariner was in the harbour of Buchanan in December 1999 and that the witnesses who saw that ship at the time now testify about it calling the ship by its current name, even though they are speaking about the ship in an era that it was bearing a different name. If true, the witness statements do, after all, refer to the same ship.[66]

She believes that the Appeal Court failed to understand the context of Liberia in wartime, and the problematic nature of presenting evidence from a foreign war-torn country in the comfortable courtrooms of the developed world. She cites another example of evidence that the court labelled problematic. In describing how weapons were unloaded from the *Antarctic Mariner* one witness statement claimed that much of the arms cargo was unloaded by hand and with the use of step ladders. This, the court believed, was an implausible assumption. 'True, it is quite unlikely that such cases would be offloaded by manpower alone in a developed country like The Netherlands,' van den Herik concedes. 'But is it really that incredible when account is taken of the status of Liberia as belonging to the category of Least Developed Countries?'[67]

The consequence of the judgment was that Kouwenhoven, two years after being found guilty, was now a free man, cleared of all charges against him. His loud protestations of innocence had to be taken at face value, despite this jarring with the reality that he had, in his own testimony, admitted to materially supporting one of the world's fiercest warlords in return for monetary gain. The Dutch Campaign Against the Arms Trade lamented that:

> Dutch arms dealers guilty of brokering outside the Netherlands have little to fear from the Dutch authorities. . . . International initiatives and requests from parliament for more adequate legislation have been delayed by this government. Even with adequate legislation it will continue to be very difficult to bring arms brokers to justice, because, for example, cooperation is needed from countries to which the arms are sold in the first place.[68]

His freedom, however, might be short-lived. After the 2008 judgment the Public Prosecutor appealed once more. At the heart of this appeal was the Appeal Court judge's refusal to admit damning testimony that had been heard after the 2006 judgment by the Special Court for Sierra Leone. In 2010, the Supreme Court found the judge's decision unreasonable, arguing that the evidence should have been admitted for consideration by the Appeal Court. The Appeal Court decision was overturned and a retrial was ordered for Gus Kouwenhoven.[69]

If the Bout and Kouwenhoven cases typify two of the major problems in prosecuting arms dealers – a lack of political will and the difficulty of gathering evidence from war-torn and chaotic territories – the case of Leonid Minin exemplifies the pre-eminent obstacle to justice: jurisdiction.

Minin was arrested *in flagrante* on 4 August 2000. The police tackled his indiscretions one at a time. The first charge to be prosecuted was for the illegal possession of drugs. Considering the large quantity of cocaine in his possession and his previous arrests on narcotics charges, Minin was swiftly found guilty and sentenced to two years in prison.[70] Walter Mapelli, the Italian prosecutor in charge of the case, then turned his attention to the accusations of arms dealing. In June 2001, Mapelli successfully argued for Minin to be retained on pre-trial detention on the basis of documents found in his possession, photographs of his plane in action in Liberia and the testimony of a number of interviewees. This pre-trial evidence alone seemed damning. One photograph, for instance, showed a series of bags next to Minin's plane in Liberia. The weapons, which were clearly visible in the bags, were identical to weapons detailed in brochures and a catalogue that was in Minin's possession.[71] The prosecutor also produced the end-user certificate used by Minin to transport weapons to Liberia, which was signed by the Ivorian President, Robert Guéï.[72] When Italian investigators contacted the Ivorian authorities, it was confirmed that the certificate had never been issued and was fraudulent, clear evidence that Minin had been trafficking arms illegally.[73] Finally, Mapelli presented a detailed summary of the various financial transactions that Minin had arranged to facilitate the deals.

The determined and thorough prosecutor was understandably confident of a successful prosecution when one adds to this Minin's confession, the evidence of his one-time partner, Fernando Robleda, and one of Minin's pilots, and the exhaustive work of the UN investigator Johan Pelemann.[74] His case did not suffer the same problems as Kouwenhoven's. In Minin's case, the public prosecutor had 'solid' evidence in the form of extensive documentation and money flows and didn't need to rely on sometimes tricky witness statements.

It also seemed that Minin was bent on undermining his own defence. By 2002, he had fired four different lawyers, one of whom, Pierre Traini, described Minin as 'a difficult, difficult client. I represented him for three months only and I am very tired.'[75] Minin's own testimony under questioning was frequently contradictory and contained bold assertions that often did not tally with the documents that had been seized from him. Walter Mapelli described Minin during questioning: 'He was often changing in his mood and behaviour, passing from a collaborative and talkative approach to aggressive and pressing speeches. I felt Minin's words were not fully faithful [sic].'[76] Given this erratic behaviour and his criminal past, Minin was unlikely to have made a credible witness. His future looked bleak.

But in September 2002, Minin appealed against his pre-trial detention. The judges found in his favour, not pronouncing on Minin's guilt or innocence but instead ruling that the court had no jurisdiction over the crimes.[77] Minin was freed, two years after his initial arrest. Mapelli attempted to have the judgment reversed and appealed the matter all the way to Italy's highest court. In 2004, the Supreme Court of Cassation confirmed that jurisdictional concerns prevented Minin's prosecution. The crime, they pointed out, had taken place in an overseas country by a foreign national. In addition, there was no evidence that the arms had ever entered or flown over Italian territory from their source in the Ukraine, or that

Minin had conducted any important brokering meetings in Italy.[78] The only charge on which he could be found guilty was possession of unregistered diamonds, for which he was fined €40,000.[79]

The decision was galling but not surprising. Minin had been a resident of Italy for many years and was married to an Italian woman. Some of the proceeds of his crimes were certainly utilized in Italy. But I was told that in the days leading up to his successful appeal Minin's legal team had been bolstered by the arrival of a posse of high-powered lawyers from one of Italy's leading arms companies.[80]

As Italy is a UN member state, one would imagine that an Italian court would look unfavourably on a local resident breaking UN arms embargoes. But Minin's case highlights the weakness of international enforcement efforts. UN sanctions and weapons embargoes are pointless if national legislative frameworks do not allow some sort of universal jurisdiction. For the most part, the law and its enforcers have to police multinational crimes with legal instruments that have failed to keep pace with modernity. 'Jurisdiction is one step behind criminality today, because criminality is operating globally and continues to do so all the more,' Mapelli complained during the proceedings. 'Whereas each state is very jealous of its own sovereignty and its own prerogatives within its borders, the consequence of this is that each state only sees one little segment of the whole business.'[81]

Mapelli based his case on Article 10 of the Italian Criminal Code, which states that a non-citizen who is physically in Italy may be charged for a crime undertaken in another country which is punishable by at least three years in jail, at the request of the Minister of Justice. The initial judge was of the same opinion but the Supreme Court cancelled the arrest warrant, claiming that illicit arms trading is an exception to the rule of Article 10. Mapelli clearly disagrees with this interpretation and is worried that there has never been a conviction in Italy for a serious case of arms trafficking.[82] I was told by a source close to the investigation that the Ministry of Justice was not keen to grant permission for the trial to take place and that informal political pressure was applied to the courts.[83] But I was unable to verify this with a second source.

When considering the cases described in this section, and their unacceptable legal outcomes, one cannot but conclude that the tragic reality is that arms companies, large and small, and arms dealers and agents, get away with corruption and bribery on a massive scale, complicity in crimes against humanity, and even murder. They operate in a shadow world, taking advantage of gaps in the international legal system and hiding behind the protective cover of powerful politicians and intelligence agencies, as they continue to grease the wheels of dictatorships and other unaccountable governments, allowing the intensification of conflicts and mass human rights violations. As a consequence our world is a more dangerous place for the majority of us to live but a more lucrative place for the small group of criminals and their protectors who have become fabulously wealthy through the immiseration of others.

SECTION III
Business as Usual

BAE's Al Yamamah deal, the largest and most corrupt weapons trans-action in history, was not an isolated incident. It was part of a pattern of doing business that the company employed from Pretoria to Puento Alto via Prague. With the tacit support of the British government, BAE's brib-ing of officials and politicians and their efforts to cover up the corruption undermined democracy and the rule of law and inhibited socio-economic development in the purchasing countries, which were much poorer than Saudi Arabia. Judging by their behaviour in the late 1990s, the only lesson BAE learned from the Al Yamamah experience was how to work the sys-tem: bribe and corrupt as necessary and then rely on your political friends for protection.

9. Things Fall Apart – with Help from BAE

Destroying Dreams in the Rainbow Nation

I experienced BAE's pernicious impact on developing countries at first hand. In 1994, as South Africa became a democracy after over 300 years of racism and injustice, I was elected an ANC Member of Parliament. I had first come into contact with the ANC in the squatter camps of Cape Town in the mid-1980s where I worked as head of a student welfare agency.

In the early years of the new South Africa, under the inspirational leadership of Nelson Mandela the country defied the tawdry politics of much of the world to become a bastion of reconciliation, unity of purpose, progressive human rights and good governance.

However, as Thabo Mbeki succeeded Mandela, non-racism was replaced by a less inclusive Africanism, a sense of the national interest superseded by the needs of the party. Open accountability gave way to a closing of the ranks in which loyalty to the party and its leader became the crucial political currency.

At the time I was the ranking ANC member on Parliament's Public Accounts Committee, a body which vigorously and in a non-partisan manner reviewed government spending and instigated action against the misappropriation of public funds. We were at the apex of the accountability chain, a role in which I revelled.

It was also a role that would bring me into direct contact with the arms trade for the first time. With the end of apartheid the ANC had undertaken to reduce spending on the military in favour of the country's dire socio-economic needs. So it came as something of a surprise when the government announced a massive purchase of military equipment in 1999. Estimated to cost roughly $3bn at the time – although this disguised the true cost of the deal by at least 250 per cent – it secured South Africa a range of military hardware, including Hawk and Gripen jets from BAE and Saab, submarines and frigates from Germany, and helicopters from

Italy. By far the largest portion of the deal in terms of cost – over 50 per cent – was the purchase of the jets.

The procurements, known collectively as the 'arms deal', were wracked by allegations of corruption from the start. When the country's Auditor General presented the Public Accounts Committee with a damning report into the deal, replete with allegations of malfeasance, we set in motion a series of public hearings and investigations.

I was approached by myriad sources, some apparently reliable and well intentioned, others with clear agendas and a few bordering on the mentally troubled. After countless overt and covert assignations and the receipt of thousands of pages of evidence from the Auditor General and intrepid journalists, a close colleague and I pieced together a frightening tale of corruption and deceit, with BAE the main villain of the piece.

We established that, at the time he was claiming the government had insufficient resources to provide life-saving medication to the millions of South Africans living with Aids, Thabo Mbeki had entered into contracts for arms that by their conclusion in 2018 will have cost the country over $6bn.[1] This, despite the reality that South Africa faced no external threat.

About $300m was paid in commissions and bribes to middlemen, senior politicians, officials, their associates and the ANC itself. The bribes were a key motivator in the deal, especially the need to finance the party and upcoming elections.[2]

From the time of the country's constitutional negotiations, which started in late 1991 and in which I acted as a facilitator, international defence companies began to interact with key people in the ANC, including Mbeki and the former head of the ANC's armed wing, Joe Modise. In December 1993, Modise and the head of the state arms company, Armscor, were invited to the UK as guests of Britain's Defence Export Services Organisation (Deso).[3] It was a brazen move – Modise had not yet been installed as the Defence Minister. During official visits successive UK Prime Ministers punted British weapons to the new government. In 1994, during John Major's first visit to the newly democratic South Africa, he handed a private letter to Mandela asking him to consider arms purchases from the UK.[4] British officials set about persuading the South Africans that a big arms deal was not only a good way to keep the apartheid generals happy but was also useful to raise party and personal funds. Unless seen in this way, many of the decisions made defy logic, especially the awarding of the largest contract to BAE and Saab for the supply of trainer and fighter jets.

The decision-making process comprised three main tiers: technical committees; an Arms Acquisition Council (AAC) on which the then Defence Minister, Joe Modise (assisted by his political adviser, Fana Hlongwane), and the head of procurement in the Defence Force, 'Chippy' Shaik, were the key players; and a Ministers' Committee chaired by the Deputy President, Thabo Mbeki.

With respect to the jets contract the joint British and Swedish bid, which was heavily punted by Tony Blair on visits to South Africa, by the Swedish Prime Minister on a special trip and even by the British royal family, did not make the initial shortlist which the relevant technical committee sent to the AAC. It failed to meet certain of the technical criteria and was over-specified in other respects. The Hawk trainer jets and Gripen fighter planes were also unfamiliar to South African pilots, who had flown mainly Cheetahs. Not unimportantly for a country facing a multitude of socio-economic challenges, the BAE/Saab option was two and a half times more expensive than the Italian Aermacchi jet favoured by the technical committee.

Beyond cost, BAE faced another major hurdle. When the South African Air Force (SAAF) reviewed its needs in the mid-1990s, it decided that it had to cut its clothes to fit the cloth. Knowing that South Africa needed to reduce defence spending, it suggested that only one type of plane be bought. This plane would serve a dual function: it would act as a training jet and could also be used in conflict.[5] This, however, immediately disqualified BAE/Saab from the running as they were offering separate training jets (the Hawk) and fighting jets (the Gripen). BAE could offer no plane that could both train and fight. Other suppliers could, especially Aermacchi, the Italian plane-maker, which offered a dual-fighter at a much lower cost.[6]

In November 1997, however, under the strict instruction of Joe Modise, the Air Force was compelled to drop this approach. Instead, as per Modise's directive, the SAAF announced that it needed two discrete planes: one to train new pilots and one in which to fight.[7] BAE could now become a contender, as it was in prime position to submit both types of jet for consideration. Beyond benefiting BAE, it was an incredibly strange decision. In effect, the Air Force had agreed to purchase more jets without

increasing combat capacity. In addition, as a series of auditors were later
to discover, every single supplier that had been approached confirmed
that pilots could make the transition from the training planes South Africa
already had to a fully functional jet fighter – meaning that there was absolutely no need for the additional training rung on which BAe would
eventually hang the Hawk.[8]

Even with this gerrymandering, BAE faced another obstacle. After
receiving the bids, a shortlist drawn up by a technical committee listed the
Hawk and Gripen as the least desirable planes of their respective types:
for trainers the Air Force preferred the Aermacchi MB339FD, and for
fighter jets Daimler-Benz's AT2000.[9] In each case, the fact that the Hawk
and Gripen were by far the most expensive options, did little to help their
cause.

The Gripen, however, was able to sneak through on a technicality. A
major part of the bid was the proposal to finance the deal, which was
weighted at 33 per cent of a final score given to each bidder. When review-
ing this, the members of the selection committee claimed that only BAE
had submitted a full financing proposal, despite repeated calls to the other
bidders to do likewise.[10] This fatally hamstrung the other bidders, and the
Gripen moved into first place by default,[11] despite being the most expensive and least technically suitable option. It stretches credulity to believe
that BAE's competitors would not have submitted such important information if asked. And when auditors looked into the deal they could find
no evidence that any of BAE's competitors had been informed of the
need to submit the financing proposal.[12] Here, selective silence had
worked in favour of BAE.

To select the Hawk, a more gauche approach was taken. When the
shortlist was presented to the AAC, placing the Hawk last, the minister,
Joe Modise, was furious. So, in what was later described by his Cabinet
colleagues and cowed investigators as 'a visionary decision', Modise
decided to exclude cost as a procurement criterion on the single largest
contract in the democratic South Africa's history. There were now two
parallel shortlists. One factored in cost and ranked the Hawk last. Another
excluded cost, which, while not placing it first, gave the Hawk enough
points for it to be able to win with a considerable offsets bid. The non-
costed option, which was the only shortlist considered, kept the Hawk in
play when the SAAF had demanded the opposite.

To improve their prospects even further, BAE/Saab were then asked to make an improved economic offset offer, an opportunity not given to the other companies.[13] They came up with a package roughly ten times larger than that of any of their competitors. However, when the offset proposals were reviewed by the South African Department of Trade and Industry it was discovered that their value had been 'grossly inflated' by the evaluation committee, from $245m to $1.6bn.[14]

Offsets, sometimes known as countertrade, are programmes in which the supplier company agrees to invest in the industry of a purchasing state, to offset the economic impact of the transaction. Case studies and the literature on these so-called benefits suggest they are so much economic sophistry: useful for politicians to justify spending billions on weapons but very seldom delivering the promised benefits, especially in developing countries. They are also a clever way to channel bribes and benefits to key decision-makers. So controversial are they, that the World Trade Organization bans the use of offsets as a criterion for contract evaluation in all markets other than the arms trade.[15]

The South African experience of offsets has largely chimed with that elsewhere in the world. When the arms deal was announced it was promised that offsets would create 65,000 jobs in the country and generate R104bn (roughly £10bn) in economic activity. Despite the fact that 65,000 jobs was actually an incredibly poor return for such a huge investment of money and implied an absurdly high cost per job, even these expectations were unfounded. In 2010, the government department overseeing offsets – the Department of Trade and Industry (DTI) – confirmed that only 28,000 direct jobs had been created,[16] roughly £107,000 per job at the underestimated stated cost of the deal, or £214,000 per job at the close to £6bn (at current exchange rates) that the arms deal will actually cost by 2018. By comparison, it cost on average £3,870 a year, as of August 2010, to employ a South African teacher.[17] The staggering figure of fifty-five teachers could thus be employed for a year for the same price as a single direct job created by the offsets programme.[18]

Even the paltry number of jobs created by the offsets programme has to be taken with a large pinch of salt. The DTI has denied any review of how companies have been awarded credits under the offset system. The department claims that the activities of the arms deal companies are embargoed due to 'commercial confidentiality'.[19] Even the investigatory team that examined the arms deal with Parliament's blessing but Executive interference was not allowed to review the details of the programme.[20] Clearly, DTI is concerned that the realities of the offset programme will make for underwhelming reading.

The offsets credit system is applied in such a way that arms deal companies can be granted hundreds of millions of dollars of credits based on minuscule investment and an only tangential relationship to economic activity. The example of McArthur Baths makes the point graphically. In 2001, Saab spent R15m (roughly $3m) upgrading a set of heated pools in the coastal town of Port Elizabeth and undertaking marketing activities in Sweden to attract tourists to the South African town.[21] For this tiny investment Saab had claimed $218m in offset credits by 2005 alone.[22] The company was able to do so by claiming $3,830 for every Scandinavian visitor to South Africa and not just Port Elizabeth. Saab received this credit for every Scandinavian visitor until 2011 – effectively meaning that the company was granted offset credits for each Swedish tourist who travelled to South Africa to watch the football World Cup in 2010.[23] How many offset credits have been awarded subsequent to 2005 has yet to be disclosed, but if the programme was managed along the same lines, Saab would be in line for offset credits in the high hundred millions for an investment of a paltry $3m.

Despite the inherently suspect nature of offsets, by including a massively improved offset offer, BAE/Saab's bid nudged into first place on the non-costed shortlist.

Clearly unsure of their ground, Modise and his accomplices arranged an informal meeting of a few of the members of the Ministers' Committee. Two Defence Force representatives who were at the get-together were shocked the following morning when 'Chippy' Shaik asked them to sign minutes of the meeting, confirming that it had been formally decided to buy the Hawks and Gripens. The officials argued that the meeting was not formally constituted, that alternatives to the BAE/Saab offer had not even been discussed and that no decision had been made.[24] Nevertheless, despite these procedural irregularities and the South African Air Force making clear that it would only accept the Hawk/Gripen if forced to do so by politicians,[25] the British–Swedish joint venture was awarded the prized contract.

Our investigations on the Public Accounts Committee made clear that

South Africa had been taken for a ride. The arms companies had persuaded political leaders and military officials that they needed far more equipment than had originally been envisaged. They charged a premium, in one instance 35 per cent more than others paid for the same equipment, and promised unrealizable economic benefits from the contracts.

There was immediately clear evidence of conflicts of interest and possible corruption. For instance, we were made aware that the Defence Minister had acquired shares in a company called Conlog in 1997 through a complex transaction that resulted in him paying nothing for the shares.[26] Conlog was identified by BAE during the bidding process as a potential recipient of substantial offset contracts.[27] Using insider information Modise purchased Conlog shares, anticipating that their value would increase in the aftermath of the arms deal as a result of BAE's offset commitments.[28] This gave Modise considerable inducement to ensure BAE's selection. On retiring from government in early 1999, Modise was appointed chairman of Conlog.[29]

Fortified with this information, myself and the committee chairperson, an opposition MP, won the support of the Public Accounts Committee for a massive investigation by a multi-agency team to get to the bottom of the deal. We pushed a resolution approving the proposal through Parliament. When the ANC leadership realized what we had done, they reacted angrily. We were called to a meeting of the party's senior leadership at which President Mbeki's closest ally in Cabinet screamed at me across the meeting room table: 'Who do you think you are, questioning the integrity of the President, the cabinet and the government.'[30]

They developed a strategy to prevent further meaningful investigation. It included the ANC members of the Public Accounts Committee using the party's majority to water down our resolution, excluding any investigators who were not sympathetic to the ANC and unconstitutionally instructing the others as to who and what they could and could not investigate. These agencies were also severely hamstrung in their efforts to work with international investigators.

I refused to cooperate with the cover-up and continued to pursue more information. A number of senior party members tried to persuade me to fall into line. One told me that this was a battle I could not win, that the party would close ranks around the deal because we had received money from the successful bidders which was used to fund our election campaign in 1999. The Minister of Finance suggested to me privately: 'We all know Joe Modise [who had a history of corruption, even during the ANC's years in exile]. Of course there was shit in the deal. But they're not that stupid. No one will ever uncover it. Just concentrate on the technical aspects of the deal, which were sound.'[31]

Thabo Mbeki and his inner circle were happy to undermine key institutions of the new-won democracy, including Parliament and important components of the judicial system, in order to safeguard the interests of the party and to protect some of its senior leaders.

I was removed from the Public Accounts Committee. My attempts to continue to investigate the deal were met with constant disciplining from the party leadership until, under the terms of South Africa's proportional representation system, I was forced to resign my parliamentary seat.

On arriving in the UK in November 2001 I was besieged by people from all over the world who had followed the South African arms deal. I began to understand that this event was just one in a long history of systematic bribery and corruption by arms companies. The SFO was, at the time, engaged in multiple investigations into BAE. In addition to the Al Yamamah deal and a more modest investigation into South Africa, it was also examining similar transactions in Tanzania, the Czech Republic and Hungary.

After telling investigators all I knew about the South African deal it was clear that BAE used similar routes and methods to pay off South Africans as it had others.

Together with South Africa's anti-corruption unit, the Scorpions, which was subsequently disbanded by the government, the SFO revealed the web of companies used to pay the bribes. In an affidavit submitted to South African courts in an application for search warrants, the agencies claimed 'reasonable suspicion that BAE devised a system of payments . . . designed as bribes to achieve success . . . and to seek to obtain undue advantage over its competitors in the bidding process'.[32] This was done through a system of 'overt and covert' advisers. The SFO alleged that Red Diamond Trading Ltd was created 'to ensure that corrupt payments could be made and that it would be more difficult for law enforcement agencies to penetrate the system [of covert payments]'.[33]

The SFO investigation revealed that £115m of commissions had been

paid by BAE to agents and key political leaders and officials in South
Africa. From 2002 to 2007, Fana Hlongwane, Modise's political adviser,
received significant payments from BAE, including a total of £10m paid
in instalments between September 2003 and January 2007 directly from
BAE shell companies, with a further amount of £9.15m to be paid by
other BAE shell companies or in the form of bonuses.[34] These payments
were made through BAE itself, via Sanip – a company in South Africa
established by BAE and Saab to manage their offset obligations – and two
covert entities: Arstow Commercial Corporation, registered in the British
Virgin Islands, and the Jersey-registered CIC (Commercial International
Corporation). It appears that CIC was bought by financial consultants 'as
a vehicle for use by Fana Hlongwane'. BAE 'could not produce any significant records . . . of work done that could reasonably justify [such]
compensation [to Hlongwane]'.[35]

The company tried to suggest that it only became involved with
Hlongwane after it had won the contract, but the SFO then seized documents indicating that it was working with him during the contract
negotiation phase.

The affidavits also revealed a scramble by BAE to make two highly confidential commission payments to seal the deal prior to the signature of the
final contract with the South African government in December 1999. On
2 December, the day before the contract was signed, BAE approved payment of $4m to Huderfield Enterprises Inc., a covert company set up by
BAE's agent, Richard Charter, alongside his overt consultancy. A special
payment of £100,000 had been made to Arstow on 5 October 1999, after
the South African government announced the purchase of the Hawk and
Gripen aircraft. These two payments were approved through an extraordinary 'ex-committee' procedure attended by only a handful of BAE's
most senior executives. It is assumed these payments, or a part thereof,
were intended for Hlongwane and others.[36]

Besides the Briton Richard Charter, the Zimbabwean John Bredenkamp
was identified as one of BAE's covert agents on the deal. A former Rho-
desian international rugby captain, Bredenkamp, who admits to breaking
arms sanctions in place against Rhodesia's racist Ian Smith government,[37]
is alleged by EU and US authorities to have been close to Robert Mugabe
or people within his inner circle.[38] Bredenkamp denies this, instead claiming

he has not met Mugabe since 1981, has been subjected to false arrest and imprisonment by the regime, before being cleared, has had his passport rescinded and had his farm listed for seizure on two occasions.*

It was alleged in court documents submitted by the SFO that Kayswell Services Ltd, one of Bredenkamp's commercial vehicles, was paid more than £37m by BAE on the South African deal.[39] Allan McDonald, a former BAE executive, claims that Bredenkamp and his team's only contribution towards the selection of BAE as preferred bidder was to advise the company which 'key decision-makers' needed to be identified with a view to 'financially incentivising' them to make the right decision with regard to the Hawk/Gripen contract. He was told that Bredenkamp's team had boasted that 'we can get to Chippy Shaik' and that they had actually been speaking to him about the Hawk. Bredenkamp's UK operations chief spoke of the 'Third World procedures' required to win the South African bid – an assumed reference to bribery.[40]

The obvious conclusion drawn is that at least part of these exorbitant alleged payments were used by Hlongwane and Bredenkamp to bribe others. The Scorpions concluded their submission in support of the warrants as follows:

> In view of the huge sums of money involved, there is at the very least a reasonable suspicion that Bredenkamp and/or BAE's South African representative Richard Charter, used some of the money they received to induce or reward Fana Hlongwane and/or certain other officials involved in the evaluation of the various bids . . . Alternatively, there is at the very least a reasonable suspicion that Fana Hlongwane may have used some of the huge sums of money he received, either directly or through the various entities which he controlled, to induce and/or reward such officials for such assistance.[41]

This would account for the complete undermining of the procurement criteria, at the insistence of Joe Modise and his henchmen, that led to BAE being awarded the contract to supply the Hawk over the Aermacchi jet.

* At the time of writing, Bredenkamp was residing in Zimbabwe, facing no apparent legal or political difficulties. In addition, as stated in Chapter 19 below, Bredenkamp is on the United States' Foreign Assets Control (OFAC) sanctions list and the EU's financial sanctions list and is described on both as a Mugabe crony. You can see Bredenkamp's detailed defence of himself at www.johnbredenkamp.co.za.

Bredenkamp denies paying bribes or providing covert assistance to BAE. He stated in correspondence with the author that he was simply an investor in companies which assisted BAE in their bid.

In late 2010, it was reported that Hlongwane had granted a sizeable home loan to Siphiwe Nyanda, the chief of the South African National Defence Force (SANDF) at the time of the deal. Allegedly Nyanda only paid back a fraction of the loan before it was written off when he was appointed Minister of Communications in 2009, suggestive of a deal to transfer funds to Nyanda with a minimal paper trail.[42] After leaving the SANDF in 2005, Nyanda became chief executive of Hlongwane's group of companies, Ngwane Defence.[43] Nyanda was the SANDF chief during the selection and negotiation process and also, crucially, during a 2004 review of the purchase that resulted in the decision to pursue additional tranches of the BAE–Saab deal. The bonus payment to Hlongwane in 2004 was conditional on South Africa agreeing to the additional tranches.[44]

Around the same time as they raided the homes and offices of Hlongwane and Bredenkamp, investigators froze five bank accounts belonging to Hlongwane in Switzerland and Liechtenstein, blocking funds of more than R160m. The Swiss initiated their own money-laundering inquiry.

Other alleged recipients of arms deal largesse suffered mixed fates initially. South Africa's then Deputy President – now President – Jacob Zuma was fired for corruption in relation to the deal after his financial adviser, Schabir Shaik – the brother of the head of procurement in the Defence Force, 'Chippy' Shaik – was sentenced to fifteen years in jail for fraud and corruption for paying Zuma to further his business interests.

The ANC's Chief Whip in Parliament, who attempted to stop me investigating the deal, also served a brief prison sentence for offences linked to gifts from EADS, a French–German arms company which also bid for contracts. He was carried shoulder-high into prison by senior leaders of the ANC and, on his premature release, was greeted as a hero. Today he serves on the highest decision-making body of the party and runs the ANC's influential Political School. 'Chippy' Shaik had to flee the country after evidence emerged that he had received $3m from ThyssenKrupp, which was part of the consortium that won the contract – in highly controversial circumstances – to build frigates. The work was effectively awarded to a Spanish company before the then Deputy President, Thabo Mbeki, made a visit to Germany. Thereafter the tender was reopened. The third Shaik brother, an intelligence operative called 'Mo', was briefly deployed to Hamburg, where the German Frigate Consortium was headquartered, as the country's Consul General. The consortium was awarded the contract, allegedly paying $25m in bribes. The awarding of a submarine deal to a consortium led by Ferrostaal was also highly contentious.[45]

Jacob Zuma was charged with 783 counts of racketeering, fraud and corruption, for receiving payments related to the deal through Schabir Shaik. In return South Africa's current President intervened to ensure the businessman won a lucrative subcontract through the French company Thomson-CSF, now Thales. When Thomson-CSF was considering dumping Shaik as its partner in 1998, the businessman flew Zuma to London to meet the company, where he reassured them that Shaik was well regarded throughout the ANC, including by Mandela and Mbeki – an untrue statement. Subsequently, in an encrypted fax, the company agreed to pay Zuma R500,000 a year to further the interests of the company and to protect it from any possible inquiry into their role in the arms deal. South Africa's Constitutional Court, when deliberating on Schabir Shaik's appeal against his conviction, stated:

> Counsel for the appellants [Shaik and his companies] very properly conceded in argument that, given the criminal conviction of Mr Shaik, it must be accepted for the purpose of these proceedings that Mr Shaik did pay bribes to Mr Zuma . . .
>
> The payments were made by Mr Shaik in order to influence Mr Zuma to promote Mr Shaik's business interests and, in attending the meeting [with Thomson-CSF] in London in July 1998, Mr Zuma did, as a matter of fact, promote Mr Shaik's interests.[46]

After unseating Thabo Mbeki as ANC President and just ten days before he was elected South Africa's President, the charges against Jacob Zuma were controversially dropped by a prosecutor who was made an acting High Court judge after the election. The statement announcing his decision drew heavily – in some sections, near verbatim – from a judgment delivered by Justice Conrad Seagroatt in a commercial case in Hong Kong. Seagroatt later pointed out that his own judgment was made under a different legal system, in a commercial not criminal case and, most importantly, was overturned on appeal, making it an invalid legal precedent. He even went on record saying that the Zuma trial should have gone ahead.[47] Schabir Shaik was released from jail less than two years into a fifteen-year sentence on compassionate grounds, using legislation intended for prisoners in the final stages of a terminal illness. He was suffering from high blood pressure and depression. Since his release he has been spotted in a nightclub and playing golf, and has been accused of two separate assaults.[48]

South Africa continues to pay for this deal in lives. A Harvard University study conservatively estimated that, over the five years following the deal, 365,000 South Africans died avoidable deaths because the state, in thrall to Thabo Mbeki's Aids denialism and fiscal discipline on everything but the purchase of unnecessary weapons, would not provide the antiretroviral medication they needed to live.[49]

It is estimated that the arms deal will have cost the country up to R71bn by 2011.[50] This figure dwarfs what has been spent on what were and remain far more pressing priorities. By 2008, South Africa had spent a paltry R8.7bn in its HIV/Aids and STI programme;[51] for every rand spent on keeping South Africans with Aids alive, an equivalent R7.63 was spent on the arms deal.[52] In the same period R41bn had been spent to provide housing to the millions of South Africans left homeless by apartheid, R30bn less than spending on the arms deal.[53] South Africa could have built close to 2 million houses with the money spent on the weapons or employed 1.1 million maintenance workers and cleaners for a year – the equivalent of 100,000 jobs per year for ten years, in a country with a formal unemployment rate of close to 30 per cent.[54]

South Africa's prosecutorial and investigative bodies were left in disarray by the arms deal and have continued to deteriorate sharply. Parliament has never recovered from being turned into a rubber stamp which approves all important executive decisions without meaningful interrogation. The deal and its cover-up were the point at which the once-proud ANC lost its moral compass. It heralded the start of a series of similar corrupt transactions that have continued to benefit the ANC, and some of its key leaders, while undermining the provision of basic social services. Even the country's Deputy President lamented the pervasive corruption that infects the ANC and all levels of government.[55] As the country's premier political newspaper opined: 'much of what is going wrong [in South Africa] has its roots in the arms deal'.[56]

As for the weaponry, only eleven of the twenty-four Hawks have ever been operational. The Air Force can only afford to let the Gripen squadron, comprising the eleven planes so far delivered, fly for a paltry 250 hours a year, or just over twenty hours for each operational plane a year – 250 hours is the minimum a combat pilot needs to fly in order to retain accreditation.[57] The Hawks, while cheaper to fly, have only been granted 2,500 hours per year due to cost, roughly half of what the Air Force believes is needed in order to maximize its use of the planes.[58] Remarkably, the Air Force has confirmed that the lack of flying hours for the Hawk means that some pilots are without the flight time needed to graduate to flying the Gripens, a problem that could have been avoided if the original decision to purchase only a single type of jet had been kept to.[59]

In addition, South Africa continues to pay millions for maintenance on the aircraft. For the Hawk alone, South Africa has shelled out R268m for maintenance to BAE since 2006.[60] Other equipment has also struggled to live up to the hype. In the most high-profile case, one of the three submarines purchased from German suppliers has been beset by a 'litany of problems'. As a result, it has spent much of its life in South Africa waiting for repair on a dry-dock.[61]

On 1 October 2009, the Serious Fraud Office announced that it was seeking permission to prosecute BAE for overseas corruption in Africa and Eastern Europe. A plea bargain was offered to the company in terms of which BAE would have to admit guilt and pay penalties of around half a billion pounds. The shocked company rejected the deal as its share price plummeted.

Poverty No Barrier

As the SFO charge sheet illustrates, South Africa was not the only African country afflicted by BAE. While trumpeting his Commission for Africa's recommendations for improved governance on the continent, Tony Blair persuaded the President of Tanzania, one of the world's poorest countries,[62] to purchase an air radar system for military aircraft at a cost of over $40m. At the time Tanzania had an air force of eight planes, most of which were in various states of disrepair. Bribes of almost $10m were allegedly paid on the deal.[63]

In 1997, BAE bought a company, Siemens Plessey Systems (SPS), which had been negotiating with the Tanzanian government since 1992 for a deal to sell radar equipment. As part of the transaction BAE took on SPS's agent, Sailesh (or Shailesh) Vithlani. At the time the agent requested amendments to his consultant relationship because of 'commitments' and 'promises' made to Tanzanian government officials.[64] The original deal, an unaffordable £110m,[65] had been blocked by the World Bank and the UK's Overseas Development Administration.[66] In 2000, the deal re-emerged with BAE splitting the project into two phases to make it appear cheaper.[67] Clare Short, the UK's Secretary for International Development at the time, recalls that 'It came back as half a project. The thing was so grubby from beginning to end and, of course, it was so old that the technology was overtaken. Tanzania didn't have military aircraft. It needed civil air traffic control improvement in order to improve its tourist industry.'[68]

Despite vigorous opposition from Short and the Foreign Secretary, Robin Cook, the deal went through in 2001 with BAE selling Tanzania a £28m Watchman air traffic control system.[69] The radar was transportable and packed with anti-jamming devices.[70] The sale was funded through a loan from Barclays Bank, the bankers on BAE's South African deal.[71] In October 2001, a report by the UN's International Civil Aviation Organization (ICAO) made clear the absurdity of the deal:

> The system as contracted is primarily a military system and can provide limited support to civil air traffic control purposes. The purchase of additional equipment . . . would be required to render it useful for civil air traffic control. However, if it is to be used primarily for civil air traffic control purposes, the proposed system is not adequate and too expensive.[72]

BAE accused the ICAO of making false cost comparisons,[73] but a World Bank spokesman confirmed the folly: 'We are concerned that such a large expenditure is going to purposes who's [sic] justification is not clear to us. To put it in context, $40m is about one third of basic national education expenditure in Tanzania. So it really is a large amount of money and it is competing with priority programmes such as education and health.'[74]

Norman Lamb, a Liberal Democrat MP and the party's spokesman on international development at the time, said a modern system could have been provided for 10 per cent of the cost. He claimed: 'The Department of Trade and Industry, with the apparent support of the prime minister, has colluded with British Aerospace and Barclays Bank in foisting an expensive and unnecessary arms deal on the desperately poor people of Tanzania.'[75] Lamb's outrage never dimmed. In 2009, he called the deal 'morally indefensible', adding: 'it's outrageous that it's gone on for so many years. We had the inquiry launched by BAE Systems, in the name of Lord Woolf, which was a complete whitewash. What we need is decisive action by the SFO, to make it clear that that culture is no longer acceptable. I also believe we need a public inquiry into how this export licence was allowed to be granted.'[76]

Clare Short was particularly angry about the deal she had opposed in Cabinet. A £35m aid package for education development in Tanzania was effectively wiped out by the expenditure on the air traffic control system. She placed the blame squarely at the door of the Prime Minister, Tony Blair: 'Tony was absolutely dedicated to all arms sales proposals,' she says. 'Whenever British Aerospace wanted anything, he supported them 100 per cent. He didn't seem to understand that there are matters of principle concerned. He had also been duped and bought the argument that it's always good for the British economy, which is absolutely not so.'[77]

Cabinet discussion on the deal had been heated, especially after it was revealed that the Ministry of Defence had given BAE the go-ahead before the export licence process had decided on the legality of the deal.[78] So intense was the Cabinet dispute that in late 2001 an ad-hoc committee was set up to analyse the deal and adjudicate whether an export licence should be granted. John Prescott, at the time Deputy Prime Minister, chaired the committee. Clare Short hoped for support from the Chancellor, Gordon Brown. 'I talked to everybody individually and he [Gordon Brown] said he would back me. But then, when it came to the meetings convened by John Prescott, he sent a junior minister and didn't stand. The press was briefed that Gordon was supporting me but, when it came to the crunch, he didn't make an issue of it with Tony.'[79] Blair argued that the 280 British jobs at stake on the Isle of Wight were more important than the government's international anti-poverty goals.[80] He was supported by the Trade and Industry Secretary, Patricia Hewitt, the Defence Secretary, Geoff Hoon, and the Foreign Secretary, Jack Straw,[81] all known for their uncritical support of BAE.[82]

Colonel Gaby Komba, military attaché to the Tanzanian embassy in London, who was surprised by the vehemence of the debate, defended the deal: 'It is wrong to say it is basically a military system because it's not. It is going to be used for both (military and civilian) purposes,' adding: 'You can get a cheaper system, but for the purposes of what we want this would have been the best.'[83] He admitted there was a 'military element' to the equipment but the system as a whole would be used to 'maintain the integrity of Tanzania's airspace'.[84] The deal was expected to help Tanzanian tourism and raise $3m to $5m per year in air traffic charges.[85] Defenders of the deal failed to mention that Tanzania only possessed eight, unsophisticated, underutilized military planes.[86]

The deal was financed with a $39.5m loan from a commercial bank, Barclays,[87] which was strange as Tanzania had recently received $2bn of debt relief, under the terms of which it could not borrow money except on concessional terms, such as those available from multilateral development banks.[88] Barclays claimed that the loan was at a concessional rate, explaining that the financing had been in place since 1999, that it was 'not involved' in the debate surrounding the sale, and that any loan it made had to conform with export-licensing laws.[89] But Clare Short assumes that the bank merely inflated the original price of the deal and then dropped it a little so it could be called concessional.[90] Indefensibly, a loan was available from the European Investment Bank to install a state-of-the-art radar system for Tanzania and its two neighbours that was less than half the price of the BAE system.[91] In 2002, Short delayed £10m in aid money to Tanzania, arguing that the country had breached its commitments to alleviate poverty.[92]

Norman Lamb also criticized the financing, suggesting in the House of Commons that 'The more sinister explanation [of the financing] is that the contract price was fiddled – artificially inflated so that it looked to the outside world as if Barclays were providing a concessional loan. If this is correct then it seems to me that there has been fraud. When you have the secretary of state alluding to corruption, surely it is time that the financing of this deal be thoroughly investigated. I have also been told that bungs have been paid to oil the wheels.'

Alan Johnson, then a junior trade minister, responded that the Department of Trade had 'absolutely no evidence that there had been any fraud or bungs offered'.[93] Benjamin Mkapa, the Tanzanian President, was adamant: 'No one has given me an iota of evidence about corruption.'[94] The reliability of his denial was inevitably questioned by his inappropriate purchase in 2002 of a brand-new Gulfstream jet for $40m, in a country in which the poorest third of the population live on less than a dollar a day.[95]

The agent on the jet deal was Tanil Somaiya, a business tycoon who owned the Shivacom Group of Companies with interests in tele-communications, construction, advertising, promotion, real estate and, the ubiquitous catch-all, 'security'.[96] His associate, the BAE agent Sailesh Vithlani, is a plump 42-year-old of Indian extraction. He has a UK pass-port and a mother and brother in south London, but in Tanzania 'he is a power in the land'.[97] Somaiya and Vithlani grew up together in Mwanza on the southern shore of Lake Victoria, before moving to Dar es Salaam, where they registered a company called Merlin International Ltd in 1986.[98]

When BAE's nemesis, David Leigh, investigated the radar deal, the trail led him to these two men. He discovered them in an obscure office in the old Avalon cinema building down Samora Avenue in Dar es Salaam, just across from the ferry terminal to Zanzibar. He first interviewed Somaiya, who acknowledged that two parallel arrangements were made with BAE. In the first, a conventional agency agreement was signed. This above-board contract stated that 1 per cent commission was to be paid to Merlin International if the deal went through. But in terms of a second, under-the-table agreement, BAE's Red Diamond Trading Ltd deposited £6.2m, representing 30 per cent of the contract price, in Switzerland.[99] That money was controlled by the other BAE agent, Vithlani. The mid-dlemen insist that this Swiss cash did not go to public officials in Tanzania. They refused to comment when asked if the money went to third parties outside Tanzania.[100] Officials close to the Tanzanian investigation, how-ever, confirmed that it was Vithlani who negotiated payments with senior government officials and made arrangements for the transfer of kickbacks from the Swiss bank account.[101] A secret consultancy contract was held with a firm registered in Panama called Envers Trading Corporation, which acted as a 'consultant' for BAE on the deal. A legal power-of-attorney document allowed both Vithlani and Somaiya to act as agents of Envers, which was effectively their covert 'dirty' company.[102]

Vithlani eventually admitted that he arranged for the £6.2m to be paid secretly into the Swiss bank account by BAE.[103] But the company, as always, protested its innocence: 'We won the contract in open competi-tion and it was completely above board. We operate a global company in a very above-board manner, which is the way we have to work nowadays. Everything is becoming more transparent.'[104]

In August 2007, an international arrest warrant was issued for Sailesh Vithlani and a criminal case filed in Tanzania charging him with perjury and lying under oath. The SFO had been looking into the case since mid-2004 and in July 2009 interrogated him.[105] It is unclear why they didn't have him arrested but speculation suggests that he might have agreed to turn state's witness. Vithlani is reported to be enjoying a comfortable life in Switzerland. Somaiya, who belatedly withdrew from Merlin in 2007 after the corruption allegations first hit the headlines,[106] has since denied any involvement in the deal.[107]

Somaiya and Vithlani had been making serious money from arms deals for many years before the radar purchase. They were involved in public procurement contracts worth well over $240m.[108] In 2004–5, they won a multimillion-dollar tender from the defence ministry for the supply of around 650 trucks and buses for the Tanzania People's Defence Force (TPDF). While the government paid the suppliers the full amount of the purchase price in 2006, only 350 of the vehicles had arrived in the country by 2009.[109] In applying for the tender, Somaiya and Vithlani fraudulently claimed to be the owners of INCAR Tanzania Limited, the authorized dealer for IVECO trucks from Italy. It was not until 2006 that they actually bought the company. The INCAR company file has meanwhile mysteriously vanished from the Business Registration and Licensing Authority offices in Dar es Salaam. Concerns were raised in military circles that the fleet of IVECO trucks might not be appropriate to replace the army's ageing vehicles, citing the high unit price, uneconomic fuel consumption and high maintenance costs.[110]

Somaiya and Vithlani are also alleged to have been involved in the provision of helicopters to the ministry, which they supplied even though they were not the chosen agents of the manufacturer, Agusta Bell. Two of the four helicopters have already crashed, leading to the loss of several lives. Apart from being overpriced, the helicopters were actually designed for civilian use.[111] Inevitably, Somaiya and Vithlani were involved in the $40m purchase of the top-of-the-range Gulfstream business jet from the US in 2002 for the use of President Makapa.[112]

In April 2008, Tanzania's Infrastructure Minister, Andrew Chenge, who was Attorney General at the time of the radar deal, resigned following allegations that £500,000 in a Jersey bank account belonged to him. Chenge did not dispute the money's existence, but denied it came from BAE. As Attorney General he gave advice on key aspects of the transaction, which ultimately led the Tanzanian Cabinet to approve the deal. In particular, he advised that the commercial financing of the purchase was compatible with Tanzania's application for debt relief.[113] It was alleged that Sailesh Vithlani even sent a copy of Chenge's legal opinion to Barclays. A payment to Chenge's account coincided exactly with the delivery of his opinion in favour of the deal.[114]

According to a draft SFO report Chenge received six credit transfers totalling $1.5m between June 1997 and April 1998 from a Barclays Bank branch in Frankfurt. They were paid into a Barclays account in Jersey,[115] owned by Franton Investment Limited, a company owned by Chenge for the sole purpose of transferring the money.[116] In May 1998, he authorized the transfer of $600,000 to an account owned by Langley Investments Ltd, which was operated by the former Tanzanian Central Bank Governor, Dr Idrissa Rashidi. Rashidi was responsible for approving the financing arrangements of the radar deal, under the terms of which the Bank of Tanzania pledged its gold reserves to secure the Barclays loan. Rashidi was also responsible for Tanzania agreeing that English law, and not Tanzanian law, would prevail in the event of any litigation arising out of a possible default on the loan. On 20 September 1999, Chenge personally authorized the transfer of $1.2m from the Franton account to Royal Bank of Scotland International in Jersey.[117]

Displaying remarkable insensitivity, Chenge referred to the money in his account as 'pocket change'.[118] His foreign lawyers in the US and UK[119] admitted that he gave legal advice to the government on some aspects of the deal, though they maintained that he in no way promoted the purchase from BAE.[120] That he was able to retain the services of expensive British and American law firms in itself fuelled media speculation about the extent and origins of his personal fortune.[121]

The investigations into Chenge and the deal in the UK took an alarming turn in autumn 2006, when Norman Lamb had a meeting with SFO and MoD investigators in Portcullis House, where some British MPs have their offices. An SFO investigator suggested to Lamb that they should meet in the atrium because Lamb's office might be bugged. The outraged MP wrote to the SFO's Carl Brown on 5 June 2008: 'You explained that

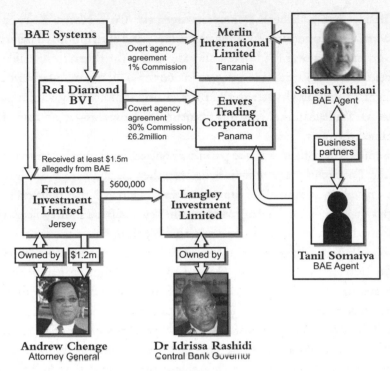

Figure 3: BAE's web of payments in Tanzania

during the course of your investigations . . . BAE Systems appeared to be aware of key findings and key information that you received as a result of interviewing witnesses. You indicated that you were left with the impression that they were able to listen to your interviews with potential witnesses.' The SFO responded: 'At that time, we were operating with an abundance of caution . . . it was considered prudent to take such precautions.' The MP was left 'pretty incredulous' at the allegation: 'My hope was it wasn't true and that my office wasn't being bugged. I didn't [have it swept] because it might have alerted BAE that I knew they were bugging it. But I had hoped that it wasn't true. Extraordinarily, the concern the SFO expressed was that they believed that their investigation was being monitored, that conversations were being bugged.'[122]

BAE called the allegations 'preposterous',[123] after which Lamb added: 'The suggestion the SFO had concerns [that] a company was bugging them is so serious it must be part of a public inquiry.'[124] It seems less far-fetched when taken together with BAE's history of dirty tricks against its opponents, such as the Campaign Against the Arms Trade.

Besides Lamb's Liberal Democrats, even the Conservative Party, not known for its commitment to fighting bribery and corruption, challenged the government over the bribery allegations and the threat to sustainable development in Tanzania in a debate in 2007.[125] This is particularly ironic in light of the party's offer to the BAE chairman, Dick Olver, of a position as Trade Minister when it returned to government in 2010. He declined the offer.[126]

Lamb's fears of surveillance paled by comparison with the experience of the Tanzanian prosecutor investigating the case. Edward Hoseah told US officials in 2007 that 'his life may be in danger' and that politicians in Tanzania were 'untouchable' over what he termed BAE's 'dirty deal'. He despaired of being able to prosecute the 'big fish' but was sure that 'it involved officials from the Ministry of Defence and at least one or two senior level military officers'. Hoseah told them that he had received threatening text messages and letters and was reminded every day that he was fighting the 'rich and powerful'. Hoseah, in a hushed voice, explained that 'If you attend meetings of the "inner-circle", people want you to feel as if they have put you there. If they see that you are uncompromising, there is a risk.' Hoseah made it clear that if the threat against his life rose he would be forced to flee the country.[127] His personal safety and future, as well as the crucial investigation which was having a deleterious impact on Tanzanian democracy, depended on the SFO and the British justice system.

After the Wall: Capitalism BAE-Style

Vienna's first district retains much of the Hapsburg city's imperial grand-eur. At its centre lies the Ring Straße, encircled by imposing facades and regal statues of Emperor Franz Josef. It exudes aristocratic power and wealth. 14 Kärtner Ring is nestled between Belvedere Palace in its baroque splendour, the Musikverein, which has been home to some of the world's greatest classical musicians, and the ultra-luxurious Hotel Imperial. The building's cavernous vestibule leads to a grand staircase. On the first floor an innocuous small white door bears the large black letters 'MPA' on a brass background, underscored with the name 'Mensdorff-Pouilly'.

The interior reflects its surroundings: ornate high ceilings, deep, aged leather chairs, expansive canvasses of demure young noblewomen along-side the stuffed heads of animals vanquished on the rural hunting estates of the aristocratic tenant. A severe assistant greets me and tells me she will inform the Count I am here.

Count Alfons Mensdorff-Pouilly, 'Ali' to his innumerable friends, is taller, thinner and more handsome than he appears in pictures. He is of imposing height and aristocratic bearing in a green baize alpine jacket and somewhat audacious pink tie. He is charming in a slightly roguish way. As we lower ourselves onto the sumptuous leather, the austere Magister Luka perched beside me blinking at her poised notebook, the 56-year-old *bon vivant* cuts through my awkwardness at asking inconvenient questions about his career as BAE's most notorious agent in Eastern and Central Europe, by regaling me with stories of his two brief spells in jail.

'Five weeks in an Austrian jail was far easier than five days in a British prison. I couldn't get anything from the British authorities, not a toothbrush, a comb, nothing. I befriended all the prisoners,' he says with a hint of macho pride, 'and a black man offered me his comb and toothbrush. I washed and used the comb, but I couldn't use the toothbrush.'[1] After his spell in Penton-ville prison, north London, Mensdorff-Pouilly complained that his human rights had been abused because his prison underpants were too small.[2] 'I wasn't given decent underwear despite having asked for it several times.'[3]

He describes MPA as a consulting company through which he provides strategic advice about Central and Eastern Europe to between thirty
and forty clients in a variety of sectors, mainly healthcare. He claims that
BAE was his only client in the defence industry. He came into contact
with the British company through the husband of a cousin, Tim Landon.
A notorious character, Landon was known as 'the White Sultan' for his
close links to Oman, where he assisted in a coup in which his friend from
Sandhurst, Sultan Qaboos bin Said, overthrew his father. Landon made
hundreds of millions of dollars out of his business dealings with Qaboos.
He earned his early money breaking the oil embargoes of South Africa
and Rhodesia and smuggling Bofors cannons to Oman in the 1980s.[4]

Mensdorff-Pouilly speaks with fondness of Landon, who died in 2007.
He explains that Landon had told BAE that to win business in Central
and Eastern Europe they needed somebody who was well-connected in
the region. Landon introduced them to the Count, who claims to know
everybody who is anybody in Austria, the Czech Republic and Hungary,
the former Austro-Hungarian Empire of his aristocratic lineage – he even
claims a cousin related to Queen Victoria. Mensdorff-Pouilly, who is
married to Maria Rauch-Kallat, a former Austrian Cabinet minister and a
senior member of the conservative ÖVP, says he can talk to all the key
politicians in the region whenever he wants to. He contends that he was
always paid by BAE on a monthly retainer for his political and economic
insights into these countries.[5]

The authorities argue that in the late 1990s BAE made payments of
more than £19m to companies associated with the Count, most of which
were connected to 'solicitation, promotion or otherwise to secure the
conclusion of the leases of Gripen fighter jets to Hungary and the Czech
Republic. . . . BAE made these payments even though there was a high
probability that part of the payments would be used in the tender process
to favour BAE.'[6] Put more explicitly by a UK court: 'BAE adopted and
deployed corrupt practices to obtain lucrative contracts of jet fighters in
Central Europe.' The barrister Tom Forster described the company's
activities as 'a sophisticated and meticulously planned operation involving very senior BAE executives . . . [who] spent over £10m to fund a
bribery campaign in Austria, the Czech Republic and Hungary'.[7] Three
offshore entities were created in Switzerland to prevent them 'being penetrated by law enforcement' agencies, with 'the underlying purpose to

channel money to public officials'.[8] About 70 per cent of the BAE money transferred to Mensdorff-Pouilly went into accounts in Austria.[9] There were 'significant cash withdrawals', often within days or weeks of important defence procurement decisions. BAE executives were alleged to be present at meetings where 'so-called third party payments or down-the-line payments' were discussed.[10]

More than £19m was transferred to the Count, but all he officially did in return was produce his 'marketing reports'.

Havel's Nightmare

Vaclav Havel, Czechoslovakia's remarkable dissident playwright turned President, suggests that 'politics is work of a kind that requires especially pure people, because it is especially easy to become morally tainted'.[11] BAE tested this maxim to the limit.

The Czech Republic, as it became after the split with Slovakia in 1993, joined NATO in 1999, necessitating an upgrade in military equipment. That year, companies were invited to submit proposals for the purchase of fighter aircraft. Five companies tendered bids, including Saab, which had entered into a deal with BAE in 1995 to help with the marketing of the Gripen aircraft. The Gripen had recently suffered severe setbacks with a dramatic accident during testing and another crash during the Stockholm Water Festival before tens of thousands of spectators.[12]

From 1997, the partnership started an intensive campaign to persuade the Czech government to buy the plane. It was primarily run by two BAE men, Steve Mead and Julian Scopes. Eventually, in December 2001, the government resolved to buy twenty-four Gripens for a price of approximately £1bn. All four of the other competitors withdrew from the competition, alleging corruption in the process.[13] The deal met with substantial resistance in both houses of the Czech parliament, where it was narrowly voted down.

The summer of 2002 brought devastating floods to the Czech Republic and the election of a new government, putting the Gripen purchase on hold. The costly clean-up from the natural disaster and the excessive cost of the new fighter aircraft led to the creation of an 'expert committee' to resolve the tender.[14] At the time, the UK offered to provide fourteen used

Tornado jets as a stop-gap measure while another tender could be organized for the aircraft purchase. (Though it was reported as a free offer, it is likely that BAE would have profited from the provision of training and spare parts.[15]) Tony Blair made a very public lobbying visit to the country in 2002 as part of the BAE/Saab campaign.[16] The committee, however, decided on a ten-year lease of fourteen Gripens for £400m, without a public tender. The deal was signed in June 2004, immediately reigniting allegations of corruption.[17]

After the US Defense Department, along with the contractors Lockheed and Boeing, had withdrawn from the competition, the US government accused BAE and the British government of 'corrupt practice' in a meeting with Sir Kevin Tebbit, the Permanent Secretary at the Ministry of Defence.[18] During the meeting US officials 'underscored our concern about persistent allegations that BAE Systems pays bribes to foreign public officials to obtain business'.[19] They also 'emphasize[d] a consistent pattern of alleged behaviour, over time. Press accounts reinforce material from more sensitive sources.'[20] They asked what the British government had done to investigate allegations of bribery by BAE, not only in connection with recent projects, but also older ones 'for which bribe payments may still be ongoing'.[21] They suggested that 'in the US, this volume of allegations about one company would have triggered a Department of Justice Criminal Division investigation long ago'.[22]

American officials nicknamed Tebbit 'Sir Topham Hatt', after the Thomas the Tank Engine character, because of what they described as 'his almost haughty disdain for the allegations of bribery involving BAE' and the orotund manner in which he challenged them to detail evidence of wrongdoing.[23]

Tebbit may have been feigning ignorance because the Czech police had already confirmed attempts by BAE to corrupt Czech politicians.[24] Two senior opposition MPs separately reported efforts to bribe them and their parties to vote in favour of the Gripen when the deal originally came before Parliament. Jitka Sietlova, an opposition Senator, recounted: 'I was contacted by an acquaintance who told me it would be to my advantage if I voted for the Gripen project. I reacted negatively, you don't do things like that, I was dismayed that someone thought you would do something like that.'[25] The other politician, Premysl Sobotka, described how 'there were strangers who approached me in the street. They said that if I voted in favour, they would make investments in my constituency. I refused to speak with them, I don't like that.'[26] A third, Michael Zantovsky, also had an offer by telephone, of SEK 10m to his party. Zantovsky and the other seven Senators in the ODA party, of which he was leader, did not vote against the Gripen. But he did go to the police, who traced the call to a telephone booth just outside a government building, a stone's throw from the Senate. The police investigation concluded that a crime had been committed but closed the case six months later after failing to identify the caller.[27]

The promised investment in Sobotka's constituency probably referred to the offset investments, which were a crucial element of the BAE/Saab campaign to sell the Gripen. On the original deal to sell twenty-four of the aircraft, contracts worth 150 per cent of the cost were to be placed with Czech companies.[28] The generosity of the offsets was put forward as one of the most important reasons for buying the Gripens. The offset programme for the lease deal was similarly extravagant and much larger than any competitors, at $950m, approximately 130 per cent of the value of the aircraft.[29] However, the offset contracts incorporated a confidentiality agreement that veiled any actual economic activity in mystery. Only the company was able to reveal details of the promised investment. So they claimed that the programme was to be directed at regions with high unemployment, including north Bohemia – slated to receive 38 per cent of total offset investment – and north Moravia, which was to reap 33 per cent.[30] By mid-2005, senior representatives of the north Bohemian and north Moravian regions said they had no information about offset projects. 'Lots of promises have been made public, but I'm not aware of any offset project so far. . . . I was always rather sceptical about the offset program,' said Evzen Tosenovsky, Governor of the Moravia–Silesia region, which had an unemployment rate of 14.5 per cent at the time.[31] According to the Trade and Industry Minister, Milan Urban, sixteen projects had been identified and 'some of them are already running', though he refused to elaborate.[32] Opposition politicians raised concerns about why the offsets would be kept secret and why representatives of the regions involved would not know about the supposed investment in their area. Even the head of the Armaments Industry Association seemed confused: 'That's not sensitive data that needs to be classified.'[33]

The true nature of the deal was exposed when journalists from Swedish

Television, Sven Bergman, Joachim Dyfvermark and Fredrik Laurin, tracked down an anonymous whistle-blower involved in the BAE sales campaign and a host of secret documents obtained from the Czech police investigation. The anonymous source told them:

> Everyone wanted to achieve so much, the project was so important, we just got carried away . . . But after I stopped going to corrupt Prague I realized it was all wrong, very wrong. . . . The Gripen campaign had a huge exclusive office on the heights of Prague, with a view over the whole town. Steve Mead's room was in the inner part of the office. There was a desk, a couple of chairs, and on the wall a board. Steve Mead surveyed Czech politicians. On the board there was something like 50–100 pictures. Photos of members of the government, key people in the parliament, senators, members of the opposition, and other important people, for example from the Ministry of Defence. There were names and positions and handwritten details of each person, and most of them were marked; green, amber or red – for, in between, or against the Gripen.[34]

When the journalists visited the plush offices the landlord confirmed that BAE were the previous tenants. The keys were still labelled with the name of the company. The landlord told them excitedly that in the 'particularly fine room' that belonged to Steve Mead 'He has boards, with pictures of all members of government and House of Deputies. Because it was the biggest business in new Czech history.'[35]

The whistle-blower continued: 'The most important object was Ivo Svoboda, who, at that time, was the Finance Minister. Mead also spoke of the importance of taking care of the opposition in the same way. They worked on key people, who were to enrol the other party members later.'[36] Svoboda was forced to resign in 1999 over an unrelated fraud scandal and was sentenced to five years in prison. The source explained what happened then: 'When Svoboda went to prison, Mead was forced to rearrange the deal and the contacts were then handled by another member of the government.'[37] It was clear that the matter at hand was bribes: 'Steve Mead spoke of the contact in Austria that took care of the payments for the Czech government. He was responsible for the payments, paying the bribes. The Austrian contact could distribute the money to those in the government who were not already "onboard", and also to those who were already on our side. It was enough to focus on a few key people in the government to get approval to pass the decision.'[38]

The secret agency agreements for the deal confirmed the corrupt behaviour and the identity of the Austrian contact. The first was a contract from BAE:

```
        In Strict Confidence
   Proposal: appointment of advisor


Date: 5 November 1999
Territory: Czech Republic
Products to be included in the agreement:
  Gripen
Name of advisor: Alfons Mensdorff Pouilly
Address of advisor: MPA Vienna³⁹
```

The journalists recognized the Count's name from another BAE scandal. In 1995, he was identified on a tape recording as the conduit for secret payments from BAE to party funds in Austria in return for the sale of aircraft. If the deal was concluded the two political parties stood to share 70m Schillings ($7m in 1995 or £4.4m). The secret tape contained the following conversation:

Herman Kraft: (an Austrian ÖVP MP) A few hundred million for the plane and a few billion for the helicopters.
SD: (An unidentified Social Democrat MP) How much are we talking about?
HK: Two Percent.
SD: Two Percent of 3 billion?
HK: 3.8 billion
SD: Two percent is 70 million. How would it be shared?
HK: We split it
SD: Who will transfer the money?
HK: Our Count.
SD: What's his name?
HK: Mensdorff.

SD: That's his name, Mensdorff? And he represents the English?

HK: He's their consultant

SD: How will the money get to Austria?

HK: The English will fix that.[40]

Herman Kraft was convicted for attempted bribery, but Mensdorff-Pouilly was acquitted as the reference to him was not considered sufficient evidence. Both BAE and the Count denied any involvement.[41]

In relation to the Czech aircraft deal there was also a secret agreement promising Mensdorff-Pouilly a massive commission if the deal went through. It identified the contract value as up to £1bn with a commission rate of 4 per cent.[42] This would have worked out to £40m, an extraordinary sum for any legitimate help a local adviser might provide. Mensdorff-Pouilly refused to speak to Swedish TV but admitted to the *Guardian* that 'my company, MPA, has a contract with BAE since 1992 for consultancy services in Eastern Europe. According to this contract I'm paid on a monthly basis.'[43]

However, he was not the only agent. At the bottom of the contract was a sentence reading: 'Details of other representatives in the same territory: Hava.'[44] Richard Hava was the director of the Czech state arms company, Omnipol, in which BAE had bought a stake in 2003.[45] Omnipol was to be used openly by BAE in their Gripen campaign but a further covert agreement revealed more:

```
BUSINESS SECRET


Region: Czech republic
Concerns: Gripen programme
Agent: Richard Hava
c/o Legal Advisor Remo Teroni, Geneva
Estimated contract value: £1.5 billion
Commission: 2%[46]
```

This implies that Hava would be paid up to £30m if the Czechs bought the Gripen. Interestingly, Hava's address is not given as Omnipol. He was allegedly to be paid via an entity called Gabstar.[47] Hava denied any role, telling Swedish TV: 'I am not a secret agent, not now, not before.'[48]

Hava's agreement, in turn, contained the name of yet another agent: 'Additional representatives in region: Jelinek.'[49] Otto Jelinek is a former world champion figure skater and Ice Capades star turned politician. He became a minister in Brian Mulroncy's Tory government in Canada before returning to his native Czech Republic, where he became well-known in business circles. Jelinek admitted to having BAE as a client: 'British Aerospace was one of numerous clients that I had.'[50]

Jelinek and the other agents were paid through offshore accounts in BAE's usual intricate manner. The company made payments via Red Diamond's account at Harris Bank in New York to Jelinek International and Dubovy Mlyn, companies controlled by Jelinek. He was also paid via a Bahamian entity called Fidra Holdings.[51] Additional money was sent from Harris Bank to another Bahamian entity called Manor Holding, a company Jelinek was said to represent.[52] When asked about the payments through the offshore companies Jelinek responded: 'It is personal, like my sex life.'[53]

There is no doubt though that Mensdorff-Pouilly was the primary agent, responsible for disbursing money. While the arrangements for the leasing deal that actually eventuated may have differed from the earlier attempt to sell the Gripens they are just as damning. They document a series of payments from Tim Landon's company, Valurex, to Mensdorff-Pouilly, who then distributed some of the money onwards. (See p. 206.)

Valurex paid Mensdorff-Pouilly as a consultant. He then made payments using another British Virgin Islands entity, Brodman Business, whose managing director had been a friend of the Count's since school. Brodman was used as a hub for the payments received from Landon from 2002 until his death in 2007.[55] Money was paid out through 'significant cash withdrawals, often in the range of 100,000 pounds, often within days or weeks after important decisions of military procurement, in which BAE had a strong interest'.[56] Mensdorff-Pouilly described Brodman as a mechanism to spread his investment capital, though it seems a fiendishly complicated investment scheme. As always, he claims the payments were for 'marketing reports', which consisted of 'a compilation of newspaper clippings and information available to everyone'.[57] Contradicting this explanation, the Count boasted in an email to his accountant, Mark Cliff, that he used 'aggressive incentive payments to key decision-makers' on transactions.[58]

The money trail from BAE to Valurex is unsurprisingly complicated, with Red Diamond allegedly paying another British Virgin Islands entity,

---

**Gripen Aircraft interim five year
deal/lease**

```
Government of contracted authority:
  Czech Republic
Advisor: Valurex International SA
  succersale de Genève
Payments: €5.33 million, $1 million,
  £2 million
The fee schedule will be paid in
  instalments as detailed:
1,125 M Euros 31/8 2004 PAID
1,125 M Euros 31/12 2004 PAID
1,125 M Euros 31/7 2005 PAID
1 M US $ 31/8 2005
1,2 M £ 31/8 2005
800 000 £ on delivery of the final 8 air-
  craft
1,125 M Euros 31/12 2006


Count Mensdorff-Pouilly is the primary con-
  tact for the provision of the services
  under the terms of this agreement.[54]
```

Prefinor, which in turn held consulting contracts with Foxbury and Valurex, both companies controlled by Landon.[59] Investigators identified €6.3m which passed through Prefinor and Brodman. Of this, 30 per cent, €1.9m, was thought to be the commission to be divided between Mensdorff-Pouilly and Landon. This money passed into another secretive financial vehicle, a foundation in Liechtenstein called 'Kate'. Authorities established that Mensdorff-Pouilly was involved in the foundation, which was named after Timothy Landon's widow and Mensdorff-Pouilly's cousin Katalin Landon, known to friends and acquaintances as Kate.[60]

In 1995, when BAE was constructing its infrastructure of offshore companies for covert payments, the company had identified Liechtenstein as the best European region for its devious purposes. Foundations such as 'Kate' registered in the principality are not subject to normal accounting or transparency requirements. They can also be rapidly set up and shut down. Austrian investigators attempted to find out more about 'Kate' but lawyers for the foundation appealed against any disclosure.[61]

Where the payments flowed from Mensdorff-Pouilly is not certain, but according to research by an Austrian magazine, a Russian deputy called 'Tishchenko' received €3m. A Vienna-based company called Blue Planet was also named as a recipient, as were the mysteriously named projects 'Singapore', 'Russia' and 'India'. €4.7m also flowed to a Viennese businessman, Wolfgang Hamsa, a specialist in offshore companies.[62]

The use of so complex and discreet a method for diverting funds suggests that these were proceeds from the covert dimension of Mensdorff-Pouilly and Landon's work for BAE.[63]

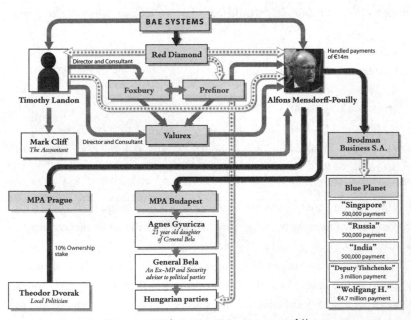

Figure 4: BAE's Eastern European network[64]
Key: Dotted grey lines = payments; grey = consultancy agreements; black = ownership; dark boxes are companies

Joachim Dyfvermark (as James Kershaw) and Rob Evans (as Dr Miller) went undercover to unearth more about the deal. Posing as representatives of a fictitious British company, ESID, they claimed to be working for a

client, presumed to be BAE. They explained that their client was attempting to assess exactly what had transpired on the Gripen deal in order to
plan a strategy in case the story broke in the media. They visited a former
senior civil servant who worked for Mensdorff-Pouilly. He told them
about the connection between the Austrian and Svoboda, the Finance
Minister in the 1990s. 'I bring Svoboda to Mensdorff, I introduced him.'
The civil servant said that he had heard nothing about bribes but then
admitted that he works for BAE on offset deals. He ended the interview
abruptly: 'I don't know who is your client. I don't want to know it. My
contractor is Mensdorff – I can speak only with Mensdorff. . . .'[65]

After communicating with him by phone, the undercover reporters met
with a former Czech Foreign Minister, Jan Kavan, in a central Prague hotel.
They gained the trust of the minister by citing information that would
only be known to an insider on the Gripen deal. They asked what Kavan
thought the consequences would be if the police investigated the deal:

> **Kavan:** That could be quite disastrous.
> **Undercover Reporter:** Sorry?
> **K:** That could be quite disastrous.
> **UR:** Oh, you mean so . . .?
> **K:** If Steve Mead would tell the police everything that he knows, and he
> was himself involved in. That could involve a large number of important
> people here. Yes.[66]

Kavan, denying that he ever took money, acknowledged that other high-
ranking politicians were bought by Steve Mead in the Gripen campaign.

> **K:** I was never part of any discussions, or approached about the kick backs.
> Because they [both] knew I was basically so pro British. They were much
> more interested in the people in the middle. Who had no views or had to
> be persuaded or bought. But the fact that money changed hands in the par-
> liament at least was a pretty well known secret shared by a large number of
> people.
> **UR:** Because we are talking about both ODS and . . .
> **K:** The Social democrats . . .
> **UR:** Yes.

K: It went across the political spectrum. And also Christian Democrats.
UR: Yes.
K: We are talking about all three [parties] . . .[67]

Kavan was Foreign Minister and later Deputy Prime Minister in the Social Democrat government elected in 1998. His tenure, a full four-year term, was not without scandal, after a large sum of money was found in his office and his senior civil servant was charged with hiring a hitman to liquidate one of the country's best journalists.[68] He was posted to the UN between 2002 and 2003, at one point working as President of the UN General Assembly. The reporters got the experienced statesman talking about Julian Scopes and Steve Mead. Scopes was BAE's head of Eastern Europe, Steve Mead's boss.

K: Julian Scopes was also involved but he was more careful, Mead was everywhere.
UR: Yes.
K: Julian was kind of overseeing, but Julian Scopes also had the information. I had secret meetings with both of them but Mead was the one who did the nitty-gritty work on the ground, yes.[69]

Kavan knew about Valurex and became visibly concerned when told that the police were aware of the company.

K: They received this from the Austrian or from Switzerland?
UR: Don't know for certain, they are very good.
K: So they would have all that?
UR: Yes!
K: (Big sigh)
UR: How many know of the Valurex?
K: I have no idea, but not few.
UR: Sorry?
K: It will not be just few.
UR: It could be widespread?
K: (Nods)
K: If they investigate thoroughly the Pre-Gripen negotiations led by Steve

Mead primarily, it will send shivers down the spine of many . . . My hunch
is that it will involve dozens.[70]

Kavan offered to ring round a few friends, senior politicians who might
know more. In a subsequent telephone conversation he also mentioned
that he might try to delay any police investigation:

UR: Would it be possible to have an effect on the police investigation?
K: Aah, I would think that that is not out of the question, but let's discuss
that directly and not necessarily on the phone . . .
UR: But it could be possible?
K: I think so yes.[71]

The reporters had so convinced Kavan of their bona fides that even after
they left Prague he continued to talk to them. Communicating via the email
and phone of the fake company the journalists had set up, Kavan tells them:

K: Since you left I made some inquiries from my close friends. Most of
these questions can be fairly easily answered by a friend of ours who runs
a consulting firm which had a contract, but not a signed one, an informal
contract, with Steven. And cooperated with him for quite a long time.
UR: Based in Prague?
K: Based in Prague and who has a fair amount of the information. We
could meet anywhere, London, Paris . . . whatever. No problem.[72]

They met up with Kavan and 'the consultant', Petros Michopulos, in a
hotel just outside London on 17 January 2007. Michopulos told them of
his work with Mead:

Petros Michopulos: With us, Steve Mead was always very open. But he
didn't tell week by week whom he bribed and not bribed. But we were in
contact with him daily, we saw each other about three times a week. In
some cases he told us like it was, in some cases you could tell from people's
changed attitude.
K: His main activities was against the ODS and the social democrats.
UR: In terms of paying kick-backs?
K: Yes, that's what he is talking about.

Michopulos turned to Kavan and said in Czech: 'I don't know how many names to give them.' Kavan responded: 'Don't give them all at once.' Michopulos agreed, before continuing:

> **PM:** The other group he communicated with economically, I'm sure they were civil servants, not only politicians. Above all people from the Department of Defence and the Defence Command. The Department of Industry, of Trade, . . . and of Finance.[73]

He maintained that he took no part in the bribing and reiterated that Mead was key:

> **PM:** Steve was the central figure in this whole deal.
> **K:** Nothing was done without Steve knowing about it.
> **PM:** To judge from what I heard or can guess he did it rather intelligently. It's like that, the corrupt person always will have someone at his side, be it a physical person, a company or an institution, who does business with someone else, and from that deal will finance this bribe. I don't think that you can find one instant where the money goes directly to some politician's, statesman's or official's account.[74]

Michopulos confirmed that BAE spent large sums of money on the underhand Gripen campaign:

> **PM:** BAE gave out much more money on these things than what Steve actually spent.
> **K:** The amount of money allocated by BAE for kick-backs, the volume of expenditure in the Czech republic in connection with this project, was larger than the amount of money actually spent by Steve Mead.[75]

This was deeply incriminating information. However, when Kavan eventually realized that the two people he was meeting were not working for BAE but were journalists, he changed his story. He told Swedish TV:

> When in fact I acquired the suspicion, not the suspicion that they were journalists, but suspicion that this is about corruption and that they are involved in something which I consider illegal, I went to the Czech police

and informed them about this and gave the names Mr Kershaw and Mr Miller (their pseudonyms) and the name of this organisation and described in detail my suspicion that they actually want us to circumvent or slow down police investigation of corruption.[76]

Though Kavan claimed he spoke to Czech police in early January, no police contact was made with the journalists or their front company. Even if he was telling the truth, he still waited a month after the meeting at which he told the reporters that he could slow down a police investigation. He tried to justify attending the meeting in London:

> **K:** I had contacts with the journalists even after we had the suspicion and informed the police because I was hoping that we could acquire from the conversation more information.
> **Swedish TV:** Mr Kavan, the camera does not lie, and you are heard on the tapes saying that money changed hands, that this will send chills down the spine of many important people, that a number of people were bribed, that BAE's manager in Prague was handling the kickbacks. Now you are saying something else. Are you taking a responsible position here? Are you upright about this?
> **K:** I'm absolutely honest and straightforward. I'm saying that I was sharing with them what I described as rumours and speculation that abounded in the parliamentary corridors about certain kickbacks that might have taken place. I'm not denying that those speculations were heard and that I passed them on to those two gentlemen. I'm saying that I personally can't prove it, I have no evidence that any such corruption has taken place.[77]

Petros Michopulos added: 'Your reporters raised the corruption issue and claimed to have the evidence. I hope I'm not that evidence, because that would be serious manipulation.'[78] Kavan wrote to the *Guardian* after the publication of an article about their undercover sting:

> Let me make it clear that I did not 'admit' anything. I only shared with two undercover journalists, posing as representatives of a British security organisation, rumours and speculation that abounded some years ago around the Czech parliament. I made it clear to them that I had no real evidence of any bribery. . . . If I had known they were journalists, I would

obviously have been more cautious but also more precise. They would have obtained a result which was less sensational but more reliable.

Jan Kavan

Former foreign minister, Czech Republic[79]

Saab was not an innocent bystander while BAE was weaving its nefarious webs. The deepthroat who exposed the corruption commented that 'the Swedes, Per Andersson among others, were also talking about bribes, but they were less specific'.[80] Per Andersson was the head of Saab's campaign for the Gripen Czech Republic deal. Several people at Saab heard Steve Mead talking about how politicians were bribed:

> Steve Mead spoke openly about it with quite a few people. Both Swedish and British people heard it, because Steve was pretty dictatorial, and he wanted to enrol all of us. Per Andersson, Saab's campaign leader, was a part of the inner circle that discussed the whole arrangement – which political contacts were on 'our' side, which were on the 'other' side and which members were in the 'middle' – marked with amber on Steve's board – they needed to be approached and persuaded.[81]

When asked for an interview, Andersson responded: 'No, this is nothing I have any knowledge of whatsoever. I have left Saab, and I don't work with this at all anymore. I have no comments to make or anything to say about this, other than that it's nonsense, preposterous.'[82]

The whistle-blower's account was not the only evidence of Saab's involvement. Mensdorff-Pouilly's contract was signed by a senior Saab executive as follows: 'I approve the terms of this appointment on behalf of Saab, Signed Lars Göran Fasth, vice-president Export, 5/11/99'.[83]

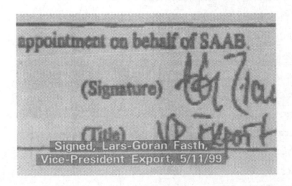

Fasth was clearly rattled when approached for comment:

Lars Göran Fasth: I have no idea what you are talking about.
Swedish TV: I sit here with your signature in front of me. Was it you who took decisions like this yourself?
(Long pause)
LGF: No, I must say that I . . . don't have . . . the picture you describe clear to me.[84]

Saab's official anti-bribery policy did not cover the agreement with BAE; therefore, corruption by agents employed by the British would not violate Saab's policy, even if the bribes were for the Swedish company's benefit and even though notes from BAE meetings showed that Gripen International was directly involved in decisions around payments.[85] Gripen International made clear in a series of meetings that they found the original commission rate of 4 per cent for Valurex too high: 'Gripen International are uncomfortable with indemnifying BAE to this level because the basis of the deal may change, i.e. the Swedish government may supply used aircraft direct and the deal may become government-to-government.'[86] Anders Frisén, Saab's commercial director, was the Gripen International representative at the meetings. The note reveals that Saab and BAE wanted to lower Valurex's commission and try to make it a fixed sum rather than a percentage. But as the document puts it: 'The fee will be confirmed at a later date . . .'[87]

Josef Bernecker, a former chief of the Austrian Air Staff, confirms working with Mensdorff-Pouilly for Valurex on behalf of BAE and Saab:

Swedish TV: You two work together for Valurex?
Josef Bernecker: Yes, as consultants. I do it on the military level, since –
I know all my people from the past and Mensdorff on the political level . . .
STV: So he is kind of doing the lobby work on the politicians?
JB: Right. Right. I started with Mensdorff when I retired.
STV: Yes.
JB: And at that time the deal was done already, so I was more or less in the aftermath of the whole thing. He was doing some political or social lobbying . . .
STV: For?
JB: Yes, for the deal . . .

STV: For the lease deal . . .

JB: But on behalf of Valurex.

STV: But Mensdorff is Austrian, how come . . . I mean Czech Republic is Czech Republic?

JB: You know, these noblemen, they are well connected, well netted all over Europe, so it's just that he knows a lot of people.

STV: Was that on behalf of BAE and Saab?

JB: Yes, I think so, yes, or at least they knew about it.

STV: Saab?

JB: Yes, yes!

STV: Alright, because . . .

JB: . . . or Gripen International.[88]

The involvement of the Count's third cousin, the lyrically named Michael Piatti-Fünfkirchen, illustrates how well-connected 'these noblemen' are and how they strive to keep business in the family, which often ends in tears.

In the 1990s, Piatti-Fünfkirchen was close to a range of luminaries within the Czech government. Mensdorff-Pouilly offered his cousin a commission of €1m if he used these contacts to ensure the Czech government bought the Gripen.[89] A number of high-level meetings in the summer of 1998 involving Czech officials, a BAE manager and finally the Czech Finance Minister, Ivo Svoboda, came to nothing. The Count determined that because the proposed sale was scrapped in favour of the lease deal, Piatti-Fünfkirchen was not entitled to a commission.[90] The irate cousin later filed a fraud complaint against Mensdorff-Pouilly, accusing him of 'suspicion of serious fraud' in his efforts to convince the Czech government to buy the Gripen.[91]

This is what landed the Count in a Viennese prison for five weeks from late February 2009, where he was kept in preventive detention on bribery charges. The judge detained Mensdorff-Pouilly because of the danger of 'obfuscation and additional crimes' by the lobbyist.[92] Mensdorff-Pouilly complimented the wardens and food in the Viennese prison and recalls: 'Sometimes I stood in front of the mirror saying to myself: "Ali, you're in jail – accept it!" '[93] During my conversation with him, he described how the arresting officers, prosecutors and prison officials always treated him with respect, addressing him as 'Count' despite Austria's banning of the use of aristocratic titles from 1919.[94]

★

The SFO had begun investigating BAE in July 2004 for allegations of corruption in the Czech Republic, along with South Africa, Tanzania, Chile, Qatar and, in 2006, Romania.[95] Czech police reopened their inquiries following the screening of the zetetic Swedish TV documentary in 2007. At the request of the SFO, Austrian police raided Mensdorff-Pouilly's home in late September 2008, seizing a large quantity of documents.[96] In October, the SFO interviewed the Count. Julian Scopes was interviewed by UK police. In February 2009, Mensdorff-Pouilly was arrested by the Austrian authorities and questioned about an £11m payment allegedly made to him by BAE.[97] He was charged by the SFO on 29 January 2010 with conspiracy to corrupt in connection with BAE's deals with Eastern and Central European governments, including the Czech Republic, Hungary and Austria.[98] However, after a bail hearing in which the patrician Conservative MP John Gummer (now Baron Deben) gave Mensdorff-Pouilly a glowing character reference, the Count was granted bail of £500,000 deposited with the court and £500,000 in surety, during which he was allowed to stay in a Belgravia flat wearing an electronic tag, under curfew between midnight and 6 a.m., and was made to surrender his three passports.[99]

Austrian prosecutors continue to scrutinize the Count's activities.[100] The FBI initiated an examination of the Czech Gripen deal as a consequence of the bureau's interest in Erste Bank, one of the largest financial services providers in Central and Eastern Europe, through which cash may have flowed as part of bribes in the transaction.[101] The Czech authorities have played the investigative equivalent of musical chairs, opening and closing inquiries into the deal with startling regularity. At the time of writing their investigation remains open.[102]

A Swedish inquiry into the Gripen deals in the Czech Republic, Hungary and South Africa started in March 2007[103] but was dropped two years later when the Swedish chief prosecutor, Christer van der Kwast, concluded that:

> The inquiries showed that BAE, using a sophisticated payment arrangement, has hidden large payments that can be linked to the campaigns in the Czech Republic, Hungary, and South Africa and have made it possible to bribe the decision makers in these countries. It is very serious, both in terms of the systematics and the amount. It involves hundreds of millions of Swedish crowns in hidden payments in several countries, and there is

strong reason to believe that bribery also has occurred. But I cannot fully verify that Saab participated in the bribery payments. But I have made the judgement that in court I could not prove that some representative for Saab has intentionally participated in the payment of the bribes.[104]

He questioned over thirty people within Saab without receiving a reasonable explanation as to why vast amounts of Swedish crowns were passed to middlemen. 'No, I have not got that [explanation],' van der Kwast said. When asked how believable he found Saab's contention that it was normal business activity, he replied: 'I do not want to answer that except to say in my opinion the collected evidence is not enough to prosecute any representative of Saab.'[105]

Due to the statute of limitation in Swedish law, van der Kwast was not able to prosecute for what had taken place prior to 1 July 2004. He also believes that Sweden does 'not have laws that effectively cover this type of arrangement between middlemen and consultants'.[106]

The Swedish inquiry was criticized by the OECD due to the very limited resources devoted to it – one investigative policeman. Van der Kwast was also subject to inappropriate, albeit indirect, pressure. 'They have emphasized that these inquiries are of course damaging to Swedish business,' he said. When asked who says that, the prosecutor responded: 'I don't want to go into that. I don't want to say more than that. But from my position, from the policeman's position, it is understood as a sort of indirect hint to take it carefully.'[107] Christer van der Kwast's findings were reported the day before he retired as chief of the National Agency Against Corruption.[108]

Vaclav Havel was shocked by the revelations that emerged years later and by the corruption 'in the army sphere'.[109] His dream of a politics of morality appears more distant than ever.

Hungary: 'The Happiest Barrack'*

Lieutenant General Tome Walters Jr, former head of overseas sales for the Pentagon, claimed that the problems in the process to sell fighter aircraft to

---

* During Soviet times Hungary was described as 'the happiest barrack' for its 'Goulash Communism', a form of socialism that allowed some free market activity and displayed a far better human rights record than the other Soviet satellite states.

the Czech Republic were mirrored in efforts to sell American jets to the government of Hungary. Ultimately BAE secured the Hungarian contract as well, with American officials claiming that both the Hungarian and Czech governments were influenced by improper payments. They cite a CIA briefing during which they were told that BAE paid millions of dollars to the major political parties in Hungary to win the contracts there.[110]

In 1999, the Hungarian Cabinet issued a tender for the purchase of used fighter aircraft. In June 2001, the government announced that the American arms behemoth Lockheed Martin had won the contract. Hungarian military experts considered the American F-16 superior to the Gripen and recommended it for lease and eventual purchase in a document dated 6 September 2001. The decision was endorsed by János Szabó, the Minister of Defence.[111] A few days later, at a small gathering of the National Security Cabinet chaired by the Prime Minister, Viktor Orbán, the Swedish Gripen was chosen in an unexpected *volte-face*. All government documents pertaining to the decision-making process around the startling deal were destroyed.[112] In 2003, Hungary finalized a contract to lease fourteen Gripen fighters for Ft.210bn (approximately €823m) for ten years, after which the planes would become Hungarian-owned.[113] The first of the aircraft was delivered in January 2005 at a ceremony attended by the two countries' defence ministers.

Hungary cited as one of the main reasons for its selection of the Gripen Sweden's offer of 100 per cent offset for the $500m lease deal, which included 30 per cent in investments in Hungarian industry.[114] This justification was given in spite of the evidence that these offsets obligations are rarely fulfilled.

In both the Hungarian and Czech deals, the Lockheed Martin F-16 was thought to be the favourite, fuelling suspicion of underhand activity. In an SFO report submitted to the Austrian investigation into Alfons Mensdorff-Pouilly, an extract concerning the Hungarian deal suggests that 'the references to making political payments are much more unequivocal. This becomes clear from a minute over a conversation with BAE personnel, Julian Scopes and David White . . . [It refers] to "payment to the socialists 7.5%".'[115] At the time, Scopes and White were BAE executives for Central Europe, the former having served as Private Secretary to the former Conservative Defence Minister, Alan Clark.

In agency documents labelled 'Strictly confidential, Gripen Europe', Mensdorff-Pouilly is listed as the agent for Hungary, with a success commission of 3 per cent. In addition, the Austrian received a fixed annual remuneration from BAE, plus expenses for his company, MPA. But the enormous commission was to be paid via Prefinor International in the British Virgin Islands.[116]

Even though the deal was ultimately not a sale but a state-to-state leasing contract, Mensdorff-Pouilly was still paid. In a secret agreement of March 2002, three months after the state-to-state deal was signed, payments amounting to $8m were identified 'for 8 years of services to the Gripen project'.[117] The money was to be routed through Red Diamond to Prefinor and from there to Mensdorff-Pouilly in Austria.[118] When questioned about these arrangements, the Count's spokesman responded: 'Alfons Mensdorff-Pouilly or any one of his companies have never received any commission from BAE or Saab. . . . neither Alfons Mensdorff-Pouilly, nor one of his companies were contracted by BAE or Saab as agent to promote the sale of Gripen.'[119]

In June 2007, following the airing of the allegations on Swedish Television, the Hungarian Defence Minister announced that the authorities would look into the 'alleged improprieties'.[120] But the Hungarian committee examining the contracts was not authorized to investigate corruption and, therefore, 'declined to pursue the possibility of it', the director of the committee said. Ágnes Vadai, who is also a State Secretary for the Ministry of Defence, added that a new parliamentary committee would have to be formed to investigate corruption.[121]

When I met Count Mensdorff-Pouilly in Vienna, besides repeating that he only ever received a retainer from BAE, he claimed credit for the leasing arrangements, saying that in conversations with government officials in the Czech Republic and Hungary he understood that their economic and political circumstances would not allow them to purchase the jets. He claims to have suggested the leasing arrangement, explaining that he then had to persuade BAE, and finally Saab, of the proposed approach. The latter were particularly wary of the proposal because of fears of not being paid. The Count used this as an example of the type of service he provides, stressing, somewhat disingenuously, that he would never explicitly suggest to government representatives with whom he had such regular contact that they buy a specific plane from any company, let alone the one from which he was receiving a retainer.[122]

Contradicting his denial that he had pitched for BAE/Saab business, he remarked that if only the partnership had used him in Poland they would have won that contract as well. He claims that the Americans paid bribes to win the Polish deal, which was why they were so keen for bribery to be revealed in the deals they lost out on. 'A type of insurance,' he suggested, 'so that the British and Swedes wouldn't be minded to expose American corruption.'[123]

After a few hours of discussion, primarily denial, I asked the Count why it was necessary to direct his retainer payments through a fiendishly complicated web of companies in the BVI, Liechtenstein, Switzerland and elsewhere. He shrugged his shoulders: 'I don't know. I just receive my money in Austria, sometimes via Switzerland for personal reasons.'[124]

Finally, the charming Count admitted that he'd done some bad things in his life: 'maybe too much wine, too many women . . . but I have never paid bribes. I talk to all sorts of influential people, I can talk to anyone in my party [the ÖVP], but would never tell them to buy Gripen rather than . . . I would never pay a politician to make a decision.'

But in response to my question about why commissions are paid, such as those he suggested were disbursed by the Americans in Poland, he explained how when he was in the game and poultry business: 'one had to give presents, benefits, incentives. This [rubbing his thumb and index finger together] applies to all business.'[125]

'This' has certainly done well by the very comfortably off Count Mensdorff-Pouilly.

A Very Swedish Paradox

Arguably the most famous Swede of all time, Alfred Nobel, claimed that 'I should like to invent a substance or a machine with such terrible power of mass destruction that war would thereby be made impossible for ever.' His life, and his view of the world, reflected this continuous dichotomy. He was a poetic idealist and a pacifist, but also a ruthless financier, obsessed with the science of explosives. Isolated and tormented, Nobel invented dynamite, then later in life bought the Swedish gun manufacturer Bofors and created the annual peace prize.

That duality lives on after him, both in the disputes over the awards of his peace prize and in the ambivalence of Sweden itself, which is still both an inventive manufacturer and exporter of arms and a persistent campaigner for world peace.[126] The country boasts an arms industry that has consistently been among the ten largest weapons exporters in the world, led by Saab, which produces, on average, 70 per cent of all weapons manufactured in Sweden. At one point BAE owned 20 per cent of Saab, as well as Hägglunds and Bofors. As Swedish military spending has dropped over recent years to 1.2 per cent of GDP so Saab's exports have grown to account for over 65 per cent of all sales.[127]

While governments of all political persuasions once argued that a thriving home-grown weapons manufacturing capability was vital for Sweden to maintain its 'credible neutrality', now the main reason for its weapons industry is to make money. And export sales are crucial to this. This accounts for the very weak enforcement of the country's strict regulations. As Henrik Berlau of the Seaman's Union in Copenhagen, which monitors international arms trafficking, has said: 'Sweden has a very strict law, but a very relaxed attitude toward enforcing it.'[128]

Just as the Nobel Peace Prize will always carry a sense of ideals thwarted, so too does the Swedish arms industry, which has been mired in controversy, corruption and double-dealing for decades.

Saab opened an office in New Delhi in order to sell Gripen jet fighters worth $10.2bn to India, but failed to make the competition shortlist.[129] This came after the successful conclusion of a controversial SEK 8.3bn deal to sell six Erieye airborne radar systems to Pakistan in 2006, intended as a precursor to the sale of Gripens.[130]

Controversial arms sales from Sweden to South Asia are nothing new. When Olof Palme, Sweden's Prime Minister, made his second visit to India in 1986, he and his Indian counterpart, Rajiv Gandhi, were at many levels political soul-mates. Palme was widely revered as a global socialist icon and a champion of world peace. Gandhi, standard-bearer of Nehru's Congress movement, had been elected as 'Mr Clean' on a promise to eradicate the insidious corruption that had plagued democratic India since its birth.

However, during the course of their discussions the two leaders agreed an arms deal that would blight their countries for decades to come. India's military was desperate for powerful, high-tech howitzers to counter the state-of-the-art artillery that the US was selling Pakistan. Palme wanted the contract for Bofors, the historic Swedish gun-maker, part of Nobel Industries, which badly needed the business if it was to avoid layoffs that would be politically costly for Palme's government.[131]

Bofors got the business: a huge $1.4bn order, even though India's military preferred a French artillery piece which was cheaper, had a longer range and was regarded as more reliable – the French equipment prevailed in eight consecutive evaluations. $250m in bribes was paid to secure the deal.

Having publicly stated that India would not utilize any agents and that no commissions would be paid, Gandhi privately informed Palme that the deal would be awarded to Sweden on condition that Bofors changed their Indian agent. Bofors made use of Gandhi's preferred agent, AE Services, but retained their original agents, renaming them consultants to the project. One of these, Svenska Inc., received $29.44m, while AE Services received a remarkable success fee of $168m.

Despite extensive efforts in Sweden and India to cover up this corruption, investigative journalists in both countries published revelatory accounts that led to them receiving death threats, court orders and even, in the case of the Indians, being forced into exile. Crucially they established that AE Services was owned by one Ottavio Quattrocchi, an Italian and a close family friend of Gandhi's wife, Sonia. Neither Quattrocchi nor his company had any prior experience in the arms business. This devastating exposé contributed to Rajiv Gandhi's defeat in an election in late 1989 that was fought on the issue of corruption. Quattrocchi spent years attempting to block Indian access to his Swiss bank accounts. Despite many of those involved dying, and some being reprieved by the courts when Congress returned to power, the main issues remain.

In December 2005, the Indian Congress government unfroze Quattrocchi's British and Swiss bank accounts. However, a few days later the Indian Supreme Court demanded that the Indian government ensure Quattrocchi be prevented from withdrawing further money from the accounts. In 2007, the court issued a warrant for his arrest. In late September 2009, the recently re-elected Congress government told the Supreme Court it was dropping the case against Quattrocchi.

In early 2011, the Bofors phoenix rose again from the ashes. An Indian tax tribunal ruled that the son and heir of one of the Bofors agents, W. N. Chanda, was liable for tax on the commissions received. The tribunal concluded in a damning verdict for the Congress Party that 'there is enough material on record to hold that the payments were indeed made by Bofors to Svenska, AE Services and Moresco through foreign bank accounts, in connection with the defence deal with the Government of India'.[132] Ottavio Quattrocchi was named by the tribunal as one of the beneficiaries of kickbacks.[133]

The *Hindu* newspaper argued that 'Unlike other corruption scandals, Bofors has refused to go away as a national issue – because the deep-seated political, moral, and systemic issues it raised won't go away. . . . [The case illustrates] how various institutions perform in relation to corruption. With the executive branch resorting to flagrant cover-up and obstruction of justice, Parliament, the Central Bureau of Investigation, and the judiciary failed to do the right thing by the people of India.'[134] The main opposition party called for a Special Investigating Team to reopen and again investigate the Bofors 'kickback scam'.[135]

While the scandal continuously re-emerges in Indian politics more than twenty years after the deal was signed, the guns have not been used extensively. Though they performed ably in the Kargil conflict, wear and tear and a lack of spare parts led to many of them being cannibalized, leaving only 200 operational.[136] One account suggests that a number of them were mothballed as they overheated when fired.[137]

Some in Sweden speculate that his involvement in this and other arms deals might have been behind the still unsolved assassination of Olof Palme. These theories are lent credence by the Social Democrats' complicity in allowing the sale of arms to Iraq and Iran during the conflict between those two countries. In the early 1980s, during a period in opposition, Palme had been acting as the UN's peace mediator between Iran and Iraq. After his return to power in 1984 he was deeply embarrassed by revelations that arms shipments were being made to the region from Sweden through Singapore, Dubai or Bahrain. Directors of Bofors insisted that this was done with the full knowledge of the government. Palme then stopped the shipments and received enraged delegations from Iran and Iraq just three weeks before his murder.

A year after Palme's murder a former admiral, Carl-Fredrik Algernon, who was the foreign-ministry officer responsible for approving all arms exports, either fell or was pushed in front of an underground train in Stockholm's Central Station just after he had come from 'a very revealing meeting' and six days before he was to appear before a special prosecutor investigating the illegal arms shipments.

Today the reputation of the Swedish arms industry, and Saab in particular, is inextricably linked to BAE. In South Africa, the Czech Republic, Hungary and Austria tales of inappropriate influence and corruption haunt the image of this bastion of peace.

I asked Thomas Tjäder of the Swedish Inspectorate of Strategic Products (ISP), the body that oversees the country's arms exports, whether these accounts influence his organization's decisions to grant future export licences to companies. After discounting the importance of negative socio-economic impact on the purchasing country, he added: 'All bribes are illegal but, if a Swedish company paid bribes in another country, I can't say we would do anything about it.'[138]

Perhaps this attitude isn't surprising given that Tjäder is not only a former Department of Defence official of nineteen years, a senior councillor for the Conservatives in Uppsala and the chairman of six companies, but, before joining ISP, was a director of Celsius, a defence company.[139]

When he was appointed to the ISP a number of people were shocked, suggesting 'he would rather work to increase arms exports, than to control them',[140] reflecting the contradiction at the heart of Sweden.

11. The Ultimate Cop-Out

In early 2010, I was invited, together with Sue Hawley, the widely respected anti-corruption researcher and campaigner, to meet the relatively new Director of the SFO. While the government could have appointed a pioneering outsider, Richard Alderman's long career in the deeper reaches of British bureaucracy made him a safe pair of hands. His owlish features and Mr Bean-like physical mannerisms were in contrast to his quite outspoken statements. Alderman told us that he had placed a final offer on the table for BAE, in relation to the SFO's investigation of the company's corruption-tarnished arms deals in South Africa, Tanzania, the Czech Republic and Hungary. The company rejected the offer that Alderman had let slip to the media would require an admission of guilt and a fine in the region of £200m to £500m. He insisted defiantly to us that he would not be returning to the negotiating table but instead would press the Attorney General for permission to charge the company with corruption and bribery. While the director didn't seem to grasp all aspects of his brief, his fortitude and openness were laudable.

Three days later, on Friday, 5 February, I was back at the SFO's slightly depressing offices on Gray's Inn Road near London's King's Cross station. I'd been there often over the previous few years. This time it was to provide another formal witness statement to the team investigating the South African arms deal. The team members interviewing me repeated what their colleagues had been saying for all the years I had been interacting with the investigation: that while they were struggling to get cooperation from the South African justice ministry, they were, nevertheless confident of their case.

Soon after I had left, the investigators started to receive the message from Alderman that RL102, the codename for the overall BAE investigation, had been settled. The company would pay a paltry £30m for accounting irregularities in relation to the Tanzanian transaction, while the investigations into South Africa, the Czech Republic and Hungary would be dropped unconditionally.[1] To complete the capitulation, the

SFO also gave an astonishing undertaking not to allege that BAE was guilty of corruption if prosecuting others linked to the company's nefarious activities.[2]

The investigators, who had devoted years of their lives to these inquiries, were furious and confused. One was so angry and frustrated that she couldn't hold back the tears, while another stormed out of the office and drank himself into oblivion. A third, incandescent that the senior investigators hadn't even been consulted, muttered darkly that 'Alderman knows nothing about the case. He has no idea what he's doing.'[3]

As I was driving home, at virtually the same time as the SFO staff were receiving the shocking message, I was called by a contact in the US government. He was leaving the courthouse where the US had just reached a simultaneous settlement with BAE. But in the US the company was forced to accept guilt on the Saudi, Czech and Hungarian deals and acknowledge that it paid unauthorized commissions about which it didn't inform US authorities. In addition, BAE had to acknowledge the existence of its maze of offshore companies through which covert payments were made. The company admitted writing a false letter to US authorities in 2000, denying it was paying any secret commissions. The Americans fined BAE $400m, the largest penalty ever imposed on a British company.[4]

The following day, as part of its undertaking, the UK dropped all charges against Alfons Mensdorff-Pouilly and released him from his brief sojourn in jail. He had spent a week in Pentonville prison after being charged with conspiracy to corrupt in the Austrian, Hungarian and Czech deals.

Where the US settlement was devastating, imperilling BAE's legal competence to export arms from the US, the UK settlement was derisory. It was a slap in the face for the people of the countries BAE has corrupted, the British taxpayer and the British justice system. It reinforced the belief that BAE is above the law and can effectively pay its way out of trouble, very cheaply.

The lack of action against individuals involved suggests that, in the arms business, one can act with impunity. In what other sphere of criminal wrongdoing would suspects against whom there was strong evidence be let off with such regularity? The settlement suggests that BAE doesn't have just the keys to the back door of 10 Downing Street, but those to the front door, the alarm code and a comfortable spot in the Prime Minister's bedroom.

The Liberal Democrats' deputy leader, and the UK's Business Secretary at the time of writing, Vince Cable, was angry that BAE had succeeded in ensuring key details of its arms deals would remain hidden. 'The one positive thing is we have now had an acknowledgement from BAE that unacceptable practices were being conducted. But nobody has been brought to account.' He added: 'The British government was up to its neck in this whole business. Government ministers were almost certainly fully aware of what was happening.'[5]

The former Labour minister Peter Kilfoyle remarked: 'I certainly think there is now an argument to be made for an independent judicial inquiry into the whole affair. This raises serious questions on what [Blair's] motivation was in intervening in the [Al Yamamah investigation] and what influences were brought to bear on him.'[6]

In Washington, the Deputy Attorney General, Larry Grindler, was clear: 'Any company conducting business with the US that profits through false statements will be held accountable. The alleged illegal conduct undermined US efforts to ensure that corruption has no place in international trade.'[7]

Richard Alderman described the deal as 'pragmatic'. In the days and weeks after the announcement, as criticism of the SFO mounted, Alderman tried to intimate, at least in private, that the Department of Justice had pulled the rug from under him by the size and breadth of the US settlement. I heard a very different story from two sources in America. One suggested that the US authorities were expecting the SFO's settlement figure to be similar to theirs and to contain serious admissions of guilt. When I asked why there would have been a sudden change, my source just shrugged his shoulders and shook his head. Two sources close to the negotiations confirmed that a deal of over £100m and acknowledgement of two counts of corruption had been agreed until Richard Alderman blustered into the negotiations, seriously weakening the SFO's position. 'He made these ridiculous statements in the media and took over the negotiations. He demanded a billion-pound fine because that's what he'd said to the media and BAE thought: "He's a joke."' Was he trying too hard to prove how tough he was, or did he have an agenda to close the whole thing down as quickly as possible?

After his statements in the media Alderman avoided calls from the Attorney General. His failure, or refusal, to consult all the key investigators was not just bad practice; it was contrary to the Attorney General's established guidelines.[8]

The arrest of Count Mensdorff-Pouilly a few days before the settlement showed how out of his depth Alderman was. 'You can't arrest someone while you're negotiating, then have to release him a few days later. That's just a flashing neon sign to the world that you don't know what you're doing.'[9]

As if to emphasize the mishandling of the case, it took ten months before the settlement was reluctantly approved by the courts. This was because in an unrelated case, the SFO was heavily criticized by the judge for acting as prosecutor and judge in settling with the company and presenting the court with a *fait accompli*.[10] A source close to the SFO revealed that in the months between the settlement and the court decision, the SFO parted company with two sets of lawyers brought in to assist them.

The settlement was finally brought before a judge in south London on 20 December 2010. With respect to the 'false accounting' in Tanzania, BAE and the SFO agreed that 'There was a high probability that part of the $12.4m would be used in the negotiation process to favour British Aerospace Defence Systems Limited.'[11] The SFO insisted that intentionally creating a hidden system of 'covert' and 'overt' agents was part of a 'legitimate commercial aim'. This was even though the SFO possessed a note written by BAE's head of HQMS which detailed the company's reasons for keeping payments to agents confidential:

1. Rules or regulations in the relevant country (including clauses in Government sales contracts) forbidding the appointment of intermediaries, agents etc.
2. Tax implications when the adviser wishes to pass on money to a third party but cannot declare this to his authorities
3. General embarrassment or possible press interest due to a large fee or a sensitive subject.[12]

When the judge questioned this practice, the SFO and BAE responded that 'in the arms trade, confidentiality is paramount'. After the SFO suggested there was not enough proof of bribes and that Vithlani was just a highly paid lobbyist, the judge offered the SFO and BAE the opportunity to call evidence to show that lobbying not corruption was the purpose of the money sent to Vithlani by the company. They declined.[13] The judge decided that the money passed to Vithlani was clearly for corruption, and resolved: 'I am not prepared to sentence on this basis without evidence, that these were mere lobbying payments . . . The payments were made to pay whoever needed to be corrupted. . . . on the basis of the documents shown to me it seems naïve in the extreme to think Mr. Vithlani was simply a well-paid lobbyist. . . . [BAE] were concealing from the auditors and ultimately the public the fact that they were making payments to Mr. Vithlani, 97% of them via two offshore companies, with the intention that he should have free rein to make such payments to such people as he thought fit in order to secure the Radar Contract of the defendants, but that the defendants did not want to know the details.'[14]

The SFO not only attempted to defend BAE from allegations of corruption so that it could prove a minor accounting offence, but also provided the company with a legal get-out-of-jail card on all its cases. In the plea agreement the SFO agreed to terminate all its investigations into BAE, not to prosecute any member of the BAE Group for any conduct preceding 5 February 2010, ensure that there would be no civil proceedings against any member of the group in relation to any matters investigated by the SFO, and that no member of the group 'shall be named as, or alleged to be, an unindicted co-conspirator or in any other capacity in any prosecution the SFO may bring against any other party'. Even Judge Bean was 'surprised to find a prosecutor granting a blanket indemnity for all offences committed in the past, whether disclosed or otherwise'.[15]

In the original settlement BAE were required to give £30m to the people of Tanzania, less the court's penalty. This created the perverse situation that the higher the fine imposed, the less money would be given to the victims of BAE's crime. For this reason the judge was reduced to fining BAE £500,000 with £225,000 in costs.[16]

The SFO, after more than five years of investigating, could only pull together a sham case, an inappropriate charge, a lack of evidence to fit it and a poorly thought-through plea deal. In this shameful episode, BAE, through a combination of its political power and the incompetence of those at the helm of the Serious Fraud Office, defeated justice.

The response to the settlement announcement in the affected countries was angry and profound.

Patricia de Lille, leader of the opposition Independent Democrats in

South Africa, mayor of Cape Town and the person who first made public the allegations of corruption in the arms deal, suggested that the UK had lost the moral authority to talk about good governance and fighting corruption to others: 'They are no better than any of the rogue leaders in Africa who have used funds from bribes in arms deals to stay in power,' she said.[17] The opposition Democratic Alliance spokesman, David Maynier, remarked: 'We have been shafted by the decision to reach a plea bargain agreement and not to prosecute BAE. The details of the various investigations will remain hidden as a result of the plea bargain agreement and nobody – whether they bribed or whether they took bribes – will be held to account.'[18]

A couple of years earlier an investigation into ThyssenKrupp, the main German beneficiary of the South African deal, had been launched by German prosecutors. The company allegedly tried to claim tax credits on commissions paid to secure the contract to build four frigates. The matter was settled with the company admitting tax violations and paying a fine. Despite documentary evidence of ThyssenKrupp having paid a bribe to 'Chippy' Shaik and Patricia de Lille brandishing in Parliament copies of cheques paid to the ANC and charities associated with party luminaries, the German authorities made no mention of the bribes paid by the company.[19]

The South African government made little comment on either decision. Just before his election to the country's presidency, Jacob Zuma's legal slate was cleared. The charges against him were controversially dropped despite the National Prosecuting Authority reiterating that it had a 'strong, substantive case against Mr. Zuma'.[20] His financial adviser, Schabir Shaik, who was jailed for corrupting him, was released after just two years of his sentence. 'Chippy' Shaik, the head of procurement in the Defence Force at the time of the deal, and the recipient of German largesse, is back in the country, a thriving businessman, while the third brother, Mo, is now head of the country's Secret Service. In making the appointment, it was announced that his responsibilities would include addressing the problems of gun and drug running into South Africa.[21]

The majority of South Africa's legal community was highly critical of the Zuma decision, the most brazen political manipulation of a prosecutorial decision since the demise of apartheid. Its equivocal and controversial nature ensured that Jacob Zuma assumed office with the stain of corruption upon him. He soon appointed as the new head of the National Prosecuting Authority a former Director General of Justice, Menzi Simelane, who in that role ensured that international investigators received as little assistance from South Africa as possible on their arms deal inquiries. On his first day in his new role Simelane told his stunned staff that he had been deployed as head of the constitutionally independent body to do the bidding of his political party, the ANC.[22] Soon afterwards he announced that South Africa would not attempt to maintain a preservation order freezing Fana Hlongwane's funds. Simelane came to his decision that 'there is no evidence of criminal conduct based on the investigation so far', despite hundreds of documents to the contrary.[23]

Since then the flagrantly irresponsible decision taken by Simelane has come in for severe criticism. In May 2011, the Swedish television station tv4 ran a series of documentaries that I had worked on with them about Swedish involvement in the South African arms deal. In particular the programmes caused waves by showing the consultancy agreements between Hlongwane and Sanip, the entity through which Saab and BAE were running their offset programmes.[24] Sanip, when it was formed, belonged entirely to Saab, although Saab claims that the operation of the company was handed over to BAE in 2004.[25]

Initially Saab denied that there had been payments to Hlongwane via Sanip. Soon after and following an internal investigation, Saab quickly changed its tune. In June 2011, the company admitted that Hlongwane had been paid via Sanip.[26] Saab, however, claimed that the agreement with Hlongwane had been reached by a BAE employee working at Sanip who had failed to disclose the matter to Saab.[27]

Unsurprisingly, the payments were made furtively, with funds being transferred to Sanip by BAE and then onwards to Hlongwane but without being reflected in Sanip's financial statements.[28] The admission by Saab was the first time that payments to Hlongwane by BAE/Saab had ever been officially acknowledged. Their secretive nature has given further credence to the suspicion that they were made with corrupt intent.

Only a few days later the MP David Maynier announced that he had access to amendments to consultancy agreements between the companies and Hlongwane.[29] The documents include one amendment in which Hlongwane's tasks were updated to include the facilitation of 'face-to-face' meetings with South African officials on BAE's behalf, as well as advising on a 'contact map' of 'key Customer [SA] personnel and in particular the decision-makers with respect to the selection of products and services'.[30] This only intensified suspicions that part of the payments to Hlongwane had been intended for the key political and military leaders and officials with whom he worked.

The Tanzanian anti-corruption unit, the Prevention and Combating of Corruption Bureau (PCCB), continued to investigate the deal for a while even after the SFO decision. While the UK investigation was in progress, the PCCB was kept waiting for key evidence from the SFO. The plea bargain meant that the SFO also dropped its charges against Andrew Chenge, Tanil Somaiya and Sailesh Vithlani.[31]

After the settlement Edward Hoseah of the PCCB wrote to the SFO demanding details of Britons involved in the radar deal, namely Michael Rouse, Dick Evans, Mike Turner and Julia Aldridge.[32] Rouse has been BAE's marketing director since 2002 and Aldridge his deputy.

The intention is to pay a significant part of the £30m fine to Tanzania. However, this is the subject of controversy in the country, where some feel the state should be reimbursed while others believe the payment should be made to humanitarian charities unsullied by any suggestion of corruption. BAE too would like to avoid a payment directly to the government which might be seen as an admission of guilt or part refund for the deal. If the money is paid to a third party, BAE will be able to claim that it implies no liability in any court case in Tanzania. Sue Hawley, now of Corruption Watch, suggests 'this is a trick chosen by BAE to avoid being implicated directly by a third party'.[33]

On 4 November 2010, Andrew Chenge was elected to the Tanzanian Parliament again and announced his intention to pursue the position of Speaker. Three days later, the PCCB, itself an organization in peril, announced that it had found no evidence to link Chenge to corruption in the radar deal, in a decision that shocked Tanzanian anti-corruption campaigners.[34]

The decision, and the statement announcing it, threatened the credibility of the PCCB, with some people doubting the way the investigations had been conducted. The national chairman of the Civic United Front (CUF), Professor Ibrahim Lipumba, said he doubted the PCCB's integrity because cleansing suspects was not among the core functions of the bureau. 'With the PCCB background of protecting some government "big wigs" who have been involved in several scandals, I may conclude that I don't have trust with PCCB,' Professor Lipumba said. He continued: 'Chenge has still failed to explain how he obtained the money found in his off-shore account, which is incomparable with his salary as public servant.'[35]

Alfons Mensdorff-Pouilly's release angered some Austrian MPs, who felt he was being protected. As he returned to the country, arguments were put forward to prevent him facing trial in Austria. His supporters claimed that he was protected by the Schengen Agreement, which stipulates that a suspect who has faced investigation in a member country can only be convicted or acquitted on that charge once within the Schengen area.[36] However, Mensdorff-Pouilly was not acquitted as the charges against him were dropped without a court adjudicating on his guilt.

When CAAT and the Corner House attempted unsuccessfully to challenge the settlement, the SFO argued that it had 'received advice from counsel to the effect that in a prosecution of Count Mensdorff . . . it would not be possible to proceed without making an allegation of corruption against BAE'.[37] Lawyers familiar with the case questioned the logic, with one describing it as 'startling' and another suggesting: 'I don't think they needed to give it [the explanation]. I think it's silly.'[38] CAAT and the Corner House pointed out a glaring contradiction in the SFO's view: '. . . the defendant [the SFO] maintains that the prosecution of Count Mensdorff could not go ahead because it would have involved unacceptable allegations of corruption being made by the prosecution against BAE Systems. This strongly suggests there was evidence to show corporate liability, or such allegations could have been legitimately made in Count Mensdorff's case.'[39] So the SFO had the Count charged because it suspected him of being involved in corruption on behalf of BAE. A week later, having settled ignominiously with the company, the SFO released him because to pursue a case against him would have led to allegations of corruption against BAE, which is why it charged him in the first place. So the SFO's motivation for dropping the case against Mensdorff-Pouilly, just a few days after jailing him, was clearly to ensure that the Count's case in no way undermined their risible settlement with BAE. I'm not sure who is the biggest ass in this instance, the law or the SFO.

As Sten Lindström, the Swedish police officer who pushed his government to investigate the Bofors affair, said: 'The primary lesson of the Bofors story is that the truth will always come out. It may take years, in this case over a decade, but you cannot hide the truth.'[40]

The truth in the case of BAE's arms dealing, with the active connivance and protection of the British government, is that it brings immiseration and suffering to many parts of the world that can least afford it. It is not the well-paid company executives or the politicians or government functionaries who have to suffer the consequences. It is the ordinary citizens of the buying and selling countries who are made to pay for the wasted fiscal resources and the diminution of democracy and the rule of law.

While the fate of the brave and committed anti-corruption officials, such as Helen Garlick, Matthew Cowie, Edward Hoseah and countless others, is usually to be fired, to leave their jobs in frustration, to face professional marginalization, even exile, they, like me, cling to the hope that the truth will ultimately out.

SECTION IV
The Arms Superpower

12. Legal Bribery

It was President Roosevelt, in the early years of the Second World War, who recast America as 'the great arsenal of democracy'. Before the attack on Pearl Harbor the US had been supplying its allies with arms and matériel behind the scenes. Between 1939 and 1945 America became an arsenal of unprecedented scale, first supplying others and then, in the wake of the Japanese attack, using force herself.[1] Not only were America's population, resources and industrial capacities marshalled to this end, but the war effort became the driving force in a far-reaching transformation of American society.[2]

The historian D. W. Brogan suggested in 1944 that 'war is a business, not an art . . . and the US is a great, very great, corporation.'[3] The Second World War witnessed an industrial explosion in the US, with manufacturing output doubling between 1940 and 1943. Arms production increased eightfold between 1941 and 1943, to a level nearly that of Britain, the Soviet Union and Germany combined. As the film-maker Eugene Jarecki observed, the conflict wove the idea of war inextricably into the American way of life. It saw an ever-increasing proportion of national resources diverted into the military and engendered unprecedented closeness between the federal government and corporate America. This gave the defence apparatus a life of its own in influencing public policy and exerted damaging influence on the separation of powers. It produced a symbiosis between the executive branch and corporate America in which each simultaneously shelters and empowers the other, producing a climate of decreased transparency and accountability and, ultimately, of unchecked executive power. During his years in the White House FDR transformed the executive branch into an office of far greater power, secrecy and autonomy than had ever been contemplated before.[4]

The bombings of Hiroshima and Nagasaki ordered by President Harry Truman, strategic efficacy aside, were an extreme case of a kind of self-perpetuating militarism. The US-driven victory in the war unleashed the forces of executive overreach and militaristic aggression that would shape

American policy and society for decades to come.[5] Since this time defence industry executives have played powerful roles in influencing both domestic and foreign policy in directions that suit the needs of their companies.

After the boom years of the war, defence spending plunged from $908bn in 1945 to $141bn in 1947.[6] Yet the growing Soviet threat would soon compel a renewed military build-up. The US replaced the UK as the pre-eminent Western global power. And the domino theory set the Truman Doctrine in motion, the most significant expansion of American foreign policy since the Monroe Doctrine of 1823. Truman argued that in the shadow of communism, a threat to free people anywhere was a threat to the United States and that the US should protect these free people anywhere at any time. In so doing he blurred the lines between peacetime and war, calling for permanent military preparedness. And through the National Security Act of 1947 increased war-making power was concentrated in the executive branch.[7]

The creation after 1947 of a national security state, which shifted power from the State Department to the Department of Defense, was a godsend to the arms industry. Since 1947, the Department of Defense has become the gravitational centre of a vast system of recruitment centres, military bases, laboratories, testing grounds, command centres, defence-related corporations and academic institutions. And the Cold War brought the military and industry into an unprecedented level of cooperation with one another, compounding their cumulative level of influence over policy: the military-industrial complex (MIC) as described by Eisenhower.[8]

Speaking to the American Society of Newspaper Editors on 16 April 1953, less than three months into office and as the US started again to spend more on defence than on human needs, President Eisenhower delivered his 'Chance for Peace' speech: 'Every gun that is made, every warship launched, every rocket fired, signifies a theft from those who hunger and are not fed, those who are cold and are not clothed.'[9]

Despite these sentiments, Eisenhower's administration conducted several covert operations in foreign countries, most notoriously Guatemala and Iran. While the intention was to gain geo-strategic ground in the struggle against communism, with increasing frequency the economic interests of corporations were also involved. Major General Smedley Butler, two-time Medal of Honour recipient and the most decorated marine in US history, said of his own participation in profit-driven US military action around the world: 'I spent 33 years and four months in active military service and during that period I spent most of my time as a high class muscle man for Big Business. In short, I was a racketeer, a gangster for capitalism.'[10]

What was new in the covert operations initiated under Eisenhower was the use of the CIA to invisibly implement the plans hatched in private consultations between the executive, select advocates in Congress and their cronies in industry, especially the weapons business. The establishment of the CIA in 1947 helped to create a new layer of secrecy and reduce accountability, blurring the line between America's national interest and the private interests of corporations friendly to the US government.[11]

This same nexus of interests accused Eisenhower, despite his remarkable military career, of being soft on the Soviets and falling behind the USSR in the arms race. This criticism took the form of two lines of negative propaganda, known as the 'bomber gap' and the 'missile gap', both of which showed the insidious intertwining of the interests of the military, Congress and the defence-industrial sector.

The bomber gap was a political canard promoted by an alliance of Air Force brass and defence contractors seeking money to build more bombers. They claimed that the USSR was surpassing the US in its production of jet-powered strategic bombers, and that these bombers were capable of delivering a nuclear attack on the US. Despite evidence refuting the claim, it was popularized by members of Congress, especially Missouri's Democratic Senator, Stuart Symington, who had served as the first Secretary of the Air Force. He is the prototype of the role played by many members of Congress today in lobbying and fear-mongering for the desires of the military-industrial complex, leading Eisenhower to suggest that 'each community in which a manufacturing plant or a military installation is located profits from the money spent and jobs created in the area. This constantly presses on the community's political representatives to maintain the facility at maximum strength.'[12] Despite being shown to be false, the bomber gap achieved its desired effect, with a massive expansion of the Air Force's air power.

The notion of a missile gap emerged after the launch of Russia's first spacecraft, *Sputnik 1*. Again it began with Senator Symington and a defence contractor executive – who had been his PA when Symington was Secretary to the Air Force – whose company wanted to produce missiles at

$1.5m a piece to overcome the gap. As the defence contractor Boeing and Douglass (as it then was) fanned the missile gap flames, Eisenhower was moved to remark that he was 'getting awfully sick of the lobbies by the munitions . . . You begin to see this thing isn't wholly the defence of the country, but only more money for some who are already fat cats.'[13] Kennedy used the missile gap claim to embarrass Eisenhower and then Nixon. Later, as President, Kennedy would have to admit it was a myth. Having run on a platform of Eisenhower being soft on the Soviets, Kennedy adopted a more hawkish global posture and oversaw 'the most far-reaching defence improvements in the peacetime history of this country'.[14] This resulted in an increase in spending from $371bn to $388bn between 1961 and 1962 – the largest single peacetime increase in US history up to that point.[15] And he committed the US to Vietnam.

It was Eisenhower, the former military man, who best understood the US arms business as systemic collusion between not only the munitions manufacturers and the military, but also Congress. His granddaughter, Susan, a prominent Cold War scholar, argues that her grandfather felt that 'clearly Congress is part of a triangle here'.[16] This symbiotic relationship prompted some critics to use the term military-industrial-congressional complex (MICC), or the iron triangle.[17] A senior Capitol Hill aide described this connivance to me as legal bribery.

The controversial and sometimes intersecting careers of two men in their mid-seventies who died within two days of each other in early February 2010 reflected much of what is wrong with the formal arms trade in the USA. One was a Congressman serving his nineteenth term, the other a former twelve-term Representative. Their careers thrived in the system built on a circle of patronage between defence companies, lobbyists, law-makers, the White House and the Pentagon: a scheme of mutual back-scratching that is not necessarily illegal under US law, but in some parts of the world would constitute illegal bribery.

John Murtha, who died on 8 February 2010 at the age of seventy-seven, was the first Vietnam combat veteran to serve in Congress after winning a special election to the House in 1974.[18] His victory as a Democrat in a district with a strong conservative tradition was taken in part as a rejection of President Richard Nixon. Murtha's campaign slogan, 'One honest man can make a difference', played to the grave doubts voters held about Nixon's ethics.

Ironically, by the time of his death John Murtha had become the pre-eminent symbol of the congressional practice of earmarking, the process by which lawmakers add federal money to the budget of often unrelated pieces of legislation to give no-bid contracts (contracts that are awarded to a company without any competition) to pet projects and companies of their choosing. He faced a drumbeat of questions about possible ethical conflicts, as executives and lobbyists for the firms receiving the contracts were among his most generous campaign contributors.

Murtha, who in 1989 had become Chairman of the powerful House Appropriations Subcommittee on Defense that controls Pentagon spend-ing, was dubbed the 'King of Pork' for the volume of taxpayer money he directed to the area around his home town of Johnstown: $192m in the 2008 budget alone.[19] Most of this largesse came in defence and military research contracts he steered to companies based in his district or with small offices there.[20] Murtha was regularly ranked by watchdog bodies as among the most corrupt Representatives in the House.[21]

The PMA Group, a powerhouse lobbying firm, whose founder, Paul Magliocchetti, was a close friend of Murtha's and his former subcommit-tee staffer, achieved unique success in winning earmarks from Murtha for its clients. In return, these companies and PMA staffers made generous campaign contributions to the Congressman.[22]

In October 2008, the FBI raided PMA's Arlington offices as part of an investigation into improper campaign donations to lawmakers. Magliocc-chetti was charged with eleven counts of corruption and conspiracy, including making illegal payments; in essence, funnelling illegal dona-tions to friendly lawmakers. A year later, the Office of Congressional Ethics decided to discontinue its investigation of Murtha's actions on behalf of PMA Group and recommended that the House ethics commit-tee take no action against him. In September 2010, Magliocchetti pleaded guilty to federal campaign finance violations.[23]

Murtha's power also reaped benefits for his family. His brother, Robert C. 'Kit' Murtha, built a successful lobbying practice around clients seek-ing defence funds through the Appropriations Committee and became a senior player at KSA, a lobbying firm whose contractor clients often received multimillion-dollar earmarks directed through the committee Chairman.[24] The Congressman's nephew – Kit's son, Robert C. Murtha Jr – for years made an excellent living working with companies that relied on Pentagon contracts over which his uncle held considerable sway. His company, Murtech, received millions in no-bid Pentagon contracts.[25]

Documents obtained by the *Washington Post* show Robert Murtha using his influential family connection as leverage in his business dealings and holding unusual power with the military. For instance, in 2001, Murtha Jr told a business partner that there were conditions for 'keeping funds flowing'. Part of the federal work, he said, must be channelled to Johnstown. 'This has been a requirement for what I do to get dollars through.'[26] A former employee at Murtech claims that the company did virtually no work on some of the contracts it won with larger contractors.[27]

In July 2010, a former executive of a Pennsylvania defence firm with close ties to John Murtha pleaded guilty to taking bribes from a partner defence company. Richard Ianieri, the former president of Coherent Systems International, admitted that he took $200,000 in bribes from officials at a firm the company hired as a subcontractor. The firm to which bribes were paid was Kuchera Defense Systems in Murtha's congressional district. Ianieri and other Coherent officials donated a total of $92,000 to members of Congress from 2003, with $34,700 of that going to Murtha's re-election campaigns or political action committee.[28] Kuchera, a company that Murtha had helped grow with more than $100m in military contracts and earmarks, was suspended from receiving further Navy contracts pending an investigation into allegations that it had defrauded the government in its billing.[29] Company officers contributed $60,000 to Murtha's campaigns. The company was not a client of PMA, but it relied for several years on lobbying work by the Congressman's brother, Kit.[30]

A year before his death, Murtha had told the *Pittsburgh Post-Gazette* that every lawmaker looks out for his own: 'If I'm corrupt, it's because I take care of my district. . . . Every president would like to have all the power and not have Congress change anything. But we're closest to the people.'[31]

The John Murtha Johnstown–Cambria County Airport sits on a windy mountain two hours east of Pittsburgh, a 650-acre expanse of smooth tarmac, spacious buildings, a helicopter hangar and a National Guard training centre. It is a fitting monument to its benefactor's career. The airport only exists because of the $200m in federal funds that Murtha steered towards its construction and development over a decade. When the economic stimulus package was agreed in 2009, Murtha's airport was the first to win funding from it: $800,000 to repave a backup runway. On an average weekday about four passengers board each of its three commercial flights to Dulles International, often outnumbered by the seven security staff members and supervisors. When Johnstown native Bill Previte arrived one morning, he lamented that his plane was half empty and that the terminal was deserted. 'Doesn't it seem kind of ridiculous to have a motorized carousel for the baggage claim when 15 people get off the airplane?' he said. 'It's obvious: There's not enough population to justify this place.' The little-used commuter airport doubles as a wartime preparedness facility for the Pentagon, after $30m was invested in improvements and expansion.[32]

Murtha's earmarks, while undoubtedly saving his economically depressed home town, have not delivered the number of jobs promised. A *Washington Post* analysis showed that of sixteen local companies the Congressman had helped win federal earmarks, ten have generated far fewer jobs than forecast, and half of those have closed operations in his former district.[33]

But there was another side to the ultimate crony insider: John Murtha, the tough former combat veteran who would not back down in a fight against powerful adversaries if he believed passionately in something. So, despite having been a crucial informal adviser to Dick Cheney when he was first made Secretary of Defense in 1989 and didn't by his own admission 'know a blankety-blank thing about defense', in 2005, when Murtha reached the conclusion that the Iraq occupation had turned into a quagmire where Americans should not be serving, let alone dying, he vociferously called for the troops to be brought home. Cheney accused him of losing his backbone, to which Murtha responded: 'I like guys who got five deferments [from serving in the military] and (have) never been there and send people to war, and then don't like to hear suggestions about what needs to be done', referencing the Vice President's history of draft avoidance in the 1960s. Murtha's call to bring the troops home, and the ensuing tussle with Cheney, was a critical turning point in the debate about the war. Even more so, it was crucial in exposing George W. Bush and Dick Cheney for what they were: crude and frequently ignorant ideologues who cared more about pursuing their own agendas than about doing right by America or its soldiers.[34]

On his death, Lockheed Martin took out a full-page ad memorializing John Murtha. On the bottom, under the Lockheed Martin logo, was the company's tagline: 'We never forget who we're working for'.[35]

When in the autumn of 1980 an FBI sting operation to trap corrupt public officials started to move against John Murtha, his friend and powerful Democratic Speaker of the House, Thomas 'Tip' O'Neill, asked the flamboyant Congressman Charlie Wilson to take up a position on the House Ethics Committee to help shut down any inquiry into Murtha. While Murtha hadn't been prosecuted for his role in the Abscam bribery scandal, in which an FBI agent disguised as an Arab sheikh lured six Congressmen and a Senator into performing political favours in return for money, the internal watchdog committee was looking into whether he broke House rules by not reporting the bribery attempt.[36]

Given his reputation as a philandering hedonist, Wilson was hardly an obvious choice. When a puzzled reporter asked the Congressman why he, of all people, had been selected for this sober assignment to the committee that acts as the conscience of the House, he replied roguishly: 'because I'm the only one of the committee who likes women and whiskey, and we need to be represented'.[37] In addition to being persuaded onto the committee with a lifetime box at the prestigious Kennedy Center, Wilson also admired Murtha, whom he worked with on Defense Appropriations and saw as a fellow anti-communist and a decorated war veteran.[38]

Wilson went to work as the wrecker-in-chief on the normally staid committee, forcing the Murtha investigation to be closed down and the special prosecutor to resign.[39] Murtha would never forget Charlie Wilson's rescue operation on his behalf and when he became chair of the Appropriations Subcommittee on Defense always deferred to Wilson on his driving political passion, Afghanistan.

Charlie Wilson was a 6 foot 4 inch Texan, square-jawed, with an all-year tan and a deep, booming Texas baritone. He was a dashing dresser – loud striped shirts set off with equally bold braces – who staffed his Congressional office almost exclusively with tall, beautiful women, known to everyone as 'Charlie's Angels'. Whenever asked about his staffing practices, Wilson would respond: 'You can teach them how to type, but you can't teach them to grow tits.'[40] The ultimate political hedonist, his indulgent apogee came in 1980 at Las Vegas's Caesar's Palace, when he was photographed in a jacuzzi snorting cocaine with two naked strippers.[41]

In the early summer of the same year Wilson walked off the floor of the House of Representatives into the Speaker's Lobby, where he read a story off the teletype datelined Kabul. The article described hundreds of thousands of refugees fleeing Afghanistan as Soviet helicopter gunships levelled villages, slaughtered livestock and killed anyone suspected of harbouring guerrillas resisting the occupation. Wilson, a fervent anti-communist, was taken with the report's description of how the Afghani resistance was murdering Russians in the dead of night with knives and pistols, or hitting them over the head with shovels and stones. Wilson immediately called the Appropriations Committee staffer who dealt with 'black appropriations', i.e. CIA funds for covert operations. He asked the staffer how much was being given to the Afghans. 'Five million,' came the reply. 'Double it,' said the Texan.[42] 'The mysterious force in the US government that was destined to hound the Red Army with a seemingly limitless flood of ever more lethal and sophisticated weapons was about to be activated,' according to Wilson's biographer, George Crile.[43]

No Congressman prior to Charlie Wilson had ever moved unsolicited to increase a CIA budget. From the beginning of the Cold War, Congress had granted that exclusive right to the President. But as dramatic as the doubling might sound, it had no visible impact on the war.

Two years later, on a trip to Peshawar instigated by his wealthy, right-wing mistress, Joanne Herring, Wilson 'lost his heart to the Afghans' at a Red Cross hospital overflowing with guerrillas wounded by the Soviets. They all asked for weapons so they could bring down the Soviet Mi-24 Hind helicopters tormenting them from the skies.[44] And they got them, in huge quantities, as Wilson increased their funding from the initial $5m to $750m a year. In addition to persuading his colleagues on Appropriations to stump up, Wilson also persuaded the Saudis – in the form of the Al Yamamah-linked Defence Minister, Prince Sultan, and his son, Prince Bandar – to match the American funds dollar for dollar.[45] Prince Bandar, a most willing accomplice in the funding of the secret war, often entertained Wilson and Herring in the desert kingdom.[46]

To keep American prints off the operation, Wilson ordered anti-aircraft guns from Israel, bullets from Egypt and cut-price AK-47s from China. When faced with resistance to providing the Afghans with lethal Stinger missiles, Wilson pushed on every possible door until the weapons that changed the course of the war were sent. When the 'muj', as he referred to them, ran into transport problems, Wilson shipped out mules from Tennessee. When the CIA would not get them field radios, he spent $12,000 buying them from Radio Shack. He travelled to the region thirty-two times, astonishing Afghan warlords and General Zia of Pakistan by showing up with attractive women called 'Snowflake' or 'Firecracker', clad in tight pink jumpsuits.[47]

In the course of a decade, billions of rounds of ammunition and hundreds of thousands of weapons were smuggled across the border on the backs of camels, mules and donkeys. At one point over 300,000 Afghan warriors carried weapons provided by the CIA, and thousands were trained in the art of urban terror. By the time they left in early 1989, 28,000 Soviet soldiers had been killed.

Throughout the 1980s, the Afghan *mujahideen* were America's surrogate soldiers in the brutal guerrilla war that became the Soviet Union's Vietnam, a defeat that played some role in the subsequent collapse of the Soviet empire. It was the biggest secret war in history, fought without debates in Congress or protests in the streets.[48]

When the Soviets were forced out of Afghanistan there were many who echoed the words of Pakistan's military leader, General Zia ul-Haq: 'Charlie did it.' Not least of these was the CIA itself, which awarded Wilson the seldom-bestowed title 'Honoured Colleague'.[49] When Wilson travelled to Saudi Arabia he was treated as an esteemed guest, being told on one trip as he was shown his lavish suite: 'We want you to know, Mr. Congressman, that these are larger quarters than we provided for George Bush [snr]. Mr. Bush is only the vice president. You won the Afghan war.'[50]

George Crile's account of Wilson's devotion to the Afghans inadvertently confirms the view of the Pulitzer Prize-winning writer Steve Coll that Wilson 'saw the *mujahideen* through the prism of his own whiskey-soaked romanticism, as noble savages fighting for freedom, as almost biblical figures'.[51] But Wilson's activities in Afghanistan were not simply a romantic fight against evil, but also 'led directly to a chain of blowback that culminated in the attacks of September 11, 2001, and to the United States' [then] status as the most widely hated nation on earth'.[52]

The warning signs were there, but Wilson's less than informed romanticism continued to drive his actions. With the departure of the Soviets, Afghan guerrillas quickly returned to the centuries-old feuding of war-lordism, but now armed with hundreds of millions of dollars' worth of weapons and explosives of every conceivable type. The Russians continued to pump an estimated $3bn a year into the mountainous country to prop up the puppet government they'd left behind, while the CIA, with Saudi support, maintained the enormous flow of weapons to the feuding warlords. The Russians suggested that the brand of militant Islam emerging in the region was just as dangerous to America as it was to the Soviet Union, a point Wilson had heard frequently from his own side, but chose to ignore.[53]

Over the next two years thanks to the money Wilson continued to deliver and the matching Saudi funds, the *mujahideen* received almost half a billion dollars a year to wage war. In addition, they were gifted a cornucopia of new weaponry after the United States decided to send them the Iraqi weapons captured during the Gulf War. The Afghans responded with increased internal conflict and, in some cases, public support for Saddam Hussein when he invaded Kuwait in 1990. Wilson's response was to drink more and more: he would not acknowledge what was becoming of his pet 'freedom fighters'.[54]

Under the umbrella of the CIA's programme, Afghanistan had become a gathering place for militant Muslims from around the world. As early as the First Gulf War, a *mujahideen* leader who had greatly impressed the Americans, Gulbuddin Hekmatyar, articulated the belief that the United States was seeking world domination and control of Muslim oil. Jalaluddin Haqani, a man Wilson had described as 'goodness personified', had long been a magnet for extremist Saudi volunteers. Osama bin Laden was one of the volunteers who could frequently be found in the same area where Wilson had been Haqani's honoured guest. As the CIA's favourite commander, Haqani had received bags of money each month from the station in Islamabad.[55]

The ten-year commitment of the CIA had turned a primitive army of tribesmen into highly armed warriors, imbued with the spirit of jihad and the belief that, having brought down one superpower, they could just as easily take on another.[56] It was some of these people or their successors who in 1996 killed nineteen American airmen at Dhahran, Saudi Arabia; bombed the US embassies in Kenya and Tanzania in 1998; blew a hole in the side of the USS *Cole* in Aden Harbour in 2000; and on 11 September 2001 flew hijacked planes into the World Trade Center and the Pentagon. The Afghan freedom fighters of the 1980s were the forebears of the militants of Al Qaeda and the Taliban of the 1990s and 2000s.[57]

Immediately after 9/11 Wilson took comfort in pointing out that the perpetrators 'were all Arabs, not Afghans. It didn't register with me for a week or two that this thing was all based in my mountains.'[58] For most other Americans, the events of 9/11 were immediately tied to Afghanistan when it was learned that the hijackers had all spent time there. Much was made of this by the Bush administration, which assailed the Taliban for harbouring Osama bin Laden and for allowing Afghanistan to become a breeding ground for international terrorists. The American public rallied behind the President when he launched his War on Terror. Barely a word was spoken of America's role in arming their attackers, even when the CIA attempted unsuccessfully to assassinate not only Osama bin Laden, but also Hekmatyar and Haqani.[59]

When it was suggested to him that he was an early facilitator of bin Laden's Al Qaeda movement, Wilson continued to claim that the defeat of the Soviet Union in Afghanistan was 'glorious and changed the world. . . . And then we fucked up the endgame.'[60] But the reality is that 9/11 was the ultimate example of blowback in the arms trade: the unintended consequences of supplying arms, especially through covert means.

For the cavalier manner in which he continued to supply his 'noble savages' with sophisticated weaponry even after he was warned of their anti-American militancy, Charlie Wilson was undoubtedly 'the King of Blowback'.

As a respected academic, Chalmers Johnson, suggested, the real victor in Afghanistan was the military-industrial complex, for 'the billion dollars worth of weapons Wilson secretly supplied to the guerrillas ended up being turned on ourselves',[61] requiring more and more weapons and services to be sourced from the very same suppliers in order to protect America.

Charlie Wilson died just two days after his close colleague, John Murtha. He was seventy-six. 'He was a rascal but he was our rascal,' the mayor of his home town of Lufkin said after Wilson's death.[62]

A month before he died, John Murtha had chuckled when asked about President Obama's assertion that he was going to freeze all discretionary spending, all earmarks, and bring about greater transparency in defence spending. 'Well, he can call for it, but we're the guys who make the decision. I always remind them of that.'[63]

President Obama inherited the most powerful fighting force in the world. It is also the most expensive and arguably the most systemically corrupt.

The US is by far the world's largest manufacturer, seller and buyer of arms and weapons. It sells about 40 per cent of the world's armaments with a high of 61 per cent in 2008.[64] Military spending has increased by 81 per cent since 2001, and now accounts for 43 per cent of the global total, six times that of its nearest rival, China. At 4.8 per cent of GDP, US military spending in 2010 represents the largest economic burden outside the Middle East.[65] Thus, unlike in Europe, US domestic defence spending is more important to arms companies than foreign deals. While corruption in export deals has declined since the toughening of legislation and enforcement, the importance of the domestic market, combined with elected representatives' dual need to deliver jobs to their constituents and to raise money for biennial elections, has led to systemic legal bribery:

> Our corruption is legal. It's legal bribery. Whatever the Pentagon wants it gets. And we're happy to sell to pretty much anyone and we're not that interested in what happens post-sale. Pakistan, Colombia, Taiwan, the Middle East, the Saudis. Often we don't even sell them, we give them weapons. We are buying political influence and American jobs. It's the most powerful lobby there is. I don't think Obama will be able to withstand it.[66]

US militarism – which a retired army colonel, Andrew Bacevich, describes as the thrall in which Americans hold military power and its perpetuation – has become the largely unchallenged underpinning of the country's national identity.[67] It is a complex network of economic and political interests tied in a multitude of different ways to American corporations, universities and communities, the so-called MICC which, true to Eisenhower's prescient words, has come to 'exercise misplaced power [which] endangers our liberties and democratic processes'.[68]

Until the late 1970s the major US arms companies could, with the assistance of their government, bribe and strong-arm their way to pre-eminence around the world.[69] The favoured Lockheed Corporation was extremely close to the CIA, selling to its client states and actively involving itself in some of the less reputable actions of the Agency in Latin America – described as a free-for-all for arms salesmen – and the Far East.[70]

The company, the world's largest defence contractor, dominates the weapons business along with fellow American giants Boeing and Northrop Grumman and Britain's BAE. After a volatile early history that saw the company teeter in and out of financial crisis, it was bought by Robert Gross in 1932.[71] Under his leadership the company became influential in the corridors of power. It built the Electra transport plane which featured as the getaway plane in the iconic Humphrey Bogart film *Casablanca*. But the Electra was insufficient to make the company profitable, so Gross turned to 'government contracts for war machines' despite preferring 'not to have to depend on the light and shadow of politics'.[72] His concerns about military business were not grounded in morality, as evidenced by his sale of Electras to the Japanese army which strengthened the fascist regime in the run-up to war. From 1934 to 1938 US aircraft sales to Europe amounted to over $42m, with the UK, Nazi Germany and the fascist regime in Italy each receiving over $2m of these sales. Japan received $15.5m. In 1938, the UK's Royal Air Force ordered 200 Hudson bombers from Lockheed. With the passing of legislation in September 1939 preventing any US citizen from delivering military goods to countries engaged in war, Lockheed bought an airfield that straddled the US border with Canada. The Hudsons were flown to the American side, and pulled into Canada before being flown to Britain. The deal transformed Lockheed into a major power in the weapons industry.

The end of hostilities posed a threat to the company's well-being. So Gross set about insinuating himself into the political process to engender permanent high spending on military aircraft. Before a Senate committee investigating national defence he argued: 'I find it very difficult to talk about the airplane as a weapon of war. It is a cause I would not be selfish enough to plead as a businessman, but it is my duty as a citizen to plead for it.'[73]

As Bill Hartung, author of a book on the company and its role in the making of the MIC suggests, this conflating of the company's and industry's interests with the national interest was to serve Lockheed and its rivals well in the decades to come. But ultimately it was not the words and arguments that opened the military spigot, but war – the Korean War. Lockheed not only supplied the US military with goods and equipment, at a substantial profit, but also with the means to transport it.

The Cold War also served the company well. Lockheed produced missiles, space vehicles and sophisticated spy planes to enable the CIA to keep track of the military capabilities of the Soviet Union. Despite this windfall, by 1960 the company was once again in financial difficulty, relying on the Kennedy administration's military build-up to return to health.

But even with this build-up, Lockheed, mirroring the history of many weapons manufacturers, was soon in trouble once more. At the centre of its difficulties lay the largest military aircraft ever built, the C-5A Galaxy. The Air Force decided it needed a colossal plane to move large numbers of troops and equipment anywhere in the world within days: hence the Galaxy, over 260 feet long, with a 223-foot wing span and a tail wing that is six storeys high. Despite its size it needed to be able to land on a dirt runway of just 4,000 feet.[74]

This gargantuan plane, which would enable the US to have an instant military base wherever in the world it needed to, was criticized early in its conception. William Fulbright, the Senate Foreign Relations Committee Chairman, argued in 1969 that such capacity would tempt the US to intervene in every conflict that broke out anywhere.

The Galaxy would never have been built if Air Force procurement officers had their way. A Boeing design was deemed superior to Lockheed's, but had an additional $400m price tag. But Lockheed held the lobbying upper hand, to the extent that when its original design exhibited faults, it was allowed to fix them. Senator Richard Russell, from Georgia, where the plane would partly be built, chaired the Senate Armed Services Committee and the Appropriations Committee's defence subcommittee. He was also a close friend of President Lyndon B. Johnson. Lockheed also placed a sub-assembly plant for the plane in the district of the House Armed Services Committee chairman, L. Mendel Rivers, an unapologetic practitioner of pork barrel politics in the Murtha mould. Legend in South Carolina held that if Rivers got one more military base for his Charleston area, it would sink into the Atlantic ocean.

When it became clear that the C-5A had enormous cost and performance problems, Rivers ensured that the House Armed Services Committee never made serious inquiries into them.

But the most important factor in Lockheed winning the contract was the Pentagon's desire to keep the company's Georgia operation in business as part of the defence industrial base. As Hartung notes:

> The practice of doling out contracts according to the financial needs of the arms makers rather than the merits of a particular weapons design is a long standing practice in the MIC, where the investments needed to keep factories at the ready to build modern armaments can run into the billions of dollars. As a result, a symbiotic relationship has developed between the Pentagon and its top contractors in which each needs the other to survive and prosper.[75]

The Air Force overruled its own selection board and opted to buy the C-5A rather than the Boeing design. The Pentagon went so far as to draw up a new form of contract for the project, requiring the company to estimate R&D and production costs up front, and commit to explicit timing and performance yardsticks. Slipping up on the schedule would bring fines up to a maximum of $11m, a minuscule amount in relation to the size of the project budget, reflecting the loopholes that riddled the contract. The government was on the hook for the vast majority of any overspending. Crucially, there was a repricing formula that would allow the overruns on the first batch of C-5As to be folded into the costs of the second batch. So the rewards for ramping up costs actually far outweighed the penalties.

Ernie Fitzgerald, a courageous cost estimator in the Air Force, repeatedly blew the whistle on the problems with the programme, until he could no longer be ignored. After his initial misgivings were concealed within the Pentagon, Fitzgerald finally discovered that the projected costs for the programme had increased by almost $2bn, since the initial estimates. It was the most expensive aircraft project ever undertaken by the US, and set records for excess costs as well. The Air Force continued to tell Congress that all was well and few on Capitol Hill were interested in asking tough questions of a scheme that was delivering billions in pork barrel projects for their constituents.

Senator William Proxmire of Wisconsin, a fitness fanatic and former journalist with a legendary reputation as an opponent of government waste, was an exception. He refused to accept campaign contributions and turned down several large projects for his own state on the grounds that he viewed them as a waste of money. His Joint Economic Committee's sub-committee on Economy in Government called Fitzgerald to give evidence, during which the whistle-blower acknowledged the possibility of the multibillion-dollar overrun.

Fitzgerald was immediately excluded by his superiors from any serious work on cost assessment or acquisitions. Investigations were launched into all aspects of Fitzgerald's personal and professional life and eventually he was fired, a year after his original testimony. He was told that his unit was being eliminated as a cost-cutting measure. The irony of removing the organization's premier cost-cutter to make savings was lost on the Air Force bureaucrats whose primary concern was to be rid of Fitzgerald so they could continue to offer sweetheart deals to Lockheed and other defence contractors.[76] Four years later, after an extensive lawsuit, Fitzgerald was allowed to return to the Pentagon in a circumscribed role. The most frightening revelation in his lawsuit was that the decision to fire him went all the way to the Oval Office, where Nixon admitted he had issued an instruction 'to get rid of that bastard'.[77]

Fitzgerald nevertheless managed to access key documents to fight the Air Force's propaganda machine. He revealed not only the extent of the overruns, but also that top officials in the Air Force had known about them for years and had misled Congress. The cover-up was eventually acknowledged under pressure from a handful of Congressmen, leading to an SEC investigation, which discovered that senior executives in Lockheed had also sold off shares at about the time misgivings were being expressed about the C-5A, without informing other shareholders. Remarkably, the SEC decided that no law had been broken and no insider trading had occurred.

An internal Pentagon study in 1969 suggested that buying the second batch of C-5As – which would help Lockheed recoup the money it had lost to cost overruns on the first batch – was unnecessary. In 1971, the General Accounting Office (GAO) revealed that the Air Force was accepting the planes with major deficiencies to the landing gear, wings and avionics. It also noted that the plane was unable to land on unpaved runways as required. Twenty-five defects were identified, including that it could only carry half of the projected capacity.

Since 1966, when the problems had been known about, the fixes proposed sometimes caused more harm than the original problem. Henry

Durham, a production supervisor on the C-5A, blew the whistle from inside the Lockheed plant. He described 'mismanagement and waste' in all parts of the factory and saw 'what appears to be collusion with the Air Force to receive credit and payment for work on aircraft which had not been accomplished'.[78] Durham's job and life were threatened, requiring federal marshal protection for him and his family. Threats notwithstanding, Durham testified before Senator Proxmire's committee in 1971 and set out Lockheed's pricing policies, including charging $65 for a simple bolt along with dozens of other examples which cost the taxpayer millions of dollars. He suggested that this practice characterized Lockheed's production processes and contributed to the massive cost overruns. Describing planes being rushed through the production line with crucial parts missing so that the company could receive progress payments from the Air Force, Durham raised a host of safety issues with the aircraft.

As the C-5A scandal was unfolding, Lockheed's finances continued to crumble. The Air Force attempted to bail the company out by buying additional C-5As on even more relaxed terms. In terms of the absurd contract formula, because the first fifty-three planes cost 100 per cent more than estimated, so the second run of planes would cost 240 per cent of the original projected cost. Lockheed was, in effect, being rewarded for its own enormous cost overruns. The Air Force rammed through the order for the second batch of planes in January 1969 without notifying Congress or the incoming Nixon administration, just hours before Senator Proxmire was to hold hearings on the deal. At this point, only four of the original run of planes had been delivered and seventeen others were in bits and pieces.

When Congress attempted to stop the programme at eighty-one planes, rather than the planned 120, Senator John Stennis argued against the cut, claiming it was part of an effort to 'cut the bone and muscle out of our military capability' rendering America 'a second rate nation' that would be 'second best to the Russians'.[79] During the debate, Mendel Rivers, the arch-supporter of the C-5A, limited some critics of the plane to as little as forty-five seconds' speaking time.

Even after Ernie Fitzgerald revealed that the overruns on the C-5A were being used to finance Lockheed's troubled commercial airliner business, Congress continued to support payments to the company. As Fitzgerald remarked: 'advocates of infinite contributions to Lockheed reacted as if [a] pallid little amendment [to hold back some payments] would have wrecked the national economy and ensconced Bolsheviks in the Pentagon in one fell swoop.'[80]

But the Pentagon's profligacy was insufficient to restore Lockheed's financial health, so the company was dependent on a $250m loan guarantee from the federal government. This came after the company was reimbursed $757m in cost overruns on the C-5A and several other projects. Ernie Fitzgerald described it as 'the great plane robbery'.[81]

In the midst of the C-5A foul-up, Lockheed had another disaster on its hands, the Cheyenne helicopter. Described as an aircraft that could take off and land like a helicopter, the Cheyenne experienced a tripling of costs and constant technical problems, resulting in the crash of a prototype in March 1969, killing the pilot. Lockheed was unable to fix the problems and the contract was cancelled, with nearly half a billion dollars in public money washed down the Lockheed drain. This debacle was made worse by the revelation that Lockheed's selection was the result of a significant conflict of interest. Willis Hawkins, the army official whose office awarded the contract, had only left the company's executive suite two years previously. Hawkins had sold his stock in the company when he joined government but continued to receive deferred compensation. This conflict appears even more damaging when considering that Lockheed had never built a helicopter before. As the Cheyenne programme was imploding, Hawkins returned to Lockheed along with his assistant, General W. Dick Jr. Mendel Rivers defended Hawkins, arguing that Congress should not find 'guilty every businessman who comes down here'.[82]

This instance of the revolving door between government and defence contractors was just the tip of the iceberg: a 1969 report released by Senator Proxmire's office found that over 2,000 military officers had gone to work for major defence contractors as of that year. Lockheed led the way with 210 former military officers on its payroll. Proxmire described this practice as 'a real threat to the public interest because it increases the chances of abuse. . . . How hard a bargain will officers drive when they are one or two years away from retirement and have the example to look at over 2,000 fellow officers doing well on the outside after retirement.'[83]

Lockheed's CEO, Dan Haughton, in arguing for the federal bailout of the company, described the C-5A programme as an unqualified success that resulted in 'the greatest airplane that had ever been built, without question'.[84] The successful lobbying for the loan guarantee, in which the Nixon administration played a crucial role, was driven as much by pork barrel politics as ideology or the merits of the case. An otherwise liberal Democrat, Alan Cranston of California, the centre of Lockheed production of its commercial airliner, sang the company's praises. He extolled the virtues of the relationship between the Pentagon and defence contractors, whom he described as 'quasi-governmental companies dependent largely on defence contracts . . . [just as] our country is dependent on them in this world of deadly, sophisticated weapons, for national defense and security'.[85]

And herein lies a key ambiguity about large defence contractors: they are pillars of the free market economy whose shareholders are supposed to provide oversight, while receiving extensive state support which insulates them from market vagaries and meaningful oversight. One thing, however, is constant: this either-or status has resulted in companies that are often badly managed and regularly find themselves in financial difficulties, despite their government's efforts, sometimes illegal, to find them business.

Human nature being what it is, the MICC comprises avaricious individuals who seek to gain private benefit at public cost. But the idea that all the players knowingly conspire to mastermind so intricate a system is difficult to prove, and unnecessary. Instead corruption among defence contractors, Representatives in Congress and the military brass is standard operating procedure camouflaged by an incestuous labyrinthine system and the primacy of 'national security'. Not only do the corrupt actors need to be held to account but, as importantly, the system needs to be untangled.[86]

To further understand this entanglement, I met Chuck Spinney, a lifelong Pentagon insider who experienced this labyrinth on a daily basis for over two decades. He produced a vast body of work explaining how the Pentagon really operates. His efforts culminated in the wrath of all participants in the MICC but saw him featured on the cover of *Time* magazine. In retirement, he now travels the world on a yacht. I managed to see him on a couple of his brief stopovers in the US. We met first at the tidy apartment he and his wife keep in Alexandria outside Washington DC.[87] A shortish, pugnacious man with light-brown hair, Spinney has a face that exudes determination: a tough jaw, Roman nose and searching eyes. He describes himself as an outsider, prone to be critical and unorthodox, driven by his belief in the Socratic method. To describe him as feisty would be an understatement, while the term maverick underplays his contempt for overbearing authority, sense of conviction, steely determination and personal courage.

Franklin 'Chuck' Spinney was born into the military, quite literally. He took his first breaths at the Wright-Patterson Air Force Base in Ohio, the son of an Air Force Colonel. A mechanical engineer by training, he worked in the flight dynamics lab at the base before leaving military life for two years. In 1977, he joined the Pentagon as a civilian analyst in the Office for Systems Analysis working under his mentor, a famous fighter pilot and iconoclastic military reformer, John R. Boyd. Boyd was not only the best fighter pilot the Air Force had, but also developed a theory on air tactics which is still used today and a hugely influential thesis of aeroplane design. He was known variously as 'the Mad Major' for his intense intellectual passion, 'Genghis John' for his abrasive and confrontational interpersonal communication, and 'the Ghetto Colonel' for his extreme, spartan lifestyle. Boyd once said to Spinney: 'the most important thing in the world is to be free. There are two ways to be free, you can be rich or you can crank down your needs to nothing. I am never going to be rich so I am going the other way.'

Boyd had a massive influence on the young Spinney, who was a fast learner. In 1975, the Pentagon was trying to figure out what to do with the B1 bomber, the costs for which had already gone through $100m. Spinney realized they were going to have to pretty much give up everything, destroy the Air Force, to keep 'this high-cost turkey'. When he presented his report to General Chapman, who led the team undertaking the review, the General went through the roof, exclaiming: 'You can't show this.' Spinney responded: 'Well that's what the numbers show.' The senior officer put his foot down: 'You're not going to show this because I have better information than you and we are going to get more money than you say we are going to get. You just understand, Captain! I am giving you a direct order, you are doing it my way not your way.' In the presentation to the senior decision-makers, Spinney laid out every possible option, including the forbidden doomsday figures he had calculated. When asked which option he would go for, the 24-year-old chose his own scenario. Chapman went berserk. Chuck immediately called Boyd to tell him he was in trouble with the General. 'There is silence on the end of the line, and all of a sudden Boyd starts roaring with laughter. He pulls the phone away and I hear him shouting: "My captain just fucked Chapman."'[88]

Eventually, because of the budget implications he had raised, the Pentagon wanted to find a way to get rid of a plane they had been saying was essential to the survival of the Western world. When he became President, Jimmy Carter saved them, by killing off the B1. Up to that point its manufacturers had been working with the Governor of California, Ronald Reagan, and their Congressional allies, to keep it alive using money intended for the space shuttle. When Reagan was elected President they reinvented the B1 as a sub-sonic plane.

John Boyd was the intellectual ring-leader of what became known as the Military Reform Movement (MRM). The MRM were the only insiders who believed that the Pentagon, not the politicians, had lost Vietnam. Their intention was to move beyond the primitive perspective of war held by the military. They wanted to develop weapons that worked from a tactics and strategy perspective, but also provided a defence capability that was affordable.

To do this they had to reveal the inner workings of the Pentagon and the influence of the MICC as a force that corrodes US policy making, leading not just to misbegotten expenditures but ultimately to war:

> The MICC is incredibly complex with each component textured by competing interests: interservice, corporate and congressional rivalries respectively. They then interact in more complex ways than a simple co-conspiracy. At times they collaborate, at others compete. It is a system in which the components of the Complex evolve through their competition toward a state of heightened voracity whose cumulative effect accrues to the benefit of the system as a whole.
>
> The sponsors of any specific weapons programme are a diffuse alliance of people in Congress, the Pentagon and the defense industry. Each has his own agenda. The defense contractor wants the programme to sell for obvious reasons. The program manager at the Pentagon wants it to happen for career reasons. And the Congressman wants it because it will increase his political clout or bring him some other kind of benefit.

The contractor and service arm talk about what is needed and develop products to match. But then the contractors add all sorts of bells and whistles, with which the Pentagon is seduced. The collaboration in getting to this point unfortunately increases the risk that the public interest represented by the service arm becomes blurred by the private interest of the contractor.[89]

For instance, a commander at the Pentagon described his relationship with Lockheed Martin in matrimonial terms: 'Whenever we find a new way to improve the processes, Lockheed is involved. We are wedded to the factory and the company. They are our prime source of parts and expertise. And they are a part of all we do. It is a wonderful marriage of industry with military.'[90]

Working in matrimony, the service arms and the company develop a proposal for a weapons system and then work together to win the support of those in the Pentagon and Congress who control the purse strings. The Pentagon has developed two basic power games. Spinney calls them front loading and political engineering.

In front loading they over-promise what the system is going to do and underestimate the kind of economic and other burdens it's going to impose. When the benefits don't materialize and the burdens are higher than predicted a safety net is created that makes it impossible to shut off the money flow. This is political engineering, in which the defence contractor intentionally spreads contracts and subcontracts for a particular system to a wide range of Congressional districts in order to build a constituency in Congress that provides long and lasting support for that system, with the elected officials effectively becoming representatives of the producer to his colleagues on Capitol Hill and to the executive. It actually benefits a very small percentage of the American people, but they are strategically placed to ensure enough members of Congress have to commit to the system.

Most of the people who are making the decisions are benefiting from them. That's why I call it 'Versailles on the Potomac.' It's very similar to Versailles: You've got people who are parasitic, they feed off the masses while of course keeping the masses in ignorance. I think one of the things you have to realize is that the majority of people that are doing this are not evil-intentioned people, they are not ripping the system off consciously.

In the government, like in the Pentagon, it's not to say there are not rotten apples, there are a lot of them. But you are also dealing with a lot of dedicated, hardworking people. In fact, one of the central questions to me has always been: how can so many well-intentioned people create such a mess?

In 1977, I was trying to kill this program, which I actually did. It wasn't a big programme, about 6 or 800 million dollars. The guy I was working with was a good engineer and obsessed with bringing this thing in. He got diagnosed with terminal brain cancer and took early retirement. He heard that I was being successful at canceling the program. He came in to put a stop to it. He got off of his early retirement, came back on active duty for the last days of his life to take me out. This guy had nothing to gain, absolutely nothing!

The mentality they have is: 'we got to do this to save the country.' They sit around saying this to each other and they really believe it.

The defense contractors are a little different because, first of all, their survival is much more directly related to it. The higher ups in the defence contractors are uniformly more venal. And over in congress you have got a system that is so overwhelmed by information. The staffers are flooding the information in. A lot of these staffers wanna go work for a K street lobbyist or become an Assistant Secretary over at the Pentagon or wherever.

Let me give you a concrete example. I have a friend who is a congressional staffer for a guy who represented a district in Florida. My friend was a really moral guy. The Senate had decided to terminate the production of the F-16. The House then decides they are going to fund this fully. The whole idea is you are gonna negotiate a compromise in the middle and keep the line open. So as soon as the Senate zeroes it, the lobbyists let loose and they start spreading letters around the Hill. They've got a letter from General Dynamics saying 'The F-16 is absolutely essential for national security and accounts for so many jobs.' My friend was incensed. He called me up and says, 'this is nothing but extortion.' The benefits were supposedly going to about 44 states, one in every congressional district. I remember this one district in Alabama, it had something like 132 dollars going to it. And by the way, these jobs, if you wanna make jobs, defence spending is about the worst way to do it.

What you have is huge economic distortion taking place because when these guys go and work for defense contractors, the engineers learn cost plus economics – where basically your profits are a function of your costs.

The higher your costs, the more you make. These companies are insecure, they are basically welfare queens. They have to live on the government dole. That's another reason why we can't turn this off, because you've got a disproportionate size of the shrinking manufacturing sector tied up in defense. So we've got this real monster on the loose, it's Eisenhower's nightmare writ large. You have a lot of people scratching each other's back and they are making out like bandits.[91]

Crucially, this dependence manifests itself in a greater belligerence in foreign policy too. To keep defence spending high and thus the defence contractors growing, it is essential that the US continue to fulfil the role of the world's policeman, the defender of freedom wherever it may be threatened, at home and abroad. So every President enters the Oval Office with enormous pressure, from the industry and its lobbyists, from both sides of Congress and from the military, to keep this 'virtuous circle' spinning through continual increases in defence spending and constant expansion of the imperial role of the US military around the world while always ensuring homeland security.

13.   In the Name of Uncle Sam

The domestic practice of legal bribery in the US arms business is supplemented by an external dimension of support for the industry in relation to foreign weapons sales. It takes various forms, including subsidies, American aid specifically for the purchase of US weapons, generous loans to purchasers and overt and covert pressure on foreign governments and companies to buy from American arms manufacturers.

Export sales are important not only for geopolitical reasons but also to bring down the production costs of domestic weapons systems and to increase profitability. Overseas sales are more lucrative for weapons manufacturers because the R&D costs have already been paid for with taxpayer dollars and they can charge whatever the market will pay for follow-on maintenance contracts and upgrades to the weapons sold. Some Pentagon critics contend that the armed forces and prime contractors also lobby for arms sales abroad because they artificially generate demand for new weapons at home that are better than those sold.[1]

In the case of the US, loans are made not only to the contractors, but also to their customers. For instance, during the 1970s, US government loans to Chile bankrolled a tripling in military spending under the authoritarian General Pinochet, whom the Americans helped bring to power in a brutal coup against the elected government of the leftist Salvador Allende. The General maintained a web of 125 secret, personal foreign bank accounts, most of which were unsurprisingly held at Riggs Bank, where he secreted $27m.[2] It is no wonder the Merex network benefited from his regime.

In Argentina under its military junta in the 1970s, $10bn of the money borrowed by the generals went to military purchases, most from the United States. Transcripts from a meeting between the Secretary of State, Henry Kissinger, and the junta's Foreign Minister make clear that the administration knew loans would be used for weapons bought from the US, in the midst of a campaign of terror on its own people.[3]

In the 1970s, Japan was again the site of flagrant violations of ethical business and government practice. The lengths Lockheed and Rolls-Royce went to in order to secure deals for their TriStar plane illuminated the darkest aspects of interaction between business and government and the central role of bribery in it. It led to a political upheaval unparalleled in Japan's post-war history.

Japan was a country in which the relationship between money and politics could not be ignored, for money was politics. Corruption in Japan had always been closely associated with deals with arms companies, as Basil Zaharoff discovered to his advantage. But the nature of the deals and the power of the middlemen were concealed behind what the Japanese called the *kuromaku*, or 'black curtain'.[4]

The key agent used by Lockheed in Japan was one Yoshio Kodama, aka 'The Monster'. After spending three years in prison on war crimes charges after the Second World War, Kodama was set free by the US occupying forces on the grounds that he would make a good ally in the Cold War fight against communism. He then took his fortune – earned by supplying Japanese troops during the war and looting diamonds and platinum from areas conquered by Japan – and put it to work in his country's politics. Variously described as an organized crime boss and a CIA asset, he helped found and fund the dominant Liberal Democratic Party.[5]

In the late 1950s, Lockheed paid bribes of about $1.5m to $2m to various officials and a fee of $750,000 to Kodama to secure an order for 230 Starfighter planes. The details of the bribes were passed on to the CIA, which confirmed that every move made was approved by Washington. Lockheed was seen to be conducting a deep layer of Washington foreign policy.[6] This marked the high point of the Starfighter. It was sold to the German air force, and over a ten-year period crashed 178 times, killing a total of eighty-five German pilots. It earned the nickname 'the Flying Coffin', and a group of fifty widows of the pilots sued the company.[7]

Over ten years later Lockheed again utilized Kodama to fend off four other bidders and secure a massive deal to sell TriStar planes. Kodama was paid $5m for disbursing $7m of bribes including $1.7m to the Japanese Prime Minister, Kakuei Tanaka. Richard Nixon intervened personally, as did the British Prime Minister, Ted Heath, on behalf of the TriStar's engine-maker, Rolls-Royce. It was later alleged that Lockheed donated a million dollars to Nixon's 1972 campaign within weeks of winning the contract. Five years later, after leaving office, Tanaka was jailed for accepting the bribe.[8]

Lockheed executives claimed not to know or care where their money went, as long as they won the contract. Dan Haughton, the CEO, had the following to say under questioning by Senator Proxmire:

THE CHAIRMAN: Do you or don't you have accurate information as to payments that have been made, where your money goes, the officials who receive it?

MR. HAUGHTON: We have accurate information that we paid the commissions. We do not have accurate information to the point as to where the money finally went.

CH: You pay out millions of dollars from your corporation without knowing where it goes?

HA: We know where it goes. Insofar as the contracts with the consultants are concerned. Where it winds up finally, we do not know. . . . If payments have to be made and you are doing it to get a contract and payments are made and you get the contract, it is good evidence that you needed to make the payments, I think.[9]

Japan may have been the costliest front in Lockheed's bribery operation, but it was far from the first. Going back to the late 1950s, the use of well-connected agents who could sway the decisions of key government officials was already a common practice.

In Germany, Lockheed deployed a huge lobbying force with the aim of winning over the German Defence Minister, Franz Josef Strauss, who would later work with Merex's Gerhard Mertins. In 1958, Strauss recommended the Starfighter to the Bundestag. It was widely assumed that Lockheed had paid off Strauss and other officials or made contributions to their political parties, but nothing could be proved, as Strauss destroyed all defence ministry documents related to the deal. Ernest Hauser, a Lockheed representative who had been hired because of pressure from Strauss, claimed that the company contributed $12m to Strauss's political party. Fred Meuser, a Dutchman who was then Lockheed's director for Europe, received a commission of almost $1m. It is assumed he passed some of this on to German officials.[10]

In the Netherlands, Lockheed aimed higher. With Meuser's help the company recruited none other than Prince Bernhard, the husband of Queen Juliana and father of the current monarch, Queen Beatrix. He had started commercial life as a salesman for IG Farben and was supposedly always kept on a very tight financial rein by his wife and the Dutch Parliament. His financial needs were great as he attempted to keep a mistress and their love child in comfort in Paris. Importantly, he was Inspector General of the Armed Forces and a director of the state airline, KLM. With Bernhard's help, Lockheed sold the F-104 to Holland in late 1959. After the sale, the Prince requested $1m from Lockheed's CEO, Robert Gross, with the money to be paid to him via Switzerland.[11]

The link between Bernhard and Lockheed continued into the mid-1970s, when an investigation by Senator Frank Church's Subcommittee on Multinational Corporations revealed the relationship. From 1964 through to 1974 Bernhard claimed to be working hard to persuade the Dutch to purchase the Lockheed P-3C Orion aircraft. Just as the company seemed to be well placed to win the deal, Bernhard wrote two angry missives to Roger Smith, the company lawyer, seeking a commission of between $4m and $6m to be disguised as a donation to the World Wildlife Fund, of which Bernhard was the founding president. It later emerged that Bernhard and Meuser had simultaneously been working for Lockheed's rival, Northrop.[12] Clearly, there is little honour among arms agents.

In Italy, Lockheed hired a well-connected agent, Olvidio Lefebvre, who told the company president, Carl Kotchian, that he was 'embarrassed' to say that he would have to 'make some payments if you want to sell aircraft in this country'. He suggested $120,000 per plane. A handwritten letter from Roger Smith that emerged at the Church Committee noted that a contact referred to as 'Antelope Cobbler' would provide the final figure on what Italian officials would require to ensure the deal. It was established that 'Antelope Cobbler' was code for the Italian Prime Minister. Unfortunately for the subsequent investigation, Italy had three different Prime Ministers during the two years that negotiations took place. Ultimately, bribes of $2m were paid to secure the contract, including $50,000 to the Defence Minister, with much of the balance going to his political party and its leading members.[13]

During this period, the company also paid bribes in Turkey, Indonesia, Colombia and, of course, Saudi Arabia. In Indonesia in 1965, Lockheed disbursed bribes of $100,000 per plane. However, soon afterwards the CIA assisted the right-wing General Suharto to overthrow the Sukarno government. Lockheed worried that its agent, Isaak Dasaad, might not be sufficiently well connected to the new regime to be of use. Illustrating the extent of US government complicity in controversial foreign arms sales, the company's marketing executive noted that a Lockheed official 'went to the US embassy in Jakarta and asked them specifically whether Dasaad could continue, under the new regime, to be of value to Lockheed'. The embassy said yes, leading Lockheed to record that 'apparently Dasaad has made the transition from Sukarno to Suharto in good shape.'[14]

The company continued to use Dasaad for a few more years before it was instructed by the Indonesian air force to pay directly. This raised concerns within the company, not about the ethics of paying bribes, but the practicalities. It was noted that using a third party established 'at least a nominal buffer. If such payments should someday become public knowledge, the repercussions could be damaging to Lockheed's name and reputation.' The company was also concerned that without a middleman it would 'have no legal means of charging off these commissions. Thus, they may not be considered allowable deductions by the Internal Revenue Service.'[15]

The biggest commissions were paid on sales to Saudi Arabia, which was at the centre of the early-1970s arms-buying spree driven by increased oil revenues. Lockheed's agent was the flamboyant Adnan Khashoggi. Just twenty-six in 1964 when Lockheed hired him, Khashoggi was already a slick operator with extensive relationships with key Saudi officials. Khashoggi's father had been one of the personal physicians of the Saudi King Ibn Saud, and Adnan had been at school with King Hussein of Jordan. Khashoggi was also close to Prince Sultan, the future Defence Minister, and Prince Fahd, who would later rule the kingdom.

He befriended influential Americans as well, including Richard Nixon, in his years of political exile, during which Khashoggi not only wined and dined him in Paris, but ensured too that he was well received in Arab capitals. This all paid dividends when Nixon was elected President in 1968, after which the friends continued to have private meetings. Khashoggi was rumoured to have funnelled millions of dollars to Nixon's 1972 re-election campaign.[16]

Khashoggi represented Lockheed on numerous sales worth billions of dollars. Between 1970 and 1975 he was paid $106m in commissions, although how much he passed on or kept is unknown. Lockheed's vice-president for International Marketing at the time described Khashoggi as 'for all practical purposes a marketing arm of Lockheed. Adnan would provide not only an entrée but strategy, constant advice and analysis.'[17] Khashoggi regularly demanded increased rewards for his role. He pushed up his commission on the sale of C-130 aircraft from 2 per cent to 8 per cent, claiming he needed the extra money 'due to more players getting involved, and the necessity to meet their requirements'.[18] A Lockheed executive noted that 'we have no way of knowing if the so-called "under the table" compensation is ever disbursed to Saudi officials, or stops at our consultant's bank account.'[19] For instance, in August 1968, a Saudi official was 'completely disenchanted with Khashoggi . . . [as] he never received the $150,000 that was agreed to'.[20]

As with Prince Bernhard in the Netherlands, Khashoggi became an agent for Northrop as well in 1970. He was recommended to the company by Kermit Roosevelt, the grandson of Theodore, and a key player in the 1953 US–British coup that brought the Shah of Iran to power. Kermit also successfully represented Northrop in the sale of Tiger aircraft to the Saudis. Both companies knew that Khashoggi was working for the other, but quietly accepted the unusual arrangement, as there was more than enough business for all in the Saudi kingdom.[21]

By the early 1980s, Khashoggi's personal wealth was estimated at $4bn, making him one of the richest men in the world. He was thought to own twelve homes – including a house in 2,000-hectare grounds in Marbella and others in Paris, Cannes, Madrid and Monte Carlo. His property on Fifth Avenue, Manhattan, was sixteen flats knocked into one. He had a stable of Arabian horses and 200 exotic animals, 100 limousines and a $75m yacht, the *Nabila*, which was used in the Bond film *Never Say Never Again*. He also boasted a South Korean martial arts-trained bodyguard, named Mr Kill. His lifestyle certainly brought him into contact with the rich and famous. His sister married Mohammed Al-Fayed, the tycoon and former owner of Harrods, and was the mother of Dodi Al-Fayed, who died in a car crash with Princess Diana.[22]

This lifestyle was largely funded by the Saudi commissions – and the bribes flowing from them – which were well-known to the US authorities long before the Church Committee. The Pentagon was aware of them as they were being carried out. In 1973, Northrop arranged for Khashoggi to meet key Pentagon officials responsible for brokering and monitoring US arms sales. He explained the commission system in some detail, suggesting the payments were meant to build up the kingdom's limited economic infrastructure. Money for the princes, he claimed, was not for material gain, but as a sign of loyalty. By the end of the meeting, David Alne, the Department of Defense's Director of International Sales Negotiations, described Khashoggi as 'an honest and astute businessman [who was running] an inexpensive economic aid program'.[23]

When, as a consequence of the Church Committee and SEC investigations, the defence industry's bribing habits were exposed, Lockheed's president, Carl Kotchian, and the CEO, Dan Haughton, saw no problem with their behaviour, believing that it was quite justified to pay bribes in pursuit of increased sales. Lockheed's initial reaction was to provide as little information as possible. Eventually, under pressure from the SEC, the company acknowledged paying $22m in bribes, but refused to name the recipients, as to do so might hurt future business opportunities and damage foreign officials. Haughton would not even use the word 'bribe', describing them instead as 'kickbacks', on the advice of his lawyers.[24]

The company's lead legal representative was William P. Rogers, former Secretary of State and Attorney General in the Nixon administration. Rogers urged his former colleague, the Secretary of State, Henry Kissinger, to intervene on behalf of the company. As Sampson records, Kissinger obliged, sending a note to the Attorney General, Edward Levi, in which he argued that the information in the Lockheed documents was 'uncorroborated . . . and potentially damaging' and would do severe harm to US relations with the countries concerned. The Church Committee proceeded to release all the details it had anyway.[25] While the media published the revelations, they were largely treated as just the latest examples of corporate and political malfeasance in the post-Watergate moment.

In Japan, however, the revelations were their Watergate. More than 3,000 investigators were deployed to the investigation, searching two dozen homes and offices, including those of an ailing Yoshio Kodama, senior former politicians and Lockheed executives. More than a dozen officials and agents were indicted for their roles in the bribery schemes. The US, following Kissinger's lead, was uncooperative, refusing to make available all the documentation on the scandals. The Japanese were furious, with one observer commenting that 'the United States has told us we have a thief in the house but won't tell us who he is.'[26] The former Premier, Kakuei Tanaka, was arrested in July 1976, becoming the first Japanese Prime Minister to be indicted for bribery that occurred while he was in office. Seven years later he was found guilty and sentenced to four years in prison and fined $2.1m for accepting $1.6m in bribes from Lockheed.[27]

Surprisingly, given Italy's reputation, two former defence ministers were indicted while efforts to lift the immunity of a former Prime Minister failed by only a single vote, thanks to the support of the Socialist Party.[28] In the Netherlands, Prince Bernhard faced a threat to his reputation, but not his liberty. A Dutch government inquiry failed to find evidence of criminal wrongdoing in the Prince's dealings with Lockheed. It criticized him harshly though, stating that Bernhard had 'allowed himself to be tempted to take initiatives which were bound to place himself and the Netherlands' procurement policy . . . in a dubious light. . . . He showed himself open to dishonorable requests and offers.' Bernhard was stripped of virtually all of his business, military and government posts, and was no longer allowed to wear Dutch military uniform. He was widely seen to have brought shame on himself and the Dutch royal family.[29]

In most of the other countries involved in the bribery scandals, there was no accountability of any sort. Adnan Khashoggi continued to make lucrative deals as a middleman between the Saudi government and its major customers, and government officials in Turkey, Indonesia, Colombia and Singapore faced no consequences for their actions.[30] In the case of Indonesia, Henry Kissinger, serving President Gerald Ford, who had replaced the disgraced Nixon, authorized the sale of arms to the Indonesian dictator, Suharto, which were used against the people of East Timor, in direct violation of Congress's Arms Export Control Act. And despite the litany of scandals the head of the Pentagon, Donald Rumsfeld, still wanted Lockheed in business and continued to go to great lengths to persuade foreign governments of the company's credentials.[31]

Daniel Haughton and Carl Kotchian were forced to resign their posts in an effort to keep the company from losing too many contracts in the wake of the bribery revelations. Both men were offered lucrative consulting arrangements with Lockheed after they stepped down, but the offers were rescinded two months later in the face of a public outcry. Neither of the men expressed remorse for their actions. In a July 1977 interview with *The New York Times*, Kotchian described himself as a 'scapegoat' in the affair, comparing himself to Richard Nixon: 'My experience has some of the elements of Watergate. I can compare it because a lot of the things that came out in Watergate were things that were going on previously – and all of a sudden there's a different set of standards.'[32] Not only had it gone on before, argued Kotchian, but any reasonable person would have done what he did in the same circumstances: 'For any businessman who is dealing with commercial and trade matters, would it be possible to decline a request of certain amounts of money when the money would enable him to, like myself, get the business award?' He even dismissed the language of bribery itself: 'Some call it gratuities. Some call them questionable payments. Some call it extortion. Some call it grease. Some call it bribery. I looked at all these payments as necessary to sell a product. I never felt I was doing anything wrong. I considered them a commission – it was a standard thing.'[33] In the defence industry it certainly was, but that didn't make it ethical or correct.

A litany of scandals came to public attention in the wake of the political fallout from Watergate, uncovering slush funds for domestic and foreign bribery.[34] The SEC offered an amnesty for companies admitting to questionable or illegal payments; over 450 US companies admitted making such payments worth over $300m to government officials, politicians and political parties.[35] Over 117 of the self-reporting entities were Fortune 500 companies.[36] Many of the payments were justified as 'facilitation payments' or 'commissions'.[37]

Despite the lurid accounts of not only Lockheed's activities around the world, but similar schemes by scores of other companies,[38] there was no re-imagining of ethics in the violent, corrupt world of the arms dealers, but there was a dramatic recognition of the scale and damage of corruption in the US. The demand for stronger regulation and banning of bribery was resisted by corporate interests which argued that it would put the US at an economic disadvantage.[39] The protestations were largely ignored and the Foreign Corrupt Practices Act (FCPA) was passed by unanimous vote in 1977.[40] The Act was intended to force companies to police themselves into a cleaner capitalism, to compel them to avoid bribery for fear of the shame of getting caught. The focus was on transparency towards shareholders with anti-bribery penalties as a back-up. A commissioner of the SEC, A. A. Sommer Jr, said in 1976, a year before enactment of the FCPA, that:

there are moral problems as well as legal problems that go far beyond simply the question of illegal payoffs to foreign officials. There are questions concerning the role of multinational corporations, the extent to which they have obligations to the countries in which they conduct their business, the extent to which they should seek to raise the standards of conduct there, the respect which they should show the laws of other countries.[41]

Until the 1990s the US was the only country to ban overseas bribery.[42] In America, opposition was substantial and corporate interests, including the defence sector, still work against the strong enforcement of the FCPA today: *Forbes* magazine published a cover story in May 2010 effectively accusing FCPA prosecutors of imposing numerous and high fines in order to create a good market in the private sector for themselves when they leave the Department of Justice.[43]

The FCPA contains anti-bribery as well as record-keeping and accounting provisions. The former prohibit payments to foreign officials or political parties to 'obtain or retain business'. Payments seeking to obtain 'an improper advantage' are not formally outlawed, though the effect may well be the same with the courts applying the definition widely. However, 'facilitation payments', or grease payments as they're sometimes called, are allowed in an exception to the law. A facilitation payment is defined as a bribe for 'routine governmental action . . . which is ordinarily and commonly performed by a foreign official'.[44] This somewhat lessens the moral force of the statute.

The record-keeping and accounting provisions are intended to create a paper trail and prevent concealment of bribery. However, this second part of the FCPA only applies to corporations registered in the US which have to file periodic reports with the SEC.[45] The anti-bribery clause applies to all issuers, domestic concerns and related individuals. Therefore privately owned companies, ones not listed on the stock exchange that is, do not have to comply with the record-keeping provisions. It is, therefore, likely that a great deal of foreign bribery goes undetected, especially among smaller companies.

Another weakness of the Act is its limited scope when it comes to foreign subsidiaries not wholly owned by a US parent. A foreign company or person is subject to the FCPA if they play any role in a corrupt payment while within the US.[46] The Act only applies to the bribery of 'public officials'. Pertinent to the BAE case, the term includes members of the royal family.

The legislation, which is primarily enforced by the DOJ and the SEC, undoubtedly changed the behaviour of US companies abroad. However, the loopholes left in the Act were exploited. For example, the use of non-majority-controlled joint ventures overseas is a major method for US companies to pay bribes in Saudi Arabia. While American companies have instituted a culture of compliance plans domestically, international surveys suggest that often these are not communicated to foreign subsidiaries or implemented where bribery is most likely to take place.[47]

For many years after the introduction of the Act, enforcement seemed minimal amid significant push-back from both corporate interests and the administration, especially during Ronald Reagan's tenure. As the Act went through Congress and in later 1981 hearings, corporations argued that the SEC should not have any enforcement role in the FCPA, fearing intervention in global trading norms.[48] The executive branch under Reagan claimed that the SEC was improperly using the FCPA '. . . as a Trojan horse to get an extension of accounting standards to all companies when they do foreign business at all or not [sic]'.[49] The administration attempted to highlight examples of lost trade and increased costs of business caused by the Act. However, these arguments were contradicted by trade figures supplied by the Department of Commerce showing that US exports had increased in the years following the promulgation of the FCPA. In a 1981 survey by the GAO, of the 200 Fortune 1000 company respondents, two thirds said that the FCPA 'had little or no affect [sic] on business'.[50]

14. Taking the Mickey, the Toilet Seat and the Hammer . . . in a Galaxy Far, Far Away

The attitude to the FCPA reflected the Reagan administration's general support for business and the defence sector in particular. By the end of Jimmy Carter's administration, military spending was at its lowest level since 1951, consistent with US security needs. The US was not involved in any major conflict and détente with the Soviet Union had resulted in rough nuclear parity. However, to conservative hawks, including California's Governor Reagan, the Soviet Union was a military colossus in whose shadow the puny US was cowering.

George H. W. Bush, then Director of the CIA, constituted a panel, called Team B, to revise the official intelligence assessments of Soviet military strength. It included the hardline hawk Paul Wolfowitz. Armed with this information Reagan savaged the Carter administration throughout the presidential campaign of 1980 on its wimpishness in the arms race. Reagan, of course, had spent much of the 1950s giving anti-communist speeches as a representative of the General Electric Company.[1]

On assuming office, Reagan delivered on his rhetoric. With his hardline Defense Secretary, Caspar Weinberger, he pushed through $75bn in additional military spending in 1981 and 1982 alone, hitting a top line of $185bn in the fiscal year 1982 – a 39 per cent increase over 1980 levels. By the end of Reagan's second term military spending doubled, marking the largest peacetime military build-up in US history. This was a massive windfall for the MICC, with, for instance, Lockheed's Pentagon contracts doubling to $4bn a year from 1980 to 1983.[2]

Resistance to this massive build-up was slow in coming, partly because of its popularity among ordinary Americans. But towards the end of Reagan's first term, criticism was voiced of both the excessive size of the build-up at a time of growing deficits and social needs, and fear that the massive increase in nuclear weapons could exacerbate the risk of a superpower nuclear confrontation. The latter led to the nuclear freeze campaign, one of the most inspiring citizens' movements of the twentieth century, while the former forced at least a slow-down in the military build-up.

Among the most effective tools of Reagan's critics were two vastly overpriced items: a $600 toilet seat and a $7,662 coffeemaker. At a time when Caspar Weinberger was telling Congress that there wasn't 'an ounce of waste' in the largest peacetime military budget in the nation's history, the spare parts scandal opened the door to a more objective – and damning – assessment of what the tens of billions in new spending was actually paying for. It also opened up Weinberger to ridicule, symbolized most enduringly in a series of cartoons by the *Washington Post* cartoonist Herblock in which the Defense Secretary was routinely shown with a toilet seat around his neck. Appropriately enough, the coffeemaker was procured for Lockheed's C-5A transport plane, the poster child for cost overruns and abject performance.[3]

A young journalist, who had been mentored by the Pentagon whistle-blower Ernie Fitzgerald, was central to exposing the scandals. Dina Rasor fingered the aircraft engine makers Pratt & Whitney for thirty-four engine parts that had all increased in price by more than 300 per cent in a year. A procurement official noted in the memo which revealed the scam that 'Pratt & Whitney has never had to control prices and it will be difficult for them to learn.'[4] The Air Force responded that the increases were justified, confirming Fitzgerald's view that 'Generally the public relations people [in the Air Force] lie instinctively, even when the truth would serve them better.'[5] This profiteering at the taxpayer's expense was surpassed by the Gould Corporation, which provided the Navy with a simple claw hammer, sold in a hardware store for $7, at a price of $435. The Navy suggested the charges – $37 for engineering support, $93 for manufacturing support and a $56 fee that was clear profit – were acceptable.[6]

Further revelations included Lockheed charging the Pentagon $591 for a clock for the C-5A and $166,000 for a cowling door to cover the engines. The exorbitant coffeemakers were exposed as poorly made and needing frequent repairs. Lockheed was also billing the taxpayer over $670 for an armrest pad that the Air Force could make itself for between $5 and $25. Finally, it was discovered that a $181 flashlight was built with twenty-year-old technology and a better one could be bought off the shelf for a fraction of the cost.[7]

Lockheed defended itself by pointing out that spare parts were only 1.6 per cent of the defence budget, suggesting that those uncovering the fraud, waste and abuse were the enemies of peace and freedom and should remain silent in the interests of national unity in the face of global adversaries. Ernie Fitzgerald again brought sanity to bear, by suggesting that an overcharge was an overcharge, and that the same procurement practices used with toilet covers and coffeemakers when applied to whole aircraft like the C-5A made the planes 'a flying collection of spare parts'.[8]

Rasor also revealed that the Air Force planned to pay Lockheed $1.5bn to fix severe problems with the wings on the C-5A that the company itself had created. The wing fix was little more than a multibillion-dollar bail-out for Lockheed.[9]

Despite this litany of disasters, the Air Force engaged in illegal lobbying to help Lockheed win the contract to build the next-generation transport plane. In August 1981, a McDonnell Douglas plane was selected for the project, with the Air Force concerned about Lockheed's proposed C-5B. Two weeks later the Air Force reversed its decision. Rasor could not believe that the Air Force 'would want to have an updated version of one of its most embarrassing procurements'.[10] She and Ernie Fitzgerald concluded that this had to be yet another bailout of the company.

When Boeing then put forward an impressive and much cheaper alternative and Henry Jackson, known as 'the Senator from Boeing', persuaded his Senate colleagues to support it, the Pentagon, Air Force and Lockheed leaped into action. A ninety-six-page lobbying plan detailed the use of generals, the Senate majority leader Howard Baker, the Secretary of the Air Force, the Deputy Secretary of Defense and President Reagan himself to secure the votes of lawmakers. The civil rights leader and Atlanta mayor, Andrew Young, was drafted in to lobby members of the Congressional Black Caucus.[11]

The Pentagon and Lockheed coordinated assignments with the manufacturer calling the shots, to the extent of drafting the Defense Secretary's position paper on the C-5B,* while the Air Force provided customized pictures for use in a full-page ad in the *Washington Post*. But the heart of the lobbying effort was pure pork barrel politics. The House Speaker 'Tip' O'Neil, Representative Glenn Anderson and Senator Carl Levin of Michigan were brought onside by subcontractors with the prospect of jobs in their areas.[12]

---

* The Department of Defense's Congressional liaison office, a body only providing information, drafted a 'Dear colleague' letter which is meant to be a communication from one or more members of Congress to their legislative colleagues.

Once the lobbying scheme was exposed, the Air Force and Lockheed were unapologetic, with Lieutenant General Kelly Burke, who oversaw the C-5 programme, claiming: 'You're just wrong if you think this is a highly unusual happening . . . all you're seeing is democracy in action. This is how the system is supposed to work.'[13]

Not everyone agreed. A General Accounting Office report called for investigations of possible criminal violations of the law restricting lobbying activities by executive branch officials and whether the coordination with contractors also violated the law. On the second point, the report noted: 'Since the Air Force is prohibited from directly mounting a grass-roots lobbying campaign . . . it follows that it may not engage in a network of defense contractors to do the same thing.'[14] The GAO felt strongly that salaries paid to Air Force and Defense Department officials during the joint lobbying campaign with Lockheed were an improper use of public funds. Ernie Fitzgerald was highly sceptical whether the referral of these matters to the Justice Department would go anywhere, suggesting it was like 'asking the King's lawyers to prosecute the King's men for doing the King's business'.[15] Calls for a special prosecutor to investigate the case were ignored. Fitzgerald was proved right.

This incident captured the structural malaise that continues to affect the procurement process. As Bill Hartung points out:

> All the same elements are present when weapon systems are up for debate: Industry and Pentagon lobbyists swarm Capitol Hill; pressure is ratcheted up on members of the Armed Services and Defense Appropriations Committee in the House and Senate, many of whom have had key production facilities placed in their states or districts; key members receive generous political contributions from the producer of the system and its subcontractors; and official reports and testimony are created that make a one-sided case for the weapons system in question, often with the aid of the contractors.[16]

This is the iron triangle in action, leading to gargantuan defence budgets and questionable weapons purchases.[17] Even liberal lawmakers who often denounce waste and abuse in the military budget are transformed into military budget boosters when the possibility of weapons being built in their areas arise. For instance, an attempt to kill the F-18 project due to extreme cost overruns and performance problems was strongly countered by the prominent liberals Ted Kennedy and Alan Cranston, just as Cranston had supported the Lockheed bailout a decade earlier.

Reagan's pet project, however, was the missile defence programme. In March 1983, in response to dire approval ratings and with 57 per cent of the country worried that he might involve the US in a nuclear war, Reagan pledged to find technologies that would render nuclear weapons 'impotent and obsolete' in what became known as his 'Star Wars' speech.[18] The Secretary of State, George Shultz, regarded the notion, which had been championed by the conservative 'Prince of Darkness' Richard Perle, as ludicrous. Lockheed was responsible for, and benefited financially from, one of the myriad technologies that comprised the Strategic Defense Initiative (SDI). Its Homing Overlay Experiment – interceptor warheads that would unfurl umbrella-like spokes – was tested successfully in June 1984, after three failed tests had threatened the future of the initiative. To this day the company brags about the test which, it turns out, was rigged. A decade later the GAO reported that the mock warhead used in the test had been 'enhanced' to make it easier to hit. By that time $35bn had been spent on Star Wars. So, displaying its customary lack of ethics, the company cooperated with the Army to once again dupe the American taxpayer out of billions of dollars.

The Reagan administration that was so desperate to reward defence contractors, and particularly Lockheed, was equally determined to remove as many regulatory restraints on the private sector as possible. And this included weakening the provisions of the FCPA. In 1988, in response to business lobbying, amendments were made to the Act that weakened its effectiveness. The 'grease payment' exception was widened from the original definition including just officials 'whose duties are essentially ministerial or clerical' to all officials where the purpose was for a 'routine governmental action'. According to Senator Heinz, one of the principal sponsors of the amendments, the changes embodied an effort to eliminate some exportation obstacles facing US firms in the era of a burdensome trade deficit.[19]

And a clause prohibiting any payment to a third party 'while knowing or having reason to know that all or a portion' of the payment would be used to bribe foreign officials was amended to exclude the 'reason to know' phrase, so that liability only applied where the payment was made with 'knowledge' that it would be used for bribery. This is a much harder test to prove. Also added were two defences, to wit: if payment was lawful under the laws and regulations of the foreign country, and if the payment was reasonable expenditure on behalf of a foreign official for promotion of a transaction or contract with a foreign government or agency.[20] This is of course highly relevant when dealing with pervasively corrupt countries such as Saudi Arabia.

There is also a national security exception to the FCPA which the CIA added as it was adopted. This exemption means that any company taking part in what the CIA has designated a national security operation does not have to inform the SEC of foreign payments. A memorandum from a meeting between the CIA general counsel and a Congressional investigator, Peter Stockton, in 1998 showed that there were a 'whole series' of US companies exempted from notifying the SEC, as they were CIA fronts. Stockton wrote: 'How does the SEC assume that there are no abuses by companies with these exemptions . . . is it a license to bribe?'[21] This was a massive boon for the arms trade, both the formal companies and the many dealers contracting business in or with the US. For instance, the massive payment of bribes to facilitate the Iran–Contra fiasco was exempt from the jurisdiction of the FCPA.[22]

Iran–Contra, which in the words of the independent counsel in the investigation, was 'a conspiracy that drew in the chief actors of the [Reagan] administration',[23] violated the Arms Export Control Act and contravened at least one other Act of Congress. The scandal and its cover-up, which also involved the Saudis and Israelis, eventually led to the conviction of eleven members of President Reagan's administration, including the Defense Secretary, Caspar Weinberger. George H. W. Bush, Vice President at the time, pardoned all eleven when he became President. Iran–Contra remains one of the most egregious examples of the illegal use of the arms trade in pursuit of political objectives, and profit. It also reiterates the extent to which arms-trading activities, in pursuit of covert goals, are above the law, including the FCPA.

For the Pentagon insider Chuck Spinney, the Reagan years marked the apex of military madness. Informed by his involvement in the small group around John Boyd, in 1980 Spinney produced a document entitled *Defense Facts of Life* which sharply criticized defence budgeting. It explained how the pursuit of complex technology produced expensive, scarce and inefficient weapons. Like an addict destroying his life, the Air Force had spent so much on its addiction to expensive and technologically overcomplicated systems that it couldn't maintain those systems. The technology tail was wagging the dog. He believed that a propensity towards expensive high-tech product development and acquisition was weakening America's defences from within. The folly of this approach was displayed in the Iran hostage crisis, in which the mission to free the hostages held by Iranian revolutionaries in April 1980 failed miserably due to a series of technical equipment failures, including a crash involving two of the US helicopters.[24]

Senator Sam Nunn became interested in the work of the Military Reform Movement and asked to see Spinney. The Pentagon said no. Nunn threatened to use a subpoena before it relented. The Senator requested an unclassified report on the material. Spinney spent that Christmas writing it up.

The new year heralded the arrival of the Reagan administration and the new Defense Secretary, Casper Weinberger. Spinney describes Weinberger's Senate confirmation as 'a big love-in because all these guys in the Armed Services Committee want to do is throw money at the Pentagon'. And Sam Nunn was thought of as one of them by Spinney. As he tells it:

> Nunn is considered to be a wholly-owned subsidiary of the Pentagon. No one is expecting anything from him. But he said: 'I have this report in my hands, the more money you spend the worse things are going to get and this report is being squelched in the Pentagon.' The press went berserk, demanding the report. It caused a run on the Pentagon, they printed over 2,000 copies. So all of a sudden I am *persona non grata* big time and I get the order 'you are not working on this any more.' So I said 'OK.' I had already figured out that going specifically into the procurement programme was the next step, so I just started working on that.[25]

Spinney commenced work on what he called *The Plans/Reality Mismatch*,[26] which revealed the disparity between what the defence sector had promised at the time it sought Congressional appropriations for certain programmes and what was ultimately delivered. It showed that when quantities went down, costs went up. Explosively, Spinney exposed the vast gulf between the amount requested for the defence budget and the actual amount spent: Reagan's real defence spending was at least $500bn more than the five-year total he had projected in his request for the 1984 budget. 'But, of course, no one wanted to see that type of thing.' To thwart Spinney his bosses commissioned an evaluation of his work. Because they refused to release his findings, Spinney started to give briefings on his work to the press in motel rooms in the evenings.

> Out of the blue I get a call from an acquaintance in the office of the Defense Secretary. 'I have got something I want to show you.' He shows me an Air Force study and while I am reading this thing he says: 'You know this study is saying the same thing you are saying, saying it differently, but it is basically in agreement.' And I am saying, 'yeah, yeah, I would sure like to get my hands on this.' And he says, 'well it's yours.' So here we have this unclassified document put together by a bunch of retired 3 and 4 star generals and it basically says they are in a melt-down.
>
> The Pentagon is starting to go bonkers because all the reporters want my report, which most of them have seen now. We unleashed the Air Force report, and then the Heritage report came out [saying something similar].
>
> Senator Grassley, who was a freshman Senator from Iowa, very conservative, heard about this and was really interested. Bear in mind this is at the height of Reagan's popularity and Grassley decides he is going to take Reagan on. Which was gutsy. He decides he wants to have a meeting with me, but they are telling me that I can't have a meeting with him. But John [Boyd] tells me: 'OK, Chuck, I am not going to tell you anything but you just be in your office for the next couple of hours.' What I did not know was that Grassley got into his car and drove over to the Pentagon, walked up to the Secretary of Defense's office, barged in and says 'I want to meet Chuck Spinney.' So they say to Grassley that I am not available. Grassley knows, of course, that I am available, so he is pissed and thinks: 'I am a senator and he can't do that to me.' So he goes back and uses the stonewalling to build-up momentum for a hearing. By March [1983] he had built support for the hearing and they were going to subpoena me. Weinberger said: 'just let him go over, they'll forget about it in a couple of weeks.'
>
> Now *Time* decide they want to do a story on it. They are trying to decide what to put on the cover. They were talking about Boyd, but he didn't want to do it. John basically said to them: 'Look, you've got to put Spinney on the cover and the reason is very simple. From your standpoint it's David versus Goliath and he is going to need protection because when they have this hearing his ass is grass.' They said 'OK' and he says 'I will see if Spinney

will go along.' So the next day Boyd says to me, 'Do you want to be on the cover of *Time*?' And I said 'fuck no!! Jesus Christ!!' He says 'listen, when we have this hearing you know what is going to happen, this is the best insurance you can possibly get. You think about it and let's talk tomorrow.' I thought about it and he was right, there was no choice, I had to do it.

Meanwhile the Pentagon convinced Senator John Tower, Chairman of the Senate Armed Services Committee and another of their wholly-owned subsidiaries, to hold the hearing on a Friday because everyone leaves town on a Thursday, and you get a little coverage in the weekend papers and it's over. This is a standard tactic of the Pentagon's. They were going to put it in a little tiny room. Grassley went berserk. He says 'we are having a joint hearing.' It's the only time they have ever had a joint hearing of the Senate Budget and the Senate Armed Services committees. It ends up being in the Caucus room where they had their Oliver North and the McCarthy hearings. It's a standing room only crowd. To give you an idea as to how stupid the Pentagon was, the *Time* guys that week are lathering up all the people in Congress, going around the hill saying: 'listen we are putting Spinney on the cover, we are going to make a big deal about this hearing.' So all the members want to show up at the hearing. The Pentagon did not have a clue. It's just incredible.

Finally, I give the presentation for two hours in front of eight TV cameras.

Time came out on the following Monday. Before it had been delivered to the Pentagon there was a staff meeting in Weinberger's office. I had a friend who was there and he told me that John Layman, Secretary of the Navy said, 'Well that Spinney thing is taken care of. There was a couple of blurbs at the weekend but that's the last we are going to hear of that'. Then the *Time* story was released and all hell broke loose. They had to take several truckloads of copies to the Pentagon. Walt Mossberg, the *Wall Street Journal* reporter, calls me up and he says 'I was on the phone to the Assistant Secretary for Public Affairs and he is reading me the riot act about an article I wrote which didn't have anything to do with you. They are just complaining about what I wrote and all of a sudden the Assistant Secretary goes, 'Oh my god, oh my god.' Mossberg goes 'what's the matter?' 'I just got hold of *Time* Magazine and Spinney is on the cover.' And Mossberg says 'ahh that's just a joke, they are just jerking your chain.' And he says 'no, no it's true, it's true, I got to go.'

My buddy Ray Leopold came in with a whole stack of them and handed them out. He gave one to Boyd, who was sitting there with his feet up on the desk, leaning back and he looks at it and just threw it over in the corner and says, 'well that's done.' By his action he was telling me in effect 'look this is just business, don't let it go to your head.' But it caused a huge ruckus and really gave a big boost to the reform movement. Grassley has said in several speeches on the Senate floor that it was that hearing, and our work, that enabled him to put together the coalition that froze the Reagan budget in 1985. So it had a big impact.

After this momentous intervention, Spinney was left alone. He continued to work on inefficiencies within the defence system. But they were afraid to even look at it seriously. 'The long and short of it,' says Chuck, sitting in his Alexandria apartment, 'from 1988/89 I was never given anything to do. Until I retired in 2003 I was not given one official task. But I was a busy guy. I produced more stuff than anybody in my organization.'

Reagan's profligacy continued under George H.W. Bush, whose military spending breached \$450bn in 1989.[27] Hardly surprising given that both Bush's grandfathers were present at the creation of the MICC and its intelligence-gathering adjunct, the American International Corporation.[28] The Walker and Bush families have epitomized and risen alongside the emergence of the complex, the post-1945 national security state and what the dynasty's chronicler, Kevin Phillips, describes as the twenty-first-century imperium.[29]

Crucial to the Bushes' rise to fortune, if not fame, has been their business relationship with the Saudi royal family. Craig Unger, author of *House of Bush, House of Saud*, calculates that approximately \$1.4bn was transferred between individuals and entities connected to the House of Saud and those connected to the Bushes. The House of Bush is defined here as George W. Bush, George H. W. Bush, James A. Baker III, Dick Cheney and the major institutions they are tied to, including the George H. W. Presidential Library, the Carlyle Group and Halliburton. The House of Saud includes members of the royal family, companies controlled by them and members of the merchant elite such as the bin Laden and bin Mahfouz families, whose fortunes are closely tied to the royal family.[30]

An Air Force mate of George W.'s, James Bath, acted as a gatekeeper to provide the Saudis with access to the Bushes. He was very close to the bin Laden business empire, especially Salem bin Laden and another Saudi businessman, Khalid bin Mahfouz, whom the CIA, probably erroneously, identified as a half-brother of Osama bin Laden. Bath was also connected with a number of those involved in the Iran–Contra scandal. He invested $50,000 in one of George W.'s early oil companies.[31] When the company was bought by Harken Energy, with George W. becoming a Harken board member, a Saudi investor, Abdullah Taha Bakhsh, became the company's third-largest investor.[32]

The controversial Carlyle Group is the other major string in the links between the Bush family and the House of Saud. The group was, at its inception in 1987, a new business model in private equity investing. It was effectively built from the ground up to specialize in taking advantage of the revolving door mechanics of governments.

The story of Carlyle exemplifies the MICC in one company, with the coming together of an expansive US military, big business and high-power politics. Carlyle has targeted companies to invest in, whose business is largely determined by the actions of government; whether through regulatory change, because the government provided the company's contracts or as a consequence of Carlyle's big political names opening doors around the world. By having special knowledge of the political future or being able to change the political present, Carlyle was ranked the largest private equity firm in the world, mastering the art of 'access capitalism'. The firm's Washington offices are at 1001 Pennsylvania Avenue, at the heart of US power. In 2010, the company had $90.5bn under management.[33]

The Carlyle political glitterati have included Bush senior, his Secretary of State, James Baker III, who was reported to have introduced Carlyle to members of the Saudi royal family,[34] and George W., who in 1990 was appointed to the board of directors of one of Carlyle's first acquisitions, an airline food business. Bush left the board in 1992 to run for Governor of Texas.[35] After his election Governor Bush appointed the members of the board responsible for the Texas teachers' pension funds, which a few years later chose to invest $100m in Carlyle.[36] Frank C. Carlucci, the Carlyle chairman and chairman emeritus from 1989 to 2005, was a former Secretary of Defense,[37] while Arthur Levitt, Chairman of the SEC under Bill Clinton, has been a Carlyle Senior Advisor from 2001.[38] The former British Prime Minister, John Major, joined Carlyle as an adviser in 1998, and was chairman of Carlyle Europe from 2002 until 2005.[39] Fidel V. Ramos, former President of the Philippines,[40] and Thaksin Shinawatra, twice Prime Minister of Thailand and thereafter found guilty of corruption, *in abstentia*, were both members of Carlyle's Asia Advisory Board.[41] The company has also boasted a former White House Chief of Staff to Clinton,[42] a former Under Secretary of the US Treasury under George W.,[43] a retired four-star US General, who is also on the board of BAE Systems Inc. (BAE's US subsidiary),[44] and a two-term Chairman of the Joint Chiefs of Staff in the Clinton administration.[45]

The Carlyle Group has established a number of firsts in the US, including the first time a former President has toiled on behalf of a defence contractor and the first time a former President advised his son, while the latter was holding office, on foreign policy decisions that had a direct impact on the financial fortunes of them both.[46]

'It's not possible to get closer to the administration than Carlyle is,' asserted Charles Lewis, Director of the Center for Public Integrity during the administration of George W. Bush. 'George Bush senior earned money from private interests that worked for the government of which his son was President. You could even say that the president could one day profit financially, through his father's investments, from the political decisions he himself took.'[47]

Carlyle has a prominent role in the arms business. At one time, Carlyle's combined investments in the arms industry made it the US's eleventh-largest defence contractor and a major arms exporter to Turkey and Saudi Arabia.[48]

In the UK it was involved in the highly controversial privatization of the arms research company QinetiQ, from which the group and a number of civil servants made enormous profits after acquiring a stake in the company before it was floated on the Stock Exchange. The top ten managers gained a return on investment of 19,900 per cent. Accusations were levelled that the initial stake sold by government was significantly undervalued.[49]

In October 1997, Carlyle acquired United Defense Industries.[50] It went public on the New York Stock Exchange in December 2001 with Carlyle retaining a stock ownership position. United Defense primarily supplies the US military and is known for the Bradley Fighting Vehicle, and purchased the Bofors heavy-weapons division in 2000.[51] Carlyle completed the sale of all of its United Defense stock and exited the company in April

2004.[52] The next year BAE purchased United Defense.[53] Carlyle sold another significant arms business, Vought, in March 2010 for $1.44bn.[54] It makes components used in the F-22 , the F-35, Black Hawk helicopters and the Global Hawk UAV.[55]

Through a 51 per cent joint venture with the Saudi government, Carlyle's United Defense provided tactical training and maintenance for the thousands of Bradley Fighting Vehicles purchased by the Royal Saudi Land Forces after the Gulf War.[56] Carlyle was also, for a time, the official offset adviser to Saudi Arabia,[57] in charge of the programme in which US companies dealing with the Saudi military were supposed to invest 35 per cent of earnings from every sale into the kingdom.[58] This programme was described as 'a disaster' by a Saudi official.[59]

The closest link between Carlyle and the Saudi military establishment occurred shortly after the appointment of Frank Carlucci to the company's board. In 1990, he spearheaded the $130m acquisition of BDM Consulting. BDM was a specialist in the defence-contracting business and had a formidable network of contacts thanks to its CEO, Earle Williams, a close friend of Carlucci. At the time, defence contracts were being slashed as the Cold War ended and cheap buyout opportunities were everywhere. Carlyle identified a target, Vinnell, arguably the first modern mercenary corporation hired by the US government.

Vinnell started out building airstrips during the Vietnam War, but by the 1970s was training Saudi troops to protect oilfields. Traditionally, the US government provided military training to foreign governments directly. However, in 1975 Vinnell won a $77m contract to train the Saudi Arabian National Guard, the first time an American civilian company obtained an independent contract to provide a foreign government with military services. The contract has been renewed ever since for a total estimated value of almost $500m.[60] Another five-year contract, awarded in 1998, has an estimated value of $831m and involves 280 US government personnel and 1,400 Vinnell staff at various locations in Saudi Arabia.[61]

Carlyle sold its interest in Vinnell in 1997.[62] It is currently owned by Northrop Grumman and has raised eyebrows around its profligate political giving. Between 1990 and 2002, Vinnell gave $8,517,247 in US campaign contributions, a close second to General Electric's $8,843,884.[63]

But the most profound connection between Carlyle and Saudi Arabia is in the direct investments placed by the royal family in the private equity house. When the group started working in Saudi Arabia in the early 1990s, it operated through Prince Alwaleed bin Talal bin Abdul Aziz Al-Saud,[64] a nephew of King Fahd.[65] Alwaleed bin Talal has become one of the biggest foreign investors in the United States with investments in Citicorp, Compaq, Disney and Kodak. A 2001 CNN report identified him as the sixth-wealthiest man in the world.[66] The source of all of the Prince's wealth is not known but he acted as a middleman linking foreign construction businesses and Saudi companies. In 1991, when Citicorp was close to collapse after the savings and loans crisis, the Prince invested $600m in the company in a deal facilitated by Carlyle, which handled the political and regulatory ramifications of a massive Saudi investment in a US bank.[67] The funding was viewed by some as a *quid pro quo* for the US intervention against Iraq in the Gulf War.[68] 'The deal gave us an enormous profile in Saudi Arabia,' says Stephen Norris, one of the founders of Carlyle.[69] Thanks to that deal and the access provided by Prince Alwaleed bin Talal, Carlyle expanded its business in the kingdom exponentially. The following year Carlyle bought Vinnell.

Investors in Carlyle have included Princes Sultan and Bandar. In addition, they encouraged other wealthy Saudis to invest as a favour to George H. W. Bush.[70] Carlyle claims that Saudi citizens have invested less than 1 per cent of the capital that it manages. However, a former Carlyle employee suggests that the firm doesn't know the origin of some funds invested from offshore havens such as the Cayman Islands. The firm denied this.[71] One of the most important Saudi investors in Carlyle was the bin Laden family, who invested at least $2m in 1995.[72] A significant factor in the deal was the drawing power of James Baker, who 'knew them very well' and was the family's 'favourite politician' according to Charles Schwartz, a Houston lawyer who represented bin Laden family interests in Texas.[73] Shafiq bin Laden was the family's representative at Carlyle conferences and at a group investors' conference in Washington DC when the 9/11 attacks occurred.[74]

The end of the Cold War, a watershed for the defence industry, and the denouement of the Reagan era, heralded not only the indictment of Oliver North and his cronies – including arms agent Sam Cummings, who had links to the Merex network – but also ultimately saw the sobering corporate collapses of Enron, Worldcom and others. Defence spending started to reduce at the beginning of the nineties, as the US, in the words of the head of the Joint Chiefs of Staff, Colin Powell, 'was running out of enemies'.[75] The consequent defence cuts, which saw arms procurement and research fall to half the levels attained at the height of the Reagan military build-up, led to significant restructuring of the sector.

Lockheed used the opportunity of consolidation to transform itself into the world's largest weapons manufacturer through a series of mergers and acquisitions. The most significant was with Martin Marietta in 1995, creating Lockheed Martin and installing Norm Augustine as the merged entity's CEO. The following year, Augustine paid a massive $9.1bn for the defence electronics company Loral Corporation. The behemoth, which topped the list of Pentagon-financed companies year after year, became the number one recipient of funds from NASA, number two on the Department of Energy's list of nuclear weapons contractors and a major supplier of goods and services to the IRS and the US Postal Service. During the 1990s the company also diversified for a few years into the provision of social services.[76]

Under Augustine's leadership Lockheed Martin intensified its lobbying efforts to unparalleled heights. As Hartung has noted, the CEO was not just wired into the Washington policymaking process, 'for much of his career he had been one of a handful of people drawing up the blueprints for American defense policies and deciding where the wiring should be placed'.[77] In addition to running the world's largest defence contractor, Augustine served on the Defense Policy Advisory Committee on Trade (DPACT), part of the network of little-known organizations 'that often outrank Congress in their influence over the size and shape of the [defence] budget'.[78] DPACT provides confidential advice to the Secretary of Defense on arms export policies. Augustine also chaired the Defense Science Board – a Pentagon advisory panel with the power to approve or reject nascent weapons programmes – and was president of the Association of the US Army, made up of retired army personnel and major contractors.

He had turned down an offer from President George H. W. Bush to serve as his Defense Secretary but was a long-time business associate of William Perry and John Deutch, who went on to become Defense Secretary and CIA Director respectively in the Clinton administration. Augustine used his connections quite blatantly not only to influence all manner of public policy but also to help his company win new contracts and subsidies.

These personal links and the organizations in which Augustine played so prominent a role exemplify why the arms business in the US is a closed shop that cannot operate in the best interests of taxpayers but rather serves the contractors and the military hierarchy.

In the first three years of Clinton's term Augustine vigorously promoted a series of major initiatives that yielded billions of dollars for the company. His boldest move was the creation of a government policy that subsidized the arms industry mergers of the time with taxpayer dollars, yielding billions of dollars for the merged Lockheed Martin. He was also pivotal in creating new subsidies for arms merchants and their preferred customers – a $15bn loan guarantee fund to finance US arms exports and a $200m-plus tax break for foreign arms purchasers. And he was key in persuading the Newt Gingrich-led, Republican-controlled Congress to add billions in funding to key Lockheed Martin projects, ranging from the F-22 combat aircraft to the 'Star Wars' missile defence programme. The F-22 was built in a factory adjacent to Gingrich's Georgia district.

The intense lobbying of Augustine and his successors, and the welcoming attitude of lawmakers, made it virtually impossible to reduce the military budget to reasonable levels, even in times of reduced threat such as the immediate post-Cold War period.[79]

Augustine's *modus operandi* was laid bare in Congressional scrutiny of Bill Clinton's decision to implement the policy that yielded billions of dollars in Pentagon 'restructuring costs' to companies like Lockheed, Martin Marietta and Boeing. A one-page memo from John Deutch, then Under Secretary of Defense, authorized federal funding for closing plants, relocating equipment, severance payments, and 'golden parachutes' for board members and executives. The memo was approved by the Deputy Defense Secretary, Bill Perry. Because of their business links to Augustine, both Deutch and Perry had to receive special conflict of interest waivers to approve the policy change advocated by their associate.[80]

It was revealed that Perry's firm, Technology Strategies Alliances (TSA), had a contract with Martin Marietta until just a few months before his appointment to the Clinton administration. Deutch pocketed $42,500 in 1992 as part of a nine-year consulting arrangement with Augustine's firm. In his letter justifying lifting the conflict of interest ban on Perry and Deutch *vis-à-vis* Martin Marietta, the Defense Secretary at the time, Les Aspin, argued that 'for both Perry and Deutch the interest of the government outweighed the concern that a reasonable person would question their impartiality'.[81] As if to emphasize the questionable nature of the arrangement, it was rushed through without notifying Congress and without publishing it in the *Federal Register*, where many significant government decisions are recorded.

The idea of the complex subsidies was that the costs the government put into restructuring would be recouped later from contracts for weapons systems. In reality, as a Reagan Pentagon official, Lawrence Korb, has noted, there is no evidence that any weapon system got cheaper as a result of the merger subsidies. In fact, weapons costs increased in their wake. Lockheed Martin benefited by as much as $1.8bn from the policy, while Augustine himself was the biggest beneficiary of the 'golden parachute' payments, in spite of ending up as CEO of the merged entity. He netted $8.2m in bonuses for 'leaving' Martin Marietta, of which almost $3m was paid for with taxpayer dollars.[82] The more than 19,000 workers who were laid off in the merger received little assistance. No officials were willing to testify against the subsidies because, as one of them put it, 'Norm Augustine really wants this' and no one wanted to cross him.[83] The 'payoffs for layoffs' scandal illustrated that a company like Lockheed Martin has too many resources and too influential a network for the average elected official to contend with.

Under Augustine, Lockheed had set a goal of doubling its arms exports within five years. A real obstacle to achieving this was that few countries could afford the multibillion-dollar cost of the company's sophisticated weaponry. As Chairman of the DPACT Augustine led the effort to create a new arms export subsidy; a $15bn fund that would provide low-rate US government-backed loans to potential arms-buying countries. With the arrival of Newt Gingrich's conservative revolution in Congress the fund was approved and signed by President Clinton in December 1995.

Armed with this new 'open chequebook for arms sales', Augustine and Lockheed's vice-president for International Operations, Bruce Jackson, determined that their best hope of new business lay in an extended NATO. New entrants to the military alliance would be required to replace their Soviet-era weapons with systems compatible with NATO's dominant

Western members. Augustine toured Eastern Europe. In Romania he pledged that if the country's government bought a new radar system from Lockheed Martin, the company would use its considerable clout in Washington to promote Bucharest's NATO candidacy. In other words, a major defence manufacturer made clear that it was willing to reshape American international security and foreign policy to secure an arms order.

After stepping down as CEO in 1998, but remaining as chairman for another six years, Augustine went on to serve as an adviser to the CIA in forming its own venture capital company, In-Q-Tel. He was also an influential member of a panel established by the Defense Secretary, William Cohen, to assess whether the Marines should proceed with the production of a troubled aircraft, the V-22, produced by Boeing. Despite two crashes during testing that resulted in the deaths of twenty-three marines, Augustine opined that 'the V-22 will turn out to be a very fine flying machine'.[84] In typical Washington style, no one raised any questions about the conflict of interest in Augustine's role in bailing out the project, given that his company and Boeing had been partners on multibillion-dollar projects such as the F-22. Augustine was awarded an honorary doctorate from Princeton in 2007. No one mentioned the damage done to the American taxpayer by the ease with which Augustine could use his government access to earn billions for his company.

Augustine's successor, Bruce Jackson, was no slouch either when it came to influencing government policy to favour Lockheed Martin. He served as a Director of the neocon Project for the New American Century (PNAC), which, during the Clinton years, called for a 'Reaganite policy of military strength and moral clarity', active intervention against recalcitrant regimes like Saddam's Iraq, not to say massive defence budgets.[85] Jackson's similarly hawkish confrères at the PNAC included Paul Wolfowitz, Donald Rumsfeld, Dick Cheney, former Congressman Vin Weber, who became a Lockheed Martin lobbyist, and George W. Bush's brother, Jeb. While Jackson influenced direction from outside government, a troop of Lockheed Martin executives accompanied Cheney and Rumsfeld into the Bush administration. Cheney's wife, Lynne, served on Lockheed Martin's board from 1994 to 2001, earning $120,000 a year, before stepping down shortly before her husband took office with his own inextricable ties to Halliburton.[86]

Bruce Jackson, however, was also a Republican Party activist of standing. Prior to the party's 2000 convention that nominated George W. and for which Jackson drafted the foreign policy platform, he was allegedly overheard telling colleagues from other arms firms that they had 'nothing to worry about. I'll be drafting the platform.'[87] During the 1990s, Jackson chaired the US Committee to Expand NATO . . . and defence contractors' market opportunities. The company spent furiously to influence votes in favour of expansion in the Senate. In the 1995/96 election cycle alone, the company and its executives distributed $2.3m in political donations.[88]

This all paid off when in late 2003 Lockheed Martin sold F-16s worth $3.8bn to Poland. The sale was accompanied by a subsidized loan that covered 100 per cent of the cost at a below-market rate and with no payments required for the first eight years. The cost to the US went beyond the subsidized loan. It included about $3bn in offsets, including an agreement to produce the planes' engines in Poland, among other things. The reality is that while the deal may have been good for Lockheed Martin, it was not for other US firms and workers.

Bidding for the Polish deal was marred by corruption from the outset. On 7 July 2001, the Deputy Defence Minister, Romuald Szeremietiew, was suspended. His assistant, Zbigniew Farmus, was arrested on 10 July trying to flee the country on a ferry to Sweden. Farmus was charged with illegal access to state and NATO secrets, which were sold to bidding competitors, and soliciting bribes in exchange for contracts. Szeremietiew, who was in charge of weapons procurement, was suspected of complicity in the bribe taking and the leaks.[89]

Thereafter, in a revised process, Lockheed Martin's F-16, Dassault's Mirage 2000 and BAE/Saab's Gripen were considered. A Polish commentator claimed that 'Lockheed Martin didn't win the contract, the US government did, with pressure and support coming from the very highest levels. They created a program that, politically and economically, was very hard to say no to.'[90]

A source with links to Lockheed's competitors claims that the US tactics in the deal were not all above board, and allegedly included electronic eavesdropping of the European consortia and access to confidential competitor information. Threats were also supposedly made to curtail future procurement opportunities and the maintenance and upgrade of existing US equipment previously donated to Poland if the deal was not awarded to the Americans. Blocking multilateral financial assistance as well as limiting Poland's role in NATO and US military planning in Europe and the Baltics were also allegedly threatened. I have been unable to verify this account with other sources, but assume that there may be kernels of truth amid the competitor hyperbole.

As the Polish News Agency has reported, since the completion of the deal, the F-16s have been dogged by problems. On two occasions jets have been forced to make emergency landings due to avionics failures. And, according to *Newsweek Polska*, 'since the Polish Air Force began operating the F-16s in December last year, dozens of faults and defects have been detected in the fighter planes' equipment. All repair costs are borne by the Polish military, because the Polish government failed to include clauses on guaranteed repairs and services in the purchase agreement. As of today, the defense ministry has ordered spare parts for the F-16 jets for $123m that are to satisfy demands until 2010.'[91]

So while on the home front Lockheed Martin and the MICC were taking the mickey, abroad the same actors were acting tough to get their way. But the good times were only just beginning.

As George W. and his Cabinet took up their posts in January 2001 the need for new sources of growth for US corporations was urgent: the tech bubble had burst and the Dow tumbled 824 points in their first two and a half months in office. Bush's solution was to reduce taxes and grant lucrative government contracts.

Military thinkers and actors dominated the new White House and the key departments of state, both military and civilian. Over thirty senior arms industry executives, consultants or advisers were placed in key positions in the military and across government.[92] To some it seemed they were there to disburse contracts back to their companies. This practice reached its zenith when the former COO of Lockheed Martin, Peter Teets, became Under Secretary for the Air Force and Director of the National Reconnaissance Office, a former Enron executive became Secretary of the Army, a vice-president of General Dynamics Secretary of the Navy and a Northrop executive Secretary of the Air Force.[93]

More than half a dozen important policy positions in the Bush administration were occupied by Lockheed Martin executives, lobbyists or lawyers, reflecting the influence of defence contractors across the breadth of government. They included Michael Jackson, who occupied the number two slot at the Department of Transportation, before becoming Deputy Secretary of the Department of Homeland Security (DHS). Jackson's industry-friendly tenure at DHS 'set the tone for a laxity in terms of contract oversight' according to the department's former Inspector General, who criticized the 'undue use of no-bid contracts, [and] contracts that fail to deliver what's promised even though billions of dollars have been spent'.[94] During Jackson's time at DHS, which ended in 2007, Lockheed Martin received in excess of \$650m in contracts.[95]

In October 2001, with this coterie of arms industry executives firmly in place, the Pentagon awarded Lockheed Martin what could amount to a \$382bn contract[96] – the largest in US history – to build a strike fighter jet, the F-35, that might have been useful during the Cold War but is largely irrelevant to the military needs of the twenty-first century.[97]

When the Bush administration left office a number of these appointees went straight back into the defence industry, including the head of procurement at the Pentagon who went onto the Lockheed Martin board the day he left government. Bill Hartung stopped keeping records of people who went into the industry from the Bush administration, because there were so many of them.[98]

George W. Bush named the deeply unpopular Donald Rumsfeld Secretary of Defense, while the most senior apostle of a new militarism was undoubtedly Vice President Dick Cheney, who had served as Bush senior's Defense Secretary before becoming CEO of the notorious Halliburton. The two hawks and other influential players in the administration, such as Paul Wolfowitz and Richard Perle, the leading neoconservatives, had for years been arguing for an extension of the Truman Doctrine and the wholesale privatization of warfare. From the early 1990s they spoke of 'a world dominated by one superpower' and a strategy 'to prevent the re-emergence of a new rival'.[99] In the most radical expansion of the Truman Doctrine, Paul Wolfowitz recommended that America commit herself 'to protect a new order . . . deterring potential competitors from even aspiring to a larger regional or global role. Such deterrence would include, when necessary, the use of pre-emptive force.'[100] They advocated military intervention in Iraq 'to assure access to vital raw materials, primarily Persian Gulf oil'.[101]

The conservative think-tank PNAC, in a report entitled *Rebuilding*

America's Defenses, called for a 'Pax Americana' and a revolution in military affairs, changing the military force of the US from one of cumbersome brutality to manoeuvrability, speed and flexibility, dominated by precision-guided munitions.[102] Many signatories to this document found their way into the Bush administration, including seventeen out-and-out neocons who championed these views. Much of the report became administration policy between 2002 and 2006.[103]

The report was written by Thomas Donnelly, who went on to work as a vice-president at Lockheed Martin in 2002. It called for an increase in military spending, by $75bn to $100bn over five years. It strongly endorsed spending more on the over-priced, troubled F-22. The underlying ideology was that America, rather than enjoying a post-Cold War peace dividend, should capitalize on the weakness of its potential rivals to 'run up the score', as the Secretary of Defense, Robert Gates, put it later in the context of the F-22 debate.[104]

One of the most vociferous of the neocons, Robert Kagan, defended this aggressive foreign policy, arguing that America has from birth been a more aggressive, imperialist country than many believe, and it should simply continue to do what has made it a great nation. While it is true that in its history America has formally declared war only eleven times, it has deployed its military and used force on over 100 occasions. Though some contend that America has always been ambivalent about its militarism, the Bush Doctrine would liberate the US to start wars with far less evidence of danger and with little scrutiny of the potential consequences.[105]

The PNAC report suggested that the process of transforming the military would 'be a long one without some catastrophic and catalysing event – like a new Pearl Harbor'.[106] 9/11, the ultimate blowback, was that event. The tragedy was, at one level, a godsend for the fledgling administration, allowing the nation to be placed on a perpetual war footing. While the nascent new militarism had already seen a significant increase in defence spending by the time 9/11 occurred, the neocons actively seized on the tragedy to realize their goals, believing that the promotion of American hegemony could now be pursued by any means necessary.

As Jarecki suggests: 'a nation forged in a war of revolution against an empire has over time come to repeat the very errors from which it sought to learn – the runaway expansionism combined with weakening commitment to founding principles, the growing military that spirals on itself, thrusting the nation into conflicts of ever-increasing scope and depth'.[107] The most obvious example of this was the willingness to exploit the sentiment evoked by 9/11 to distort the threat posed by Saddam in order to gain the nation's support for war. This was achieved with rhetoric eerily reminiscent of the fear-mongering propagated during debate about the bomber and missile gaps decades earlier, and strongly supported by the defence industry.

The security failures that led to 9/11 further convinced the Bush administration that only private firms had the intelligence and innovation to meet the new security challenge. Bush's New Military Deal transferred hundreds of billions of public dollars a year into private hands, mostly awarded with a lack of competition – so-called no-bid contracts. As Andrew Bacevich has noted, the White House first used 9/11 to massively increase the security powers of the executive in what he has called 'a rolling coup' and then outsourced these functions.[108]

The 9/11 moment supposedly altered everything, neatly disguising that the only thing that changed for free market fundamentalists and corporations was the ease with which they could pursue their agenda. Rather than enduring fractious debate in Congress, the Bush White House could use the patriotic alignment behind the President to further militarize the society into a utopia for weapons manufacturers. As the *New York Times* observed, 'without a public debate or a formal policy decision, contractors have become a virtual fourth branch of government'.[109] The Bush team devised a new role for government, one in which the job of the state was not to provide security but to purchase it at market prices.

The newly created Department of Homeland Security (DHS) was the clearest expression of this outsourced form of government. As Jane Alexander, Deputy Director of DHS, said: 'If it doesn't come from industry, we are not going to be able to get it.'[110]

This new militarism was encapsulated in the declaration of the permanent, all-encompassing 'War on Terror'. Every aspect of the way in which the War on Terror was defined has served to maximize its profitability and sustainability as a market. The document that launched DHS declares: 'Today's terrorists can strike at any place, at any time and with virtually any weapon' – which means that the security services must protect against every conceivable risk in every conceivable place at every possible time. This is epitomized by Dick Cheney's 1 per cent doctrine, which holds that if there is a 1 per cent chance that something is a threat, it requires that the US respond as if the threat is a 100 per cent certainty. So while the War on Terror was unwinnable, from an economic perspective it was an unbeatable proposition.[111]

It ensured that after 9/11 the defence-related revenue stream became a bottomless supply of tax dollars funnelled from the Pentagon. This included $270bn a year to private contractors, an increase of $137bn over the year before Bush took office. US Intelligence paid $42bn a year for outsourced intelligence, double the 1995 level; and the DHS spent $130bn on private contractors. In 2003 alone, the Bush administration spent $327bn on contracts to private companies – forty cents of every discretionary dollar.[112]

As a consequence US military spending now exceeds that of all other defence budgets on earth combined. The national defence outlay for 2008 reached $709bn, the highest spending on defence at any time since the Second World War.[113] Altogether, different security-related agency budgets and the proliferation of national security installations around the world raise this expenditure to almost a trillion dollars.[114] Nick Turse illustrates, alarmingly, how the military metaphysic is abroad, infiltrating all aspects of everyday life. He reveals that Starbucks is now a major contractor to the US Defense Department and documents the work that the super-cool Apple Corporation has done for the US military.[115]

The privatization of many of the activities previously performed by the armed services included not just supplying the military with its gear but also serving as manager for its operations and even participants in warfare. This significantly expanded opportunities for their allies in the sector, such as Bruce Jackson, with arms companies seeing their profits rise significantly. In total, business to the Pentagon's top ten contractors jumped from $46bn in 2001 to $80bn in 2003, an increase of nearly 75 per cent. Northrop Grumman's contracts doubled, from $5.2bn to $11.1bn, and Lockheed Martin saw a 50 per cent increase, from $14.7bn to $21.9bn.[116]

According to a 2006 study, since the War on Terror began the CEOs of the top thirty-four defence contractors have enjoyed average pay levels that are double the amounts they received in the four years leading up to 9/11. Average CEO pay went up 106 per cent, while in other large US companies this averaged 6 per cent over the period 2001 to 2005.[117]

And for this money executives such as Augustine and Jackson influenced many levels of public policy through their institutional involvements in think-tanks, NGOs and government agencies and boards, as well as the lobbying and campaign contributions of their company, which then reaped the financial benefit. However, the impact of the policy interventions had ramifications for the US far beyond just Lockheed Martin.

Halliburton and its former subsidiary Kellogg Brown & Root (KBR) are possibly the worst exemplars of the symbiotic relationship between business and politics.[118] Lyndon Johnson was known as 'the Senator from Brown & Root', as it then was, because of its political contributions to him. Once he became President, the company was awarded lucrative contracts to build military bases in Vietnam.[119]

In 1992, a $9m contract was awarded by the Pentagon to study the efficacy of using the private sector more aggressively. The Secretary of Defense at the time was Dick Cheney. He awarded the contract to KBR. Its report suggested aggressive privatization, identifying all sorts of tasks that the private sector should undertake, leading directly to a new Pentagon contract known as the Logistics Civil Augmentation Programme (LOGCAP). It involved not just supplying the military with its equipment and matériel, but also serving as manager for its operations.

A select group of companies was invited to bid for vaguely defined unlimited logistical support for the US military. No dollar value was attached to the contract: the winning company was simply assured that whatever it did for the military, its costs would be covered plus a guaranteed profit. At the end of Bush senior's term of office the contract was awarded . . . to Halliburton, the parent of the company that drew up the plans. And over the next ten years it received 700–800 government contracts.[120]

When Dick Cheney left office in 1993 he became CEO of Halliburton, until elected Vice President in 2000. During this period the company doubled the number of federal contracts it received, while its federal loans and loan guarantees increased fifteen-fold. The company also doubled its lobbying spend and campaign contributions. It donated considerable sums to right-wing think-tanks that gave a veneer of academic respectability to the no-bid contracts with the Pentagon, the vast expenditure on missile defence, and the crucial work on *Rebuilding America's Defenses*. Cheney was involved in all of these initiatives, seeing his personal wealth rise from about a million dollars to $60m or $70m.[121]

Over the seven years that Cheney served as Vice President, Halliburton was awarded more than $20bn in contracts.[122] Many of these were on the no-bid basis. During this time the company was fined for overcharging government and for using misleading accounting practices, which as we've seen in the case of BAE is a hold-all for a variety of transgressions.[123]

While in office Cheney regularly praised Halliburton, giving the company free publicity and endorsement. As Vice President he held 1.2 million Halliburton stock options from which he collected millions every year in dividends and was paid an annual deferred income from the company of $211,000. Halliburton's stock price rose from $10 before the war in Iraq to $41, a 300 per cent jump mainly due to soaring energy prices and Iraq contracts, both of which were down to Cheney's steering the country to war in Iraq. The war has been the single most profitable event in Halliburton's history. So who was Cheney representing? The government or his former employer in which he still held financial interests?[124] The retired US Air Force Colonel Sam Gardiner suggested of Cheney that 'He doesn't see the difference between public and private interests.'[125]

His political colleague and ideological soul-mate, Donald Rumsfeld, was no different. When Rumsfeld accepted George W. Bush's nomination as Defense Secretary he was so weighed down with holdings in defence-related companies that he tied government lawyers and their ethics rules in knots trying to hang on to everything he could. He sat on the board of the aircraft manufacturer Gulfstream and was paid $190,000 a year as a board member of ABB, the Swiss engineering giant that was revealed to have sold nuclear technology to North Korea. He sold off directly owned stock in Lockheed Martin, Boeing and other defence companies and put up to $50m of stocks in a blind trust. But he was still part or complete owner of private investment firms that were devoted to defence and biotech stocks. He continued to hold these interests six months into the job. The frequency with which he had to excuse himself from meetings for this reason in his first year in office was described as embarrassing.[126]

Both men could easily have divested themselves of their holdings but then they would have missed the boom years they created. What would they have made of FDR's injunction against war profiteers: 'I don't want to see a single war millionaire created in the US as a result of this disaster [the Second World War].' In the Bush administration the war profiteers weren't just clamouring to get access to government, they were the government.

Rumsfeld – of whom Nixon famously said: 'He's a ruthless little bastard, you can be sure of that'[127] – joined the Cabinet in 2001 with a personal mission to reinvent warfare for the new century. His controversial transformation project was a catch-all for a wide array of technological advances that comprised a twenty-first-century vision of how the US would wage war. In spite of asking for increases in defence budgets every year, he wanted less spent on staff and far more public money transferred directly into the coffers of private companies. He, Cheney and Bush believed that the job of government is not to govern but to subcontract the task to the more efficient and generally superior private sector. Rumsfeld saw this as a world-changing crusade on a par with defeating communism.[128]

In 1998, he had chaired the Rumsfeld Commission, which, contrary to official intelligence sources, published an alarmist assessment of the North Korean missile threat that was used to push a pro 'Star Wars' amendment through Congress, despite continuing disagreement about whether a missile defence system is either workable or affordable. The whole 'Star Wars' notion is a kind of military opportunism at the heart of government, with military men paying court to the pet schemes of inexperienced politicians in preparation for lucrative post-retirement positions in the arms industry or military think-tanks. Scientists who saw the system for the deluded, money-grabbing enterprise that it was were quickly marginalized.[129]

The findings of the commission, that a nation with 'Scud-based' technology, such as Iraq and North Korea, could achieve the first flight of a long-range ballistic missile within five years, were based on the testimony of Lockheed Martin engineers. So the opinions of employees of a company that stood to benefit from the perception of a greater missile threat were allowed to overrule the consensus of the US intelligence community. The Rumsfeld Commission was used to give credibility to the madness. Where Bush senior had spent over $2bn per annum on 'Star Wars', the Rumsfeld report resulted in the Clinton administration stepping up missile defence funding from $3bn to $5bn a year by the end of his second term, leading to well over $1bn in missile defence contracts for

Lockheed Martin alone. Reverting to the Reaganite model, George W. doubled spending on missile defence to $10bn.[130]*

Rumsfeld, who had been the youngest Secretary of Defense in history during the presidency of Gerald Ford, became the oldest person ever to serve in the role under George W. 'He was a walking MIC with a mission to transform the Department of Defense', according to the defence expert Josef Cirincione, who suggested that Rumsfeld's plan was a case study in 'how the military industrial forces not only prove disfiguring to the nation's balance of power and its spending priorities but also distort US strategy in the field. They fuel a self-perpetuating cycle of overzealous militarism and gross miscalculation. The ambitious notion of a push-button war launched from high altitudes is a direct extension of the rise of the MIC and its influence on the very concept of American war.'[131] This led to the failure in Iraq, where Rumsfeld's transformational vision actually produced a clumsy, unwinnable battle of old ideas delivered with the hollow sound and fury of high-tech weaponry.

As the war was failing the opportunities for profits were plentiful. While Rumsfeld believed that 9/11 had provided impetus for transformation, Chuck Spinney reckons that 'transformation was just a buzzword put together by a bunch of people in the Pentagon who are trying to protect the status quo'.[132] Cirincione agrees:

> After September 11, every single weapons programme that should have been cancelled (as it was now obsolete) was just relabelled. Instead of trimming or reorganizing the military we just threw money at it. Everything was funded. Even though we're talking about fighting a war against terrorists in caves, we're buying weapons designed to pulverize an advanced industrial nation. So suddenly, things like the B-2 bomber – a bomber that costs $2 billion a copy and was designed to penetrate Soviet radar – was being justified as an anti terror weapon. You re-label an F-22 fighter aircraft from something that would kill Soviet aircraft to something that will

* As Hartung points out, the cumulative projected costs of missile-defence-related programmes have now reached over $100bn. As of 2008 there was still at least $63bn left to be spent, including over $23bn for Lockheed Martin's SBIRS satellite programme. Despite deploying prototype interceptors it is still not clear whether the initiative is viable or practical, one of the reasons why President Obama was recently prepared to abandon the idea of a missile defence shield in Europe.

kill terrorists. You just repackage it as the 'new military thinking' weapon. Wrap the flag around it. Keep the program going.[133]

So transformation, far from being a revolution in military affairs, became an excuse for more of the same, repackaged to seem appropriate to the new War on Terror, while maximizing the profits of the manufacturers. The figures are mind-boggling: in 2003, the US government handed out about 3,500 contracts to companies to perform security functions; in a twenty-two-month period to the end of 2006 DHS issued 115,000 such contracts. The global homeland security industry is now a $200bn sector. In 2006, US government spending on homeland security averaged over $550 per household.[134]

Chuck Spinney suggests that this has been allowed to happen because the US's Christmas Tree politics has resulted in a Congress of Special Pleaders characterized by constant horse trading, currying favour with the executive for future needs or trading between Congressional members. 'The intersection of economic and political interests gives licence to the militarist tendencies of the executive in what should be called the corporate-congressional-military-executive complex.'[135]

This accumulation of executive power ultimately culminated under George W. Bush in what Colonel Lawrence Wilkerson, Chief of Staff to Colin Powell, described as a self-acknowledged cabal led by Dick Cheney and Donald Rumsfeld, whose insular and secret workings resembled the decision-making process associated more with a dictatorship than with a democracy.[136] 'It has come to a point where the MIC is so influential on the fateful decisions a President makes that it's dangerous for the republic.'[137]

This occurs in a number of ways. Decisions made by defence contractors with their patrons in the Pentagon, as Spinney describes, are effectively pushing attitudes to defence, security and war in particular directions. Think of the impact of the development of the atom bomb or more recently drones and remote weapons on the ways in which wars are fought. These weapons give an omnipotence to the Commander-in-Chief that makes it almost inevitable that he will continue to pursue an ever-expanding American empire predicated on force which requires ever larger military budgets.[138]

The same MICC provides the means and the motivation for a continuous state of war. The Second World War was a discrete event, whereas the

Cold War and the War on Terror have ensured growing security measures, increased government secrecy and surveillance, and the continual
increase of executive power.[139] The MICC, and particularly defence contractors, through their role in the media, public pronouncements and
massive support for bellicose think-tanks, creates a continuous drumbeat
of fear and insecurity, which allows and maintains the national security
state, permeating every aspect of life.

The revolving door brings militarism to the government from the defence
industry, both into the White House and into government departments.
Alexander Haig, Colin Powell, and Cheney and Rumsfeld are only the
most obvious emblems of the military metaphysic influencing the Oval
Office. It is not coincidental that the two generals led the State Department, thus militarizing the corridors of diplomacy. For arms sales abroad
are not just an instrument of foreign policy in the hands of the executive,
but crucially result in a situation where captains of the defence industry
are pushing, with a great deal of money, certain foreign policy approaches
that favour their needs, be it the expansion of NATO, specific approaches
to the Middle East and certainly the nature of relations with Saudi Arabia.
Often these dovetail with the views of the executive, but not always, as
seen in President Obama's initial attitude to Israel.

The infusion of military-minded people into government departments
affects the mind-set with which projects are managed, the types of contracts that (under-)regulate them and the way in which they are assessed.
This applies not only to defence-related arenas, but even the postal service, the IRS and the census.

This military metaphysic was having its most profound impact at a
time when economic ideas were changing. Historically, economic wisdom held that sustainable growth requires stability and peace. The War
on Terror turned that assumption on its head. The world was becoming
less peaceful while accumulating more profit, at least until the credit
crunch. Today global instability benefits not just shady arms dealers but
the whole of what Naomi Klein has called 'the disaster capitalism industry' (i.e. those companies that benefit from natural and man-made
disasters, especially war) and of course the defence contractors. Since 9/11
it appears that terrorist attacks are perceived by markets as good for business. While the Dow plummeted 685 points in the wake of 9/11, after the
7/7 attacks on London less than four years later, the US markets were up

that day thanks to soaring homeland security stocks and the London Stock Exchange picked up again the next day.[140]

The post-9/11 outsourcing of military functions, especially homeland security, also gave birth to an army of new lobbyists, increasing the number of homeland security lobby firms from two in 2001 to 543 by mid-2006.[141] These firms, together with their clients in the weapons-making and military service provider businesses, ensure that the world is ceaselessly portrayed as a dark and menacing place, its troubles responsive only to force. Not only do they fund think-tanks which extol this view but they are also becoming entwined with media corporations. For example, GE owns NBC and now a company specializing in bomb detection devices.[142] It is disconcerting to the nature of American democracy that those who benefit most from war are becoming more and more influential in creating the atmosphere in which politicians feel honour-bound to take the country to war. At the Paris Air Show in 2009, it was noticeable that every defence company invariably started each presentation with a slide depicting just how dangerous a place the world is, and will continue to be, before presenting their weapons systems that will keep us all safe.

Naomi Klein concludes that the architects of the War on Terror are corporate politicians, notorious for conflating corporate interests with the national interest, and are themselves incapable of drawing the distinction. A startling example is a long-time neocon and Rumsfeld confidant, Richard Perle, whom Rumsfeld appointed to chair the influential Defense Policy Board (DPB). Taking a leaf out of his mentor's book, Perle used his position to persuade the arms dealer Adnan Khashoggi to arrange a meeting with Saudi industrialists, from whom he solicited $100m for his recently established security-oriented investment firm, Trireme. He also attempted to use his position to persuade the government to approve the sale of a division of the corrupt, bankrupt telecommunications firm Global Crossing to a Chinese buyer for a fee of almost a million dollars; and was retained by a company that had been charged with the transfer of secret satellite information to China to plead their case with the US government.[143]

He was eventually forced to resign as Chairman of the DPB after being charged with abusing his position as an adviser to Rumsfeld for personal gain. He, however, continued as an ordinary member of the board. When he stepped down from the chairmanship, Rumsfeld described Perle as a man of 'deep integrity and honour'.[144] The Center for Public Integrity found that nine of the board's thirty members had relationships with weapons contractors that together had received over $76bn in contracts from the Pentagon in the most recent financial year.[145]

The DPB, like a number of defence-related public bodies, blurs the distinction between the public and the private, resulting in the situation where activities undertaken with public money display minimal transparency and accountability. This is consistent with American capitalism, in which the activities of a corporation are seen as the province of that corporation, and neither the public nor Congress has a fundamental right to access information about them. Most notably, the US Freedom of Information Act doesn't apply to private companies, leading a Democratic representative from Illinois to suggest that 'it's almost as if these private military contractors are involved in a secret war'.[146]

By allocating so much public sector work to private companies, the Bush administration created a condition in which the nature and practice of government activities could be hidden under the cloak of corporate privacy. This severely limits both financial and political accountability. The financial activities of these companies are scrutinized primarily by its shareholders if it is a public company and occasionally by government auditors on a contract-by-contract basis. And of course, at a political level, it is not just feasible but common for the government to claim that a contractor had promised to do one thing but then did another, thus absolving government of responsibility.

This opaque operating environment, in addition to the secrecy afforded by national security, makes it extremely difficult to critically analyse and hold to account the massive military-industrial complex that drives the country's predisposition to warfare and the increasing militarization of American society. What analysis there is tends to focus on the few corruption scandals that see the light of day.

And the Bush Jr years yielded a plethora of shameful ones.

15.   Illegal Bribery

There are precious few examples of the MICC being punished even when its members stray outside the 'accepted' parameters of this system of legal bribery. Where they do exist they serve not only as a salutary warning that there are some legal limits, but also as a reminder of the extent to which immoral behaviour is regarded as standard operating procedure in the alternative universe that is the MICC.

In December 2001, Congress approved the lease of 100 Boeing KC-767 in-air-refuelling tankers in a deal worth $26bn for ten years.[1] In-air-refuelling tankers are built to gush fuel to other aircraft while flying, using what is essentially a long pipe joining the two planes in mid-air, allowing the recipient aircraft to fly further and for longer.

The decision to lease the aircraft was a remarkable one. The Congressional Budget Office (CBO) determined that the decision to lease with an option to buy later would cost taxpayers $5bn more than buying the aircraft outright. Senator John McCain slammed the deal, claiming: 'this is war profiteering'.[2]

The 100 new aircraft were intended to replace the 126 KC-135 'E' tanker aircraft in the US Air Force armoury, despite the Air Force already having 410 upgraded versions of the 'E',[3] which are intended to stay in service until 2030 or 2040. Air Force studies of its tankers concluded that the cost of maintaining the fleet as it was would rise by only $23m per year over the next forty years but that there might be capacity shortfalls under certain – classified – circumstances. The Air Force had no plans to start updating the tanker fleet until 2013 but 9/11 increased concern about the fleet's age.[4] Quite how newer refuelling tankers could prevent terrorist attacks is not apparent.

In its prioritization process released in October 2001, the Air Force listed sixty budget priorities, but the 100 new tankers did not feature.[5] The studies found that the fleet as it was remained in good condition and examined four options:

The first option was to do nothing, thus accepting the cost of $23m per year over forty years, and accepting some risk of shortfall. The second option was to upgrade the 126 'E' tankers, increasing the capacity of the fleet a little and costing $3.2bn.[6] The Chairman of the Joint Chiefs of Staff commented that the tanker fleet was 'relatively healthy' with 'lots of flying hours left on them'. The General Accounting Office shared this view and expressed serious concerns about the third and fourth options.[7] The third was the direct purchase of 100 Boeing 767 tankers, while retiring the 'E' model fleet, at a cost of around $150m per aircraft.[8] The total cost was approximately $18bn, with the process of bringing them into service taking eight or nine years. The advantage would be a more modern aircraft with possibly a longer life, though the actual capacity of the fleet would be slightly reduced.[9] So none of the shortfalls identified in the Air Force studies would be resolved.

The final option was to lease the 100 Boeing 767 aircraft in their commercial configuration. They would have to be converted and then converted back again at the end of the lease. The total cost of this option, which would last for only ten years, would be $26bn. The option would provide the same tanker capacity and take the same amount of time to bring into service as the direct purchase of the aircraft, with slightly lower immediate costs, but lasting only ten years, suggesting that the actual cost was much higher.[10]

The leasing solution was not subject to public scrutiny as it was added by the Senate–House Conference Committee to the 2002 Defense Authorization Bill. There was no discussion of the programme in the committee process. The Chairman of the Senate Committee on the Budget, Kent Conrad, proposed to waive government rules determining when leases can be used instead of outright purchases. These rules were put in place to minimize costs, but, as the Office of Management and Budget (OMB) pointed out, in the tanker case the costs were greatly increased with minimal benefit from leasing.[11]

The deal was clearly intended to benefit Boeing, which had complained that since 9/11 orders for its commercial aircraft had dried up while its biggest rival, Lockheed Martin, had won a major competition to build the Joint Strike Fighter, the F-35.[12] The Defense Authorization Bill which contained the earmark for the aircraft lease specified that the Air Force was authorized to lease 100 tankers but only if they were leased from Boeing. Boeing could not have written the earmark better itself and as was later discovered, it pretty much did.

This favouritism was subject to inquiry on 12 February 2002 at a Senate Armed Services Committee hearing on the defence budget. John McCain asked the Air Force Secretary, James Roche, if the prospective contract had been discussed with Boeing's main competitor, EADS (which owns Airbus). Roche answered: 'Yes, sir. Back as far as October I made the point that if Airbus could come in and do something, we would be delighted to have that happen. . . . I have met with Philippe Camus [CEO of EADS] and have opened up the door for him if he wished to do something.' McCain responded: 'But doesn't the legislation say the loan can only be Boeing 767s?' 'Yes, sir. But if Airbus did something that was particularly good, I would come back to the Congress, sir.'[13]

A week later, possibly stung into action, the Air Force did put out a request for information on the contract for both Boeing and EADS, giving two weeks for a response. Predictably enough, Boeing was judged the winner based on its answers.[14]

John McCain tried to stop the lease deal by exposing the intensive influence peddling that had gone on. He released documents detailing a high-level lobbying campaign by Boeing and the Air Force to fend off critics and competitors to gain what McCain characterized as 'corporate welfare'.[15] Boeing and Air Force email messages and internal memos culled from some 8,000 documents showed that the Air Force and the company assisted each other in structuring the programme, promoting it in Washington and setting requirements so that no other competitors could qualify. The Air Force went so far as to rely on Boeing to provide it with arguments that would play well with influential members of Congress, in the White House and with the news media.[16]

Rudy DeLeon, a former Under Secretary for the Air Force and Deputy Defense Secretary who became the head of Boeing's Washington office in July 2001, felt that the emails released by McCain simply showed that 'people who believed in the program' were working hard to get it completed. The *Washington Post* reported that another Boeing official defended the lobbying effort as common practice, suggesting the only unusual thing about it was having it on public display in the emails.[17]

James Roche also had a revolving-door past. He left the military in 1983 as a Captain, then served as a Staff Director of the US Senate Armed

Services Committee from 1983 to 1984 before joining Northrop Grumman. He went on to hold several executive positions with the arms giant until being brought back into government by the Bush administration in 2001. At the time of his appointment Roche was on the Board of Advisers of Frank Gaffney's hardline Center for Security Policy. The Center's 2002 annual report title page included a quote from Donald Rumsfeld: 'If there was any doubt about the power of your ideas, one has only to look at the number of Center associates who now people this administration – and particularly the Department of Defense – to dispel them.'[18]

In December 2001, language authorizing the deal but providing no money had emerged in legislation in what Capitol Hill veterans refer to as a 'virgin birth', meaning it was inserted into the Defense Appropriations Bill after the bill had passed the House and Senate, during closed negotiations between conferees. It was then approved on the House and Senate floors as part of a compromise bill. Ordinarily, costly military systems are bought after being included in formal budget proposals, which lead to Congressional hearings and votes in committees and on the House and Senate floors. In this case, no hearings were held or committee votes taken before the deal was approved.[19]

The Chairman of the Senate Appropriations Committee, Ted Stevens, a long-time supporter of expanding federal leasing, claimed credit for inserting the language. Stevens was also responsible for ensuring that the funding be only for the leasing of Boeing aircraft and no others. A month before he did so, Stevens received $21,900 in campaign contributions from thirty-one Boeing executives at a fundraiser in Seattle, where Boeing is headquartered. In total the company directed $34,000, the largest contribution, to Stevens's 2002 re-election campaign.[20] Stevens was intimately involved in many aspects of the campaign for the deal. A senior Air Force official, Darleen Druyun, noting that Stevens could 'work' a former employee of his, who was then at the OMB, asked Boeing to help produce briefing charts, which the Air Force took to Stevens's office for his use. Boeing also sought to solidify support from John Murtha by agreeing to explore a subcontract to a firm in his district.[21]

Boeing and the Air Force jointly planned a campaign 'to educate the media' on the merits of the deal. This public education included an op-ed article touting the 767 tankers in five publications by a retired Admiral, Archie Clemins. The piece was actually written by Boeing. Soon after,

Clemins became a consultant to the company.[22] Richard Perle, the controversial Chairman of the DPAB, was also the co-author of an op-ed in the *Wall Street Journal* in favour of the tanker deal. Boeing had invested $20m in Perle's defence-related venture capital firm. The investment was not disclosed in the article.[23]

The Boeing tanker was initially selected in 2002 and the contract for the leasing deal awarded in 2003.[24] However, after protests by Senator McCain and others, the Air Force was forced to compromise by purchasing eighty tankers and leasing the remaining twenty.

But in December 2003, this compromise deal was frozen after allegations surfaced around the behaviour of Boeing and Darleen Druyun.[25]

Druyun had been Principal Deputy Assistant Secretary of the Air Force for Acquisition and Management from 1993. She oversaw the contract negotiations for Boeing's leasing of tanker aircraft for the Pentagon.[26] In a meeting on 1 April of Air Force and Boeing officials after the company had been selected, Druyun told Boeing to 'keep in mind' that the Airbus bid was $5m to $17m cheaper per aeroplane than a basic Boeing 767. Back in 2003, Boeing attempted to explain away Druyun's comments as her negotiating strategy, describing her as a 'truly tough negotiator' who was 'send[ing] us a clear message that we needed to sharpen our pencil'.[27]

Druyun, known as 'Dragon Lady', had a reputation for being tough. However, Boeing were clearly exempt from her fire-breathing antics. After one meeting, a Boeing executive wrote in a document released by McCain: 'Meeting today on price was very good. Darleen spent most of the time bringing the USAF price up to our number . . . It was a good day!'[28] According to Boeing emails Druyun was exploring how to get Congress to approve a special waiver of federal accounting rules and was advising the company on how to win over key lawmakers. McCain said the emails demonstrated that 'the Air Force appeared not so much to negotiate with Boeing as to advocate for it, to the point of giving Boeing unusual control over pricing, and other terms and conditions'.[29]

In November 2001, the Air Force had drafted a document detailing what capabilities the new tankers needed. Colonel Mark Donohue, an official in the air mobility office, promptly sent it to Boeing for private comment, and the company sought and received concessions so the requirements matched what the 767 could do. Most importantly and extraordinarily, the Air Force agreed to drop a demand that the new tankers match or exceed the capabilities of the old ones.[30]

Boeing's lobbying campaign had to be persuasive to bring round politicians and officials when the case for any replacement of tanker aircraft seemed so shaky. An internal Boeing email from one of their lobbyists reflected this. Reporting on a meeting with Roche and Druyun's boss, the Air Force's Chief of Procurement, Marvin Sambur, the lobbyist reported that Sambur had turned to Boeing for help: 'He indicated that the USAF is desperately looking for the rationale for why the USAF should pursue the 767 tanker NOW . . . It was clear he was looking to find a path forward.' Another memo showed the complicity of Roche in encouraging lobbying. The lobbyist documented a meeting with the Air Force Secretary and other Air Force officials in which they had 'urged us to have our friends on the Hill, think tanks, etc. get more visible/vocal with pro-tanker arguments'. He continued that Roche was particularly keen on anything Boeing could do 'especially if it helps drown out McCain'.[31]

The lobbying operation targeted both Congress and the White House. Boeing planned to have the House Speaker, J. Dennis Hastert, a Republican from Illinois and a strong supporter of the deal, talk to President Bush and other White House officials. Several Air Force officers took chunks of a corroded tanker wing in the trunk of a car to Capitol Hill, where an Air Force General had been flown in from Oklahoma to brief members of Congress on tanker ageing. A Boeing lobbyist wrote: 'We are in touch with Andy Card [White House Chief of Staff] and White House political operation. They see increased pressure and realize a political downside to not moving forward with tankers.'[32]

Another of the company's lobbyists noted the increasing help from the Deputy Defense Secretary, Paul Wolfowitz, and his boss, Donald Rumsfeld. Roche told Boeing that more involvement from Rumsfeld provided 'necessary "top cover" for Air Force', adding that it 'works better in White House and will help on Capitol Hill'.[33] The White House Chief of Staff, acting at what officials said was the direction of President Bush, told the Air Force and OMB to resolve their differences. Bush had been lobbied hard by the House Speaker, Hastert, and Representative Norman Dicks, whose districts were in states that included respectively Boeing's headquarters and a key production facility.[34]

Druyun actively encouraged the placing of work in the districts of key politicians. A memo written by Boeing staff after a meeting between Druyun and Boeing executives noted that 'She [Druyun] also said "work placement could help" [promote the deal], meaning that Boeing should ensure that subcontracts were awarded in the districts of key Congress members.'[35]

Boeing was rightly concerned about the illogicality of the deal for the taxpayer. Bob Gordon, a Boeing vice-president, worried in an August 2002 email that the company could have a 'PR risk' because the idea that leasing was preferable to buying 'won't make sense in the newspapers'. He continued that neither Boeing nor an investment banking firm familiar with the deal 'would ever put its hand on a bible and say [it] makes economic sense'.[36] The problem was exacerbated by a report from the Institute for Defense Analyses (IDA), an independent think-tank, which told the Pentagon after a detailed study that the Air Force was overpaying by at least $21m per plane and that the lease violated federal accounting rules. 'The concern remains that we are not giving the [US government] a fair deal. This continues to be driven by the IDA study and OMB,' the Boeing Defense Systems president, Jim Albaugh, noted at one point. Another Boeing executive wrote that Roche asked Boeing to pressure other Pentagon bosses to squelch the study. The IDA did not back down.[37]

Boeing executives also contacted key subcontractors and 'urged them to be part of the debate' by calling Card and other administration officials. Boeing's tame politicians, Hastert and Dicks, directly reached Bush in late September 2002. According to a Boeing email, Bush then instructed Card to be 'on point' for the deal. A month later Card called Roche and others to the White House and asked them to detail how many jobs the leasing deal would create. This was a key issue for an administration which had seen 2.5 million jobs lost, and a typical MICC argument, justifying any project however inefficient and unnecessary as a way to stop job losses. The next day Boeing executives wrote in an email to Druyun that the lease would support 25,000 to 30,000 jobs, including both existing and new workers.[38] The following day Roche sent a letter to Card that overstated this tally. Citing Boeing as his source he said the deal would create about 39,000 new jobs alone, more than 11,000 at Boeing and 28,000 among suppliers. Card led other meetings about the deal, met Boeing officials and took calls from Dicks and Boeing lobbyists.[39]

After the OMB continued to speak out against the deal, Boeing agreed to cut the price of the tankers, bringing it closer to the IDA figure. But this was accomplished by further scaling back the tankers' capabilities. The company was motivated in part, according to its emails, by the looming retirement of the Pentagon's chief weapons buyer, the Under Secretary of Defense, Edward C. Aldridge Jr, a supporter of the deal. His replacement had already pressed the firm aggressively for a large price cut. On 23 May, Aldridge's last day at the Pentagon, he announced an agreement with Boeing on most terms of the lease, calling it a way to get new tankers 'delivered much faster' than if they were purchased – even though there was no rush to retire the old tankers and there was no sign that leasing would provide new tankers quicker than purchasing.

The deal put in place by Aldridge included a $5bn sole-source maintenance contract for the new tankers and allowed Boeing to earn a 15 per cent profit on the deal, more than double what the company makes from commercial aircraft orders.[40] Aldridge was the former president of McDonnell Douglas Electronic Systems, which later became part of Boeing. After leaving the Pentagon he took a job with Lockheed Martin.[41] In total, during Aldridge's forty-six-year career he held twelve high-level positions – six with arms companies, five with the Defense Department and one stint with the OMB. During his next job at Lockheed Martin, Donald Rumsfeld appointed him to the blue-ribbon panel that advises the Pentagon about weapons purchases.[42] Despite this constantly revolving door, Aldridge has never been charged with wrongdoing.

Nepotism and cash were key ingredients used by Boeing to win contracts. While examining a deal worth $4bn for Boeing to update C-130 Hercules transport aircraft, Darleen Druyun rang Boeing's chief financial officer, Mike Sears, and asked him to arrange a job for her daughter's fiancé, Michael McKee. Boeing gave him a job immediately. Three months later, while the contract was still on the table, Druyun contacted Sears again, this time requesting a job for her daughter, Heather. Again Boeing acquiesced without question or pause. Absurdly, this was not forbidden under Pentagon rules, illustrating the leeway for blatant corruption within the MICC.[43]

At the height of the tanker negotiations, Heather emailed Sears informing him that her mother planned to leave the Air Force and that her new job 'must be challenging, tough, lots of responsibility. She is very interested in talking to us, but we would have to give her something that would blow her out of the water. She also mentioned that Boeing has her most admired quality: honest values.'[44] Sears discussed potential employment at Boeing with Druyun while she was still overseeing Boeing contracts at the Pentagon. They met secretly for half an hour at Orlando airport in October 2002 to discuss her salary, bonus and starting date at the company, as well as the F-22 contract which Boeing was involved in. In November 2002, she accepted a position as vice-president and deputy general manager of Boeing's Missile Defense Systems[45] with a salary of $250,000 per year and a signing-on bonus of $50,000.[46]

According to Paul McNulty, who prosecuted Druyun, landing jobs for her family was not against the law but getting a job for herself was a felony, violating conflict of interest laws.[47] Druyun's boss, Marvin Sambur, had outlined the ethics rules governing what jobs Druyun could take after leaving government employment. The two had a handshake agreement that Druyun could join Lockheed Martin as an executive. But shortly after leaving government employment she reneged on the job plan with Lockheed, if that was ever her intention, to go to Boeing.[48]

Druyun's position at Boeing was short-lived. She was fired in November 2003 after an internal investigation.[49] Initially, she attempted to cover her tracks, but, disgraced and facing five years in jail, she soon decided to tell all she knew about misconduct at the company and cut a deal with prosecutors.[50] Initially after her arrest Druyun admitted that she had talked to Boeing about a job while in government, but denied favouring the company. She then admitted to advantaging the company and doctoring a personal journal to hide the conflict of interest.[51] Under the terms of her plea agreement she was sentenced to nine months in prison in October 2004 for giving Boeing preferential treatment.[52] Druyun served her prison term from January to October 2005 at a minimum security jail in Marianna, Florida.[53] She was also given a $5,000 fine, 150 hours of community service and seven months of community confinement upon release.[54]

In her plea agreement Druyun admitted that, in addition to the tanker case, she had awarded $100m to Boeing as part of a NATO contract in 2002. She admitted that the payment could have been lower, but favoured Boeing because her daughter and son-in-law worked there and she was considering working there as well. She also oversaw a $4bn award to Boeing to modernize the avionics on C-130J aircraft in 2001. In this instance, she favoured Boeing over four competitors because the company had just employed her son-in-law. And she agreed to pay $412m to the company as settlement over a dispute in a C-17 aircraft contract in 2000, at the time when her son-in-law was seeking the job.[55]

Druyun was also found guilty of manipulating other Air Force contracts to be given to Boeing over competitors.

Despite her disgrace, and the billions involved in her corrupt behaviour, Druyun is still thought to be receiving a government pension.[56] Boeing's Mike Sears, who had agreed with Druyun to lie about their discussions, was fired in November 2003 and sentenced to four months in prison.[57]

A big question remains as to how much other Boeing staff knew about the relationship with Druyun. Knowledge of their meeting at the airport was disseminated by Sears in an email to 'The Office Of The Chairman'. It read: 'Had a "nonmeeting" yesterday . . . Good reception to job, location, salary. Recommend we put together a formal offer.'[58] This suggests that senior executives knew what was going on. Whatever he knew or didn't know, this evidence cost Boeing's CEO, Phil Condit, his job. He resigned in December 2003.

The fingerprints of the Air Force Secretary, James Roche, were all over the scandal. Ultimately he was cited for two ethics violations. While he may have been driven by a desire to ease the immediate budget woes of the Air Force by avoiding the upfront costs of a purchase rather than a lease deal, he went further than secretly aiding Boeing in persuading the public, Congress, the Pentagon and the President to support the deal. Roche and the OMB's Associate Director, Robin Cleveland, had an email exchange in 2003 in which Cleveland, who oversaw the budgeting of national security programmes, sent Roche a CV for her brother on 9 May 2003, saying: 'I would appreciate anything you can do to help with NG [Northrop Grumman]', the arms firm where Roche had been a senior executive. Her request came as the administration was deciding on whether to go ahead with the leasing plan, which other top OMB officials had called a waste of money. Roche forwarded Cleveland's email to a senior Northrop lawyer, with his own endorsement of her brother. He told Cleveland what he had done, adding: 'Be well. Smile. Give tankers now (Oops, did I say that? . . .).' As it turned out, Northrop did not hire Cleveland's brother. Roche protested later that his note to the Northrop official was a personal communication to a friend. However, his endorsement had been sent officially from the Air Force. Roche was cited for misusing his public office for someone else's private gain and violating Pentagon rules governing the personal use of email systems.[59]

Roche resigned in January 2005, shortly before a report on the tanker scandal concluded that he had broken ethics rules.[60] In 2003, he had been nominated as Secretary of the Army. John McCain attacked his nomination suggesting that 'Secretary Roche, contradicting Air Force studies, has been relentless in exaggerating aerial tanker shortfalls and problems in order to win approval of the [Boeing] lease. If this represents the kind of acquisition reforms and defense transformation we can expect from Secretary Roche if he is confirmed as Secretary of the Army, then God help the Army and the American taxpayer.'[61] Roche was not confirmed in the post.[62]

On resigning Roche immediately joined the board of Orbital Sciences Corp., a company involved in the development of space-based weapons.[63] In September 2008, Roche joined the board of Compudyne, which calls itself 'an industry leader in sophisticated security products, integration, and technology for the public security markets'.[64]

While the Air Force long maintained that Druyun was the lone gunman on the Boeing scandal, investigations fingered other culprits at the Pentagon such as Roche, while a wide cross-section of Pentagon officials, political appointees, White House politicos and Congressmen were involved in pushing for the leasing deal regardless of value to the taxpayer. They included the Air Force's top acquisitions official, Druyun's boss Sambur, who had been appointed to the role in 2001, after managing the $1.5bn arms business of ITT Industries. He resigned in January 2005 in an attempt to escape criticism over his role in the Boeing debacle.[65]

Boeing paid $615m in settlement in May 2006 for its actions in the tanker scandal and the illicit possession of thousands of pages of proprietary documents from its rival Lockheed Martin that it used to win contracts.[66] A week after the settlement was announced, an uncensored version of a 2005 Defense Department Inspector General's report on the deal showed that the original report had concealed significant information. The Inspector General, Joseph Schmitz, submitted his report to the White House before its release, whereupon it was scrubbed of damning information, including forty-five deletions of references to White House officials.[67] The original public release had redacted Boeing emails and several references to the company. Freedom of information requests revealed that Boeing and government agencies, in addition to the White House, had been allowed to see the unredacted report before its release. References to members of Congress and staff were also redacted and replaced with vague identifiers. Some of the deletions referred to an agreement between the White House and Congress to shield information from the public and were justified with the following note: 'The Report does not include full verbatim text of this email because staff of the White House Counsel has indicated its intent to invoke an agreement between Members of Congress and the White House covering the production of tanker-related emails – the inclusion of which full verbatim text in the Inspector General's independent judgment would have circumvented the agreement.'[68]

Schmitz's report did not include any of the comments of either Donald Rumsfeld or Paul Wolfowitz because, according to Schmitz, they had not said anything 'relevant'. The *Washington Post* editorialized that 'If so, investigators must not have asked the right questions. To offer just one example: Mr Roche recounted that Mr. Rumsfeld called him in July 2003 to discuss his then-pending nomination to be Secretary of the Army and "specifically stated that he did not want me to budge on the tanker lease proposal."'[69] A transcript of the Office of the Inspector General's interview with Rumsfeld revealed that when asked by investigators whether he had approved the deal despite widespread violations of procurement rules, Rumsfeld answered: 'I don't remember approving it. But I certainly don't remember not approving it, if you will.' He was also asked about the fact that in 2002 President Bush had asked Andy Card to intervene in the Pentagon discussions with Boeing: 'I have been told,' Rumsfeld said, 'that discussions with the President are privileged, and with his immediate staff.' Much of the rest of the transcript was blacked out and none was included in the public report.[70] Schmitz's team also failed to interview anyone outside the Department of Defense, despite the involvement of several lawmakers, administration officials and even the President.[71]

Senator Chuck Grassley wrote to Schmitz questioning his 'decision to submit an Inspector General (IG) report to the White House Counsel for review'. Grassley wrote that the legal authority Schmitz cites 'appears to be inapplicable and invalid', that the White House–Congressional agreement has 'no legal standing whatsoever' and that Schmitz was 'not bound by the protocols'. Furthermore, Grassley argued that because of the White House's redactions 'potential targets were shielded from possible accountability'.[72]

John McCain lambasted Schmitz in a Senate hearing on the scandal. In relation to Edward Aldridge, the Pentagon's chief weapons buyer who approved the deal as he retired and failed to get proper approvals despite suggesting that they were in place, McCain suggested to Schmitz: 'Mr Aldridge basically lied.' Schmitz replied: 'We know generally that . . . he and others within the Air Force and [the Office of the Secretary of Defense] were trying to treat the appropriations language as if it had waived a whole bunch of legal requirements.' An incredulous McCain retorted: 'Don't you think it would have been important to have his testimony?' To which Schmitz responded: 'My staff couldn't reach him.' 'You couldn't get hold of him through Lockheed Martin?' asked McCain with more than a hint of irony. 'I don't think it's a mystery,' Senator John Warner chipped in, 'he's on the board of a major defense contractor, it seems to me he's locatable.'[73] It was even easier than Warner might have supposed, given that Schmitz's brother, former deputy counsel for George H. W. Bush, worked as a registered lobbyist for Lockheed Martin at the time of the Boeing deal and probe.[74]

In 2005, Joseph Schmitz resigned as Inspector General for the Department of Defense under a cloud of allegations that he had allowed inappropriate political interference by the White House in not only the Boeing probe but other politically sensitive investigations as well. At other points during his tenure Schmitz had failed to address documented evidence of KBR engagement in human trafficking, seizure of workers' passports, threatening workers that their food and water would be cut off to force them to go to Iraq, and lying to workers about their safety or contract terms.[75] Soon after resigning Schmitz went to work for Blackwater, one of the largest and most controversial contractors operating in Iraq.[76]

The tanker competition was restarted in 2007 and was awarded a year later to a bid by Northrop Grumman and EADS, based upon the Airbus 330 aircraft. Boeing protested at the result, claiming that the competition had unfairly favoured the larger Airbus aircraft, that there had been manipulation of evaluation criteria, and the application of unstated and unsupported priorities among the key system requirements.[77] The GAO sided with Boeing and recommended the competition be rebid.[78] It was briefly reopened in July 2008 for an 'expedited recompetition' before being cancelled again in September due to uncertainty that the process could be completed before the end of the year. It was put on hold until after the US general election.[79]

In September 2009, the bidding process was restarted once again, this time for 179 aircraft for $35bn over forty years. On this occasion Northrop withdrew in protest, claiming that the set-up of the competition favoured Boeing.[80] Despite Northrop's departure, EADS continued with the contest.[81] Both sides accused the other of benefiting from illegal subsidies. The World Trade Organization (WTO) first ruled that Airbus had received illegal financial aid and then released an interim ruling that Boeing had also received illegal subsidies, though at a lower level than those received by Airbus.[82]

This farcical deal highlights the conflicts of interest that are implicit in an MICC dominated by a rapidly revolving door between government and the defence sector. It also serves as a reminder that even in the rare cases when anyone is brought to book, they get off so lightly that there is little disincentive for the illegal practices to continue.

At the Paris Air Show in 2009, as the bidding process was restarting for the third time, I suggested to the head of Boeing's tanker division that their corruption in the first tender would surely count against them now. The tall former military officer went puce and looked as though he might answer me physically, before a rotund media officer placed himself between us.

In June 2005, news broke that Congressman Randy 'Duke' Cunningham of California, a war hero and member of the House Defense Appropriations subcommittee, had received more than a million dollars in payments from defence contractors for whom he had secured favourable treatment from the Pentagon. He resigned from Congress and was sentenced to just over eight years in prison for conspiracy to commit bribery and fraud. The media delighted in salacious stories of lavish, champagne-drenched parties aboard luxury yachts involving numerous female guests and prostitutes. His is hardly the only tale of corrupt politicians in the US seduced by militarized money but it is among the most colourful.

Cunningham sped to instant stardom on 10 May 1972 when he shot down three MiGs, which, together with the two kills he had already made meant that he had become the first fighter ace since the Korean War.[83] At the tail end of an unpopular war this small victory and new title made him a celebrity and changed the course of his life. The 'Duke' persona – attention-seeking, self-righteous, with an outsized sense of entitlement – stuck firm. 'In my opinion, Randy stopped developing as a person on 10 May, 1972,' said Jack Ensch, a fellow pilot who flew with Cunningham and spent seven months as a POW after being shot down. 'He was frozen in time, and he never advanced from there. . . . I always say it was part of my life, it wasn't my life. With Randy it became his life. And you could say it was the end of his life.'[84]

Cunningham turned the event into a myth that defined him. He published an autobiography in which he so embellished his opponents that his ghost-writer wrote a correction for the historical record after more research.[85] As a fighter ace Cunningham was a hit with the press in Saigon. He returned home to the US and planned a two-week speaking tour that turned into a five-month-long, three-city-a-day media campaign.[86] Cunningham loved the attention and continued seeking it: he bought personalized numberplates for his sports car reading 'MIG ACE' and invited a photographer along to capture him affixing them. The picture was printed in fifty newspapers around the country.[87]

He was transferred to Miramar, the Navy fighter pilot training school made famous by the movie *Top Gun*, where he eventually commanded Fighter Squadron 126. He was a talented pilot but a poor leader, with an entrenched sense of entitlement and immunity.[88]

This attitude, together with material greed, had revealed itself early in Cunningham's career. After his third dogfight victory he was to be awarded the Navy Cross, the highest honour the Navy can bestow. Just before the ceremony Cunningham confronted the base commander and told him that he and his co-pilot were boycotting the ceremony to hold out for a higher award, the Medal of Honor. The base commander spat back: 'The way you get the Medal of Honor is you don't hold out for it – you die for it. You ain't going to get the Medal of Honor. Here's what's going to go down: First, both of you are going to go get a haircut. Then you're going to get your blues cleaned and pressed with gold braid and make sure you've got a good shine on your shoes. And tomorrow, at ten o'clock, a grateful nation is going to heap praise on two of its lofty heroes and give you the Navy Cross. And you're going to accept them and be gracious and charming. Anything less than that and I will personally rip your tits off. Now get out of my office.'[89] Cunningham told the commander: 'Well I was counting on getting that money' – the $100 a month stipend and small tax breaks given to Medal of Honor awardees.

'Duke' made the frequent assertion that the film *Top Gun* was based on him. It even appeared on his Congressional website. The movie's scriptwriter, Jack Epps, laughs at Cunningham's self-serving assertion: 'That is a myth. We didn't spend two minutes thinking about Randy Cunningham. . . . I never talked to Randy Cunningham – not once. And I never really paid attention to him or his story.' In 1988, Cunningham nevertheless formed a company, Top Gun Enterprises Inc., to sell his book and other souvenirs, piggybacking on the success of the film.[90]

Cunningham's fame, including as a CNN commentator, enabled him to give speeches for $10,000 a time,[91] and to interact with prominent people, including several Republican politicians, leading to a run for Congress in San Diego's 44th Congressional district in 1990. He wrapped himself in the flag, campaigning in his bomber jacket and describing his opponent, Jim Bates, as a 'MiG to be shot down'. Bates had faced allegations of sexually harassing his staff, so Cunningham labelled him 'a sexual pervert who's guilty as sin'.[92] During the contest, it was discovered that Cunningham had not been registered to vote between 1966, when he was twenty-five, and 1988. His first wife later explained that Cunningham had forbidden her from registering to vote over fears that he would be subject to higher state taxes. Despite this, Cunningham managed a narrow win by 1,659 votes.[93]

As a Congressman, Cunningham was distinguished by a propensity to tears: days after being sworn in he cried over a vote to authorize the Gulf War. He bawled when Newt Gingrich stepped down as Speaker of the House, wept at the impeachment of Clinton, blubbered at the death of Ronald Reagan, shed tears when his son was convicted of drug dealing, choked up talking about his mother and sobbed when the United States recognized Vietnam. Cunningham's recollection of his actions on 10 May 1972, which he frequently invoked on the House floor, on television and profitably at lobbyist, campaigning and fundraising events, always led to copious tears.[94]

He was also known for personalizing political arguments, frequently brow-beating opponents with his remarkable virtue built on his heroic military career. Patronizingly he would explain things to 'the people who have never been in the military', which by his definition included all Democrats and anyone who opposed a Republican defence budget. Early in his Congressional career he castigated Beverly Byron, a Democrat from Maryland who opposed the budget: 'Mrs. Byron has never strapped herself into it [a military jet]', she lacked 'the background she needs' to talk about the plane. Byron, however, was from a military family and had flown new equipment as a test pilot. She retorted: 'Let me assure him that I have, indeed, been strapped into a jet. . . . I need not say that I have eleven trap shots and eleven cattle shots from the USS *Kennedy* on A-6s and F-14s. I also happen to be the only female who has ever flown in an SR-71 over Mach 3.2.' The cheers that greeted this put-down had little impact on Cunningham, who was widely seen as a taunting bully, boorish and not particularly bright.[95]

At an event for cancer survivors Cunningham, referring to his own experience of a rectal procedure for prostate cancer, described it as 'just not natural, unless maybe you're Barney Frank', the highly respected, openly gay Congressman who later responded that Cunningham 'seem[ed] to be more interested in discussing homosexuality than most homosexuals'.[96] Cunningham gave the finger to an elderly cancer patient at the event after the 74-year-old had called for cuts in the military budget. 'Fuck you,' Cunningham shouted at him.[97]

One thing 'Duke' did excel at was fundraising for fellow Republicans, boasting that he had raised over $1m for the 'Grand Old Party' in 1996 when he campaigned for sixty candidates. He was desperate to be appointed to the Appropriations Subcommittee on Defense. Newt Gingrich engineered the move in 1997 despite the protests of the committee Chairman, who felt Cunningham was jumping over more senior colleagues. He also inveigled his way onto the Select Committee on Intelligence in 2001. And the following year he found himself a safer Republican seat, moving to California's 50th district after it had been gerrymandered.[98] Thanks to his committee appointments, Cunningham was well placed to supply his constituents with pork from earmarks. But trouble was brewing.

In mid-May 2005, Marcus Stern, a news editor for the small local Copley news service, was looking through a recently released report on privately funded Congressional travel. The report had caused quite a stir, showing travel worth $50m on corporate jets and to posh hotels and resorts paid for by special interest groups, lobbyists and arms companies. Cunningham, as the Copley news service's local politician, was Stern's focus. The Congressman's travel figures were not bad compared to others; he had taken six trips between January 2000 and June 2005 valued at $25,572.04. Two of them intrigued the reporter, trips to Saudi Arabia paid for by a Saudi businessman living in the US, rather than by the Saudi state as might be expected of a trip to promote Saudi political and business relations. Stern attempted to investigate the trips but finding no obvious links between Cunningham and the Saudis he decided to undertake a lifestyle audit to check if the Congressman had more money than he ought to. What he found would spark a major political scandal.[99]

The reporter came across a national real estate database which showed that Cunningham had bought a mansion in the extremely wealthy neighbourhood of Rancho, Santa Fe. It was assumed the Congressman was living on his $154,700 per annum salary and his wife's earnings as a high school administrator. But he had bought the house for $2.55m with two mortgages, one for $500,000 and another for $595,000, leaving a significant down payment of $1,455,000. Cunningham probably realized some money from the sale of his previous home, which he had bought for $425,000 in 1988 with financing of $315,000 and sold fifteen years later for $1.675m. That might have been the source of the down payment on the mansion. But Stern noticed something curious in the paperwork: the house had been sold to a company and not an individual or couple.

It was sold to 1523 New Hampshire Ave. LLC, which had a Mitch Wade listed as its president. Wade was also president of another company, MZM Inc., which was located at 1523 New Hampshire Ave. in Washington DC. MZM had, from nowhere, become a top 100 defence contractor since 2003. The company had gone from having no prime government contracts to contracts worth $100m in two years.[100]

A more intensive look into the real estate data revealed that Wade had bought Cunningham's old house and almost immediately put the place back on the market at an asking price of $1.68m, slightly more than he'd bought it for. The house sat on the market for eight months before selling for only $975,000, a $700,000 loss for Wade. Clearly Wade had paid Cunningham much more than the house was worth. The overpayment, while interesting, was not illegal nor damning evidence of anything nefarious. Evidence was needed of a *quid pro quo* from a Congressman on powerful committees dealing with military and intelligence contracts to a remarkably successful defence contractor.[101]

When Stern called Mitch Wade to ask him directly about the house deal, his press secretary responded that the company had been looking to move to the San Diego area and that the best price had been obtained in both the buying and the selling of the house. Cunningham claimed he had sold the house for as much as he could get, noting that his estate agent had set the price. However, he acknowledged that he had supported contracts for MZM, but claimed it was no different to other arms companies he had supported due to their ties to San Diego, such as Qualcomm, Titan, SAIC and TRW. Cunningham suggested that all he had done for these companies was to 'write letters of support, saying, hey, I support this program of General Umptiump or Admiral Uptiump supports this program. But I don't make the decisions on what's going to be funded or not. It's based on what the military wants. National Security.' Of course in the case of earmarks this was untrue. In fact, Cunningham even chatted to the reporter about Charlie Wilson and his success in pushing his pet project.[102]

The discovery of the unusual house purchase led to numerous reporters, bloggers, amateur researchers and law enforcement officials turning their attention on Cunningham and his campaign donations, valuations of the house and even other lawmakers who benefited from Mitch Wade. Reporters received tip-offs which led them to two boats: the newer of them was registered to Wade, but named the *Duke-Stir* and by all accounts was used solely by Cunningham. It transpired that Wade also paid everything for the boat, including the yacht club membership and slip fees. Within a matter of days of the first allegations being published, Cunningham was under investigation by the FBI. Mitch Wade soon agreed to cooperate in exchange for a reduced sentence.[103]

Cunningham tried, cack-handedly, to cover up evidence of the long-running bribery and kickback schemes he had been running. He attempted to coach the owner of an antiques store where he had been a regular customer to say that while Wade paid Cunningham's bills, he was always paid back. And the Congressman asked the owner to store away some of the many expensive items he had bought. His estate agent was asked to lie about who set the price of his house and whether it was fair market value. And Cunningham forged a letter purporting to show his astonishment at Wade making a loss on the deal in what prosecutors described as 'repeated and egregious attempts to both fabricate evidence and influence witnesses'. Even the night before he was locked up Cunningham left several suitcases and duffel bags in his soon-to-be-ex-wife's driveway, containing dirty underwear and $32,000 in cash.[104]

Despite his disingenuous efforts to conceal it, the evidence against Cunningham was overwhelming. He was sentenced to eight years and four months in prison. He was also fined $1,804,031.50 in back taxes on his corrupt gains, which he would have to pay out of the Congressional and Navy pensions that he still received despite his disgrace.[105]

Mitch Wade, who helped put Cunningham in prison, was sentenced to thirty months in jail and a fine of $250,000. He benefited from over $150m in corrupt defence contracts, a tab the taxpayer will be picking up.[106] Before he set up MZM in 1993, Wade had worked in a variety of civilian, military and intelligence jobs at the Pentagon. He had a high-level security clearance, contacts, and excellent knowledge of the military and intelligence worlds.[107]

In 1998, he was part of a contract run by Brent Wilkes, who had worked as a tax specialist for Deloitte and Arthur Andersen before setting up his own business, World Finance Group Ltd, in 1984. While the company handled real estate transactions and equipment and aircraft leasing, its name was suspiciously similar to a CIA front involved in the Bay of Pigs fiasco. One of his biggest clients was South Pacific Islands Airlines, which ferried US and other military personnel around the Pacific. Wilkes also did business in El Salvador and Honduras, gaining access to the upper levels of Honduran society.[108] He also regularly escorted Congressmen and contractors who were visiting Central America, providing lavish parties and prostitutes to relieve the tedium of working travel.[109]

Wilkes's best friend from childhood, Kyle Foggo, better known as 'Dusty', became a high-ranking CIA official. Foggo was posted in Honduras and Panama as a CIA money man, handling contracts, logistics and financial dealings. It was widely rumoured that Wilkes was connected to the CIA, where he worked with Foggo, who had been involved in the Contras' campaign to overthrow the Sandinista government of Nicaragua.[110]

Wilkes's mysterious trips to Central America had ended in 1987, around the time of the Iran–Contra scandal and he shut down his World Finance Group Ltd business. By 1992, he was making a very good living as a political consultant, distributing bundles of campaign contributions on behalf of his clients. Some of the contributions turned out to be illegal. On behalf of a digitizing company he was involved in persuading a legislator to earmark a project into a bill to force the California Department of Transport to digitize its maps and blueprints. He had lobbied and made contributions to Cunningham's predecessor in his second Congressional seat, and made contributions to other notable names, such as John Murtha, to earmark similar projects for military use of the technology. Wilkes had other Congressmen in his pocket, earmarking projects. In 1995, he bought the rights to a rival company's document digitizing system, hired engineers and created a new company called ADCS Inc. He began courting Cunningham as a sponsor, taking him to posh restaurants and in 1997 bought him a jet boat for $11,255. Cunningham pushed ADCS, winning them an increase in their contract with the Pentagon.[111]

Cunningham used the return of control of the Panama Canal to Panama, which was scheduled for December 1999, to promote a project to digitize strategically useful documents on the canal. As ADCS was not yet qualified to be a prime contractor for the government, it worked through a qualified contractor for the Department of Veterans' Affairs. Despite the department having nothing to do with the digitization of the Panama documents, Wilkes arranged for a friendly Congressman in charge of the Veterans' Affairs Appropriations Subcommittee to be given campaign money. Soon afterwards, ADCS and its partner won a contract for the work. Cunningham's role was then to bully and cajole programme managers at the department to sign off on unsubstantiated, dodgy and outright fraudulent billing for the projects, threatening any civil servants who objected.[112] Mitch Wade was hired in 1997 to provide high-level, security-cleared staff for ADCS's project. This enabled Wade to get to know 'Duke' Cunningham.

After 9/11 and the declaration of the War on Terror, there was virtually no limit on contracts in the military-intelligence field. With Cunningham's help MZM garnered $163m in contracts, nearly all sole-sourced and classified.[113] The company also won a so-called blank-purchase agreement worth $225m. This was a controversial contracting method meant to simplify high-volume business with the government for everyday requirements, but it had little oversight, competition or transparency.[114] MZM extracted huge profit margins on the dubious contracts. For example, 850 per cent profit on a $6m earmark attached by Cunningham for storage devices for Counter Intelligence Field Activity, which had not requested the devices and did not need them. Wilkes and Wade bought the devices off the shelf for $700,000. MZM was also involved in contracts in Iraq for translators, and countering improvised explosive devices (IEDs), though the details are classified.[115]

MZM and Wade gave thousands in bundled campaign contributions to Congressmen, with Wade often illegally paying back MZM employees who were pressured into making individual political contributions.[116]

Since 1996 Wilkes had been plying Cunningham with prostitutes, private jet travel and limousine services. He gave the war hero $700,000 in gifts and cash in exchange for millions in contracts. The bribes from Wade and Wilkes were passed both directly and through sham purchases such as the house and boats, as well as antiques and a Rolls-Royce.[117]

The *quid pro quo* was explicit. When Cunningham's home and boats were raided a document was found with Wade's cooperation: the bribe menu. While sitting in a restaurant for lunch, Cunningham had bargained with Wade over his prices for contracts. Written on Congressional notepaper, cryptic to the uneducated eye, the menu showed that Cunningham wanted a $140,000 yacht for the first $16m in contracts, then $50,000 for each additional million dollars. After $340,000 in payments for contracts worth $20m, the cost of each further million would be dropped to $25,000.[118] (See p. 327.)

In addition to his involvement with Cunningham, Mitch Wade also pleaded guilty to making illegal campaign contributions to other politicians, though supposedly without their knowledge, and to bribing a Defense Department official and other employees in return for their help in awarding contracts. The Pentagon employees were not named in court filings.[119] Brent Wilkes was serving a twelve-year sentence for bribery, conspiracy, fraud and wiretapping but maintains his innocence. He was granted bail in January 2009 while he appeals his conviction. He is still out on bail, and in July 2010 won a poker tournament, earning $10,000.[120]

Kyle Foggo rose to become an Executive Director at the CIA, responsible for all the agency's external contracts. He was described as a freewheeling

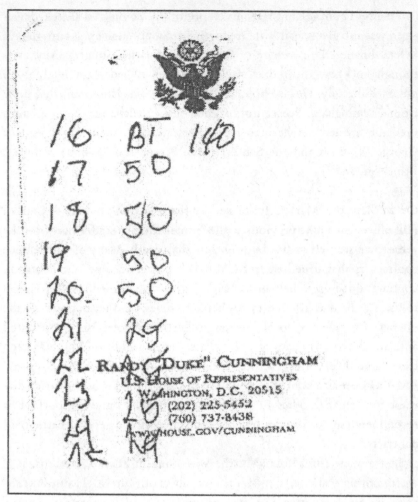

Figure 5: Randy Cunningham's bribe menu

covert logistics officer, credited with organizing the secret supply pipelines that fanned out from Europe at the onset of war to remote regions of Afghanistan and Iraq.[121] In 2008, Foggo pleaded guilty to directing CIA contracts to his friend Wilkes. They included a $2m to $3m contract for supplying bottled water to Iraq and Afghanistan, despite Wilkes's company having no experience in the area. Foggo received bribes from Wilkes and a trip to a Honolulu estate, and had been offered a high-ranking job at one of Wilkes's companies.[122] He was sentenced to thirty-seven months in prison in February 2009.[123]

Finally Thomas Kontogiannis, a politically connected Greek developer, was also given a jail sentence for bribing Cunningham. Kontogiannis helped finance the purchase of two homes for the Congressman, even though he knew the money for the purchases had most likely been obtained illegally. He also bought a yacht at a considerably inflated price from Cunningham. Prosecutors argued that in exchange, Kontogiannis used the former war hero to meet world leaders, including President George W. Bush and the Saudi Crown Prince and Defence Minister, Prince Sultan.[124]

On 20 May 2010, Mark Critz picked up the keys to his old boss's Capitol Hill office. Two days previously, the former Murtha staffer had won the Johnstown seat left vacant by John Murtha's death. Many of the defence contractors that benefited from Murtha's power to dole out Pentagon contracts lined up to help elect Mark Critz, who immediately promised to work as hard as his mentor to shepherd federal money and jobs to the district. Contractors, local business officers and lobbyists contributed $142,400 in the early days of Critz's campaign, in addition to the $21,400 from large defence contractors. Four former lobbyists of the disgraced PMA Group also contributed to his campaign.[125] As local district director for Murtha's office in Johnstown, Critz was vitally important in recommending to Murtha which companies should receive earmarked contracts.[126]

Lest anyone think John Murtha was alone in his indiscretions, it is worth noting that twelve of sixteen members of Murtha's House Appropriations Subcommittee on Defense mimicked the Chairman's pattern of earmarking, providing targeted military funds to specific contractors represented by former staffers and friends.[127] Despite President Obama's vow to sharply reduce them, as Critz took over from his former boss it was confirmed that the value of Congressional earmarks increased to almost $16bn in fiscal 2010.[128]

The use of earmarking has exploded since the Reagan years. When Reagan took office in 1981 there were fewer than ten earmarks in the Transportation Bill according to the conservative Heritage Foundation. In 1988, Reagan vetoed the bill because of the 121 earmarks in it. In 1991, earmarks grew to 538, then 1,850 in 1998 and in 2005 reached 6,373, costing $24.2bn according to Taxpayers for Common Sense.[129] In 2009, the total earmarks listed by the official OMB database numbered 11,124, worth \$15.2bn.[130] Along with the increased support in one's district, earmarks for corporate use elicit support in return, normally as campaign contributions. While the pretence can be maintained that there is no direct *quid pro quo* for earmarks, the reality allows the system of legalized bribery to thrive in Washington. John Murtha would implicitly acknowledge the connection, according to an unnamed lobbyist: 'His basic pitch was: "Thank you for helping me so I can continue to help you."'[131]

Attempts have been made to roll back aspects of this corruption. In March 2010, the rules were agreed to ban earmarks for for-profit organizations, though this still leaves the door wide open for money to be diverted through non-profit ones. There have also been moves to increase the transparency of earmarks. The Earmark Transparency Act would force all sponsors and co-sponsors of earmarks to be publicly identified along with their earmarks on a public website. The Act is currently in the Congressional process.[132]

This focus on John Murtha, Charlie Wilson, Darleen Druyun, Randy Cunningham and the scandals they have been involved in, while important, must be seen for what they reveal about the political and economic system: that they are not the exception but part of business-as-usual for Congress and defence contracting. What is never mentioned, for obvious reasons, are the countless scandals, conflicts of interest and abuse that do not result in publicity or prosecution. Hucksters like Cunningham, Murtha and Druyun make the system safer for the more systemic legal bribery and corruption that takes place in the day-to-day practices of the MICC.

16.   Beyond Utopia, Hope?

The transition from the defence contractor utopia of George W. Bush to the potentially more difficult Obama administration has been fairly seamless for the weapons business in the US.

While during his campaign and the early months of his presidency, Barack Obama talked tough on the need for fundamental change to the way the defence industry and the Pentagon operate, the reality is that there has been only very small, peripheral change. On the whole it is business as usual for the MICC.

Pentagon budgets suggest that the amount of money available to defence contractors has undergone little change. In fact, in 2011 basic funding levels – not including money set aside for the wars in Afghanistan and Iraq – were in line with the last Bush administration budget, right down to prospective further increases. The overall figure for the 2011 Pentagon budget was actually $513bn; that is higher than Bush's last base budget. The preliminary figure for war-fighting in 2011 was $159bn, which represents a slight increase from the $155bn that went to military operations in 2010. Add that to the base Pentagon budget and you get a subtotal of $662bn for 2011 military expenditures. If the estimated costs of military spending lodged in other parts of the federal budget (like funding for nuclear weapons, which falls under the Department of Energy), as well as miscellaneous non-Defense Department defence costs – about $17bn last time around – are also included, then President Obama's most recent military budget comes in at around $689bn.[1]

Unsurprisingly, after the preliminary budget figures were released the Secretary of Defense, Robert Gates, who was kept in post after Obama assumed office, told reporters: 'In our country's current economic circumstances, I believe that represents a strong commitment to our security.'[2] The administration's request for 2012 is $703bn.[3]

Any attempt to cut the overall defence budget will be fought tooth and nail in Congress and within the military, backed by all the lobbying power of the weapons-makers and service providers. The extent of the abiding power and influence of the MICC was evident in relation to the F-22 Raptor, Lockheed Martin's major weapons system and the most expensive jet fighter in history to date, costing $350m per plane with over 1,000 parts suppliers across forty-four states.[4] On 20 January 2009, 200 members of the House and forty Senators signed a 'Dear Mr. President, Save the F-22' letter, meant to be waiting for Barack Obama as he entered the Oval Office. The letter asserted that the F-22 programme 'annually provides over $12 billion of economic activity to the national economy'. Twelve Governors signed a similar letter. Even if that dubious claim were substantiated, the economic activity comes at a high cost: almost $70bn for a fighter that lacks a role in any imaginable war-fighting scenario the US might actually find itself in.[5]

The letters were accompanied by an advertising blitz from Lockheed Martin, proclaiming '300 MILLION PROTECTED, 95,000 EMPLOYED'.[6] When asked where the jobs were located, the company claimed the information was proprietary and refused to provide it. As Hartung remarked: 'Never mind that Lockheed Martin gets almost all its revenues and profits from the federal government – when it's time to come clean about how it is using our tax money, it's none of our business.'[7]

The company had to back away from the 95,000 jobs claim, clarifying that more than 70 per cent of those jobs are only indirectly related to the F-22 and that just 25,000 workers are employed directly on the plane's construction.[8] The irony is that almost any other form of spending – even a tax cut – creates more jobs than military spending. In fact, if the F-22 is funded and spending on other public investments goes down accordingly, there will be a net loss of jobs nationwide.[9]

Efforts to promote the plane as a critical tool in the War on Terror floundered when Gates said in 2008: 'The reality is we are fighting two wars, in Iraq and Afghanistan, and the F-22 has not performed a single mission in either theater.'[10] In fact, it has never been used in combat.[11] Williamson Murray of the Army War College believes that 'The F-22 is the best fighter in the world, no doubt about it. But there ain't any opposition out there. It's sort of like holding a boxing tournament for a high school and bringing Mike Tyson in.'[12]

This was not the first attempt to stall the F-22. In 1999, John Murtha and the Republican Jerry Lewis surprisingly teamed up to withhold production funding in protest at the programme's huge cost overruns.

They had no intention of killing the F-22, but wanted to get the company's and the Air Force's attention. Lockheed Martin pulled out all the stops, deploying a range of ex-Congressmen as lobbyists. From a luxury box at a Baltimore Orioles baseball game to the steam room of the House gymnasium, which ex-members are allowed to frequent, the message went out that allowing funding to slip by even a few months would strike a devastating blow to the country's security and economy. Former Senator Dale Bumpers described the company's campaign as 'one of the most massive lobbying efforts I've ever witnessed'. The Air Force, technically prohibited from lobbying Congress, formed a 'Raptor Recovery' team 'to tell our leadership in Congress that we believe the Air Force and the country need this'.[13] The Air Force described its intervention as 'informational' activity, suggesting it is pretty much able to lobby as it pleases.

The Air Force's intention at this point was to buy 339 planes for a projected cost of over $62bn – up from an initial proposal to buy 750 planes for $25bn. That's less than half as many planes for more than double the price. This absurd situation arose because initially Lockheed Martin put in a low bid, knowing that the planes would cost far more than their initial estimate. This practice of 'buying in' allows a company to get the contract first and then jack up the price later. Then the Air Force engaged in 'gold plating' – setting new and ever more difficult performance requirements once the plane is already in development. And finally Lockheed Martin messed up aspects of the plane's production, while still demanding costs for overheads and spare parts from the Pentagon. As Hartung observes, this is a time-tested approach that virtually guarantees massive cost overruns.[14]

From inside the Pentagon, Chuck Spinney described the process as follows:

> When you start a programme the prime management objective is to make it hard to cancel. The way to think about this is in terms of managing risk: you have performance risk and the bearers of the performance risk are the soldiers who are going to fight with the weapon. You have an economic risk, the bearers of which are the people paying for it, the tax payers. And then you have programmatic risk, that's the risk that a programme would be cancelled for whatever reasons. Whether you are a private corporation or a public operation you always have those three risks. Now if you look at

who bears the programmatic risks it's the people who are associated with and benefit from the promotion and continuance of that programme. That would include the military and civilians whose careers are attached to its success, and the congressman whose district it may be made in, and of course the companies that make it. If you look at traditional engineering, you start by designing and testing prototypes. To reduce performance risk you test it and redesign it and test it, redesign it. In this way you evolve the most workable design, which in some circumstances may be very different from your original conception. This process also reduces the economic risk because you work bugs out of it beforehand and figure out how to make it efficiently. But the process increases the programmatic risk, or the likelihood of it being cancelled because it doesn't work properly or is too expensive.

But the name of the game in the Pentagon is to keep the money flowing to the programme's constituents. So we bypass the classical prototyping phase and rush a new programme into engineering development before its implications are understood. The subcontractors and jobs are spread all over the country as early as possible to build the programme's political safety net. But this madness increases performance and economic risk because you're locking into a design before you understand the future consequences of your decision. It's insane. If you are spending your own money you would never do it this way but we are spending other people's money and because we won't be the ones to use the weapon – so we are risking other people's blood. So protecting the programme and the money flow takes priority over reducing risk. That's why we don't do prototyping and why we lie about costs and why soldiers in the field end up with weapons that do not perform as promised.

In the US government money is power. The way you preserve that power is to eliminate decision points that might threaten the flow of money. So with the F-22 we should have built a combat capable prototype. But the Cold War was ending, and the Air Force wanted that cow out of the barn door before the door closed.[15]

The Army sided with Lewis and Murtha against the Air Force, in an example of inter-service rivalry, which is one of the complexities of the MICC, where different parts of the military are divided not about how much to spend but about what to spend it on. But in October 1999 Lockheed Martin won $2.5bn more for the F-22 programme.[16]

Cost concerns lingered into the early months of the George W. Bush administration, but after 9/11 the massive increase in military spending and the new attitude to security saved the F-22 and other threatened projects. As a senior Boeing executive said: 'the purse is now open and any member of Congress who doesn't vote for the funds we need to defend this country will be looking for a new job after next November [elections]'.[17]

It was assumed Lockheed Martin's lobbying power would ensure the survival of the F-22 even when the Obama administration took office. But, in April 2009, the Defense Secretary, Robert Gates, announced that production of the F-22 would be halted when the last of 187 planes are delivered in 2011. He announced a $13bn increase in spending on military personnel and an extra $2bn for unmanned drone aircraft. He also announced increases in weapons spending, including an additional $4bn for the F-35, another Lockheed Martin product.

Despite this extra money Congress responded angrily. First, the Senate Appropriations Committee demanded that the Air Force study the viability of creating an export version of the fighter jet to sell to Japan and Australia.[18] And the House Armed Services Committee provided $369m over two years to purchase parts to construct twelve more of the jets.[19]

But two weeks after the announcement Lockheed Martin itself seemed to accept that the decision was made. Bill Hartung reveals that in the weeks leading up to his announcement, Gates had met with the company's CEO, Robert Stevens, and essentially said: 'If you oppose me on this, I'll eat your lunch.' Lockheed's top management decided to back off on lobbying for the F-22 for fear of alienating their biggest customer.[20] Gates also played the jobs card effectively without ever questioning the faulty innate logic of the argument. The acceleration of the F-35 programme would more than offset any F-22 job losses. He claimed that while F-22 jobs would fall by 11,000 between 2009 and 2011, the F-35 programme would gain 44,000 over the same period.[21]

This didn't make the Congressional battle any less nasty. The opposition to cutting the F-22 was bipartisan, pork-driven and led by Senators whose home states had the biggest stake in the programme. The Armed Services Committee voted to build seven additional planes in order to keep the production line operating, opening the door to the provision of more funds the following year. The 13–11 vote reflected the domestic politics of the programme. A pork-driven vote in the House Armed Services Committee led to a further $369m to help keep the programme going. And so it went to the Senate floor for a dramatic and conclusive vote.

President Obama announced that he would veto any defence budget that included additional funding for the F-22, a virtually unprecedented and bold move, which he then backed up with some heavyweight lobbying by his administration. Gates himself delivered a speech in Chicago less than a week before the vote in which he lambasted Congress, reminding his audience in the Windy City and Washington that the defence budget was an increase over the last one of the Bush administration and that the US spent more on defence than the rest of the world combined: 'Only in the parallel universe that is Washington DC could this be considered "gutting" defence,' concluded the combative Defense Secretary.

In the debate itself, the F-22 was stoutly defended by, among others, Senator Daniel Inouye, a Hawaii Democrat who has spent over two decades on the Appropriations Subcommittee on Defense and describes himself as 'the #1 guy for earmarks'. In 2009 alone Inouye had brought home over $206m, in return for which he received over $117,000 in campaign contributions from companies that benefited from his earmarks, with half coming from Lockheed Martin.[22] As Hartung remarks: 'Inouye never met a weapon system he didn't like.' Obama's former election opponent, John McCain, dispatching his campaign flip-flopping to return to his reforming roots, argued persuasively that 'it boils down to whether we are going to continue the business as usual of once a weapons system gets into full production it never dies or whether we are going to take the necessary steps to reform the acquisition process in this country'.[23] The vote was carried by a surprisingly large majority of 58 to 40.

Lockheed Martin's lobbying power had kept the F-22 alive against the odds for so long in a battle that they ultimately lost, but in a war they continue to win. In fact the company will come out ahead of the game under Gates's budget package, with the F-35 Joint Strike Fighter likely to be the largest programme in the history of military aviation. Sold to Congress with a promised price tag of $62m per aircraft, that has already risen to $111m, an 81 per cent increase per plane.[24] An extra $4.4bn was added to the F-35 project in Obama's first defence budget.[25] Although cheaper per plane than the F-22, it is intended that over 3,000 will be bought by the US and UK alone, with another 600–700 bought by partner countries.

A Lockheed Martin executive, Mickey Blackwell, described it as 'the Super Bowl, the huge plum, the airplane program of the century'.[26] Northrop Grumman and BAE will have significant roles in the production process, moves that garnered wider US pork and British support for the project.

The usual litany of problems have beset the F-35: 2,000 pounds over-weight with inadequate pre-testing and so far behind schedule that it could cost an extra $16.6bn over five years, bringing the total project cost to over $380bn.[27] In addition, over the lifetime of the jet, maintenance and running expenses will cost the American taxpayer $1 trillion.[28] Chuck Spinney was moved to suggest that 'the F-35 will be a far more costly and more troubled turkey than the F-22'. In an even more damning indict-ment of the company and its products, a former Pentagon aerospace design engineer, Pierre Sprey, described Lockheed Martin as 'always the sleaziest [of the defence contractors] and they make crappy airplanes. The F-35 is a total piece of crap, far worse than the planes it's replacing.'[29]

The Bush presidency and the first year of the Obama administration were good times for US arms-exporting activity as well. Major foreign arms deals by US companies more than doubled from 2001 to 2008, reaching a total of over $31bn. The US lead in the overall global weapons market increased dramatically as well. In 2008, more than *two thirds* of all new arms sales agreements worldwide went to US companies.[30]

Significant amounts of money continue to be made available to coun-tries buying weapons from the US. So, in addition to the record levels of defence spending and foreign military cooperation funding (that is often used to buy US weapons and totalled around $5bn in 2003),[31] the State Department and Pentagon spend an average of over $15bn per year in security assistance funding, a large share of which goes to finance purchases of US weapons and training.[32] In addition, low-rate, US government-backed loans are made available to potential arms-purchasing nations. Such a loans programme existed in the 1970s and 1980s but was closed down after loans worth $10bn were either forgiven or never repaid, i.e. the programme became a further giveaway for US contractors and their foreign clients.[33] Despite this history, in 1995 another $15bn loan guaran-tee fund was signed into law by President Clinton. This followed six years of lobbying by the arms industry, led by Lockheed Martin's CEO, Norm Augustine.[34]

Direct pressure from the Pentagon and the White House is often used to close a sale. For instance, in 2002 the US government demanded that South Korea award a $4.5bn contract to Boeing rather than a French company. Leaks from the South Korean defence ministry indicate that the French plane outperformed its American rival in every area and was $350m cheaper. But the Deputy Defense Secretary, Paul Wolfowitz, told the Koreans that they risked not only losing US political support but the American military would refuse to provide them with cryptographic systems that allow aircraft to identify one another or to supply the American-made air-to-air missiles that the plane uses. Boeing was awarded the contract.[35]

When Colombia considered buying light attack aircraft from Brazil rather than a US manufacturer, the senior American commander in the region wrote to Bogotá that the purchase would have a negative impact on Congressional support for future military aid to Colombia. The deal with Brazil fell through.[36]

Of all the monies spent today in the US on foreign affairs, 93 per cent passes through the Department of Defense and only 7 per cent through the State Department. This both reflects the support given to the weapons manufacturers and is indicative of why the US so often turns to the military option in solving international problems.[37]

And, of course, Lockheed Martin is the biggest beneficiary of this trend, and one of its biggest export items is the F-16 fighter plane. Since 2006, the company has entered into agreements to sell F-16s worth nearly $13bn to Romania, Morocco, Pakistan and Turkey. A relatively new, even more lucrative development is the large-scale export of current-generation Lockheed Martin missile defence systems. During 2007 and 2008, the company made agreements to sell one or more of these systems to the United Arab Emirates, Turkey, Germany and Japan for a total of over $24bn. Its C-130J military transport planes are destined for Israel, Iraq, India and Norway in deals worth nearly $5bn. Additional sales of Hellfire missiles, Apache helicopters, and various bombs and guidance systems are earning the company billions more.[38]

One of the most controversial recent sales of Lockheed Martin equipment was a $6bn deal with Taiwan that included 114 of the company's PAC-3 missiles at a cost of $2.8bn.[39] The deal sparked an angry response from China, which threatened to cut off military-to-military cooperation with the United States and impose sanctions on US firms whose equipment was part of the deal. As of this writing, the threatened sanctions had not been imposed and military relations were pretty much reinstated.

Lockheed Martin argues that its weapons exports provide stability by deterring war, but critics suggest that weapons exports fuel arms races and make war more likely: does Romania need to spend $4.5bn on F-16s? Isn't Pakistan more likely to use its F-16s against India than against Al Qaeda or the Taliban? Does buying missile defence technology to a value of over $15bn protect the United Arab Emirates or is it just making this purchase to curry favour with Washington?

In Turkey, for example, Lockheed Martin-supplied F-16s didn't just sit on a runway: they were used in a brutal fifteen-year war against Kurdish separatists affiliated with the Kurdish Workers Party (PKK) that left thousands of villages bombed, burned and abandoned, and tens of thousands of people dead. Of the people driven from their homes during the conflict 375,000 have yet to return.[40] Although the F-16 was far from the only weapon used in suppressing the Kurds, it was featured in air strikes – both within Turkey and in raids against alleged PKK sanctuaries in Iran and northern Iraq – that helped set the stage for more intensive raids using attack helicopters, armoured personnel carriers, rifles and anti-tank weapons. Joel Johnson, then a lobbyist for the Aerospace Industries Association, of which Lockheed Martin is an active member, tried to justify Turkish bombing of Kurdish areas by essentially saying that everybody does it:

> It must be acknowledged that the Turks have not invented Rolling Thunder. We used B-52s to solve our guerrilla problem [in Vietnam]. The Russians used very large weapons platforms [in Afghanistan]. And Israelis get irritated on a reasonably consistent basis and use F-16s in Southern Lebanon. One wishes it didn't happen. Sitting in the comfort of one's office, one might tell all four countries that they're wrong. It's a lot easier to say that here than when you're there and it's your military guys getting chewed up.[41]

Israel has been another major user of Lockheed Martin products and is a good example of how difficult it is to control the use of exported weaponry once it is delivered, even when the recipient is a close ally (see Chapter 17).

The company's involvement in virtually every facet of missile defence was underscored by President Obama's September 2009 decision to scrap a Bush administration plan to place missile defence components in Poland and the Czech Republic. Although Boeing, which is responsible for the radar system that would have been deployed in the Czech Republic under the Bush plan, stood to lose from President Obama's change in course, it appeared that Lockheed Martin might actually come out ahead. This unexpected outcome is tied to the fact that the Obama administration did not abandon missile defences in Europe – it just restructured them. Leaked Pentagon documents indicate that the number of Lockheed Martin interceptor rockets deployed in Europe could quadruple under the Obama plan.[42]

And in January 2010, just three months after Obama announced the restructuring, plans for the deployment in Poland of Lockheed Martin-made PAC-3 missiles were announced. Then, in early February, Romania's President Traian Basescu announced that his country was entering talks with the Obama administration to place PAC-3 missile interceptors there. The fact that Lockheed Martin should benefit from a change in missile defence policy is not so surprising given the company's extensive role in the roughly $10bn per year missile defence programme. As with the termination of the F-22 programme, the company is big enough and diversified enough to weather the cuts. For Lockheed Martin, what the Pentagon takes away with one hand it usually gives back with the other (and then some).

But the company's biggest source of future growth is likely to be on the home front, where it is involved in everything from homeland security to the 2010 census. Lockheed Martin's rapid move into the homeland security arena led to the company's biggest fiasco in years, when it attempted to rebuild the US Coast Guard in the aftermath of 9/11. The programme to urgently upgrade the important but neglected Coast Guard was known as Deepwater, a $17bn initiative to build a small navy with over 90 new ships, 124 small boats, nearly 200 new or refurbished helicopters and aeroplanes, almost 50 unmanned aerial vehicles (UAVs), and an integrated surveillance and communications system.[43]

The first round of Deepwater failed so badly that it left the Coast Guard weaker and less capable. The winners of the Deepwater competition were Lockheed Martin and Northrop Grumman. The companies were to work in partnership not only to build their own aspects of the contract but to supervise the work of every other company involved in the programme. This 'innovative' approach was touted as a way to reduce bureaucracy and increase efficiency compared with a system in which the Coast Guard itself would retain primary control. What it ended up proving was that contractors can be far *less* efficient than the government at running major programmes. Anthony D'Armiento, an engineer who worked for both the Coast Guard and Northrop Grumman on the project, called it 'the fleecing of America. It's the worst contract I've seen in my 20-plus years in naval engineering.'[44] Initially eight ships were produced for $100m. They were unusable: the hulls cracked and the engines didn't work properly. The second-largest boat couldn't even pass a simple water tank test and was put on hold. The largest ship, produced at a cost of over half a billion dollars, was also plagued by cracks in the hull, leading to fears of the hull's complete collapse.

In May 2005, Congress cut the project's budget in half, leading to the usual battery of letter writing, lobbying and campaign contributions that resulted in not only the avoidance of cuts to the disastrous programme but an increase to the budget of about $1bn a year, bringing the total project budget to $24bn. Finally, in April 2007, the Coast Guard took back the management of the project from the defence contractors. The first boats are expected to be ready for launch sometime in 2011, ten years after the 9/11 attacks that prompted the modernization effort in the first place.[45]

As is the way of the MICC, Lockheed has a chance to redeem itself through another ship-building project, the Littoral Combat Ship (LCS), a vessel designed to operate in offshore waters and to deal with 'asymmetric threats' such as pirates, drug runners, terrorists and small attack boats. After costs on early versions of the ship more than tripled, Robert Gates, the Secretary of Defense, restructured the programme to create a competition between Lockheed Martin and Northrop Grumman to win the rights to build the next ten ships. Ultimately, in December 2010, Lockheed Martin and Austal USA, the US branch of an Australian company, were awarded the contracts to build four ships initially, probably rising to ten ships by 2015.[46] The total cost is estimated to be around $37bn.[47]

Deepwater is by no means Lockheed Martin's only project concerned with domestic security. The company is the eighth-largest contractor to the Department of Homeland Security, including projects on airport screening and biometric technology. The latter is also used by the IRS, so that Lockheed not only keeps track of fingerprints but is also involved in processing tax forms, counting individuals in the census and sorting the mail.[48]

In 2010, the company received a $5bn contract to provide logistics services to US Special Forces in their deployment to Afghanistan and other areas of current or potential conflict. It is also getting a foothold in the market for UAVs, with a system based on blimps loaded up with cameras and sensors that can hover over an area and do surveillance without putting a pilot at risk.[49]

Lockheed Martin remains the US's leading government contractor, with $36bn in federal contracts in 2008 alone, roughly $260 per taxpaying household – what Bill Hartung terms 'the Lockheed Martin tax'. It is obviously the largest weapons contractor, with over $29bn in contracts from the Pentagon. And it has more power and money to defend its turf than any other weapons-maker. It spent over $15m on lobbying and campaign contributions in 2009 alone (excluding the contributions of its 140,000 employees), and the same again in the 2010 election cycle. The company ranks number one on the database of contractor misconduct, with '50 instances of criminal, civil or administrative misconduct since 1995'.[50]

In 2004, Lockheed Martin's CEO, Robert Stevens, told *The New York Times*: 'Our industry has contributed to a change in humankind.' The question is whether for good or ill.

Despite President Obama's acknowledgement that oversight of contractors to the government is inadequate, he has been unable to do much about it. One of the primary reasons is that, under the privatized military model, many of the outsourced contracts are managed by contractors as well, down to drafting the contracts and assessing the performance of other contractors. As a consequence, oversight of the hundreds of billions of dollars spent by the US military and its contractors is woeful.

Meaningful Congressional oversight of the Defense Department and defence contractors is severely undermined by the combination of cronyism, executive pressure on foreign purchasers, the revolving door and elected representatives' desperate desire for defence companies in their states. In addition, national security is invoked to limit public scrutiny of the relationship between government and the arms industry. The result is an almost total loss of accountability for public money spent on military

projects of any sort. As *Insight* magazine has reported, in 2001 the Deputy
Inspector General at the Pentagon 'admitted that $4.4 trillion in adjust-
ments to the Pentagon's books had to be cooked to compile required
financial statements and that $1.1 trillion was simply gone and no one can
be sure of when, where and to whom the money went.'[51] This exceeds the
total amount of money raised in tax revenue in the US for that year.

Remarkably the Pentagon hasn't been audited for over twenty years
and recently announced that it hopes to be audit-ready by 2017,[52] a claim
that a bipartisan group of Senators thought unlikely.[53] If a developing
country was run like this it would be prevented from receiving money
from USAID or the UK's DiFID.

A study by government auditors in 2008 found that dozens of the
Pentagon's weapons systems are billions of dollars over budget and years
behind schedule. In fact ninety-five systems have exceeded their budgets
by a total of $259bn and are delivered on average two years late.[54] A
defence industry insider with close links to the Pentagon put it to me that
'the procurement system in the US is a fucking joke. Every administration says we need procurement reform and it never happens.' Robert
Gates on his reappointment as Secretary of Defense stated to Congress:
'We need to take a very hard look at the way we go about acquisition and
procurement.' However, this is the same official who in June 2008
endorsed a Bush administration proposal to develop a treaty with the UK
and Australia that would allow unlicensed trade in arms and services
between the US and these countries. The proposal is procedurally scandalous and would lead to even less oversight but has generated little media
coverage. In September 2010, with Robert Gates in office, the agreement
was passed.[55]

The rigour of procurement accountability undoubtedly weakened in
the post-9/11 environment and especially during the conflicts in Iraq and
Afghanistan, where there has been a proliferation of non-traditional
security programmes whose implementers believe they are exempt from
normal requirements. The US Inspector General has said that with respect
to Iraq and Afghanistan countless weapons and vast amounts of money
are simply not accounted for. At least $125bn has been misused or is
unaccounted for in the reconstruction of Iraq alone.[56]

In the past two years Iraq has signed arms deals worth more than $3bn.
Amnesty International claims that there was no clear audit trail for 360,000

small arms to Iraqi armed forces, many from the US and the UK. In addition, about 64,000 Kalashnikov assault rifles have been sent from Bosnia to Iraq, while thousands of Italian Beretta pistols have been dispatched via the UK, many of which landed up in the hands of Al Qaeda insurgents in Iraq.[57] A defence industry insider, who wished to remain anonymous, said to me: 'The whole Iraq programme is corrupt to the core. There is no accountability. People are involved there because of connections not competence. These are connections in Republican circles. Just look at KBR.' He continued: 'Pakistan has also been given billions of dollars for fighting the Taliban, and there are huge transparency issues there as well.'

As a consequence of this lack of accountability and the Bush administration's zeal to privatize as much of the military as possible, a number of fly-by-night operators landed huge defence contracts in Iraq and Afghanistan. The chaotic state of defence contracting reached its nadir with the procurement of ammunition for the Afghanistan security forces.

AEY Inc. was run out of a nondescript single room in Miami Beach, Florida, by Efraim Diveroli, a 21-year-old with a forged driving licence who had previously been arrested for domestic violence. His sidekick, David Packouz, was four years older, a drifter who had trained as a masseur. The two were serial party-goers, regular pot smokers who also dabbled in cocaine and acid.[58] The company and its young president were on the State Department's Arms Trafficking watch list. Nevertheless, in January 2007, AEY received a $298m contract with the US military as the main supplier of ammunition to the Afghan security forces.[59]

The US Army had asked for an independent evaluation of the company from a private individual, Ralph Merrill, who produced a glowing endorsement of AEY and Diveroli. It turned out that Merrill was a financial backer and a vice-president of AEY.[60] The contract was vaguely written and contained few restrictions.[61]

Diveroli, wanting to purchase the ammunition as cheaply as possible, investigated Eastern European options, and found the cheapest prices and most malleable environment was Albania. As its post-war idiosyncratic, autarkic communist regime started to crumble in the early 1990s, Albania's per capita quantity of weapons and ammunition was among the largest of any European country's. The nation's paranoid dictator, Enver Hoxha, gripped by the illusion of 'an imperialist-revisionist invasion', spent more on defence than anything else. Albania was completely militarized, awash with weapons and matériel and dotted with 600,000 concrete bunkers and fortifications for a population of just over 3 million. A great part of this armoury was of Soviet production. But in the 1960s and 1970s large quantities of Chinese weapons and ammunition reached Albania, Beijing's close ally at the time. From the 1960s the country also produced its own ammunition.[62]

As the country emerged from communism, the State Security Service collaborated for years in weapons trafficking with the Italian mafia, Palestinian and Irish groups, among others. In 1991, Albania created an 'autonomous' enterprise to sell its stockpiles. Called MEICO (Military Export–Import Company) and headed by Ylli Pinari, it worked very closely with an iron merchant, Mihal Delijorgji, who was also the president of the Dinamo football club. Delijorgji had a history of problems with Customs and the courts. In 2004, he was arrested in the VIP section of the Dinamo stadium on charges of tax evasion. While under investigation he won a defence ministry tender to dismantle tanks and armoured vehicles. He eventually paid compensation of 122 million leks to Customs, and was found guilty of forgery of stamps and documents, for which he paid a fine. However, he engineered a 'declaration of innocence' from the Military Court of Appeal a year later.

He was always proposed by Pinari as a partner for foreign companies. The Army was Delijorgji's golden goose, providing for senior individuals in the military and the defence ministry, as well as for Pinari, who owns real estate and apartments in Albania and a 'luxurious house' in Philadelphia.[63]

Albanian weapons were transported to Rwanda the year before the genocide, and sold into the Democratic Republic of Congo in 2005, and Sudan between 2004 and 2006. Albania sold weapons to the Israelis during the 2009 Gaza incursion and to Armenia, Georgia and Iran.[64] While the amounts of arms may have been relatively small, this history displays a cavalier approach to the illicit arms trade which Efraim Diveroli was happy to exploit.

In 1997, when the country descended into anarchy after the collapse of a series of pyramid schemes in which many had invested their meagre savings, a number of the old arsenals were looted. The weaponry was used by organized crime gangs within the country and abroad, causing problems for Europe and the world. The UN and NATO, which was then contemplating Albanian membership, ran projects to dismantle, neutralize and destroy the arms and ammunition proliferating in the country. The most successful was conducted by a US firm, SAIC, a global leader in the decommissioning process and a company supported by Randy Cunningham. MEICO was involved in these efforts but, according to a senior worker in the main factory used, it was only there 'for reasons of corruption'.[65]

MEICO realized there was significant money to be made in decommissioning, so contacted an American firm, Southern Ammunition Company Inc. (SAC). It is a small firm specializing in sporting guns. It can only be assumed that it was approached because an American firm offers good political cover in Albania and it happened to have initials very similar to the established US decommissioner, SAIC. Its president, Patrick Henry III, visited Albania a number of times, where he agreed on MEICO's instructions, to form a joint venture with Mihal Delijorgji to create a company called Albademil. In return, SAC demanded that prices for ammunition should be fixed and the military should bear the cost of transporting the ammunition to the disposal site, which should be located close to Tirana.[66]

Albania's Defence Minister, Fatmir Mediu, had met Patrick Henry in Tirana, and then pushed a decision through the Cabinet to allow a private company to take over the dismantling of the state's ammunition. The Finance Minister at first opposed the decision, requesting a proper tendering process for the contract, but his opposition was overcome with assistance from the Prime Minister's Office. When the Prime Minister signed the notice, it transgressed at least two Albanian laws. Mediu also created a state pricing authority which approved selling at the price Henry had agreed, although no payment was received from the company for the ammunition.[67]

In steamrolling the decision through Cabinet, Mediu made no mention of his and the businessmen's plan to mobilize the army to collect and transport the ammunition at no cost. This would set the state back at least half a million dollars. Nor did he mention that the private contractor, with his approval, had refused to provide any guarantee of security against accidents, by far the most expensive aspect of disposal work. Mediu was accused of profiting from the contract. When this was revealed it caused little surprise. Close to the country's President, and later Prime Minister,

Sali Berisha, Mediu had been detained by Italian police at Milan airport in 1998, for harbouring among a delegation of MPs heading to an EU meeting on organized crime, and supplying with a bogus identity and a diplomatic passport, an Albanian underworld figure wanted in Italy for trafficking in prostitution and his leading role in an international drug-trafficking organization. Mediu was sentenced to three years in prison for assisting a fugitive from Italian justice. His sentence was confirmed in the Milan Appeals Court before being overturned by the Italian Supreme Court. Mediu was appointed Defence Minister by Berisha after elections in July 2005.[68]

The minister issued an order to allow the adaptation of an old tank base into a decommissioning factory at a densely populated village called Gerdec, situated conveniently between the capital and its international airport. The order made no mention of the transport requirements and the safety measures necessary for such a site. It had no licence for the storage and disposal of ammunition. Even the commander of the Joint Armed Forces suggested the site was inappropriate. Work at Gerdec was delayed by a few weeks, supposedly because of a visit to Tirana by George W. Bush. Albanian authorities seemed reluctant to alert the Americans to the operation that involved a US company. In April 2007, a company owned by Mihal Delijorgji began work to convert the site.[69]

Meanwhile Efraim Diveroli, having identified Albania as the cheapest and most conducive location for sourcing ammunition for Afghanistan, negotiated the knockdown price of $22 per 1,000 bullets with MEICO. When Diveroli pointed out that he was forbidden by US law from dealing in Chinese ammunition, he received photographs showing how easily the 'Made in China' markings could be removed. He would have to repackage the bullets, while MEICO would issue false certificates guaranteeing their Albanian origin. Pinari and Diveroli were fully aware that the bullets to be sent to Afghanistan would be up to forty years old, partly decomposed and largely unusable, and that many of them would be Chinese-made. A hundred million bullets were contracted for purchase.[70]

Diveroli entrusted the crucial repackaging process to the local packaging supremo, Kosta Trebicka. However, in June, as work was about to start at Gerdec, Pinari informed Diveroli that he would have to buy the bullets at $40 per 1,000 from a Cyprus-based firm, Evdin Ltd, and that Trebicka's firm had to be replaced by Delijorgji's company. Trebicka, who bravely revealed documents of the various transactions, showed that Evdin was a phantom company whose only purpose was to divert money to Albanian officials. The purchases were a flip: Albania sold ammunition to Evdin for $22 per 1,000 rounds and Evdin sold it to AEY for much more. The difference, he suspected, was shared with Delijorgji and Albanian officials, including Pinari and the Defence Minister, Fatmir Mediu.[71] Importantly, the son of Sali Berisha, the Prime Minister, was alleged to have been involved in at least one meeting with Delijorgji and Pinari, leading to speculation that he too was in on the deal.[72]

Evdin was a company created by a Swiss arms dealer, Heinrich Thomet, who has been accused in the past by groups, including Amnesty International, of arranging illegal arms transfers under a shifting portfolio of corporate names. Thomet and Evdin are on the US State Department's Defense Trade Controls watch list. Hugh Griffiths, of the Arms Transfer Profile Initiative, describes Thomet as a broker with contacts in former Eastern bloc countries with stockpiles and arms factories.[73] An arms dealer since his teens, Thomet has been accused of smuggling arms into and out of Zimbabwe and was also under investigation by US law enforcement for shipping weapons from Serbia to Iraq.[74] His proximity to AEY's purchases raised further questions about whether the Pentagon was adequately vetting the business done in its name. 'Put very simply, many of the people involved in smuggling arms to Africa are also exactly the same as those involved in Pentagon-supported deals, like AEY's shipments to Afghanistan and Iraq,' Griffiths said.[75]

Diveroli, aware of the corruption, went along with the new arrangements. In a conversation with Trebicka, Diveroli admitted: 'Pinari needs a guy like Henri [Thomet] in the middle to take care of him and his buddies, which is none of my business. I don't want to know about that business.' Diveroli then recommended that Trebicka try to reclaim his contract by sending 'one of his girls' to have sex with Mr Pinari. He suggested that money might help, too. 'Let's get him happy; maybe he gives you one more chance. If he gets $20,000 from you . . .' At this point, Diveroli appeared to lament his dealings with Albania: 'It went up higher to the prime minister and his son,' he said. 'I can't fight this mafia. It got too big. The animals just got too out of control.'[76]

While these machinations were being worked out, Delijorgji's brother-in-law, Dritan Minxolli, the newly appointed supervisor at Gerdec, began employing people, including children. None of the employees received social security or health insurance. That summer through to October, Gerdec dismantled about 60 million bullets and removed from decades-old crates, washed, repackaged and dispatched to Afghanistan thirty-six consignments of falsely labelled bullets.[77]

Trebicka provided his revealing documents about the case to a *New York Times* journalist based in Tirana, Nick Wood. As Wood started ferreting around, all hell broke loose. Fatmir Mediu, seeking to cover his tracks, even visited the US ambassador for advice. The military attaché at the US embassy in Albania claimed that the ambassador, John L. Withers II, assisted the attempted cover-up of the Chinese origins of the ammunition. The ambassador met Mediu hours before Nick Wood was to visit the contractors' operations in Tirana. The attaché, Major Larry D. Harrison II, attended the late-night meeting on 19 November 2007. He claims that Mr Mediu asked the ambassador for help, saying he was concerned that the reporter would reveal that he had been accused of profiting from selling arms. The minister said that because he had gone out of his way to help the United States, a close ally, 'the US owed him something', according to Major Harrison. Mr Mediu ordered the commanding general of Albania's armed forces to remove all boxes of Chinese ammunition from a site the reporter was to visit and 'the ambassador agreed that this would alleviate the suspicion of wrongdoing', according to Harrison's testimony to a House committee. The ambassador denied the allegations, claiming that all he advised Mediu to do was to issue a denial when any article was written.[78] The Department of Justice cleared the ambassador, who has since retired, of involvement in covering up allegations of illegal activity.[79]

The *New York Times* stories led to an investigation of the scam and Diveroli was accused of a criminal scheme to sell banned Chinese munitions to the Pentagon and was indicted on federal fraud and conspiracy charges. He pleaded guilty in 2009 to a single conspiracy count and was sentenced to four years in jail.[80] However, Miami federal prosecutors allowed the return of $4.2m of Diveroli's property – including a new Mercedes S550 – that had been confiscated.

Because much of the equipment used by Iraqi and Afghan forces is of Soviet design and has to be sourced from a variety of former Soviet bloc countries, the standards applied to the procurement process by various US military commands and agencies, including the State Department,

vary, as does the quality of the weaponry. Despite this reality, the granting of such a huge contract to so obviously unsuitable a company and
individual beggars belief. Lax standards, virtually no vetting and contracting officers' limited understanding of munitions all but ensured that
the Army would end up with a disaster on its hands. The consequences
for innocent Albanians would ultimately be far more deadly.

Feruzan Durdaj has lived in Gerdec since 1993 when he moved from an
ancient village in the south of the country. His three children were all
born in the village. He was proud of the house he had built them on the
back of years of hard work. The village is poor, but close-knit, a community who rely on each other to get by. On the hill above Gerdec are five
low bunkers of dirty concrete, Hoxha's legacy. They are now used to
house sheep and goats.[81]

On Saturday, 15 March 2008, Erison Durdaj, Feruzan's seven-year-old
son, could not sit still at home. He had finished his homework and
rechecked it to the point of boredom. He was a bright child, chatty and
full of energy. He loved nothing more than to career around the village
on the sparkling new bike he had been given for his seventh birthday. His
father was at work, his mother busy cleaning up the house. And his sister
was annoyingly engrossed in a book. After one more glance at his homework he decided to visit his cousins, so grabbed his bike and set off for
their house only fifty yards away. As he arrived at their gate his cousins
Roxhens and Erida were just leaving to take their mother her lunch. He
happily fell in beside them.

Erison's aunt, Rajmonda, worked at the new factory in the village. In
April 2007, work had begun at the dilapidated military base in the middle of the village and by June a prefabricated structure surrounded by a
rickety fence had been built. Military trucks started to drive into and out
of the site twenty-four hours a day. It was only when villagers were
employed to work in the factory that they discovered its purpose, which
was being undertaken in contravention of a number of environmental
and safety laws and regulations. The villagers assumed it was a state-run
factory, even though in the early days there were a number of Americans
supervising the use of machinery. Dozens of unqualified men, women
and children were soon employed. Every day crowds of unemployed
people would congregate at the fence, anxious for work. The site manager
would point to his selected candidates, those who appeared strongest,

with a long stick, like a plantation owner at a slave market assessing the latest cargo from Africa.

It was dangerous work. One employee described how sometimes the bullets exploded, and the machines would catch fire. At first because the site only handled small-calibre ammunition, the fires could be easily extinguished, with only minor burns to a few workers. The casings and gunpowder were easy to take away.

Through the summer of 2007 and into September and October, about 60 million bullets were dismantled at Gerdec. Tens of millions of bullets were also repackaged into new boxes. In late 2007, the government granted permission for the factory to dismantle large-calibre ammunition, something at which none of the companies involved had any experience. The granting of this permission violated a host of further safety regulations, especially in relation to the distance of the operation from inhabited areas. In January 2008, the first 55 tons of large-calibre shells arrived at the factory. By mid-March, 8,900 tons of ammunition had been delivered to the site by a twenty-four-hour stream of military vehicles. One tenth of the entire ammunition arsenal of the Albanian armed forces was dumped at Gerdec.

Workers came from surrounding villages to take advantage of the increased activity. The work involved removing the component parts of the shells from the crates, setting to one side the fuses and projectiles, and then opening the casing, from which the detonators and gunpowder were removed. This was all undertaken in the most primitive way, by hand. The only mechanized equipment at the site was a military bulldozer, which pushed the piles of projectiles towards the nearby field. They filled two fields of about 2,000 square metres. The gunpowder was put into sacks, the detonators into crates and taken to one of the buildings of the old military base. The shells were washed with detergent and oil. The women who cleaned them were also responsible for cleaning assembled shells, which were so ancient that workers found mould and mice inside the crates in which they arrived. These cleaned, assembled shells would then be taken from Gerdec, while hundreds of tons of gunpowder and thousands of detonators and dismantled shells were left behind.

On 12, 13 and 14 March, army trucks had unloaded more than 460 tons of shells at Gerdec. There were more than 1,000 tons of gunpowder, over 286,000 detonators and almost 4,400 dismantled or intact shells, containing about 800 tons of TNT. Thousands of projectiles had been pushed aside by the bulldozer or carried to the field, and those that the women in the cleaning shed had recently washed were stacked there in piles. Gunpowder filled all the available containers and a large part of the main shed and was left in unsealed plastic bags around the open area where workers were dismantling shells. The casings hadn't been removed for ten days.

The Durdaj cousins set off towards the factory, which was not 200 yards from where they played. They arrived at the gate within five minutes. The guard told them they couldn't go into the factory but that he would give Rajmonda her lunch. 'Be careful not to spill anything,' Roxhens told the guard, 'because there are some olives in brine.' The guard nodded and walked away. The children set off to play. Erison jumped over a ditch in the field and stopped to mount his bicycle. Roxhens turned round to see why his cousin had fallen behind. He saw a huge ball of smoke and fire, resembling a gargantuan rose, opening behind Erison's back with a deafening roar. 'Eri, Eri, Eri,' he screamed, as the deadly flower enveloped them all.

Feruzan was at work in Tirana, when at 11.55 his wife called to say there had been an explosion. He screamed into his phone: 'Run, run far away with the children.' His wife told him that she had two of the children, but Erison was out playing with friends. He raced to the village. The police stopped him entering the village, so he found another route to his home. On the road he met his wife and two older children. His daughter was crying still because of a projectile that had exploded in front of them. He crammed eight people into his car and took them to the hospital, then raced back to find his son. They wouldn't let him back into the village. He returned to the hospital to look there for Erison.

At 4 p.m. a cousin told him that his son was in hospital in Tirana. He sped to the capital and scoured the hospital. He walked straight past his youngest child without recognizing him. His wife found the little boy. 'I was playing. I don't know where the fire came from,' he managed to say, between sobs. When Feruzan saw him, he lost all hope. He was so badly burned. 'I'm really sorry I went out without permission,' Erison said, quietly. The next day Feruzan took Erison to a hospital in Italy. He was only allowed to watch his son's agony through glass. At 3 a.m. on the morning of the eighteenth day, they told Feruzan that his son had died. He never heard him speak another word.[82]

In the explosions, which continued until 2 a.m. the following day and were heard more than 100 miles away, Feruzan also lost his sister-in-law, Rajmonda, along with twenty-four other villagers. One member of the extended family who lived in the house nearest the factory miraculously survived. Uran Deliu lost his mother, father and three-year-old son, his pregnant wife, his brother and his brother-in-law, who was only at the house by chance. Over 300 people were injured, 318 houses were completely destroyed and almost 400 others damaged.[83] The figures would have been even worse had many villagers not been out and about, and if hundreds of others had not managed to flee up the hill, some into Enver Hoxha's surreal bunkers.

Six months after the Gerdec explosion, the body of the whistle-blower Kosta Trebicka was found near Korçë. He appeared to have died in a car accident. However, contradictory evidence surfaced to cast doubt on this claim, especially given the threats he had received since exposing the corruption and criminal negligence at Gerdec.[84] Whatever the cause of his death he too was a victim of this criminality.

Standing on the hill above the village, where the skeletal remains of two houses stand unmended by the villagers as symbols of their suffering, I asked Feruzan what life was like in Gerdec over two years after the explosion. With goats wandering into and out of the derelict concrete bunkers and villagers nodding in agreement, this handsome, dignified and pained man replied: 'It is like living every minute of every day in a cemetery.'

If the Departments of Defense and State are so patently inadequate at vetting and controlling contractors and Congress is abject at oversight because of its own compromised position, that leaves the Department of Justice (DOJ), its sub-agencies, and the Securities and Exchange Commission (SEC) as the bulwark against arms trade anarchy. The DOJ has limited resources and varying levels of enthusiasm for investigations into arms deal corruption.

I gathered this when meeting a senior anti-corruption officer in the FBI in late 2008. I waited for him outside the J. Edgar Hoover Building on Pennsylvania Avenue, an imposing, if dour edifice. He had approached me as a consequence of my work on the South African arms deal to ask if I knew anything about corruption in the US defence industry. A tallish man, younger than I had imagined from his telephone voice, approached the bench I was sitting on and indicated for me to follow him. We walked six long blocks before he stopped outside a small, obscure coffee shop.

We sat in a dark corner. He was nervous. He spoke in a torrent, his frustration palpable. 'Look at Nigeria. Look at an American company called W. They engage in corruption but it's regarded as small scale. They never sign a contract of more than $50m to $70m. On each one they pay bribes of between $1m and $2m. Deals of this size are never investigated, we don't have the capacity. It's only if they do ten or fifteen deals like this that we will get interested. We can only focus on the big contracts because there are never enough people working on FCPA [Foreign Corrupt Practices Act] cases on arms or the military broadly.' He suggested that, despite the legislation, corruption in arms contracts is substantial.

We agreed to remain in touch and to exchange information on a regular basis.

As the source confirmed, the FCPA was not rigorously enforced for its first two and a half decades. From 1977 to 2001, only twenty-one companies and twenty-six individuals were convicted for criminal violations of the legislation.[85] In 2002, the Organisation for Economic Co-operation and Development (OECD) concluded that 'the number of prosecutions and civil enforcement actions for FCPA actions has not been great'.[86] However, since 2002 there was an increase of cases as a consequence of improved resources and the formation of a new dedicated five-member FCPA enforcement team, which has expanded several times since.[87] At one point there were sixty cases being investigated. Even if they were not all carried through, it suggests greater enforcement than thirty cases prosecuted in almost thirty years. At the end of 2009, the DOJ and SEC were between them investigating 120 FCPA cases.[88] There has also been an increase in consolidated investigations, where multiple companies are investigated for multiple activities.[89] While this is a definite improvement it is still a very small number.

In enforcing the FCPA, both criminal and civil sanctions are used. The SEC uses fines and often disgorgement of profits for corrupt deals, while both the SEC and DOJ have moved towards settlements and deferred and non-prosecution agreements in dealing with offenders. They argue that this is more effective than the long, complex and expensive court processes in establishing the guilt of offenders and that such agreements are effective in obtaining structural reforms within offending organizations.[90]

An FCPA prosecution can, but seldom does, result in loss of export priv-ileges and debarment from US government contracts.[91]

For the 1978–2002 period, of a total of thirteen cases initiated by the SEC, two were dismissed or disposed of without sanctions. Indeed between 1978 and 1996 in seven of the thirteen cases no fines or penalties were imposed, most were resolved with an injunction, a legal slap on the wrist. For a period of at least ten years no actions were brought by the SEC under the accounting and record-keeping provisions of the FCPA.[92] Where fines were imposed they were generally very small.[93] Corporate fines for 1978–2001 ranged from $1,500 to $3.5m, with the exception of Lockheed, whose settlement amounted to $21.8m in 1994. Individuals in the same period received fines of between $2,500 and $309,000 and until 1994 no jail sentences were imposed.[94]

Lockheed's settlement related to its operations in Egypt, where between 1980 and 1990 Dr Leila Takla was their consultant, responsible for the development of markets and sales. In 1987, Takla became a mem-ber of the Egyptian Parliament, where she used her influence with the Ministry of Defence to direct business to Lockheed, specifically to ensure it received a contract for three C-130 aircraft. During the contract nego-tiations, Suleiman Nassar, the regional vice-president for Lockheed International, agreed to make monthly payments to Takla. The payments, which totalled $129,000, were wired from Lockheed to a corporation known as Takla Inc. whose signatory was Takla's husband, a police gen-eral. In addition, the company submitted fraudulent statements regarding the bribes to the Defense Security Assistance Agency. Ultimately, Lock-heed was awarded a contract worth $78,983,575. After it was signed, the company paid Takla $1m as a commission.[95] She was a board member of the Suzanne Mubarak Women's International Peace Movement, chair-person of the UN Voluntary Fund and President of the Union of the World's Parliament.

The corporate collapses of Enron, Worldcom, Tyco International, Peregrine and Adelphia as well as the bursting of the dotcom bubble com-pelled legislators, in response to a backlash from their constituents, to attempt to clean up both the US's illicit extra-territorial adventures and the corporate shamanism that had come to dominate markets. This led to the International Anti-Corruption and Good Governance Act of 2000 to stop US companies bribing foreign governments or officials and the

Sarbanes Oxley Act (SOX). The government announced that white-collar crime would be a greater focus of the 'War on Crime', causing a sea-change at the SEC and DOJ. An increased focus on money laundering in the War on Terror and enhanced powers for surveillance and tracking of money movements made possible by the Patriot Act also contributed.

While this legislation didn't amend the FCPA, it significantly increased possible penalties. It also enhanced the transparency requirements for corporate accounts and imposed higher levels of due diligence and better auditing standards. CEOs and CFOs face penalties of up to $5m and twenty years' imprisonment for serious violations. The threat of these penalties certainly had some impact.

In recent years there has been an increase in investigations and prosecutions under the FCPA, and big corporations seem not to be immune. Large companies have been investigated and joint investigations more willingly carried out. Recent large FCPA investigations by the US government have also been likely to include parallel investigations in other countries, such as the UK in relation to BAE and France and Nigeria with respect to Halliburton. There have also been increases in the severity of penalties. In early 2009, KBR was hit with a $402m fine and along with its former parent company, Halliburton, a $177m disgorgement payment.[96] And, as we know, BAE finally agreed to pay $400m for lying to the US government over its corrupt dealings in Saudi Arabia and Eastern Europe.

The penalties for these offences, while far higher than was historically the case for FCPA violations, have never been truly commensurate with the scale of the corruption. For example, BAE's bribery campaign for Al Yamamah in Saudi Arabia may have involved as much as £6bn in corrupt payments, as part of a deal worth an estimated £43bn. By comparison, a $400m fine is negligible. Just days after the BAE settlements were announced, the company received a £261m pension windfall, almost compensating for the value of the entire fine. BAE also announced profits of £2.2bn on sales of £21.5bn for the year.[97] Mike Koehler, a business law professor at Butler University, noted wryly: 'Any time someone settles a case for $400 million or $180 million, you're like "Wow – they really got hammered!" But when you go through the DOJ's own allegations and add up the amount of the bribe payments and the amount those bribes caused the companies to get in business, you're still in a situation where they come out net positive.'[98]

What is the aim of these penalties? Should the intention be to penalize the company even if it could precipitate its collapse? To what extent is it fair that shareholders and employees who knew nothing of any bribery should lose their money or jobs? Should governments debar companies from future public sector contracts for periods of time linked to the severity of the offence even though it may threaten the industrial base or in the case of the MICC the perceived national security interest? To what extent should companies bear responsibility for the actions of individual employees and how much should an employee be penalized for their part in corporate corruption?

Judging the severity of a penalty is made even trickier by the lack of information available on FCPA cases. They are rarely aired in public, most being settled out of court so that the companies do not have to deal with weeks of bad headlines and large lawyers' fees. Instead, most companies choose to come clean and at least appear to make a fresh start, firing anyone clearly tied to a crime and requesting lenience for the company, as Lockheed did with Kotchian and Haughton. While arguably making the lives of investigators and companies easier, this inhibits transparency, making external scrutiny by the public impossible. There is a compelling argument that without an ongoing understanding of the application of the law, no democratic process can be sufficiently informed to improve or change the law for the better.

Companies often plead guilty and cooperate with FCPA investigators once it's clear that investigators are able to substantiate allegations against them. The opposite is remarkably rare but occurred in the BAE case. Investigators reacted to the company's lack of acknowledgement of guilt or cooperation by apprehending BAE executives Mike Turner and Nigel Rudd at US airports and copying the contents of their laptops, phones, PDAs and papers before allowing them to proceed. This power to examine and copy any data brought into the country was granted to US investigators under War on Terror rules to facilitate detection of potential terrorism plots, as well as other crimes such as child pornography and copyright infringement.[99]

The FCPA operates on the principle of *respondeat superior*; that is, if one employee is guilty of bribery, even an employee acting only at a low level or against official company policy, then the entire company can be found guilty of the crime. This requires only a minimum of evidence to substantiate a claim of bribery on which to convict the company.[100] The Financial Reform Bill – officially called the Dodd–Frank Wall Street Reform and Consumer Protection Act – passed in July 2010, contains provisions for whistle-blowers to receive a cut of any settlement or penalties from companies violating the FCPA. The SEC will pay whistle-blowers at least 10 per cent and up to 30 per cent of monetary sanctions in excess of $1m, awarded in a successful enforcement action. Given the size of recent FCPA settlements, the incentive to inform on a corrupt company has been greatly increased.[101]

It is obvious that there are more instances of bribery and corruption in the arms trade than ever make it into the media. Most malfeasance remains hidden behind the veil of national security while some companies do self-report and put in place remedial steps that cause the DOJ or SEC to decide that justice has been served.[102] But in the cases of BAE and KBR/ Halliburton there was definite intention to hide the illegal behaviour.

BAE's Mike Turner famously told the SFO that the reason for the company's extensive web of secret offshore companies used to launder bribe money was to ensure commercial confidentiality and to avoid intrusion by the media and anti-arms campaigners.[103] This systemic, intentional and long-running effort to hide payments with the complicity of executives who clearly knew what they were doing was illegal, and deserved a far greater penalty.

In the KBR case, Technip paid bribes to Nigerian officials using agents via shell companies in Gibraltar and Japan with the authorization of senior executives.[104] Technip was fined $240m in settlement and $98m in disgorgement of profits.[105] While this was again a significantly larger fine than in the earlier years of FCPA enforcement, it was hardly damaging to the company, as Technip made a profit of €417.3m in 2009.[106] The corporate structure was, according to investigators, 'part of KBR's intentional efforts to insulate itself from FCPA liability for bribery of Nigerian government officials through the Joint Venture's agents'. The company's executive chairman, Albert 'Jack' Stanley, received a seven-year jail sentence. Two UK citizens, Jeffrey Tesler and Wojciech Chodan, who were indicted in the United States for their alleged participation in the scheme and arrested in the UK, face extradition to the US. Why there was the motivation to prosecute individuals in the KBR case but not BAE is perplexing.

While there has been an increase in prosecutions of individuals – in

2009 there were three trials of four individuals in FCPA cases, equalling the number of trials in the preceding seven years[107] – this still unimpressive figure does not include anyone from the large defence companies, suggesting that bribery and corruption are still more tolerated when it comes to the commanding heights of the weapons business.

The closest a company has come to debarment was the temporary suspension of BAE's US export privileges while the State Department considered the matter.[108] Specific measures seem to be taken to avoid applying debarment rules to major arms companies, in particular by charging companies with non-FCPA charges as in the case of BAE.[109] A legislative effort was undertaken to debar Blackwater (Xe) from government contracts due to its FCPA violations. Legislation was introduced in May 2010 to debar any company that violates the FCPA, though with a waiver system in place that would require any federal agency to justify the use of a debarred company in a report submitted to Congress.[110] The mutual dependence between the government, Congress and defence companies means that, in practice, even serial corrupters are 'too important' to fail. For example, the US could not practically debar KBR, a company to which it has outsourced billions of dollars of its military functions. Similarly, debarring BAE would threaten its work on new arms projects and the maintenance of BAE products that the US military already uses.

Some argue that it would be unfair to impose so massive a penalty on companies that depend almost entirely on government contracts, as arms companies do. Within these huge companies, very few are guilty of involvement in bribery and workers and shareholders should not be punished for the crimes of a few executives. However, the status quo is, in a way, a golden get-out-of-jail card for the arms business, and suggests that even serial corrupters are immune from punishment that will seriously threaten their business.

Smaller operators are far more likely to face grave consequences for illicit arms dealing, especially since the enforcement of the FCPA underwent a revolution a few years ago with the use of sting operations in arms cases. Stings have generally been associated in the public mind with catching drug dealers. However, while they have been used against arms dealers for many years by journalists, more recently the Drug Enforcement Agency (DEA) and DHS have adopted the practice.

*

Sting operations by US law enforcement agencies have been used in the cases of Monzer Al-Kassar, Viktor Bout and Amir Ardebili, an Iranian arms procurer.[111]

The sting against Ardebili was planned and undertaken over four years by Immigration and Customs Enforcement (ICE), a division of DHS, which set up a number of mock arms businesses to trap the Iranian arms procurement network.[112] The operation was driven by a 32-year-old agent, Patrick Lechleitner, a former Virginia cop, Navy analyst and National Security Agency investigator, who floated easily among the law enforcement, military and intelligence communities. He acted as an undercover arms broker, trawling internet bulletin boards for smugglers and fielding queries from shady foreigners. Elsewhere in the Philadelphia area, he interviewed American contractors who called in tips about suspicious overseas requests. On 20 April 2004, he met a local factory owner who'd received a query, supposedly from Dubai, for jet-fighter parts. 'He seemed almost offended by the bluntness of the email,' Lechleitner recalled, especially the dubious point of origin. 'We both knew that it had to be Iran.' 'Tell him to contact me,' the agent said, handing the man a card from his undercover company. 'Tell him we might have what he needs.'

Iran is desperate for American-made weapons and technology because its crumbling military infrastructure is largely American – the legacy of billion-dollar US arms sales during the 1960s and 1970s. But Iran isn't on the prowl merely for spare parts. The country seeks to outfit its military with all the vital components required to fight a twenty-first-century war – radar, sonar, Kevlar vests, night-vision scopes, cockpit computers and missile guidance technology. US officials also say Iran is furnishing America's enemies, funnelling military gear to the Taliban, Hezbollah and Iraqi insurgents.

Amir Hossein Ardebili lived in Shiraz, a city of 1.2 million people in southern Iran. A freelance arms broker, Ardebili used the internet to buy and smuggle embargoed commercial and military technology from US companies. He had only one customer: the Iranian government. He was no patriot, no political ideologue or religious radical. He was a capitalist. A businessman. At twenty-nine, he was unmarried and lived with his parents, a symbol of his commitment to family but also of his paltry finances.

After graduation, Ardebili had taken a job with the state-run Shiraz Electronic Industries (SEI), placing orders with Iranian brokers who bought embargoed military goods from US and European companies. The contraband moved from the United States to a trusted port in Europe or the Middle East, perhaps Amsterdam or Dubai, then was re-labelled and re-shipped to a dealer inside Iran. He excelled at the work but earned just $650 a week. In early 2004, he struck out on his own, hoping to make more money. He opened a tiny office in Shiraz. SEI and other state-run companies began faxing requests and he sent queries to US companies. Online he called himself 'Alex Dave' and used a forwarding address in Dubai. He rarely told US companies where he was and they seldom asked. Sometimes American companies stiffed him: they'd realize he was in Iran and keep his deposit money.

Lechleitner noticed that Alex Dave was prolific, submitting so many requests for price quotes that an agent remarked of him: 'The guy's got so many quotes, he's like Shakespeare.' The name stuck. Alex Dave became known as Shakespeare, the case, Operation Shakespeare. Ardebili was more prolific than ICE agents realized. In a week around the Dubai Air Show he wired a $7,000 deposit to a New England broker for precision gyroscopes, devices that can be used to guide missiles. He also closed a $1m deal for technology to evade US submarines.

ICE decided to involve an undercover agent, known as 'Darius', who had established a fake US arms company in a Baltic country. The CIA had created eleven such overseas 'storefronts' at a cost of $100m, all but one of which failed. The Iranian, they figured, might become more trusting if he believed he was dealing with a Russian arms broker in Northern Europe. After a few introductory emails, Darius called Ardebili's mobile phone. They spoke in English. 'I send you a note about trans-shipping night vision,' Ardebili told him, according to a tape of the call. 'This is very, very serious business for Iranian armed forces.' Darius pretended to fret about the US embargo but Ardebili offered an easy solution: ship the US gear to Europe, then re-ship to Iran. Darius replied cautiously. 'What you say can perhaps be good business, but I stress to you what we are doing is ILLEGAL in US. Would original source of goods know they go to Iran? With more discussion it is possible we do good business, but patience and good planning keep us out of jail!' Relax, Ardebili told Darius, he'd done this before. 'This is long time we are in the business and working in full security. . . . Never know end user are located in Iran.'

They arranged to meet in Tbilisi, Georgia, where US agents arrived with gyroscopes – poker-chip-size avionics components the Iranians needed to help guide surface-to-air missiles – to show their 'partner' they could deliver. They filmed and recorded Ardebili acknowledging the extensive business he had done and hoped to do in the future, before arranging his arrest by Georgian police. From his laptop, agents traced thirty-three bank transfers – money sent from Tehran via Germany to the US accounts of American manufacturers. They found transactions involving seventy American companies, sixteen of which held large Pentagon contracts. They also identified two dozen Iranian procurement agents – men just like Ardebili – as well as fifty Iranian government subsidiaries buying weapons and components for the Islamic Republic's military. Ardebili was extradited and flown to the US to face trial.

With the Iranian secretly locked away in a Philadelphia prison, agents assumed his online persona, posing as the arms broker from Shiraz. They resumed negotiations with 150 US companies. Operation Shakespeare, still secret, had broadened into one of Homeland Security's largest investigations. US agents initially caught a dozen American companies agreeing to sell military or restricted technology. Soon the number would grow to twenty – companies based in Arizona, Texas, New York, California, Dubai and Europe, selling stealth technology, advanced radar and avionics needed to pilot a Predator drone.

At his eventual trial in 2009, after two harrowing years in solitary confinement, Ardebili broke down in tears and claimed he was no international arms dealer. 'I've done nothing wrong. I didn't harm my people or my government. I just tried to help myself. . . . They label me as an international arms dealer, which is really a big lie. I'm nobody.' The judge felt Ardebili showed genuine remorse and that he was unlikely ever to return to Iran: 'You are effectively a man without a country.' The prosecution described Ardebili as an Iranian procurement agent. He was sentenced to five years in prison.

Through access to Ardebili's computer, American agents identified thirty Iranian front companies, twenty Iranian brokers like Ardebili, and 100 suspect US companies, many with Pentagon contracts. Homeland Security and other agencies launched 102 investigations, two dozen of them labelled high priority. Search warrants were executed in Arizona and New York. At least four cases led to indictments. More were pending. To date only one minor case has been made public. The rest remain sealed either because the indicted were fugitives, cooperating as informants, or the evidence had led to bigger fish. In an additional three dozen cases, prosecutors decided not to file charges because they couldn't prove the American companies knew for sure that their products were headed to Iran. Instead of indictments, federal agents paid quiet visits to corporate executives, issuing informal warnings and soliciting help in the future.

In a very different case on home soil, 250 FBI agents were involved in an operation in January 2010 to arrest twenty-two people who had all agreed to pay substantial bribes in exchange for fictitious contracts to equip the presidential guard of Gabon.[113] In the sting, which was termed 'the shot show showdown'[114] inside the FBI and 'Catch-22' by others,[115] investigators ran a 2½-year operation that culminated in the dramatic arrest of twenty-one of the dealers at a shooting and hunting trade show in Las Vegas on 17 January 2010. The twenty-second was arrested in Miami.[116] FBI agents secretly filmed the arms dealers agreeing to commissions of 20 per cent to an agent supposedly representing Gabon's Defence Minister. The arrested individuals were managers for small or medium-sized arms companies. As they were arrested in Las Vegas, FBI agents spread out across the country to carry out search warrants at the individuals' companies.

The sting represented the first ever use of undercover techniques in an FCPA investigation and the largest case against individuals ever. It also made use of international cooperation, the FBI working with City of London police to execute seven search warrants in the UK.[117]

The arms dealers were told that in order to win a contract, they had to add a 20 per cent 'commission' to price quotes, half of which would go to the purported Minister of Defence for Gabon and the rest would be split between others in government. Three of the defendants were associated with British arms companies and another worked for an Israeli company.[118] The dealers attempted to sell everything from pistols to grenade and tear gas launchers to explosive detection kits.[119]

One of the defendants managed to get bail. Saul Mishkin, a Peruvian citizen, was determined by a judge to be no flight risk despite representations to the contrary by prosecutors. In the bail hearing prosecutors presented recordings of Mishkin talking about bribes involving government officials in Peru, Colombia, Georgia and Botswana in return for contracts to sell tear gas, armoured personnel carriers, Humvees and food rations. He claimed on tape to have contacts with the President of Bolivia and with high-level officials in Peru. In the sting, Mishkin agreed to pay the requested commission in order to obtain a contract to sell riot control gear. He created two price quotations: one showed the true cost of the goods and the other included the bribes.[120]

Pat Caldwell, a veteran of twenty-seven years in the US Secret Service, was head of sales and marketing for Protective Products of America Inc. (PPA), a Florida firm that sells body armour, for just five months before the sting. He hoped to win a contract with the African country for about $15m and went along with the 20 per cent commission. After $18,000 was wired to a PPA bank account as a test purchase, the first batch of fifty body-armour plates was shipped off – on 16 July, the same day Caldwell was promoted to CEO. It was a very short stint as PPA chief, as he was arrested in January.[121]

The sting was based on the cooperation of one arms company executive facing FCPA charges in a different matter. Richard Bistrong, a former vice-president for international sales at Armor Holdings – acquired by BAE in 2007 – is accused of paying bribes from 2001 to 2006 to get contracts to supply law enforcement equipment to United Nations peace-keeping forces and government agencies in the Netherlands and Nigeria. Bistrong's assistance in the sting operation probably means he will receive a lenient sentence if convicted. One of those arrested in the sting, Jonathan Spiller, was Bistrong's boss at Armor Holdings. Bistrong was married to Nancy Soderberg from 2004 to 2008. Soderberg was the third-ranking official on the National Security Council under President Clinton from 1993 to 1997 and served as US ambassador to the United Nations from 1997 until January 2001.[122]

Bistrong's central role in the sting was to give a character reference for the two undercover FBI agents posing as defence officials. Starting in May, meetings were held at the Mandarin Oriental hotel in Miami and at Clyde's restaurant in Washington,[123] and payments were soon made to the Gabonese 'officials' by cheque and wire transfer.[124] All twenty-two arms dealers gathered at Clyde's, where they raised their glasses to toast the man who had brought them together, while being secretly videotaped by the FBI.[125] In total the FBI recorded over 5,000 phone calls and literally every meeting between the defendants and undercover agents.[126]

The defendants will argue that they were entrapped. The entrapment defence focuses on the defendant's subjective predisposition to commit the crime, whether the person was willing to engage in criminal conduct when presented with the opportunity or was persuaded to act in a way he otherwise would not have.[127] The prosecutors allege that the arms dealers all acted as part of a single conspiracy. They face up to five years in prison for each FCPA charge and up to twenty years for alleged money laundering.[128] Their defence team will call into question the trustworthiness of Bistrong and have requested that the prosecution hand over his tax returns, internal DOJ–FBI communications about his handling and any export licences he had been given by the federal government.[129] It is also possible that the case will fail as no foreign public official was bribed.[130]

Another of the dealers, Daniel Alvirez, a former president of the arms-maker ALS Technologies Inc., will plead guilty to paying bribes to secure contracts for the sale of ammunition, grenades and grenade launchers.[131] Alvirez and Lee Allen Tolleson, director of acquisitions at ALS, sent a wire transfer for $16,200 to a bank account purported to be controlled by the African country. Two days later, the two executives sent a wire transfer of the 20 per cent commission to a bank account controlled by one of the undercover FBI agents. In October, Alvirez and Tolleson again met the undercover agents at Clyde's in DC to set up a second, more lucrative, transaction.[132]

At the time of writing, several other defendants have pleaded guilty, four are currently on trial, while the majority are still awaiting trial. The lawyers of the first four defendants focused on the character of Bistrong, with his FBI handler acknowledging use of drugs and prostitutes.[133] Whatever the ultimate outcome, the case will have consequences for FCPA enforcement.[134]

At the time of the sting there were twenty agents reportedly working full-time on FCPA cases.[135] In June 2010, a bureau official said that the FBI was expanding its FCPA team by increasing the number of supervisory special agents from three to seven, each being responsible for an area of the world.[136] In the DOJ there are now eight full-time FCPA prosecutors supplemented by fifty-four other prosecutors in the fraud section.[137]

Clearly, sting operations that have netted Monzer Al-Kassar, Viktor Bout and the 'Las Vegas 22' are to be welcomed. Nevertheless, for the behemoths of the arms industry, the FCPA may well be viewed as merely a cost to business. The loopholes are glaring and are likely to be taken advantage of. The potential penalties for major corporations close to power are eminently bearable. While the economic system is predicated on a constant increase in profits, the proviso of being within lawful, not to mention moral and ethical, bounds is sometimes secondary, especially in the arms trade. In such an environment the self-regulatory light touch largely followed in FCPA enforcement will never be effective in stamping out the scourge of corruption.

The enforcement environment will also need to be cognisant of important changes to the industry.

On 2 December 2002, as Donald Rumsfeld signed the infamous torture memo that 'sanctioned' the behaviour at Abu Ghraib and elsewhere, President Bush was also at the Pentagon signing the biggest defence budget ever. This was part of a seven-year run of increases in the defence budget, the most since the Second World War. Can the military be forced to make do with less? In the last Congress of the George W. era only Representative Barney Frank, and a smattering of others, were keen on major cuts.

It is still unclear whether President Obama is willing or prepared to take on the most established and powerful interest group in the country. The President's pronouncements on the role of the US in the world are a far cry from the triumphalist narrative of the Bush administration. But this discourse has not altered the seemingly sacrosanct status of the arms industry. In the midst of economic hardship, is Ronald Reagan's dictum, 'Defense is not a budget item', still valid?

For generations no administration has considered seriously reducing defence expenditure. Robert Reich recalled that it was made clear to him as head of Bill Clinton's economic transition team that cutting defence spending was simply not a political option.[138]

The arguments most commonly used to justify the scale and nature of the weapons industry in the US are firstly national security and secondly jobs. Jobs created in the sector are far more expensive than any others, and are more heavily subsidized by government. An authoritative study by economists at the University of Massachusetts in 2009 found that a billion dollars spent on a variety of domestic priorities – clean energy, education and healthcare – would each produce more jobs than the same amount spent on the military.[139]

For every billion dollars invested in defence, 8,555 jobs are created. By contrast, the same billion invested in healthcare would create 12,883 jobs and in education 17,687 jobs or more than double the defence stimulus payoff.[140]

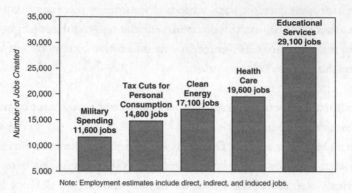

Note: Employment estimates include direct, indirect, and induced jobs.

Figure 6: Comparative job creation figures for defence and other sectors in the US

Nevertheless, the defence industry was awarded its own stimulus package in the form of Obama's first budget for 2010, in which the Department of Defense received just under $700bn. It seems that despite the dire economic times the defence industry remains almost impervious to budget cuts, insulated by an enduring conviction that war spending stimulates the economy.[141] It has often been said that the Second World War – and the production stimulus it offered – lifted the United States out of the Great Depression. Today, the opposite seems to be the case. The 'war economy' helped propel the US into the current ongoing economic morass. During the boom years the US spent its way into severe financial crisis, in significant part by launching unnecessary, profligate wars. President Bush Jr cut taxes at more than a peacetime pace and borrowed 'like an addicted gambler on a losing streak to underwrite his wars of choice, including the global War on Terror'.[142] So that, unlike in 1929, the US is already on a global war footing. In a more enlightened polity, the state of the US economy would surely reignite the guns versus butter debate that has been silent for two generations.

While the good times rolled, the defence contractors ranking first, second and third on the Pentagon's list of top ten contractors, Lockheed Martin, Boeing and Northrop Grumman, had a ball, on a similar scale to the big banks and sub-prime mortgage giants. In 2002, the first full year of the War on Terror, for instance, those three companies split $42bn in contract awards, more than two thirds of the $67bn distributed among the top ten Pentagon contractors.[143] In 2007, the last year for which full contracting data is available, the same Big Three split $69bn in Pentagon contracts, which was more than the total received by the top ten companies just five years earlier. The top ten divvied up $121bn in contracts in 2007, an 80 per cent increase over 2002. Lockheed Martin graduated from $17bn in awarded contracts in 2002 to $28bn in 2007, a leap of 64 per cent. Given such figures, it's easy enough to understand how the basic military budget – excluding money for actually fighting the war – jumped from about $300bn to more than $500bn during the Bush years.[144] While the defence giants briefly endured difficulties at the height of the financial crisis, at the time Lockheed Martin alone was sitting with $81bn of orders, enough to keep going for another two years without a single new contract.[145]

If such war spending had been an effective stimulus for the economy, there would have been no recession during the recent, banker-induced economic meltdown. But increasingly this kind of spending mainly stimulates corporate shareholders, stock prices and, of course, war itself. The new defence budget ensures that for the defence industry some version of good times will continue to roll, even if the economic impact of these huge military investments proves negligible and the need in other areas is staggering.

When he first came to office, President Obama instructed his Office of Management and Budget to undertake a line-by-line analysis of the Pentagon budget. In speeches he focused on wasteful and unnecessary defence spending. On his own website on 5 March 2009 he insisted that 'the days of giving defence contractors a blank cheque are over'. To underline that assertion, he cited the 2008 General Accounting Office study that found ninety-five military projects over budget by a total of $295bn. He pledged to end such egregious practices, and the no-bid contracts that often go with them.[146]

However, his first Pentagon budgets suggested that the real amount of money available to the defence contractors was unlikely to change significantly. Unfortunately, this spending is a drag on the prospects of an economic recovery, despite the claims of the defence industry and its publicists and lobbyists. For example, the Aerospace Industries Association (AIA) stated in January 2009 that 'Our industry is ready and able to lead the way out of the economic crisis.' AIA estimates that defence and aerospace manufacturers contribute $97bn in exports a year, while maintaining 2 million jobs. The US Bureau of Labor Statistics (BLS) suggests this is a hugely inflated claim, putting the figure for the number of people who work in industries where at least one fifth of the products are defence-related at below 650,000 in 2006.[147] Where the defence sector does boost employment figures and continue to spend a fortune is on lobbyists. In 2010, the industry spent almost $150m on lobbying firms to get its points across to Congress and the administration.[148]

But why would government subsidize such expensive job creation? Is it because of the national security imperative? Of course there are geopolitical issues that affect weapons exports and domestic political imperatives. Charles 'Chuck' Lewis, of the Center for Public Integrity, suggests that 'all of the big manufacturers use Political Action Committees through which every officer in the corporation gives money, often getting it back with a little extra in their next pay packet. Under George W. Bush these contributions-for-influence were paid in cheques that were clearly numbered so that there was no doubt about who had given what.'[149] As Rumsfeld's biographer, Andrew Cockburn, put it to me: 'most campaign contributions are bribes by another name.'[150]

While this process serves the interests of politicians, the manufacturers, lobbyists and the armed forces, it is questionable whether it provides value for money for the American taxpayer or meets the standards of accountability expected of the world's dominant democracy.

Chuck Lewis suggests that the defence system is part of the currency of power. To survive and prosper not even Obama at his most popular could annoy the defence contractors, 'because they'll crush you politically'.[151] Chuck Spinney has described the way in which the MICC takes care of itself as 'a self-licking ice-cream'.[152] Spinney believes that it is largely business-as-usual under Obama:

> You see, these 'think-tanks' and the contractors are essentially holding pens for the political appointees in the administrations and so basically what you will see is people that you have seen before or clones of those people, protégés of those people. Bill Perry is a classic case. He was in the Carter Pentagon, then he was in the Clinton Pentagon, and many of the people in the current Pentagon are protégés of his, like Ashton Carter, the Under

Secretary for Acquisition, and Michèle Flournoy, the Under Secretary for Policy. Usually the constancy between the administrations has to do with the money and the people who are benefiting from the money go back and forth between industry, think-tanks, and the Pentagon – this is especially true of the so-called policy wonks, who, usually in my experience, are the people who write these great global tomes without having screw-all to do with the reality. Obama has been particularly vulnerable to their pernicious influences.[153]

The Obama administration has painted a mixed picture on the issue. The initial retention of Robert Gates as Defense Secretary was a pointer towards the status quo. As Spinney said: 'Gates is a slick bureaucrat, and no reformer, not even close.

Bill Hartung has suggested that Gates's approach mostly involved moving money around, not actually cutting weapons spending. Similarly, Gates and his team announced a new efficiency drive meant to save $100bn over five years (i.e. $20bn per year out of a $700bn annual budget for military spending). The $100bn was supposed to come from cutting bureaucracy (fewer generals and admirals, eliminating the Joint Forces Command, reducing use of private contractors). But even if the savings were achieved, Gates's plan was to plough the money back into 'the warfighter', which will mostly translate into more weapons spending. This is change the weapons companies can believe in.[154]

Gates's approach will make sense to his successor: cut waste if possible, make a big deal about how you're seeking 'efficiencies' and spending every penny wisely, then use that to try to slow the decline in spending – if there is a decline in real terms; Gates spoke about a 1 per cent per year increase on top of the largest military budget since the Second World War – hardly 'austerity'.[155]

On assuming office with the hope of change still fresh, Obama said that he would look at everything. He wanted to beef up oversight, slow down the revolving door, get rid of no-bid contracts and build better accountability in procurement. As one of his advisers on Capitol Hill, who wished to remain anonymous, put it at the time: 'His people feel it's gone too far, but whether they can roll it back is unclear politically.'

Afghanistan and Iraq are two obvious targets for cutting back no-bid, outsourced contracts. But when Afghanistan's President Karzai, a figure hardly untainted by corruption, suggested outlawing all private security firms in his country, many of which had been involved in egregious economic scandals and human rights abuses, the Obama administration flew to their defence, saying that while their functions should ultimately be handed over to the Afghan government, the timing was inappropriate.[156]

Finally, when confronted by a conservative tide demanding a slashing of the deficit, President Obama, in announcing plans to cut the deficit by $4tn over twelve years, acknowledged that there would need to be cuts to military spending. He ordered a comprehensive review of 'missions, capabilities and America's role in the world'.[157] However, a seasoned Pentagon budget analyst, Winslow Wheeler, pointed out that just such a review occurred, with little effect, in 2010, suggesting that the Pentagon would conduct another 'sham' to fulfil this latest request.[158]

The appointment of Leon Panetta, former Director of the CIA, to replace Gates in the summer of 2011 was an interesting one because of his extensive experience of budget negotiations. What remains to be seen is whether he will reduce the defence budget by cutting personnel costs, healthcare and other 'soft' targets', or whether there will be the political will to slash unnecessary weapons programmes.[159]

At the dramatic denouement of the debt stand-off in late July and early August 2011, some claimed that the debt-ceiling deal will result in reductions in the defence budget of anywhere between $350bn and $600bn. Critics of excessive defence spending pointed out that the lower figure wouldn't even represent a real cut in Pentagon spending, just a slowing of its rate of growth. While Wheeler was quick to pour cold water on any optimism regarding real reductions in military spending. He makes clear that the two-year cap on 'security' spending will actually extend to ten years and that the creation of the 'security spending' category – which includes the Department of Energy/nuclear weapons, all State Department security-related spending, Veterans Affairs and Homeland Security – was designed to lessen the impact on the Department of Defense. Finally, he points out that rather than the 'sequestration process' contained in the deal which would lead to across-the-board spending cuts if spending caps weren't achieved, it is much more likely that the joint Congressional committee to be established to produce a proposal to reduce the deficit by at least $1.5tn over ten years will recommend a selection of cuts that do not hit the Department of Defense hard. In fact, in the bill the House proposed,

Republicans included a specific protection for defence spending. Wheeler estimates that the reductions under this debt deal will be to the very generous level of spending that President Obama has in his pre-existing ten-year Department of Defense budget plan, as described above.[160]

This continuing exorbitant level of defence spending led the commentator Tom Engelhardt to wonder why 'for months Americans have been focused on raising that debt ceiling, [while] [i]n the process, few have asked the obvious question: Isn't it time to lower America's war ceiling?'[161]

The problematic rotation of corporate officials into senior positions in the national security administration has been pared back, but still occurs. Obama has not prevented generals and admirals getting jobs lobbying for defence contractors. While the introduction of new ethics rules was commendable, their implementation is less so. For instance, in apparent contravention of the rules' requirement for a two-year hiatus between working as a lobbyist and serving in a related government role, William J. Lynn III was appointed Deputy Secretary of Defense despite having worked as a lobbyist for eight years for the weapons manufacturer Raytheon, which received $10bn in contracts in 2008 from the agency he now manages.[162] Larry Duncan, one of Obama's most important and longest-serving fundraisers, has earned a fortune as a lobbyist for Lockheed Martin. So too the fundraiser Mark Alderman, whose law firm earned almost a million dollars in Washington in 2007, representing clients including Lockheed Martin.[163]

The Democratic think-tank the Center for a New American Security (CNAS) was funded by defence contractors, including Lockheed Martin. Its founders, Michèle Flournoy and Kurt Campbell, were appointed Under Secretary of Defense for Policy, the third-ranking position in the Pentagon, and Assistant Secretary of State for East Asian and Pacific Affairs, respectively, in the Obama administration. When Campbell was questioned about potential conflicts of interest during his confirmation hearing, he argued that there was no problem with CNAS's defence contractor funding because its critically acclaimed reports never talk about weapons systems. Bill Hartung has shown this to be untrue. In a February 2010 report, *Arsenal's End: American Power and the Global Defense Industry*, CNAS argues for a significant Pentagon weapons budget for items such as the Lockheed Martin F-35, while absolving the company of any responsibility for cost overruns on the system. Hartung concludes that 'it is hard to imagine a better analysis from Lockheed's point of view.'[164]

Chuck Spinney probably echoes the views of many who are critical of the MICC, on the subject of Obama: 'I have been very disappointed. He has been a total disappointment on defense.'[165] 'He is continuing his predecessor's war-centric foreign policy . . . he is continuing the establishment's business-as-usual practices including the grotesque diversion of scarce resources to a bloated defense budget that is leading the United States into ruin.'[166] I asked Chuck what he thought of the Pentagon now. 'It's worse now. Things are worse today than they've ever been.'[167] He says that the corruption he sees today is an extension of the corruption he fought for thirty-three years.

If President Obama is to emerge from his first few cautious years in office as the force for change that he embodied as a candidate, he has to confront the MICC, accustomed to multibillion-dollar budgets based on exaggerated global threats, unsubstantiated economic claims and entrenched profligacy. Key to this will be not just reductions in defence spending but also far greater transparency in procurement, lobbying and performance. What is clear is that the weapons business profoundly undermines American democracy, representing the ultimate beneficiary of the legalized bribery that proliferates on Capitol Hill. It does this largely under a veil of secrecy that prevents accountable and transparent governance. Obama's approach to the industry and the arms trade it spawns will determine the success or failure of his stated wish 'to change the way we do politics'.

17. America's Shop Window

The Israeli arms industry plays a unique role in that it is a manufacturer as well as a large client and also acts as an intermediary for other countries, particularly the US. Ronen Bergman, an Israeli journalist with sources in the country's intelligence community, describes Israel as the 'long arm' of the US in the Middle East and the 'primary testing ground for American weapons and ... combat tactics'.[1] In effect, a shop window for the American weapons industry.

The Israeli defence industry is an impressive showcase. While the government has not released figures for the value of its arms exports in 2007 and 2008, the country did reveal that it signed arms contracts worth over $6.3bn in 2008, the seventh-highest of thirty-two countries for which there is information available.[2] It was the eleventh-largest importer of arms between 2005 and 2010, when its imports rose 102 per cent.[3] All of these figures are most likely much higher than the official information provided.

Large parts of the Israeli military budget, including the procurement figures, are classified, only ever seen by a small group of people who have the relevant security classification, so no one knows its true size. Israel spends 8 per cent of GDP on the military, to the US's 4.5 per cent.[4] Most countries spend around 1 per cent. In Israel defence spending is always the biggest budget item, even though it excludes the Shabak (Israel's internal security service) and Mossad, whose budgets are entirely secret. In the 1980s, an economist, Tal Wolfzon, claimed that Israel wasn't calculating the cost of defence correctly and that the country was spending 12.3 per cent of its GDP on defence, which would make it the largest *per capita* defence spender in the world.[5]

For the first two decades of Israeli statehood, what there was of an arms industry was in government hands, but it is now substantially privatized, with a few large companies still in state control or run jointly by the state and private interests. During these early years the country was primarily an importer with some limited production. 1967 saw the need for a domestic industry as a consequence of the occupation of Palestinian land and a French arms embargo. The occupation lacked international support, which encouraged greater self-sufficiency, especially in the production of weapons. From 1973 the US started to provide Israel with aid, mostly military, to the tune of $3bn annually.[6]

Israel set about the creation of a $3bn armaments industry. But internally focused production was extremely expensive and unable to meet the country's defence needs in full. The most high-profile example of this failure was the Lavi jet fighter, which was eventually scrapped in 1987 because of its exorbitant cost. With the realization that it would not be able to sustain production entirely for its own use, the Israelis began to develop an industry for export, in order to fund its own war machine. By the late 1970s/early 1980s Israel was ranked between eighth and tenth among exporters, with massive sales to Central and South American military regimes, the Shah's Iran and South Africa. The industry declined in the 1980s due to the Reagan administration's massive sales to Central and South America and the fall of the Shah. During the 1980s, as its economy tumbled, Israel lost markets but large investments made during the middle part of the decade saw its high-tech industry become one of the world's most advanced. This was aided by 'normalization' during the Oslo process whereby Israel, less of a pariah, was a more acceptable partner for military relations.

By the 1990s, Israel was firmly established as the tenth-ranked arms exporter in the world but the fourth-largest to developing countries, including rogue states in Africa, Latin America and even the Middle East.[7] India has been the largest recipient of Israeli arms for much of the last decade, along with Turkey, China and the US. Currently, Brazil is becoming a more important recipient than Turkey, with Russia starting to be important. Singapore has been a big market for decades now, relative to its size, with Israel's first drone export going to the country in 1978. Switzerland is a significant purchaser.

A theme common to Israel's largest weapons customers is that they have used the weapons to repress civilians and small-scale guerrilla groups. This is largely a consequence of Israel, as an often marginalized state, being less concerned about the diplomatic consequences of selling to those countries and because the Israeli industry has specialized in equipment designed to control civilians.[8]

Initially, retiring army officers came to dominate the emerging arms companies, creating an elite that controlled public and private life in Israel. Economic analyses suggesting that the industry was not as well run as it could be and the advent of globalization led to the privatization and professionalization of the arms industry.[9]

The Israeli economy is among the most militarized in the world. Defying accepted economic wisdom, over the past decade and prior to the credit crunch, wars and terrorist attacks have been increasing in Israel while the Tel Aviv stock exchange has risen to record levels. Israeli companies pioneered the homeland security industry and continue to dominate the sector today. The Israeli security industry includes over 600 companies, employing about 25,000 people, with over 300 of these companies exporting products and services.[10]

At the Paris Air Show in 2009, Elbit Systems Ltd – which, among other activities, was partly responsible for the separation barrier with the occupied territories, at a cost of $2.5bn, and which with Boeing was contracted to build the proposed wall between the US and Mexico, before the abandonment of the project in late January 2011 – was among the most sought-out exhibitors. Using a massive IMAX screen the company spooled continuous footage of a simulated attack on a Palestinian village in order to showcase its unmanned drone surveillance and attack aircraft. A flock of hawk-like salesmen regaled potential clients with stories of 'our decades of testing weapons in real conflict situations'.

After the dotcom crash of 2000, when the Israeli economy experienced its worst year since the early 1950s, the government again intervened with a 10.7 per cent increase in military spending and encouraged tech industries into the security and surveillance fields.

After 9/11, the Israeli state openly embraced the idea of a homeland security boom. By 2004, the economy had recovered and by the following year was outperforming most Western economies.[11] It had become a shopping mall for homeland security technologies. The industry's pitch was simple: 'We have been fighting a War on Terror since our birth, we'll show you how it's done.'[12]

The War on Terror industry was crucial in saving Israel's faltering economy. A prominent Israeli investment analyst told *Forbes* magazine that security matters more than peace. Naomi Klein asserts that it is no coincidence that the decision to put defence and counter-terrorism at the centre

of its economic strategy coincided with the abandonment of peace negotiations and the reframing of the conflict against Palestinians not as a battle
against a nationalist movement but as part of the global War on Terror.[13]

This does not minimize the reality that there would a massive peace
dividend for Israel: while the economy would suffer short-term adjustment shocks, peace would enable resources to be redirected to more
productive activity and trading with Arab nations would increase exponentially.

But peace is far from the minds of arms company executives. While the
ill-fated Lebanon invasion of 2006 was a somewhat tarnished showpiece
for Israeli and US weaponry, Israeli companies didn't just support the
attacks but sponsored them, running ads promoting the war together
with corporate branding. The stock market rose in August 2006, the
month of the war. In that year which had seen a bloody escalation of hostilities in the West Bank and Gaza, Israel's economy grew by almost 6 per
cent. The bombings of Gaza in late 2008 and early 2009 were a better marketing tool, demonstrating the immense destructive powers of Elbit's
unmanned drones which minimized Israeli Defence Force (IDF) casualties while maximizing Palestinian fatalities and the destruction of much
of Gaza.[14] After the Gaza invasion Israel held a closed arms fair to demonstrate how well its new weapons for urban warfare had worked.[15]

Despite it being the mainstay of Israel's economy, the defence sector is
still unable to meet all the country's weapons needs, with all planes, larger
boats and submarines imported. The US is unsurprisingly the biggest
supplier, on very favourable terms. Israel has been the largest recipient of
US security assistance since the early 1970s, when the Nixon administration dramatically increased military aid to the country and cemented the
close relationship that endures to this day. Henry Kissinger was supposed
to have quipped that 'for every tank we give to Israel, its neighbours buy
four from us'.[16]

In recent years both US military aid and weapons transfers have
expanded. At the same time, the intensity and ruthlessness of Israeli military operations have also increased, with US weapons and military
hardware of every size on lethal display.[17] Between 2002 and 2007, Israel
received over $19bn in direct military aid from the Bush administration
and in August 2007 the US and Israeli governments signed a ten-year
Memorandum of Understanding (MoU) for the provision of $30bn in US

military aid.[18] At the signing ceremony the Under Secretary of State for Political Affairs, Nicholas Burns, characterized the $30bn as 'an investment in peace' and emphasized America's 'abiding interest in the security of Israel'.[19] Arms sales from France, Germany and the UK are on a smaller scale but nevertheless significant.[20] In the first quarter of 2008 the British government licensed weapons sales worth almost £19m to Israel.[21]

Israel receives most of its US military assistance through what is known as Foreign Military Financing (FMF) – US grants for weapons purchases. At least as valuable is the special treatment that comes with the billions of dollars in grants. Israel is the only country allowed to use its US military aid to build its domestic military industry, a privilege that includes developing indigenous weapons systems based on US designs and using FMF funds to purchase materials, as well as research and development, from Israeli firms. Additional US funds are spent on joint military research and production such as anti-ballistic missile defence systems and even fighter jets. While other countries get their FMF doled out in quarterly allotments, Israel receives all of it in one lump sum early in the year – a practice that creates a loan burden for the US government, as it necessitates borrowing from the US Treasury long before Congress actually releases the monies promised. Along with a handful of other countries, Israel enjoys 'fast-track' status for weapons sales, meaning that it can essentially bypass the Pentagon's intermediary role, involving cumbersome procedures and delays, to make deals directly with manufacturers.

Between 1998 and 2008, it is estimated that the Israeli government devoted $75bn to its military budget. During that same period, FMF alone accounted for nearly $25bn, essentially covering a third of Israel's defence budget. According to an August 2008 memo by the American Israel Public Affairs Committee (AIPAC), Israel plans to double its military budget in the coming decade to $150bn.[22]

The billions of dollars in US military aid to Israel have bought a stunning array of US weapons and military hardware for the IDF. Israel has 226 F-16 fighter and attack jets, more than 700 M-60 tanks, 6,000 armoured personnel carriers,[23] and scores of transport planes, attack helicopters, and utility and training aircraft, not to mention innumerable bombs and tactical missiles of all kinds. The IDF also has a wide array of munitions at its disposal, including cluster bombs and incendiary devices like white phosphorous. Israel is a more regular customer than almost any other nation; over the last ten years for which full data is available (financial years 1997–2007), Tel Aviv signed agreements for US weapons imports worth $10.59bn. Of the six biggest importers, only Saudi Arabia, with $10.7bn in US weapons purchased over the same period, signed agreements worth more.[24]

The arms trade relationship with the US is about far more than just the purchasing of weapons. It is about the politics of the Middle East, and it touches on a range of geopolitical issues. As a source in the industry who is sympathetic to Israel told me: 'Israel gets at least $2bn to $3bn a year from the US to buy US-made weapons. It uses some of them itself and also arms countries the US couldn't, with a nod and a wink.' The most extreme manifestation of this was the selling of arms to Iran.

It is well known that Israel had joined the US in supporting the Shah of Iran politically and militarily. Shortly before the fall of the Shah, Israel agreed to the sale of substantial arms to Iran and was paid for them. However, after the triumph of the revolution led by Ayatollah Khomeini, Israel refused to deliver. Khomeini broke off all relations with Israel and sued for $5bn. International arbitration on the matter has continued since 1983.[25]

It is not common knowledge, though, that while the West, and for a time the Soviets, supported Saddam Hussein's Iraq against the Islamic Republic of Iran, the Israeli government and its arms agents, on behalf of the US, transferred hundreds of tons of weapons and equipment to Iran, shoring up a weak Iranian army as it faced defeat at Saddam's hands. A few years after halting sales to Iran, Israel was approached by a French go-between, and agreed to sell arms to Khomeini's regime in a secret operation codenamed 'Seashell'. The Israelis believed that such sales would bring them closer to Iran's rulers and weaken both Iran and Iraq. But, as important, the weapons industry wanted to make money. As one key figure in Operation Seashell recalls: 'I do not remember even one discussion about the ethics of the matter. All that interested us was to sell, sell, sell more and more Israeli weapons and let them kill each other with them.'[26]

Weapons worth $75m reached Iran through a Portuguese arms dealer, George Pinole, who arranged false bills of lading and bribed officials of an Argentinian airline to transport the equipment. After one of the planes crashed, Pinole arranged alternative transport by sea. The Iranian impresario behind the operation was Dr Sadeq Tabatabai, a distant relative of Khomeini's and one of his confidants in sensitive matters. Ironically his success with Operation Seashell led to Tabatabai being promoted through the ranks until he became a top Iranian representative in Lebanon and one of the midwives of Hezbollah, Israel's bitter foe. It was Tabatabai who would later push for the abduction of two Israeli soldiers by Hezbollah that led to the war in the summer of 2006. But the ultimate irony was that after the strengthened Iranians forced a stalemate in the war with Iraq, they started to supply some of the arms Israel had shipped to them on to Hezbollah.[27]

Ronen Bergman has revealed new information about the Iran–Contra affair that reflects on the gullibility of the Israelis and the Americans in their involvement with arms dealers.[28] Hashemi Rafsanjani, the moderate head of the Iranian legislature, and future President of the Islamic Republic, believed that Iran should adopt a more pragmatic foreign policy that would enable it to enlist Western support for its war against Iraq, including access to Western arms. In 1984, the Reagan administration rebuffed the Iranian overtures. As an alternative Iran approached Israel through two go-betweens: Manucher Ghorbanifar, an Iranian arms dealer and swindler who was close to Rafsanjani, and Adnan Khashoggi, the billionaire Saudi arms dealer. The Iranians wanted Israel to sell them arms and to mediate between them and the Americans. Ghorbanifar travelled to Israel on a Greek passport to conclude the $50m sale of combat equipment to Iran. Some of those involved on the Israeli side admitted that among their motives was financial gain.

The Americans became interested in the operation because of a desire to staunch the wave of abductions of Americans in Lebanon by the Iranian-backed Hezbollah. They envisaged acting on a number of parallel tracks: US Intelligence had set up a company called GMT as a cover both for its efforts to undermine the Iranian regime from within, as well as to foster anti-Soviet forces in South and Central America. The latter included the Nicaraguan Contras, the conservative rebel group opposed to the Sandinista government which had overthrown the Somoza dictatorship before winning elections in 1984. The CIA trained the Contras and acquired weapons for them through GMT, but wanted to intensify the operation. By transferring surplus NATO equipment from Europe to Israel to replace the Israeli arms that were to be sold to Iran at prices significantly higher than their true market value, the US could use the profits to finance the Contras. At the same time they would be improving relations with Iran and getting the hostages in Lebanon freed.[29]

A deal was signed between GMT and Israel at the Negev farm of the Defence Minister, Ariel Sharon, that determined how the operation would be implemented and the division of profits and commissions. The Director of the CIA, William Casey, was briefed about the deal and how the money would be funnelled through secret Swiss bank accounts. In the summer of 1985 the Israeli government gave the go-ahead. It was decided to leave the implementation to unofficial middlemen involved in the arms trade. Ghorbanifar was to represent the Iranians and Khashoggi was laying out the cash. The shipments began in August 1985. However, the missiles sent by Israel were faulty, having passed their sell-by dates. It still remains unclear who gave the instruction for faulty weapons to be delivered. Nevertheless, in exchange for the weapons delivered, Israel received replacement supplies from the US. One American hostage was released.[30]

What is clear is that under the umbrella of concern for the hostages, innumerable other undisclosed deals were happening between the US, Israel and Iran. About 600 tons of ammunition, weapons and equipment was shipped to Iran. A person involved in the deals said: 'There were very few Israeli companies with anything to sell to Iran, [sic] which were not selling. The entire government-owned military industry and the privately owned military industries were involved in it, very deeply.'[31] Ronen Bergman's access to the internal documents of the Israeli side of the operation reveals that Israel also supplied arms directly to the Central American rebels for additional profit.

The failure to gain the release of more than one hostage led the Israelis to appoint Amiram Nir, the Prime Minister's counter-terror adviser, to take charge of the operation, in what became the second stage of the Iran–Contra affair. His opposite number in the US was Colonel Oliver North, the gung-ho official of the National Security Council. Nir decided that it should be agreed with the Iranians exactly how much equipment would be supplied for the release of specific numbers of hostages. Added sweeteners included the promise of dialogue between the Iranians and the Americans and the release of thirty-nine Shi'ite prisoners held by the pro-Israeli South Lebanon militia. This gesture could also be used to explain the release of the hostages by the Iranians, while hiding the arms transactions.

Nir met with North and then Ghorbanifar and Khashoggi. President Reagan gave the go-ahead. Front companies and bank accounts in Switzerland and Liechtenstein were set up. Ghorbanifar deposited $10m in the Swiss bank account and, on 16 February 1986, 1,000 missiles were flown into Israel, transferred to an El Al cargo plane whose markings had been painted over, and flown on to Tehran by an American crew. Two days later, and in violation of the carefully crafted agreement, two Israeli soldiers were abducted by Hezbollah in Lebanon, apparently to spur the Israelis to supply more weapons to Iran. After an exchange of letters between the Prime Minister of Israel and the US President – delivered by Nir to North – and the deposit of a further $15m, the second shipment began. Documents reveal that not only was Israel supplying Iran with faulty weapons, but it appears the US was trying to do the same to Israel for reasons that remain unclear.[32]

When George H. W. Bush ran for the presidency he strenuously denied that he had any knowledge of this sordid affair which took place while he was Vice President. However, intelligence documents reveal that in July 1986, as US Vice President, he was personally briefed by Nir on the whole operation. In his later report on the meeting to the Prime Minister, Shimon Peres, Nir stressed that Israel was doing everything to provide cover that would protect the US from exposure for the whole operation, which was, after all, undertaken at the explicit request of the Americans. He described Bush's tone in the meeting as supportive and optimistic.[33]

However, in 1986 word leaked about the secret transactions. The Lebanese magazine *Ash-Shiraa* published a series of articles in November that exposed the weapons-for-hostages deal. It was soon revealed that the huge profits from the arms sales to Iran had been used to fund the Contras. There was outrage in Congress, which had explicitly forbidden such support. Reagan's spokesperson quickly blamed the Israelis, who were furious. They decided not to respond publicly as they were still maintaining a link to Ghorbanifar in the hope that it would lead to the release of the hostages, thereby bolstering Reagan's position *vis-à-vis* the planned Congressional inquiry and serving to vindicate the entire operation.

But then the *Washington Post* discovered that at the same time as it was dealing secretly with Iran, the CIA had supplied Iraq with intelligence about key targets in Iran. The Iranian regime broke off all contact. Nir was thrown to the press as the fall guy in the US and Israel, where he remained in relative seclusion until he died in a mysterious crash in 1988, allegedly on a plane belonging to the CIA front that had flown weapons to Iran.[34]

The intersection of intelligence agents and arms dealers is common. Ronen Bergman describes the Israeli situation: 'Arms dealers naturally have access to sensitive information, much more than a regular business-man would have. The Israeli intelligence community knows how to use these dealers, now and again, for its purposes. Since the intelligence community is involved in the official procedures for giving these dealers their export licences, it can easily create an unhealthy dependence on its approval. The consequences are often disastrous.'[35]

Nahum Manbar, who had links to Mossad while making millions in the arms business, sold chemical weapons to the Iranians, leading some in the CIA to believe that while encouraging the US to take strong meas-ures against Iran, the Israelis were conducting an operation behind their backs.[36]

Manbar, codenamed 'Termite' by Mossad, was born on a kibbutz which his family had helped found. He served in the IDF during the 1967 and 1973 wars before entering the arms business. He linked up with Bari Hashemi (alias Farschi), an Iranian defence ministry purchasing agent who headed a Vienna-based company. Initially, Manbar bought weap-onry, often from the Polish army, which he sold on to the Iranians. He also sold them protective gear against atomic, biological and chemical arms, soon setting up a plant in Poland to manufacture the products. He claims that the relevant Israeli authorities were fully informed of his activities. When approached by the Iranians to provide them with chem-ical weapons, Manbar is adamant that he reported the requests to the appropriate Israeli 'factors'. They instructed him to get more details about what the Iranians wanted. 'I asked the Iranians to submit more blueprints and sketches. Everything was conveyed to Israel.'[37]

Manbar had become wealthy through arms trading. Many people and companies wanted part of the action. Through Brigadier General Amos Kotzer, Manbar offered to supply Israeli Intelligence with information on military subjects, as well as on the missing Israeli airman Ron Arad. Arad had been captured by Lebanese Shi'ite militia in October 1986 after being forced to eject while on a mission to bomb PLO targets. Manbar believed that with his excellent contacts in Iran he might be able to bring the air-man home. His leads on the Arad case ultimately proved worthless.[38]

In late 1990, Manbar signed a contract with Dr Majid Abbaspour, a spe-cial assistant to the Iranian President and still one of the key figures in Iranian arms procurement, to supply the know-how for the production of substances used in chemical weapons, to set up a production plant with the necessary equipment and to train teams of employees. Manbar was to be paid $16.23m. In 1992, Israeli internal security agents met Manbar and ordered him to cease all activities with Iran and hand over all documents connected to them. For the next six years he enjoyed his multimillions, with villas on the Swiss–Italian border and the French Riviera, where he entertained many in the Israeli power elite, showering them with the best of everything. He visited Israel regularly, investing in Israeli basketball teams and being photographed with, among others, Shimon Peres, now the Israeli President, the future Prime Minister Ehud Olmert and Yitzhak Rabin's wife, Leah.[39]

Britain's MI6 tried to exploit Manbar's network in order to penetrate the Iranian arms industry. A young agent named Richard Tomlinson was given the mission. He claims that 'We never intended to interfere with Manbar's work. On the contrary, the whole thing was a classical British intelligence operation: to allow authentic private businessmen to enter into relationships with hostile countries and later to penetrate their net-works in order to gather information on the target country.'[40] Tomlinson, who was jailed for trying to publish a sensational book on his experiences, is absolutely certain that Manbar acted on behalf of Israeli Intelligence in his arms deals with Iran: 'We had no doubt about it. Officially, the Mos-sad never admitted that Manbar was acting on its behalf, but it was clear that the Israelis knew about everything that he did.' He further claims that 'Mossad kept trying to disrupt our work and didn't hand over all the documents that it had.'[41] The CIA shared MI6's conviction that Manbar was working for Mossad, casting a shadow over the relationship between the two agencies.

Manbar claims he ended all connections with Iran in 1993 after being 'spoken to by the Israelis'. But he admits that in 1995 he gave Abbaspour's calling card to the Foreign Minister at the time, Peres, who 'took the card and told me that the matter was being dealt with'.[42] Two weeks later Man-bar contributed $200,000 to Peres's campaign funds.

He was eventually arrested in Israel in March 1997. A blanket gagging order prevented the media from reporting the details of the case. His trial was held behind closed doors and much of the testimony was classified. Manbar's lawyers asserted that the Israeli arms industry – including Israeli businessmen who functioned with the ostensible permission of the security authorities – had sold and were still selling vast quantities of material to Iran. The judges partially accepted this argument and levelled sharp criticism at the state's conduct. He was sentenced to sixteen years in prison. Richard Tomlinson suggests that 'Just as it happens often in intelligence services, the Israelis decided to get rid of Manbar, break off the connections and make him a scapegoat. The Mossad kept all the documents that could have proved his innocence to itself.'[43]

Iran was not the only beneficiary of Israel's lax approach to arms control. The Georgian conflict with Russia was fuelled by Israeli arms, which many speculate were provided with American backing.[44]

At the time of the Russian invasion in August 2008, the Georgian defence establishment was dominated by Israelis, notwithstanding that a number of Israeli arms companies had simultaneous contracts with the Russians.[45] This dominance was a consequence of the number of Georgians who have emigrated to Israel and work in the defence sector and the fact that Georgia's Defence Minister at the time, Davit Kezerashvili, is a former Israeli. According to a well-placed Georgian source, deals with the Israeli defence industry 'were conducted fast, mainly due to the Defence Minister's personal involvement'.[46] Among the Israelis providing some $500m of military equipment to Georgia were an ex-mayor of Tel Aviv, Roni Milo, and his brother Shlomo, a former director general of Israel Military Industries, Brigadier General Gal Hirsch and Major General Yisrael Ziv.[47] Hirsch had commanded Israeli forces in the second Lebanon war, and resigned after being accused of poor leadership. He then formed his own company and became an agent for arms sales to Georgia. He persuaded the Georgians that Israeli equipment would enable them to defeat the Russians.[48] While Hirsch doesn't describe himself as an arms dealer, but rather as a military trainer, he made clear to the Georgians exactly what equipment they should buy and where to source it.[49]

Aeronautics Defense Systems provided equipment to both the Georgian and the Russian security forces prior to the war and, in Russia's case, afterwards. Israelis' activities in Georgia, and the deals struck, were all authorized by the Ministry of Defence. However, Israel Aerospace Industries refused to participate in activity with Georgia as the company felt it would anger the Russians, with whom it was involved in a project to improve fighter jets produced in the former Soviet Union. This led to an Israeli decision to sell Georgia only non-offensive weapons systems. The difficulty of this delicate diplomatic balancing act was illustrated by the comments of another Jewish Georgian minister who, in the wake of the invasion, called for help 'from the UN and from our friends, headed by the United States and Israel'.[50]

In mid-2011, Ziv's firm, Global CST, solicited business from the Georgian breakaway republic of Abkhazia, which is supported by Hamas, among others.[51] Should a contract emerge, Global CST will have trained both the Georgian forces and those of the Abkhazian breakaway republic in the next war. Israeli access to Abkhazia comes, not coincidentally, as military relations with Russia continue to warm. Abkhazia has Russian patronage and would have been inaccessible to Israelis previously.

What happened in Georgia is by no means exceptional. Former Israeli officers train people all around the world, in deals often arranged by arms merchants. All manner of ruses are used to get to the bottom line: the selling of weapons and security equipment. In one example, an entity called New Horizons Consultants (NHC) developed a service to help the democratization of African countries. Its members include the General Manager of the Likud Party, who was a former campaign manager for Ariel Sharon and Binyamin Netanyahu, a retired commander of the Counter-Terrorism Unit of the Israeli Police and a former Commander of the IDF Ground Forces. They offer the ultimate service: from how to start a political party to the running of an election campaign, which 'may lead to instability', requiring the strengthening of the 'police establishment', and, of course, 'a strong democracy also needs a strong army to protect its borders'. NHC provides training and equipment through a unique one-stop shop that includes all requirements for riot control, ground forces, homeland security, counter- and anti-terror, K9 dogs, and identification of and protection against nuclear, biological and chemical weapons. And, of course, the providers of this one-stop shop specialize in 'the sale and distribution of defense systems & equipment to the Israeli Government & the international community'.[52]

Israel's aggressive exporting of weapons and know-how has consequences for America because of the technology- and production-sharing
between Israel and the US. This poses the constant risk that US technologies will be transferred to other, 'non-friendly', countries. To cite
just one example, the Chinese air force flies a Jian-10 fighter plane that is
very similar to the Israeli Lavi, a joint Israeli–US design based on the
F-16. Although the joint production of this fighter plane was cancelled in
1987 because of cost overruns, and to prevent the Israelis becoming direct
competitors for exports, the design and technology ended up in Beijing.
Indeed, Israel is China's second-largest weapons supplier after Russia.[53]

Despite close US–Chinese economic ties, the two nations remain military
rivals, and most future nation-state war scenarios imagined by Pentagon
planners involve China as an adversary in some way. That Washington's
closest ally is assisting a 'near peer' rival to obtain high-tech weaponry should
be a major worry. China's own role as an arms dealer is well known and
has been roundly criticized in Washington. Just over a decade ago, the
UN Register of Conventional Arms disclosed that China had passed on
technology that was co-developed by Israel and the US to Iran and Iraq,
among other nations.[54]

The shadow world, as we have seen, is replete with Israelis operating as
middlemen, agents and dealers. The country has also provided citizenship –
and thus the ability to travel and bank with discretion – to an alarming
number of shady arms agents and brokers, primarily from the former Soviet
Union. A veteran Israeli investigative reporter, Yossi Melman, tells a joke
that the Israeli business community is divided into two: 'Those who are
arms dealers and those who don't admit they're arms dealers.'

President Teodoro Obiang has ruled Equatorial Guinea since a bloody
coup in 1979. He is believed to have ordered the deaths of thousands of his
citizens during his tenure as head of one of the most corrupt regimes on
the continent. US law enforcement agencies revealed several years ago
that Obiang held accounts at Riggs Bank's Washington DC branch containing some $700m. The accounts were frozen on suspicion of Obiang
having received bribes. An Israeli businesswoman, Yardena Ovadia,
befriended Obiang after a visit to his impoverished nation. In 2008, Ovadia operated as a mediator in arms sales to Equatorial Guinea for sums of
up to $100m. The deals involved Israel Shipyards Ltd and Israel Military

Industries Ltd. In the past Ovadia has been connected to deals with Obiang involving Brigadier General Shlomo Ilia and Boaz Badihi, an Israeli who operates from South Africa.[55]

It is always difficult to know whether arms agents are operating as renegade dealers on their own account or with a degree of state backing. Rumours abound of their relationships with senior political leaders or their utility to the country's intelligence agencies. The nature of the Israeli state, its permanent war footing and its legendary engagement with pariah regimes – apartheid South Africa on weapons and nuclear technology, Pinochet's Chile, Mugabe's Zimbabwe and all three sides in the Angolan civil war[56] – makes it even more difficult to assess this in the case of Israeli arms dealers such as Ovadia, Arcadi Gaydamak, Leonid Minin, Yair Klein, Shimon Yelenik and others. Jimmy Johnson describes the involvement of Minin, Klein, Yelenik and Israeli diamond dealers in Africa and beyond as a picture 'not only of war crimes, profiteering, massive environmental destruction, corruption and greed, but one of Israelis, Hezbollah and Al Qaeda all working together in mutually profitable enterprises, regardless of principle or ideology.[57]

Israel's relationship with apartheid South Africa was particularly bizarre, given the Nazi sympathies of the leaders of the racist state. The sight of South Africa's Prime Minister and brutal former Justice Minister, B. J. Vorster, paying his respects at the Yad Vashem memorial to victims of the Holocaust was especially surreal, given that Vorster had been interned during the Second World War for his strong Nazi sympathies. In a recent book, Sasha Polakow-Suransky has documented how Israel's booming arms industry and South Africa's isolation led to a semi-hidden military alliance that continued even after Israel passed sanctions against South Africa in 1980. The unlikely allies exchanged billions of dollars of extremely sensitive material, including nuclear technology, which boosted Israel's struggling economy and strengthened the beleaguered apartheid regime. The documents that Polakow-Suransky unearthed of the myriad deals confirm that Israel has been a nuclear power for decades, a truth that Washington dare not speak.[58]

There are two reasons why Israel dominates the shadow world: the first is the right of return to Israel for any Jew,[59] and the second is the deeply militarized and sometimes corrupt nature of the society. It therefore provides a desirable bolt-hole for arms dealers who might be in legal difficulty elsewhere, while providing a conducive environment for continued arms trading.

Israel struggles with corruption: for instance, when the former Prime Minister Ehud Olmert was indicted for fraud in August 2009, he was the fourth senior politician to face criminal charges in twelve months; while his three predecessors also faced corruption allegations, none culminated in criminal charges. The Movement for Quality Government in Israel commented that 'Governmental corruption has reached the point that it represents a strategic threat to Israel.'[60] 'Official illegality' in covert operations, including the use of false or stolen identity documents, untraceable weapons, etc., is also common practice.[61] This increases the country's appeal for illicit arms dealers.

Israel's militarization has created not a revolving door between military and civilian activities, but an open doorway. This is reflected in the ease with which former army officers become arms dealers once they have left the military. As Shir Hever, a leading, critical economic analyst of the Israeli military, has noted, the permit system is so lax that senior officers in the IDF almost always have the connections to get permits to trade in arms. The IDF has a very young retirement age – forty for combatants, forty-five for non-combatants and officers. So, at forty-five they are looking for other jobs, often becoming mayors or CEOs of defence companies.

For most of them, their primary skills are combat and control, so many set up an arms company.[62] They invent a product and then ask their friends in the army to buy even just a few of it. The fact that the IDF uses it is a key marketing tool. 'Wherever we try and sell they want to know if it's been used by the Israeli army.' And they are willing to sell to anyone, driven exclusively by the profit motive. In 2006, soldiers captured in Lebanon were shot with weapons showing Israeli markings. The weapons had been sold to Iran and were then sent to Hezbollah. Because individuals get permits so easily, the system gets out of hand and they end up selling weapons to Hezbollah, even if indirectly.[63]

Yossi Melman suggests that dodgy deals occur 'because Israel is a small country based on an old boys' network and there is insufficient supervision of the system. For a former officer, a small dodgy deal changes his life. Officials won't say no, as they may want to work for them in the future.' The licence is his main asset, as he could sell 'battle-proven Israeli arms'. Before the changes, the department in the Ministry of Defence responsible for marketing weapons exports was also tasked with licensing and supervising arms dealers. Melman shrugs: 'You can't supervise arms deals if you're promoting them!' In 2007, supervision and marketing were separated and in theory there is now extensive supervision. However, the new regime is not implemented with great conviction.[64] 'It's still a revolving door, so the problems continue. And there is apathy towards corruption. Israel won't fight military-security corruption because of the old boy network.'[65]

A former weapons salesman for an Israeli company told me that in a society as militarized as Israel, all the key people in the defence industry are ex-officers. The defence ministry is, therefore, under huge pressure from the industry not only to give contracts but also to ensure that it can operate unhindered and unscrutinized. Such is the extent of malfeasance that there is double-dealing even within companies: my source recounts how an arms dealer he knows is a legitimate agent for a large weapons-maker but also circumvents the licence process to undercut the company's price by 20 per cent in illicit deals about which the company knows nothing. In Israel, like the UK and the US, the big weapons companies are rarely properly investigated. They very seldom land up in court.[66]

As Mearsheimer and Walt have argued in their book *The Israel Lobby and US Foreign Policy*, Israel wields an inordinate amount of influence on US foreign policy, not always in the best interests of America. In fact, they argue that by encouraging unconditional financial and diplomatic – and I would add military – support for Israel, the lobby jeopardizes America's and Israel's long-term security.[67] But that military support, even connivance, has intensified in the last five years, just as the intensity and ruthlessness of Israeli military operations have increased.

Israel used US-supplied weapons, including Lockheed Martin's F-16 fighter planes and Boeing's GBU-39 bombs, in its July 2006 war in Lebanon and its December 2008 to January 2009 operation in Gaza to devastating effect, with civilians overwhelmingly bearing the brunt of the attacks. In the summer 2006 intervention in Lebanon, F-16 fighters were used to bomb Lebanese targets, while Lockheed's Multiple-Launch Rocket System (MLRS) sprayed cluster bombs across the countryside. A cluster bomb is essentially a large canister – as long as thirteen feet and weighing up to 2,000 pounds – packed with hundreds of 'bomblets' that can have an explosive impact on an area the size of three football fields, spreading shrapnel along the way.[68]

Although it is important to note that Hezbollah forces also fired missiles into northern Israel, including 100 or more Chinese-made rockets packed with cluster munitions, the issue has been the extent to which Israel's attack was disproportionate, and whether it put civilians at risk unnecessarily. The Israeli air force launched more than 7,000 air strikes during the conflict. The bombs hit roads, bridges, airports, factories and power plants, killing over 1,000 people, injuring over 4,300 and driving nearly a million more from their homes. At least 860 of the dead were civilians. Hezbollah's rockets were responsible for the deaths of fifty-five Israelis, of whom forty-three were civilians.[69] The attacks were devastating and indiscriminate enough to elicit Amnesty International's assertion that 'war crimes had been committed', and the UN's Undersecretary General for Humanitarian Affairs and Emergency Relief, Jan Egeland, called them 'a violation of international humanitarian law'.[70]

In Israel's 2008–9 intervention in the Gaza strip, which by one account killed over 1,400 civilians, F-16s were used to run bombing raids as part of the overall military operation, known as Operation Cast Lead.[71] At least 121 women and 288 children were killed. By contrast the total toll of thirteen Israeli deaths included two civilians. Of the eleven IDF soldiers killed, four died from 'friendly fire'.[72]

As devastating as the aerial attacks in Lebanon and Gaza were, it has been the use of US-supplied cluster bombs that has drawn the most international attention. Their military uses include attempting to slow down advancing troops, destroying airfields and taking out surface-to-air missile sites. Because cluster bombs can kill or wound anything in a large area, there is a high risk of hitting civilians as 'collateral damage' in the initial attack. They can also leave large numbers of unexploded 'bomblets' on the ground that blow up later on impact – when stepped on inadvertently, or picked up by a child, or run over by a plough. After Israel dropped millions of cluster bomblets during its thirty-four-day war in Lebanon, hundreds of thousands were left unexploded. Human Rights Watch estimates there have been at least 200 fatalities caused by leftover cluster munitions, and hundreds of injuries.[73]

The bomblets can be as small as a fizzy-drink can or a torch battery, and they don't look particularly menacing to someone unfamiliar with what they are. The results of this confusion can be devastating. Eleven-year-old Ramy Shibleh lost his right arm when he picked up a cluster bomblet that had got in the way of a cart that he and his brother were using to carry the pine cones they were collecting. The bombing also had a crippling effect on agricultural production in southern Lebanon, where unexploded cluster munitions rendered fields and orchards unusable, making them the equivalent of mine fields. A commander of an Israeli rocket unit told the Israeli daily *Haaretz* that the saturation bombing of Lebanon was 'monstrous; we covered entire towns in cluster bombs'.[74] The outrage at the use of this inhuman weapon was intensified when it came to light that Israel was launching more cluster munition volleys into Lebanon even while a ceasefire was being negotiated. According to Jan Egeland, '90 percent of the cluster bomb strikes occurred in the last 72 hours of the conflict, when we knew there would be a resolution'. Egeland called the strikes 'shocking and immoral'.[75]

The Lockheed Martin MLRS played a central role in the cluster-bombing of Lebanon. Researchers who went to the country after the war found large numbers of M-26 rockets that had been fired from MLRS systems. Each time the MLRS was used, it spread more than 7,700 cluster bomblets over the Lebanese landscape.[76]

The Israeli case is a telling example of how difficult it is to control the use of weaponry once it is sold, even when the purchaser is an ally. The non-governmental advocacy group Landmine Action uncovered a secret US–Israeli agreement governing the use of US-supplied cluster bombs which indicated that they should be used 'only for defensive purposes, against fortified targets, and only if attacked by two or more Arab states'. It also limited them to being used only against 'regular forces of a sovereign nation'. A preliminary State Department investigation found 'likely violations', but the ultimate findings of the review have been classified.[77]

Despite Israel violating the secret agreement with the US, Congress did not push for a full investigation. In fact, as the civilian death toll rose in Gaza, the House and Senate passed resolutions overwhelmingly supporting Israel's offensive. The validity of the self-defence rhetoric employed by Israel and parroted by the US is undermined by the disproportionate use of force and the reality that military action was premeditated and awaiting a trigger. A letter from Representative Dennis Kucinich in January 2009 to the Secretary of State, Condoleezza Rice – the only call for an investigation by an American lawmaker – made clear that 'Israel's attacks neither further internal security nor do they constitute "legitimate" acts of self-defense. They do, however, "increase the possibility of an outbreak or escalation of conflict," because they are a vastly disproportionate response to the provocation, and because the Palestinian population is suffering from those military attacks in numbers far exceeding Israeli losses in life and property.'[78]

Premeditation also nullifies any claim to self-defence. The March 2007 testimony of the Israeli Prime Minister at the time, Ehud Olmert, to the Winograd Commission set up by the Israeli government to investigate Israel's prosecution of the Lebanon war, states explicitly that his administration had decided 'at least four months in advance' of the [2006] operations that any kidnap of Israeli troops on its borders would trigger war. As for the 2009 Gaza War, the evidence that Operation Cast Lead was planned well in advance and just awaited a strike from Hamas to set it in motion is similarly convincing. Writing in *Haaretz*, the analyst Barak Ravid cites sources within the Israeli defence establishment stating that 'Defense Minister Ehud Barak instructed the Israel Defense Forces to prepare for the operation over six months ago, even as Israel was beginning to negotiate a cease-fire agreement with Hamas.'[79]

The US has, on occasion, briefly suspended weapons transfers to Israel, such as in 1982 at the time of an earlier Israeli invasion of Lebanon, when the Reagan administration suspended all military aid and transfers to Israel after determining that Israel may have violated the terms of a 1952 Mutual Defense Assistance Agreement (which included a commitment that US military matériel and other assistance would be used only to 'maintain its internal security, its legitimate self defense . . . and not to undertake any act of aggression against any other state'). A ten-week investigation into whether Israel was using weapons for 'defensive purposes' was inconclusive and the ban was lifted. This was the firmest US rebuke to Israeli military action in the last quarter-century.[80]

The former Israeli weapons salesman I spoke to told me that in 2007 there was a ban on the delivery of night-vision equipment from a US manufacturer, ITT.[81] Even goggles already ordered were not allowed to be delivered after the ban. But US soldiers in Afghanistan found US night-vision goggles in a cave after a fight with the Taliban. The serial numbers indicated that they had been delivered to the IDF in defiance of the ban, and had found their way to the Taliban, probably at a huge premium. He says this is an example of arms-exporting laws passed in the US which, when it comes to Israel, are just ignored.[82]

The United States is simply unwilling to hold Israel to account for transgressions of the laws regulating the use of US-supplied weaponry or even of special bilateral agreements on their use, as in the case of cluster munitions. While in the army, my source was using ammunition that wasn't yet approved in the US. It came from the American company ALS, where it was still in the testing phase and, thus, not legally usable in the US. But it was being used against people in the occupied territories by the IDF.[83]

In this and other ways, the US doesn't just accept Israeli illegality in weapons use, but actively supports military missions using US weaponry that kills civilians. During the Lebanon assault, the Pentagon complied with an Israeli request for military fuels worth up to $210m. Two days after Operation Cast Lead was launched, the *Jerusalem Post* reported that the Israeli air force was using recently delivered GBU-39 bombs – 250-pound GPS-guided bombs manufactured by Boeing, capable of piercing more than three feet of reinforced concrete – to penetrate Hamas's underground rocket launcher sites. The US also tried to transfer new weaponry in the midst of the operation: according to a 9 January 2009 Reuters report, the US had tried to hire a merchant ship to transport hundreds of tons of US arms from Greece to Israel.[84]

Barack Obama initially set out to depart from the foreign policy path set by his predecessor. For a few brief months he was critical of the Israeli right-wing government under the Likud hardliner Binyamin Netanyahu. But in March 2010, as the Israeli Prime Minister was at the White House supposedly experiencing the full wrath of the Obama administration about his refusal to countenance a permanent cessation of illegal settlement building in the West Bank and East Jerusalem – identified as a major stumbling block to peace talks – the administration was finalizing details of a $3bn arms deal with Israel. In terms of the deal, Israel will purchase three new Hercules C-130J aircraft designed and built specifically for their needs by Lockheed Martin.[85] In October 2010, it was announced that Israel will also purchase twenty F-35s from the same company, with a further option for seventy-five more.[86]

★

Today Israel is at the forefront of high-tech military development, and undertakes a massive amount of R&D on behalf of not only its own companies but also US companies and the Pentagon. Shir Hever believes that Israel is the only country that buys from its own companies using US aid money, by setting up US subsidiaries. So technology seeps both ways.[87]

My arms salesman source suggests that 'the latest, state of the art equipment is never sold, but is only for the IDF and the US'. Among other things, Israel has pioneered unmanned bulldozers, jeeps, drones – in which it is the global leader – surveillance equipment and ships. The separation barrier is equipped with unmanned, armed observation points that, through personnel in a distant, secure location, identify and fire on anyone who comes too near to the barrier. This is the creation of a robotic warfare that accelerates and intensifies the process of dehumanization and non-culpability for death – the very factors that have enabled mass killings and genocide to occur from Auschwitz to Kigali.

As the son of a Holocaust survivor I desperately wish that the US and Israel would consider that one of the ways to pay tribute to the suffering of Jews during the Holocaust is to condemn the atrocities caused by the trade in arms, whether they involve Jews or non-Jews, whether perpetrated by or against the state of Israel. A more transparent, honest arms trade can contribute to a reduction in the oppression of one people by another, the persecution of one group by another.

18.   Making a Killing: Iraq and Afghanistan

The decision to go to war in Iraq was the culmination of the life's work of many people in the Bush II administration: an outcome prompted by the exhortations of Prince Bandar and the unwavering support of Tony Blair. It had enormous consequences for the US, for the Iraqi people, for geopolitics and for the arms trade. Arguably, they were mostly negative, except for the bonanza it provided to arms dealers, weapons manufacturers and the providers of military services. They made a killing.

Iraq and its 'liberation' unsurprisingly interested Lockheed Martin's Bruce Jackson, both as a neocon and as a businessman. Although he left Lockheed Martin in 2002, his ten years with the company shaped his approach to national security as he continued to take actions that benefited his former employer. As a co-founder of the Committee for the Liberation of Iraq (CLI), Jackson worked directly with the Bush administration in marketing the war. In fact, he claims that the White House asked him to 'do for Iraq what you did for NATO'.[1] He drafted a letter signed by ten Central and Eastern European leaders endorsing an invasion of Iraq, right after Colin Powell's misleading presentation on the US case for war to the UN.

He was so wired into the hawkish think-tanks that one prominent neocon described him as 'the nexus between the defense industry and the neo-conservatives. He translates them to us and us to them.'[2] His job was eased by the number of his Project for the New American Century colleagues in prominent roles in the Bush administration, all of whom were early proponents of the invasion and misled the American public to justify it.

In addition to building up the PNAC's advocacy for greater military might and bigger budgets, Jackson's efforts to promote intervention in Iraq were substantially aided by the CLI, which he had helped found. One of the most vociferous media supporters of intervention was the retired General Barry McCaffrey, who worked as a consultant for NBC in the lead up to and after the invasion. He appeared over 1,000 times extolling the necessity of invasion and the virtues of the war. What was never mentioned was that he earned hundreds of thousands of dollars as a consultant to defence contractors seeking to profit from the Iraq War. An exhaustive *New York Times* investigation put McCaffrey at the centre of a Pentagon-orchestrated plan to get retired military officials – many with ties to the defence industry – to use their numerous media appearances to promote the administration line on the war. They received special Pentagon briefings to inform their commentary. In mid-2007, McCaffrey signed up with a company, Defense Solutions, to help it lobby for a contract to deliver used armoured vehicles from Eastern Europe to forces in Iraq.[3]

Despite this media onslaught the administration was not able to convince the majority of Americans of the purported link between Saddam and Al Qaeda, let alone convince them of the Weapons of Mass Destruction (WMD) argument, which Paul Wolfowitz admitted in *Vanity Fair* was the approach decided on because it was considered the best way to sell the war to the American people.[4] Even after definitive proof that the WMD did not exist in Iraq the PNAC clung to the justification, publishing a report in April 2005, *Iraq: Setting the Record Straight*, which argued that there might still be WMD in Iraq.

Chuck Spinney argues that the intertwining of defence companies like Lockheed Martin, their allies in government, think-tanks and the Pentagon not only results in profligacy from $600 toilet seats to the $70bn spent on unrequired F-22s, but it also makes war more likely, due to the combination of interests and the dominance of the executive over the legislature. The President has gained more and more power, which gives him ever increasing patronage. The executive branch is able, in myriad ways, to control money going to Congressional districts, directly (through supporting weapons programmes) or indirectly (through all of the government agencies). And patronage is now crucial given the cost of elections. It is extremely difficult for a Representative with defence production in his or her constituency to oppose a President going to war. It is for this reason that West Virginia's Senator Robert Byrd remarked in February 2003, as the Iraq War inexorably approached:

> As this nation stands on the brink of battle, every American on some level must be contemplating the horrors of war. And yet this chamber is for the most part ominously, ominously, dreadfully silent. You can hear a pin

drop. Listen. There is no debate. There's no attempt to lay out for the nation the pros and cons of this particular war.[5]

Lockheed Martin and Halliburton were the two biggest beneficiaries of the war. The former received 25 billion US taxpayer dollars in 2005 alone. This sum exceeded the GDP of over 100 countries and was larger than the combined budgets of the Departments of Commerce, the Interior, Small Business Administration and the entire legislative branch of the government. Lockheed's stock price tripled between 2000 and 2005. The Defense Index went up every year from 2001 to 2006 by an average of 15 per cent, seven and a half times the S&P average, and these companies were among the most resilient in the credit crisis. Lockheed was also the biggest spender on political campaigns among the arms manufacturers who contributed almost $200,000 to the Bush '04 campaign.[6]

The US, and other allies in the invasion, had a long history of support for Saddam, including providing him with financing, weapons and matériel. This despite his authoritarian, repressive rule since assuming absolute power in 1979, symbolized by his brutal genocide of Kurds in the north of the country which led to between 50,000 and 100,000 deaths, and included the largest chemical attack on civilians in history, at Halabja.[7]

The Arab Socialist Baath Party had overthrown the country's military government in 1968, with Saddam becoming President in 1979. He was supported by the US and the West because of his government's secular nature and general friendliness towards Western companies. He was also a crucial bulwark against the theocratic regime in Iran which had overthrown the American-supported Shah.

Saddam's Iraq, where Sunni occupied most positions of power over a Shi'ite majority, was concerned when the ruling Sunni minority was overthrown by the Shi'ite majority in Iran. In 1980, using claims over a disputed waterway,[8] Iraq declared war on what was believed to be a weakened Iran so soon after its revolution.[9] The Iran–Iraq War lasted from September 1980 to August 1988, claiming the lives of at least half a million people.[10] The war ended in a stalemate, partly due to covert and overt arms sales from Germany, Britain, France and especially the United States.[11]

On 4 August 1989, FBI agents raided the Atlanta offices of Banca Nazionale del Lavoro (BNL), which is headquartered in Rome. On a tip-off from two company insiders, the FBI seized thousands of documents that, when stitched together, would conclusively prove that the US had been funnelling money to Saddam Hussein.[12] Over the next three years, Representative Henry B. Gonzales sifted through the documents attempting to reconstruct exactly what had happened, despite the constant intervention of the George H. W. Bush White House, terrified of the implications of the scandal. By 1992, the picture had become clearer: BNL had become Saddam Hussein's largest creditor, sending over $5.5bn in loans to Iraq from 1985 to 1989 with the help and complicity of the CIA and Washington power players.[13] The loans had been guaranteed by the US government, using the cover of the Commodity Credit Corporation, an agricultural loan facility used to promote the export of US food produce around the world. When Iraq later defaulted on the loans, it was the US taxpayer who picked up the tab.[14]

The money raised from the BNL scandal was central to the military ambitions of Saddam Hussein's regime – and that of the US itself. During the drawn-out war between Iraq and Iran, Washington claimed neutrality. Covertly, however, deals were made with both sides. Under the auspices of Oliver North's illegal Reagan-supported, Israeli- and Saudi-aided project the US diverted weapons to Iran, in what would become known as the Iran–Contra scandal. But, for the most part, the administration's decisions tilted to Iraq and Hussein, as the US worried about the implications of Iran's religious aversion to the West. Certainly the monetary support Hussein received was far in excess of that given to Iran. With the money at its disposal, Iraq embarked on a weapons-buying spree, purchasing billions of dollars in arms, mostly from Europe.[15] The US not only made the money available, but also allowed tons of 'dual-use' items into Iraqi hands, including valuable virology material that aided in the production of biological weapons.[16]

From 1980 to 1990, Saddam spent at least $50bn on conventional weapons and close to $15bn on covert weapons programmes, both nuclear and biological.[17] While the US was careful not to export any conventional arms, it did provide about $1.5bn in dual-use items, many explicitly for use in these covert programmes. Between 1985 and 1989 alone, the General Accounting Office found that the US Commerce Department approved 771 dual-use exports to Iraq.[18] The list of dangerous chemical concoctions that were sold at the time makes for chilling reading: 'Sarin,

Soman, Tabun, VX, Cyanogen Chloride, Hydrogen Cyanide, blister agents and mustard gas', according to the journalist Stephen Brown. 'Anthrax, Clostridium Botulinum, Histoplasma Capsulatum, Brucella Melitensis, Clostridium Prefingens and E Coli' rounded out the list of biological agents.[19] A more conventional deal was the purchase of sixty helicopters for Saddam from manufacturers Bell, McDonnell Douglas and Hughes. Technically, the choppers were sold for use in agricultural spraying. In reality, they were militarized as soon as they entered Baghdad. Perhaps their intended use would have become clearer to the Department of Commerce if they had paid attention to the man who was brokering the deal on behalf of Iraq: Sarkis Soghanalian.[20]

Sarkis Soghanalian was one of the most notorious arms dealers of the Cold War era. Born in Syria in either 1929 or 1930, Soghanalian was raised in Lebanon. He later joined the French army in 1944, working in a tank division. He was to spend the rest of his life around sophisticated weapons. He started his arms-dealing business in earnest in the early 1970s, becoming actively involved in supplying US weapons to the Lebanese government. Soon after, Soghanalian moved to the US, where he settled permanently and made a number of key connections in the CIA and FBI. Prior to working in Iraq, he provided weapons to numerous regimes with the active support of the CIA. These included Nicaragua, Ecuador, Argentina and Mauritania. Other notable clients included Libya's Muammar Gaddafi, to whom Soghanalian sold a C-130 transporter plane in 1987, and Zaire's Mobutu Sese Seko.[21]

His biggest deals, however, were in Iraq, where he was reported to have overseen $1.6bn in arms deliveries to the country. Despite claiming he was acting with the blessing of the CIA, he was arrested and convicted in 1991 of exporting arms to Iraq without federal licences. Initially given a six-year sentence, Soghanalian had his term reduced to two years after agreeing to help the FBI bust a counterfeiting ring in Lebanon producing $100 notes. One of his most notorious post-Cold War deals involved an air drop of 10,000 AK-47s into Peru, allegedly with the knowledge of the CIA. The arms were subsequently transported into Colombia where they were sold to the FARC. In 2001, he was convicted once more for cashing fraudulent cheques, although he was released immediately on the advice of the US Attorney General, who claimed that Soghanalian was assisting with an unnamed investigation.[22]

The UK, too, played its part in supplying multiple dual-use items to Iraq. Technically, the UK had banned the exportation of 'lethal' items to the country from 1984 onwards, although it allowed many questionable 'non-lethal' products through Customs. These sales included sophisticated electronics, military Land Rovers, uniforms, military radars and machine tools.[23] Trading relations were good enough for Iraq even to buy into UK companies. In 1989, Iraq purchased the Coventry-based Matrix Churchill, whose board then featured two members of the Iraqi security forces. Matrix Churchill was one of the most respected machinist firms in the country and supplied sophisticated parts and machines that helped Iraq establish its own indigenous arms-manufacturing capacity.[24] In 1992, two directors of Matrix Churchill were prosecuted for violating Customs regulations. The case, however, collapsed when it was discovered that the company had been making the sales with the knowledge and implicit help of the Conservative Party.[25] In 2001, the two directors received substantial payouts in compensation for being wrongfully prosecuted.[26]

For its conventional weapons, Iraq was able to enlist the services of nearly every country. Answering the question: 'Who armed Saddam?', Anthony Cordesman, an expert on the Iraqi military, answered bluntly: 'everybody who has arms'.[27] By far the largest numbers of weapons – the basics such as AK-47s – were imported from the USSR, which accounted for just over 50 per cent of the trade with Iraq.[28] The rest was made up from various countries, with France and Germany the two most important European suppliers. German companies and scientists were deeply involved in Iraq's ballistic missiles programme, providing technical goods and specialist advice. French companies such as Dassault, Thomson-CSF and Aérospatiale, meanwhile, made considerable sums of money by selling a vast array of weapons to Saddam.[29] Between 1979 and 1990, France exported dozens of Mirage F-1C fighters, 150 armoured cars, numerous Puma and Gazelle helicopters, 2,360 surface-to-air missile systems and over 300 super-powerful Exocet anti-ship missiles.[30] In 1989, Saddam hosted the first ever international armaments fair in Baghdad. France mounted the largest display of French weaponry seen outside the country for decades.[31]

But, a year after the BNL scandal erupted, Saddam Hussein invaded Kuwait, a staunch US ally. The man the US and the world had helped arm was now enemy number 1. Arms trade blowback once again.

The US, led by President George H. W. Bush, repelled Iraq's army, sweeping away Saddam's million-man force with remarkable ease. Thirteen years later, George W. Bush took on Saddam again, launching an invasion that, it was hoped, would remake the world. The two wars could not have been more different: the US operation in Kuwait in 1990 was backed by the international community and undertaken with a UN mandate. In 2003, much of the world looked on in horror as Bush Jr ignored the protestations of the UN. Millions marched around the world beseeching the US to change its mind. Most importantly, it was a war fuelled by an ideological impulse to assert American hegemony and remodel the world to its strategic imperatives. And it was undertaken largely by private companies.

The result has been a windfall for the companies involved in the business of war, but at the cost of a world that is less safe, less secure and less amenable to the supposed ideals of the United States of America.

The wars in Iraq and Afghanistan were driven, in addition to the lure of black gold, by the dual ideological impulses of the Bush administration: a muscular neoconservative belief in the power and right of the US military to shape the world; and a near-religious faith in the efficiency and productive power of the unfettered free market, both fervently held and actively promoted, for its own benefit, by the US defence industry.

These two strands were woven together in 1997 with the publication of the PNAC's *Statement of Principles*, which lamented the certainties of the Reagan years and argued for the need 'to accept responsibility for America's unique role in preserving and extending an international order friendly to our security, our prosperity, and our principles'.[32] And, consequently, the 'need to increase defense spending significantly if we are to carry out our global responsibilities today and modernize our armed forces in the future'.[33]

The signatories of the *Statement* were many of those who would lead the path to the wars in Iraq and Afghanistan: Jeb Bush, the brother of George W. Bush, Dick Cheney, Donald Rumsfeld, Paul Wolfowitz, 'Scooter' Libby and Zalmay Khalilzad, the US ambassador to both Afghanistan and Iraq in the years following the US invasion.

Three years later, the hubristic logic of this neoconservative call to arms would become the guiding light for the new rulers in the White

House. In September 2000, the PNAC published the defining report, *Rebuilding America's Defenses* (see Chapter 14). Coming as it did only months prior to the 2000 US election, it had a significant impact on George W.'s defence policy. It warned that states were deterred from threatening American supremacy and the values it holds dear by the capability and global presence of American military power. But it warned that if that power declined, 'the happy conditions that follow from it will be inevitably undermined'.[34] The upshot was a clarion call for a massive increase in defence spending.

The 2000 report did not specify exactly who was the largest threat to American security. But it was clear that Iraq was in the crosshairs. On 26 January 1998, the PNAC sent an 'open letter' to Bill Clinton, signed by many who had signed the *Statement of Principles*. The open letter highlighted Saddam Hussein's alleged nuclear and biological weapons programmes – that had once been helped along by the US but totally destroyed after the 1990 Kuwait debacle – and pushed hard for a policy of regime change. It was, in other words, a dry run for the future war in Iraq.[35]

At the same time as the future Bush administration was outlining its foreign policy principles and badgering for an invasion of Iraq, most of those who signed the *Statement* were making fortunes in business, as we've seen. Dick Cheney was CEO of Halliburton while Donald Rumsfeld was amassing an estimated $12m from his forays into the private sector.[36] They were the standard-bearers of both the politician-entrepreneur and the emerging disaster capitalism industry.

Unsurprisingly, when America finally went to war, it would be done with the firm belief that subcontracting out its functions to the private sector was not only efficient and rational, but the essence of patriotism.

The attacks on the World Trade Center and the inauguration of the War on Terror galvanized George W. Bush's presidency and provided fertile ground for the new militarism that Cheney and Rumsfeld had spent years evolving. Within a month of the tragedy the US was attacking Afghanistan, hoping to dislodge the Taliban government whose predecessors it had once so aggressively championed with Charlie Wilson at the forefront. Faced with the might of the American military, the Taliban melted into the hills from where they would fight an ongoing low-intensity guerrilla war for much of the next decade. At the time, however, what impressed many in the US was the ease with which the Taliban were swept aside. American military might seemed unassailable and the prospects for future campaigns seemed certain. The time had come to fulfil the neocons' dream of kicking Saddam out of power.

On 20 March 2003, the US, accompanied by small contingents from the absurdly named 'Coalition of the Willing', invaded Iraq. In just under fifty days the US military marched through the country and seized the capital, Baghdad. Saddam Hussein, later captured in a muddy hole near his home town armed only with a solitary pistol, was whisked away to face trial and execution. On 1 May 2003, in a photo-op that would come to define his faintly ridiculous presidency, Bush Jr addressed a global television audience aboard the USS *Lincoln*. 'Major combat operations in Iraq have ended. In the battle of Iraq, the United States and our allies have prevailed.'[37] In reality, the war had just begun.

The ease of the US's apparently quick victories in Afghanistan and Iraq suggested that it had run a tightly controlled and efficient military campaign. In reality, while the first 'surges' into the respective countries were carried out with remarkable force, only the most basic planning had been undertaken as to how the countries would be run in the aftermath of the military successes. It soon became clear that the Coalition Forces would have to prepare to dig in for the long haul. Without clear plans in place, those in control of Iraq had to fumble for solutions, moving from one crisis to another. The US administration in the country became an 'adhocracy',[38] with short-term solutions used to quell a thousand different fires without the requisite thinking through of all the consequences. With a small invasion force the Coalition Provisional Authority (CPA) and those that followed were forced to turn repeatedly to the private sector to fill in the gaps, ballooning the costs of the war while ensuring a massive flow of income to those lucky enough to be on the inside track – a state of affairs that delighted Cheney, Rumsfeld and their acolytes, who had aggressively punted the privatization of conflict.

Far more than had been anticipated or fantasized about by the dogmatic privatizers, the wars in Iraq and Afghanistan would be contractor wars. They are easily the largest privatized conflicts the world has ever seen. Contractors have been used in previous wars undertaken by the US but never on this scale. During the First World War for example, the US deployed 1 contractor for every 20 soldiers, 1 for every 7 in the Second World War and 1 for every 6 in Vietnam.[39] As of March 2010, there were 207,553 contractor personnel active in Iraq and Afghanistan compared to 175,000 troops — a ratio of 1.18 contractors per soldier in the region. Afghanistan was even more heavily dependent on contractors: 112,000 contractors supported 79,000 troops, a ratio of 1.42 contractors to every soldier.[40] Remarkably, a full 11,610 contractors were employed in Iraq as of March 2010 to supply security — a tacit admission that the US Army could not control the country without relying on a sizeable mercenary force.[41]

While estimating the total amount awarded to contractors in Iraq and Afghanistan is difficult, some figures are indicative. Between 2003 and 2007, US agencies had placed over $85bn in contracts with private suppliers in Iraq.[42] Other figures suggest that the values of contracts have increased exponentially since then. In one study the GAO reported that during the fiscal year 2008 and the first half of 2009, $39bn had been awarded via 84,719 contracts in the two countries: over $2bn per month or $26bn a year.[43] Taken together, this would suggest that contractors had earned considerably more in Iraq and Afghanistan than the $100bn by 2010 that has previously been estimated.

Easily the largest contract was awarded to KBR, the engineering and logistics subsidiary of the Texas-based Halliburton, until June 2007, when it was sold. By March 2010, KBR had earned $31.4bn via its hugely controversial LOGCAP, which Dick Cheney had been instrumental in developing and awarding.[44] This figure excludes the largest contract placed by the US Army Corps of Engineers in Iraq, a $7bn deal with KBR to reconstruct Iraqi oilfields damaged in the conflict. In return for this brazen cronyism, Halliburton/KBR made hay out of the cost-plus contracts as they mismanaged projects, inflated prices, overspent and double-billed the government they were serving.[45]

After Cheney left the Defense Department in 1992, his appointment as CEO of Halliburton in 1995 led to a remarkable improvement in the company's fortunes, especially with regard to federal contracts. In the five years prior to his arrival, Halliburton had received a paltry $100m in government credit guarantees. Under Cheney's five-year leadership, Halliburton received fifteen times that amount — $1.5bn.[46] Cheney was paid well for his services: for fifty-eight months he received $45m.[47] As we've noted, some of these payments were made to him while he was Vice

President.[48] Charles 'Chuck' Lewis, the Executive Director of the Center for Public Integrity, was vituperative:

> This is not about the revolving door, people going in and out. There's no door. There's no wall. I can't tell where one stops and the other starts. They're retired generals. They have classified clearances, they go to classified meetings and they're with companies getting billions of dollars in classified contracts. And their disclosures about their activities are classified. Well, isn't that what they did when they were inside the government? What's the difference, except they're in the private sector?[49]

Further muddying the waters was the fact that Halliburton was one of the largest contributors to the Republican election campaign that propelled George W. Bush to the presidency. Between 1998 and 2003, the company donated $1,146,248 to the Republican Party. The Democrats, in the same period, received a comparatively risible $55,600 from Halliburton's lobby fund.[50]

The first major scandal erupted only months after the Iraq War began in earnest.[51] As the years went on it became clear that KBR's mismanagement and misconduct was systemic, omnipresent and, perhaps most importantly, seemingly hardwired into the corporate culture of the company. It reflected the contradiction at the heart of the hawks' privatizing zeal: support for free markets and private enterprise were portrayed as the essence of patriotism, but players in these markets act only on the basis of maximizing bottom-line profit and not out of any idealistic vision of patriotic duty.

This was certainly the impression gained by David Wilson, a fifty-year-old Vietnam veteran who went to work for KBR. He was shocked at his corporate induction by an extraordinary pep talk in which the recruits were told they were going to Iraq 'for the money'. The trainer told them they were not going to help the troops, not going to help the Iraqi people, not going for America, but 'FOR THE MONEY', a slogan they had to chant repeatedly. And once in Iraq his worst suspicions were confirmed as mismanagement, ineptitude and wastage eventually cost the lives of six KBR drivers and two soldiers.[52]

KBR could only get away with this behaviour because they were allowed to. The US Army and government could barely keep tabs on what the contractors were doing. In 2009, the bipartisan Commission on

Wartime Contracting – established as a means to prevent future contractor debacles – published an interim report indicating that, while the US was happy to pour hundreds of billions of dollars into the hands of contractors and the military, it was far more stingy when it came to employing people to monitor or regulate these activities. One staff member was responsible for overseeing nineteen contracts, over and above his normal military duty.[53] Similarly worrying was the fact that the Defense Contract Audit Agency (DCAA), responsible for monitoring and auditing contracts placed by the DOD, has run for much of the Afghanistan and Iraq wars without sufficient staffing, with numbers remaining the same while contracts increased by 328 per cent.[54]

When the DCAA reviewed the various contracts awarded during the War on Terror it found literally billions of dollars had been frittered away on wasteful and excessive spending. In total by the end of the 2008 fiscal year, the DCAA had recommended reductions in billed costs of $7bn – over and above a further $6.1bn where 'the contractor had not provided sufficient rationale for the estimate'.[55] A partial audit of KBR's LOGCAP contract found $3.2bn in dodgy expenditure and an additional $1.5bn that the contractor could not support.[56]

Even more galling was that, in many instances, contractors hired by the US in Iraq and Afghanistan didn't do a particularly good job, critically undermining the US missions in each country.[57]

Of course, this is not to suggest that only KBR and Halliburton could be criticized for undermining the reconstruction of Iraq. Equally damaging to US legitimacy in the broader region was the role of private security contractors, or, to use a more loaded but accurate term, 'mercenaries'. Just as advertising was once characterized as 'the pimple on the arse of capitalism', so mercenaries could be appropriately described as the vultures circling the Grim Reapers of the arms trade. Given the nature of their activities it is unsurprising that they sometimes get involved directly and indirectly in the arms trade itself.

The invasion of Iraq unleashed boom years for mercenaries around the world.[58] Contractors were needed to fill the gaps caused by the US force in the country being smaller than needed. They were employed *en masse* to protect bases, embassies and, bizarrely, local and foreign dignitaries. Indeed, the first US proconsul in Iraq, Paul Bremner III, was protected by a crack team of hired guns from perhaps the most controversial security company of all, Blackwater.

Equally important in boosting the numbers of contractor security staff was the fact that the US military had proved unable to protect the other private contractors, forcing them to hire mercenary outfits to protect themselves. Soon, the cost of hiring private security was swallowing at least 10 per cent, and perhaps up to 25 per cent, of many reconstruction budgets.[59]

In addition, mercenaries were so involved in fighting the war itself that by September 2010 contractor deaths in Iraq and Afghanistan constituted more than 25 per cent of all fatalities afflicting the US and its allies.[60] In *Blood Money*, his study of waste, greed and lost lives in Iraq, T. Christian Miller notes that 'contractors, for the first time in US military history, were not only supporting the war, they were in the middle of it, fighting and dying alongside soldiers'.[61]

Unfortunately, with mercenary services came chequered pasts and questionable motives. The type of hired guns employed by private security contractors at salaries as high as $200,000 a year soon raised eyebrows. They included South Africans drawn from the country's notoriously vicious apartheid-era security forces[62] and Serbian ex-special force operatives, many of whom were alleged war criminals who had honed their skills during the genocidal Balkans conflict.[63] A British company by the name of Aegis was awarded a security contract worth just under $300m in 2004.[64] The company was headed by Colonel Tim Spicer, a controversial former British Army officer who also ran Sandline International, a mercenary group that was involved in numerous contentious conflicts and arms trading. In 1998, Sandline had been hired by Sierra Leone's President Ahmed Kabbah to help restore him to power following a coup. Sandline imported 35 tons of Bulgarian AK-47s despite Sierra Leone being under an arms embargo at the time.[65] Spicer was to claim that he had imported the weapons with the approval of the British Foreign Office, a view later upheld by a number of government inquiries.[66] According to an investigation by the UK House of Commons Committee on Foreign Relations, Spicer's cargo had been given a 'degree of support' by Peter Penfold, the UK's High Commissioner to Sierra Leone. Penfold ridiculously claimed that the shipment did not violate the terms of the arms embargo. The diplomat was released from his position and placed in a different department.[67]

Once Spicer's background became public, Democrats in the US wrote to Donald Rumsfeld asking him to cancel Aegis's contract in favour of a less controversial candidate. Rumsfeld and the DOD rejected the request.[68]

Given that mercenaries are generally viewed with suspicion, one would have expected that they would be subject to intense oversight. The exact opposite is true. On 27 June 2004, in one of his last acts as proconsul, Paul Bremner decreed Order 17 into law,[69] under the terms of which all staff associated with the Allied forces and the contractors they hired were exempt from Iraqi law.[70] Order 17 would remain in effect until explicitly struck down by the Iraqi government. This placed contractors such as Aegis and Blackwater in a legal lacuna, especially as they did not operate under the terms of the Uniform Code of Military Justice that governed the behaviour of all US troops[71] and it also wasn't clear that US courts would have jurisdiction over crimes committed by contractors on foreign soil. They had been given a *de facto* 'licence to kill'.[72]

The author of Order 17 was one Lawrence Peter, who at the time was in charge of overseeing the activities of Iraq's Ministry of the Interior.[73] Soon after the controversial Order was passed and the CPA ceased to exist as power was handed over to the newly elected government, Peter found employment elsewhere: as a lobbyist and liaison for the Private Security Company Association of Iraq. 'The new Iraq,' noted the respected journalist Sidney Blumenthal, 'included a revolving door.'[74]

Blackwater, among others, thrived in this lawless environment. Formed in 1996, the company was led by a former Navy Seal, Erik Prince, a man with impeccable Republican connections.[75] As Blackwater grew following the September 11 attacks, it was assiduous in adding well-connected individuals to its board, such as J. Cofer Black, appointed vice-chairman after a twenty-eight-year career in the CIA, latterly as head of the CIA Counter-Terrorist Center, from where the policy of extraordinary rendition emerged.[76] Another influential appointee was the COO, Joseph Schmitz, who joined the company in September 2005. A month previously Schmitz had resigned as the Defense Department's Inspector General overseeing all contracts placed by the Pentagon, after allegations that he had inappropriately intervened, or allowed political intervention, in suspiciously awarded contracts, including the Boeing tanker refueller debacle and millions that were directed the way of Blackwater.[77] Incredibly, in September 2010 Schmitz was awarded a sole-source contract to independently monitor the Special Inspector General for Afghanistan Reconstruction's (SIGAR) efforts to alleviate deficiencies in its investigative division.[78]

With such connections, perhaps Blackwater's growth is understandable. Prior to 9/11, the company had a $1m federal contract; by 2009 it had received roughly $1.5bn from the Pentagon to supply mercenary services in Iraq and Afghanistan, as well as other conflict zones.[79] The company's name became synonymous with the use of excessive force after it was embroiled in the unjustified killing of at least eighteen Iraqi civilians in two separate incidents in Iraq.[80]

Shortly after Blackwater was banned from operating in Iraq for its involvement in the shooting of innocent civilians in Baghdad, it was reconstituted as Xe Services and was still bidding for US government contracts to operate in areas besides Iraq, including Afghanistan. It was discovered that Xe had committed 289 violations of the Arms Export Control Act, for which it faced possible prosecution.[81] Fortunately for Blackwater/Xe, it escaped with a mere slap on the wrist: a civil fine of $42m paid as part of a settlement agreement with the State Department in August 2010. This was considerably less than the maximum $288m fine that could have been levied.[82] By avoiding court, Xe would remain eligible to receive further government contracts.[83] Business as usual then for the contractor whose legacy to Iraq's struggling democracy is mayhem, murder, massive wastage and an undermining of whatever rule of law may exist.

Despite mounds of evidence pointing to mass illegality, misconduct and corruption, no contractors employed in Iraq have faced the threat of debarment. In fact, KBR could earn $50bn over ten years from a slightly amended LOGCAP IV alone.[84]

The boom years for private contractors that followed 9/11 were as good for the conventional defence industry: weapons manufacturers, dealers and brokers. While the activities of the likes of KBR and Blackwater have dominated news cycles and analysis, little attention has been paid to the super-profits earned by the formal defence trade or the shadow world, some of whom emerged from the network of brokers, dealers, thugs, money launderers and gangsters linked to Merex.

While uncertainties and difficulties exist in estimating exactly how much the US military has spent on defence procurement specifically related to the Iraq and Afghanistan wars, what is clear is that it is an extremely large amount. By far the largest procurement costs directly linked to the wars in the Middle East are those associated with the practice of 'reset', the policy whereby the US military continually repairs, upgrades or simply replaces military equipment that has been used on the field of combat. This 'resets' the equipment and units that use them to their operational level as it existed prior to the conflicts. It has been a massive and ongoing programme, especially since 2005. As of 2006, it was reported by the Congressional Budget Office that roughly 20 per cent of the entire inventory of the US military had been deployed in Iraq, Afghanistan and surrounding areas.[85] The Army alone had $30bn worth of equipment stationed in the two theatres by early 2007.[86]

The harsh conditions have meant a high rate of attrition, repair and replacement. As a result the US Army has estimated that a considerable amount of the weapons deployed in Iraq and Afghanistan would need to be replaced every year to keep stocks at pre-war levels – not repaired, but actually replaced. It has been estimated that 6 per cent of the total helicopter force deployed would have to be replaced annually; roughly 5 per cent of fighting vehicles, and 7 per cent of trucks.[87] If equipment levels remained the same, by 2020 every helicopter deployed in Iraq and Afghanistan would be due for replacement. Whether forces will remain in the country until 2020 is unsure, especially as President Obama announced, in mid-June 2011, a newly revised timeline for withdrawal from Afghanistan and Iraq that should see the bulk of forces moved out by 2014.[88] This, in turn, has been muddied by reports of a 'secret pact' between the US and Afghan governments, committing thousands of trainers, contractors and secret forces agents to the country until 2024.[89] Nevertheless, if the conflict rumbles on – which the 2010 budget cautioned, with temporary plans until 2020 – a full 20 per cent of the entire military might of the US would be replaced, a mouth-watering prospect for the MICC.

When repairs to vehicles and equipment are included it becomes a truly gargantuan undertaking, which would see thousands of pieces of equipment sent to the mechanics of large defence contractors. The CBO has reported that after two years of operations in Iraq, it was necessary for *every* Abrams tank and Bradley Fighting Vehicle that returned home to be sent for repairs. Repairing each Bradley costs $500,000, each Abrams tank

$800,000.[90] The total annual cost for simply cleaning sand and dust from the Bradley vehicles and Abrams tanks is between $700m and $1.2bn.[91]

As one would expect looking at these figures, the costs related to procurement and reset in Afghanistan and Iraq have skyrocketed. In 2004, the total amount set aside for procurement in the supplemental budgets that funded the wars was $7.2bn. In 2008, at its peak, a massive $61.5bn was set aside. For the six years between 2004 and 2010, $215bn had been budgeted, with a further $21.4bn requested for 2011.[92]

From 2004 onwards, the cost of war in Iraq grew steadily. That year, it cost roughly $4.4bn a month; in 2006, $7.2bn a month; and, in a sudden leap, $10.2bn and $11.1bn a month in 2007 and 2008 respectively.[93] The leaps between 2006 and 2007–8 – about a 40 per cent increase in the cost – occurred at a time when troop levels remained stagnant. Almost the entire increase in the cost of war was thus due to reset-related procurement that began in earnest in 2007.[94] To reiterate: once resetting and replacing equipment really started, it increased the total cost of war in Iraq by at least 40 per cent. Once troop drawdown in Iraq is finally completed, the reset of equipment in the field as of 2010 is estimated to cost at least $40bn and take roughly two years to complete – over and above the annual reset requirements described above.[95] As a result, of all the factors that have contributed to the 'spiralling' costs of war, reset has been 'perhaps . . . the most significant', according to the Nobel laureate Joseph Stiglitz and Dr Linda Bilmes of the Kennedy School of Government.[96]

The amounts described were incurred *over and above* the existing DOD budget, which mushroomed during the War on Terror, under George W. Bush and for at least the first two fiscal years of the Obama administration.

In 2007, the CBO conducted a study of reset costs incurred in Iraq and Afghanistan. It discovered that more than 40 per cent of the costs requested for reset in the two wars was actually being spent on either upgrading existing systems, rather than resetting them to pre-war levels of operation, or, crucially, 'buying new equipment to eliminate shortfalls in the Army's inventories, some of which were long-standing'.[97] So, far from merely retaining operating levels, the DOD undertook massive expenditure that would improve the stock of the entire military and paid for it out of the budget for the Iraq War. In 2006, for example, under the rubric of 'reset', it was decided to replace the entire Pentagon fleet of 18,000

Humvees with vehicles better able to resist improvised explosive devices (IEDs).[98]

In another instance, the Pentagon inserted a request for two Joint Strike Fighter jets from Lockheed Martin into the 2007 requisition for funds for the wars in Iraq and Afghanistan – even though the fighters would never be ready in time to see action in either conflict.[99] By restock-

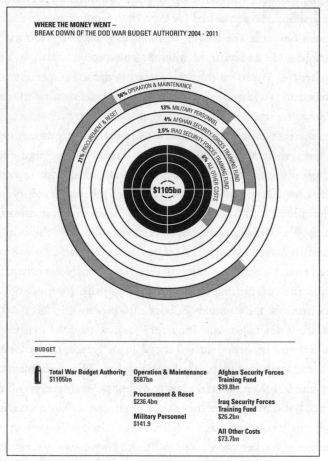

WHERE THE MONEY WENT –
BREAK DOWN OF THE DOD WAR BUDGET AUTHORITY 2004 - 2011

56% OPERATION & MAINTENANCE

13% MILITARY PERSONNEL

4% AFGHAN SECURITY FORCES TRAINING FUND

2.5% IRAQ SECURITY FORCES TRAINING FUND

21% PROCUREMENT & RESET

6% ALL OTHER COSTS

$1105bn

BUDGET

	Total War Budget Authority $1105bn	Operation & Maintenance $587bn	Afghan Security Forces Training Fund $39.8bn
		Procurement & Reset $236.4bn	Iraq Security Forces Training Fund $26.2bn
		Military Personnel $141.9	All Other Costs $73.7bn

Figure 7: US Department of Defense budget and spending on the wars in Iraq and Afghanistan

ing inventories on the war tab, the Army was able to fund purchases that it was not able to undertake within the already huge amounts dedicated to the military in the DOD budget. Even the budgets for the wars in Iraq and Afghanistan have been padded with pork barrel projects: 'It's a feeding frenzy,' an Army official involved in budgeting complained: 'Using the supplemental budget, we're now buying the military we wish we had.'[100]

What makes this even more concerning is that, by being included in the supplemental budgets for the wars, these pork barrel projects could effectively pass under the radar, without any accountability. This is a function of the absurd budgeting process for the wars in the Middle East. Supplemental budgets are passed by Congress – emergency budgets that appropriate money for needs outside the usual budgetary process. These budgets are passed fast and hard, the exigencies of war demanding that many line items be taken on faith: in one instance, a $33bn request under the Iraq Supplemental included a meagre five pages justifying the expenditure.[101] 'In my opinion as a budgeting professor,' Dr Linda Bilmes commented: 'this is not the best way for the US budget system – or any budget system – to operate. The purpose of the emergency supplemental facility is to fund a genuine emergency. . . . The late transmittal of supplementals during the budget process leads to less congressional review and lower standards of detailed budget justification than regular appropriations.'[102] The GAO concurred: 'The use of emergency funding requests and budget amendments for ongoing operations of some duration reduces transparency, impedes the necessary examination of investment priorities, inhibits informed debate about priorities and trade-offs and, in the end, reduces credibility.'[103]

Each of the major defence contractors was well placed to provide the weapons used in the wars. As detailed above, Lockheed Martin offered a massive range of products suited to the War on Terror. These included Multiple-Launch Rocket Systems used to launch cluster bombs against Iraqi opponents, leaving behind deadly fragments of unexploded bomblets that killed or injured both Iraqis and US soldiers.[104] Its F-16 jets were heavily involved in the initial bombings, and its Hellfire air-to-ground missiles were used extensively to attack Iraqi armoured vehicles.[105] The company's communication equipment was also widely used and replaced on a regular basis.[106]

Lockheed had also made the prescient and lucrative move into supplying privatized services to the military. The company had become, as a result, a vertically integrated war industry of its own accord. 'Lockheed Martin is now positioned to profit from every level of the War on Terror from targeting to intervention, and from occupation to interrogation,'

Bill Hartung commented in 2005.[107]After Lockheed purchased Sytex in March 2005, and acquired a portion of Affiliated Computer Services (ACS), it supplied interrogators and analysts for use by the DOD. Some of the interrogators were deployed to Abu Ghraib, others involved at Guantanamo Bay. Lockheed was well positioned to receive a sizeable chunk of the 'Intelligence Industrial Complex' market, which received $50bn from US intelligence agencies every year – nearly three quarters of which was spent on private contractors.[108] The company was the largest private intelligence contractor employed by the US government, making it jointly 'the largest defence contractor and private intelligence force in the world'.[109] After KBR, Lockheed Martin was the second-largest contractor to the US in Iraq and Afghanistan.

BAE, meanwhile, provided almost all of the US's Bradley Fighting Vehicles, for which it received a new $2.3bn contract in 2007.[110] After BAE acquired Armor Holdings for $4.532bn in 2007, it was also in line for contracts related to the Pentagon's plan to replace its 18,000 Humvees with mine-resistant vehicles in which Armor specialized.[111] Northrop Grumman's products were also in high demand, in particular its B-2 strike bomber that was used continuously to effect 'shock and awe'.

It has also taken the lead, along with Israel's Elbit Systems, in building unmanned aerial vehicles and militarized drones – the unmanned aircraft that controversially fly the deserts and mountains of Iraq, Afghanistan and Pakistan searching for, and eliminating, insurgents and terrorists.[112]

The startlingly roughshod manner in which budgets were passed has made it almost impossible to track the exact amounts flowing from the war budgets and those of the intelligence services into the coffers of the formal defence industry. There is little doubt that the years since 9/11 have been extraordinarily lucrative. Some indication is given by the explosion in share prices of the largest defence contractors. In January 2003, for example, the monthly average price for a BAE share on the London Stock Exchange was £1.13. Its September 2010 monthly average was £3.41. Similarly, Lockheed Martin's share price in January 2000 was $15.32. As of September 2010, the monthly average price for a Lockheed share was $71.28. So too Northrop Grumman – its share grew from $19.76 to $60.63 over the same period.[113] Both BAE and Northrop Grumman reported share price increases of over 300 per cent, while Lockheed Martin's was a virtually unheard of 465 per cent increase since the inauguration of the War on Terror.[114]

The largest 'reset' costs budgeted during the Middle East wars were inserted in the years 2007 and 2008 – with over $60bn budgeted in the latter year.[115] Almost without exception, the share price of the major defence

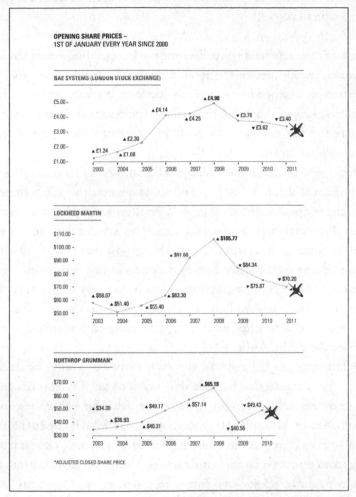

Figure 8: Share price movement in BAE, Lockheed Martin and Northrop Grumman

companies reached a decade-long peak in this same period. BAE's shares, for example, rocketed above £4 a share in December 2006 and remained there until October 2008. Its historical peak was in December 2007, where it reached £4.98 a share, or a full 440 per cent increase on its January 2003 price.[116] Lockheed Martin's shares also bulged, soaring from $65 in May 2006 to a decade-high of $109 in August 2008.[117] Both BAE and Lockheed's shares dropped substantially in October 2008 and fell consistently thereafter – a month before Barack Obama took control of the White House promising a withdrawal from Iraq and, most importantly, the procurement costs in the supplemental budget were slashed from $61.5bn in 2008 to $32bn in 2009.[118]

The lack of oversight and control over defence spending – and the haste with which major projects were undertaken – meant that Iraq and Afghanistan also turned into extremely lucrative markets for arms dealers and brokers. Indeed, some of the earliest operations in Iraq opened the floodgates for the one man most closely associated with questionable practices: Viktor Bout.

In 2003, shortly after the invasion of Iraq, the US military faced a major problem. While it had successfully taken control of a number of key landing strips, conditions remained perilous for civilian contractors. Baghdad International Airport, for example, was subject to repeated mortar fire from the surrounding suburbs, almost universally off-target, and planes flying over Baghdad's suburbs often had to dodge anti-aircraft fire. As a result, US civilian cargo operators were advised against running supplies into the country. This left a major hole, as cargo planes were desperately needed to help the US undertake the largest air cargo operation since the Berlin Airlift.[119]

To fill the gap, the US and its contractors turned to a range of air cargo suppliers operating around the world. From 2003 until at least the end of 2005, one of the most consistent operators was Irbis Air – an airline owned and controlled by Viktor Bout. In 2003–4 alone, Irbis Air conducted hundreds of runs to Baghdad and other high-security airports, carrying items ranging from tents and boots to military hardware and ammunition. Irbis landed in Baghdad ninety-two times from January to May 2004, while also conducting deliveries to other Iraqi airports. Between March and August 2004, the Defense Logistics Agency confirmed that Irbis Air had refuelled 142 times in Baghdad alone.[120] The income Bout earned from his flights in Iraq was not inconsiderable. At $60,000 per return run, he was estimated to have earned $60m between 2003 and 2005 – over and above the free fuel regular cargo operators were given by the US military.[121]

Bout's client list in Iraq made for intriguing and damning reading, given his status as 'the merchant of death':

[US military] officials explained that Irbis had been hired repeatedly as a secondary military subcontractor, delivering tents, frozen food and other essentials for American firms working for the US Army and US Marines. The Bout flagship also was a third-tier contractor for the US Air Mobility Command, flying deliveries for Federal Express under an arrangement with Falcon Express Cargo Airlines, a Dubai-based freight forwarder. And Irbis was also flying . . . under reconstruction contracts with the petro-chemical giant Fluor, and with Kellogg Brown and Root.[122]

For Chris Walker, the man in charge of Baghdad airport's civilian cargo control, Bout's involvement was an embarrassment, and a blindside, as he had assumed that all airlines that operated in the months after the invasion had been properly vetted. As it turned out, the CIA had flagged Bout's operations – but the email failed to reach the appropriate person at the CPA offices.[123] Walker was caught in a real bind: even though Bout was likely to be placed on the Asset Freeze list and was wanted by both the FBI and the CIA, stopping his flights would have fatally disrupted stretched supply lines. As a result, as of mid-2005 Bout's planes were still flying into Iraq. When it was confirmed that the US Treasury was placing Bout and his airlines on an Asset Freeze list and the Foreign Assets Control (OFAC) list that outlawed the use of certain contractors, the US military's Central Command asked for a week's reprieve. It was granted, allowing Bout to deliver a final shipment of arms, ammunition and other supplies. 'It ensured that private contractors continued paying Bout's network despite the fact that any other American firm doing the same would have been subject to prosecution.'[124]

While the Russian was able to make a fortune from his contracts directly with the US, the wars provided other opportunities for arms dealers. One of the most pressing needs was to restock the military supplies of the Iraqi security forces, which had largely faded into the shadows during the initial invasion. Re-equipping the de-Baath'd forces was crucial as the Coalition Forces hoped that Iraqis would assist in fighting the insurgency and retaining law and order. Millions of tons of small arms and ammunition flooded into the two countries, and Iraq in particular. Between 2003 and 2007, roughly 115 orders were placed for arms deliveries to the Iraqi security forces at a total cost of $217m.[125] As of July 2007, the US training command confirmed that 701,000 weapons had been imported for Iraq's security forces.[126] Most of these were 'Soviet-type infantry weapons', including AK-47s, portable machine guns, RPGs and pistols. Unfortunately, these deals were often undertaken with the help of brokers with dubious track records – and may, in fact, have ended up supplying weapons to the very people the Coalition Forces were fighting.[127]

One of the most consistently used primary contractors has been Taos Industries, currently a subsidiary of Agility and Defense Services[128] and a recent joint recipient, with Dyncorp and one other company, of a $643.5m one-year task order under LOGCAP IV.[129] Taos specializes in 'the procurement of non-standard matériel, including equipment for security forces, foreign military systems and hard-to-find components'.[130] In one deal, the company was contracted by the US to deliver 99,000 kilograms of AK-47 rifles to the Iraqi security forces.[131] The weapons were to be sourced from Bosnia, where a considerable stockpile of surplus weapons remained following the Balkans wars of the mid-1990s. To fulfil the order Taos employed a cargo company by the name of Aerocom.[132]

As of 2004, Aerocom did not have a valid air operator licence after it had been involved in a particularly dodgy deal only a year previously. In 2003, the UN reported that Aerocom had been involved in supplying Charles Taylor with tons of small arms and ammunition. According to the report, the company had been hired by Temex Industries to effect the delivery of weapons from Serbia to Monrovia in violation of the UN arms embargo still in force against the country.[133] Aerocom also had connections to Viktor Bout. Records showed that Aerocom and Jet Line – a part of Viktor Bout's delivery empire[134] – had frequently leased each other's jets or used each other's licences to conduct deliveries.[135]

Another Taos acquisition brought attention to the fact that a substantial number of arms bought for the Iraqi security services may have been diverted to the insurgents fighting against the US. In 2004, Taos was asked by the US to arrange a separate consignment of weapons for the Iraqis. It in turn contracted a London-based outfit by the name of Super Vision International,[136] which decided to source the arms from Italy, acquiring 20,318 Beretta 92S handguns from the Beretta company itself.[137] The consignment was shipped to Exeter, from where it was delivered to Baghdad. Italian police, however, were not happy with the deal when they discovered that Beretta had sold the weapons without the appropriate licence. The weapons were old and sourced from the Italian interior ministry before being refurbished and sold on to the UK. But Beretta did not have the appropriate registration to sell refurbished arms. The company had also listed the guns as 'civilian' products in their export papers, even though the 92S had been declared a 'weapon of war' by the Italian legal system. Registering the handguns as civilian made the deal subject to far fewer checks than if they had been registered as military matériel.[138]

Although the weapons were delivered to Baghdad in July 2004, they were only officially accepted in Iraq on 18 April 2005.[139] It is uncertain why the delay occurred. However, the CIA informed the Italian police in February 2005 that Al Qaeda operatives who had been captured in Iraq were in possession of Beretta 92S weapons – allegedly from the very same batch that Beretta had exported to Exeter on behalf of Super Vision and Taos Industries.[140] The captured insurgents were fighting on behalf of Abu Musab al-Zarqawi, Al Qaeda's principal leader in Iraq. It is not entirely clear how the weapons were passed on to Al Qaeda, although it had long been rumoured that Iraq's police had been infiltrated by insurgent elements. The Italian police service acted quickly and seized the thousands of Berettas still in Italian warehouses awaiting shipment to the UK.[141]

The Beretta deal illustrated that systems to ensure weapons bought by the US for the Iraqi military didn't fall into insurgent hands were inadequate if they existed at all. In July 2007, the GAO published a report that didn't generate much interest, despite its explosive content. Auditors and investigators from the GAO travelled to view *in situ* how the handover of weapons had been managed in Iraq, and how the US had kept track of the weapons it had bought for the security services. It found that until December 2005 the body responsible for training and arming the Iraqis 'did not maintain a centralized record of all equipment distributed to Iraqi security forces' and that, as a result, the same body had 'not consistently collected supporting documents that confirm the dates the equipment was received, the quantities of equipment delivered, or the Iraqi units receiving the equipment'.[142]

A mountain of weapons was missing. By September 2005, the Iraqi security forces had received 185,000 AK-47 rifles, 170,000 pistols, 215,000 items of body armour and 140,000 helmets. The US entity responsible for their distribution could not account for 110,000 AK-47 rifles, 80,000 pistols, 135,000 items of body armour and 115,000 helmets[143] – more than 50 per cent of all the equipment that had been delivered at great cost. Not being able to account for the weapons did not necessarily mean that all of them had found their way to the black market – some were probably just 'lost in the system'. But, as David Isenberg, US Navy veteran and senior analyst with the British American Security Information Council, commented after the 2007 GAO report was published: 'it seems fairly likely that some of the missing weapons are being used against US forces in Iraq. Given that the most readily accessible black market for those stolen weapons is in Iraq, some of those are going to be bought by the insurgents.'[144]

Considering the size of the weapons procurement for the Iraqi forces – and the quantity of logistics and reconstruction contracts – it is not surprising that dealers tied into the Merex network have operated in Iraq. Merex and the Mertins family have been at the rock face of the weapons industry during America's two great wars of the last five decades: the Cold War and the War on Terror. Joe der Hovsepian has been there with them.

Despite his involvement with a menagerie of unsavoury arms dealers and his participation in a number of illegal weapons transactions throughout his career, der Hovsepian profits from American largesse in Iraq and Afghanistan. Having described the Americans as 'the biggest terrorists on the planet' at the outset of our conversation, he wore an ironic grin as he showed me his US Department of Defense ID and a USAID identity document enabling him to operate as a contractor in Iraq. He also showed me a letter from USAID dated 6 April 2005, confirming his appointment as a security consultant in Iraq. While der Hovsepian said both had expired, the USAID ID seemed to be valid until 2011. Both the Department of Defense and USAID were unwilling to confirm the name of consultants they use in conflict zones.

He worked for KBR in Iraq, as 'they always get contracts to do all the work. They even sign up for projects that don't exist.' He is a security adviser for four other companies in the country: Najran Co. Ltd; Dahab Al E'amar Co. Ltd; Jawhart Al-Eman Co. Ltd; and Jawharat Al Mahabba Co. Ltd.

He explained how he gets equipment into Iraq without it being captured by insurgents. He will have a truck of one colour take goods and matériel up to the border post. Then, because there are informants at the borders, he surreptitiously changes vehicles on the other side, so the insurgents waiting to ambush are looking for a different colour truck. He also spends a lot of time meeting tribal leaders, wearing traditional dress. He does this to reduce the possibility of raids on his vehicles and sometimes buys their protection.

During my interview with der Hovsepian, he was adamant that Helmut Mertins, the son of Merex's founder, Gerhard, was operating in Iraq. Der Hovsepian invited me to check for myself and gave me an email and physical address for Helmut. While Mertins was unwilling to see me, the address itself made for interesting reading. The email address der Hovsepian had on file suggests that Mertins was working for a company called Sweet Analysis Services Inc. (SASI). SASI is headquartered in Alexandria, Virginia – the current home of Helmut and the town from which the US branch of Merex operated.

SASI is named after its founder, Patrick Sweet, a self-proclaimed US Army veteran. The company, founded in 1990, currently has additional offices in Kiev in the Ukraine and Bucharest in Romania. Sweet has made some powerful friends in the Ukraine. A press release from 2009 confirmed that he served on the board of the US–Ukraine Business Council.[145] According to its corporate website, SASI runs a dedicated department handling 'Foreign Material Acquisition and Foreign Military Sales'.[146] The list of weapons SASI procures for clients is impressive, including thermobaric munitions, rocket-propelled grenades, anti-ship cruise missiles, tanks, infantry weapons, small- and large-calibre ammunition, radar systems and unmanned aerial vehicles.[147]

Patrick Sweet previously worked for Vector Microwave Research Corp., which performed secret tasks for the CIA and the US military, 'using guile, experience and connections, including those of its president, retired Lt. Gen. Leonard Perroots, a former director of the Defense Intelligence Agency'.[148] Vector was contracted to acquire foreign missiles, radar and other equipment for US intelligence agencies. So complex was the web of connections surrounding the company, that its founder, Donald Mayes, became a business partner with China's state-owned missile manufacturer while secretly buying Chinese weapons for the US government. But when Vector went out of business in the late 1990s, papers revealed that it had been doing its own illicit business as well. The firm bid on its own account for a batch of North Korean missiles, and in trying to sweeten the deal provided China with sensitive technical specifications on the US Stinger anti-aircraft missile.[149]

Information available from the DOD shows that the US has made use of SASI's services, and supposedly those of Helmut Mertins, on at least sixteen occasions during its wars in Iraq and Afghanistan. Between 2000 and 2009, SASI won contracts from the DOD worth $45m, mostly for ammunition and small arms. By far the largest contract was placed in 2004 and ran until February 2007: at a total cost of over $35m, SASI was contracted to deliver 'miscellaneous weapons' to the USA Material Command Acquisition Center headquartered at Fort Belvoir in Virginia.[150]

But of all the weapons dealing in the US wars in Iraq and Afghanistan, none was more intriguing and lurid than that of Dale Stoffel. On 8 December 2004, Stoffel, a strapping arms merchant with an insatiable appetite for adventure, was shot dead on the outskirts of Iraq. His colleague, Joseph Wemple, driving the vehicle in which they were travelling, was shot once in the head at distance – possibly by a sniper.[151] Stoffel was shot repeatedly in the front and back. His laptop and other personal effects were stolen. The crime scene was grisly: blood drenched their car, the front of which had crumpled like paper as it careened to a sudden stop, the windscreen, pocked with gunshot, cracked.[152]

Theories abound as to who killed Dale Stoffel. His tragic story will remain a symbol of the violence and flux of post-invasion Iraq, and the undertow of corruption and double-dealing that so often accompanies arms dealing amid the chaos of conflict.

Dale Stoffel lived his life in the military and in the murky world of intelligence and arms dealing. Entering the military as a means to pay for college, he swiftly rose through the ranks as a respected technical specialist with a highly prized mathematics degree. In 1987, he cemented his credentials when he examined the wreckage of USS *Stark*, which had been sunk in the Persian Gulf. Looking through missile fragments like tea leaves he was able to divine that the ship had been struck by two missiles rather than one – suggesting a premeditated attack rather than a simple accidental misfire.[153] By 1989, Stoffel had left the employ of the military and had begun working for a number of defence contractors, including Raytheon and Mesa/Envisioneering.[154] He filled a unique niche as a result of his training – he was knowledgeable about Eastern bloc weapons and able to procure sophisticated weapons systems, available following the fall of the Berlin Wall. The systems would be aggressively studied for any technical tips, as well as providing the military with valuable information about their capabilities before they entered the free market.

Six years later, Stoffel decided to enter the arms market on his own account. In 1995, he formed a company called Miltex, through which he was able to continue his niche purchasing. He was forced to drop the name in 1999 when Human Rights Watch reported on a shipment of Bulgarian weapons to an unnamed African country that was then under embargo.[155] The shipment, stopped before it was able to leave Bulgaria, had papers listing Miltex as the broker.[156] Stoffel denied ever being involved in the deal, claiming that another dealer must have used his name and company stamp to undertake the deal[157] – a not unreasonable claim considering Stoffel's daily contact with sometimes unscrupulous brokers in Eastern Europe. He dropped the Miltex name and reformed his enterprise as Wye Oak Technologies.

It was under that name that Stoffel attempted to make his fortune in Iraq. In 2003 he hired the services of BKSH,[158] a powerful lobbying group based in Washington that was part of Burson-Marsteller, the largest public relations company in the US.[159] BKSH had a number of clients certain to be influential in post-invasion Iraq. They included the Iraqi National Congress (INC), led by Ahmed Chalabi, one of Iraq's most powerful politicians in exile. Chalabi had, throughout his period in exile, cultivated strong links with Republican leaders and intelligence agencies in the US, who believed that Chalabi could assume the reins of the country once Saddam fell. As a consequence, Chalabi's INC received roughly $40m in support and aid from the US government – and motivated Chalabi to push fervently for a US intervention in the country.[160]

Chalabi's importance to the Bush administration was made clear in February 2003 when Colin Powell delivered his ill-fated 'call to war' speech to the UN in which the US outlined its intelligence that Iraq had weapons of mass destruction.[161] A crucial piece of evidence was the testimony of Mohammad Harith, an alleged Iraqi defector who claimed to have invented mobile labs that could research and produce biological weapons. But Harith, according to the investigative journalist Aram Roston, was a 'known fabricator' who had been served up to the US by Chalabi, who, at the time, was desperate for 'intelligence' that would motivate the invasion of Iraq.[162] 'Mr Chalabi and his cronies gave phoney information about weapons of mass destruction to the White House and the Defense Department bought it hook, line and sinker,' Democrat Representative Jay Inslee would dramatically inform the House in 2004.[163]

In January 2004, Stoffel was convinced by BKSH lobbyist Riva Levinson to travel to Iraq in search of lucrative contracts. A few weeks later, he arrived in Baghdad to be looked after by Margaret 'Peg' Bartel, who had an agreement with BKSH to help newly arriving Americans with transport and board. Stoffel quickly fell in with the BKSH–Iraqi National Congress set, and was frequently seen with Ghazi Allawi[164] – a relative of Ahmed Chalabi and a member of the powerful Allawi family, who came to fill numerous Cabinet posts in Iraq's post-invasion government. In May 2004, for example, Ayad Allawi, Ghazi's cousin, was appointed Iraq's interim Prime Minister. Another brother, Ali Allawi, would serve as Minister of Defence in a Cabinet appointed by the Interim Iraq Governing Council between 2003 and 2004 and as Minister of Finance from 2005 to 2006. Ayad emerged again as a crucial power broker, as leader of the largest party after the disputed March 2010 elections.

Ghazi Allawi was, at some stage in his career, involved in a Panamanian business with Leonid Minin's one-time partner, Erkki Tammivuori. The company was the Central Iraq Trading Company, suggesting that the Finn was also interested in doing business in Iraq.[165]

Despite these connections, Stoffel struggled to crack the Iraqi weapons market. It took six months to secure his first deal. In June 2004, the Multinational Security Transition Command–Iraq (frequently referred to by its nickname 'Mitskey') was investigating options related to Iraq's existing weapons stockpile.[166] Large amounts of it had rusted and decayed in Iraq's deserts, sitting useless and unusable, while some was salvageable. An idea was developed to refurbish the items that could be saved, defraying the cost by selling the unusable items as scrap metal. The earnings potential was huge: Stoffel had estimated the value of all scrap metal from Iraqi arms to be worth roughly $1bn, if not more.[167] With the go-ahead of General David Petraeus, who headed Mitskey, the Iraqi Ministry of Defence proceeded with the deal. Stoffel was granted access to various bases to inventory the equipment and, in August 2004, he signed an agreement with the Iraqi defence ministry to undertake the job. For his services as broker, Stoffel was to receive 10 per cent of the cost of refurbishment and any scrap sales[168] – an income of $100m or more, even though US, but not Iraqi, regulations outlaw contracts with such percentage payments.[169] Regardless, Stoffel had hit the jackpot.

But things soon started to go wrong. As part of the agreement, the Iraqi Ministry of Defence claimed that Stoffel could not be paid directly. Instead, a third party would be paid by the ministry, which would, in turn, pay Stoffel. The third party was the General Investment Group,[170] headed by a Lebanese businessman, Raymond Zayna, and staffed by Mohammed abu Darwish, the one-time foreign affairs attaché for the Lebanese political party Lebanese Forces.[171] Darwish would later be black-listed by the Pentagon for running a scheme to defraud the US of millions of dollars.[172]

In October 2004, Stoffel submitted his first invoice to the Iraqi government, charging just under $25m for refurbishing services he had undertaken and would continue until January 2005. He never received the money. Furious and fretful, he travelled back to the US and petitioned his local representative, the Republican Rick Santorum. Santorum fired off a letter to Donald Rumsfeld, the result of which was a meeting between Stoffel and Rumsfeld scheduled for December 2004.[173] A few days later, Stoffel was 'invited slash ordered' to travel back to Iraq by the Coalition military.[174] On 5 December, a further meeting was arranged in Baghdad to sort out the payment issues, attended by a range of Iraqi and US brass. The meeting was tempestuous but the outcome was that Stoffel would receive an immediate $4m payment from Zayna with more to follow. 'He left me a message on my voicemail,' an associate recalled, 'in which he was exuberant. Everything was solved.'[175] Three days later, Stoffel was dead.

A few months later an Iraqi group calling itself 'Rafidan – the Political Committee of the *Mujahideen* Central Control' released a video claiming responsibility for Stoffel's assassination. Asserting that 'the devil Stoffel' was a 'shadow CIA director' in Iraq, Rafidan drip-fed documents from Stoffel's stolen laptop via its website. The group claimed that Stoffel had been assassinated to prevent him from raping the treasury and assets of the Iraqi people. One document in particular painted Stoffel in a less than flattering light. It was a memorandum of understanding (MoU) dated 20 June 2004 entered into between Stoffel, Ghazi Allawi, Mohammed Chalabi and the Turkish arms dealer Ahmet Ersavci.[176] The MoU stated that 'the parties to this MoU are endeavouring to establish Mr. Stoffel as the exclusive broker to the Iraqi Ministry of Defence with respect to the disposition of all military arms and weapons, including inventories, acquisitions and procurements'.[177] Stoffel, in other words, would be the sole weapons broker to Iraq. It was envisioned he would operate via a company, Newco, established by Ahmet Ersavci.[178] Newco, in turn, would earn a 10 per cent 'brokerage fee' on the value of all transactions – a potentially astronomical sum.[179] Of this fee, 50 per cent would be retained in the company, while the remaining 50 per cent would be split, with Stoffel taking 60 per cent and the rest of the partners dividing the balance.[180] If the MoU was accurate, it meant that Stoffel was involved in a contract that would have netted both himself and a series of politically connected Iraqis vast amounts of money.

With Rafidan claiming responsibility, the mystery of Stoffel's death appeared solved. But many were not convinced. Nobody had heard of the Rafidan *mujahideen*. They had not claimed any other attack before Stoffel's death and have never claimed one since. The 'lawyerly' manner in which the documents were presented online – replete with a video walking the audience through the documents – was most unlike what one would expect from a rag-tag group of insurgents and street fighters. Ghazi Allawi had also been taken hostage for twelve days, the month before Stoffel was killed, again by a formerly unknown group, Ansar al-Jihad ('Partisans of Holy War'). After his release the matter was quickly forgotten about.[181]

What is certain is that Stoffel had more enemies in Iraq than just an unknown group of insurgents.

Frustrated by his exclusion from contracts in the first half of 2004, Stoffel had started to blow the whistle on companies and the US administrators doling out contracts on behalf of the CPA. What he witnessed in the chaotic days following the invasion confirmed to him that Iraq and the CPA were riddled with corruption: he would frequently complain of deliveries of cash hidden in pizza boxes from contractors to administrators at the CPA. In fact, according to affidavits submitted by his family, Stoffel had been 'working and cooperating with Mr. [Stuart] Bowen'[182] of the Office of the Special Inspector General for Iraq, the independent watchdog with powers to investigate corruption in Iraq. In 2009, the *New York Times* reported that, on 20 May 2004, Stoffel had signed an agreement with the Special Inspector General giving him limited immunity from prosecution in return for information.[183] Curiously, Stoffel was due to meet Bowen on 10 December to discuss matters relating to his contract in Iraq – only two days before he was gunned down.[184]

In 2009, cryptic clues emerged as to who Stoffel may have been planning to finger. In February, the *New York Times* reported that the Special Inspector General had started to look more seriously into allegations of corruption levelled at members of the CPA. This included, according to officials in Iraq, revisiting the allegations of corruption levelled by Stoffel.[185] At the same time it was reported that two senior and high-ranking members of the CPA had been subpoenaed to provide their bank statements as part of an investigation into bribes and kickbacks. One of these officials was Colonel Anthony Bell, who worked as the contracting officer for the CPA in Baghdad from June 2003 until March 2004.[186] Attached to court papers supporting the subpoena was a statement from James J. Crowley, a 'Special Agent' for the Special Inspector General for Iraq Reconstruction, confirming that 'SIGIR received information from a confidential source that Anthony Bell and another individual were improperly receiving kickbacks in connection with certain contracts entered into in Iraq. The confidential source was killed in Iraq after he met with US officials.'[187] It is assumed that this is a reference to Stoffel.

The suspicions aroused by Dale Stoffel's death and the questions that remain unanswered reflect that the days after Iraq's liberation were, like the shadow world of the arms trade, defined by greed, corruption, opportunism, deception and violence. There were stratospheric profits to be made but in seeking them you were likely to put yourself in a position to pay the ultimate price.

In June 2011, President Obama announced a new timeline for troop withdrawal. Over 33,000 troops, who had been redirected from Iraq to Afghanistan in a 'surge' in 2009, would be returning home by 2012.[188] This would leave roughly 70,000 troops in the country. The stated plan is to remove all troops by 2014,[189] but this claim has been undermined by more recent reports of the 'secret pact' between the US and Afghan governments to keep thousands of service members in the country until 2024.[190] Either way, the US will still be involved for a few years yet, adding to the costs of war with every passing day.

The most quantifiable of these costs is the financial outlay on the wars.

In September 2010, the Congressional Research Service estimated that the wars in Iraq and Afghanistan have cost $1.092tn.[191] The war in Iraq received the bulk of the money, $751bn, while Afghanistan accounted for $336bn.[192] This did not include a supplemental budget request for 2011 worth $171bn, which would push the costs to a staggering $1.3tn.[193] Troop drawdown in Iraq brought no savings – the money was merely diverted to Afghanistan, which is set to receive 60 per cent of all funding.[194]

In 2011, a twenty-strong group of economists and social scientists at Brown University confirmed that, when these additional costs were taken into account, the total actual outlay of costs to 2011 was, conservatively, $3.2tn ($3.9tn in a 'moderate estimate'). Partially, this was made up of the cost of additional veterans' care packages that there was an obligation to run until 2051. A larger portion, just over $1tn, was made up of interest on the loans taken out to finance the wars in Iraq and Afghanistan ($185bn), additions to the Pentagon's base budget ($326bn), additions to the US Aid and State Department budgets ($74bn), amounts disbursed by 2011 to disabled veterans ($32bn) and, most notably, additions to the Homeland Security budget for spend on the War on Terror ($401bn). In total, the Brown team calculated that the cost of the wars by 2020 would reach or exceed $4tn.[195]

This still ignores the opportunity cost and the long-term indirect costs of war. One of these is the impact of a growing US national debt, as 'This was the first time in American history that the government cut taxes as it went to war,' Stiglitz and Bilmes point out. 'The result: a war funded completely by borrowing.'[196] Between March 2003 and 2008, just before the bailout of US banks, US debt had grown from $6.4tn to $10tn.[197] The inference was that, when financial markets went belly-up in 2008 causing a worldwide recession, the US was severely hamstrung in how it could deal with the crisis. Stiglitz and Bilmes have argued that the severity of the global downturn, and the limitation in the range of US responses to it, could be directly and indirectly traced to the wars in Iraq and Afghanistan:

> The global financial crisis was due, at least in part, to the war. Higher oil prices meant that money spent buying oil abroad was not money being spent at home. Meanwhile, war spending provided less of an economic boost than other forms of spending would have. Paying foreign contrac-

tors working in Iraq was neither an effective short-term stimulus (not compared with spending on education, infrastructure or technology) nor a basis for long-term growth . . . As a result of two costly wars funded by debt, our fiscal house was in dismal shape even before the financial crisis – and those fiscal wars compounded the downturn.[198]

What has been explicitly avoided in such discussions is the opportunity cost of such expenditure – what could have been bought or achieved if the money had been spent elsewhere. According to estimates from Brown University's *Costs of War* project, 8.3 jobs were created for every $1m (in 2011 values) in military spending, an incredibly poor return in terms of jobs for cash outlay. The same amount of spending on public education would create 15.5 jobs, '14.3 jobs in healthcare, 12 jobs in home weatherization,* or about the same numbers in various renewable energy technologies. A million dollars spent on construction (residential and non-residential structures) creates 11.1 direct and indirect jobs.'[199] If the same amount of money spent on the wars in Iraq, Afghanistan and Pakistan had been spent on other sectors, considerably more jobs would have been created. If the money had been spent on construction, for example, 936,000 jobs would have been created per year. If the same amount had been spent on healthcare, it would have created 780,000 jobs. Expenditure on energy efficiency projects, including public transport, renewable energy programmes and weatherization of homes, would have created an estimated 500,000 jobs every year.

But it is the human cost that will exact the longest and most wounding toll on both the US and the Middle East. Calculating the exact number of deaths has, however, proved incredibly difficult. The most recent estimate, published in June 2011, is provided by the same team from Brown University. By their estimates, a total of at least 137,000 civilians have been killed in Iraq, Afghanistan and Pakistan. Pakistan, often ignored in the broader War on Terror and which relies extensively on US funding for its military operations, has experienced roughly the same number of fatalities as Afghanistan. While only 6,000 US soldiers have died in the war, considerably more have been injured: Veterans Affairs had received

* 'Weatherization' involves improving the energy efficiency of homes by making upgrades to the electrical system, heating and cooling (insulation and weatherproofing), and consumer appliances.

550,000 disability claims by the autumn of 2010. Large numbers of enemy combatants have also been killed. In total, it is estimated that 225,000 people, in uniform and out, have been killed as a result of the wars in Iraq, Afghanistan and Pakistan. Moreover, at least 7.8 million people have been internally displaced or are seeking refugee status abroad: equivalent, as the authors point out, 'to all the people of Connecticut and Kentucky fleeing their homes'.[200]

In addition, 'the two countries are now awash, as never before, with the tools to bring further death and immiseration – weaponry, ammunition and minefields'.[201]

The political cost, less easily quantifiable, has also been severe. The attempt to remould the Middle East has, as all such efforts tend to, backfired. Residents of the region are even more wary of the US than they had been in the past. Polls in Iraq in 2004 suggested that 51 per cent of the population opposed US occupation.[202] Three years later, 78 per cent wanted the US to withdraw.[203]

The two countries are mired in corruption and rendered sclerotic by political in-fighting and inadequate state institutions. Afghanistan labours under constant corruption scandals and political torpor.[204] President Obama has announced an accelerated timetable for withdrawal from Afghanistan. Its implementation and consequences remain to be seen.

In Iraq, specifically anti-US parties have increased their share of the political market place. As recently as October 2010, Muqtada al-Sadr emerged as a king-maker in the post-election Iraqi government. The firmly anti-US cleric was the sole politician to gain rather than lose seats in the March 2010 elections. The consequences for nearby Pakistan have also been dire. The state is close to collapse, the impotent government wracked by corruption, and the army and secret services – mentored and largely paid for by the US – continue to play a double-game, supporting, both tacitly and on occasions more overtly, the militants who control the Frontier regions. The American intervention has made the region less stable: Iraq has become a magnet for militant Islamists, Pakistan is a less reliable ally in the War on Terror, as evidenced by the eventual killing of Osama bin Laden in an outlying suburb of the capital Islamabad after he avoided detection for almost a decade. President Obama's chief counter-terrorism adviser commented that it was 'inconceivable that bin Laden did not have a support system' in Pakistan that allowed him to live comfortably with his family near Islamabad.[205]

The War on Terror has severely undermined American democracy. Key features of the US constitutional dispensation have been rewritten, discarded or ignored. Power has been further centralized in the executive, the military has been largely privatized, but is if anything more wasteful and less efficient. Oversight mechanisms have been purposefully weakened or marginalized. Black sites, extraordinary rendition and redefinitions of torture have torn up the international legal rule book, placing enemies of the US in legal black holes that defy international monitoring and allow for mass violations of human rights. Individual freedoms in the US, too, have suffered as the Patriot Act drastically empowers the US government to pry into the lives of ordinary Americans. As Patrick Cockburn has acutely observed: 'Iraq has joined the list of small wars, as France found in Algeria in the 1950s and the Soviet Union in Afghanistan in the 1980s, that inflict extraordinary damage on the occupiers.'[206]

The neocons were right in one sense: the wars in Iraq and Afghanistan have transformed the world and the Middle East. But it is a world that is fundamentally more unstable, more dangerous, less democratic at home and abroad, poorer and, most importantly, increasingly hostile towards the US and those Western powers, such as the UK, that have supported the wars. Stiglitz and Bilmes spoke the one incontrovertible truth: 'the only winners in this war, have been those in the defense industry making excessive profits'.[207] They put huge amounts of money into encouraging the wars and, together with the inhabitants of the shadow world, they have made an exceptional return. They have laughed all the way to the bank.

The Killing Fields

19. Cry, the Beloved Continent

The global arms trade is a sprawling web of networks. Links between the innumerable actors are sometimes close and durable, at other times tenuous and transitory. Companies, dealers and middlemen may compete on one deal while cooperating on another.

I have so far described a number of such networks: that which had its roots in the German entity Merex, and the more formal networks driven by BAE and the British government and Lockheed Martin and the MICC in the unique environment of the US arms trade. They are indicative examples. In reality there are thousands of these loose structures, constantly in flux, as circumstances warrant. Wherever there is conflict these networks will appear and morph into the most expedient shape for the deal.

Unsurprisingly, Africa has been among the shadow world's most fertile ground. The continent's colonial history, independence struggles, Cold War battles, weak state formations and 'big men' rulers willing to plunder their nations to retain power and enrich themselves have ensured continuous conflict, violence and poverty. While the ready availability of small arms and mobile weapons systems is undoubtedly a consequence of some of this violence, it is also a precipitating cause. The easy supply of weapons makes these conflicts exponentially more violent and deadly; in some cases it elevates small tussles into fully fledged wars and it is no coincidence that some of the most egregious acts of violence have been preceded by massive inflows of weaponry. The arms trade in Africa has militarized social conflict, and, when that happens, mass deaths, poverty, widespread displacement and human rights violations are sure to follow.

Africa's most notorious conflicts – Liberia and Sierra Leone, Rwanda, the Democratic Republic of Congo, Angola, Somalia and the Sudan; as well as the recently volatile Egypt, Libya and Ivory Coast – reflect these dynamics and act as a profitable stage for networks similar to, and sometimes interacting with, those already described. As the US is the world's only arms superpower, its role in Africa is crucial, reflected in the creation

of the US Africa Command (Africom) in early 2007, leading to fears of a
further militarization of US engagement with Africa.[1]

'Death to the cockroaches': The Rwandan Genocide

The Rwandan genocide, pitting government supporters against perceived
opponents who included all Tutsis and some Hutu from the 'wrong'
background, was one of the bloody twentieth century's most brutal
moments and a tragic exemplar of arms directly enabling and exacerbat-
ing conflict.

The genocide had long historical roots. A pre-existing social fluidity
was replaced by what was effectively a colonial Belgian and Tutsi ruling
alliance which emphasized ethnic identity. In 1959, the Tutsi ruling monarchy was overthrown by Hutu resistance. Belgium quickly changed
allegiances and supported the Hutu right to rule. In 1962, when Belgium
departed its colony, it left behind a society riven by ethnic conflict, simmering tension and a new Hutu government with a great deal of
resentment towards its Tutsi brethren.[2]

In the first decade of independence the new Hutu-led state oversaw the
deaths of nearly 20,000 Tutsi and the mass exodus from the country of a
further 300,000 – refugees who settled in neighbouring countries and
bred a series of resistance movements vowing to reclaim Rwanda.[3] By
1994, the number of Tutsi Rwandan refugees was estimated to be about
500,000.[4] When anti-Tutsi rebellions were launched once more in 1973,
Juvénal Habyarimana took power by military coup, citing the need to
keep order. He promised a policy of balance, where power and resources
would be shared between Tutsi and Hutu. In reality Habyarimana ran
Rwanda as his personal fiefdom, dispensing jobs and resources to family
and clan members. It became a militant one-party state, with power centralized for the next two decades in the hands of Habyarimana's
MNRD – the National Republic Movement for Democracy and Development.[5]

By the late 1980s, things were beginning to look precarious for Habyarimana, as the economy foundered due to plummeting coffee prices.[6]
Average Rwandan citizens bore the brunt of economic collapse and started
militating for political change, believing that Habyarimana was unfit to

rule the country.[7] In June 1990, Habyarimana announced that he would convert Rwanda into a democracy within two years, a move forced by both the internal ructions and severe international pressure. Equally threatening to his regime was a new alliance struck in Uganda between Rwandan exile movements and the government of President Yoweri Museveni. When Museveni, previously involved in the war against Idi Amin, sought to take power in 1985, he was aided by Rwandan exile fighters, known as the *Banyarwanda*. In return, he allowed the largely Tutsi *Banyarwanda* to join the Ugandan national army and provided them with weapons and training.[8] With an invasion of Rwanda in mind, the predominantly Tutsi Rwandan Patriotic Front (RPF) was formed in 1987.

In October 1990, the RPF invaded Rwanda, making quick headway. However, their assault was halted after Rwanda received military assistance from Mobutu Sese Seko's Zaire and, most importantly, France. By March 1991, the RPF and the Habyarimana regime signed a ceasefire in which the President agreed to work towards a multi-party democracy. Habyarimana was hardly energetic in this task. After a two-year hiatus the RPF launched another invasion in February 1993, this time reaching the edges of the capital, Kigali, where it halted. Under considerable international pressure, a peace agreement – the Arusha Accords – was signed, providing a roadmap towards Rwanda becoming a fully fledged democracy.[9]

The likelihood of a peaceful transition to democracy was always slim. The response of the ruling Rwandan elite – in particular the AKAZU, a secret group of political heavyweights including Habyarimana's wife[10] – was to resist any change in the status quo. No power would be transferred, and especially not to the hated Tutsi. Instead, with the support of senior political figures and extremists in the army, Rwanda was slowly prepared for genocide: the final confrontation that would, once and for all, eliminate the Tutsi 'threat'.

This had two dimensions. The first was a propaganda war, a concerted effort by media outlets with links to the state to demonize the RPF and all Tutsi in Rwanda. Rumours were spread that the RPF's ultimate plan was to exterminate the Hutu; to defend themselves, the Hutu needed to exterminate the Tutsi first. The Tutsi were described as a cancer, an illness, a threat to the body politic, that needed to be purged. The extremist *Kangura*, the most popular journal in the country, which was read by nearly all literate Rwandans and read out in public meetings, whipped up fears of the Tutsi threat. A notorious issue contained the Hutu Ten Commandments, all of which were related to how the Tutsi had to be avoided. 'A traitor is anyone who befriends, employs or marries a Tutsi,' proclaimed one commandment.[11] It was a chilling precursor of how the genocide would be undertaken – anyone considered friendly to Tutsi citizens, including numerous Hutu who either opposed the genocide or showed insufficient enthusiasm for its horrors, would be dispatched with the same efficiency and cruelty as the Tutsi. The journal also popularized the term 'cockroach' to refer to Tutsi Rwandans: 'A cockroach gives birth to a cockroach. . . . the history of Rwanda shows us clearly that a Tutsi stays always exactly the same, that he has never changed. . . . the *inyezzi* [RPF and all Tutsi] who attacked in October 1990 and those of the 1960s are all linked. . . . their evilness is the same.'[12]

Rwanda's first non-state-owned radio station, Radio Télévision Libre des Mille Collines (RTLMC), fuelled the flames of hatred. Established in 1993, RTLMC espoused a vitriolic extremism. Daily programming and editorial content emphasized the evilness of the Tutsi; terms like 'cockroach' were repeated *ad nauseam* and potted history lessons were woven in between ad jingles and pop songs, to stress the timeless perfidy of the Tutsi. The largest shareholder was President Habyarimana himself, along with businessmen, politicians, bank managers and army generals who formed his most solid support base, the AKAZU.[13]

The second dimension to maintaining the status quo was the rapid militarization of Rwandan society between 1990 and 1994. Without this, it is unlikely that the genocide could have occurred on the scale it did. In response to the RPF attacks in October 1990, the ruling elite implemented a 'Civil Defence Plan'. The Civil Defence would be created by providing military training and supplies to all corners of the country in order to build a ready-trained militia with leaders in each of Rwanda's communes and communities. It was from this programme that the infamous *Interahamwe* emerged, a youth militia that was part of Habyarimana's ruling party and which would constitute the genocide's shock troops.[14] At the same time the Rwandan army was rapidly expanded from just under 10,000 troops in 1990 to 35,000 by 1993.[15]

But these plans faced a major obstacle: a paucity of weapons. Between 1980 and 1988 the Habyarimana regime spent a paltry $5m on arms imports.[16] Between 1990 and 1994 tons of arms and ammunition were bought and disbursed throughout the country. So large was the buying spree that Rwanda, a continental minnow in weapons terms, became Africa's third-largest importer of arms between 1992 and 1994, spending over $112m, twenty times what had been spent in the entire 1980s.[17] In the four years from 1990 Rwanda spent 70 per cent of its annual state budget on arms, increasing its national debt by over 100 per cent.[18] By 1994, an estimated 85 tons of arms and ammunition had been distributed throughout the country; a huge amount considering Rwanda had a population of only 7 million.[19] Militia commanders in the countryside filled in requisition slips for AK-47s and ammunition; grenades required no paperwork at all. By 1994, grenades were so widely available that they could be purchased from local vegetable markets for $3 apiece.[20]

Rwanda had a number of sources for its weapons. South Africa's state-owned armaments company, Armscor, supplied arms and ammunition worth $5.9m to the Habyarimana regime in 1992 and 1993.[21] Not only did the transfer of South African arms help Rwanda militarize on its path to genocide but it was conducted in violation of the arms embargo placed on South Africa, which would only be lifted after democratic elections in the country in 1994.[22] In addition to 3,000 R-4 automatic rifles and ammunition, the South Africans supplied SS-77 machine guns, heavier Browning machine guns, 1 million rounds of ammunition, 70 hand-held grenade launchers with 10,000 grenades, 100 60mm mortars and a further 10,000 M-26 fragmentation grenades.[23] Between October 1990 and June 1992 Rwanda bought $12m of weapons from Egypt, including 6 powerful towed guns, 70 mortars of various calibres, including 10,000 shells; 2,000 RPG rockets, 2,000 landmines, 450 Egyptian Kalashnikov rifles, 200kg of plastic explosives and 3.2 million rounds of ammunition.[24]

This entire arms-buying spree was directed from the country's embassy in Paris, 'a seven-floor building in the 17th *arrondissement*, on orders from Kigali'.[25] France was not only the largest supplier to Habyarimana's regime, but also played a role in securing the arms from South Africa and Egypt. The Egyptian weapons were paid for with a bank guarantee from Crédit Lyonnais, and the French, who had been secretly supplying the apartheid regime for a long time, acted as an intermediary during the South African deal.[26]

France saw in Rwanda the opportunity to expand French influence in Africa. It was unconscionable to the French that a reliable francophone ally such as the Rwandan government could come under such severe military pressure from a Tutsi resistance movement funded and supported by English-speaking Uganda.[27] The French had run African affairs directly from the Office of the French Presidency since the beginning of the Fifth Republic. In the late 1980s, the head of this office was François Mitterrand's son, Jean-Christophe.[28]

France became an active participant in the war against the RPF, sending troops to bolster and train Rwandan government forces. French involvement was 'directly responsible, through arming and training, for the exponential growth of the Rwandan Government Army (FAR)'.[29] The French were also said to be involved in the ideological brainwashing that preceded the genocide. Corporal Jean Kuburare of the *Interahamwe* recalled that 'They [the French] told recruits that the enemy was the Tutsi. After the training lasted a few days, they provided each of the trainees with a gun.'[30]

In addition to the much-needed training, French troops provided considerable firepower. In the early phases of the civil war, for example, French artillery units were considered largely responsible for halting RPF advances. The use of helicopter gunships piloted by French soldiers to disrupt and attack RPF supply lines dramatically undermined the rebels' effort during the fierce battles in early 1991. It was the success of these helicopter attacks that forced the RPF to drop its traditional military approach in favour of guerrilla warfare.[31]

While Belgium refused to supply any weapons that could further destabilize Rwanda, the French had no such compunction. Between February 1990 and April 1994, France exported arms and ammunition to a total value of 136 million French francs.[32] They also made direct transfers of weapons, i.e. arms taken from existing French supplies and paid for by the French Ministry of Defence or the Ministry of Cooperation, at no cost to Rwanda. With fewer administrative obstacles, these transfers could take place quickly and more frequently. In the four years preceding the genocide France undertook thirty-six direct transfers worth FF43m.[33] What was additionally transferred for free makes for sober reading:

> France agreed to transfer – and presumably delivered – the following
> weapons: three Gazelle helicopters, six Rasura radar systems, one Alouette
> II helicopter, six 68-mm rocket-launchers (with 1397 68-mm rockets; for

the helicopters), two Milan anti-tank missile launchers, 70 12.7-mm heavy machineguns (with 132,400 rounds of ammunition), eight 105-mm cannons (with 15,000 shells), six 120-mm mortars (with 11,000 shells), 3,570 90-mm shells (for AML-90 armoured vehicles already in service), 8,850 60-mm mortar shells, 4,000 81-mm mortar shells, 2,040 rounds of 20-mm, 256,500 rounds of 9-mm, 145,860 rounds of 7.62-mm and 1,256,059 rounds of 5.56-mm ammunition, as well as many small arms and spare parts for helicopters and armoured vehicles.[34]

France's *laissez-faire* approach to arming Rwanda was linked directly to the event that triggered the genocide. On 6 April 1994, the Rwandan presidential plane carrying Juvénal Habyarimana and the Hutu President of Burundi, Cyprien Ntaryamira, was brought down by missiles outside Kigali's airport. A day later the Rwandan genocide began in earnest: a 'retaliation' against what was portrayed as a cowardly Tutsi attack on the Rwandan political establishment. It is still unclear who brought down the plane. Hutu militias and the political establishment claimed Tutsi guilt. Others argued that the plane was actually destroyed by extremist Hutu factions who believed that Habyarimana could not be relied upon to forcefully reject moves towards power-sharing with the RPF.[35] A report by a Rwandan panel of experts in January 2010 – drawing on advice from the UK Defence Academy – found that the missiles fired into Habyarimana's Falcon Dassault jet could easily have been of French origin. The Mutsinzini Report added that 'there is additional information to suggest that France provided the FAR [Rwandan army] with SA-16s purchased by Iraq in 1988 and which France later recovered during the Gulf War. The Committee also obtained documentation showing that between 1992 and 1993 Rwanda specifically requested that France provide 150 mid-range surface-to-air missiles along with 12 launchers.'[36] France, needless to say, has denied any involvement. A number of experts, however, have provided evidence to suggest that the RPF was definitely involved: a mystery that will most likely remain unresolved for some time.[37]

That the international community was slow to respond to the situation in Rwanda is an extreme understatement. It was only in May 1994, a month after the genocide started, that the UN imposed a mandatory arms embargo on the country. For the Rwandan *génocidaires*, however, this did not mean a reduction in the flow of arms. Instead the government turned to the ever-present shadow world of arms dealers to fulfil its needs. In particular, a company based in Sussex in the UK was highly successful in breaking the arms embargo on Rwanda's behalf.

In November 1996, a bus near a Hutu stronghold in the Democratic Republic of Congo was searched by journalists.[38] Among the debris was a paper trail revealing that an entity called Mil-Tec had supplied the Rwandan army with arms from mid-April 1994 until mid-July 1994 – the exact time that the genocide was being conducted.[39] Mil-Tec was run by Anoop Vidyarthi, a Kenyan Asian, from a 'dingy office above an aromatherapy shop' in the north London suburb of Hendon.[40] In total the company transferred over $5.5m worth of arms to Rwanda during these three bloody months. Most were sourced from Bulgaria and Israel.[41] Among the weapons delivered were ammunition worth $1.3m, 2,500 AK-47s, 2,000 mortar bombs and 100 rockets for RPG-launchers.[42] Vidyarthi went underground as soon as the story broke. But Mil-Tec had not violated any UK government rules, as it was registered in the Isle of Man. Due to sloppy legislation the UK had failed to extend the UN arms embargo to British crown protectorates, of which the Isle of Man is one. This was only done in December 1996, a month after the Mil-Tec story erupted in the international media.[43]

On the day that President Juvénal Habyarimana's plane was downed, organized militias armed with farming implements and firearms spread throughout the country, systematically killing Tutsis and any moderate Hutus who resisted the genocide. All the while, local radio exhorted further violence and greater destruction. Over the course of just three months somewhere between 800,000 and 1,174,000 people were killed, at least 400,000 of whom were children.[44] This was over 10 per cent of Rwanda's population of 7 million and a substantial part of the Tutsis, who had made up 14 per cent of the country's populace.[45] For 100 unremitting days at least six men, women and children were killed every minute of every day.[46] Against women, rape was the weapon of choice: between 100,000 and 250,000 women were raped, 67 per cent of whom contracted Aids as a result.[47] Of the children who survived, over 75,000 were orphans, many forced to raise younger siblings.[48] Penury was virtually assured for survivors of any age.

And yet these statistics barely do justice to the horror that played out in the country. When the RPF finally overthrew the Kigali regime in July

1994, the full magnitude and ferocity of the slaughter became clear: mass killings in churches, entire families slaughtered by their neighbours, rotting corpses filling mass graves or left to fester in the street. A systematic bloodletting of incomprehensible proportions.

The popularized images of the Rwandan genocide suggest a primal orgy of slaughter, a frenzy of bloodlust and carnage. The exact opposite, however, was true. The genocide was meticulously organized in order to kill as many people as efficiently as possible.[49] The mountains of weapons that had been imported into the country were crucial to achieving this aim. Guns and firearms, as opposed to the more widely distributed machetes, were used specifically to kill young men with community standing who could resist the *génocidaires*, and to exterminate large numbers of people in quick massacres. The slaughter of thousands of Rwandans in schools and football stadiums was done almost exclusively with firearms and grenades in order to achieve the highest kill-rate possible.[50]

The importation of arms into Rwanda may not have caused the genocide. But it certainly enabled and intensified it, militarizing the country's social conflicts in a devastating spiral of violence. Above all, the imported arms made the genocide exponentially more efficient. It can only prompt the question: how many hundreds of thousands of lives may have been saved if the tools for ruthless and efficient killing were not so easily acquired?

'The Vilest Scramble for Loot': The Democratic Republic of Congo

Over the last century and a half the Democratic Republic of Congo (DRC), a country the size of Western Europe, has been bedevilled by oppressive dictatorship and violent conflict and has only experienced democracy once. Predator countries, both from the region and from Europe, and individuals, including the BAE agent John Bredenkamp and Viktor Bout, have armed the Congo, or militias within it, in pursuit of its abundant natural resources, which range from large forests to deposits of diamonds, gold, uranium and the minerals that have enabled the information technology revolution to happen, coltan primary among them. The country's first free and fair election where the result was honoured for more than a short while was held in 2006 – 119 years after King Leopold declared Belgian control over the Congo Free State.[51] The election came at the only partial conclusion of the most bloody war since the Second World War; a war that continues to rage in the eastern part of the country, fuelled with a virtually limitless supply of small arms and weapons.

The DRC, then known simply as the Congo, achieved independence from Belgium in June 1960 after a wave of nationalist protests had rendered the country ungovernable. The most popular politician at the time, and the man elected Prime Minister, was Patrice Lumumba.[52] A fierce democrat and one of the most articulate politicians of his time, Lumumba was viewed with deep hostility by Belgium and the US, who also had vested interests in the country.[53] A month after Lumumba gained power the armed forces mutinied, causing widespread unrest. A major province, Katanga, announced its secession from the Congo with the support of a Belgium eager to protect its mining interests in the area. Lumumba appealed in vain for help from Western powers. In frustration, he turned to the Soviet Union and quickly received considerable supplies.[54] It was a move that locked Lumumba and his country firmly into the great Cold War struggle and the inevitable inflow of weapons. The American ambassador in the capital, Leopoldville, disparaged the Prime Minister by calling him 'Lumumbavitch'.[55] The links to the Soviet Union also strained relations between Lumumba and the Congolese President, Joseph Kasa-Vubu, with whom he ruled in coalition. In September 1960, Kasa-Vubu ended Lumumba's short reign by presidential decree, which Lumumba rejected. Both men appealed to the head of the Congolese armed forces, Joseph-Désiré Mobutu, to intervene. Mobutu, an intelligent former journalist appointed by Lumumba, had maintained close ties to the West, and viewed Lumumba with suspicion.

On 14 September, Mobutu placed Lumumba under house arrest. He escaped but was arrested and brutally murdered in January 1961. It is still unclear who undertook the killing, although evidence points strongly to the involvement of the CIA and Belgium.[56] Congo's first democracy limped on for another four years, although power now rested with the country's well-armed military. In 1965, this was formalized when Joseph-Désiré Mobutu took power in a bloodless coup. With the support of the West he was to rule the country for much of the next three decades. Political activity was banned. His eccentricities and failures were legion.

Clothed in leopard-skins and sporting a cane topped with a soaring eagle, he adopted a policy of 'authenticity', a cack-handed African nationalism.[57] In 1974, he renamed the country Zaire, dubbed himself Mobutu Sese Seko[58] and nationalized most industry. Three years later he was forced to reverse the decision as the country's economy virtually collapsed.[59] By the time he finally left power sick and in disgrace in 1997, he had plundered a reported $5bn, secreted in tax havens around the world.[60]

With Western support, Mobutu's regime had seemed impregnable. The US provided nearly $300m in military aid, primarily arms, partly so that Zaire could be used as a base from which the UNITA rebel movement in Angola could be supported. In reality Zaire gradually disintegrated into a failed state.[61] He dealt brutally with any opposition, with a penchant for having his opponents thrown out of airborne helicopters.[62] He exacerbated ethnic tensions, filling most government posts with members of his own clan.[63] His traditional support base, the military, was wracked with internal conflicts. The desultory pay offered to ordinary soldiers rankled, particularly while Mobutu's special presidential guards were lavished with luxuries. As Western support faded after the fall of the Berlin Wall, Mobutu's power structure creaked.

His regime limped on until 1996, when regional events, particularly in Rwanda, and ill-health sealed his downfall. As the RPF swept to power in Kigali, many Hutu in the country, particularly the *génocidaires*, fled Rwanda via its western border into Zaire, bringing their weapons with them. By 1996, nearly a million Hutu had settled in the eastern part of Zaire, most in hastily constructed refugee camps. Worryingly for Rwanda and Uganda, which had supported the RPF's invasion, the rump of the Hutu *Interahamwe* survived in eastern Zaire. Carrying the weapons that had been so generously given to them by France, the *Interahamwe* started to regroup and vowed to attack the Rwandan government of Paul Kagame. Mobutu, a long-time ally of Juvénal Habyarimana's regime, turned a blind eye to the attacks initiated by the newly arrived Hutu refugees on elements of the Tutsi population that had historically settled in the Kivu provinces of eastern Zaire. It has been suggested that the attacks were undertaken with the active support of some Kivu politicians and the Zairean armed forces (FAZ), although the evidence is sketchy.[64]

In September 1996, the oldest Tutsi group in the eastern Congo, the *Banyamulenge*, launched a 'pre-emptive' strike against the newly arrived

Hutu migrants. Rwanda's new government and Museveni's Uganda soon joined in the attack. The Rwandan government, basking in the moral high ground following the genocide, claimed at the time that the attack was launched in self-defence. Recent reports suggest that they were motivated by revenge and ethnic hatred. Accounts of RPF atrocities in the Congo were fairly numerous over a period of years,[65] but it was only in 2010 that a leaked UN report alleged that the sweep of Rwandan and Ugandan forces through the eastern Congo was almost equal in horror to that of the Rwandan genocide. The report claims that Rwandan forces rounded up Hutu men, women and children in large groups and killed them with hoes, axes, hammers and guns, concluding that 'the systematic and widespread attacks have a number of damning elements, which, if proved before a competent court, could be described as crimes of genocide'.[66] Rwandan authorities rejected the claims and the UN was reported to have toned down the subsequent version of the report.[67]

A second genocide or not, the attacks marked the death knell of Mobutu's regime. His armed forces, poorly trained and their morale low, melted away in the face of the Rwandan and Ugandan troops. As they fled west, Mobutu's troops unleashed a wave of terror, looting freely as they went. Although it was initially only a sortie into eastern Zaire, Rwanda and Uganda used Laurent Kabila, a small-time bandit and smuggler, as their front-man. Kabila had been able to maintain a basic fighting force in South Kivu for much of Mobutu's presidency: a reflection of his cunning, the weakness of the Zairean state and the easy availability of weapons. The joint forces of Kagame, Kabila and Museveni undertook a 'long march' through Zaire, reaching the capital, Kinshasa, which was taken with remarkably little fighting. By May 1997, only six months after Ugandan and Rwandan forces had entered the country, Zaire was no longer. On seizing the capital, Kabila renamed the country the Democratic Republic of Congo and appointed himself transitional president.

Initially Kabila's reign was greeted with high hopes among the Congolese. Very quickly his government frayed. He won few plaudits by adopting the same practices he had used during his time in Katanga, which included a political re-education campaign that irked many Congolese.[68] His glacial moves towards an election also rankled, as did the alliance that brought him to power. Only a few months after greeting Rwandan and Ugandan troops as liberators, the Congolese, especially in Kinshasa, viewed the foreigners with increasing suspicion, concerned that their one-time liberators might turn into their oppressors.[69] Rwanda and Uganda started to believe that Kabila was becoming too independent from them and was insufficiently committed to dealing with the threats to their countries from eastern Congo, where guerrilla groups and a secessionist movement, the Mai-Mai, fought on. By mid-1998, Rwanda believed that the lack of progress fighting the *Interahamwe* was due to political protection and even claimed that Kabila was recruiting *Interahamwe* troops into the new Congo army, the FAC.[70]

In August, Rwandan and Ugandan forces launched an insurrection against Kabila, marching on Kinshasa. Unable to resist the attacks of a superior army, Kabila appealed to regional partners for help. Zimbabwe, Namibia and Angola agreed to send troops to fight off the attack. Sudan, Chad and Libya also came to Kabila's aid. Although the combined troops saved Kinshasa, Rwanda and Uganda took control of the eastern part of the country nearest to their borders. In 1999, the Rwandan and Ugandan leaderships fell out, largely over control of mineral resources, and began to fight each other. Three sides were thus locked in triangular battle. None of the forces was powerful enough to press for a full military victory, and even within each group's area smaller militia units vied for control.[71]

From 1998 to 2003, the DRC was devastated by what became known as Africa's 'Great War'. The human suffering was grotesque: by the end of 2003 it was estimated that 3.3 million people had died as a result of violence, starvation or disease.[72] Those left alive were barely able to scrape together a living. In parts of the eastern Congo the average citizen lived on less than eighteen US cents a day.[73] More than 2.3 million Congolese were compelled to move within the country, while a further 330,000 took refuge outside its borders.[74] Nearly 400,000 children were forced to flee the violence.[75] Troop behaviour was brutal: tens of thousands of women were raped by all the different militias.[76] Girls as young as ten were forced into sexual or domestic slavery – those that resisted had limbs amputated or were sliced to pieces as a warning to others.[77] Much as in Sierra Leone, extensive use was made of child soldiers, dragooned into combat at gunpoint. The sight of ten-year-old boys wielding AK-47s was not unusual.[78] Celebratory rituals in which soldiers wore the entrails of the vanquished were not uncommon.[79] It was hell on earth.

Waging such an extensive conflict across a country as big as Western Europe was only possible because of the unrestrained flow of weapons paid for by the industrial-scale exploitation of the DRC's natural resources. The massive sums of money made by all sides became one of the pre-eminent reasons for continuing the war, providing both the means for further conflict and avenues for self-enrichment. Rwanda, for example, raised 80 per cent of its entire military budget between 2003 and 2006 from resource exploitation in the Congo.[80] All parties to the conflict used the chaos and their armed strength to seize mines in their regions of control. Eventually 'war fronts were concentrated around localities housing gold and coltan mines'.[81]

These were run by 'elite networks' in each of the three regions of the country controlled by the warring parties. These networks were made up of senior political figures, military commanders and prominent business-people who diverted billions in revenue that should have gone to the coffers of the DRC into their own pockets. They ensured the 'viability of their economic activities through control over military and other security forces that they used to intimidate, threaten violence or carry out selected acts of violence'.[82] The arms trade was central to this: it provided the means to intimidate, and was operated with a network of smugglers and transporters used not only to procure arms but also to trade the minerals themselves. Two prominent individuals – John Bredenkamp and Viktor Bout – were alleged to be providing a one-stop shop for mineral extraction and arms supplies.

Bredenkamp had been granted six concessions in the country by Gecamines, the state-owned mining company.[83] His company, Tremalt Ltd, stood to exploit 2.7 million tons of copper and 325,000 tons of cobalt over the twenty-five years of the concessions, which were estimated to be worth $1bn in total. For this Tremalt paid a risible $400,000 – a mere 1 per cent of what would be earned from the concessions each year.[84] Kaba-bankola Mining Company, which undertook the extraction, was said to be 80 per cent owned by Tremalt and 20 per cent by Gecamines. According-ing to a secret memorandum sent from the Zimbabwean Defence Minister to the country's President, Robert Mugabe, the profits from the conces-sions would be split three ways: Tremalt would receive 32 per cent of net profits and the DRC and Zimbabwean governments 34 per cent each.[85] Tremalt also agreed to purchase cars, trucks and buses, as well as provide cash payments, to the Congolese and Zimbabwean militaries. These costs would be deducted from their share of the profits.[86] So important was Bredenkamp to Zimbabwe that Tremalt met in a monthly 'forum' to discuss military strategy in the DRC with Zimbabwe's Brigadier Moyo and General Zvinavashe, along with other representatives from the Kababankola Mining Company.[87]

But Bredenkamp, who as we saw has been a major agent for BAE, is no ordinary businessman. Initially a tobacco magnate and thought to be one of the 100 richest men in Britain,[88] he made his initial fortune helping Rhodesia break arms sanctions.[89] When Rhodesia became the newly independent Zimbabwe, Bredenkamp switched allegiances and became a confidant of Robert Mugabe or his circle.[90] He is deeply involved in the arms trade. Aviation Consultancy Services (ACS), a company in which he has a share and which many believe he controls, has worked as an agent not just for BAE, but also Dornier of France and Agusta in Italy.[91] The UN suggests that he provided significant help to Zimbabwe during their war effort in the DRC: 'Mr. Bredenkamp's representatives claim that his companies observed European Union sanctions on Zimbabwe, but British Aerospace spare parts for [Zimbabwe Defence Force] Hawk jets were supplied in early 2002 in breach of those sanctions.'[92] The UN also notes that, even if he had not helped Zimbabwe get spare parts, he had 'offered to mediate sales of British Aerospace military equipment to the Democratic Republic of Congo' in discussions with senior officials.[93]

Bredenkamp has vigorously denied any involvement in supplying arms to the DRC and has taken umbrage at the claim that he underpaid for his concessions. In a further UN report in 2003, he and his companies are listed as having 'resolved' the substantive issues raised in the earlier report, subject to monitoring by the OECD[94] – a decision he has trumpeted as clearing his name. He claims further in correspondence with the author that the UN panel encouraged him to continue investing in DRC, although he quit the country in 2003.

What constitutes 'resolution' was kept vague in the report, although it most often recorded that 'resolution' involved an agreement to stop any further illegal activity and to increase the transparency of business operations.[95] The report also contained a vital caveat: 'It should be stressed that resolution should not be seen as invalidating the Panel's earlier findings with regard to the activities of those actors. Rather, it signifies that there are no current outstanding issues. . . .'[96] Thus, Bredenkamp may have resolved issues to the UN's satisfaction, but this did not mean he was not implicated in the actions described by the 2002 report.

A more damning indictment of Bredenkamp's business ethics came in 2008 when the US placed him on the Foreign Assets Control (OFAC) sanctions list, freezing both his personal and his company assets.[97] The announcement described Bredenkamp as a 'Mugabe regime crony' who was 'involved in various business activities, including tobacco trading, grey-market arms trading and trafficking, equity investments, oil distribution, tourism, sports management and diamond extraction. Through a sophisticated web of companies, Bredenkamp has financially propped up the regime and provided other support to a number of its high-ranking officials.'[98] He is also on the EU's financial sanctions list.

Bredenkamp argues that his presence on these lists is a purely administrative measure, ought to be provisional and interim, and is not indicative of any criminal finding. He says he is contesting both listings as unfair and unjustified. At the time of writing Bredenkamp was still on both of these lists.[99]

While John Bredenkamp was only connected with one side in the conflict, Viktor Bout has been linked in various ways to all the participants. In 1999, after the Ugandan and Rwandan forces had split, he was alleged to have organized Israeli trainers for the Ugandan Air Force. He may also have been involved in mass transfers of arms, supplies and minerals. Between 1998 and 2002, ninety-seven outbound flights arranged by Bout's companies were tracked leaving Entebbe in Uganda and entering the DRC.[100] The planes had flown under the banner of Okapi Air, an outfit that Bout had purchased and which shared flight times and slots with Planet Air, a Ugandan air freighter owned by the wife of one of Uganda's most prominent generals.[101]

Bout was thought to be in contact with the Rwandan Patriotic Army's Chief of Staff from at least 2000. According to a UN report in 2002, Bout's planes had been used by Rwanda 'for a number of purposes including transportation of coltan and cassiterite, the transport of supplies to mining sites and the transport of military supplies and equipment'.[102] Again, Bout had set up a bespoke airline, Bakavu Aviation Transport.[103] The UN even located invoices sent from Bout's companies to the Rwandan government.[104] Completing his triangular supply chain, Bout was also alleged to have arranged a shipment of Bulgarian arms to the DRC government in Kinshasa in 2000. This time using San Air – yet another of his many incarnations.[105]

The alleged activities of Bout and Bredenkamp were only the tip of the iceberg in the DRC. There was a constant flow of cheap and plentiful small arms, from rocket launchers to the ubiquitous AK-47, mostly sourced, as with the majority of Africa's post-Cold War conflicts, from surplus stocks in Eastern Europe. Between June 2002 and June 2003, for example, when the war was supposedly winding down, Rwanda alone imported 400 tons of ammunition from Albania.[106] Mugabe's Zimbabwe also imported tons of arms to do battle on the side of the DRC government. Some had been produced or acquired by Zimbabwe's own defence parastatal, Zimbabwe Defence Industries (ZDI), which in 2001 had formed a joint venture with a Congolese company to 'facilitate the shipping of arms and foodstuffs'.[107] In one documented deal a Czech company, Arms Moravia, agreed to supply 1,000 RPGs and 500 machine guns for $1.2m to the Zimbabwe and Congolese armies.[108] BAE Hawk jets have been used by Zimbabwe in the DRC.[109] Zimbabwe is highly dependent on arms and military equipment from China. In 2008, this amounted to 39 per cent of all imported arms, followed by 35 per cent from Ukraine and from Libya 27 per cent.[110]

With a seemingly endless supply of arms and companies desperate to assist in mineral extraction, it was feared that the Second Congo War would continue in perpetuity. However, in 2001, the DRC's President, Laurent Kabila, was assassinated by one of his own bodyguards. His son, Joseph, was drafted in to replace him. Acknowledging the weakness of his own position, Joseph Kabila inaugurated his presidency by embarking on a massive round of diplomacy, aided by a posse of international observers. In December 2002, the majority of the warring parties in the DRC met at the once-glitzy Sun City resort in South Africa, where they signed the 'Global and All-Inclusive Agreement on Transition in the Democratic Republic of Congo'. The Global Agreement committed most of the parties to the conflict – including the proxy forces run by Uganda and Rwanda – to ending all hostilities and the neighbouring countries to withdraw their troops from the DRC.[111] It also provided for the creation of a transitional government leading to democratic elections, which were duly held in 2006.[112]

Unfortunately, the agreements, while ensuring a limited peace in the heartland of the Congo, did little to change the situation in the combustible eastern region. Both Uganda and Rwanda, via their allied militias – most notably the large RCD-Goma group tied to Rwanda – continued to operate in the provinces of North and South Kivu. The much-feted troop withdrawals by both countries proved chimeric: proxy militias had been trained to remain in the eastern Congo to protect and monitor rebel-held mines.[113] In January 2010, it was estimated that 50 per cent of all mines in the eastern Congo remained in the hands of non-government militias.[114] The violence that accompanied the continuing conflict was bloody. By 2010, 5.4 million people had died in the DRC since the beginning of the Second Congo War in 1998,[115] with 2.1 million of those deaths occurring since the official end to the war in December 2002.

And the conflict shows little signs of abating. In January 2010, a UN observer mission reported that the DRC armed forces were engaged in a protracted mission against the Forces Démocratiques de Libération du Rwanda in the eastern Congo.[116] Over 160,000 refugees from the eastern Congo have sought shelter in the neighbouring country of Congo-Brazzaville alone.[117] In September 2010, the UN released a report detailing the rape of at least 303 civilians in four days in eastern Congo. The 'scale and viciousness' of the brutal mass rape of 235 women, 52 girls, 13 men and 3 boys by mainly Mai-Mai militiamen 'defy belief', said the UN's human rights chief, Navi Pillay.[118]

The length and intensity of the conflict have left the country awash in small arms, and weapons deliveries continue to the various warring parties. These occur despite a UN arms embargo imposed on the country in 2003. Remarkably, the UN saw no reason to impose an arms embargo during the Second Congo War itself, allowing all forces involved to import arms with impunity. The current embargo is virtually unenforceable because considerable areas of the country remain ungoverned and ungovernable. Its implementation was also badly mismanaged. All parties who were not signatories to the 2002 Global Agreement were banned from importing arms, leaving key fighting groups such as the RCD-Goma, free to bring in weapons.[119] In addition, the embargo only covered deliveries to the Kivus and the nearby province of Ituri. Arms could be freely delivered into the rest of the DRC, from where they were transported into the conflict areas.[120]

In 2005, the UN realized the futility of such an embargo and extended its reach to encompass all weapons deliveries into the DRC, except those to DRC government forces.[121] This too held little hope of success, as the embargo placed no restrictions on either the Rwandan or Ugandan governments. As a result their forces are able to buy arms on the international market without limitation – using minerals extracted in the DRC – which can be easily smuggled back into the DRC, where effective policing is non-existent. The omission of the DRC government is also problematic, as it is alleged it has been making military supplies available to non-governmental militias in the Kivus, most notably the Mai-Mai.[122]

The DRC remains condemned to a cycle of extreme violence and poverty, with an endless supply of arms fuelling a persistent and brutal conflict funded by the industrial exploitation of mines – many of which are staffed by contingents of virtual slave labour forced to toil at the end of the barrel of a gun. Kabila *fils* has developed some of Mobutu's old instincts, showing little determination to bring good governance to the areas he controls, while dealing brutally with political opponents.[123] As in so many African conflicts, the suffering has been immense. There is little doubt that the misery inflicted could have been drastically mitigated if arms were not so widely and easily available.

'Money Corrupts, Money Kills, Money Rots Men's Consciences': Civil War in Angola

Angola is a victim of the oil curse. Its vast reserves of 'black gold' have contributed to a history of debilitating conflict followed by the rule of a kleptocrat who numbers among the world's richest men, while his citizens remain mired in poverty. 'The scale of corruption and mismanagement in Angola has been immense.'[124] Billions of dollars of oil revenue have disappeared without a trace, diverted from any effort to develop the impoverished country. Between 1997 and 2002, for example, an estimated $4.7bn disappeared from Angola's treasury: equal to all foreign aid assistance that had been delivered in the same period.[125] Despite the fact that, since 1997, the country's GDP has increased tenfold to $83.4bn in 2008,[126] Angola remains one of the least developed countries in the world: it sits at 143 out of 182 countries on the UN's Human Development Index.[127] The life expectancy of a healthy newborn is only forty-seven and 70.2 per cent of the population live on less than $2 a day, even though per capita GDP is $5,385.[128] The arms trade has played a central part in this tragic tale of greed and violence.

Angola suffered under the harsh colonial rule of the Portuguese, only to become a battlefield for Cold War rivalry. The passing of Cold War enmities did not end the devastating civil war, which was now driven by a lust for oil and, to a lesser extent, diamonds. The easy availability of arms and the complicity of the international community in feeding the ruling kleptocracy have rendered Angola a festering sore on the international body politic, confined to the status of one of the most underdeveloped nations on the planet despite its immense natural endowments.

From as early as the fifteenth century Portuguese traders conducted business with indigenous Angolans. Local Angolan leaders made a fortune selling slaves to the traders to be used throughout the world, but most often in Portugal's other major international satellite, Brazil.[129] From the sixteenth century Portugal maintained a permanent presence in Angola, although it was only at the end of the nineteenth century that the Berlin Conference – a massive divvying up of Africa between European powers – fixed Angola's borders and confirmed Portuguese control. By 1951, Angola was declared an official province of Portugal itself.[130]

In the late 1950s and early 1960s three main resistance movements fought a nationalist revolution in Angola. The first was the Movimento Popular de Libertação de Angola (MPLA), which was formed in 1956. The second, the Frente Nacional de Libertação de Angola (FNLA), was formed in 1961, and the União Nacional para a Independencia Total de Angola (UNITA) was created in 1966.[131] The three groups made limited gains in the struggle for independence, until the April 1974 revolution in Portugal overthrew the fascist dictatorship of Marcelo Caetano and initiated the process of giving independence to all the country's colonies.

Angola was ill prepared for independence in 1975, with no history of democratic practice.[132] Each of the resistance movements had a specific regional base. After an initial round of fighting, the MPLA, led by Agostinho Neto and with the largest support base in the country, was able to establish a quasi-government based in the capital, Luanda. With support drawn from urban areas more than rural, the MPLA had slowly adopted Marxist ideological trappings and, as such, received military support from the USSR. It achieved international diplomatic recognition, except from the US and apartheid South Africa.[133] The FNLA, under Holden Roberto, harboured its own nationalist ambitions, was opposed to the MPLA's Marxist leanings, and initially seemed in a position to challenge for the capital.

Over time, however, the main challenge to the MPLA came from UNITA, led by the charismatic Jonas Savimbi, whose ideological leanings were fluid and deliberately opaque. Savimbi was once an avowed Maoist and UNITA's official motto was 'Socialism, Democracy and Negritude',[134] not exactly what one would expect of an organization receiving support from the US. Unwilling to accept defeat or a position of less prominence than undisputed President of Angola, Savimbi was adept at portraying himself so as to maximize support from various quarters: 'When seeking military aid from China he claimed to want to build a Maoist state that would somehow accommodate local culture,' the *Economist* wrote on his death. 'To his South African allies he presented himself as a bulwark against communist imperialism. When wooing Reagan he posed as a democrat and an avid fan of the free market.'[135]

The three would be at war for fifteen years, with their strings pulled by the Cold War powers. The MPLA's Marxism ensured that it received considerable support from Russia and Cuba, with the latter contributing most to the government's war effort. From 1975 onwards, Cuban troops flooded the country, providing training, military equipment and soldiers on the ground. In 1975, Cuba sent 5,500 troops to Angola,[136] increasing to 50,000 by the time of a major MPLA offensive against UNITA in 1988.[137] In 1984 alone, the USSR supplied Angola with $2bn in military aid.[138]

UNITA and the FNLA, meanwhile, relied on the support of anti-communists. In 1975, in the direct aftermath of independence, the administration of Gerald Ford started a covert supply of military aid to UNITA. In three months Savimbi's men received just under $40m of such aid from the US.[139] They would have received even more if the undercover aid had not been discovered by journalists and politicians, which led to the Clark Amendment in January 1976 that prohibited arms transfers from the US to any military units in Angola. In 1985, Ronald

Reagan oversaw the repeal of the Clark Amendment and resumed secret military assistance. Over the next three years UNITA received an estimated $250m in chandestine aid and arms transfers.[140] The USA's covert support mission in Angola was the second-largest in its history, bettered only by US support for the *mujahideen* in Afghanistan.[141]

However, by far the biggest supporter of UNITA and the FNLA was the apartheid regime in South Africa. Apartheid's rulers viewed MPLA success in Angola with deep concern. Not only was the MPLA avowedly communist but it was sympathetic to apartheid's main enemy, the African National Congress (ANC) of Nelson Mandela and the South-West African People's Organization (SWAPO). The latter was fighting a vicious war with the apartheid government in South-West Africa/Namibia, which the South Africans controlled. Over the next fifteen years, Angola was a staging post for both the ANC and SWAPO, a country in which they could receive military assistance and some security from which to launch attacks on South African forces. The greatest regional threat to the apartheid state was the possibility of the MPLA controlling all of Angola, including the south, where at present UNITA dominated.

South African support had two dimensions. The first was the supply of substantial military aid and weapons. By the mid-1980s the South African government was providing roughly $200m a year to UNITA in weapons and ammunition.[142] The second was the mobilization of South African troops in Angola to fight with UNITA forces and to undertake destabilization campaigns. For thirteen years from 1975, South Africa engaged in a number of ambitious military campaigns, the most brutal of which was Operation Protea, launched in 1981. The aim of Protea was to consolidate southern Angola as a UNITA stronghold. Deploying its largest mechanized force since the Second World War, South Africa invaded and captured Cunene province – an area of roughly 50,000 square kilometres. Villages that resisted South African control faced an initial long-range artillery bombardment, followed by carpet bombing by the Air Force and a final rush-and-seize invasion by infantry troops. Protea devastated Cunene, forcing over 120,000 Angolans to leave their homes. SWAPO and MPLA troops suffered about 2,000 losses. The South Africans, who possessed overwhelming military superiority, recorded only fourteen deaths.[143]

Roughly 100,000 Angolans died between 1980 and 1985 as a direct result of war. Between 1981 and 1988, over 333,000 children alone died of unnatural causes.[144]

As Mikhail Gorbachev's transforming Soviet Union started to withdraw support for its military proxies in the late 1980s, South Africa reduced its support of UNITA following a failed military attack on Cuito Cuanavale in 1988, and the US rolled back its covert-aid budget. As a result, UNITA's Jonas Savimbi agreed a ceasefire in 1989 which led to an election in September 1992. The MPLA swept the board, with a large majority in Parliament, and its leader since September 1979, Eduardo dos Santos, defeated Savimbi for the presidency by 49.6 per cent to 40.7 per cent.[145] This should have meant a run-off vote, as a successful presidential candidate was required to receive more than 50 per cent.[146] Savimbi cried foul, disputing the fairness of the election despite the international community's conviction that it was largely free and fair. Sensing that he would have no hope in a run-off, Savimbi reignited the conflict. The MPLA was recognized as the official government of Angola, even by the US under the Clinton administration. In 1993, the UN imposed a mandatory arms embargo on UNITA, outlawing any supplies of weapons or petrochemical goods to Savimbi. This created a massive opportunity for rapacious arms dealers.[147]

The violent destruction wreaked on Angola between 1992 and 1994 was beyond anything the country had experienced. UNITA laid siege to already destitute villages that refused to accept its rule. In response the MPLA employed bombing runs that did little to discriminate between civilians and soldiers.[148] The result was social dislocation and suffering that exceeded, in two short years, the carnage of the entire fifteen-year civil war that had preceded it.[149] Between October 1992 and the end of 1994, 300,000 people died as a result of the conflict, many from starvation and disease. This was over 2 per cent of the entire population.[150] From May to October 1993, more than 1,000 Angolans died every day – far more than during any other conflict at the time.[151] Survivors faced extreme hardship and deprivation. The widespread use of landmines, popular during both the original and second civil wars, made it likely that any Angolan citizen not killed by military action would be maimed by its hidden debris. In 1994, there were roughly 70,000 amputees who had lost their limbs to landmines.[152]

The easy availability of weapons in the region, and UNITA's

continued access to war matériel, was crucial to the combustibility and intensity of the conflict. The arms embargo on UNITA, and the international opprobrium it faced, posed little danger to its ongoing operations. UNITA forces were extremely well stocked with arms that had been delivered by its previous US and South African supporters, and were able to raid weapons from the new Angolan army's stocks.[153] These seizures consisted of more than just light weapons. The rebels captured a number of tanks from MPLA forces and, by buying spare parts and accessories on the open market, were able to rehabilitate them to battle-readiness.[154]

After a major military victory in the diamond-rich Cuango Valley in late 1992, UNITA could also rely on a number of shady dealers for any new arms it required.[155] While diamond production was initially limited by UNITA's lack of capacity, it soon allowed international players to industrialize the diamond-mining operations. UNITA offered security and the use of diamond plots in return for 50 per cent of all diamonds found.[156] The yield was astonishing. Between 1992 and 1997, diamond mines controlled by the rebels constituted 10 per cent of global diamond production.[157] The South African mining giant De Beers admitted that it had purchased diamonds from UNITA to the value of $500m in 1992 alone.[158] In 1996, its most profitable year, Savimbi's outfit earned an estimated $730m from diamond sales.[159]

In the early years of its diamond operations, UNITA fell in with two brothers who seamlessly united the rebels' diamond selling with the purchase of weapons. The South Africans, Ronnie and Joe De Decker, were responsible for the majority of UNITA's weapons purchases in the two-year civil war from 1992.[160] Ronnie was in charge of the acquisition of weapons, while Joe, a former De Beers sightholder and owner of De Decker Diamonds, took care of the diamond sales. The brothers would travel together to a UNITA base in Andulo in a Lear Jet. Ronnie – known as 'Watson' – would meet with UNITA commanders first to discuss their arms requirements. Joe would then step in to value the diamonds, which were handed over in $4m to $5m parcels. 'Watson' acquired most of the weapons from Eastern Europe, including 'mortar bombs, anti-tank weapons, anti-aircraft weapons, grenades, ammunition of various kinds and a variety of small arms and light weapons'.[161] Angola thus had the dubious distinction of being the first African conflict to draw heavily on the massive amounts of surplus weapons available in Eastern Europe after the end of the Cold War.

The MPLA's activities were not uncontroversial either. In 1993, the Angolan/MPLA government negotiated a deal that would create major international ructions. Angolagate, as it became known, had its roots in the Bicesse Accords signed between UNITA and the MPLA in 1991. The MPLA was more committed to the demobilization envisaged in the accords.[162] Large numbers of their troops demobbed and put down their weapons, with little effort expended in keeping the new army's soldiers battle-ready. In addition, valuable arms flows and expertise from Cuba and the Soviet Union had evaporated with the fall of the Berlin Wall. Thus, when UNITA broke the accords and resumed fighting, the Angolan government was horribly under-prepared. As a result UNITA made enormous gains, seizing at least five of Angola's provincial capitals and a number of valuable diamond-producing areas.[163]

In a panic, President dos Santos made a direct appeal to France to procure weapons for his beleaguered forces. Dos Santos contacted Jean-Bernard Curial, the French Socialist Party's former Southern Africa expert, who travelled to Luanda to assess the situation. Curial was keen to help, but the political situation in France was delicate, with a 'cohabitation' arrangement in place between centre-left and centre-right parties. François Mitterrand's leftist presidency relied on the support of the government of the conservative Prime Minister, Édouard Balladur. And while Mitterrand and his party were sympathetic to the cause of the Angolan government, rightists in France were not. François Léotard, the French Defence Minister at the time, was, for example, a massive supporter of UNITA.[164] Curial approached Jean-Christophe Mitterrand, the President's son, who, until 1992, had been his father's point-man on African affairs. Mitterrand suggested that Curial make contact with Pierre Falcone.

The highly controversial Falcone was born in Algeria and accumulated a vast fortune in everything from advertising to oil . . . and weapons. He married a stunning Bolivian, Sonia Montero, at the nineteenth-century home of the Rothschilds, where the guests included his good friend, Jean-Christophe Mitterrand. Falcone cuts a slightly disappointing figure in the flesh: plump, balding, he resembles an insurance salesman rather than a jet-setting, covert operative.[165] He served as a consultant for SOF-REMI, a state body set up to sell abroad French expertise in the security fields and police equipment. SOFREMI fell under the jurisdiction of Charles Pasqua, the Minister for the Interior. Pasqua feared that, with the fall of the Berlin Wall, Angola's massive oil deposits could be overrun by Anglo-American interests, and was therefore in favour of anything that would promote French interests in the African country.[166]

Falcone moved quickly to secure a deal with Angola, signing an initial contract worth $47m in November 1993 to supply ammunition, mortars and artillery.[167] By 1994, the deal had grown exponentially so that the total price of weapons transfers to Angola organized by Falcone stood at $633m.[168] To pay for it, Angola agreed to a complicated pre-financing arrangement based on oil extraction. Oil companies would lift the equivalent of 20,000 barrels a day for four years to pay for the loan.[169] For its massive outlay Angola received a veritable feast of arms: six warships, twelve helicopters, 420 tanks, 150,000 shells, 170,000 landmines, large numbers of small and light weapons, and millions of rounds of ammunition.[170] The matériel was sourced from Eastern Europe and funnelled through a Slovakian company, ZTS-Osos. To negotiate the contracts with ZTS, Falcone joined forces with another hugely controversial figure, Arcadi Gaydamak.[171] A Russian with Israeli, French and Canadian passports, Gaydamak has been indicted for fraud and money laundering. He was a close ally of the Israeli Prime Minister, Binyamin Netanyahu, and in 2008 launched an unsuccessful bid to become mayor of Jerusalem.[172] Gaydamak's Russian connections – he was chairman of the Russian Credit Bank and closely connected to the Chief of Staff of the Russian armed forces – were very useful in negotiating the deal with the Slovak supplier.[173]

Falcone and Gaydamak became intimate cronies of President dos Santos, whose systematic pilfering of the state treasury has made him, by some accounts, one of the world's fifty richest men. The two men were given a stake in virtually every key sector of the Angolan economy, from food to diamonds to oil. They also wielded enormous political influence in the country. According to Gaydamak, both he and Falcone were granted Angolan citizenship and given diplomatic passports, served as advisers to the government and were named as senior employees of the Ministry of Foreign Affairs.[174]

The arms deals, however, were in violation of the Angolan peace agreements and the UN arms embargo which came into effect two months before the first Angolagate deal.[175] While the mandatory embargo was mostly focused on UNITA, it also stated specifically that 'all states shall prevent the sale or supply, by their nationals or from their territories or using their flag vessels or aircraft, of arms and related matériel of all types . . . to the territory of Angola other than through named points of entry on a list supplied by the Government of Angola.'[176] In addition, the Secretary General of the UN was supposed to be notified of all weapons deliveries to any force in Angola. Needless to say, the UN was not notified of the delivery at all and considerable effort was expended to ensure that the deal remained as secret as possible.

Although the weapons did not transit through France, most of the substantive contracts were signed in Paris. The deals were thus conducted under French jurisdiction, and broke a number of French laws. Two of these stipulated that all arms exports from the country needed to be approved by the Ministry of Defence, and that, to act as a weapons broker, one needed to be registered.[177]

It later emerged that Falcone and Gaydamak may also have been guilty of large-scale tax evasion as they did not declare earnings on the deals to French tax authorities.[178] In addition, during the Angolagate trial in which forty-two people, including Falcone and Gaydamak, were indicted, it became apparent that Falcone had made payments to French politicians to secure their continued support for the deals and, perhaps, to further the interests of Angola on the international stage. One recipient was Jean-Christophe Mitterrand, who was paid $2.2m by Falcone, although Mitterrand contends that the payment was related to another matter. Charles Pasqua was alleged to have received money for his election campaign to the European Parliament: a claim that Pasqua has suggested was circulated by Jacques Chirac and others as a political ploy to sully his reputation.[179] It also emerged that Falcone and his wife were contributors to the Republican Party in the US and had a soft spot for George W. Bush.[180]

The Angolagate trial was a sensation in France, with high-profile politicians and businesspeople having to sit by while their nefarious dealings around the world were uncovered. In October 2009, the court handed down judgment. In total thirty-six people involved in the deal were convicted on various charges. Jean-Bernard Curial, the man who had responded to dos Santos's initial plea for help, was sentenced to two years' probation and fined €100,000 as an accomplice to an illegal deal.[181] Jean-Christophe Mitterrand was cleared on arms-trafficking charges, but given a two-year suspended sentence and fined €375,000 for the misuse of corporate funds.[182] Pierre Falcone was found guilty on most of the charges brought against him: arms trafficking, influence peddling and the misuse of corporate assets. He received a six-year prison sentence.[183] Arcadi Gaydamak received the same sentence on being found guilty *in absentia* for arms trafficking, tax fraud, money laundering and influence peddling. Well connected in Israel, where he lived unhindered at least until late 2008, and Russia, he has evaded arrest. Charles Pasqua received a three-year prison sentence, twenty-one months of which were suspended, as an accomplice to the deal and for influence peddling.[184]

Ironically, it was the French President, François Mitterrand, who had said in 1971 at the third annual congress of the French Socialist Party: 'Money corrupts, money buys, money crushes, money kills, money ruins, money rots men's consciences.'[185] Little did he know that his words would prove prophetic when it came to arms dealing, not only about his son and his associates, but also with respect to his own, and other, French administrations.

Partially as a result of the arms supplied via Angolagate, dos Santos's government was able to force back UNITA's advance and retake the territory that had been lost. By 1994, both sides were at a stalemate and agreed to a further peace process, known as the Lusaka Protocols. It enforced a ceasefire and pushed for the demobilization of UNITA troops, who would be integrated into the Angolan army. The UN arms embargo put in place against UNITA in 1993 was upheld and continued.[186] In reality, both sides made use of the ceasefire to rebuild troop levels and weapons caches. The government did so via the Angolagate contracts that began delivering in large quantities from the end of 1994. It also turned to another notorious source, Viktor Bout, who had initiated a relationship with the Angolan government in 1994. For four years Bout supplied weapons and matériel worth $325m to the Angolan air force, using a company by the name of Air Charter in Belgium.[187] Of course, he was not only supplying the Angolan government. An equally important client of his was UNITA. Once Bout's double-dealing was discovered he was cut off by the Angolan government, but still remained a supplier to UNITA.[188]

Despite the embargo, dos Santos's regime, as the legitimate government of Angola, was able to undertake numerous deals without much hindrance. Between 1994 and 2002, for example, the government purchased weapons from fifteen different countries.[189] The scale of the weaponry verged on the absurd: between 1994 and 2002, the government bought 349 tanks, all of them from Eastern European countries, bar three purchased from South Africa. It also purchased 393 infantry fighting vehicles from Eastern Europe. Ninety-two towed guns with calibres ranging from 122 to 152mm were acquired, as were eighty-six multiple-rocket launchers – all, once more, from Eastern Europe.[190] How much all of this cost is not entirely clear; but it was certainly an astronomical amount compared to the money spent on ameliorating Angola's dire socio-economic situation.

UNITA was also able to secure its arms with little fuss, as the revenue from industrialized diamond mining was more than sufficient to both buy weapons and grease a considerable number of palms. Savimbi's quest for weapons was supported by Mobutu Sese Seko. From late 1994 until Mobutu's overthrow in 1997, UNITA stockpiled its weapons in Zaire, from where they were transported as needed to Angola: 'most of these planes arrived at night and military cargo was offloaded and then put in bags to try to disguise it as food or clothing. Some of the cargo was stockpiled in warehouses in Kinshasa ... and transported to Andulo [in Angola].'[191]

Mobutu also supplied fraudulent end-user certificates (EUCs) to arms dealers on UNITA's behalf, which would stipulate Zaire as the ultimate destination for deliveries.[192] In 1995, Mobutu introduced Savimbi to Imad Kabir, a Lebanese arms merchant who formed part of Mobutu's entourage. Until 1999, Kabir was UNITA's 'primary broker for importing arms and military equipment'.[193] The system they devised was remarkably simple: Savimbi would inform the dictator of what weapons he needed and request EUCs. In return Savimbi gave Mobutu a large stash of diamonds and hard currency. The EUCs were handed to Imad Kabir, who then arranged to acquire the arms from Eastern Europe and transported them to Kinshasa for onward delivery to Angola.[194]

Many different cargo companies were involved in the delivery flights, but by far the most active were Air Cess and Air Pass – both owned by Viktor Bout.[195] According to one former employee of Air Pass in South Africa, Kabir frequently visited Bout's offices, where he was treated with 'exceptional deference'.[196] At the time, Bout operated from Lanseria airport near Johannesburg. To disguise the end-point of his runs, he often directed his pilots to fly over Zambian airspace before diverting to drop-off points in Angola.[197]

Kabir's relationship with Bout didn't last. By 1998, Savimbi had grown wary of the Lebanese dealer's reliability, fearing that he was skimming some weapons off the top of consignments.[198] Savimbi requested a personal meeting with Bout, which took place in February 1998 in Andulo, UNITA's main base of operations. Thereafter, Kabir was out and Bout dealt directly with Savimbi and UNITA as the mainstay of their gun-running operations.[199]

Savimbi had also set up a back-up plan, lest his Zairean ruse unravelled. In 1993, he dispatched one of his key lieutenants to meet President Eyadema of Togo. In return for Eyadema's providing EUCs and a safe haven for the UNITA leader's children, Savimbi agreed to share some of his imported weapons with the cash-strapped state. Eyadema agreed, and received an envelope of diamonds from the Angolan in gratitude.[200] From 1997, after the fall of Mobutu, the majority of weapons transfers to UNITA were conducted via Togo, with Eyadema skimming 20 per cent of the weapons off the top.[201] At least one of the shipments was transported by Bout's Air Cess operation with a Togolese EUC.[202] Bout also used EUCs from other countries. In 2002, for example, he made a number of deliveries from arms manufacturers in Moldova by the name of Joy Slovakia. The stated end-user was Guinea. The arms ended up with UNITA.[203]

With this continuous supply of weapons UNITA contested the war against the Angolan government for four years. Eventually the bitter, personalized conflict ended simply. On 22 February 2002, Jonas Savimbi was assassinated by Angolan government forces.[204] His second-in-command died fourteen days later of diabetes.[205] With its charismatic leadership dead, the UNITA forces agreed to end their bloody war. Six weeks after Savimbi's death a ceasefire agreement was signed, bringing the war in Angola to an end.[206] It was testament to Savimbi's strength of character, and his manic energy, that he was able to single-handedly run a brutal militia movement that had devastated one of Africa's most resource-rich countries for over four decades. While his energy may have carried UNITA through such an extended conflict, it was his collaborators, first in the West and then in the shadow world of arms dealers, thugs and corrupt Presidents, who allowed him to act as such a destructive sociopath. Without so many willing to supply arms to UNITA and the MPLA, the Angolan conflict would have killed fewer than 500,000,[207] would not have maimed over 70,000,[208] and would have displaced only a fraction of the 4.5 million who were forced to flee their homes in terror and fear.[209]

'The Open-Air Arms Bazaar': Somalia

Somalia has virtually ceased to exist. Following a brutal civil war and the overthrow of the incumbent regime in 1991, the country has failed to form a unitary government.[210] Instead, multiple local warlord-businessmen control chunks of the country, running mini-states based almost entirely on banditry and dispossession. Complex clan and family-based associations, which carry more weight than national identifiers, are the *de facto* groups to which Somalis mostly claim allegiance.[211] It is not easy to understand the multiple forces and pressures causing a country the size of Somalia to implode and atrophy. But the veritable explosion of small arms in the region has accelerated the process, allowing militias to be formed with little money and scant logistical support. The impact on ordinary civilians, cowed by roving private armies with no state for protection, has been exponentially magnified by the proliferation of weapons of war. Somalia's militarized lawlessness and a failure to even cursorily abide by UN arms embargoes have produced their own threats to international order: violent piracy and growing support for Al Qaeda.

In 1960, as decolonization swept the African continent, two territories previously controlled by Britain and Italy were granted independence: in an effort to achieve unity, British Somaliland in the north and Italian Somaliland in the south agreed to form a new country, a union that produced the modern state of Somalia.[212] The new state was a combustible formation from the outset. Somalis in the north worried that the Somali government, with its seat in Mogadishu, favoured southern interests and ignored their needs. Southern clan families, such as the Hawiye and

Darod, also feared that power was being centralized in Mogadishu and that their voices were no longer being heard. Despite the gloss of unity, no such thing could be said to exist in Somalia: differing ideologies and power groups were so rampant that when the first election was held in the country, sixty parties participated.[213]

This heterogeneous polity came to a brutal end in 1969 when a military coup brought the dictatorial Mohamed Siad Barre to power. He ruled the country until his overthrow twenty-two years later. Somalia's geographical location on the east coast of Africa, adjacent to major shipping routes and a stone's throw from the Mediterranean, made it a vital Cold War asset. From as early as 1962 the country was backed by the Soviet Union, which provided considerable aid, mostly of a military nature. Military support was stepped up once Barre became President and the country was soon awash in arms. Between 1973 and 1977 alone, the Soviet Union was estimated to have provided $260m in arms to Barre's regime.[214] Soviet assistance ended in 1978 when Somalia switched allegiances, largely as a result of Soviet support for Ethiopia during the Ogaden War between the two countries. Stung by Soviet perfidy, exaggerated by their embarrassing military reverse in Ethiopia, Somalia turned to Western powers to stock its war machine. Despite considerable evidence of Barre's brutality and repression, the US provided $154m in arms between 1981 and 1991.[215] By far the largest contributor, however, was Italy, which had long historical ties to Somalia. In the four years from 1978, Italy delivered $380m of weapons to Barre, nearly $100m each year.[216] As a result, Somalia had one of the largest and most powerful military forces on the African continent.

Barre's regime was a shambles. During the first phase of leadership, with Soviet support, he experimented with his own brand of scientific socialism together with the full panoply of dictatorship.[217] The security sector, bolstered by Soviet aid, was rapidly expanded. The result was devastating: he held power with military force alone, and oversaw a famine in 1975 that killed 20,000 and forced 20 per cent of the entire pastoral population of Somalia to make for relief camps.[218]

When Barre switched allegiances to the West – repaid with handsome donations of aid – his economics went from the doctrinaire to the erratic. Through the late 1970s and 1980s Somalia's state withered and collapsed.[219] In a tacit acknowledgement of state failure, Barre's regime liberalized the economy, abandoning even foreign exchange controls: traders were allowed to import and export goods with whatever foreign exchange they could lay their hands on through informal networks.[220] The regime survived primarily as a result of foreign military and humanitarian aid. But 80 per cent of the aid, which accounted for 25 per cent of the country's GNP, was diverted to military expenditure.[221] The state, such as it was, existed purely to maintain power and extract what it could from an ailing populace.[222]

Despite the free flow of arms to Somalia's dictatorship, numerous resistance movements began to contest power from the late 1970s. By the late 1980s Barre's regime was on its last legs. Clans in the north and south of the country drew on copious military aid from Ethiopia, which had tired of his continued claims to Ethiopian land. As the Cold War drew to a close, Western support for Barre shrivelled, eliminating his major source of income and military support. From 1988, battles raged throughout Somalia until Barre's overthrow in January 1991.

Once Barre was ousted, the disparate clans who claimed victory fought against each other for the spoils of war. Local 'Big Men' used their positions of relative power to build large militias. Major asset stripping occurred, as state institutions were dismantled and sold to private interests.[223] The money, needless to say, was funnelled into ever-expanding war machines, all of which accelerated Somalia's precipitous decline from failing to failed state.

The impact of the war, fuelled by internationally supplied stockpiles of weapons, was particularly severe on the population of Somalia. During the fighting from 1988 to 1991, roughly 100,000 people were killed in northern Somalia alone, largely as a result of the indiscriminate aerial and artillery bombardment of cities.[224] Hargeisa, the capital city of the self-declared (but not widely recognized) independent state of Somaliland in the north of Somalia, reported 50,000 dead over the three years.[225] Livelihoods faltered as economic infrastructure was targeted for attack: wells were poisoned with corpses, reservoirs shelled and trading markets shut down. Between 1988 and 1992, roughly half the livestock in Somalia was killed – devastating for a mostly agrarian economy.[226] To make matters worse, a drought in the region around the city of Baidoa claimed 300,000–500,000 lives. Those affected received no meaningful aid, as three competing warlords hemmed in the territory, which became known as the 'triangle of death'.[227] Refugees flooded out of areas affected by the war. In the war-ravaged south over 1.7 million people, a third of the region's population, fled the war. Some settled in Mogadishu, where limited aid supplies were available. When the warring parties later converged on the capital, the refugees were forced to up sticks again.[228]

By 1992, Somalia was drowning in guns, a situation that has still not been reversed despite a UN arms embargo placed on the country that year. Weaponry is commonplace, with 64 per cent of Somalis possessing one gun or more.[229] This weapons glut has even encouraged open-air arms markets, the biggest of which is the Huwaika market in Mogadishu.[230] At any one time roughly 400 arms dealers operate in Huwaika, selling masses of weapons at affordable rates: $25 for hand grenades, $100 for landmines and various models of AK-47s ranging from $140 to $600.[231] It is an extremely lucrative trade. 'I have only been in the weapons business five years,' one open-air trader admitted to a Reuters reporter, 'but I have erected three villas. I have also opened shops for my two wives.'[232]

The consequence is that clan leaders can form and equip militias quickly and cheaply, without needing to engage in any unnecessary subterfuge. Many militias operate on the principle of plunder: they steal enough to support themselves and to buy their next load of ammunition and arms from the local arms market.[233] They often institute ad-hoc roadblocks or demand tithes, and control the lucrative trade in khat – a highly addictive chewed plant that is ubiquitous in the country.[234] It is the archetypal war economy and provides considerable inducements to continued violence and a rejection of any central authority.

Unlike in other more clandestine conflicts, the sources of Somali weapons are relatively well-known. Following the civil war in the early 1990s, the largest source of weapons was the existing stockpile of the overthrown Barre government.[235] As the state atrophied, armouries were looted while impoverished soldiers and officers often sold their weapons to dealers to make ends meet. The enormous gifts of military aid from the West served to arm the various bandits and militias that now dominate the country. Since 2006 large quantities of weapons have also been supplied by Ethiopia, mostly to militias willing to tackle the Islamists known as Al-Shabaab.[236] UN troops, intermittently posted to keep the peace in different parts of the country, have also been observed selling their UN-issued weapons to local dealers.[237]

The lack of any policing in Somalia makes it easy for freelance international arms dealers to arrange for new weapons to be brought into the country in contravention of the UN arms embargo, which is still in effect. 'There have been numerous and regular violations [of the arms embargo] – by individuals, factions and political leaders, local and regional administrations and outside state actors,' a 2002 UN report complained. 'In fact, the violations are so numerous that any attempt to document all of the activities would be pointless.'[238]

Two deals, however, provide some flavour of how this trade operates. In June 1992, barely six months after the arms embargo was instituted, Monzer Al-Kassar, one of the world's most notorious arms dealers, organized and sponsored a large shipment of weapons to the war-torn region.[239] Al-Kassar had established a close relationship with Polish arms producers in the 1980s. Many of the arms he organized to supply Nicaraguan rebels during the Iran–Contra affair were sourced from Poland.[240] In the 1990s, Al-Kassar was involved in smuggling weapons from Poland to Croatia in violation of the arms embargo in place on the Balkans at the time. His main contact in Poland was one Jerry Dembrowski, a director of the Polish arms company CENREX.[241] Dembrowski, according to UN investigators, supplied weapons to Al-Kassar, who was then able to smuggle them into Croatia using falsified EUCs from the People's Democratic Republic of Yemen – despite the fact that, by May 1990, the People's Democratic Republic had ceased to exist![242]

In May 1992, Al-Kassar planned a second shipment of weapons, this time to Somalia. But the situation was complicated by the fact that his usual roster of documents had started to invite scrutiny in Poland. Luckily for Al-Kassar and Dembrowski, Poland agreed to donate a substantial amount of arms to the newly created Latvian armed forces at the same time as their deal. Dembrowski befriended Janis Dibrancs, the Chief of Procurement for the Latvian armed forces. Dibrancs agreed to help Dembrowski and supplied documents showing that the weapons for Somalia were destined for Latvia. In return, Dembrowski undertook that even more surplus Polish weaponry would find its way to Latvia. On 10 June 1992, Polish Customs cleared the ship, MV *Nadia*, for departure, whereupon it landed in Latvia. A small portion of the arms were unloaded in Latvia, with Dibrancs signing a receipt that suggested all the weapons had been disgorged. The majority of the cargo continued its onward journey – 1,000 sub-machine guns, 100 hand grenades, 300 AK-47s, 160

RPG launchers, 10,000 mortar bombs and 3,450,000 rounds of AK-47 ammunition. From Latvia, the MV *Nadia* travelled to a location off the coast of Somalia, where the weapons were collected by another ship and transported to the Somali mainland.[243]

The weapons were delivered to Ali Mahdi Mohamed, an archetypal post-civil war Somali militia leader. Prior to the war Mohamed had made a fortune in construction. He was also seriously politically connected: after Barre was overthrown, Mohamed was appointed President of Somalia. While in this position he sold off a wide range of state assets, all to raise money for himself and his militia, which sought to control substantial sections of southern Somalia.[244] In 1991, he sold the entire Somali state shipping fleet: five ships that had sailed under the banner of the Somali High Seas Fishery Corporation (SHIFCO). The fleet, which had been donated by Italian dockyards to Somalia in the 1980s, was sold for a paltry $500,000 to Omar Munye, a Somali politician with links to Yemen.[245]

It was a SHIFCO vessel that collected Al-Kassar's shipment off the coast and delivered it into the country.[246] Considering the close connection between SHIFCO and Ali Mahdi Mohamed, it is not inconceivable that Al-Kassar's shipment made it into Mohamed's hands.

This deal is a microcosm of the tragedy of the Somali state and the impact of the arms trade on the country. To buy arms, large portions of the state were sold off and destroyed, and, when delivered, the arms were put to use to further destroy the country's fragile political order, preventing any semblance of a state emerging.

A second deal illustrates that violations of the UN arms embargo have continued, virtually unabated, since 1992. In June 2010, US courts in southern Florida indicted two men known to be in the arms trade, Chanoch Miller and Joseph O'Toole. O'Toole, a US citizen, had supplied arms during the Iran–Contra scandal.[247] Miller is a well-known Israeli arms dealer who worked as an executive for Israel's Radom Aviation.[248] O'Toole and Miller worked together from their separate bases in the US and Israel to organize an air drop of roughly 24 tons of small arms and ammunition from Bosnia into Somalia.[249] One of Miller's key roles was to organize fraudulent EUCs – the delivery, on paper, was destined for Chad, where no arms embargo was in place. O'Toole was promised a small commission of just over $4,000 for facilitating the contact between Miller and a transit company.[250]

The man they contacted to transport the weapons was a US Customs informant. Over a period of two months, O'Toole and Miller exchanged a series of emails with the informant, sending contracts to seal the deal, for which the informant would receive a payment of $142,000 per trip.[251] Miller bragged in one email that he had 'enough cargo for 100 flights' if the first flight was successful.[252] This suggested that he had about 1,200 tons of matériel ready for delivery. When the first shipment was delayed, Miller contacted the Customs informant and organized another deal, in which he planned to purchase AK-47s directly from the informant, which would then be delivered to Somalia via Panama.[253] Both men were arrested in mid-June 2010 and were charged with seven counts related to arms trafficking. If found guilty Miller and O'Toole could have received fines of $500,000 and a maximum prison sentence of twenty years.

In October 2010, Joseph O'Toole and Chanoch Miller entered into a plea agreement with the US authorities. In return for having most of the charges dropped, O'Toole and Miller acknowledged their guilt in 'export[ing] defense articles from the United States to Somalia, an embargoed nation, without having first obtained a license or written approval from the United States Department of State'. In their guilty pleas, O'Toole and Miller acknowledged that they had failed to source 700 AK-47 rifles from Bosnia to send to Somalia using a falsified end-user certificate from Chad. When they failed, they turned to the informant, who promised to provide the weapons from stockpiles in Panama and the US itself. As a result of their plea agreements, O'Toole and Miller were liable to a maximum five-year prison sentence. In fact, O'Toole received a sentence of one year and one day and was ordered to pay a fine of $100. He will serve two years' probation.[254] Miller received a sentence of eighteen months, and was also ordered to pay a $100 fine. He will be on probation for three years.[255]

The failure of the Somali state, and the proliferation of weapons that has both underpinned and typified it, has had major global ramifications that extend beyond the humanitarian outrage of its own politics. The first, and perhaps most notorious, such threat is that of piracy off the Somali coast. From 2007, the number of pirate attacks on international shipping near to Somalia escalated dramatically. From an already substantial base, the attacks increased by 220 per cent between 2007 and 2010.[256] This rise was associated with an increasing sophistication on the part of the pirates and a willingness to attack larger ships, even those weighing over 10,000 tons such as oil tankers and major cargo vessels.[257] The emboldened pirates also ventured beyond the Somali coastline, on occasion travelling 1,000 nautical miles to the Seychelles.[258]

On 25 September 2008, a group of sixty-two men boarded a Ukrainian cargo ship sailing under the name MV *Faina*.[259] The pirates demanded a ransom of $20m to release the ship, which was carrying 2,320 tons of military equipment and ammunition, including thirty-three Russian-made tanks.[260] International observers blanched at the thought of these tanks being used in any number of Africa's conflicts, making the MV *Faina*'s release a top priority. After months of tense negotiations the pirates agreed to release the ship in February 2009 for a reported $3.2m ransom.[261] It is not entirely clear where the arms were to be delivered. Kenya claimed that it had bought the cargo through legal channels; manifests, however, suggested that the weapons may have been on their way to southern Sudan.[262]

Piracy and smuggling, while always a part of Somalia's maritime economy, increased massively after the collapse of Barre's government in 1991, as the ports were now easily accessible and became a focus of contestation for military forces.[263] Given that many of those fighting were little more than criminal militias, pirates were able to operate with impunity. The arms which have flooded Somalia since 1992 have 'tremendously enhanced the capabilities of pirates'.[264] As a piracy expert, Rob de Wijk, points out: 'where in the past pirates used knives and guns, today they can be equipped with M-16 and AK-47 assault rifles and rocket-propelled grenades'.[265]

Like most of Somalia's competing criminal clans and militias, pirates are able to rely on arms shipments from Yemen or purchases from the local Somali arms markets to stock their arsenals. Some of the market operators have even assisted in transporting the cargo. Mogadishu arms dealers take deposits from the pirates via the *hawala* system and truck the arms up to the pirates' hideouts, mostly in the province of Puntland. On receipt, the remainder of the payment is made.[266] Besides ensuring a constant flow of weapons, the actions of the Mogadishu dealers mean that pirates do not need to travel to areas where they might face capture or punishment.

The second major threat to international peace and security in Somalia is the rise of Al-Shabaab, 'the youth'. Al-Shabaab had constituted one part of Somalia's Islamic Courts Union (ICU, which formed a rival administration in the south) but split and created a distinct group in 2006. One of the reasons cited for the schism was ICU's lack of radicalism, a remarkable statement considering the ICU had already attracted international opprobrium for its consistent human rights violations and insistence on the universal introduction of sharia law. From 2007 onwards Al-Shabaab grew in strength. By 2010, numbering close to 10,000 fighters, it was in control of most of southern and central Somalia.[267] Al-Shabaab is now 'the most powerful single armed faction in the country, controlling more territory than any other group'.[268] In August 2010, Al-Shabaab militias captured the majority of the capital, Mogadishu. In late August they marched on the Presidential Palace, where they were only rebuffed by African Union forces dedicated to maintaining the ICU's rule.[269] In a remarkable development, the Obama administration agreed to supply 40 tons of arms to the ICU to defend itself – despite the group's anti-democratic and hardline Islamic policies.[270] Al-Shabaab is seen as such a severe threat to international peace that the ICU supposedly pales by comparison.

As with most militias in Somalia, in addition to the internal arms markets, Al-Shabaab can rely on a ready supply of weapons from across Africa's porous borders. One of its largest suppliers has been Eritrea, motivated by a desire to undermine the efforts of Ethiopia, which invaded Somalia in 2006, with a resultant increase in Al-Shabaab's internal nationalist support.[271] Eritrea and Ethiopia have a long-standing conflict in which Somalia is just another front.[272] Al-Shabaab's links to international Islamist groups have also enhanced its access to arms. In 2010, it appeared to be getting arms from Libya, Iran and Qatar, although this could not be definitively verified.[273]

Life under Al-Shabaab control is harsh. While some Somalis are thankful for the order and relative safety provided by the Al-Shabaab rulers, it has come at the cost of freedom of association, religion and expression. Spies are widespread, informing on any infraction from serious political activity to smoking. Those found to be breaking Al-Shabaab's rules face harsh punishment – flogging, public stoning and executions. Hardline sharia regulations prohibit women from working in any public space and they are forced to wear Islamic dress on pain of beating. This has devastated many Somali families whose men have been abducted or killed, leaving women as the only breadwinners.[274]

But Al-Shabaab's rule over large parts of Somalia doesn't just threaten Somali lives. The group has been frequently linked to Al Qaeda. While not all members of Al-Shabaab are radical Islamists – some are motivated, instead, by more parochial nationalist aims – a number of the leadership core have articulated the link,[275] most vocally in 2009. On Christmas Day a US-bound airliner was subject to a failed bombing attempt. Responsibility was claimed by an Al Qaeda affiliate in Yemen. When it was feared that the US might retaliate with attacks in Yemen, representatives of Al-Shabaab offered fighters to Al Qaeda's Yemeni cell.[276] Osama bin Laden frequently mentioned Al-Shabaab in his various communications, proclaiming the good that the group has done. While this may be nothing more than bluster, it has alarmed Western observers. Al-Shabaab is now a listed terrorist organization in the US. There is a fear that it may act as a feeder and training body for terrorists. This concern is fuelled by the fact that a small core of Al-Shabaab fighters are not from Somalia at all but have been drawn from radical Islamist movements in countries such as Pakistan and Afghanistan.[277] In September 2010, UK intelligence chiefs publicly expressed concern that Al-Shabaab is housing anti-UK terrorists. According to a statement by the head of MI5, over 100 UK residents had travelled to join Al-Shabaab and received training in order to undertake attacks in the UK.[278] By 2010, nearly 50 per cent of all terrorist threats against the UK emanated from Somalia and specifically Al-Shabaab.[279]

Amid the worst drought in the region for sixty years, parts of Somalia were plunged into famine at the time of writing. Getting aid to these areas was complicated by the formal designation of the group as a terrorist organization by the US government. Susan Rice, the American ambassador to the UN, blamed Al-Shabaab, which, until a recent about-face, had made humanitarian work in the country dangerous, if not impossible.[280]

Might the situation have been different if the international community, particularly the UK and the US, had shown greater concern for the plight of ordinary Somalis and made some effort to stop the continuous flow of weapons into the country? According to a senior US official who knows the region well: 'Somalis in the Gulf states are multimillionaires. Some have links to the Saudis. The authorities [in the US] allow the guns to pour in sometimes because they don't know how to intervene and other times because they have no interest in intervening for intelligence reasons. They favour their chosen people and won't disrupt them. Somalia is a prime example of blowback for the Western powers.'[281]

'Without a Kalash You're Trash': Sudan and Darfur

International attention has focused on the conflict in Darfur since 2003 because of the scale of the war crimes and crimes against humanity committed with virtual impunity in this southern region of the Sudan.

The conflict stems from the complex and violent politics of modern Sudan. The country, which is home to a multitude of different ethnicities, achieved full independence from British rule in 1956.[282] The north is predominantly Muslim and its political elite largely self-identify as Arabs, while the south is made up largely of Africans, many of whom are not Muslim.[283] The east and west contain a range of different populations. In Darfur the population is mostly of Fur origin, hence the name, which means 'Land of the Fur': self-identified black African pastoralists who, unlike those in the south, are mostly Muslim.[284] The colonial boundaries were an absurdity, with communities cutting across state lines into countries such as Chad. This has meant that Sudanese conflicts often become embroiled in larger regional power politics and vice-versa.[285]

The northern political elite dominated government positions after independence, largely as a result of British colonial policy that actively encouraged the north to assume administrative and political control over the south. This outraged the population of the south, who referred to themselves as 'internally colonized people'.[286] After independence the government refused demands for southern autonomy or greater federalism. The discovery of oil in the south only hardened this position.[287]

The stand-off led to two brutal civil wars between 1955 and 1972 and again from 1991 to 2005. Many worry that the ceasefire brokered in 2005 is fragile and may not last.[288]

The wars were devastating: the second civil war is estimated to have left almost 2 million people dead from conflict, disease and starvation, mostly in southern Sudan, where the majority of the fighting took place. The conflict created nearly 350,000 refugees who fled to other countries while 80 per cent of Sudan's southerly population have been internally displaced at one time or another since 1983.[289]

As with Somalia, the war was perpetuated by the Cold War nations. Initially Sudan received large-scale Soviet assistance although this had ended by 1976 as the relationship cooled. Thereafter, Sudan relied on military aid from a number of states, the most notable of which was the US. Despite its atrocious human rights record for a period until the late 1980s, Sudan was, according to the US Department of State, the 'single largest recipient of US development and military assistance in sub-Saharan Africa'.[290]

Notwithstanding the aid, the Sudanese government in Khartoum struggled to finance the continual war which was sapping the morale of its fighters. As a result a new militia strategy was adopted and implemented in 1985 by General Abdel Rahmen Suwar al Dahab. It was based on the Sudanese government locating and arming groups in southern Sudan who were hostile to claims for southern independence. They would be the government's shock troops with orders to 'devastate communities' who were supporting the southern Sudanese rebels.[291] In a chilling precursor to Darfur, the militias thus created focused on 'ethnically targeted killings' in a context of 'total impunity'.[292] This, combined with the fact that they were encouraged to loot in lieu of salaries, made the militias – known as *murahaliin* – brutal, ultra-violent and devastatingly effective. In an echo of Somalia, weapons and military aid from the West found its way into the hands of barely governable militias responsible for gross human rights violations.

The war between north and south Sudan set the mould for future internal conflicts in the country. Much the same confluence of factors converged in Darfur: local Darfurians protesting at northern control and perfidy, a violent response on the part of the Sudanese government, the creation and arming of local outsiders to form brutal militias, and an international response that, at times, actively aided the conflict and, in rare moments of contrition, did little to stop it.

Darfur is ethnically heterogeneous. The Fur, who comprise the majority, are self-identifying black African Muslims. The Zaghawa are also indigenous Africans who lay claim to land in Chad, as do the smaller Massalit group. These three African groups are farmers or pastoralists, raising and selling cattle, and most are Muslim.[293] The minority population in Darfur are Arab herders and nomads who travel freely throughout the country, either looking after large herds of livestock or taking advantage of their mobility in other ways. Tensions have long existed between the Arab nomads and the agrarian African population in Darfur, mainly around land use for grazing and sources of water. Historically, most of these conflicts, which are exacerbated during times of drought, were resolved by mediation and conciliation.[294]

By the late 1980s the conflicts increased in frequency and violence. This was partly due to the decreasing availability of land as Saharan desertification continued to spread. Equally important though was the intervention of Libya and the resulting massive flows of arms into Darfur. Colonel Gaddafi had frequently dreamt of a pan-Arab swathe across a large portion of Africa.[295] In 1975, he started to realize his vision by annexing a northern strip of Chad and mounting attacks on the rest of the country, with little success. Ten years later he approached the government of Sudan to use Darfur as a staging post to attack Chad. The Sudanese government, while sympathetic to Gaddafi's pan-Arabian vision, was more likely motivated by the offer of oil and arms. Gaddafi drew on Darfurian Arabs who were open to his vision and armed them extensively. A select group received military training in Libya and were exposed to the doctrine of Arab supremacy. Many commanders trained in Libya would later emerge as leaders of the militia responsible for much of the violence in Darfur.[296]

Libya's involvement made weapons ubiquitous in the region. By 1990, it was possible to purchase an AK-47 in a Darfurian market for $40. A popular jingle at the time captured the spirit of the new weapons culture and its impact on politics in the region: 'The Kalash brings cash', the jingle promised, before warning that 'without a Kalash you're trash.'[297] Tragically for Darfur, arms flows into the region coincided with a belief that, even if Africans in Darfur were Muslim, they were still ethnically inferior to Arab Muslims. In the late 1980s, a diatribe called 'Qoreish 1' was first distributed in Darfur by Al-tajammu Al-Arabi, 'the Arab Gathering', who were known to have sympathetic ears in government. It was a 'war cry', a statement of intent against African 'dominance' of Darfur, drawn from resentment at a lack of Arab representation in local Darfurian government: 'Should the neglect of the Arab race continue, and the Arabs be denied their share in government, we are afraid that things may escape the control of wise men and revert to ignorant people and the mob. Then there could be catastrophe, with dire consequences.'[298] A decade later, in

1999, 'Qoreish 2' was published, outlining a plan to take over large parts of Sudan and Chad for Arabian herders and nomads by 2020.[299]

With arms swamping the area and a new militant ideology taking hold, it was inevitable that violence would increase. The local African population, in particular the Massalit, complained of being targeted by violent Arab raiders with the complicity of the Sudanese government. They formed resistance movements, with the government responding by supplying more arms to local Arab militias, fuelling a further escalation of violence. In 2000, Sudan's President Omar al-Bashir declared a state of emergency in Darfur, which led to a massive crackdown on Darfurian dissidents.[300]

The local African population was distraught and increasingly came to believe that Khartoum was purposefully neglecting their demands and the plight of those attacked. By the early 2000s two embryonic resistance movements had formed in Darfur to protest against al-Bashir's northern military and political elite: the Sudan Liberation Movement/Army (SLM/A) and the Justice and Equality Movement (JEM).[301] As in Somalia, the resistance was able to arm itself extensively from local arms stocks.[302] The weapons provided by Libya to Darfurian Arabs would now be used against a government that was a Libyan ally. In early 2003, the resistance movements launched attacks on the Sudanese government. In April, armed only with one large machine gun and a single rocket launcher, the rebels destroyed two Antonov cargo planes, used to drop bombs and transport oil, and five helicopter gunships.[303]

The government in Khartoum panicked, fearful of facing an additional military threat while still engaged in conflicts in southern Sudan. Al-Bashir's government responded by approaching Darfurian Arab groups hostile to the SLM/A and JEM, in particular the nomadic Rezeigat, who had previously been used by Khartoum to fight its wars. Collectively, the Arab fighters came to be known as the *Janjaweed*,[304] which was variously taken to be a conflation of the terms for a G3 rifle and a horse,[305] or a traditional term usually applied to bandits. At the same time the Sudanese military, with its overpowering collection of conventional weapons, was mobilized *en masse* in the region. Together, the *Janjaweed* and government forces were formidable. Attacks were often started with government forces bombing enclaves of Darfurians. *Janjaweed* militias would then move into the area, killing, mutilating and raping the remaining civilians.[306]

Both main elements of the arms trade were thus brought to bear on the Darfurian population: large-scale military systems, most often bought in government-to-government contracts, were used alongside light weapons and mobile mounted guns that are the stock-in-trade of shadow world arms dealers and itinerant warlords.

From 2003 onwards the bloodletting was beyond comprehension. Estimates suggest that as many as 300,000 people have died as a result of either direct action or starvation over the last seven years.[307] Since 1991, as a result of the Darfur conflict and the civil war in Southern Sudan, 2.2 million Sudanese citizens have died, making Sudan a contender for the most violent and desperate place on earth. In Darfur roughly 2.7 million people have fled their homes, nearly half the population of a region roughly the size of France.[308] And while the atrocities have slowed down in recent years, especially since the SLM/A rebel group signed a ceasefire agreement with Khartoum in 2005, violent clashes are still commonplace.

The scale and near-genocidal impact of the Darfur conflict were intensified by Khartoum's easy access to weapons. The ferocity of the early stages of the fighting was influenced by the fact that, from 1999, Omar al-Bashir's regime dramatically increased its weapons purchases, using money obtained from drilling the oilfields in the south that had previously been inaccessible because of the continuing civil war.[309]

To exploit the oilfields, Sudan forged a close alliance with China. Of the nine profitable oil blocks in the country, China holds the concession to drill eight.[310] The Asian giant supplies the infrastructure necessary to extract and process the oil, as well as investing in machinery, roads and airstrips.[311] The result has been an explosion in Sudanese oil exports to China and a massive flow of Chinese money into the country in return. In 2001, for example, Sudan exported just over $1bn in oil to China. By 2006 this had increased to over $4bn.[312] In return, China agreed to a virtually limitless supply of light arms on the cheap. Between 1999 and 2003 China and Iran were between them responsible for 95 per cent of all Sudan's small-arms imports.[313] And from 2003 to 2006 China accounted for 90 per cent of Sudan's small-arms imports, which amounted to $55m.[314]

While China's support for the al-Bashir regime has been based on economic opportunism – a chance to gain access to Sudan's valuable oil deposits – Iran seems to be acting out of a sense of ideological affinity and regional politics. Iran and Sudan have a long history of close relations. In

1991, for example, the Iranian President, Ali Akbar Hashemi Rafsanjani, paid a visit to Sudan following al-Bashir's decision to apply harsher sharia law. Rafsanjani was accompanied by 150 officials and declared that 'the Islamic Revolution of Sudan, alongside Iran's pioneer revolution, can doubtless be the source of movement and revolution throughout the Islamic world'.[315] Rafsanjani agreed to put his money where his mouth was: soon after his visit nearly 2,000 members of Iran's armed forces travelled to Sudan to train al-Bashir's troops and millions of dollars of aid were pledged.[316]

Exactly how much military aid Iran has supplied to Sudan is not entirely clear. Indicatively, Sudan had purchased $18m of military equipment and small arms from Iran between 2004 and 2006,[317] but little detail is available for the period thereafter. It is clear that arms have continued to flow. In March 2008, Iran and Sudan signed an extended military cooperation agreement that committed both sides to share expertise in various fields.[318] And, in June 2010, a Sudanese opposition newspaper reported that Iran may have set up an entire arms factory in Sudan to produce light weapons.[319] This was probably a consequence of the many difficulties Iran experienced shipping weapons from its own factories after numerous shipments had been intercepted.[320] The factory also provides Iran with the means to produce and distribute arms to allies throughout the region, particularly in Somalia. While the report of the Iranian factory remains unconfirmed, it definitely touched a nerve in the al-Bashir government as the newspaper that broke the story – *Opinion of the People* – was banned and shut down indefinitely, while its proprietor was jailed on the President's order.[321]

Two other countries have shown a willingness to transfer arms to Sudan since the early 1990s: Belarus and Russia. Russia has been a particularly useful source for more complex weapons systems. Flush with cash from oil exports, Sudan purchased thirty BTR-80A infantry fighting vehicles from Russia in 2000 and sixteen Mi-24/Hind combat attack helicopters, which were used to soften up Darfurian settlements with aerial bombardments before the *Janjaweed* attacked.[322] In 1996, Belarus reported the transfer of six MI-24V attack helicopters to Sudan, as well as the purchase of nine T-55 Belarusian tanks. In 1999, a further sixty T-55 AM-2 tanks were delivered. Twelve multiple-rocket launchers and twenty-four towed guns were ordered in 2002.[323]

One would expect that the international attention focused on the humanitarian crisis in Darfur would have halted arms sales to the Sudanese regime, especially as evidence mounted that al-Bashir was intimately involved in arming the *Janjaweed* militias. The UN Security Council imposed an arms embargo in 2004. However, it only prohibited the transfer of weaponry into Darfur. By so doing, it failed to impose any sanctions against the Sudanese regime. Khartoum was able to import weapons unabated.[324] A 2005 update to the embargo attempted to paper over this glaring omission. But all it did was ask all states exporting to Khartoum to elicit a promise from the Sudanese not to use the weapons in Darfur.[325] After two years it was realized that this was insufficient. The exporting countries would now need to acquire an EUC from Sudan stating that the weapons would not be used in Darfur. Considering the number of forged or misleading EUCs used to secure weapons transfers, the proposal was either intentionally ludicrous or astonishingly naive. In addition, no punishment was to be meted out if Sudan provided the EUC but still used the weapons in Darfur, rendering the embargo both farcical and useless.[326]

Weapons have continued to flow into Darfur without hindrance. From 2003 to 2007, Russia and China supplied a considerable number of advanced weapons systems, including cargo planes, helicopters and fighter jets. Russia has supplied two loads of attack helicopters, twelve Mi-24s and fifteen Mi-8s. These followed hard on the purchase of twelve MiG fighter jets supplied by Russia in 2004. Two loads of Antonov transport cargo aircraft have also been delivered, one in March 2004 and another in September 2006. They have a dual purpose: to transport men and goods and as blanket bombers capable of dropping massive amounts of explosives.[327]

China has provided a series of different fighter jets: K-8 jet trainers in 2006 allegedly equipped with cannons and rockets, sixteen F-7M military jets purchased in 2006 and a number of A5 'Fantan' jets, which have been spotted in Darfur since January 2007.[328] China has also continued to dominate the small-arms trade with Sudan. Since 2003, roughly 70 per cent of all small arms purchased by Sudan have been supplied by the Chinese, in addition to the less glamorous vehicles of war such as 212 military trucks purchased in 2005.[329] The UN has repeatedly discovered weapons of Chinese and Russian origin on Darfurian battlefields.[330] The precise cost of these weapons is unclear; however, it has been estimated that up to 80 per cent of Sudan's entire oil exports have been used to purchase arms.[331] Considering that Sudan earned over $4bn in oil exports to China alone in 2006,[332] it is likely that the al-Bashir regime has spent in excess of $10bn equipping its forces since 2003.

Violations of the arms embargo have continued. In October 2009, for example, the UN Security Council Panel of Experts on Sudan depressingly confirmed that 'All parties to the conflict continue to fail to meet their affirmative obligations under international humanitarian and human rights law in areas under their control . . . Almost all sides in the conflict have failed in their obligation to comply with Security Council sanctions and to cooperate with the monitoring efforts of the Panel of Experts.'[333] There is just too much money to be made. While the situation on the ground continues to mutate, there is little doubt that, if a north–south civil war were to explode once more, the Khartoum regime would be extremely confident of its ability to arm its troops to the teeth.

That is not to suggest that all international players have acquiesced so easily to Sudan's militarism. In March 2009, the International Criminal Court (ICC) issued an arrest warrant against President Omar al-Bashir for crimes against humanity and war crimes. In mid-2010, after initially rejecting the request, the ICC added three counts of genocide to al-Bashir's list of charges stating that there 'are reasonable grounds to believe [al-Bashir is] responsible' for orchestrating a wave of rapes, murders and torture.[334] Al-Bashir, despite travelling widely in the region, has not been arrested as the ICC has no independent enforcement mechanism, relying instead on the prerogative of member states, who baulk at the diplomatic fallout of such an action. In August 2010, al-Bashir controversially attended the signing of the new Kenyan constitution. Kenya, as a signatory to the ICC, was obliged to arrest al-Bashir. Nothing was done.[335]

At the time of writing, South Sudan had recently become an independent nation after a largely peaceful referendum in which over 99 per cent of the south voted to secede.[336] But structural problems still persist: most importantly, North Sudan retains control of pipelines ferrying oil from the south, raising the threat that any breakdown in the current détente could lead to a further contesting of the country's black gold and who, exactly, profits from it. And while al-Bashir continues to hold the reins of power, no one in Sudan, even in the newly created South, can sleep peacefully. With a stock of weapons that exceeds the arsenal of many of his rivals, al-Bashir has ample means to reignite wider regional conflict if the need emerges. The residents of Darfur devastated by the genocide unleashed on their area, will only feel truly safe if the international community does what it should have done decades ago: stop arming a genocidal dictator.

Blowback Writ Large: Egypt, Libya and the Ivory Coast

On 17 December 2010, Mohammed Bouazizi, a 26-year-old graduate and fruit seller, poured petrol over his head and body and set himself alight. Two weeks later, Bouazizi passed away, a martyr to those who shared his rage at Tunisia's economic stagnation, poor record on human rights and political censorship.[337] By then, his death had spurred on a revolution many had not foreseen in one of Africa's perceived stable states, attempting to throw off the chains of political corruption and the twenty-three-year rule of Tunisia's dictator, President Zine El Abidine Ben Ali. Only nine days after Bouazizi expired in hospital, the government of President Ben Ali crumbled, the President fleeing to safety in Saudi Arabia.[338]

The overthrow of Ben Ali resonated beyond his country's borders, fuelling protestors in a wide arc of North African Arab states. In Egypt in particular, the Tunisian Revolution was a clarion call to those who envisioned a future *sans* the country's longest-serving leader, President Hosni Mubarak. Eleven days after Tunisia's leadership was overthrown, mass protests were launched throughout Egypt.[339] Millions spilt from their houses, peacefully occupying public spaces, defying military curfews, refusing to be quelled until their voices were heard. In Cairo, hundreds of thousands of protestors occupied Tahrir Square, Ground Zero of the protest. After it emerged that Mubarak's support within the military had frayed, his resignation was announced on 11 February 2011 by his long-time right-hand man and Vice-President, Omar Suleiman.[340] In less than two months North African and, by extension, Middle Eastern politics had changed fundamentally.

For those unused to following Egyptian politics, it seemed like a bolt from the blue. In reality, Mubarak's regime had been creaking under the weight of its various limitations for a number of years. Born in 1928 in the Nile Valley, Mubarak had taken power following the assassination of Anwar Sadat in 1981[341] – a killing motivated by Sadat's decision to sign the 1978 Camp David Peace Accords that signalled a détente between Egypt and Israel.[342] Drawn from the military – he had served with distinction as air force chief during the Egyptian–Israeli war of 1973, despite Egypt's devastating defeat by Israeli troops – Mubarak maintained much the same political landscape as that of his military predecessors, originally outlined during the tempestuous rule of General Abdel Nasser. Nasser's 'social contract' was simple: 'political repression and limited political participation among the working class and peasantry in return for the state's delivery of basic services'.[343]

Mubarak demanded the same of his populace. When acquiescence was unforthcoming, repression was the preferred tool. By mid-2010, 17,000 political prisoners, many linked to the Muslim Brotherhood, were languishing in jail.[344] Nominal elections were held, although disruptions, repression, bans and allegations of vote rigging gave them the air of ritualized performance pieces held for their photo opportunities rather than as a meaningful contesting of the country's political direction. And yet Mubarak could not do what Nasser had set out to do: use the stability of military rule for economic gain. In 1991, following the Gulf War, Egypt agreed to a series of structural adjustment programmes guided by the World Bank. It earned plaudits among the technocratic conservatives and Friedmanites of the West but yielded poor results for the mass of Egyptian poor.[345] Unlike Nasser, who had increased access to farmland, the liberalization of agriculture forced many from farms and put power back into the hands of large landowners.[346] Unemployment remained stubbornly high at 26 per cent of the population and more than half of Egypt's wheat is now imported.[347] The economy may have exploded from 2005 onwards, growing at least 5 per cent per year, but the ordinary Egyptian has yet to benefit.

Egypt's close relationship with Israel also rankled. The sharing of intelligence between Egyptian and Israeli security forces and Egypt's alleged role in assisting Israel's assaults on Gaza infuriated Egyptians who felt kinship with Palestine.[348] Nepotism added to a general sense of grievance: from the late 1990s, Mubarak seemed to be grooming his son, the deeply unpopular Gamal Mubarak, to take on his mantle.

And, all the while, most Egyptians believed that Mubarak had been using his position of power to feather his nest, taking cuts from arms deals and the relationship with Israel. Hussein Salem, one of Mubarak's closest confidants and alleged front for the President's business activities, hit the headlines in the late 1970s, when Egypt started taking delivery of weapons from the US. Out of nowhere Salem was awarded the contract to ship the weapons – a role he was accused of using to pad the deal by $8m for his own benefit and that of his business partners.[349] A few years later, Salem was fingered by US authorities, forcing him to admit his guilt and repay $3m.[350] More recently, Salem structured a $1.5bn deal with the Israeli businessman Yosef Maiman to export natural gas to Israel. Many claim that the price paid per cubic unit was astoundingly low, thus selling Egypt's economy down the river. As protestors occupied Tahrir Square, Salem quietly slipped from the country, and was rumoured to have landed in Dubai with $500m in hard cash.[351]

Mubarak and two of his sons, Gamal and Alaa, as well as Hussein Salem, are currently facing charges for corruption.[352] Hosni Mubarak and Salem are specifically facing criminal charges related to arms exports and the shipping of arms supplied to Egypt from the US under the annual military assistance package. Interpol is pursuing them on the same charges.[353]

Mubarak's regime survived because of the support of the military and control over the feared intelligence services. As long as Mubarak was able to disburse the pleasures of patronage to the roughly 500,000 conscripted soldiers who made up the army,[354] and, in particular, the officer corps which led them, his power was assured. Fortunately for Mubarak and the military that ran the country, they were able to lean heavily on the support of the West, and in particular the US, to keep the taps running.

US support for Egypt was closely tied to support for Israel. After the 1979 Camp David Accords, Egypt became one of the few Arab states willing to enter into peaceful and friendly relations with Israel. Under Mubarak the relationship was maintained and expanded via business ties and the sharing of intelligence. Mubarak's largest internal foe was the country's Islamist movement, against which he had ordered repeated crackdowns. Sharing information with Israel served to both cement the relationship and provide important intelligence on Egypt's own enemies.

In return for its renunciation of conflict with Israel, Egypt was handsomely rewarded by the US. Since 1979, Egypt has received an annual average of $2bn in economic and military aid from America.[355] More recently, economic aid had taken a backseat to the aid directed towards the military. In 2011, the Obama administration has requested a total of $1.552bn in aid – $1.3bn for the military and a far more circumspect

$250m for the mass of Egypt's poor.[356] While total aid to Egypt has decreased annually from 1998 onwards, military aid has remained stable – only economic support has been reduced.[357] In 2010, Egypt received a total of $1.55bn in aid ($1.3bn for military matters), making it the fifth-largest recipient of US aid after Afghanistan, Israel, Pakistan and Haiti.[358] This was actually a relatively poor showing: between 1979 and 2010, Egypt was the second-largest recipient of assistance from the US, surpassed only by Israel.[359]

The US military aid, plus defence budgets that have averaged in the region of $4bn (at 2009 prices) since 1988,[360] has funded an extended bout of weapons purchases. Between 1981, when Mubarak took power, and 2010, Egypt has spent a total of $28.4bn on military equipment.[361] By far the largest supplier has been the US: its $21.17bn in sales constitutes just under 75 per cent of all arms purchased by Egypt since Mubarak assumed office.[362] Only two other countries have breached the $1bn mark: China ($2.3bn) and France ($1.5bn).[363] Russia ($878m) and the UK ($482m) are the two next-largest suppliers.[364]

This boom in spending largely benefited US suppliers, both big and small. The extent of the sales means it is impossible to list all the weapons transferred; suffice it to say that transfers of weapons systems from 1981 onwards take up six full, tightly itemized pages in the SIPRI arms transfer database.[365] Among the more notable transfers have been hundreds of US-designed Abrams tanks, now assembled in the suburbs of Cairo under the supervision of General Dynamics;[366] F-16 fighters provided by Lockheed Martin; Chinook helicopters supplied by Boeing; and Black Hawk helicopters built by Sikorsky Aircraft.[367] The earnings have been substantial. In the last few years Lockheed Martin earned $3.8bn and General Dynamics $2.5bn, while Boeing pocketed $1.7bn from its business with Egypt.[368]

Equally important have been the transfers of riot control gear, light weapons and tear gas, frequently bought from smaller US suppliers. Reporters from the US television station ABC patrolled the grounds of Tahrir Square only to find spent shells and tear gas canisters boldly emblazoned 'Made in the USA'.[369] The canisters were traced to the US supplier Combined Systems Inc. (CSI), a relatively small company based in Pennsylvania.[370] Even here, however, the tentacles of the US military giants penetrated: among CSI's many shareholders is the Carlyle Group, which bought a minority shareholding in 2005.[371] Indicative of the cosiness between Egypt, Israel and the US, tear gas used by Israeli armed forces in Gaza has been traced back to the same company.[372]

In the UK, MPs expressed outrage at the fact that the government had issued arms export licences for various questionable countries in 2009/10, including 'machine guns, imaging cameras, electronic warfare equipment [and] components for semi-automatic pistols', worth £16.8m, approved for sale to Egypt.[373] More galling was the trip to Egypt undertaken by the Tory Prime Minister, David Cameron, following Mubarak's resignation, the first such visit undertaken by a foreign dignitary. Standing in Tahrir Square, Cameron loudly trumpeted the democratic credentials of the Egyptian protestors, whom he found 'genuinely inspiring'.[374] The protestors, he gushed, were not rag-tag bands of Islamic extremists, but 'people who want to have the same sort of freedoms that we take for granted in the UK'.[375]

Failing to sense the deep irony that US and UK arms suppliers had actively assisted the Egyptian military deny these very freedoms, David Cameron was accompanied by a slew of big-wigs from the UK defence industry. Among those present were Ian King, CEO of BAE, Alastair Bisset, group international director of QinetiQ, and Rob Watson, the regional director of Rolls-Royce.[376] It was 'very much in Britain's interests', Cameron claimed, that defence relationships between the UK and countries in the region be maintained and established. Certainly, without these relationships, the UK's arms-makers would be significantly out of pocket.

Despite the softly-softly support that the US and UK provided for the Egyptian protestors, the highly publicized death of 880 of them during the three-week uprising that led to Mubarak's overthrow served as a tragic reminder of a simple fact: that Western suppliers have, since 1981, been providing the means and methods to shut down Egypt's political life, engage in human rights abuses and imprison anyone who dared to speak out. But that is not the only legacy of this relationship. After Mubarak's resignation many wondered whether the Egyptian military would willingly relinquish power. A law passed in early April signalled the worst: all protests were banned and protestors threatened with imprisonment. The existing Military Council has promised elections but given their history as colleagues and confidants of Mubarak, this cannot be taken for granted.

There are powerful incentives for the military and the West to retain the status quo: billions in aid could still be extracted from the US, mounds of weapons purchased and the greasy wheels of patronage kept turning. A civilian government – especially one which has long baulked at Egypt's friendship with Israel – threatens to unravel such a system, undoing the knot of money and pragmatism that ties Egypt and the West together.

For the new military rulers, one thing is assured: if they do decide to crack down on civilian aspirations, they have the use of a considerable stockpile of tanks, jets, helicopters, mortars, artillery, light weapons, chemical agents, tear gas and riot control gear, much of it courtesy of the United States.

Egypt was not the only country to be spurred into resisting a long-time tyrannical ruler by the fall of Tunisia's government. On 15 February 2011, only days after Mubarak relinquished his leadership of Egypt, mass protests took place in Libya. Largely peaceful, they were some of the first flickers of an anti-Gaddafi movement, and were initially repressed by Libya's armed forces. Since then, Libya's rebel forces have swept through the country, despite Gaddafi's heavy-handed response. In a see-sawing contest, Libyan forces hit back with heavy weapons, including the use of cluster bombs in civilian areas.[377] Given cover by US and NATO jets that pounded Gaddafi's heavy-weapons units and battlements, the rebels, at the time of writing, appear to have finally dispatched the eccentric self-styled 'father-President', one of Africa's longest-lasting dictators.[378] It was not an easy battle: Gaddafi had stockpiled massive amounts of weapons, many of which now sit in poorly maintained bunkers and buildings and were used to repel the forces of rebellion.

The legacy of this is threefold. First, if Gaddafi's overthrow is not followed by democracy but, instead, by in-fighting, those who would wage war for control will have a seemingly endless supply of weapons to do so. The experience of Iraq and Afghanistan illustrates, although in somewhat different circumstances, how the overthrow of a tyrant can beget a long-running insurgency or civil war, drawing in the surrounding region and increasing instability. The West, already heavily committed to the region, may yet be drawn into a conflict that lasts longer than many hoped. Secondly, even if the resistance movement in Libya results in a peaceful democracy, the country will have to deal with the rotting stockpiles of a mad dictator:[379] without proper care, Libya is a country filled with potential Gerdecs. And last, but not least, there is the deep and abiding fear that, in the aftermath of chaos, Gaddafi's stockpile of conventional and biological weapons and explosives (including 10 tons of mustard gas and 1,000 tons of uranium)[380] may enter on to the region's black market, falling into the hands of the very people who would threaten Gaddafi's most faithful suppliers: the West.[381]

Since taking power in 1969, Gaddafi had become a totemic figure, spouting the fire and rhetoric of anti-colonialism while, all the time, crushing opposition at home and abroad. Laws passed soon after he took power criminalized the formation of political parties on pain of execution.[382] The press existed only in the form of the state-run media.[383] Factions that became strategically threatening frequently disappeared into the darkness of military tribunals, torture and death. Gaddafi's monomaniacal desire to influence African affairs has left criss-crossing scars across the continent. Providing training, supplies and arms (many taken from stockpiles purchased from the West and Russia), Gaddafi has, as we have shown, birthed horrors such as Charles Taylor's NPFL and Sierra Leone's RUF. By invading neighbouring Chad, Gaddafi escalated tensions between the Muslim north and African south, fuelling a long-running battle for control of the country. As we have seen, *Janjaweed* forces that committed genocide in Darfur were frequently linked to Gaddafi: many had once been Islamic Legion members, the rag-tag mercenary army Gaddafi had created to fulfil his vision of a pan-Arabic band across North Africa.[384]

If Libya does go the way of Iraq and Afghanistan or worse, those looking for explanations need only examine the ease with which Gaddafi was able to purchase billions of dollars' worth of arms since 1969, fuelled by its massive reserves of oil.[385] Since 1970, and even with a long-term UN arms embargo in place between 1992 and 2003, Libya has spent $30bn on weapons purchases.[386] Most of this was sourced from the USSR (and, more recently, Russia): a total of $22bn. But equally important were sources of sophisticated Western weapons, which Gaddafi used as major force multipliers. France and Germany made the most hay while the sun shone, earning $3.2bn and $1.4bn respectively.[387] For once, the US features lowest on the list of major arms suppliers, its sales totalling only $227m since 1970.[388]

The sheer quantity of weapons purchased is both absurd and

frightening. From Russia alone, Libya imported over 2,000 tanks, 2,000 armoured fighting vehicles, 350 artillery weapons, dozens of ships and fleets of aircraft.[389] So many weapons were purchased that there were doubts that the majority of them would ever be used. Anthony Cordesman, an expert on military affairs, reported that Libya's 'imports vastly exceeded its ability to organize, man, train and support its forces. These imports reached farcical levels in the late 1970s and 1980s, and involved vast amounts of waste on equipment that could never be crewed and operated.'[390] Because of its absurd weapons to manpower ratio, Libya had been forced to keep most of its aircraft in storage, along with over 1,000 tanks.[391]

All of this occurred despite long-running disputes with the West that threatened to derail Gaddafi's access to international arms markets: a tale of arms embargoes put in place only after the horse has bolted. In 1986, Gaddafi, powered by his commitment to anti-colonialism, focused his attention on the US, supplying weapons, funding and training to anti-US terrorists. On 5 April 1986, Libyan terrorists planted a bomb that ripped through the La Belle discotheque in Berlin, killing US servicemen who were known to frequent the venue. The US responded by bombing Libya and imposing an arms embargo partnered by EU countries.[392] Two years later, Libyan operatives planted explosives in the hold of a Pan Am flight between Germany and America. The plane exploded over Lockerbie in Scotland, killing 270 people.[393] Only a few months later, explosives tore through the body of a French UTA airliner, plunging 171 to their deaths over the Chadian Sahara. When it also became clear that Gaddafi had secretly been developing nuclear and chemical weapons, retribution was swift. In 1992, a 'mere' twenty-three years after Gaddafi took power, he was slapped with his first UN arms embargo and widespread sanctions.[394]

It marked an eleven-year period of isolation for Gaddafi. Sanctions bit into oil revenues and the arms embargo was surprisingly effective: reports suggest that Gaddafi imported less than $10m in arms every year from 1992 to 2003.[395] This confident assertion, however, may be undermined by more recent revelations. In 2010, the Institute for Security & Development Policy claimed that Belarus – home to Europe's last true dictator, President Alexander Lukashenko – had admitted to exporting $1.1bn in arms to Libya between 1996 and 2006.[396] The tiny land-locked country in Eastern Europe is known for consistently supplying some of the world's rogue states. Sitting on a massive stockpile of Soviet-era weaponry, and blessed with one of the more modernized of former Soviet economies, it has sought export markets around the world following a drastic reduction in Russian purchases. It has consistently thumbed its nose at international treaties. Belarus has agreed to salt away what remains of Gaddafi's estimated $70bn to $100bn personal fortune, which has been frozen throughout much of the Western world, thus offering a one-stop arms, banking and transportation hub for Libya's dictator.[397] Unsurprisingly, Belarus was also the last nation to fly in supplies to Libya – assumed to be mercenaries – prior to the imposition of a fresh arms embargo in 2011.[398]

Largely as a result of economic woes – Libya estimates it lost $33bn in revenues due to economic sanctions[399] – Gaddafi started to make all the right noises by the early 2000s. In 1999, he embraced free markets and globalization, flamboyantly proclaiming that 'no more obstacles between human beings are accepted. The fashion now is free markets and investments.'[400] The following year, Gaddafi indicated that the world had not passed him by, announcing that 'now is the era of economy, consumption, markets and investments. This is what unites people irrespective of language, religion and nationalities.'[401] More concretely he pronounced that he had formally abandoned his search for chemical and biological weapons and agreed to allow those associated with the Lockerbie bombing to be tried. In 2003, he finally consented to pay compensation to families of those slain in the bombing.

It marked the end of Gaddafi's isolation. In 2003, the UN arms embargo and sanctions were lifted,[402] followed a year later by those of the EU and the US.[403] Little was said then about his persistent human rights violations in his own country or his involvement in other African conflicts. Instead, he was eagerly embraced by businessmen and politicians in Europe with what some saw as distasteful haste. In 2009, the Libyan prisoner Abdelbaset Ali Mohammed Al Megrahi, incarcerated for his alleged role in the Lockerbie attack, was released from Scottish prison on compassionate grounds and returned to Libya.[404] He was reported to have fatal prostate cancer that would kill him in three months; as of June 2011, he was still alive. Many suspect that the deal was a political sop to open up key Libyan markets to the UK. Indeed, shortly afterwards, British Petroleum signed a $900m deal with Libya to explore Libyan oilfields.[405]

Of course, it was not just oilmen who basked in the sun of the newly opened desert markets of Libya. Arms-makers, especially those from Europe, pursued Libyan deals with vigour. In 2009, only weeks after Megrahi was released, Richard Paniguan of the UKTI DSO (UK Trade & Investment Defence & Security Organisation) announced that 'there have been high-level political interventions, often behind the scenes, in places like Libya, Oman, India and Algeria',[406] presumably to aid the DSO in its campaign to market British arms. Downing Street clarified the statement by laconically pointing out that 'it's hardly surprising that UKTI DSO are seeking to promote defence exports – that's their job'.[407] Other political figures also rushed into Libya's welcoming arms. Nicolas Sarkozy, for example, flew to Libya to promote French exports and business, while in 2010 Russia announced that it had agreed to a major $1.8bn arms deal with Libya that included tanks, fighter jets and air defence networks.[408] Only two years earlier, Russia had agreed to cancel Libya's $4.5bn debt incurred on old arms deals.[409]

The size of the deal was not that different from the total EU arms exports to Libya between 2005 and 2009, the most recent years for which figures are available. In these years, EU countries reported exports of just over €834m to Libya.[410] Italy did particularly well with €276m in exports between 2006 and 2009,[411] which included a €110m deal to supply helicopters that were reportedly used to attack rebel forces.[412] France came in a close second, at a total of €210m, while UK sales reached €119.35m.[413] Of course, BAE was in on the action, in the form of 200 Milan anti-tank missiles – made by MBDA, of which BAE owns a third – that were sold in 2007 and delivered in 2009–10.[414] Ironically, it is the same Milan anti-tank missiles that were transferred to the Libyan rebels from Qatar in April 2011.[415] EU supplies to Libya also included riot control gear, small arms, ammunition, electronic equipment – such as jammers from Germany that have been presumed to be used by Libya to block mobile phones and internet access in order to deny rebels access to social networking sites and organizational tools[416] – military planes and ammunition.

In total Libya imported military planes worth €278m, just under €100m in small guns and €85m in electronic equipment from the EU between 2005 and 2009.[417] Further south, Libya was able to turn to South Africa, whose President Jacob Zuma allegedly received campaign funding from Gaddafi and initially made loud protests against the imposition of a no-fly zone, before reversing his position, twice. In 2010, South Africa exported weapons worth R70m (roughly £6.5m) to Libya, after licences were granted by the South African arms export committee in 2003–9 to the value of R80.9m (£7.5m).[418] BAE was due to benefit from a US deal to sell fifty armoured personnel carriers to Gaddafi. The Pentagon deal, estimated at $77m and approved just months before the country imploded, was to have been contracted to BAE and Turkey's Nurol. The project was reportedly cancelled in late February 2011 amid the turmoil in Libya.[419]

Despite this latter action, when a fresh arms embargo was imposed on Libya in 2011, it was difficult to take it seriously: by then, the horse had already bolted and Libya's new stocks of weapons were being used – in the end fruitlessly – to repel the rebel advance. When US, NATO and EU forces were compelled to intervene in Libya, they faced a common problem in the world of blowback: negating the very arms they had exported to the country.

But the joy at the overthrow of Gaddafi – the third dictator removed in the Arab Spring – needs to be tempered with reality. Significant weapons stockpiles remain, largely unguarded and unwatched, from which arms could easily be pilfered by Gaddafi loyalists, to engage in a long-running conflict. Even if this does not happen, the temptations of war remain for those who may see Gaddafi's overthrow as an opportunity to advance their agendas – in the process almost certainly drawing the US and NATO into further morale-sapping conflict. At the very least, those who supplied weapons to Gaddafi will have to explain themselves very carefully to Libya's new rulers, who have suffered at the sharp end of Gaddafi's reign of terror. Diplomatic blowback cannot be ruled out. Neither can more literal blowback: Gaddafi's stockpiles of arms, already identified as being targeted by smugglers and looters and which include chemical and biological weapons, could easily re-emerge on the black market, being sold to any insurgent force; any terrorist group; any madman with a plan.

As the Libyan conflict raged, another battle in West Africa showed signs of abating. After ten years of fractious rule in the Ivory Coast, Laurent Gbagbo was captured on 11 April 2011 when French Special Forces arrested him in his presidential compound and handed him to the forces under the control of the competing presidential contender, Alassane Ouattara.[420] Quickly placed under UN guard and due to face prosecution for various crimes, Gbagbo has seen Ouattara, the victor in 2010 UN-monitored elections, assume the presidency. Whether peace will be forthcoming depends in great measure on Ouattara's manoeuvres and the whims of a notoriously brutal army attached to Gbagbo's cause: an army that has had little trouble building substantial stockpiles of arms.

The roots of the Ivorian conflict are complex and deep-rooted. Following independence, the Ivory Coast – also known as the Côte d'Ivoire – was headed by the deeply influential President Félix Houphouët-Boigny, who ruled the country from 1959 until his death in 1993. For all his political failings, Houphouët-Boigny had overseen the massive expansion of the Ivorian economy, known popularly as the 'Ivorian miracle'.[421] The stability of his rule and demand for Ivorian cocoa fuelled a major boom that was leveraged by the Ivorian state to invest heavily in education and healthcare.[422] When cocoa prices took a tumble in 1978, the Ivory Coast's economic model was threatened. Although all indications were of a temporary dislocation, international financial institutions such as the International Monetary Fund would only provide the loans the country needed in return for stringent structural adjustment policies.[423] They were implemented with radical haste, presaging a long-term collapse of social services as the state retreated, while the emphasis on export-led development was undermined by flat or declining prices for the Ivory Coast's cocoa supplies that were no longer protected by government subsidies and tariffs. The 'miracle' began to unravel: while the country achieved a GDP growth rate of 3.9 per cent between 1960 and 1978, the economy contracted by an annual average rate of 3.7 per cent between 1978 and 1993.[424]

Economic decline led to pressure for political reform. With Houphouët-Boigny on his deathbed, the political settlement he had fashioned fell apart.[425] The newly installed President, Henri Konan Bedie attempted to sideline his major competitor for power, Alassane Ouattara. Proclaiming a policy of *Ivorité*, Bedie blamed economic woes on foreigners and migrants who had long lived in the country, especially in the predominantly Muslim north.[426] Only *true* Ivorians, he claimed, should be allowed to participate in the electoral process. In 1995, just as a second round of multi-party elections were to be held, the Ivorian judiciary found that Ouattara's mother was Burkinabe, and he was banned from contesting the poll. Needless to say, Bedie was returned to power, although the majority of the voting population abstained in protest.[427]

Bedie's tub thumping, however, could not save his skin. In 1999, he was overthrown in a military coup d'état by General Robert Guéï after a farcical election in which over 60 per cent of the populace again abstained in protest at Ouattara's political exile.[428] Guéï's ascendance was met with outrage, and he soon faded into the background, to be replaced by Laurent Gbagbo in 2000.[429] Since then Gbagbo has ruled the Ivory Coast along much the same lines as Bedie. When in 2010, Gbagbo finally acceded to demands for an election, he was trounced by Ouattara, but refused to recognize his defeat.[430]

In reality, Gbagbo could never lay claim to controlling the country in any real sense. In 2002, rebel groups attempted to wrest control of Abidjan. Although they failed, three separate rebel groups, later united under the banner of the Forces Nouvelles, took control of the Muslim north of the country.[431] Charles Taylor, sensing an opportunity for easy money, sent troops to overrun plantations in the west, where Liberian mercenaries exported their usual brand of extreme violence and madness.[432] From 2003 onwards the country was effectively split into northern and southern portions; a 'Zone of Confidence' sandwiched in between and policed by French forces barely managed to prevent all-out war.[433] It was not nearly enough to stop a humanitarian crisis of startling proportions. Refugees who flooded into the Ivory Coast to evade the conflict in Liberia were now complemented by thousands of Ivorians going in the opposite direction. Rape, abuse, mutilation and the use of child soldiers marked the conflict, especially in the western part of the country controlled by Liberian and Sierra Leonean mercenaries.[434] When Gbagbo refused to accept his election defeat in 2010, an orgy of violence forced an estimated 150,000 Ivorian refugees into aid camps in Liberia.[435]

To survive, rebel and government forces relied on that particularly toxic mix that has plagued African conflicts and ensured their continuation: the exploitation of raw materials, both cocoa[436] and rough diamonds,[437] which were smuggled out of the country to raise funds for truck loads of arms. In 2004, the UN imposed a mandatory arms embargo in an attempt to stop a major weapons-buying spree.[438] Coming two years after the start of conflict, it was, as usual, a tragically late step. By then most of the forces in the country had added to already existing stockpiles that had been accumulated via informal smuggling networks that linked West Africa's many conflicts. For example, Robert Guéï was able to siphon off considerable matériel by acting as a thoroughfare for weapons delivered to Liberia and Sierra Leone. In return for end-user certificates, Guéï was due half of all the weapons that transited via Abidjan which had been arranged by Charles Taylor's favourite Ukrainian, Leonid Minin. Many of these arms were added to government stores that were used to prevent Ouattara's assumption of power.

When the Chairman of the UN council created to oversee the Ivorian embargo visited in 2005, he dryly noted that 'there are serious indications that large quantities of arms are at the disposal of the population'.[439] The reason: both sides in the conflict used the period right before the imposition of the arms embargo to fortify their supporters. Between 2002 and 2004, large quantities of weapons were imported from former Eastern bloc countries such as Ukraine, Romania, Bulgaria and Belarus.[440] Frequent flights from these countries were recorded as transiting into the Ivory Coast carrying air shipments of light weapons: 29 in 2002, 35 in 2003 and 16 in 2004.[441] By far the largest supplier was Belarus, which reported exporting a number of ex-Russian combat vehicles, mortars, combat aircraft, transport aircraft and spare parts.[442]

Unsurprisingly, brokers and underhand dealers flourished in the chaos of war. One particular company, Darkwood, based in neighbouring Togo, was said to be a key source of arms for the Ivorian government. In 2008, Amnesty International had accessed a shopping list of weapons that Darkwood had proposed selling to Gbagbo's troops, some of which Amnesty believed had been delivered up to the last minute prior to the imposition of the embargo. Included in the shopping list were 5,000 AK-47 rifles, 200 machine guns, 200 rocket launchers, 100 mortars, 5 million rounds of AK-47 ammunition, 2,000 RPG rounds, two combat aircraft, an Antonov-12 cargo plane, a number of armoured vehicles and an astonishing 7,000 surface-to-air missiles.[443]

The arms flows were so substantial that, when the arms embargo was applied, little attempt was made to break it. In 2005, the UN Panel of Experts on the Ivory Coast reported that 'since the Security Council measures on Côte d'Ivoire the government has restrained procurement of weapons and munitions. This is due to the intensive procurement programme prior to the embargo and limited use of arms and ammunition during the relatively short period of intensive armed conflict in 2004. Currently there is no urgent strategic need for new procurement . . . It is the same for the [Forces Nouvelles], who, in September 2002, captured large amounts of arms and ammunition and are well equipped.'[444] A two-year shopping spree, in other words, was enough to carry all parties through eight years of war, torture and the mass violation of human rights.

Admittedly, Ivorian stockpiles began to run low in late 2010. When Gbagbo refused to accept his defeat at the polls, he therefore had an urgent need for new weapons to fill the gap. Luckily for him he could turn to two of the world's pariahs for help. In March 2011, a top-secret UN investigation revealed that Robert Mugabe had secretly been shipping arms supplies to Gbagbo's forces.[445] Exactly why Mugabe decided to aid Gbagbo is unclear, although some have speculated that it may have been a function of his instinct to undermine the UN and Western powers wherever possible.[446] At the same time, the UN reported that Belarus – that ever-reliable supplier of rogue states – had delivered a cache of arms to the same forces in late February. Included in the cargo were three attack helicopters – major force multipliers in a low-tech conflict such as the Ivory Coast's.[447] Late February was a busy time for Belarus: in roughly the same period, Belarusian freighters were hurtling supplies and support to Muammar Gaddafi in Tripoli.

With Gbagbo now behind bars, Ouattara has assumed power, finally fulfilling a mandate he believes he has had since the death of Houphouët-Boigny. But it will be a transition marked by intense challenges, none greater than convincing warring parties to finally accept civilian rule. The threat remains that disgruntled rebels or Ivorian generals may nip the country's democratic birth in the bud. With such a surfeit of arms in the region, it would be distressingly easy to do.

SECTION VI

End Game

Erison's bicycle at the place where it was thrown by the explosion

20. Bringing Peace to the World

Adnan Khashoggi, displaying the remarkable lack of self-irony that seems required of successful arms dealers, sent out a Christmas card in 1986, the year in which he made a fortune from the Iran–Contra imbroglio, probably the most cynical weapons transaction of all time. In gold lettering it read:[1]

> During this holiday season we entreat those who feel the responsibility of bringing peace to the world to raise their hearts in prayer and deed that all mankind may join hands in celebrating the brotherhood of man.

Khashoggi was never the richest man in the world, but he flaunted the myth that he was with such energy that most of the world believed him. His quarter-of-a-million-dollars-a-day lifestyle was built on a very public show of yachts, planes, a dozen houses, wives, hookers, opulent gifts, excessive parties, friendships with movie stars and other jet-setters, and his companionship with kings and world leaders. His indulgent existence outshone even that of his prime benefactors, the royal family of Saudi Arabia. Eventually his public hedonism became an embarrassment for the Saudis, leading to eventual disaffection. By the end of the indulgent 1980s, Khashoggi's fortunes were in decline: his yacht gone, his planes gone, his dozen houses gone, or going, and his reputation in tatters.[2]

On 19 July 1989, he arrived in New York from Geneva first class on a Swissair flight, accompanied by Swiss law enforcement agents and handcuffed like a common criminal. He was taken to the federal courthouse on Foley Square, where he was charged with helping his friends Ferdinand and Imelda Marcos plunder the Philippines of some $160m by fronting for them in illegal real-estate deals. When United States authorities attempted to return some of the Marcos booty to the new Philippine government, they had discovered that the ownership of four large, prestigious commercial buildings in New York City had passed to Adnan Khashoggi. On paper it seemed that the buildings had been sold in 1985, but the authorities later charged that the documents had been fraudulently back-dated. In addition, more than thirty paintings, valued at $200m, that Imelda Marcos had allegedly purloined from the Metropolitan Museum of Manila, including works by Rubens, El Greco, Picasso and Degas, were being stored by Khashoggi for the Marcoses. It turned out that the pic-tures had been sold to Khashoggi as part of a cover-up.[3] He was later acquitted in one of a series of deals with prosecutors and the SEC.

In the early 2000s he was again involved in litigation, this time in Thai-land and Los Angeles, concerning allegations of stock manipulation and fraud.[4] In 2010, Khashoggi was investigated by the SEC for a stock fraud scheme. He and the company's officers agreed to a settlement without admitting or denying the allegations. Khashoggi and the company's CEO agreed to be barred for five years from serving as an officer or director of a company that issues registered securities.[5] Donald Trump, who bought Khashoggi's yacht for a knockdown price when the arms dealer first ran into financial difficulties, commented: 'Khashoggi was a great broker and a lousy businessman. He understood the art of bringing people together and putting together a deal better than almost anyone – all the bullshit-ting part, of talk and entertainment – but he never knew how to invest his money. If he had put his [arms deal] commissions into a bank in Switzer-land, he'd be a rich man today, but he invested it, and he made lousy choices.'[6] They included a major property development in Salt Lake City that went bad and a publicly traded internet company that went bust when the tech bubble burst.[7]

But it wasn't just his bad business dealings and excessively flamboyant hedonism that led to his downfall. In the den of crooks that is the shadow world of the arms dealer, there is a strange honour code, which Khashoggi violated. According to Joe der Hovsepian, Khashoggi burned himself not only because he supplied second-hand goods and claimed they were new, but, more importantly, because in the mid- to late eighties he promised a variety of people in the trade bribes that he never paid. So he was driven out of the business, and, under threat of physical harm, had to undertake to never engage in arms dealing again. He now lives a quiet life in Mar-bella in what are reduced circumstances only by the standards he had become used to in the 1980s. Asked by *The New York Times* to reflect on his career, he responded: 'Where did I go wrong? Nowhere. . . . OK, I behaved unethically, for ethical reasons.'[8]

Der Hovsepian himself remains in good shape. Having worked for the US Department of Defense, USAID and the National Democratic Institute in Iraq, Afghanistan and Liberia, despite his antipathy towards America, he is now doing good business in volatile Yemen, a focus of concern since late 2009 as the source of much global Al Qaeda activity, and another repressive regime under pressure at the time of writing.

Over the years he has supplied the Yemenis with matériel from South Africa and the countries of the former Soviet Union. His current, lucrative work is with the Yemeni Coast Guard. He provides security to escort ships on their behalf and sells them weapons and radar systems. He is also involved in other small projects in developing countries, 'providing the Third World with weapons and ammunition for war or the police force'.[9]

For a while the American Merex was run by Gerhard Mertins's son, JT, who soon left the business and became a policeman, according to der Hovsepian. JT's brother Helmut, with whom he doesn't get on, is still in the arms business, operating out of Alexandria, Virginia. Der Hovsepian claims that Helmut does some work for the CIA, which gives him deals.*

Der Hovsepian was once bested in an arms deal in Yemen by Monzer Al-Kassar, who got his start in the trade when he did business for the government of Yemen. Al-Kassar, whose long and successful career in the arms trade included involvement in Iran–Contra, fell foul of the Americans when he began to fuel the insurgency in Iraq. In 2006, when Iraq's new government released its list of most-wanted criminals, Al-Kassar was No. 26, described by an Iraqi official as 'one of the main sources of financial and logistics support' for the insurgency.[10]

Following the sting operation that lured him from his palatial home in Marbella, in February 2009 he was found guilty of conspiracy to kill Americans. After thirty years as the Prince of Marbella, Al-Kassar – 'the Peacock' – will spend the next thirty years, or as long as he lives, not in his ostentatious Palacio de Mifadil but in an American jail cell.[11]

During the trial, Al-Kassar's lawyer wanted to introduce evidence that would demonstrate his cooperation with US authorities, but the Department

---

* I was unable to verify this claim as the CIA will not divulge details of agents or associates. Helmut Mertins did not respond to repeated requests for an interview.

of Justice objected that the evidence contained classified material. The court ultimately ruled that the evidence was irrelevant. Several of Al-Kassar's friends and associates confirm that he had indeed assisted the CIA over the years, along with his brother and mentor in the arms business, Ghassan. The agency will neither confirm nor deny such suggestions.[12]

Arms dealers are often used as an instrument of geopolitics, and Al-Kassar went to great lengths to make himself useful. Many governments, including that of the United States, make clandestine purchases from international arms brokers, because using guns from their own country might betray their involvement in covert operations. 'The Al-Kassars' ability to provide governments with access to arms and equipment through irregular channels allows them to do business with high-level government officials who wish to deal "off the record" with terrorists or other politically sensitive groups,' a 1992 investigation by the US House of Representatives concluded. 'Governments who receive such services apparently "look the other way" with respect to the brothers' trafficking activities.'[13] Ghassan Al-Kassar remained close to Monzer and active in the arms business until his death in 2009, of natural causes. It can only be assumed that Monzer went too far in his support of Iraqi insurgents for the Americans' liking, and suffered the consequences.

Another network member, Nicholas Oman, remains in an Australian jail, not for his various illegal arms deals, but for paedophilia committed in Liberia. In 2006, he acknowledged that he had molested a number of under-age children during his many trips to Liberia in the early 1990s.[14] The repulsive crime was befitting of the ethics he had employed as an arms dealer: duplicitous, depraved and completely lacking in morality. His punishment was six years in prison. The government of Slovenia continues to seek his extradition from Australia.[15]

The former Liberian President, Charles Taylor, was transferred from Monrovia to The Hague in 2006 to face charges of crimes against humanity, and violations of the Geneva Conventions and of international humanitarian law. He is still in detention in The Hague and continues to protest his innocence. His undiminished sartorial elegance and high-powered defence team suggest that he has access to at least some of his vast misbegotten wealth. The British supermodel Naomi Campbell was subpoenaed to testify that at an event for Nelson Mandela's Children's Foundation in 1997 she had received blood diamonds from Taylor as a gift. She claimed not to know what they were or who they were from, a contention refuted by a fellow guest, the actress Mia Farrow, and Campbell's agent at the time. After complaining about the 'big inconvenience' of having to appear, Campbell claimed to have known nothing of Taylor, or even to have heard of Liberia.[16] The conservative American televangelist Pat Robertson was another associate of the dictator, having lobbied for his interests in the US in return for a gold-mining concession in Liberia. Robertson's spokesman denied that his support for Taylor had anything to do with the gold mine but was rather to safeguard Christians in Liberia.[17] Taylor's claimed links to US Intelligence have never been clarified.

Viktor Bout, who also worked for the Americans before running foul of them, is in the Metropolitan Correctional Center in lower Manhattan, New York City, awaiting trial. During his last weeks in Thailand, before his deportation, I managed to contact an associate of his in Bangkok. Jeff, who runs a website supportive of Viktor, claims that the Russian was never involved in anything other than transportation. Bout is expected to stand trial in late 2011, with Andrew Smulian as the main state witness. Prosecutors will aim to show that shortly before his 2008 arrest in the FARC sting, Bout sought a missile system deal in Libya.[18]

Bout's testimony could prove highly embarrassing to his captors, who, it can be assumed, will attempt to prevent him speaking about his work for a variety of US government agencies. It is crucial that the full story of his exploits in Africa, Iraq and Afghanistan are allowed to be presented at the trial. It is also important to bear in mind that, if he is found guilty, the imprisonment of Viktor Bout will be an important step against the illicit trade, but that the formal trade remains far larger and more lucrative than and in some ways as damaging as the illicit trade in weapons.[19]

Leonid Minin is a free man in Rome. By all accounts, the years of excessive drug use have left him in a semi-vegetative state.

Roger D'Onofrio, the arms dealer and proud CIA asset, killed himself having reached his late eighties. Taylor's and Minin's associate Erkki Tammivuori is still in 'the trading business', based in Lausanne, Switzerland.

Gus Kouwenhoven awaits his retrial in Holland. A technical session was to be held in the summer of 2011 to agree how to collect additional evidence without the same problems arising as in the original trial.

Count Alfons Mensdorff-Pouilly continues to live the aristocratic life in Austria, after being awarded £372,000 in compensation from the

British government for false imprisonment – almost as much as the UK fined BAE.[20] His relationship with the arms company has ended and the possibility of Austrian, Czech, Hungarian or Swedish prosecutors charging him for his role in the litany of odious European deals is slight. In late 2010, the Czech investigation, again reopened, seemed to be reinvigorated by a request to the US for assistance[21] and the suspension of a Deputy Minister of Finance and former Defense Department official who had been mentioned in the BAE case. A former US ambassador and executive of the truck-maker Tatra claimed that Martin Bartak 'had asked for millions of dollars' to resolve problems the company had in winning a multimillion-dollar contract with the Czech army.[22]

Inquiries in Hungary seem fitful at best, according to someone close to the investigation, while Austrian prosecutors remain determined to bring charges against Mensdorff-Pouilly for bribery and corruption, money laundering and making a false statement to a parliamentary inquiry. Key to the Austrian case is assistance from the notoriously secret location of Liechtenstein. However, the Austrian, Czech, Hungarian and Liechtenstein authorities are all waiting for guidance and assistance from the SFO, which by mid-2011 had not yet been forthcoming.[23]

In May 2011, BAE struck another plea bargain, this time the State Department. In return for a guilty plea on numerous charges relating to arms export legislation, BAE was fined a total of $79m the $400m levied by the DOJ a year previously. The second settlement was effectively to halt the temporary embargo on BAE exporting military matériel from the US. Read together, BAE's admissions in the settlements largely confirm the information contained in the SFO's affidavits filed in South Africa, which outlined the company's extensive range of 'covert' and 'overt' agents and maze of disguised payments.

The 'Charging Letter' in which BAE acknowledged guilt, charged the company with over 2,591 violations of the Arms Export Control Act and the International Traffic in Arms Regulations.[24] It focused on the fact that BAE inappropriately brokered articles made in the US that were integrated into its weapons systems, in particular the Hawk and Gripen.[25] Brokering of US defence articles can only be undertaken by agents registered with the US Department of State and all brokering activities have to be declared in the form of annual reports and disclosures – virtually none of which was done by BAE between 1995 and 2007.

The Charging Letter further provided an explicit acknowledgement of BAE's covert agent system. The Letter confirmed that Red Diamond had been established in 1998 'in order, *inter alia*, to conceal [BAE] brokering relationships'.[26] It acknowledged that roughly 100 payments were made to 'brokers' directly by BAE between 1998 and 2007, while a further estimated 1,000 payments were made to 'unauthorized brokers' by Red Diamond.[27] When the US State Department investigated Red Diamond's activities, it discovered that the company had entered into approximately 350 covert agreements with 299 brokers.[28]

Importantly, BAE admitted that it had made payments to key entities that we have tracked throughout this book. With regards to South Africa, it was admitted that 'Red Diamond made payments to brokers involved in securing the sale.'[29] In a disclosure in March 2010, BAE also admitted to employing eight previously unconfirmed advisers to secure the lease/sale agreements for the Gripen to the Czech Republic and Hungary. These advisers included Alfons Mensdorff-Pouilly, Valurex, CEC, Laris Overseas, Jan Hasek, Dubovny Mlyn, Manor Holdings and Omnipol.[30]

According to the 2010 plea bargain, BAE admitted to making payments of over £135m and $14m to 'marketing advisors and agents' through Red Diamond.[31] The plea bargain also made clear that BAE was aware of the dubious nature of the payments:

> After May and November 2001, BAES made payments to certain advisors through offshore shell companies even though in certain situations there was a high probability that part of the payments would be used in order to ensure that BAES was favored in the foreign government decisions regarding the sales of defense articles.[32]

In the settlements with the US government BAE thus admitted much of what it had long denied: that it had hundreds of 'agents', 'marketing advisors' and 'brokers' to whom it had paid massive sums; that the payments were largely made through Red Diamond; that Red Diamond was established specifically in order to conceal BAE's relationships with its advisers; and that at least a portion of the payments were made despite the 'high probability' that they would be used to ensure that BAE received favourable treatment in the countries in which they hocked their wares.

The State Department further cited aggravating factors in the company's behaviour, 'including the fact that certain violations were authorized by its most senior management; that violations were systemic, wide-spread, and sustained for more than ten years; that only three of the violations were disclosed, involuntarily, at the request of the Department; and that all other violations were never disclosed, but rather identified by the Department during its investigation'.[33]

The niceties of plea bargains admitting to lesser charges precludes direct accusations of corruption and bribery. But the plea bargains confirmed more than enough to make one deeply and persistently suspicious . . . and angry that a company that behaved unethically, illegally and immorally for so long got off so lightly.

On 9 September 2010, after the publication of a book in Sweden on Saab's South African deal, a group of Swedish peace organizations filed criminal charges against Saab.[34] In November of that year I met Swedish prosecutors and gave them all the information I had on the deal. Questions from the prosecutor led to Saab's admission in June 2011 that the former political adviser to the then South African Defence Minister, Fana Hlongwane, had been paid tens of millions of rand, reigniting the storm of controversy over the South African arms deal in South Africa and Sweden. Saab's admission has been widely read as final confirmation that a contractor paid bribes on the deal,[35] although whether Saab or BAE is ultimately responsible, or whether they acted in concert, is not clear.

At the time of writing Swedish prosecutors were about to make a decision on whether to reopen an investigation into Saab. The United Kingdom authorities, and BAE, were silent.

In August 2011, a leaked investigation by US compliance lawyers into Ferrostaal uncovered a string of questionable payments relating to its submarine contracts in the South African arms deal. The investigation confirmed that Ferrostaal had paid close to €35m to various 'advisers' and consultants in South Africa, all of whom had political connections to the very top. One of the confirmed beneficiaries was Tony Georgiades, who received €16.5m from Ferrostaal between 2000 and 2004. Georgiades, as the investigation noted, 'knew a number of senior politicians, including President Thabo Mbeki and possibly Nelson Mandela, and introduced senior Ferrostaal employees to these politicians'. Moreover, investigators found that 'there is little evidence to suggest that Georgiades did work commensurate with the fee received'. Another consultant, who was also paid €16.5m, was Tony Ellingford. Ellingford was hired after Ferrostaal

executives expressed a desire for 'someone with "political connections".'
Ellingford, a former defence industry executive, was widely acknowledged to be close to the Defence Minister, Joe Modise. In total,
Georgiades and Ellingford received payments that accounted for almost
25 per cent of Ferrostaal's entire revenue stream from the project. To further rub salt in the wounds, it also emerged that Ferrostaal had entered
into a joint venture with 'Chippy' Shaik as part of its offset commitments:
a mining deal in Mozambique in 2004. Chippy, as we saw earlier, was
Chief of Acquisitions in the deal, as well as brother to Mo Shaik, currently the head of South Africa's Secret Service, and Schabir Shaik,
President Zuma's 'financial adviser' who was sentenced to fifteen years in
jail for soliciting a bribe for Zuma from another arms deal contractor. The
report also detailed bribes paid to Muammar Gaddafi, which were
included in €336m in payments made by Ferrostaal to consultants around
the world that the compliance lawyers believed 'presented serious compliance issues and significant red flags'.[36]

These revelations came on the back of a series of recent scandals involving Ferrostaal. In March 2010, it was alleged that the company had paid
just under €83m ($124)[37] to key Greek politicians to win contracts to sup-
ply Greece with submarines.[38] Similarly scandalous was the company's
supply of two submarines to the Portuguese navy at a cost of about $1bn,
a deal that has also been wracked by allegations of corruption. The most
serious of these centred on Jurgen Adolff, Portugal's Honorary Consul in
Munich.[39] In January 2003, Ferrostaal signed a consultancy agreement
with Adolff, under the terms of which he would receive 0.3 per cent of
the total value of the contract. In total, Adolff received €1.6m ($2.4m)
from the company for his role.[40] Ferrostaal also entered into dozens of
consultancy agreements, including one with a Rear Admiral of the Portuguese navy.[41] In March 2010, Portuguese authorities uncovered an
invoice for €30m ($45m) that they believe was a bogus consultancy con-
tract to facilitate the funnelling of millions of euros to Portuguese
politicians.[42] Klaus Lesker, a member of Ferrostaal's executive board, was
arrested in mid-March 2010 and two other members of the board also face
investigation for a 'particularly serious case of bribing foreign officials in
connection with international business arrangements'.[43]

And also in 2010, Thales, the French company implicated in high-level
corruption in South Africa, together with the state defence company

DCNS, was ordered to pay a fine of over $800m to the Taiwanese government after being found guilty of paying bribes to inflate the price of frigates that it supplied on a $2.8bn arms deal in 1991.[44] In addition to its involvement in DCNS's Taiwanese scandal, the company faces a separate inquiry in France over allegations that it paid kickbacks to a friend of the Malaysian Prime Minister.[45] In June 2002, DCNS concluded a €1.2bn ($1.8bn) deal to supply Malaysia with submarines.[46] It later emerged that €114m ($170m) had been paid in 'consulting fees' to a company whose principal shareholder was the wife of a close associate of the Defence Minister – now the Prime Minister.[47] There has been no investigation into the corruption allegations by Malaysia, although French prosecutors eventually opened one in 2010.[48] Moreover, a translator for the Malaysian delegation negotiating the deal, who threatened to reveal its details, was murdered by a special bodyguard unit, underscoring the damage that corrupt arms deals wreak on the rule of law.[49]

In 2009, Prince Bandar bin Sultan disappeared. Reports into his whereabouts ranged from his being in a deep depression to a rumour, beloved of Saudi dissidents, that he had been jailed for organizing an attempted internal coup within the royal family. He reappeared 'from Agadir in Morocco' in September 2010 and was met at the airport by the Chief of Saudi Intelligence, his father Prince Sultan, and other princes and staff members of the National Security Council, of which he is General Secretary.[50] We can probably conclude that he had been receiving treatment for either cancer, depression, or drug or alcohol addiction. He no doubt received the best medical care in the world available to a man worth an estimated $20bn, a significant portion of which has been contributed by the taxpayers of the United Kingdom and the United States.[51]

He appears to have recovered sufficiently to return to his international diplomacy role. After Saudi Arabia's intervention in Bahrain in March 2011, in which they used their National Guard troops (trained by the UK)[52] to put down a pro-democracy uprising in the neighbouring kingdom, Bandar was dispatched to Pakistan, China and India to gather support for the Saudis' hardline approach. While in Pakistan Prince Bandar reportedly negotiated for thousands of Pakistani troops to assist in the event of the Arab Spring spreading into Saudi Arabia.[53]

After numerous stories of British arms being used to repress Arab Spring revolutions the UK government suspended arms exports to several countries. These moves, while very late, considering the weapons were already in the hands of repressive governments, were welcome. However, despite *de facto* arms embargoes on states such as Bahrain, Saudi Arabia was conspicuously not embargoed, in spite of its National Guard's intervention in Bahrain, which also utilized BAE Tactica armoured vehicles. This position has been challenged in the courts by the CAAT.[54]

Wafic Said, who made his initial fortune from the Saudis, appears well and is living in London and Monte Carlo. He is a grandee of the British establishment. I received very polite correspondence from him but he refused to meet to discuss the arms trade.

Mohammad Safadi remains a minister in the interim government currently running Lebanon.

Mark Thatcher is regarded by many as a buffoon, and, there are grounds to suspect, a corrupt one at that. But he is, by all accounts, a wealthy man. On his release from jail in Equatorial Guinea, Simon Mann called for Thatcher to face justice for his role in the farcical failed coup attempt which Mann led and which Mark allegedly funded.[55] It is as unlikely that Mark Thatcher will face justice in the UK as it is that BAE will ever face the full legal consequences of its role in arms trade corruption.

BAE briefly became the largest defence contractor in the world in 2008, surpassing for a short time the mighty Lockheed Martin.[56] The company shrugged off its record fines as pocket change.

Soon after the controversial UK settlement with the company, a number of senior investigators left the SFO, a tacit vote of no confidence in Richard Alderman's leadership of the demoralized institution. The UK Accountancy and Actuarial Discipline Board announced in October 2010 that it was initiating an investigation into KPMG's conduct as auditors of BAE between 1997 and 2007, in relation to 'the commissions paid by BAE'.[57] While acknowledging that commissions were paid, given the board's rather passive approach to its members' role in the financial implosion of the banking sector, hard-hitting results are not expected.

The SFO has another opportunity to tackle arms trade corruption with Saudi Arabia. A whistle-blower has come forward alleging bribery in a £2bn contract held by a subsidiary of EADS for the military communications of the Saudi Arabian National Guard. The passage of the contract, administered by the UK's Ministry of Defence, was allegedly smoothed with bribes of luxury cars, jewellery and briefcases of cash given to Saudi officials.[58] Will the SFO leadership rise above its abject record on arms trade matters and pursue this case with vigour and courage, regardless of any influences brought to bear on it?

The coalition government in the UK placed under review new anti-bribery legislation, in response to concerns from business that the legislation was too tough.[59] The wishes of business seem to have won the day as the revised Bribery Act and guidance on it opens several loopholes for overseas bribes. The Director of Transparency International UK slammed the changes: 'The Bribery Act, as passed by the last parliament, is one of the best anti-bribery laws in the world. But the guidance will achieve exactly the opposite of what is claimed for it. Parts of it read more like a guide on how to evade the act, than how to develop company procedures that will uphold it. It is deplorable that changes made to the draft guidance since late last year, and now enshrined in the published version, depart from international good practice in several areas. The Ministry of Justice has exceeded its brief with this final guidance which undermines the act and will limit its effectiveness. There is now a significant risk that bribery will go unpunished.'[60]

Transparency International's (TI) authoritative annual Corruption Perception Index gave the UK its lowest ever ranking for 2010, after three consecutive years of decline.[61] Those politicians most closely associated with this decline and BAE's corrupt history have moved on to greener and more lucrative pastures, as have the senior executives who plotted and led BAE's malfeasance – to senior roles in corporations, or representing unscrupulous governments around the world. Dick Evans, now Sir Richard, is chairman of the Kazakhstan State Holding Company, Samruk. He is said to be very close to the corrupt, virtual dictator, Nursultan Nazarbayev, whose family are linked to the collective of state enterprises that constitute Samruk.[62] Kazakhstan is ranked 105th in the TI Corruption Index, with a desultory score of 2.9 out of 10.[63] Evans, who describes Kazakhstan as his second home, remarked that 'As a guy who's spent most of his career in the aerospace and defence industry, I know a lot about corruption.'[64] Julian Scopes, BAE boss for Eastern Europe, was briefly made head of the company's crucial Indian operations in 2008.[65] He retired from the company in 2009.[66]

None of them has faced justice. BAE's current corporate leaders refuse to acknowledge the depth of the company's venality or its consequences. Its chairman, Dick Olver, refused my request to put BAE's side of the story. Compelled by the US DOJ to appoint a monitor to ensure that the company does not again transgress US and UK law, the company chose David Gold, a senior partner at the law firm Herbert Smith, whose prestigious clients include Prince Bandar bin Sultan.[67]

BAE's chief salesmen and protectors, Margaret Thatcher, John Major, Tony Blair and Gordon Brown, departed public life without a moment's remorse for their role in the war business. On his retirement, John Major became a member of the Carlyle Group's European Advisory Board in 1998, and chairman of Carlyle Europe in May 2001. He stood down from the once arms-business-focused private equity house in August 2004.[68]

In 2010, Tony Blair was the most unpopular Labour Party figure of recent years.[69] This blow to his ego was surely salved by his estimated £20m net worth.[70] He has addressed the Carlyle Group a number of times, at about $250,000 a time.[71] He earns about £2,000 a minute from the hedge fund Lansdowne Partners for his thoughts on geopolitics.[72] In straitened economic times, he engineered a job with J. P. Morgan Chase on a salary of $2.5m and earns a reputed $2m with Zurich Financial Services.[73] He is *pro bono* in his rather undefined position as the quartet's Middle East peace envoy – a title that evokes thoughts of George Orwell, given Blair's role in the Iraq War and with BAE. At the same time, his own commercial consultancy, Tony Blair Associates (TBA), provides strategic advice to the Kuwait government and to Mubadala, a sovereign investment fund in the United Arab Emirates. It has also entered the boutique banking business, registering with the Financial Services Authority to 'arrange deals in investments' across Europe, including several tax havens. Jonathan Powell, Blair's former Chief of Staff and a managing director at Morgan Stanley, is registered with one of Blair's companies as an adviser.[74] Even before he left office, Blair started amassing an extravagant property portfolio. He bought a £3.65m house in Connaught Square in west London and a £5.6m eighteenth-century country house in Buckinghamshire once owned by the actor Sir John Gielgud. His wife, Cherie, spent over £250,000 on Georgian and Regency furniture for it. They also acquired an £800,000 mews house next to the Connaught Square property and could pay cash for a £1.13m mews house in London for their son.[75]

Sherard Cowper-Coles, the British ambassador to Saudi Arabia who played such an important role in ending the SFO's investigation into the

Al Yamamah deal, was appointed BAE's international business development director in February 2011.[76]

Riggs Bank, that venerable Washington financial institution, is no more. Accused of hiding the ill-gotten gains of Augusto Pinochet and Charles Taylor and laundering money for Saudi and other diplomats, the bank was eventually fined $25m.[77] In 2005, it was taken over by a young upstart financial services company, its soaring golden eagle logo replaced by the nondescript, functional badge of its new owner. Sadly, most other major banks around the world continue to make a killing from the arms trade, including, most notably, Lloyds TSB, currently effectively owned by the British government, and Barclays Bank, for whom Charles Taylor's brother once worked.

With the exception of Randy 'Duke' Cunningham, who is currently incarcerated in the minimum security satellite camp at the US Penitentiary in Tucson, Arizona, Darleen Druyun, briefly, and Efraim Diveroli, all the Americans involved in the scam that is the MICC have emerged wealthy and free.

While the fate of most of those implicated in the FCPA sting operation known as the 'shot show showdown' is not yet known, many Department of Justice luminaries crowded into a Washington DC courtroom in May 2011 to see the trial of some of the defendants.[78] Whatever the outcome, the impact on the FCPA will be deep, at a time when the legislation is under threat from the US Chamber of Commerce.[79]

Erik Prince, the seemingly untouchable king of Xe (the mercenary firm formerly known as Blackwater), has taken his millions off to the United Arab Emirates, as, according to a colleague, 'he needs a break from America'.[80] Ted Wright, a top official at KBR, was named Xe's new CEO in June 2011.[81] Xe also appointed controversial former Attorney General under George W. Bush, John Ashcroft, as its new ethics chief.[82] He was a key proponent of the US Patriot Act's sweeping surveillance powers. Since leaving government he has consulted and lobbied for over thirty homeland security company clients, including Israel Aircraft Industries International.[83]

Oliver North, Dick Cheney, Donald Rumsfeld, 'Scooter' Libby, George W. Bush and the myriad corporate grandees of the defence contractors are revered by the resurgent right wing in the country.

Lockheed Martin, with the gargantuan F-35 project among many multibillion-dollar contracts, remains the pre-eminent beneficiary of the MICC.

In February 2011, years after it had bribed its way to the original cancelled deal, Boeing was duly awarded the contract to build a new fleet of tanker refuellers, which will be worth between $35bn and $100bn.[84] Achieved with massive support from Congress and the rest of the MICC, this is damning proof of the lawlessness of the American arms trade.

A few months previously, in October 2010, President Obama announced that the US would sell Saudi Arabia weapons worth $60bn over 15–20 years.[85] It is officially the largest single arms deal ever signed by the US with a foreign country,[86] and comes amid figures revealing that in 2010 Congress was notified of $102.5bn of potential foreign arms sales by the US, four times higher than the average of the previous ten years.[87] Included in the Saudi deal are eighty-four Boeing F-15 aircraft with additional upgrades to seventy F-15s already in Saudi possession, over 150 helicopters, a range of missiles, smart, dumb and cluster bombs, and helmet mounted sight and night-vision systems.[88] While Boeing is by far the largest recipient, the deal is also due to provide orders for Lockheed Martin, Raytheon, General Electric, ITT Aerospace, MD Helicopters and Sikorsky.[89]

Not that Boeing's behaviour has changed. In July 2011 the Department of Defense's Inspector General reported that the company had overcharged the Army by about $13m on $23m of spare parts for helicopters. The Army baulked at seeking the refunds from Boeing.[90]

Demonstrating both the arrogance of the defence industry and its influence over US foreign policy, as the Saudi deal was announced, Remy Nathan, vice-president of the Aerospace Industries Association, suggested that the White House and Congress should begin 'the thinking process of international sales sooner in our foreign policy and national security planning'.[91]

The extent of change in international politics since Prince Bandar first battled the Israel lobby in order to win agreement for Saudi arms deals was illustrated in the current deal by the fact that Israel was consulted in depth at a 'high level' and gave its stamp of approval.[92] The Assistant Secretary of State, Andrew Shapiro, speaking at the unveiling of the sale, promised that the deal 'will send a strong message to countries in the region that we are committed to support the security of our key partners and allies in the Arabian Gulf and broader Middle East . . .'[93]

It was, therefore, no surprise that when President Obama responded to the Arab Spring uprisings with a major speech on the Middle East in which he warned Libya, Syria and even Bahrain that 'the status quo is not sustainable' and that 'we have embraced the chance to show that America values the dignity of the street vendor in Tunisia more than the raw power of the dictator . . . After decades of accepting the world as it is in the region, we have a chance to pursue the world as it should be,'[94] the President failed to even mention or allude to Saudi Arabia – corrupt, autocratic oil supplier and buyer of billions of dollars of US weaponry.

The Saudis responded to the Arab Spring in their own inimitable manner, by spending \$130bn to pump up salaries, build houses and finance religious organizations, in an attempt to neutralize any domestic opposition.[95]

The Saudi deal is a reminder that despite an increase in Department of Justice activity against corruption in the sector, all the major companies of the MICC continue to acquire government contracts worth dizzying amounts of money. It appears that no level of abuse, law breaking or wastage will lead to debarment. The increasing importance of anonymous and unfettered contributions to electoral campaigns in the US, together with Obama's failure to bring about meaningful reform to the procurement process, and his political difficulties caused by the resurgent right wing, will ensure that the power of the MICC will only grow, with defence companies, elected representatives, lobbyists and the Pentagon continuing to benefit from its insidious impact on American politics.

And in the tradition of John Murtha, the majority leader in the Senate, Mitch McConnell, used his considerable political influence to steer \$17m of earmarks to BAE's US operation in 2010, according to Salon.com. The company's subsidiary, United Defense, donated \$500,000 to an academic centre named for McConnell at the University of Louisville, coincidentally another major recipient of McConnell's earmarks. True to his style of 'political leadership' McConnell only finally conceded his power to award earmarks, temporarily, on the same day that Representative Charles Rangel was convicted of nearly a dozen violations of Congressional regulations.[96] Legal bribery rules.

And those political leaders around the world corrupted by the arms trade, will also be rejoicing.

It appears that Robert Mugabe will only cede power when mortality intervenes. He will be heartened to know that Charles Taylor's lawyer at the Special Court in The Hague has offered to defend the Zimbabwean despot, should he ever land up behind bars in Holland.[97] The chances of a new brief for the London-based QC look slim. Meanwhile, John Bredenkamp, who has had difficulties with authorities in the EU and the US, remains free and wealthy.[98] His role on behalf of BAE in the South African arms deal will almost certainly never be brought to court, thanks to the pusillanimous SFO and the late 2010 announcement by the South African Hawks that they were closing their investigation into the deal, a shameful decision that the ANC had been working towards for almost a decade. The memorandum justifying the decision was a rambling document full of non-sequiturs, incorrect facts and spelling errors. Its contradictions were farcical, at one point arguing that the investigation should be dropped for lack of evidence only to later claim that any further investigation would be too burdensome because there was too much evidence to sift through.[99]

The Saab revelations that commissions had been paid on the South African deal led to renewed calls for the Hawks to reopen their investigations and for a judicial commission of inquiry in South Africa. At the end of July 2011, the Hawks announced that they would seek information from the SFO and Swedish authorities to determine whether there was sufficient reason to investigate further. As this book went to print, under internal political pressure and with the country's Constitutional Court deliberating an application to force him to appoint a Commission of Enquiry into the arms deal, President Zuma announced such an appointment but without details of who would lead it and its terms of reference. These will be crucial to the Commission's integrity.

Jacob Zuma sits atop an administration that is, by its own admission, wracked with corruption and wholly ineffective in delivering the basic socio-economic needs of its citizens. He continues to erode the very institutions of South Africa's democracy for which he fought. Thabo Mbeki, the sullen President-philosopher behind the arms deal and its cover-up, who was unceremoniously deposed in a bloodless party coup, founded an Institute for Leadership in late 2010.

José Eduardo dos Santos's kleptocratic rule continues in Angola, while the convictions of the defendants most directly involved in Angolagate did not hold up for long. Soon after being found guilty the majority of the accused appealed the decision. In April 2011, a large portion of the convictions were reversed. Charles Pasqua was acquitted on all charges:[100] the seventh time he has been acquitted on serious charges relating to corruption and other crimes.[101] Both Gaydamak and Falcone had their sentences drastically reduced. The main charges against both – of illegal arms brokering – were quashed, although lesser charges – abuse of corporate assets – were retained.[102] Falcone was found to have legally represented Angola and was thus able to negotiate deals on its behalf.[103] Gaydamak's sentence was halved from six to three years, while Falcone's sentence was reduced from six years to thirty months.[104] Gaydamak, still 'on the run',[105] did not attend the appeal hearing. Falcone travelled shortly after his release to meet dos Santos in Angola, claiming that his intention 'was always to fight for this juridicial [sic] truth to be told, to attain this great day of victory for the Government of Angola, for president José Eduardo dos Santos, for my family and companions that were unfairly accused'.[106] It was not a great day of victory for the people of Angola.

In late 2010 the French establishment had been hit with another arms scandal, a kickback scheme with Pakistan. French investigators have been examining allegations around *L'Affaire Karachi*, relating to a deal, made in 1994 under the government of the Prime Minister, Édouard Balladur, to sell three submarines to Pakistan for an estimated $950m. Large bribes were allegedly paid to Pakistani politicians and military officials through commission agents, a practice that was not illegal at the time. Middlemen who worked on the deal include the Lebanese arms dealers Abdul Rahman El-Assir and Ziad Takieddine. A consultancy agreement giving Takieddine a 4 per cent commission on the deal has come to light.[107]

As part of the scheme, kickbacks amounting to €2m were allegedly funnelled to Balladur's unsuccessful election campaign in 1995. The current President, Nicolas Sarkozy, was Budget Minister in the Balladur government and in charge of authorizing the financial elements of the deal. Sarkozy also acted as treasurer and spokesman for Balladur's campaign. If such a scheme did take place Sarkozy must have known about it. A Luxembourg police investigation into the scheme found that Sarkozy oversaw the setting up of two Luxembourg companies at the time.[108]

After Jacques Chirac defeated Balladur, he dismantled the system of commissions and ordered the bribes to stop. In 2002, a bus carrying staff to the Karachi site where the submarines were being constructed was bombed, killing fifteen people, including eleven French engineers. Pakistan and France blamed Al Qaeda for the attack but in late 2010 a French anti-terrorism judge investigating the bombing suggested that the attack was as a result of the cessation of the bribe payments. Chirac's former Defence Minister recently confirmed that there were kickbacks in the deal, saying: 'For the Pakistani contract, looking at the secret service reports and analyses carried out by the [defence] ministry services, one has the absolute conviction that there were kickbacks.'[109]

When questioned about the allegations by reporters Sarkozy flew into a rage, calling the allegations 'ridiculous' and 'grotesque fairy tales'. The families of those killed in the bombings say that the investigation has been hampered by the highest levels of the state refusing to cooperate or release classified documents. Should the allegations be proven true, the French state might suffer an arms trade earthquake against which the venality of Angolagate will seem a mere tremor.[110]

Omar al-Bashir, the warlord President of Sudan, despite being indicted for war crimes in The Hague, remains in charge of his shrunken country. In 2010, the new British government, in announcing its approach to foreign policy in which commercial interests take precedence over ethical issues, declared a 'new epoch' in relations with Sudan. A trade delegation from the country, which is still targeted by US sanctions, and which included senior members of al-Bashir's political party, was met in London by high-level British government officials and business leaders. The message, as expressed by the *Independent* newspaper, was clear: al-Bashir is 'Wanted by the Hague for genocide in Darfur; [and] Wanted by William Hague [the British Foreign Secretary] as a trading partner.'[111]

In Tanzania, the Cabinet minister implicated in the corrupt arms deal for which BAE was eventually fined was re-elected to Parliament in November 2010. Andrew Chenge is also the ruling party's legal adviser and chairs the party's ethics committee.[112] Meanwhile, BAE has dragged its heels in paying compensation to Tanzania. The company took over a year to form an 'independent advisory panel' to determine to whom and to what end the money should be paid. The panel is dominated by BAE executives and people with business backgrounds, and has no discernible expertise in African development. In July 2011, a British parliamentary committee accused BAE of 'dissembling' and 'lacking legitimacy' as it ignored a plan from the UK's development ministry and the Tanzanian government to use the money to buy school desks, textbooks and teachers' accommodation in an audited and transparent system. Asked whether there was any appreciation for the 'common good' in BAE's position, the company's representative answered that 'it's not a phrase we use'.[113]

Hosni Mubarak suffered the indignity of being brought to his trial on a hospital stretcher in prisoner's clothes. He denied all charges against him. Colonel Gaddafi's fate remains as uncertain as that of his country. In addition to the significant suffering experienced by loyalists, rebels and many civilians in Libya, fears also exist of further blowback, as weapons looted from government stockpiles could circulate widely. These include heat-seeking anti-aircraft missiles that could be used against civilian airliners. These missiles, which are worth thousands of dollars, could soon be circulating in the intricate webs of the shadow world.[114]

In the Horn of Africa, development activists warn that 11 million people face starvation in the world's most vulnerable region. Jeffrey Sachs argues that in an area beset by extreme poverty, hunger and the impact of climate change, the spread of further violence, abetted by the easy availability of weapons in the region, is inevitable unless action is taken now.[115]

In Albania, Fatmir Mediu, the Defence Minister who provided and executed the political master plan for the criminal enterprise at Gerdec, to materially benefit himself, his henchmen Ylli Pinari and Mihal Delijorgji, and the American arms dealers Efraim Diveroli and Patrick Henry, resigned after the explosion. Just over a year later the Prime Minister, Sali Berisha, reappointed Mediu to his Cabinet, as Minister for the Environment. Berisha, the Commander-in-Chief of the Armed Forces, whose Cabinet approved all key stages of the Gerdec operation, accepted no responsibility for the misuse of Albania's military arsenal or the disaster. He claims he did not know of the site's existence, twenty kilometres from his office.[116]

It was the criminal corruption and negligence of the Albanian government, the systemic incompetence of the US Department of Defense procurement process, and the naked greed of the American and global arms trade that caused the deaths of Erison Durdaj and twenty-five other entirely innocent people. There has been no attempt by the US to assist the people of Gerdec to gain justice. No one in the US government has been charged in the case, 'even though' as *Rolling Stone* magazine has suggested, 'officials in both the Pentagon and the State Department knew that AEY was shipping Chinese-made ammunition to Afghanistan. The

Bush administration's push to outsource its wars had sent companies like AEY into the world of illegal arms dealing – but when things turned nasty, the government reacted with righteous indignation.'[117]

No legal action has been permitted in Albania against any of the senior politicians involved in the events that led to the deaths of the villagers. The community of Gerdec are now attempting to take their case to the European Court for Human Rights. Efraim Diveroli, who is serving a four-year prison sentence for dealing in Chinese arms in relation to Gerdec, was let out on bail while awaiting trial and continued to operate in the arms trade.[118]

In August 2010, he was again arrested and charged with possession of firearms as a convicted felon and while under indictment for another offence. The affidavit submitted with his arrest claimed that he was operating a front company, Advanced Munitions, to solicit business as an arms dealer. He has no federal licence for arms brokering and, as a convicted felon, is forbidden from handling firearms. Allegedly, in July 2010 Diveroli approached a licensed arms dealer to provide him with ammunition, magazines and machine guns for resale in the Miami area. The dealer notified the authorities, who opened an investigation. Diveroli was later recorded in conversations with undercover agents in which he said he was a consultant for a company that needed help 'with the importation of 100-round ammunition drums' from a South Korean factory, which he hoped to ship into the United States at the rate of 120,000 pieces a year. Diveroli also offered rifle cartridges for sale, including a 'trial order' to sample an available inventory of five or six million rounds.[119] After his arrest he remarked to one of the agents: 'Once a gun runner, always a gun runner.'[120]

Diveroli has yet to be tried on these charges but has been debarred from business with the federal government for fourteen years. The US Army also imposed a ten-year debarment on several of Diveroli's associates and their companies.[121] David Packouz agreed to cooperate with prosecutors and was sentenced to seven months of house arrest.[122] Ralph Merrill was sentenced to forty-eight months' imprisonment on charges of major fraud and wire fraud.[123] To date Patrick Henry has not been charged with any offence.

Among those who suffer fallout from the functioning of the arms dealers, the arms companies and the politicians who support and protect them are those who have tried to bring them and their ilk to justice – the investigators and prosecutors battling with meagre resources against powerful, entrenched interests; intrepid journalists; the whistle-blowers, or 'closet patriots' as Ernie Fitzgerald calls them, who expose the truth, almost always at considerable personal and professional cost.

The real losers are the taxpayers, who pay for the wastage, corruption and flagrant misuse of their hard-earned money, and the innocent victims of conflict, socio-economic degradation and immiseration that inevitably follow the arrival of the arms merchants' deadly cargo, from Sanaa to Ciudad Juarez, Gerdec to Gaza, Mogadishu to Mullaitivu, Rangoon to Ramallah, and Kivu to Kabul.

21.   Future Imperfect

On conclusion of this book I set about passing on the hundreds of thousands of pages of documents, archives and other source materials I have collected over the past ten years on the arms trade, to the relevant investigative and prosecuting authorities around the world. I don't hold out much hope that they will be acted on, having witnessed, at first hand, the South African arms deal investigation stymied, the SFO capitulate on BAE, and the closure of investigations into the illicit trade in Italy, Sweden, Germany, India and Albania. Israel, Angola, Russia and China barely, if ever, investigate arms trade corruption.

The arms industry receives unique treatment from government. Many companies were, and some still are, state-owned. Even those that have been privatized continue to be treated, in many ways, as if they were still in the public fold. Physical access to and enormous influence on departments of defence is commonplace. Government officials and ministers act as salespeople for private arms contractors as enthusiastically as they do for state-owned entities. Partly this is because they are seen as contributing to national security and foreign policy, as well as often playing substantial roles in the national economy. In many, if not all, countries of the world, arms companies and dealers play an important role in intelligence gathering and are involved in 'black' or secret operations.

The constant movement of staff between government, arms companies, the intelligence agencies and lobbying firms the world over only entrenches this special treatment. As do the contributions of money and support to political parties in both selling and purchasing countries. This also results in the companies and individuals in this industry exercising a disproportionate and usually bellicose influence on all manner of policymaking, be it on economic, foreign or national security issues.

It is for these reasons that arms companies and individuals involved in the trade very seldom face justice, even for transgressions that are wholly unrelated to their strategic contributions to the state. Political interventions, often justified in the name of national security, ensure that the arms trade operates in its own privileged shadow world, largely immune to the legal and economic vagaries experienced by other companies. Even when a brave prosecutor attempts to investigate and bring charges against an arms company or dealer, the matter is invariably settled with little or no public disclosure and seldom any admission of wrongdoing. And the investigator, whistle-blower or prosecutor inevitably finds their career prospects significantly diminished.

While the large defence contractors like BAE and Lockheed Martin – the formal industry working hand-in-glove with government – would have us believe they are distinct from and should not be tarred with the same brush as the apparently shadier world of the black and grey trades, the reality is different. The formal and clandestine worlds interact and intersect far more regularly than they would admit. And their dependence on each other is profound. Both form, in effect, the shadow world.

The grey and black trades provide another, less formal market for the weapons and matériel produced by the formal industry. In stock market terms, it is the AIM (alternative or smaller, less regulated exchange) to the formal industry's London Stock Exchange. The grey and black markets in arms extend the practical life of products and ensure their initial value is higher than it might otherwise be. It creates a market for goods that are defective or not of a sufficient quality to be used by the formal industry. Crucially, as we have seen, almost across the world, it sells to individuals, groups, countries and companies that the large contractors and countries are unable to, for legal, political or diplomatic reasons. Those who operate in the shadow world are often used as agents, brokers and middlemen by the companies of the formal trade. While the monetary value of the shadow trade might be small in comparison to the formal trade, its role in keeping formal prices high is crucial. So too is its ability to fuel, grow and prolong conflicts which ultimately provide new markets for the formal trade.

While some form of arms industry is required in the dangerous and unpredictable world we inhabit, its special status and its intersection with the grey or black criminal world result in enormous costs to ordinary citizens and taxpayers, as the case of Lockheed Martin and the MICC so amply demonstrates.

An inestimably large amount of public money is expended on the arms trade. This is not only in direct government expenditure, which totals trillions of dollars a year,[1] but in the massive state subsidization of R&D,

export and other incentives, wastage on unnecessary weapons systems, overspending by contractors and bailouts to badly run companies. Even the jobs produced by the trade cost significantly more to create and sustain than jobs in any other sector, with larger amounts of public money spent on them. Almost any other form of job creation would be more cost-effective.

In addition, the socio-economic opportunity costs of the arms trade, especially but by no means exclusively in developing countries, are immeasurable. South Africa's experience was stark but not uncommon. In the late 2000s, as developed countries were forced to cut back their public spending to pay for the bailout of banks and the economic consequences of their hubristic investment strategies, defence-related spending was among the least affected. Instead, benefits to the poorest, education, health and public services were hit the hardest.[2]

Moreover, the manner in which the arms trade operates has an even more fundamental consequence: the diminution of democracies where they exist, and the entrenchment of undemocratic, often barbarous states, such as Saudi Arabia and Iran. The opaque way in which arms deals are concluded, habitually among a small clique of people who share a narrow self-interest, makes it impossible for the public to adjudicate whether huge amounts of their money are being used in the best possible way. The close relationship between governments and contractors, and the national security 'imperative', even undermines meaningful judicial oversight. This is made worse by the difficulty of substantive media and civil society scrutiny. National security concerns, while sometimes legitimate, are often used to hide information about malfeasance that would in no way undermine security. Legislation overseeing the trade is inadequate and in many countries non-existent. Debate about such legislation is seldom meaningfully entertained. All of this makes our hard-won democracies less transparent, accountable and honest. And it results in citizens being unable to determine whether decisions are being made in the national interest, or in some other, narrower interest.

While, obviously, the manufacture of weapons and related matériel may contribute to our general security, it always comes with a range of undesirable consequences. One is that money misspent on inappropriate fighter jets or gargantuan transport planes that cannot fulfil their purported objectives means less money for the equipment and actions that could make us more secure. The most profound of these consequences though is the blowback we experience when weapons land up in the wrong hands, as they so often do in the secretive, double-dealing world of the arms trade. The willingness of governments to utilize unreliable, often corrupt, arms dealers for the provision of intelligence is notoriously dangerous. There needs to be an acceptance and deeper understanding by governments, the military and intelligence agencies that arms dealers and weapons companies ultimately pursue their own very narrow economic interests (and those of their shareholders where they are private companies, like BAE or Lockheed Martin).

The constant expansion in the size and sophistication of the arms trade fuels and prolongs wars and conflicts. The industry, and its excessive influence, makes it easier for our governments to wage war. The extent, nature and availability of weaponry also feed organized crime, which has seen a massive global increase over the past two decades.[3] A glance at the deadly impact of virtually unlimited American weapons on the drug wars ravaging Mexico are a case in point.

The nature of the arms trade has been changing. Just as the end of the Cold War brought transformation, so too has the ease of buying weapons and ammunition online, which has started to reduce the role of middlemen and undercut regulation further. 'The advice and interaction with clients has gone because [they] buy direct from the factory now using the internet,' claims Joe der Hovsepian nostalgically. And, since 9/11, financial and other checks have become so much more stringent. As der Hovsepian again laments: 'Business was much easier at the beginning. People would arrive with $5m in cash. Now you have to fill in hundreds of forms to deposit or withdraw more than $15,000!'[4] This has made government-to-government contracts even more important as the lifeblood of the business. So even the smaller operators have to be linked to the big government players, leading to the formal and shadow trades becoming more enmeshed than ever, as we've observed in Iraq and Afghanistan. Crucially, adds der Hovsepian, 'you have to be close to the Americans, otherwise you can't deliver to your client. And also the Israelis, who will supply anyone who pays money.'[5]

China is the emerging force in the arms business and an alarming threat to the already under-regulated trade, given its insouciance towards the abuse of human rights, as we have seen. It is estimated that the country is the second-largest spender on defence and the seventh-largest exporter of weapons and matériel.[6] In addition to being the largest supplier to Africa as part of its broader diplomatic strategy in the continent over the past decade or so, China's major customers include Pakistan, Egypt, Bangladesh and India. South America is becoming a target market for Chinese sales as well. The Burmese military junta was a large customer during the 1990s, but now favours Russian, Ukrainian and Indian suppliers.[7] China has been a long-time seller to Iran, Sudan and Zimbabwe. In addition, in the year leading up to the Sri Lankan army's massacre of tens of thousands of Tamil guerrillas and civilians between January and May 2009 – during which war crimes and crimes against humanity were most likely committed, according to the UN[8] – China 'supplied a billion dollars worth of aid, including fighter jets'.[9]

For much of the twentieth century China was unable to match the technical standard of weapons produced in the USSR and the West. Where quality was lacking, however, quantity made up for it. Billions of dollars were poured into the defence industry, creating a sprawling complex of over 2,000 firms and 3 million employees by 1993.[10] The industry has been comprehensively restructured since the late 1990s and, while problems remain, huge strides have been made in technological capacity.[11]

In 2011, in a blaze of publicity, China unveiled its new J-20 stealth jet, a major flexing of muscle considering that the US is the only country that currently has stealth jets in service.[12] Experts remain divided on whether the rapid advances necessary to produce the jet could feasibly have emerged from China's defence industry. Sceptics suggest that the technology was developed from the remains of a US stealth fighter that crashed over Serbia in 1999.[13]

NORINCO is China's best-known defence company, while 'private' companies such as Huawei are heavily involved in producing and selling dual-use technologies.[14] China sells at 'friendship prices' to make up for the still inferior quality of some of its equipment. What is certain is that China's role in the trade will continue to grow at a frightening rate, as it becomes a more and more formidable economic and political force. It is unclear whether its growing status as an emerging superpower will have a positive impact on its ethics or attitude to human rights.[15]

Despite the emergence of Dubai as an important terminus for arms deal-making, and the Emirates more broadly for transportation, Beirut remains an important fulcrum, especially for the Arab arms business. India and Brazil meanwhile are the two most attractive emerging markets for sales.

Latin America was overwhelmed by arms deal corruption during the 1970s heyday of military dictatorships. It is cleaner now, but corruption continues. Chinese arms have been turning up in Peru, Bolivia and Colombia. It is estimated that Bolivia is in the process of spending $100m on weapons from Russia. Brazil, whose own domestic industry is growing, has increased its defence spending as it has modernized and grown economically. Chile still has a law, a legacy of the Pinochet era, that dedicates 10 per cent of all copper revenues to defence spending. Mexico buys to battle the drug cartels, sourcing its equipment from the US and Central America, much like the warlords. Colombia has the fifth-largest helicopter fleet in the world, used against the FARC and to keep an eye on its rival, Venezuela. It receives vast amounts of equipment from the US as part of the War on Drugs. FARC itself receives weapons from China and various sources in the shadow world. Hugo Chavez fears attacks from unfriendly states in his immediate neighbourhood and to the north and has consequently been a big spender on helicopters, tanks and missiles, mainly from Russia. It is claimed that a Kalashnikov factory is due to open in Venezuela in late 2011.[16]

India and Pakistan are awash in armaments, including nuclear weapons. The Pakistanis have historically been supplied by the Chinese, the French and the Americans. Since 9/11, Pakistan has been the third-largest recipient of US military assistance: the three years after September 11 saw a 50,000 per cent increase in comparison with the three previous years.[17] Historically this military support has been accompanied by constant blowback, as matériel finds its way to the regions around the frontier with Afghanistan, which are populated by militants who have close links to Pakistan's intelligence services. Tensions have increased considerably between the Americans and the Pakistanis in the aftermath of the assassination of Osama bin Laden at the compound he had been living in close to an army base on the outskirts of the Pakistan capital. Arms deals in the country continue to be shrouded in allegations of massive corruption.[18]

India's new-found wealth has seen a significant increase in its recent defence purchases, with military expenditure reaching $36.6bn in 2009, excluding nuclear development. Its arms purchasing has, at times, made it the largest weapons buyer among developing nations.[19] In addition to spending $25bn on arms between 2007 and 2011, India is currently arranging to buy $42bn of weaponry.[20] This has certainly focused the minds of all the big Western manufacturers, as well as Russia, which has historically been India's largest supplier. The US has been gaining ground in recent years. It appears, though, that Russia, the US and Sweden have been sidelined in favour of the European Eurofighter consortium or the French in pursuit of an $11bn contract for jet fighters.[21] However, the endemic corruption so evident in the ill-fated Bofors deal has not disappeared, despite haphazard attempts to debar companies caught paying bribes. A source told me of a senior Indian Army General involved in procurement who would not allow a weapons salesman past his door without a box of Johnnie Walker Blue Label whisky. 'What is Blue Label?' inquired the source. 'Way beyond your means, my boy,' came the reply.*

The global desire for weapons and matériel shows little sign of abating, despite the economic difficulties of the past few years in most developed countries. Given the industry's unavoidable existence, a number of committed NGOs have attempted to ensure that this business which counts its profits in millions and its losses in lives is compelled to play by rules acceptable to the broader society, limiting the harm that it does. In recent years, led by Amnesty International, Saferworld, IANSA and Oxfam, among others, their efforts have largely focused on the achievement of a multilateral code of conduct. Due to these efforts, in 2009 the UN committed to pursue an international Arms Trade Treaty (ATT) with the goal of it being negotiated and signed in 2012. The treaty, if it is ultimately signed, will undoubtedly be an important step forward. It will refocus attention on the arms trade, a focus which has been largely missing in the national security tumult following 9/11. And it will provide an added tool for citizens to hold their governments to account.

But sadly, just like the EU Code of Conduct, which excludes consideration of government-to-government deals and is only casually implemented,

* The arms trade in China, Latin America, and India and Pakistan all warrant books of their own. For more detail and reading on the arms trade in these countries see www.theshadowworld.com.

the ATT is likely to fall far short of what is required to curb this network of greed and death. It will have no impact on the systemic 'legal bribery' that is the US arms business. It is of course unlikely that Zimbabwe, North Korea, Iran or Burma will sign any such treaty, but China, Russia, Pakistan, and possibly even India, Israel and Brazil might also refuse to sign up to anything that places real curbs on their arms-trading activity. The US has indicated in early negotiations that it wants a treaty that China and Russia will ratify. This raises the question of whether a weak, even meaningless, treaty might be more damaging than no treaty at all. In the end it might simply provide the current unacceptable activities of the global arms trade with a veneer of respectability.

To be most effective, the ATT would need to include strong, enforceable anti-corruption mechanisms; to prevent the export of arms where they may increase conflict, or have a negative effect on human rights and/ or socio-economic development; to exercise greater control over the transportation of weapons; to either ban offsets or open them to far more scrutiny; as well as to impose far greater transparency on governments and companies, including the compulsion to reveal publicly how much and for what agents, brokers, dealers and middlemen are paid. And it would need to establish a coordinated international monitoring and enforcement body to police it.

Where there is a genuine need to keep aspects of an arms deal secret, this information should be made available for scrutiny by a group of senior judges, who are given the power to determine the validity of the need for secrecy. In addition, if the industry is to be allowed to conceal aspects of its activities, then in return it should accept certain prohibitions in the interests of making it less corrupt and damaging. Because of the close links between governments and arms companies and dealers, and the sensitive nature of the product being sold, funding of political parties or payments to politicians by arms companies or those linked to them should be made illegal.

Arms companies that continually flout laws and regulations should be debarred from tendering for government contracts until they have reformed their practices to the satisfaction of independent monitors. And both international and domestic criminal law should be used to prosecute arms companies and their representatives for selling weapons that are ultimately used for perpetrating crimes, not just where the arms vendors intend the ultimate crimes, but also when they are aware of a substantial likelihood that their commerce will contribute to this type of violence.[22]

While 2010 saw the opening of negotiations on the ATT, it also marked a high point in revelations of arms trade corruption.[23] The reality is that there will be no change in the way in which the arms trade operates unless the biggest producer and consumer of weapons, the USA, is willing to change. Is it feasible for a President in modern-day America to lessen the unaccountability, the deception and the iron-like grip on power and influence that the political, military and economic interests of the military-industrial-Congressional complex exercise? Or are we destined to continue living in a world dominated by the interests of this largely unelected and deeply flawed iron triangle?

During the course of the twentieth century, the trade in arms made viable and fuelled conflicts that cost the lives of 231 million people.[24] The first decade of the twenty-first century has, if anything, been more violent.

A basic commitment to universal human rights, equality and justice, to the belief that it is better to save a life by feeding a hungry stomach than to take a life by producing another deadly weapon, demands that this trade, one of the most destructive and corrupting in human history, cannot be allowed to continue in its largely unregulated, unscrutinized current form.

Acknowledgements

This project would never have seen the light of day without David Godwin, my inspirational agent, who shaped my thinking and its presentation and ensured that the project found the best possible home. That home is Hamish Hamilton/Penguin, where Simon Prosser not only bought the book but has thrown himself into it with a commitment and passion that is beyond the dreams of any author. He has been as much a partner in the project as a publisher. His constant advice and superb, tireless editing have been invaluable.

Simon, together with Penguin's rights team of Sarah Hunt Cooke and Kate Burton, found publishers around the world with similar enthusiasm for the book. Eric Chinski and Jonathan Galassi at Farrar, Straus and Giroux have also given their time, energy, intellect and passion. My previous South African publishers, Jonathan Ball, have again done me proud in my 'home market'. Jonathan himself and Jeremy Boraine, with their courage and audacity, are the ideal publishers for a political book in a highly politicized market. In Germany Günter Berg and Jens Petersen of Verlag Hoffmann und Campe have been not just highly appropriate, but also enthusiastic and wonderfully committed publishers; as have Floor Oosting at the Dutch house Uitgeverij de Bezige Bij and Elisabet Navarro at Edicionces Paidos Iberica in Spain. It has been an honour and a pleasure to work with all of them.

At Hamish Hamilton/Penguin I would also like to thank the remarkable Anna Kelly (with tireless assistance from Sharmila Woollam) and Ellie Smith, Alex Elam, Matt Clacher and Joe Pickering for their enthusiasm, patience and skill. Similarly Gabriella Doob and Kathy Daneman at FSG and Anika Ebrahim, Ingeborg Pelser and Francine Blum at Jonathan Ball. Thanks also to the whole team at DGA. David Hirst did a masterful job of legal-reading the book in a remarkably pain-free manner. Henry Kaufman contributed similarly from the US, as did Mark Rosin in South Africa. Nicola Evans at Penguin managed and oversaw the process with great expertise and efficiency. Mark Handsley was a highly skilled, forensic and sympathetic copy-editor. Their efforts contributed significantly to the final text.

Many other people have assisted and collaborated in the writing of this book in a multitude of ways.

I could not have written a book about so vast a topic without considerable research support. I have been privileged to work with Paul Holden and Barnaby Pace, the primary researchers. Their dedication, attention to detail and indefatigability (not in the George Galloway sense) have been heroic and sustaining. Barnaby's activism and deep knowledge of the UK arms trade, as well as his determination and willingness to ferret out every bit of information, has been invaluable. Paul's skills as a historian, archivist and author in his own right were irreplaceable. Not only did he, like Barnaby, make sense of mountains of impenetrable documents and information, but he wrote early drafts of the sections on the Merex network, Africa, Iraq and Afghanistan. They, like all the others, are not culpable for any errors in the final product. That is my responsibility alone. But most of what is good in it has its roots in their work. I have loved working with them and am privileged to call them friends.

Thanks also to Ben King, who undertook research in the US. And to Mia Allers for two creative and clear graphics.

Tim Salmon translated Laurent Leger's fascinating book on the French arms trade, and Cristina Massaccesi produced superb translations of difficult Italian documents. Elisabeth Scheder-Bieschin, Judith Leeb and Bigna Pfenninger all assisted with German translations.

Michael Healy and Sally Crawford transcribed lengthy interviews.

A vast number of journalists, researchers, academics, businesspeople and activists around the world were generous with their time and information and patient with my constant queries: David Leigh, Misha Glenny, Amira Hass, Doug Farah, Andrew Cockburn, Mary Jacoby, Christopher Matthews, Ardian Klosi, Lorenc Vangjell, Leart Kola, Andi Kananaj, Yllka Lamce, Claudio Gatti, Lowell Bergman, Dina Rasor, Frida Berrigan, Ken Silverstein, Laurent Leger, Joe Roeber, Mark Pyman, Laurence Cockroft, Paul Dunne, Gary Busch, Mark Hollingsworth, Anthea Lawson, Erick Kabandera, Markus Dettmer, Martin Staudinger, Brian Wood, Brian Johnson-Thomas, Peter Danssaert, Alan Bacarese, Juanita Olaya, Matt Schroeder, Inigo Guevara, James Stewart, Adam Isaacson, Jeff Halper, Ronen Bergman, Yossi Melman, Dalit Baum, Merav Amir, Nick Wood,

Aram Roston, Reuben Johnson, David Stoffel, Rachel Stohl, Roy Isbister, Oistein Moskvil Thorsen, Magnus Walan, Rolf Lindahl, Nils Resare, Per Hermanrud, Erik Dalunde, Otfried Nassauer, Wendela de Vries, Ann Feltham, Ian Prichard, Sarah Waldron, Nick Gilby, Nick Hildyard, Sarah Sexton, Mark Pieth, Daniel Thelesklaf, Sasha Polakow-Suransky, Sam Perlo-Freeman, Paul Holtom, Hugh Griffiths, Mark Bromley, Susan Jackson, Joey Fox, Abi Dymond, Helen Close, Chris Rossdale, Pierre Sprey, Winslow Wheeler and Sue Hawley.

My thanks to Joe der Hovsepian, Alfons Mensdorff-Pouilly (and his assistant, Susanne Luka), Thomas Tjäder and others who have wished to remain anonymous who agreed to talk to me at length and engage with me thereafter, despite the very different views we hold about the arms trade.

The following not only gave of their time and wisdom but also read extracts of the manuscript, and saved me innumerable embarrassments: Bill Hartung, Lora Lumpe, Chuck Spinney, Stephen Ellis, Shir Hever, Jimmy Johnson, Fredrik Laurin, Rob Evans, Jeff Abramson and a number I cannot name.

I have drawn heavily on Bill Hartung's exceptional work, especially on Lockheed Martin. Through his books, conversation and emails he has been a source of invaluable information and constant support. I have also used Chuck Spinney's experience inside the Pentagon to paint a picture of the MICC. In addition to two long interviews and numerous emails from around the world, I have also used other interviews he has given and his own writing. Chuck has been generous with his time, ideas and contacts as well as constantly encouraging.

The South African fellow travellers who continue to struggle and to hope: Terry Crawford-Browne, Gavin Woods, Raenette Taljaard, Patricia de Lille, Richard Young, Sam Sole, Stefaans Brummer, Mzilikazi wa Afrika, Adriaan Basson, Zackie Achmat and Hennie van Vuuren.

To those who make the virtuous networks happen: Mungo Soggott, who introduced me to, among many others, the larger-than-life Paulo Fusi, who was so generous in providing me with a veritable treasure trove of material on the shadow networks, and Alex Yearsley, who was also responsible for the introduction and a couple of Tuscan adventures. To Nigel Brett, who provided a bed and encouragement in Rome.

And to Jonny Steinberg and Mark Gevisser, South Africa's most talented non-fiction writers, who are always available with advice, friendship and love.

A special thanks to the investigators, prosecutors, law enforcers and agents who were willing to talk to me.

Thank you most especially to all those I cannot name because of the secretive nature of the trade and the vindictiveness of governments and some corporations. Thank you for the information, insight, advice and mostly for your bravery. You are the 'closet patriots' to whom this book is dedicated.

And to Feruzan Durdaj and the community of Gerdec who have been so willing to talk to me, and for their strength and conviction.

I could not have completed this project or grown it beyond the original idea of the book without the generous assistance of the Open Society Institute and Foundations, with whom I had a generous Fellowship for eighteen months. The network of people within the Open Society community is quite extraordinary and enabled me to explore countries and ideas I had never thought about. Thank you to Jonas Rollet for introducing me to Albania and to the amazing office in Tirana, especially Andi Dobrushi and Llukan Tako, to the teams in Brussels, Bulgaria, Budapest, Cape Town, Johannesburg, London and, of course, New York and Washington DC. Thanks to Anthony Richter, Tom Kellogg, Sandi Coliver, Sarah Pray and Ken Hurwitz, who has become a valued colleague and collaborator. An especial thanks to the remarkable Fellowship team of Lenny Bernardo, Steve Hubbell, Bipasha Ray, Lisena de Santis and Alia Ahmed. For support, advice, thought and friendship. And to the wonderful group of Fellows they have introduced me to.

To my Cape Town family who always provide shelter, sustenance, support and love: Lesley, David, Emma and Julia Unite.

To my New York family who do likewise and are turning this project into something 'beyond a book': Anadil Hossain, Driss Benyakleef, Joslyn Barnes and Ashish Segal.

To my London family: my 'landlord' Kishon Khan, my 'tech guru' Viquar Chamoun, my baba and ma who provide unending support and love, and in Ma's case turbo networking as well.

And to my little family: Simone, Misha and Maya, who have had to sacrifice more than anyone else so that this project could be realized. Thank you for your love, understanding, patience and tolerance. You are my world without shadows.

Finally, my sincere apologies to anyone whom I might have overlooked. To try and recall all those who have assisted me over the past ten years of working on the arms trade was almost as big a challenge as the work itself. My thanks to you all.

Andrew Feinstein, London, August 2011

Notes and References

Prologue

1 This account is drawn from Daniel Bergner, *Soldiers of Light* (London: Penguin Books, 2004); Lansana Gberie, *A Dirty War in West Africa* (London: Hurst & Company, 2005); and reports compiled by Human Rights Watch.

Introduction

1 *SIPRI Yearbook 2010* (Oxford: OUP, 2010); Sipri Updates; US Census Program, 'World POPClock Projection', figure for 1 January 2011, http://www.census.gov/ipc/www/popclockworld.html; and GDP based on *CIA World Factbook*, 'World Economy', GDP (purchasing power parity) of $74.48tn, https://www.cia.gov/library/publications/the-world-factbook/geos/xx.html.

2 'FY 2012 Base Defense Budget Represents a Turning Point', Center for Strategic and Budgetary Assessments, 14 February 2011, http://www.csbaonline.org/publications/2011/02/fy-2012-base-defense-budget-represents-a-turning-point/.

3 Joe Roeber, 'Hard-Wired for Corruption', *Prospect*, 28 August 2005.

4 Quoted in Anthony Sampson, *The Arms Bazaar* (London: Hodder and Stoughton, 1977) and often ascribed to the American arms dealer Sam Cummings.

5 Andrew Feinstein, *After the Party* (Jeppestown: Jonathan Ball, 2007; London: Verso, 2009); Andrew Feinstein, Paul Holden and Barnaby Pace, 'Corruption and the Arms Trade: Sins of Commission', in *Sipri Yearbook 2011* (Oxford: OUP, 2011).

6 Roeber, 'Hard-Wired for Corruption'.

7 Bloomberg, 21 April 2011, http://www.bloomberg.com/news/2011-04-21/lockheed-martin-f-35-operating-costs-may-reach-1-trillion.html. The quotation is from an interview the author conducted in May 2011 with a former Pentagon weapons analyst and designer, Pierre Sprey.

8 C. Wright Mills, *The Power Elite* (Oxford: OUP, 1956).

9 Farewell Address, 17 January 1961.

10 Chalmers Johnson, *The Sorrows of Empire* (London: Verso, 2004); Nick Turse, *The Complex* (London: Faber and Faber, 2008).

11 I will use the American spelling 'defense' when referring to the American Department and the British 'defence' in all other cases.

12 Turse, *Complex*.

13 David Bromwich, 'The Co-President at Work', *New York Review of Books*, 20 November 2008, Vol. LV, No. 18.

14 Gary K. Busch, 'The Chinese Military-Commercial Complex: The Globalisation of the Chinese Military Corporations' (unpublished).

15 Gary K. Busch, 'A Spectre is Haunting Europe: Putin, the Siloviki and Vampire Communism' (unpublished).

16 See Chapter 19 for details.

17 'EU Arms Exports to Libya: Who Armed Libya?', dataset spreadsheet downloaded from www.guardian.co.uk.

18 See, for instance, David Hambling, *Weapons Grade: Revealing the Links between Modern Warfare and Our High-Tech World* (London: Constable, 2005).

19 Discussion with Professor James Stewart, former Appeals Counsel, Office of the Prosecutor, International Criminal Tribunal for the former Yugoslavia, and leading academic in the area of corporate responsibility for international crimes.

Section I: The Second-Oldest Profession

1. Sins of Commission

1   George Bernard Shaw, *Major Barbara* (1907; Harmondsworth: Penguin Books, 1945, 1960).

2   Ibid.

3   Anthony Sampson, *The Arms Bazaar* (London: Hodder and Stoughton, 1977), pp. 51–2.

4   This account of Zaharoff's life and times is drawn from a wide range of sources, including Sampson, ibid; Donald McCormick, *Pedlar of Death* (London: MacDonald, 1965); Bernt Engelmann, *The Weapons Merchants* (London: Elek Books, 1968); Richard Lewinsohn, *Sir Basil Zaharoff* (London: Victor Gollancz, 1929); Robert Neumann, *Zaharoff, the Armaments King* (London: Allen & Unwin, 1938); H. C. Engelbrecht and F. C. Hanighen, *Merchants of Death* (New York: Dodd Mead & Company, 1934); Guilles Davenport, *Zaharoff, High Priest of War* (Boston: Lothrop Lee and Shepard Company, 1934); George Tallas, *Peddler of Wars* (AuthorHouse, 2007). For more information on Zaharoff's life and times see www.theshadowworld.com.

5   *London Sunday Chronicle*, 29 November 1936.

6   Engelmann, *Weapons Merchants*, p. 182.

7   Ibid., p. 184.

8   Ibid., p. 183.

9   Ibid.

10 Ibid., pp. 183–4.

11 Evidence given at an official inquiry, quoted in McCormick, *Pedlar of Death*, p. 74.

12 McCormick, *Pedlar of Death*, pp. 77–9 and 88.

13 Ibid., pp. 62–8.

14 Quoted in Sampson, *Arms Bazaar*, p. 54.

15 Ibid.

16 Engelmann, *Weapons Merchants*, p. 185.

17 Lewinsohn, *Sir Basil Zaharoff*, p. 102.

18 McCormick, *Pedlar of Death*, p. 118.

19 Ibid., p. 120.

20 Ibid., p. 143.

21 Quoted in Sampson, *Arms Bazaar*, p. 57.

22 Engelmann, *Weapons Merchants*, p. 186.
23 Ibid.
24 Ibid.
25 This section draws extensively on the authoritative account of Sampson, *Arms Bazaar*.
26 Royal Commission 1935–6, Minutes, p. 544, Q3989.
27 Quoted in Sampson, *Arms Bazaar*, p. 70.
28 Summarized from the League of Nations' Six Points, quoted in Sampson, *Arms Bazaar*, p. 71.
29 J. D. Scott, *Vickers: A History* (London: Weidenfeld and Nicolson, 1962), p. 144.
30 Sampson, *Arms Bazaar*, p. 76.
31 Ibid., p. 77.
32 Ibid.
33 *Chicago Daily News*, 3–5 August 1933.
34 Sampson, *Arms Bazaar*, p. 78.
35 Quoted in ibid., p. 79.
36 Sampson, *Arms Bazaar*, p. 79.
37 Ibid., p. 83.
38 Royal Commission 1935–6, Minutes, p. 536, B3866.
39 Ibid., pp. 300–370, B3866.
40 Drawn from Sampson, *Arms Bazaar*.
41 This account of the post-Second World War arms trade draws on Sampson, *Arms Bazaar*, among others.
42 J. L. Sutton and G. Kemp, *Arms to Developing Countries 1945–65* (London: Institute for Strategic Studies, 1966), Graphs 1 and 2.
43 Sampson, *Arms Bazaar*, p. 108.
44 See *Plowdon Report on the British Aircraft Industry* (London: HMSO, 1965), Cmnd 2853.
45 Robert L. Perry, *A Dassault Dossier* (Rand Corporation, 1973), from which this portrait is drawn.
46 Charles Gardner, *British Aircraft Corporation: A History* (London: B. T. Batsford Ltd, 1981), p. 16, and from whom this analysis is drawn.
47 Ibid., p. 278.
48 'Rolls-Royce and BAE in secret plea to Downing Street', *Sunday Times*, 16 March 2008, http://business.timesonline.co.uk/tol/business/industry_sectors/engineering/article3558 484.ece.
49 History section of Heckler and Koch website, http://www.heckler-koch.de/History.
50 'Milestone for BAE as its trade with America outstrips MoD business', *The Times*, 10 August 2007, http://business.timesonline.co.uk/tol/business/industry_sectors/industrials/ article2231494.ece.
51 Robert Lacey, *Inside the Kingdom* (London: Hutchinson, 2009).
52 'Saudi Arabia', US Energy Information Administration, Independent Statistics and Analysis, http://www.eia.doe.gov/cabs/Saudi_Arabia/Background.html. There is some doubt as to whether the levels are as high as claimed. See John Vidal, 'How much oil does Saudi Arabia actually have?', *Guardian* Environment Blog, 15 February 2011, http://www. guardian.co.uk/environment/blog/2011/feb/15/oil-saudi-arabia-reserves?INTCMP=SRCH, and Paul Mobbs, *Energy Beyond Oil* (Leicester: Matador Publishing, 2005).
53 'Russia becomes leading oil producer, BP says', BBC, 9 June 2011, http://www.bbc.co.uk/ news/10275183.

54 *CIA World Factbook*, https://www.cia.gov/library/publications/the-world-factbook/geos/sa.html.

55 Daniel Yergin, *The Prize: The Epic Quest for Oil, Money and Power* (New York: Simon & Schuster, 1992), p. 300.

56 'Saudi Arabia', in *Amnesty International Report 2009*, http://thereport.amnesty.org/en/regions/middle-east-north-africa/saudi-arabia.

57 Sampson, *Arms Bazaar*, interview with Edwards, p. 158.

58 John Stonehouse, *Death of an Idealist* (London: W. H. Allen, 1975), p. 50.

59 Sampson, *Arms Bazaar*, p. 159, citing 'Multinational Hearings, part 12, 693, 697'.

60 Ibid., Chapter 11.

61 'BAE in Saudi Arabia', based upon a BAC document that can be found at http://image.guardian.co.uk/sys-files/Guardian/documents/2007/05/28/cho5doc01.pdf.

62 'How to Sell an Air Force', II, *World in Action*, Granada TV, 26 January 1976.

63 Quoted in Mark Phythian, *The Politics of British Arms Sales since 1964* (Manchester: Manchester University Press, 2000), p. 87.

64 Document published by the *Guardian* at http://image.guardian.co.uk/sys-files/Guardian/documents/2007/05/28/cho5doc01.pdf.

65 According to the *Guardian*, the documents FCO 8/2346, FCO 8/2347 and FCO 8/2345 showing this dispute are being held secretly by the Foreign Office. 'Officials claim that disclosure of the documents would damage relations between Britain and Saudi Arabia, "not least because of the competing claims between Mr Edwards and Prince [Abdul Rahman] but also they contain information about Saudi Arabia's defence capacities".' According to the Foreign Office, 'Prince Abdul Rahman's claim was struck out for want of prosecution. Mr Edwards's claim was withdrawn by agreement in 1975', http://www.guardian.co.uk/world/2007/jun/08/bae32.

66 Sampson, *Arms Bazaar*, p. 162.

67 UK Foreign and Commonwealth Office, PRO: FO 371/185496, Jeddah to FO, 1 August 1966.

68 Sampson, *Arms Bazaar*, p. 162.

69 'BAE in Saudi Arabia', *Guardian*, 'The BAE Files', http://www.guardian.co.uk/baefiles; and Phythian, *Politics of British Arms Sales*, p. 213.

70 'BAE in Saudi Arabia', letter from Douglas Henley to Frank Cooper on 12 January 1977, *Guardian*, 'The BAE Files', http://image.guardian.co.uk/sys-files/Guardian/documents/2007/05/29/cho5doc04.pdf.

71 The government auditor, Sir Douglas Henley, found that 'The transactions pass through the Ministry accounts. . . . The total consultants' fees seem likely to exceed £30m. . . . The auditors examining [BAC's] costs on the ministry's behalf have stated they have no means of ascertaining the identity of the recipients. It seems to me that the ministry's agreement to special provisions in regard to the vouching of BAC's payments, coupled with their exercising a judgement on the level of commission acceptable as "admissible costs", involves the ministry in these arrangements', ibid.

72 'The unlovable Saudis', Willie Morris's Valedictory Dispatch, *Guardian*, 'The BAE Files', http://image.guardian.co.uk/sys-files/Guardian/documents/2007/05/29/cho4doc01.pdf.

73 'The unlovable Saudis', letter from Willie Morris to H. J. L. Suffield, 11 February 1970, *Guardian*, 'The BAE Files', http://image.guardian.co.uk/sys-files/Guardian/documents/2007/05/28/cho4doc03.pdf.

74 'The unlovable Saudis', dispatch from the British embassy at Jeddah to David Owen, 3 May 1977, *Guardian*, 'The BAE Files', http://image.guardian.co.uk/sys-files/Guardian/documents/2007/05/28/ch04doc04.pdf.

75 'The culture of bribery that became government policy', *Guardian*, 8 June 2007, 'The BAE Files', http://www.guardian.co.uk/world/2007/jun/08/bae10; Cooper Directive at http://image.guardian.co.uk/sysfiles/Guardian/documents/2007/06/01/ch08doc09.

76 In response to a Freedom of Information request on the subject, the following answer was received on 18 March 2010:

> First, I can inform you that we have found no record of any further revisions of the Cooper Directive following the revision on 9th November 1994 which was issued by Sir Christopher France GCB, then Permanent Secretary of the Ministry of Defence, to the Head of the Defence Export Services Organisation (DESO). The changes made in 1994 reflected changes in the role of DESO, which differed in a number of respects from the Defence Sales Organisation, and which by then, neither engaged agents nor paid commissions.

77 James Callaghan, quoted in 'Britain blocks reform', *Guardian*, 8 June 2007, 'The BAE Files', http://www.guardian.co.uk/baefiles/page/0,,2095820,00.html.

78 *Guardian*, 23 October 1975; *Sunday Telegraph*, 26 October 1975.

79 *Financial Times*, 16 September 1977.

80 'BAE in Saudi Arabia', minute from the Head of DSO (H. J. L. Suffield) to Frank Cooper, 23 June 1976, *Guardian*, 'The BAE Files', http://image.guardian.co.uk/sys-files/Guardian/documents/2007/05/29/ch05doc06.pdf.

81 'BAE in Saudi Arabia', *Guardian*, 'The BAE Files', http://image.guardian.co.uk/sys-files/Guardian/documents/2007/05/29/ch05doc06.pdf.

82 Ibid., http://www.guardian.co.uk/baefiles/page/0,,2095814,00.html.

2. The Nazi Connection

1 John R. Boker, 'Report of Initial Contacts with General Gehlen's Organization by John R. Boker Jr., 1 May 1952', in C. Ruffner (ed.), *Forging an Intelligence Partnership: CIA and the Origins of the BND, 1945–1949*, produced for CIA History Staff, Center for the Study of Intelligence and European Division, Directorate of Operations (1999; released May 2002).

2 'Statement of Gerhard Wessel on Development of the German Organisation', undated, in Ruffner (ed.), *Forging an Intelligence Partnership*.

3 Ibid.

4 Boker, 'Report of Initial Contacts'.

5 Ibid.

6 Neal Ascherson, 'Our Man in Pullach', *New York Review of Books*, 1 June 1972.

7 'Eine "Zweite Entnazifizierung"', *Frankfurter Allgemeine*, 18 March 2010.

8 Ken Silverstein, *Private Warriors* (New York: Verso, 2000), p. 110.

9 Interview with Joe der Hovsepian, Amman, Jordan, 14 May 2010.

10 Ibid.; and 'Veterans' Attitude towards Rearmament', 22 August 1951, Information Memorandum No. 84, Office of the United States High Commissioner for Germany: Office of Intelligence – Reports and Analysis Division.

11 'Veterans' Attitude towards Rearmament' (see n. 10 above).

12 Silverstein, *Private Warriors*, p. 111. After the SRP won a shock 11 per cent of the vote in Lower Saxony, German courts, fearful of its potential impact, banned it as a subversive organization.

13 Ibid., p. 112.

14 'A mini-Krupp in Kenwood', *Washington Post*, 28 April 1968.

15 Silverstein, *Private Warriors*, p. 118.

16 George Thayer, *The War Business: The International Trade in Armaments* (New York: Simon & Schuster, 1970), Chapter 7. Available at http://alexanderhamiltoninstitute.org/lp/Hancock/CD-ROMS/GlobalFederation%5CWorld%20Trade%20Federation%20-%20105%20-%20The%20War%20Business.html.

17 Silverstein, *Private Warriors*, p. 118.

18 Ibid.

19 In reality, Mertins ran a number of companies with slight variations on the name of Merex. The initial companies established in 1963 operated in the names of Merex AG (Bonn), which was controlled by Merex AG in Vevey, Switzerland. Another branch of Merex, Deutsche Merex GmbH, was also opened at a later stage. Merex Corp was the US incarnation of Merex. Over the next three decades Mertins shifted which companies were directly associated with different transactions, each company becoming the 'main' Merex company at various points. For ease of understanding, we refer to Mertins's European presence as Merex and his US presence as Merex Corp. See *Executive Sessions of the Senate Foreign Relations Committee*, together with *Joint Sessions with the Senate and Services Committee*, Vol. XIX, 90th Congress, 1967, www.fas.org.

20 'A mini-Krupp in Kenwood', *Washington Post*, 28 April 1968.

21 Anthony Sampson, *The Arms Bazaar* (London: Hodder and Stoughton, 1977), p. 57.

22 'Samuel Cummings – Obituary', *The Economist*, 9 May 1998; and 'Samuel Cummings, 71, trader in weapons on a grand scale', *The New York Times*, 5 May 1998.

23 'Samuel Cummings, 71, trader in weapons', *The New York Times*, 5 May 1998.

24 Russell Warren Howe, *Weapons: The International Game of Arms, Money and Diplomacy* (New York: Doubleday, 1980) pp. 407–8.

25 Tom Gervasi, *Arsenal of Democracy* II: *American Military Power in the 1980s and the Origins of the Cold War with a Survey of American Weapons and Arms Exports* (London: The Book Service, 1981), pp. 120–21.

26 Thayer, *War Business*, Chapter 3.

27 Silverstein, *Private Warriors*, p. 120; 'Prozente für Pfadfinder', *Der Spiegel*, 23 March 1987; 'Fall Merex: Rechtsbruch durch Tarnung', *Der Spiegel*, 22 December 1975.

28 Thayer, *War Business*, Chapter 3; 'Prozente für Pfadfinder', *Der Spiegel*, 23 March 1987; Gervasi, *Arsenal of Democracy II*, pp. 50–51.

29 'Prozente für Pfadfinder', *Der Spiegel*, 23 March 1987.

30 Thayer, *War Business*, Chapter 3; 'Prozente für Pfadfinder', *Der Spiegel*, 23 March 1987; Gervasi, *Arsenal of Democracy II*, pp. 50–51.

31 Thayer, *War Business*, Chapter 3.

32 'Prozente für Pfadfinder', *Der Spiegel*, 23 March 1987.

33 Thayer, *War Business*, Chapter 3.

34 Silverstein, *Private Warriors*, p. 120; and 'Fall Merex: Rechtsbruch durch Tarnung', *Der Spiegel*, 22 December 1975.

35 Silverstein, *Private Warriors*, pp. 123 and 130.

36 'A mini-Krupp in Kenwood', *Washington Post*, 28 April 1968.

37 Ibid.

38 Howe, *Weapons*, p. 409.

39 Ibid.

40 Silverstein, *Private Warriors*, pp. 121–2.

41 'Lieber Christian Putsch', *Jungen Welt*, 16 July 1998.

42 See O. Abegunrin, *Nigerian Foreign Policy under Military Rule, 1966–1999* (Westport: Praeger, 2003), pp. 50–53.

43 K. J. Beattie, *Egypt during the Sadat Years* (London: Palgrave Macmillan, 2000), pp. 124–5.

44 Silverstein, *Private Warriors*, pp. 125–7.

45 See A. Delgado, *Counterfeit Reich: Hitler's Secret Swindle* (Frederick, Md: PublishAmerica, 2006), p. 147.

46 Hilton M. Linklater and Neal Ascherson, *The Nazi Legacy: Klaus Barbie and the International Fascist Connection* (London: Henry Holt & Co, 1985), p. 238.

47 Silverstein, *Private Warriors*, pp. 125–6.

48 'Special Article: Freikorps Deutschland', US Army Intelligence Report, undated. Regraded as unclassified by USAINSCOM, 13 January 1997.

49 Ibid.

50 Silverstein, *Private Warriors*, p. 127.

51 Ibid.

52 Ibid., pp. 127–8.

53 P. Levenda, *Unholy Alliance: A History of the Nazi Involvement with the Occult* (New York: Continuum, 2002), p. 319. Townley was later found guilty in the US of assassinating Orlando Letelier, a liberal economist and prominent political figure who had served as Salvadore Allende's ambassador to the US.

54 'Secrets of ex-Nazi's Chilean fiefdom', BBC News, 11 March 2005.

55 'Fugitive Nazi cult leader arrested', *Guardian*, 12 March 2005.

56 Letter from G. Bausch (Merex Corp) to Tongsun Park, 8 December 1969, in *Investigation into Korean–American Relations: Appendixes to the Report of the Subcommittee on International Organizations of the Committee on International Relations*, US House of Representatives (Washington: Govt Printing Office, 1978), p. 343.

57 'Park sentenced to 5 years in U.N. oil-for-food bribery scandal', *Washington Post*, 23 February 2007.

58 Howe, *Weapons*, p. 409.

59 Silverstein, *Private Warriors*, p. 132.

60 Howe, *Weapons*, p. 406.

61 'Die Oktoberfest-Connection', *Jungle World*, No. 48, 22 November 2000.

62 'Waffenexporte unter SPD-Regie', *Die Tageszeitung*, 22 December 1986.

63 Silverstein, *Private Warriors*, pp. 133–4.

64 Financial Statements: Merex AG, 1 January 1980.

65 Silverstein, *Private Warriors*, p. 137; and interview with Joe der Hovsepian, Amman, Jordan, 14 May 2010.

66 Evidence submitted in *Merex AG*. v. *Fairchild Weston Systems Inc.*, United States Southern District of New York, 1992.

67 'Prozente für Pfadfinder', *Der Spiegel*, 23 March 1987.

68 Letter from Gerhard Mertins to Zhao Fei (NORINCO), 10 January 1984, *Merex v. Fairchild Weston Systems Inc.*, trial records.

69 Silverstein, *Private Warriors*, pp. 134–5.

Section II: Nice Work If You Can Get It

3. The Saudi Connection

1 *Sunday Times*, 20 August 2006.

2 According to the Foreign Secretary in 1968, Michael Stewart, this had long been a tactic of the French: 'the French . . . policy of support for the Arabs has been largely designed to enable them to profit in this way'. PRO: CAB 148/38/OPD(68)/66, 'Sale of Chieftain Tanks to Israel', note by the Secretary of State for Foreign and Commonwealth Affairs.

3 *Flight*, 8 December 1984.

4 *Flight*, 16 February 1985; *Financial Times*, 12 March 1985.

5 *Flight*, 22 April 1985.

6 *Financial Times*, 22 April 1985.

7 *Observer*, 10 May 1992.

8 David Ottaway, *The King's Messenger: Prince Bandar Bin Sultan and America's Tangled Relationship with Saudi Arabia* (New York: Walker & Company, 2008), p. 67, citing interview with Prince Bandar, 4 March 1996.

9 *Observer*, 19 March 1989.

10 *The Times*, 18 September 1985.

11 Chrissie Hirst, *The Arabian Connection: The UK Arms Trade to Saudi Arabia* (London: CAAT, 2000).

12 Tim Webb, *Bribing for Britain*, CAAT Goodwin Paper No. 5, October 2007, p. 13.

13 Mark Phythian, *British Arms Sales since 1964* (Manchester: Manchester University Press, 2000), p. 221.

14 Ibid., p. 222.

15 *Jane's Defence Weekly*, 5 February 1994, p. 27.

16 *Guardian*, 8 May 1986; and Hirst, *Arabian Connection*.

17 Luke Harding, David Leigh and David Pallister, *The Liar: The Fall of Jonathan Aitken* (London: Penguin Books, 1997), p. 64.

18 *Financial Times*, 27 November 1989; and *Sunday Times*, 10 December 1989.

19 Anthony H. Cordesman, *Saudi Arabia: Guarding the Desert Kingdom* (Boulder, Colo., and London: Westview Press, 1997), p. 157.

20 William Simpson, *The Prince: The Secret Story of the World's Most Intriguing Royal Prince, Bandar Bin Sultan* (New York: HarperCollins, 2006), p. 147.

21 Quoted in Mark Hollingsworth and Paul Halloran, *Thatcher's Fortunes: The Life and Times of Mark Thatcher* (Edinburgh: Mainstream, 2005), pp. 199–200.

22 Phythian, *British Arms Sales*, p. 225.

23 *Sunday Telegraph*, 25 November 1990; Phythian, *British Arms Sales*, p. 226 and notes at p. 256.

24 *Jane's Defence Weekly*, 1 September 1990.

25 *Sunday Times*, 30 September 1990.
26 *The Times*, 25 October 1991.
27 'Secrets of Al Yamamah', in the *Guardian*, 'The BAE Files', http://www.guardian.co.uk/baefiles/page/0,,2095831,00.html.
28 *Jane's Defence Weekly*, 6 May 1995, p. 33.
29 *Independent*, 16 November 1988; *Sunday Times*, 18 January 1990; *BAE Quarterly*, Autumn 1989.
30 Terry Macalister, 'Profile: Dick Evans', *Guardian*, 5 February 2010, 'The BAE Files', http://www.guardian.co.uk/world/2010/feb/05/dick-evans-bae-arms-deal.
31 Ibid.
32 Ibid.
33 Elsa Walsh, 'The Prince', *The New Yorker*, 24 March 2003. Also at http://www.saudi-us-relations.org/international-relations/prince-bandar.html.
34 'King Abdul Aziz Al Saud', The Saudi Network, http://www.the-saudi.net/al-saud/abdulaziz.html.
35 Walsh, 'The Prince'.
36 Ibid.
37 Ottaway, *King's Messenger*, p. 25.
38 Ibid., p. 26.
39 Simpson, *The Prince*, citing interview with General Faisal Mifgai in Marrakech, Morocco, 26 June 2004, p. 15.
40 Ottaway, *King's Messenger*, p. 26, citing interview with Prince Bandar, 28 March 1996.
41 Simpson, *The Prince*, p. 16.
42 Ibid., p. 21, citing interview with Sgt Ken Adams in Leasington, Lincolnshire, 14 January 2004.
43 Ibid., p. 26, citing interview with John Waterfall in Brighton, Sussex, 26 February 2006.
44 Ibid., p. 27, citing Cranwell Course Report on Flight Cadet Sultan prepared by his flying instructor, Flight Lieutenant Tony Yule.
45 Ibid., pp. 33–4.
46 Ibid., p. 34.
47 David Leigh, 'Arms and the Man', *New Statesman*, 28 June 2007, http://www.newstatesman.com/books/2007/06/prince-bandar-saudi-mandela.
48 Simpson, *The Prince*, p. 34.
49 Ibid., p. 378, citing William Gildea, 'Saudi Prince Bandar has cowboy spirit', *Washington Post*, 20 June 1994.
50 Ibid., p. 41.
51 Ottaway, *King's Messenger*, p. 28, citing interview with Prince Bandar, 28 March 1996.
52 Ibid., p. 23.
53 Ibid., p. 24.
54 Ibid., p. 24.
55 Ibid., p. 25.
56 Ibid., p. 29, citing 'Memorandum: F-15s to Saudi Arabia – A Threat to Peace'.
57 Ibid., p. 30.
58 Ibid.
59 For further reading on the enormous power of the Israel lobby and its impact on US foreign policy, including arms sales, see John J. Mearsheimer and Stephen M. Walt, *The Israel Lobby and US Foreign Policy* (New York: Farrar, Straus and Giroux, 2007).

60 Ottaway, *King's Messenger*, p. 31, citing Daily Diary, John C. West Papers, 'Sunday, April 23, 1978'.

61 Ottaway, *King's Messenger*, p. 33, citing interview with Prince Bandar, 28 March 1996.

62 Ibid.; Bandar went on to say that the *Times* printed the story the next day with the head-line 'Reagan supports Carter on F-15s to Saudi Arabia'. However, according to Ottaway, there is no record that the *Los Angeles Times* or any other major US paper ran any such story. There is also no mention of the event in John West's daily diary.

63 Ibid., p. 35, citing interview with Prince Bandar, 30 November 2001.

64 Ibid., p. 31, citing letter from John C. West to Prince Fahd bin Abdul Aziz, 6 June 1978, John C. West Papers.

65 Ibid., p. 39, citing interview with Prince Bandar, 28 March 1996.

66 Ibid., p. 40, citing John C. West, Daily Diary, 'Wednesday, April 19, 1978'.

67 Ibid., citing 'Memorandum for: Dean Robert Osgood, the Johns Hopkins University, School of Advanced International Studies. From: David E. Long, 18 May, 1979', Box 10, John C. West Papers.

68 Ibid., p. 41, citing John C. West, Daily Diary, 'Monday, Sept 15, 1980'.

69 State Department, 'Saudi Regional Role', briefing paper, May 1977, Box 36, Staff Offices Counsel, Lipshutz's Files, Middle East: Saudi Arabia 10/77–6/78, [CF O/A 712] Jimmy Carter Library.

70 Ottaway, *King's Messenger*, p. 42.

71 Ibid., citing 'John C. West letter to President Carter', 6 July 1979, Box 10, John C. West Papers.

72 Ibid., p. 44, citing John C. West, Daily Diary, 'Friday, December 14 1978'.

73 Ibid., p. 45, John C. West, handwritten note, 8 June 1998, attached to 'Draft. Letter to Crown Prince Fahd from President Carter', 3 April 1980, Box 10, John C. West Papers.

74 Harding, Leigh and Pallister, *The Liar*, p. 36.

75 Ottaway, *King's Messenger*, p. 47, citing John C. West, Daily Diary, 'Sunday, Sept. 28, 1980'.

76 Ibid., p. 47, 'Saturday, October 4, 1980'.

77 Ibid., p. 48, 'Monday, Oct. 13, 1980'.

78 Ibid., p. 50, citing interview with Prince Bandar, 28 March 1996.

79 Ronald Reagan, *An American Life* (New York: Simon & Schuster, 1990), p. 410.

80 Richard F. Grimmett, Executive-Legislative Consultation on U.S. Arms Sales, 1982, pp. 33–5.

81 Ottaway, *King's Messenger*, p. 52, citing Melinda Beck and John J. Lindsay, 'Trying to Patch the AWACS Deal', *Newsweek*, 5 October 1981.

82 Ibid., p. 53, citing Associated Press, 25 September 1981, Adams, 'Saudi Prince, Reagan, Senators discussing AWACS compromise'; United Press International, 25 September 1981.

83 Ibid., pp. 50 and 57, citing interview with Prince Bandar, 28 March 1996.

84 Ibid., p. 60.

85 Israeli ambassador Moshe Arens, interviewed by Patrick Tyler, in *A World of Trouble: America in the Middle East* (London: Portobello Books, 2009), p. 304.

86 Lawrence Walsh, *Firewall: The Iran–Contra Conspiracy and Cover-Up* (New York: W. W. Norton & Co, 1997), p. 19.

87 Ibid., p. 390.

88 Quoted in Steve Coll, *The Bin Ladens: Oil, Money, Terrorism and the Secret Saudi World* (London: Penguin Books, 2008), p. 10.

89 Tyler, *World of Trouble*.

90 Ibid., pp. 312–13.

91 Walsh, *Firewall*, p. 390.

92 Ibid., p. 391.

93 Ibid., p. 392.

94 Ottaway, *King's Messenger*, p. 61.

95 Leigh, 'Arms and the Man'.

96 Simpson, *The Prince*, pp. 119–20.

97 Quoted in Ottaway, *King's Messenger*, p. 77, citing Samantha Sparks, 'Angola: Saudi aid to rebels may be "brother" of Irangate scandal', IPS-Inter Press Service, 1 July 1987, from which this account is drawn.

98 Bob Woodward, *Veil: Secret Wars of the CIA, 1981–87* (New York: Simon & Schuster, 1987), p. 398.

99 Ibid.

100 Ottaway, *King's Messenger*, p. 63, citing interview with William Wilson, 4 January 2002.

101 Simpson, *The Prince*, p. 100.

102 Leigh, 'Arms and the Man'.

103 Woodward, *Veil*, pp. 395–8.

104 Bill Moyers, 'Target America', *Frontline*, PBS, 4 October 2001.

105 Ottaway, *King's Messenger*, p. 64, citing 'Spotlight: Bandar Survives Casey Book, But Saudi Arms Battle Looms', *Mideast Markets*, 12 October 1987.

106 Simpson, *The Prince*, p. 123.

107 Robert Lacey, *Inside the Kingdom* (London: Hutchinson, 2009), p. 194.

108 Ottaway, *King's Messenger*, p. 79, citing interview with Prince Bandar, 30 November 2001.

109 Ibid., p. 81, citing interview with Prince Bandar, 4 March 1996.

110 Quoted in Hollingsworth and Halloran, *Thatcher's Fortunes*, p. 212.

4. In Defence of Humanity

1 This and many of the insights in this section were gleaned in a personal interview with der Hovsepian, Amman, Jordan, 14 May 2010.

2 Merex records show that in 1980 der Hovsepian was listed as owing the company DM 18,000. Financial Statements: Merex AG, 1 January 1980.

3 Financial Statements: Deutsche Merex GmbH, 1 January 1980; and interview with Joe der Hovsepian, Amman, Jordan, 14 May 2010.

4 Statuten: Deutsche Merex GmbH, UR Nr. 1254/1990, dated 12 June 1990; Statuten: Deutsche Merex GmbH, UR Nr. 1022/1990, dated 15 May 1990; Amstgericht, Merex AG and Gut Buschoff Hotel und Sport Center AG, 9 April 1979–12 March 1996, retrieved from German Company Registries (Deutsche Handelsregister), 18 February 2010.

5 Ibid.

6 Company Register for Thomasberg und Sportanlagen Betriebs Gesellschaft, accessed 8 June 2010. Also see: 'Kur Investor für eine Fünf-Sterne-Herberge in Thomasberg', *General-Anzeiger*, 16 January 2004.

7 Steve Coll, *Ghost Wars: The Secret History of the CIA, Afghanistan, and Bin Laden, from the Soviet Invasion to September 10, 2001* (London: Penguin Books, 2004), pp. 71–3.

8 Ibid., p. 79.

9 BBC News, 20 July 2005; and 'Prince Turki Al-Faisal resigns as Saudi Ambassador to US', in *Arab News*, 13 December 2006.

10 Coll, *Ghost Wars*, pp. 71–3.

11 Interview with Joe der Hovsepian, Amman, Jordan, 14 May 2010.

12 Ibid.

13 Ibid.

14 Interrogation of Lorenzo Mazzega, Tribunale Civile e Penale di Venezia, 3 February 1994.

15 Interrogation of Franco Giorgi, Torre Annunziato Investigation: Cheque to Cheque, 25 June 1995.

16 Ibid.

17 Interrogation of Lorenzo Mazzega, Tribunale Civile e Penale di Venezia, 3 February 1994; 'Report on Angelos Scordas/Merex', Bavarian State Office of Criminal Investigation, Düsseldorf, Case Ref.: Ausl 142/96, Vol. M-4581-96, 11 January 2005.

18 C. Carr, *The Security Implications of Microdisarmament*, The Counterproliferation Papers Future Warfare Series No. 5 (USAF Counterproliferation Center (Air War College), 2000), p. 14. See also Commission of Inquiry into Alleged Arms Transactions between Armscor and One Eli Wazan and Other Related Matters (The 'Cameron Commission'), 15 June 1995, Section 4.

19 Commission of Inquiry into Alleged Arms Transactions (see n. 18 above).

20 Ibid.

21 Interrogation of Franco Giorgi, Torre Annunziato Investigation: Cheque to Cheque, 25 June 1995.

22 Arms transfers to all parties of the Yugoslav conflict were banned under the terms of UN Resolution 713. See S/RES/171/1991, available for download from www.un.org.

23 Interrogation of Franco Giorgi, Torre Annunziato Investigation: Cheque to Cheque, 25 June 1995. See also *Beverly Overseas SA* v. *Privredna Banka Zagreb*, 28 March 2001, Swiss Federal Court Case 4C.172/200. Available for download from www.bger.ch.

24 Interrogation of Franco Giorgi, Torre Annunziato Investigation: Cheque to Cheque, 25 June 1995.

25 See 'The woman who paid $2bn into foreign accounts', *Nacional* (Croatia), 7 November 2006. The involvement of Martinovic was outlined by Terezija Barbaric, who had acted as the adviser to Martinovic while he was director of Privredna Bank and during his stint as Finance Minister. Barbaric recalled that roughly $2bn had been transferred to suspicious foreign bank accounts while she and Martinovic were in office.

26 Commission of Inquiry into Alleged Arms Transactions (see n. 18 above).

27 Ibid.

28 Interrogation of Franco Giorgi, Torre Annunziato Investigation: Cheque to Cheque, 25 June 1995; and interview with Joe der Hovsepian, Amman, Jordan, 14 May 2010.

29 Promissory Note: Privredna Bank Zagreb, Bearer: Instersystems Inc, Signed Martin Katicic and Jozo Martinovic, 11 May 1992. Submitted in evidence in the matter of *Beverly Overseas SA* v. *Privredna Banka Zagreb*, 28 March 2001, Swiss Federal Court Case 4C.172/200. The document can be viewed at www.theshadowworld.com.

30 Interview with Joe der Hovsepian, Amman, Jordan, 14 May 2010, and Statement of

Account: Intersystems Inc., addressed to H. E. Joso Martinovic, 4 August 1992, submitted as evidence in the matter of *Beverly Overseas SA* v. *Privredna Banka Zagreb*, 28 March 2001, Swiss Federal Court Case 4C.172/200. Available for download from www.bger.ch.

31 Interrogation of Franco Giorgi, Torre Annunziato Investigation: Cheque to Cheque, 25 June 1995.

32 Ibid.

33 Interrogation of Lorenzo Mazzega, Tribunale Civile e Penale di Venezia, 3 February 1994.

34 Ibid. and interview with Joe der Hovsepian, Amman, Jordan, 14 May 2010.

35 Interrogation of Lorenzo Mazzega, Tribunale Civile e Penale di Venezia, 3 February 1994.

36 Interview with Joe der Hovsepian, Amman, Jordan, 14 May 2010.

37 Ibid.

38 He chose Switzerland as the original promissory note stated that it was governed by Swiss law.

39 *Beverly Overseas SA* v. *Privredna Banka Zagreb*, 28 March 2001, Swiss Federal Court Case No. 4C.172/2000. Available for download from www.bger.ch. See also B. Oxman, J. Kokott and S. Patrick, 'International Decisions – *Beverly Overseas SA* v. *Privredna Banka Zagreb*', *American Journal of International Law*, Vol. 97 (2003), No. 1, pp. 177–8.

40 Interrogation of Nicholas Oman, Campania Region of Carabinieri (Vico Equense Station), Cheque to Cheque Investigation, 7 November 1996.

41 Ibid.

42 Fax from Interpol Canberra to Interpol Vienna, subject: 'Oman, Nicholas Born 28/10/1943', Ref: IP/0167/92/2-42, 4 March 1994.

43 'Informative di Reato Relativa all'operazione "Cheque to Cheque"', Regione Carabinieri Campania: Stazione di Vico Equense, 30 June 1998, pp. 455–6.

44 B. A. Cook (ed.), *Europe Since 1945: An Encyclopaedia*, Vol. I (New York: Garland, 2001), p. 433.

45 Ibid. See also P. Ginsborg, *Italy and Its Discontents: Family, Civil Society, State, 1980–2001* (New York: Palgrave Macmillan, 2003), p. 144.

46 Cook, *Europe Since 1945*, p. 433.

47 Interrogation of Nicholas Oman, Campania Region of Carabinieri (Vico Equense Station), Cheque to Cheque Investigation, 7 November 1996.

48 Ibid.

49 Interrogation of Jornej (given as 'Jerney') Cepin, Interpol: Rome, 26 July 1996, in 'Informative di Reato Relativa all'operazione "Cheque to Cheque"', Regione Carabinieri Campania: Stazione di Vico Equense, 30 June 1998.

50 Interrogation of Nicholas Oman, Campania Region of Carabinieri (Vico Equense Station), Cheque to Cheque Investigation, 7 November 1996.

51 Arrest order issued by Interpol Ljubljana, 10 February 1998. Ref: 0225-19-92IP-7456/96.

52 Interrogation of Jornej (given as 'Jerney') Cepin, Interpol: Rome, 26 July 1996, in 'Informative di Reato Relativa all'operazione "Cheque to Cheque"', Regione Carabinieri Campania: Stazione di Vico Equense, 30 June 1998. See also *Republic of Liberia Truth and Reconciliation Commission: Volume III (Appendices), Economic Crimes and the Conflict: Exploitation and Abuse*, 2009, para. 115.

53 Interrogation of Nicholas Oman (Additional Explanatory Notes), Campania Region of Carabinieri (Vico Equense Station), Cheque to Cheque Investigation, 19 November 1996.

54 Interrogation of Lorenzo Mazzega, Tribunale Civile e Penale di Venezia, 3 February 1994.

55 Table 1: 'List of individuals and corporate entities that the TRC holds responsible for economic crimes', in *Republic of Liberia Truth and Reconciliation Commission: Volume III (Appendices), Economic Crimes and the Conflict: Exploitation and Abuse*, 2009.

56 Interrogation of Nicholas Oman, Campania Region of Carabinieri (Vico Equense Station), Cheque to Cheque Investigation, 18 November 1996.

57 Ibid.

58 Ibid.

59 This was a credible origin as NATO forces had made use of the Blowpipe, which had been manufactured in the UK and featured in that country's war in the Falklands.

60 Invoice Nr. 91716 from Orbal Marketing Services (Croatia) to the Ministry of Defence (Croatia), Att: Josip Vukina.

61 Memorandum from Criminal Investigation Directorate, Ministvo zo Notransje Zadeve, Ljubljana Slovenia to Interpol Rome, Subject: 'Oman, Nicholas – Trafficking with Weapons and Military Equipment – Transfer of Data', 3 July 1996.

62 Ibid. See also 'War diplomacy – controversial armaments trade', *Aim* (Slovenia), 29 April 1998.

63 Interrogation of Fulvio Leonardi, 5 June 1996, in 'Informative di Reato Relativa all'operazione "Cheque to Cheque"', Regione Carabinieri Campania: Stazione di Vico Equense, 30 June 1998.

64 *Nacional* (Croatia), No. 352, 13 August 2002.

65 'An old tale of swindle resurfaces in Bosnia', *The New York Times*, 14 December 1997; and 'Main news summary' provided by the NATO Stabilization Force in Bosnia, 26 May 2004, available for download from www.nato.int.

66 See 'Serbs threaten to unleash deadly "secret weapon"', *Independent*, 15 February 1994.

67 'The world: here comes the clown. No joke', *The New York Times*, 6 November 1994; *Sunday Times*, 16 June 1996; *Delo* (Ljubljana), 6 April 1996; *Kurier*, 6 December 1996; and *Süddeutsche Zeitung*, 12 June 1996.

68 *Nacional* (Croatia), No. 352, 13 August 2002.

69 'Verwicklung Schirinowskijs vermutet Material für Atomwaffen', *Süddeutsche Zeitung*, 12 June 1996; 'Die Kardinal und die Dealer', *Focus*, 18 July 1996.

70 Interrogation of Franco Giorgi, Torre Annunziato Investigation: Cheque to Cheque, 25 June 1995.

71 'An old tale of swindle resurfaces in Bosnia', *The New York Times*, 14 December 1997.

72 Interrogation of Franco Giorgi, Torre Annunziato Investigation: Cheque to Cheque, 25 June 1995; and Statement by Lainovic Branislav, 17 November 1995, in 'Informative di Reato Relativa all'operazione "Cheque to Cheque"', Regione Carabinieri Campania: Stazione di Vico Equense, 30 June 1998.

73 Ibid.

74 Statement by Lainovic Branislav, 17 November 1995, in 'Informative di Reato Relativa all'operazione "Cheque to Cheque"', Regione Carabinieri Campania: Stazione di Vico Equense, 30 June 1998.

75 *Nacional* (Croatia), No. 352, 13 August 2002.

76 Commission of Inquiry into Alleged Arms Transactions (see n. 18 above).

77 Ibid.

78 Ibid.

79 Ibid.
80 Interview with Joe der Hovsepian, Amman, Jordan, 14 May 2010.
81 Commission of Inquiry into Alleged Arms Transactions (see n. 18 above).
82 Ibid.
83 Ibid.
84 Ibid.
85 Ibid.
86 Interview with Joe der Hovsepian, Amman, Jordan, 14 May 2010.

5. *The Ultimate Deal or the Ultimate Crime?*

1 Fidelity National Financial, 'Riggs Bank signs long-term agreement with Fidelity Information Services', http://fnf.client.shareholder.com/releasedetail.cfm?releaseid=112302.
2 George Washington University, 'The PNC Riggs Collection', http://www.gwu.edu/gelman/spec/exhibits/pnc_riggs/dc_community.html.
3 Ibid.
4 Professional Risk Managers' International Association, 'Riggs Bank Summary', www.google.co.uk/url?sa=t&source=web&cd=8&sqi=2&ved=0CE4QFjAH&url=http%3A%2F%2Fprmia.org%2Fpdf%2FCase_Studies%2FRiggs_Bank_Short_version_April_2009.pdf&rct=j&q=riggs%20bank%20us%20embassies&ei=x9hobKiM4PBtAb4sZiEDg&usg=AFQjCNFh9qJza3KIbusrlpYvpdNMBDmR7A&cad=rja.
5 David Montgomery, 'The Bank of Dad', in the *Washington Post*, 23 April 2004, http://www.washingtonpost.com/wp-dyn/articles/A62544-2004Jun22.html.
6 Kathleen Day, 'Web site cites Bush–Riggs link', in the *Washington Post*, 15 May 2004, http://www.washingtonpost.com/wp-dyn/articles/A28396-2004May14.html.
7 *Newsweek*, 2 December 2002.
8 'Riggs Bank fined $25M for Saudi transactions', *USA Today*, 14 May 2004, http://www.usatoday.com/money/industries/banking/2004-05-14-riggs-fine_x.htm; and Timothy L. O'Brian, 'At Riggs Bank, a tangled path led to scandal', *The New York Times*, 19 July 2004, http://query.nytimes.com/gst/fullpage.html?res=9507E4DC133AF93AA25754C0A9629C8B63&pagewanted=1.
9 The 9/11 Commission Report, 22 July 2004, p. 498, http://govinfo.library.unt.edu/911/report/911Report_Notes.pdf.
10 Professional Risk Managers' International Association, 'Riggs Bank Summary' (see n. 4 above).
11 'The CIA and Riggs Bank', *Slate*, 7 January 2005.
12 O'Brian, 'At Riggs Bank, a tangled path led to scandal' (see n. 8 above).
13 'Black Money', http://www.pbs.org/wgbh/pages/frontline/blackmoney/view/, PBS, transcript available at http://www.pbs.org/wgbh/pages/frontline/blackmoney/etc/script.html. Documents pertaining to this transaction are available at www.theshadowworld.com.
14 'Secrets of Al Yamamah', *Guardian*, http://www.guardian.co.uk/baefiles/page/0,,2095831,00.html.
15 *Panorama*, BBC, 11 June 2007; *Guardian*, 7–12 June 2007; and copies of selected Riggs Bank accounts of the Saudi Embassy and Prince Bandar.

16 'Secrets of Al Yamamah' (see n. 14 above).

17 David Leigh and Rob Evans, 'BAE accused of secretly paying £1bn to Saudi prince', *Guardian*, 7 June 2007, http://www.guardian.co.uk/world/2007/jun/07/bae1.

18 M. Hollingsworth and P. Halloran, *Thatcher's Fortunes: The Life and Times of Mark Thatcher* (Edinburgh: Mainstream, 2005).

19 This is drawn from Tim Webb, 'Bribing for Britain', CAAT Goodwin Paper No. 5, October 2007, p. 12, referencing the author's interview with Said Aburish, a Saudi specialist, for his book *The Armour Plated Ostrich* (West Wickham: Comerford & Miller, 1998), p. 101.

20 Christopher Hope, 'Twenty years of smokescreen over Saudi deal', *Daily Telegraph*, 21 June 2006, http://www.telegraph.co.uk/finance/2941537/Twenty-years-of-smokescreen-over-Saudi-deal.html.

21 *Guardian*, 21 October 1985.

22 Ibid.

23 Letter of 10 October 1985 from P. F. Ricketts, Private Secretary at FCO to Charles Powell (10 Downing Street) and Richard Mottram (MoD), published by the *Guardian* at http://image.guardian.co.uk/sys-files/Guardian/documents/2007/06/01/ch07doc05.pdf.

24 Hansard, 18 October 1994, Column 235, http://www.publications.parliament.uk/cgi-bin/newhtml_hl?DB=semukparl&STEMMER=en&WORDS=saudi%20arabia%20agent&ALL=Saudi%20Arabia%20agents&ANY=&PHRASE=&CATEGORIES=&SIMPLE=&SPEAKER=&COLOUR=red&STYLE=s&ANCHOR=Debate-8_spnew9&URL=/pa/cm199394/cmhansrd/1994-10-18/Debate-8.html#Debate-8_spnew9.

25 David Leigh and Rob Evans, 'Subcontractor corruption', *Guardian*, 7 June 2007, http://www.guardian.co.uk/world/2007/jun/07/bae16.

26 David Pallister, Richard Norton-Taylor and Owen Bowcott, 'Rolls-Royce in firing line on Saudi deal', *Guardian*, 7 February 1998, http://www.guardian.co.uk/world/1998/feb/07/bae; and Leigh and Evans, 'Subcontractor corruption' (see n. 25 above).

27 Hansard, 24 January 1996, Column 455, http://www.publications.parliament.uk/pa/cm199596/cmhansrd/vo960124/debtext/60124-51.htm.

28 Ibid.; Gerald James, *In the Public Interest* (London: Little Brown and Company, 1995), pp. 119–20; http://www2.warwick.ac.uk/fac/soc/law/pg/prospective/iel/modules/intl/mat/corruption_roleprivatesector.doc; The Statement of Facts for 786 F.Supp. 65 (1992) Thomas F. DOOLEY, Plaintiff, v. UNITED TECHNOLOGIES CORP., et al., Defendants.Civ. A. No. 91-2499. United States District Court, District of Columbia, 10 March, 1992; http://scholar.google.co.uk/scholar_case?case=4949350810948149998hl=en&as_sdt=28&as_vis=1&oi=scholarr.

29 Richard Norton-Taylor and David Pallister, 'Millions in secret commissions paid out for Saudi arms deal', *Guardian*, 4 March 1999, http://www.guardian.co.uk/politics/1999/mar/04/uk.davidpallister1.

30 Ibid.

31 Luke Harding, David Leigh and David Pallister, *The Liar: The Fall of Jonathan Aitken* (London: Guardian Books, 1999), p. 166.

32 'We did it their way', *Daily Telegraph*, 10 June 2007, http://www.telegraph.co.uk/news/uknews/1554076/We-did-it-their-way.html.

33 Ibid.

34 This account is drawn from a number of meetings with David Leigh and Rob Evans, culminating in a formal interview on 26 April 2010.

35 Quoted in Harding, Leigh and Pallister, *The Liar*, p. xiii.

36 PRO: WO 32/21301. Minute of meeting between Lord Shackleton and Sir Donald Stokes, 7 July 1965.

37 The National Archives: AVIA 65/1670 Minutes of Permanent Secretary's meeting, 14 July 1965.

38 The National Archives: AVIA 65/1670 Stokes Report.

39 Nicola Stanbridge, 'Arms deal fraud allegations', *Today*, BBC Radio 4, 12 November 2003, http://www.bbc.co.uk/radio4/today/reports/politics/bae_20031112.shtml.

40 Ibid.

41 Ibid.

42 David Leigh and Rob Evans, 'Diplomat linked to BAE slush fund claims', *Guardian*, 13 September 2003, http://www.guardian.co.uk/uk/2003/sep/13/saudiarabia.armstrade.

43 David Leigh and Rob Evans, 'Homes for executive's mistress bought from BAE fund', *Guardian*, 15 September 2003, http://www.guardian.co.uk/uk/2003/sep/15/freedomof information.saudiarabia.

44 A solicitor's letter written to Winship in 1993 stated: 'You have instructed me that the purpose of the transaction is that British Aerospace charter the boat for Mr Nasser.' However, there was no evidence that Prince Turki was aware of the transaction, and the *Guardian* assumed that his name was used without his knowledge. Ibid.

45 Letter from SFO to Kevin Tebbit (MoD), 8 March 2001, published by the *Guardian* at http://docs.google.com/viewer?a=v&q=cache:eSt1Q2DKs5oJ:image.guardian.co.uk/ sys-files/Guardian/documents/2003/09/11/wright1.pdf+kevin+tebbit+bae&hl=en&gl=uk &pid=bl&srcid=ADGEESjK6Eu7Z-milphQhvMi10VLa4D_vs9X_pDaC_NoNWydm- gPgdtvjTR BZ.q-KmSZz3quJoiDvt1cYdtagKRGdC5vGMkEyI0Ljz8AkhL Odasz8QG cxM92hnifEpoahZmuJaGYiCR4LX&sig=AHIEtbQ--7DSCLbCfoHmEF5JjKUek2g- BiA.

46 Letter from Kevin Tebbit to Robert Wardle of 12 September 2003, 'Robert Lee International Ltd – British Aerospace', published by the *Guardian* at http://image.guardian. co.uk/sys-files/Guardian/documents/2003/10/10/doc_12sept2003.pdf.

47 Stanbridge, 'Arms deal fraud allegations' (see n. 39 above). An attempt by the BBC to find other points at which BAE corruption was raised with Tebbit revealed that he was approached by the US authorities regarding BAE deals for Gripens in the Czech Republic, but took it to be an attack on British interests. It appears that Tebbit again accepted Dick Evans's assurances that any allegations were baseless. He related the US concerns in a meeting with Michael Lester, the Group Legal Adviser of BAE Systems, the Acting Head of Defence Export Services and another official of the Defence Export Services Organisation, Miss A. L. Tourle, regional marketing director. (Response to BBC FOI from the MoD, 4 January 2007, published at http://docs.google.com/viewer?a=v&q=cac he:2BeNfPKedXgJ:www.bbc.co.uk/blogs/opensecrets/TebbitWayne.pdf+kevin+tebbit+ bae&hl=en&gl=uk&pid=bl&srcid=ADGEESjnuZrv8h8kq9kuQr9ET37gSqDLMmObghi6- yfoKwnhaxnjwsXonFj33aXxZAh9aTCzkJiitzcEcZ15Rhw4upTGm6XWylmUQRCp 8VvGwp8VaBntnp1dv9DsrDaxVahO9vyu3Pkr&sig=AHIEtbQGzvxfbymSKq-6yqekri KGjcHFnA.)

48 Stanbridge, 'Arms deal fraud allegations' (see n. 39 above).

49 David Leigh and Rob Evans, 'Arms firm's £60m slush fund', *Guardian*, 4 May 2004, http:// www.guardian.co.uk/uk/2004/may/04/politics.saudiarabia.

50 'Prince Turki, the RAF Wing Commander, a secret £60m BAE slush fund . . . and me', *Daily Mail*, 7 April 2007.

51 Leigh and Evans, 'Arms firm's £60m slush fund' (see n. 49 above).

52 Ibid.

53 Ibid.

54 David Leppard, 'BAE paid for luxury Saudi honeymoon', *Sunday Times*, 17 June 2007, http://www.timesonline.co.uk/tol/news/uk/article1942914.ece.

55 *Trail of the Dove*, video, Al Jazeera, 13 May 2007, http://www.youtube.com/watch?v=lnPrbCUrHEU.

56 'Black Money' (see n. 13 above); David Leigh and Rob Evans, 'BAE chairman named in "slush fund" files', *Guardian*, 5 May 2004, http://www.guardian.co.uk/uk/2004/may/05/armstrade.politics; 'BAE chief linked to slush fund', *Guardian*, 5 October 2004, http://www.guardian.co.uk/uk/2004/oct/05/saudiarabia.armstrade; and Michael Robinson, 'BBC lifts the lid on secret BAE slush fund', BBC News, 5 October 2004, http://news.bbc.co.uk/1/hi/business/3712770.stm.

57 Leigh and Evans, 'Homes for executive's mistress'.

58 Leigh and Evans, 'Arms firm's £60m slush fund' (see n. 49 above).

59 David Leigh and Rob Evans, 'Dismay at BAE as fraud office comes calling', *Guardian*, 4 November 2004, http://www.guardian.co.uk/business/2004/nov/04/themilitary.freedomofinformation.

60 David Leigh and Rob Evans, 'MoD official took BAE gifts', *Guardian*, 6 April 2004, http://www.guardian.co.uk/uk/2004/apr/06/politics.military.

61 'Black Money' (see n. 13 above).

62 Interview with David Leigh and Rob Evans, London, 26 April 2010; and ibid.

63 *CIA World Factbook*, https://www.cia.gov/library/publications/the-world-factbook/geos/vi.html.

64 Letter to Rob Evans (*Guardian*) from BVI Financial Services Commission giving details of Red Diamond Trading Ltd, published by the *Guardian* at http://image.guardian.co.uk/sys-files/Guardian/documents/2007/05/29/cho8doc05.pdf.

65 Redacted documents showing a money transfer from Red Diamond account at Lloyds in London to Red Diamond Account at UBS in Zurich, published by the *Guardian* at http://image.guardian.co.uk/sys-files/Guardian/documents/2007/05/29/cho8doc06.pdf.

66 G. Murphy, British Serious Fraud Office, Affidavit submitted as Annexure JDP-SW12 in the High Court of South Africa (Transvaal Provincial Division) in the matter of *Ex Parte* the National Director of Public Prosecutions (applicant) re: an application for issue of search warrants in terms of Section 29(5) and 29(6) of the National Prosecuting Authority Act, No. 32 of 1998, as amended (2008), Annexure B.

67 Novelmight Limited, Directors Report and Financial Statements, 31 December 1996, published by the *Guardian* at http://image.guardian.co.uk/sys-files/Guardian/documents/2007/05/29/cho8doc02.pdf.

68 Letter to Rob Evans (*Guardian*) from BVI Financial Services Commission giving details of Novelmight Limited, published by the *Guardian* at http://image.guardian.co.uk/sys-files/Guardian/documents/2007/05/29/cho8doc04.pdf.

69 'BAE's secret money machine', *Guardian*, 'The BAE Files', http://www.guardian.co.uk/baefiles/page/0,,2095840,00.html; and David Leigh and Rob Evans, 'BAE accused of hiding cash paid to win deals', *Guardian*, 5 December 2003.

70 Ibid.

71 Ibid.

72 Ibid.

73 'BAE's secret money machine' (see n. 69 above).

74 Leigh and Evans, 'BAE accused of hiding cash', *Guardian*, 5 December 2003.

75 Ibid.

76 Letter of 24 January 2006 to Rob Evans (*Guardian*) from BVI Financial Services Commission regarding Poseidon Trading Investments Ltd, published by the *Guardian* at http://image.guardian.co.uk/sys-files/Guardian/documents/2007/05/29/ch08doc07.pdf; 'BAE's secret money machine' (see n. 69 above).

77 Leigh and Evans, 'BAE accused of hiding cash', *Guardian*, 5 December 2003.

78 'BAE's secret money machine' (see n. 69 above).

79 Nicholas Gilby, an amateur researcher with the pressure group Campaign against the Arms Trade (CAAT), unearthed documents in the British Archives that revealed the price of the Tornado jets had been artificially inflated by 32 per cent to allow for an original £600m in commission payments. An attempt to sell Tornadoes to the kingdom was first undertaken in 1984 by James Blyth, the head of DSO at the time. It was proposed that the UK would buy back the Lightning aircraft previously sold to Saudi Arabia for £1.5m each and sell twenty Tornadoes for £16.3m each and twenty-four Hawk jet trainers at £4m each. (Confidential record of meeting of January 1986 regarding negotiations for Al Yamamah deal, published by the *Guardian* at http://image.guardian.co.uk/sys-files/Politics/documents/2006/10/27/J5_40RiyadhreportconclusionJan86.pdf.) The price reflected a notable, but not unreasonable, mark-up on the £13.2m price that the RAF was paying. But by the time the Al Yamamah deal was signed the Tornado aircraft would cost £21.5m each and the other fifty-two Tornadoes £25.3m per plane. (Ibid.; and David Leigh and Rob Evans, 'Kew's al-Yamamah files', *Guardian*, 7 July 2007, http://www.guardian.co.uk/world/2007/jun/07/bae.nationalarchives.)

80 Ibid.

81 'Nobbling the police', *Guardian*, 'The BAE Files', http://www.guardian.co.uk/baefiles/page/0,,2098531,00.html; 'Black Money' (see n. 13 above).

82 *Sunday Times* Rich List 2009, http://business.timesonline.co.uk/tol/business/specials/rich_list/rich_list_search/.

83 Andrew Alderson, '"Do I deserve to be labelled a Syrian terrorist?"', in the *Daily Telegraph*, 18 March 2001, http://www.telegraph.co.uk/news/uknews/1326942/Do-I-deserve-to-be-labelled-a-Syrian-terrorist.html.

84 Giles Worsley, 'The English country house rises once more', *Daily Telegraph*, 2 November 2004, http://www.telegraph.co.uk/news/uknews/1475634/The-English-country-house-rises-once-more.html.

85 David Hellier, 'The Mark Thatcher Affair: Saudi contact named as key player: David Hellier profiles the alleged middle-man who became a friend of the Thatcher family', *Independent*, 10 October 1994, http://www.independent.co.uk/news/uk/the-mark-thatcher-affair-saudi-contact-named-as-key-player-david-hellier-profiles-the-alleged-middleman-who-became-a-friend-of-the-thatcher-family-1441988.html?cmp=ilc-n.

86 Alderson, '"Do I deserve to be labelled a Syrian terrorist?"' (see n. 83 above).

87 David Leigh and Rob Evans, 'Wafic Said', *Guardian*, 7 June 2007, http://www.guardian.co.uk/world/2007/jun/07/bae17.

88 'Mr Wafic Rida Saïd gives £25 million to Oxford', Campaign for Oxford University, 28 May 2008, http://www.campaign.ox.ac.uk/news/news/wafic_rida_sad.html.

89 John Arlidge, 'The secretive billionaire who began in a kebab shop', *Evening Standard*, 1 December 2006.

90 Hollingsworth and Halloran, *Thatcher's Fortunes*, p. 204.

91 James, *In the Public Interest*, p. 107.

92 Alderson, '"Do I deserve to be labelled a Syrian terrorist?"' (see n. 83 above).

93 Ibid.

94 Valerie Grove, 'My battle with the dons', *The Times*, 13 November 1996.

95 James, *In the Public Interest*, pp. 62 and 106–7, referencing the *Sunday Times*, 9 October 1994, and Gary Murray, *Enemies of the State* (London: Simon & Schuster, 1993).

96 Wafic Said, *Guardian*, 7 June 2007.

97 Hollingsworth and Halloran, *Thatcher's Fortunes*, p. 207.

98 Tim Kelsey and Peter Koenig, 'Scott seeks Iraq link to Al-Yamamah: Inquiry to ask for details of arms shipments', *Independent*, 12 October 1994, http://www.independent.co.uk/news/uk/scott-seeks-iraq-link-to-alyamamah-inquiry-to-ask-for-details-of-arms-shipments-tim-kelsey-and-peter-koenig-report-1442401.html?cmp=ilc-n.

99 Hollingsworth and Halloran, *Thatcher's Fortunes*, p. 216.

100 Marie Colvin and Adrian Levy, '"An opportunist on a gravy train" – how Thatcher made his millions', *Sunday Times*, 9 October 1994.

101 Stephen Castle, Paul Routledge and Brian Cathcart, 'Mark Thatcher accused: sources say he got 12m pounds from arms deal signed by his mother', *Independent*, 9 October 1994, http://www.independent.co.uk/news/mark-thatcher-accused-say-he-got-12m-pounds-from-arms-deal-signed-by-his-mother-1441851.html.

102 Hollingsworth and Halloran, *Thatcher's Fortunes*, p. 215.

103 *Sunday Times*, 9 October 1994.

104 Hollingsworth and Halloran, *Thatcher's Fortunes*, p. 208.

105 Colvin and Levy, '"An opportunist on a gravy train"', *Sunday Times*, 9 October 1994.

106 Hollingsworth and Halloran, *Thatcher's Fortunes*, p. 208.

107 James, *In the Public Interest*, pp. 105–6.

108 Hollingsworth, and Halloran, *Thatcher's Fortunes*, p. 220.

109 James, *In the Public Interest*, p. 120. I have been unable to find corroborating evidence for this claim.

110 'Profile: Mark Thatcher', BBC News, 26 August 2004, http://news.bbc.co.uk/1/hi/uk_politics/3597196.stm.

111 Kevin Maguire and Michael White, 'Scratcher, the millionaire fixer', *Guardian*, 26 August 2004, http://www.guardian.co.uk/politics/2004/aug/26/uk.southafrica.

112 Ibid.

113 David Pallister, 'Thatcher was integral to coup plot, Mann tells court', *Guardian*, 18 June 2008, http://www.guardian.co.uk/world/2008/jun/18/equatorialguinea.southafrica.

114 Ibid. In the same interview Mann also claimed that the South African President, Thabo Mbeki, had supported the planned coup, as had the South African and Spanish governments. He further claimed that the Pentagon, CIA and major US oil companies had given implicit support to the coup in the oil-rich state run by the Obiang family. The main backer for the coup, according to Mann, was Ely Calil, a Lebanese businessman and property developer living in London, who he says offered him $15m to organize the coup.

115 Hollingsworth and Halloran, *Thatcher's Fortunes*, p. 209; and Leigh and Evans, 'Wafic Said'. It is unclear whether Thatcher purchased the flat through the company or whether the company made the purchase and gave it to Thatcher, who certainly occupied it for two years before selling up.

116 Hollingsworth and Halloran, *Thatcher's Fortunes*, p. 213.

117 Webb, *Armour-Plated Ostrich*, p. 99.

118 Deirdre Hipwell, 'Investors cash in on Libya's post-sanction era', PropertyWeek.com, 5 April 2007, http://www.propertyweek.com/story.asp?storycode=3084341.

119 Holly Watt and Robert Winnett, 'Company with links to Tony Blair adviser in Libya tourism deal', *Daily Telegraph*, 7 November 2009, http://www.telegraph.co.uk/news/newstopics/politics/6515524/Company-with-links-to-Tony-Blair-adviser-in-Libya-tourism-deal.html.

120 Wafic Said website, 'Said Foundation', http://www.waficsaid.com/Said_foundation.htm.

121 FAME company searches.

122 Said Business School website, 'Our Benefactors', http://www.sbs.ox.ac.uk/about/Pages/benefactors.aspx.

123 Wafic Said website, 'Said Business School', http://www.waficsaid.com/said_business_school.htm.

124 Rachel Sylvester, 'The fixer who keeps a foot in both camps', *Daily Telegraph*, 17 March 2001, http://www.telegraph.co.uk/news/uknews/1326784/The-fixer-who-keeps-a-foot-in-both-camps.html.

125 Charlie Bain, 'Oxford dons vote against business school project', *Independent*, 6 November 1996, http://www.independent.co.uk/news/oxford-dons-vote-against-business-school-project-1350919.html?cmp=ilc-n.

126 'Climber cleared of trespass offence', *Oxford Mail*, 20 February 2002, http://archive.oxfordmail.net/2002/2/20/44121.html.

127 Centre for Lebanese Studies website, 'People', http://www.lebanesestudies.com/7/About%20the%20Centre%20%3E%20Who%20we%20are.html.

128 Wafic Said website, 'Profile', http://www.waficsaid.com/profile.htm.

129 UNESCO website, http://www.unesco.org/confgen/participants/lists/saint_vincent_et_grenadines.html; Wafic Said website, 'Profile', http://www.waficsaid.com/profile.htm.

130 Alderson, '"Do I deserve to be labelled a Syrian terrorist?"' (see n. 83 above).

131 Robert Winnett and Jonathan Calvert, 'Cameron took £100,000 from Saudi arms dealer', *Sunday Times*, 26 March 2006.

132 Rasha Said, his daughter and at the time a nineteen-year-old student, and his wife, Rosemary, reportedly donated to the Conservative Party four times in 2005. According to her father, Rasha's assets at the time amounted to £200. Robert Winnett, 'Tories face investigation into donations from Syrian millionaire's family', *Daily Telegraph*, 31 March 2009, http://www.telegraph.co.uk/news/newstopics/politics/conservative/5084166/Tories-face-investigation-into-donations-from-Syrian-millionaires-family.html; David Hencke and agencies, 'Labour MP asks Electoral Commission to investigate Tory donor', *Guardian*, 18 November 2009, http://www.guardian.co.uk/politics/2008/nov/18/conservatives-bae; the Conservative Party was forced to admit that 'In 2005 a number of donations from Rosemary were incorrectly registered with the Electoral Commission as coming from her daughter Rasha. This was an administrative error for which we take full responsibility. It occurred because of a misreading of the electoral roll during compliance checks.' Despite

these claims of a clerical error, a Labour MP has asked that a £47,000 donation from Rasha Said be investigated by the Electoral Commission.

133 Chris Blackhurst, 'Whitehall alarm over Mandelson's meetings in Syria', *Independent*, 16 February 2001, http://www.independent.co.uk/news/uk/politics/whitehall-alarm-over-mandelsons-meetings-in-syria-692007.html?cmp=ilc-n.

134 Ibid.

135 David Leigh, Rob Evans and Ewen MacAskill, 'Lebanese billionaire is drawn into BAE arms deal inquiry as "second middleman for Saudis"', *Guardian*, 2 December 2006, http://www.guardian.co.uk/world/2006/dec/02/bae.armstrade.

136 Mohammad Safadi website, translated into English using google translate, biography page at http://translate.google.co.uk/translate?js=y&prev=_t&hl=en&ie=UTF-8&layout=1&eotf=1&u=http%3A%2F%2Fwww.mohammad-safadi.com%2Fwhy.php&sl=auto&tl=en.

137 David Leigh and Rob Evans, 'Mohammed Safadi', *Guardian*, 7 June 2007, http://www.guardian.co.uk/world/2007/jun/07/bae6.

138 'Lebanon's unity government', Al Jazeera, 9 November 2009, http://english.aljazeera.net/news/middleeast/2009/11/2009119194612926893.html; 'Safadi urges boycott of Israeli goods in Arab markets', *Daily Star* (Lebanon), 28 April 2010, http://www.dailystar.com.lb/article.asp?edition_id=1&categ_id=3&article_id=114295#axzz0u7qnaQfs.

139 Leigh, Evans and MacAskill, 'Lebanese billionaire is drawn into BAE arms deal inquiry' (see n. 135 above).

140 Leigh and Evans, 'Mohammed Safadi' (see n. 137 above).

141 TAG Aviation website, http://www.tagaviation.com/TagFarnboroughAirport/tabid/84/Default.aspx; Fame entry for 'TAG AVIATION HOLDING SA'.

142 Leigh and Rob Evans, 'Mohammed Safadi' (see n. 137 above).

143 Ibid.

144 Fame entry for 'BRITISH MEDITERRANEAN AIRWAYS LTD'.

145 Leigh and Evans, 'Wafic Said' (see n. 87 above).

146 Quoted in William Simpson, *The Prince: The Secret Story of the World's Most Intriguing Royal Prince, Bandar Bin Sultan* (New York: HarperCollins, 2006), p. 149.

147 Declassified State Department Cable, 7 May 2004, published at http://www.pbs.org/frontlineworld/stories/bribe/images/pdf/helicopter.pdf.

148 Ibid.

149 Ibid.

150 'Black Money' (see n. 13 above).

151 Ibid.

6. Diamonds and Arms

1 Bavarian State Office of Criminal Investigation, *Report on the Greek Citizen Angelos Scordas/Merex*, Case Ref: 142/96, Volume M-4581-96, Düsseldorf, 11 January 2005.

2 S. Ellis, *The Mask of Anarchy* (New York: New York University Press, 2006), p. 67.

3 'Charles Taylor: Africa's monster', *Independent*, 1 April 2006.

4 Ellis, *Mask of Anarchy*, p. 67.

5 Ibid.

6 'Charles Taylor: Africa's monster', *Independent*, 1 April 2006.

7   Ellis, *Mask of Anarchy*, p. 67.
8   'Charles Taylor claims US helped spring him from Plymouth Jail', *Boston Globe*, 16 July 2009.
9   Ibid.
10 'Ex-leader of Liberia cites CIA in jailbreak', *The New York Times*, 17 July 2009.
11 Ibid.; and 'How Taylor escaped US prison', *Inquirer* (Liberia), July 2009.
12 'Ex-leader of Liberia cites CIA in jailbreak', *The New York Times*, 17 July 2009.
13 Ellis, *Mask of Anarchy*, pp. 67–9.
14 'Charles Taylor and the assassination of Sankara', *Pambazuka News*, 19 June 2008, Issue 382.
15 'Ghaddaffi, Compaore named external actors in Liberian conflict', *Daily Observer* (Liberia), 14 December 2009; D. Farah, *Blood From Stones: The Secret Financial Network of Terror* (New York: Broadway Books, 2004), p. 10.
16 Farah, *Blood From Stones*, p. 24.
17 Ibid.
18 Ibid.
19 Ellis, *Mask of Anarchy*, p. 78.
20 'Troubled past of Africa's first republic', BBC News, 12 August 1999.
21 'A bad man in Africa', *Daily Telegraph*, 29 June 2003.
22 'Liberia: the politics of brute force', *Perspective*, 17 July 2000.
23 'Liberia: TRC's most notorious', *New Democrat*, 6 July 2009.
24 *Republic of Liberia Truth and Reconciliation Commission: Final Report, Volume II*, 2009, pp. 127–8, available for download from www.trcofliberia.org.
25 Ibid., p. 128.
26 Ellis, *Mask of Anarchy*, pp. 90–91.
27 A. Adebajo, *Liberia's Civil War: Nigeria, Ecomog and Regional Security in West Africa* (Boulder, Colo.: L. Rienner Publications, 2002), p. 90.
28 G. Campbell, *Blood Diamonds* (Cambridge, Mass.: Basics Books, 2004), p. 72.
29 For a chilling account of the life of a diamond and weapons mule, see *Blood Diamonds*.
30 Ibid., p. 23.
31 Ibid., p. 42.
32 United Nations Security Council, *Report of the Panel of Experts Pursuant to Security Council Resolution 1343 (2001), Paragraph 19, Concerning Liberia*, S/2001/1015, 17 October 2001, para. 153, p. 35.
33 According to information posted via the Australian Government Information Service, www.info.dfat.gov.au. Accessed 25 May 2005.
34 Company Register: Orbal Marketing Services, Australian Securities and Investment Commission. Accessed 16 June 2010.
35 United Nations Security Council, 'Firm offers Liberian diamonds despite ban', *Rapaport*, 14 January 2003; and *Report of the Panel of Experts Appointed Pursuant to Paragraph 4 of Security Council Resolution 1458 (2003), Concerning Liberia*, S/2003/498, 24 April 2003, p. 36.
36 Interrogation of Roger D'Onofrio, Regione Carabinieri Campania: Stazione di Vico Equense, 6 December 1995.
37 'Taylor, Ghadafi, ex-CIA agent organized arms, diamonds smuggling company', Truth and Reconciliation Commission of Liberia, press release, 18 February 2009, available for download from www.trcofliberia.org.; and 'Appendix A: Chronology of Nuclear Smuggling

Incidents' in *The Continuing Threat from Weapons of Mass Destruction*, timeline/briefing document presented during 1996 Congressional Hearings on Intelligence and Security, Central Intelligence Agency (CIA), undated, available for download from www.cia.gov.

38 Interrogation of Roger D'Onofrio, Regione Carabinieri Campania: Stazione di Vico Equense, 6 December 1995.

39 P. Jenkins, 'Whose Terrorists? Libya and State Criminality', *Contemporary Crises 1988*, Vol. 12, p. 14.

40 'In Italy: a subtle mixture of intimidation and seduction', *Le Monde*, 22–23 April 1984, p. 4.

41 Ibid.; and 'The Burden of Billy', *Time*, 4 August 1980.

42 'In Italy: A Subtle Mixture of Intimidation and Seduction', *Le Monde*, 22–23 April 1984, p. 4.

43 'The Burden of Billy', *Time*, 4 August 1980.

44 Ibid.; and V. Pisano, 'Libya's Foothold in Italy', *The Washington Quarterly*, Vol. 5 (1982), No. 2, pp. 179–80.

45 'Billy Carter dies of cancer at 51; troubled brother of a president', *The New York Times*, 26 September 1980.

46 Interrogation of Roger D'Onofrio, Regione Carabinieri Campania: Stazione di Vico Equense, 6 December 1995.

47 Ibid.

48 Ibid.

49 Ibid.

50 Ibid. See also *Republic of Liberia Truth and Reconciliation Commission: Volume III (Appendices), Economic Crimes and the Conflict: Exploitation and Abuse*, 2009, paras. 113–15.

51 *Republic of Liberia Truth and Reconciliation Commission: Volume III* (see n. 50 above).

52 Bavarian State Office of Criminal Investigation, *Report on the Greek Citizen Angelos Scordas/ Merex*, Case Ref: 142/96, Volume M-4581-96, Düsseldorf, 11 January 2005.

53 'Agreement No. 002A between Swift International Business Services Canada Inc. (Montreal), Battisto Elmo (Milan) and IBC International Business Consult (Monrovia)', undated; 'Agreement No. 002A between Swift International Business Services Canada Inc. (Montreal), Battisto Elmo (Milan) and IBC International Business Consult (Monrovia)', 25 February 1994 (signed Dennis Moorby, Battisto Elmo and Dr Rudolf Meroni); 'Agreement No. 001A between Swift International Business Services Canada Inc. (Montreal), Battisto Elmo (Milan) and IBC International Business Consult (Monrovia)', 2 March 1994, Signed Dennis Moorby, Battisto Elmo, Dr Rudolf Meroni and Carlo Galeazzi. Documents gathered and collated by Italian police under auspices of the 'Cheque to Cheque' investigation.

54 'Informative di Reato Relativa all'operazione "Cheque to Cheque"', Regione Carabinieri Campania: Stazione di Vico Equense, 30 June 1998, p. 308.

55 Memo conferring power of attorney to Francesco Elmo, Swift International Business Services Canada Inc., Signed Dennis Moorby, Zurich, 8 April 1994. Documents gathered and collated by Italian police under auspices of the 'Cheque to Cheque' investigation.

56 Interrogation of Roger D'Onofrio, Regione Carabinieri Campania: Stazione di Vico Equense, 6 December 1995. See also *Republic of Liberia Truth and Reconciliation Commission: Volume III* (see n. 50 above), para. 113.

57 M. Hibbs, 'Plutonium, Politics and Panic', *Bulletin of Atomic Scientists*, November/December 2004, p. 25.

58 'A master plan drawn in blood', *The New York Times*, 2 April 2006.

59 Ellis, *Mask of Anarchy*, p. 109.

60 Jimmy Johnson, 'Israelis and Hezbollah haven't always been enemies', 11 September 2006, http://www.williambowles.info/syria_lebanon/israel_hezbollah.html.

61 Statement of Fernando Robleda, 6 June 2000, Central Examining Court: Madrid and Interrogation of Vadim Semov, 25 April 2002, Central Examining Court: Madrid and Interrogation of Leonid Minin, 8 July 2001, Monza Public Prosecutor's Office.

62 'Minin Leonid Efimovic', Anneso '1', Commando Generale dell'Arma dei Carabinieri, Ufficio Criminalita Organizzata, Roma, 17 March 1996 (Cheque to Cheque documents).

63 'Mafia Ucraina/Ukrainian Organized Crime', Servizio Centrale Operativo Della Polizia di Stato, Report of Symposium held in Rome, 7–8 October 1998.

64 Ibid.

65 Ibid.

66 Ibid.

67 Ibid. Note that this is also variously spelt as Naftna Mafija.

68 Ibid.

69 Ibid.

70 Ibid.

71 Interrogation of Leonid Minin, Busto Arsizio Prison, 7 July 2001.

72 Statement of Fernando Robleda, 6 June 2000 (see n. 61 above).

73 'Articles of Incorporation of Exotic Tropical Timber Enterprises', Monrovia, Liberia, 25 February 1997.

74 'Plantation Harvesting Rights and Investment Incentive Contract between the Government of the Republic of Liberia and Exotic Tropical Timber Enterprises', signed Mary Mamie Howe, Monrovia, Liberia, 15 May 1997.

75 Letter from Fernando Robleda to the Resident Representative, European Commission (Aid Coordination Office in Liberia), 15 January 1998, and attached 'Aide Memoire'.

76 Ibid.

77 Statement of Fernando Robleda, 6 June 2000 (see n. 61 above).

78 Interrogation of Leonid Minin, 8 July 2001, Monza Public Prosecutor's Office.

79 Minutes of the Meeting of the Board of Directors of Exotic Tropical Timber Enterprises, 10 December 1998, Hotel Africa.

80 'Forest Products Utilization Contract between the Government of the Republic of Liberia and Exotic Tropical Timber Enterprises', 14 December 1998.

81 United Nations Security Council, *Report of the Panel of Experts Pursuant to Security Council Resolution 1306 (2000), Paragraph 19, in Relation to Sierra Leone*, S/2000/1195, December 2001, para. 211, p. 35; Interrogation of Leonid Minin, 10 September 2001, Monza Public Prosecutor's Office. Minin denied any role in the deal despite the extensive records linking him to it.

82 Gberie, *Dirty War in West Africa*, p. 129; and reports compiled by Human Rights Watch.

83 Gberie, *Dirty War in West Africa*, p. 127.

84 'Anatomy of two arms dealers', *Asia Times*, 19 June 2004.

85 Amnesty International and TransArms, *Dead on Time – Arms Transportation, Brokering and the Threat to Human Rights*, ACT 30/007/2006, 9 May 2006.

86 UN Security Council, *Report of the Panel of Experts Pursuant to Security Council Resolution 1306* (see n. 81 above), pp. 35–6. See also UN Security Council, *Report of the Panel of Experts Pursuant to Security Council Resolution 1343* (see n. 32 above), para. 212, p. 47.

87 'War crimes trial resumes for former leader of Liberia', *The New York Times*, 8 January 2008.

88 'The Tammivuori family has long advanced Finnish exports', *Helsingin Sanomat*, 2 July 2002.

89 Interrogation of Leonid Minin, 8 July 2001, Monza Public Prosecutor's Office.

90 Fax from Erkki Tammivuori to Leonid Minin, 20 March 1999, Minin Archives/Docs.

91 Interrogation of Leonid Minin, 8 July 2001, Monza Public Prosecutor's Office.

92 Fax from Erkki Tammivuori to Leonid Minin (Limad AG – Zug), Ref: Consulting Agreement Structure', 24 June 1999.

93 Fax from Erkki Tammivuori addressed to 'Dear Leo', undated, headed: 'Summary Report on the Meetings with a Checklist for Items Expected from the Liberian Side'.

94 'Minin Esame Documenti Sequestri', Italian translation and summary of documents seized from Leonid Minin by Italian police in August 2000, 23 May 2001.

95 Fax from Erkki Tammivuori to Leonid Minin, Ref.: 'Konkurs' Missiles Procurement, 23 March 1999, Minin Archives/Docs.

96 Ibid.

97 Fax from Erkki Tammivuori (Met A.S.) to Leonid Minin, 27 July 1999, Minin Archives/ Papers.

98 'Finnish businessman implicated in weapons smuggling from Europe to Liberia', *Helsingin Sanomat*, 2 July 2002.

99 UN Security Council, *Report of the Panel of Experts Pursuant to Security Council Resolution 1343* (see n. 32 above), para. 218.

100 Amnesty International, *Dead on Time*.

101 Ken Silverstein, 'Comrades in Arms', *Washington Monthly*, January/February 2002.

102 'Sierra Leone: Gunrunners', transcript of PBS arms-dealing special, May 2002, www. stimson.org. Accessed 9 August 2010.

103 'From factory to firing line: the story of one bullet', *Sunday Herald* Online, 9 October 2005.

104 Silverstein, 'Comrades in Arms'.

105 Interrogation of Leonid Minin, 8 July 2001, Monza Public Prosecutor's Office.

106 Ibid.

107 Fax from Fernando Robleda to Vadim Semov, 19 March 1999, Minin Italian Case Legal Docs.

108 Greenpeace, *Logs of War: The Relationship between the Timber Sector, Arms Trafficking and the Destruction of the Forests in Liberia*, March 2001, pp. 17–18.

109 'Buyer beware: the stamps that fooled a nation', *Independent*, 13 May 2006.

110 Interview with source.

111 'The deadly convenience of Viktor Bout', *ISN ETH Zurich*, 24 June 2008.

112 '*Times* Topics: Viktor Bout', *The New York Times*, 11 August 2009.

113 'The deadly convenience of Viktor Bout', *ISN ETH Zurich*, 24 June 2008. This claim was described as rubbish by Bout's wife, Alla, who attacked 'hysterical' articles making the link: 'this is complete nonsense – my father was just an ordinary school teacher, not a KGB general!'

114 'Background: the life of Viktor Bout', *Guardian*, 6 March 2009.

115 Doug Farah and Stephen Braun, *Merchant of Death* (London: John Wiley & Sons, 2007), pp. 32–3.

116 Ibid., pp. 132–6.

117 Coalition for International Justice, *Following Taylor's Money: A Path of War and Destruction*, Washington DC, May 2005, pp. 16–22.

118 Ibid., pp. 45–9.

119 Doug Farah, and Stephen Braun, 'The Merchant of Death', *Foreign Policy*, 10 October, 2006. It should be noted that the British intelligence agency, MI5, estimated the trade to be worth slightly over half of this amount at $30m. See 'A merchant of death or decent businessman?', *Moscow Komsomolskaya Pravda*, 27 February 2002.

120 Farah and Braun, 'Merchant of Death', *Foreign Policy*, 10 October 2006.

121 Farah and Braun, *Merchant of Death*, pp. 49–51.

122 Ibid.

123 Ibid., pp. 81–2.

124 'Victor Bout: Africa's merchant of death', *Guardian*, 23 December 2000. See also United Nations Security Council, *Final Report of the Monitoring Mechanism on Angola Sanctions*, S/2000/1225, 21 December 2000.

125 Farah and Braun, *Merchant of Death*, p. 41. The Liberian aircraft registry was located in London for many years and none of the flight plans or their documents were ever properly evaluated.

126 UN Security Council, *Report of the Panel of Experts Appointed Pursuant to Security Council Resolution 1306* (see n. 81), para. 224.

127 Centre for Public Integrity, *South Africa: The Merchant of Death*, 20 November 2000, available for download from www.allafrica.com. Ruprah has denied any link with Executive Outcomes.

128 'Private Military Companies: Soldiers Inc.', *Jane's Defence Weekly*, 22 May 2002.

129 UN Security Council, *Report of the Panel of Experts Appointed Pursuant to Security Council Resolution 1306* (see n. 81 above), para. 225.

130 UN Security Council, *Report of the Panel of Experts Pursuant to Security Council Resolution 1343* (see n. 32 above), paras. 59–61.

131 Ibid.

132 UN Security Council, *Report of the Panel of Experts Pursuant to Security Council Resolution 1306* (see n. 81 above), para. 232.

133 Ibid., para. 234.

134 Ibid., para 233.

135 'The international dealers in death', *Guardian*, 9 July 2001.

136 Farah and Braun, 'Merchant of Death', *Foreign Policy*.

137 Coalition for International Justice, *Following Taylor's Money*, p. 26.

138 *Republic of Liberia Truth and Reconciliation Commission: Volume III* (see n. 50 above), para. 94.

139 Farah, *Blood From Stones*, p. 5.

140 Ibid., pp. 6 and 113–16.

141 Global Witness, *For a Few Dollars More: How al Qaeda moved into the Diamond Trade*, April 2003, p. 41.

142 Farah, *Blood From Stones*, p. 56.

143 Ibid., pp. 53–9.

144 Wanted poster for Abdullah Ahmed Abdullah, Rewards for Justice Program, US Department of State.

145 Global Witness, *For a Few Dollars More*, p. 41.

146 Ibid.

147 Ibid.

148 'Al Qaeda's growing sanctuary', *Washington Post*, 14 July 2004.

149 Global Witness, *For a Few Dollars More*, p. 47.

150 Ibid.

151 H. Anders, and A. Vines, 'Sanction and Enforcement', in *Developing a Mechanism to Prevent Illicit Brokering in Small Arms and Light Weapons – Scope and Implications* (Geneva: United Nations Institute for Disarmament Research (UNIDIR), 2007), p. 131.

152 Global Witness, *For a Few Dollars More*, pp. 53–9; Yelenik is sometimes spelled Yelnik.

153 Ibid.

154 Ibid.

155 Farah, *Blood From Stones*.

156 There is some dispute as to whether Kouwenhoven, whose first name is sometimes also spelled Guus, was born in Rotterdam or Den Bosch. Different accounts and court records do not agree.

157 'Crimes against humanity: anatomy of an arms dealer', *Independent*, 19 May 2006.

158 Ibid.

159 'Profile: Guus Kouwenhoven', BBC News Online, 10 March 2008.

160 'Crimes against humanity', *Independent*, 19 May 2006.

161 Ibid.

162 Ibid.

163 UN Security Council, *Report of the Panel of Experts Pursuant to Security Council Resolution 1343* (see n. 32 above), para. 333.

164 Ibid., para. 334.

165 *Africa South of the Sahara 2004* (London: Europa Publications, 2004), pp. 614–15.

166 Global Witness, *The Usual Suspects: Liberia's Weapons and Mercenaries in Côte d'Ivoire and Sierra Leone*, March 2003, p. 24.

167 UN Security Council, *Report of the Panel of Experts Pursuant to Security Council Resolution 1343* (see n. 32 above), paras. 334–5.

168 Judgment in the Matter of Public Prosecutors Office (Holland) vs Gus Kouwenhoven, District Court of The Hague (Criminal Law Section), LJN: AY5160/ 09/750001-05, 7 June 2006.

169 Ibid.

170 Ibid.

171 Ibid.

172 Ibid.

173 Ibid.

174 United Nations Security Council, *Security Council Committee on Liberia Updates Assets Freeze List*, SC/8570, 30 November 2005.

175 'Back to the Brink: War Crimes by Liberian Government and Rebels, Section III: Lurd Forces', *Human Rights Watch*, Vol. 14, No. 4(a), May 2002; and Stephen Ellis, email communication, 19 June 2011.

176 International Crisis Group, *Côte d'Ivoire: The War is Not Yet Over*, Africa Report No. 72, 28 November 2003; and Stephen Ellis, email communication, 19 June 2011.

177 *Africa South of the Sahara 2004*, pp. 607–9.

178 The Liberian Truth and Reconciliation Commission published its Final Report in December 2009. It can be downloaded from www.trcofliberia.org. The Final Report also clarifies the origins of the Liberian Truth and Reconciliation Commission and the legal framework in which it operated.

179 'Nigeria will end asylum for warlord', *The New York Times*, 25 March 2006.

180 'Taylor's new Nigerian home', BBC News, 11 August 2003; and 'Taylor's Nigerian gilded cage', BBC News, 28 March 2006.

181 Coalition for International Justice, *Following Taylor's Money*, pp. 16–22.

182 Ibid.

183 Ibid., pp. 6–7.

184 'Nigerian to hand over Liberian ex-leader', *Los Angeles Times*, 26 March 2006.

185 'Ex-Liberian warlord behind bars', *CBS News*, 29 March 2006; and 'Charles Taylor caught in Nigeria', BBC News, 29 March 2006.

186 'Charles Taylor "duped" by Nigeria', BBC News, 10 November 2009.

187 Exact figures for the number of dead in the Liberian conflict are hard to come by. This figure is drawn from Ellis, *Mask of Anarchy*, 'Annex A: Casualties of the Liberian War, 1989–1997', pp. 315–16.

7. Buckling to Bandar

1 'Romania', *Guardian*, 'The BAE Files'.

2 In addition to the sources cited, this chapter is drawn from conversations with a variety of people with knowledge of the investigation.

3 Christopher Hope, 'Twenty years of smokescreen over Saudi deal', *Daily Telegraph*, 21 June 2006, http://www.telegraph.co.uk/finance/2941537/Twenty-years-of-smokescreen-over-Saudi-deal.html.

4 Ibid.

5 FOIA Centre, 'Government falsely claimed that NAO report cleared "Al Yamamah" of bribery allegations', 21 June 2006, http://www.foiacentre.com/news-al-yamamah-060621.html.

6 Christopher Hope and James Kirkup, 'Extravagance uncovered during Saudi arms probe', *Daily Telegraph*, 10 April 2008, http://www.telegraph.co.uk/news/uknews/1584599/Extravagance-uncovered-during-Saudi-arms-probe.html.

7 James, *In the Public Interest* (London: Little, Brown and Company, 1995), p. 56. Bourne eventually resigned from his position, not because his credibility was fatally undermined on Al Yamamah but as a consequence of an expenses claim of £365,000 over three years on travel alone and £27,000 on food. It was also discovered that he was not averse to accepting hospitality from those he was auditing, including as a guest of BAe at the British Grand Prix (Robert Winnett, 'How unsackable Sir John Bourn sealed his fate', *Daily Telegraph*, 26 October 2007, http://www.telegraph.co.uk/news/uknews/1567357/How-unsackable-Sir-John-Bourn-sealed-his-fate.html).

8 David Leigh and Rob Evans, 'Nobbling the police', *Guardian*, 'The BAE Files', http://www.guardian.co.uk/baefiles/page/0,,2098531,00.html.

9 Robert Wardle, witness statement of 17 December 2007 in High Court case between CAAT, Corner House and the Director of the SFO with BAE Systems PLC as an inter-

ested party. CO/1567/07, published at http://www.thecornerhouse.org.uk/sites/thecorner house.org.uk/files/WardleWitState.pdf, 14 April 2010.

10 Document 3 in High Court case between CAAT, Corner House and the Director of the SFO with BAE Systems PLC as an interested party. CO/1567/07, Exhibit RW4, letter of 7 November 2005 from Michael Lester to Lord Goldsmith QC, attaching a memorandum, published at http://www.thecornerhouse.org.uk/sites/thecornerhouse.org.uk/files/SecondRedactDocsRW4.pdf.

11 Ibid.

12 Ibid.

13 Ibid.

14 Ibid.

15 Ibid.

16 OECD Convention on Combating Bribery of Foreign Public Officials in International Business Transactions, Adopted by the Negotiating Conference on 21 November 1997, http://www.oecd.org/dataoecd/4/18/38028044.pdf.

17 Document 3 in High Court case between CAAT, Corner House and the Director of the SFO (see n. 10 above).

18 Document 2 in High Court case between CAAT, Corner House and the Director of the SFO with BAE Systems PLC as an interested party. CO/1567/07, Exhibit RW4, letter of 10 November 2005 from Jonathan Jones to Michael Lester, published at http://www.thecornerhouse.org.uk/sites/thecornerhouse.org.uk/files/SecondRedactDocsRW4.pdf, 23 November 2009.

19 Document 4 in High Court case between CAAT, Corner House and the Director of the SFO with BAE Systems PLC as an interested party. CO/1567/07, Exhibit RW4, letter of 11 November 2005 from Michael Lester to Jonathan Jones, published at http://www.thecornerhouse.org.uk/sites/thecornerhouse.org.uk/files/SecondRedactDocsRW4.pdf, 23 November 2009.

20 Document 6 in High Court case between CAAT, Corner House and the Director of the SFO with BAE Systems PLC as an interested party. CO/1567/07, Exhibit RW4, letter of 15 November 2005 from Matthew Cowie to Jonathan Hitchin, published at http://www.thecornerhouse.org.uk/sites/thecornerhouse.org.uk/files/SecondRedactDocsRW4.pdf, 23 November 2009.

21 Robert Wardle, witness statement of 17 December 2009 in High Court case between CAAT, Corner House and the Director of the SFO (see n. 9 above).

22 Document 1 in High Court case between CAAT, Corner House and the Director of the SFO with BAE Systems PLC as an interested party. CO/1567/07, Exhibit RW2, letter from Jonathan Jones to Gus O'Donnell and others, 6 December 2005, published at http://www.thecornerhouse.org.uk/sites/thecornerhouse.org.uk/files/RedactedDocsRW2.pdf.

23 Robert Wardle, witness statement of 17 December 2009 in High Court case between CAAT, Corner House and the Director of the SFO (see n. 9 above).

24 Document 2 in High Court case between CAAT, Corner House and the Director of the SFO with BAE Systems PLC as an interested party. CO/1567/07, Exhibit RW2, letter from Gus O'Donnell to Jonathan Jones, 16 December 2005, published at http://www.thecornerhouse.org.uk/sites/thecornerhouse.org.uk/files/RedactedDocsRW2.pdf.

25 Ibid.

26 Ibid.

27 Document 7 in High Court case between CAAT, Corner House and the Director of the SFO with BAE Systems PLC as an interested party. CO/1567/07, Exhibit RW4, file note written by Robert Wardle dated 22 December 2005 recording conversation on 7 December 2005 with Michael Lester, published at http://www.thecornerhouse.org.uk/sites/ thecornerhouse.org.uk/files/SecondRedactDocsRW4.pdf, 23 November 2009.

28 Document 8 in High Court case between CAAT, Corner House and the Director of the SFO with BAE Systems PLC as an interested party. CO/1567/07, Exhibit RW4, email from Jonathan Hitchin to Matthew Cowie of 8 December 2005, attaching a memorandum for the Director of the Serious Fraud Office, published at http://www. thecornerhouse.org.uk/sites/thecornerhouse.org.uk/files/SecondRedactDocsRW4.pdf, 23 November 2009.

29 Ibid.

30 Ibid.

31 Document 9 in High Court case between CAAT, Corner House and the Director of the SFO with BAE Systems PLC as an interested party. CO/1567/07, Exhibit RW4, Director Brief written by Matthew Cowie, 19 December 2005, published at http://www. thecornerhouse.org.uk/sites/thecornerhouse.org.uk/files/SecondRedactDocsRW4.pdf, 23 November 2009.

32 Drawn from Document 10 in High Court case between CAAT, Corner House and the Director of the SFO with BAE Systems PLC as an interested party. CO/1567/07, Exhibit RW4, note of meeting on 11 January 2006, attended by the Law Officers and the Director of the SFO, and others, published at http://www.thecornerhouse.org.uk/sites/ thecornerhouse.org.uk/files/SecondRedactDocsRW4.pdf, 23 November 2009.

33 Robert Wardle, witness statement of 17 December 2009 in High Court case between CAAT, Corner House and the Director of the SFO (see n. 9 above).

34 Leigh and Evans, 'Nobbling the police' (see n. 8 above).

35 Freedom of Information response from the Attorney General, 4 April 2007, to the *Guardian*, p. 5, published at http://web.archive.org/web/20080407230917/http://www.attorney-general.gov.uk/attachments/Sample+SFO+&+bae+reply.pdf. (Link on the *Guardian* files, http://www.guardian.co.uk/baefiles/page/0,,2098531,00.html, is no longer active; link above is using the WebArchive website retrieving the document posted active in 2008.)

36 Document 1 in High Court case between CAAT, Corner House and the Director of the SFO with BAE Systems PLC as an interested party. CO/1567/07, Exhibit RW2, letter from Gus O'Donnell to Jonathan Jones, 29 September 2006, published at http://www. thecornerhouse.org.uk/sites/thecornerhouse.org.uk/files/RedactedDocsRW2.pdf.

37 Document 11 in High Court case between CAAT, Corner House and the Director of the SFO with BAE Systems PLC as an interested party. CO/1567/07, Exhibit RW4, letter from Helen Garlick, Assistant Director of the SFO, to Jonathan Jones, Legal Secretary to the Law Officers, 27 October 2006, published at http://www.thecornerhouse.org.uk/ sites/thecornerhouse.org.uk/files/SecondRedactDocsRW4.pdf, 23 November 2009.

38 Ibid.

39 Ibid.

40 Freedom of Information response from the Attorney General, 4 April 2007, to the *Guardian*,

p. 6 (see n. 35 above), referencing the Attorney General's answer to a parliamentary question from Lord Avebury on 22 January 2007.

41 Ibid.

42 Ibid.

43 Leigh and Evans, 'Nobbling the police' (see n. 8 above).

44 David Leppard, 'Blair hit by Saudi "bribery" threat', *Sunday Times*, 19 November 2006, http://www.timesonline.co.uk/tol/news/uk/article641360.ece.

45 Benedict Brogan, '50,000 British jobs at risk if vital defence deal is lost', *Daily Mail*, 24 November 2006, http://www.dailymail.co.uk/news/article-418481/50-000-British-jobs-risk-vital-defence-deal-lost.html.

46 David Leigh and Rob Evans, 'Brutal politics lesson for corruption investigators', *Guardian*, 16 December 2006, http://www.guardian.co.uk/uk/2006/dec/16/armstrade.saudiarabia2.

47 Ibid.

48 Christopher Hope, 'Halt inquiry or we cancel Eurofighters', *Daily Telegraph*, 1 December 2006, http://www.telegraph.co.uk/news/uknews/1535683/Halt-inquiry-or-we-cancel-Eurofighters.html.

49 Isabel Oakeshott, 'MPs demand Blair save Saudi weapons deal', *Sunday Times*, 3 December 2006, http://www.timesonline.co.uk/tol/news/uk/article658378.ece.

50 Christopher Hope, 'Pressure grows to resolve fraud inquiry into Saudi arms deals', *Daily Telegraph*, 4 December 2006, http://www.telegraph.co.uk/finance/2951813/Pressure-grows-to-resolve-fraud-inquiry-into-Saudi-arms-deals.html.

51 James, *In the Public Interest*, p. 104.

52 Ibid., p. 115; and 'Pergau dam affair: "sweeteners" row sparked trade ban', *Independent*, 8 September 1994.

53 'Black Money', *Frontline*, PBS, http://www.pbs.org/wgbh/pages/frontline/blackmoney/view/, transcript available at http://www.pbs.org/wgbh/pages/frontline/blackmoney/etc/script.html.

54 Ibid.

55 Leigh and Evans, 'Brutal politics lesson for corruption investigators' (see n. 46 above).

56 Document 2 in High Court case between CAAT, Corner House and the Director of the SFO (see n. 24 above).

57 Leigh and Evans, 'Brutal politics lesson for corruption investigators', (see n. 46 above).

58 Ibid.

59 Ewen MacAskill and Rob Evans, 'Britain "agreed in secret" to expel Saudis during £40bn arms talks', *Guardian*, 28 September 2005, http://www.guardian.co.uk/uk/2005/sep/28/saudiarabia.armstrade.

60 Richard Norton-Taylor, 'Britain and the Saudis finally sign £4.43bn Eurofighter deal', *Guardian*, 18 September 2007, http://www.guardian.co.uk/uk/2007/sep/18/saudiarabia.armstrade.

61 CAAT, Control BAE website, http://www.caat.org.uk/campaigns/controlBAE/.

62 Ian Davis and Emma Mayhew, *What Happens When a White Elephant Meets a Paper Tiger?: The Prospective Sale of Eurofighter Typhoon Aircraft to Saudi Arabia and the EU Code of Conduct on Arms Exports*, BASIC Papers, Occasional Papers on International Security Policy, No. 49, December 2005, http://kms1.isn.ethz.ch/serviceengine/Files/ISN/17188/ipublicationdocument_singledocument/ceba82f1-3083-4138-a0ee-83f6ba56e3d7/en/BASIC+PAPERS.pdf.

63 'The impact of the large cost overruns and delays', in *Select Committee on Public Accounts Forty-Third Report*, Chapter One, 2004, http://www.publications.parliament.uk/pa/cm200304/cmselect/cmpubacc/383/38305.htm#note12.

64 Hansard, 9 March 1989, Column 1055, http://www.publications.parliament.uk/pa/cm198889/cmhansrd/1989-03-09/Debate-2.html.

65 Davis and Mayhew, *What Happens When a White Elephant Meets a Paper Tiger?* (see n. 62 above).

66 Hansard, 9 July 1997, Column 855, http://www.publications.parliament.uk/pa/cm199798/cmhansrd/vo970709/debtext/70709-02.htm#70709-02_spnew0.

67 Sylvia Pfeifer, 'Oman in talks to buy Eurofighter Typhoons', *Financial Times*, 3 April 2010, http://www.ft.com/cms/s/0/9616ce7a-3eb8-11df-a706-00144feabdc0.html; and UPI, 5 April 2010; and 'Sources: Oman to buy 24 Eurofighters', http://www.upi.com/Business_News/Security-Industry/2010/04/05/Sources-Oman-to-buy-24-Eurofighters/UPI-28171270484630/.

68 Davis and Mayhew, *What Happens When a White Elephant Meets a Paper Tiger?* (see n. 62 above), quoting US Department of State, *World Military Expenditures and Arms Transfers*, table III, 1999–2000.

69 'BAE steps up Saudi effort', *Flight International*, 21 June 2005, http://www.flightglobal.com/articles/2005/06/21/199774/bae-steps-up-saudi-effort.html.

70 Davis and Mayhew, *What Happens When a White Elephant Meets a Paper Tiger?* (see n. 62 above).

71 Leigh and Evans, 'Brutal politics lesson for corruption investigators' (see n. 46 above).

72 Witness statement of Dr John Jenkins (FCO) in High Court case between CAAT, Corner House and the Director of the SFO with BAE Systems PLC as an interested party. CO/1567/07, published at http://image.guardian.co.uk/sys-files/Politics/documents/2008/07/09/JenkinsStatement.pdf.

73 *Sunday Times*, 10 June 2007.

74 David Leigh and Rob Evans, 'BAE: secret papers reveal threats from Saudi prince', *Guardian*, 15 February 2008, http://www.guardian.co.uk/world/2008/feb/15/bae.armstrade.

75 Michael Settle, 'French connection to axed inquiry. Fears Paris could snatch a new deal lay behind the U-turn, finds Michael Settle', *Herald Scotland*, 16 December 2006, http://www.heraldscotland.com/sport/spl/aberdeen/french-connection-to-axed-inquiry-fears-paris-could-snatch-a-new-deal-lay-behind-the-u-turn-finds-michael-settle-1.1971.

76 Corner House, 'Documents reveal that Blair urged end to BAE–Saudi corruption investigation', 21 December 2007, http://www.thecornerhouse.org.uk/item.shtml?x=559591. The minute can be viewed at www.theshadowworld.com.

77 Document 7 in High Court case between CAAT, Corner House and the Director of the SFO with BAE Systems PLC as an interested party. CO/1567/07, Exhibit RW2, first attachment to the Prime Minister's minute: letter and note from Sir Richard Mottram, Permanent Secretary Intelligence, Security and Resilience, 23 November 2006, published at http://www.thecornerhouse.org.uk/sites/thecornerhouse.org.uk/files/RedactedDocsRW2.pdf.

78 Document 8 in High Court case between CAAT, Corner House and the Director of the SFO with BAE Systems PLC as an interested party. CO/1567/07, Exhibit RW2, second attachment to the Prime Minister's minute: letter from Sir Peter Ricketts to Oliver Robbins Esq., Principal Private Secretary, 10 Downing Street, 24 November 2006, published

at http://www.thecornerhouse.org.uk/sites/thecornerhouse.org.uk/files/RedactedDoc sRW2.pdf.

79 Leigh and Evans, 'Nobbling the police' (see n. 8 above).

80 Corner House, 'Documents reveal that Blair urged end to BAE–Saudi corruption investigation' (see n. 76 above).

81 Document 9 in High Court case between CAAT, Corner House and the Director of the SFO with BAE Systems PLC as an interested party. CO/1567/07, Exhibit RW2, letter from Sir Oliver Robbins to Jonathan Jones, 12 December 2006 published at http://www. thecornerhouse.org.uk/sites/thecornerhouse.org.uk/files/RedactedDocsRW2.pdf.

82 Document 12 in High Court case between CAAT, Corner House and the Director of the SFO with BAE Systems PLC as an interested party. CO/1567/07, Exhibit RW4, note, dated 14 December 2006, of meeting on 13 December 2006, attended by the Law Officers and the Director, and others, published at http://www.thecornerhouse.org.uk/sites/thecornerhouse. org.uk/files/SecondRedactDocsRW4.pdf, 23 November 2009.

83 Ibid.

84 Freedom of Information response from the Attorney General, 4 April 2007, to the *Guardian*, p. 7 (see n. 35 above), referencing the Solicitor General's answer to a written Parliamentary Question from Susan Kramer MP on 19 January 2007.

85 Gleaned from sources interviewed regularly from 2004 to 2010. The author requested a response from Lord Goldsmith but received no reply to a series of email messages.

86 Freedom of Information response from the Attorney General, 4 April 2007, to the *Guardian*, p. 7 (see n. 35 above).

87 Ibid., p. 8.

88 Hansard, 14 December 2006, column 1712, and Hansard, 14 December 2006, Column 1119.

89 Mark Milner, 'City shrugs off investigation into bribery allegations at BAE as earnings soar to £1.2bn', *Guardian*, 23 February 2007, http://www.guardian.co.uk/business/2007/ feb/23/politics.freedomofinformation.

90 'Arms and the man', *Guardian*, 15 December 2006, http://www.guardian.co.uk/comment isfree/2006/dec/15/labour.partyfunding.

91 'MI6 and Blair at odds over Saudi deals', *Guardian*, 16 January 2007.

92 'Blair: I pushed for end to Saudi arms enquiry', *The Times*, 15 December 2006.

93 *Guardian*, 13 March 2007 and 14 March 2007.

94 *Guardian*, 24 April 2007.

95 *Guardian*, 11 June 2007.

96 *Guardian*, 7 June 2007.

97 'Police hunt arms trail in Downing Street', *The Times*, 20 May 2007.

98 The letter can be seen at www.theshadowworld.com.

99 'Hermes enters BAE probe fray', *Financial Times*, 22 December 2006.

100 'F&C express concern over dropping of BAE case', *Guardian*, 22 December 2006.

101 Case No: CO/1567/2007, The Queen on the Application of Corner House Research and Campaign against Arms Trade and The Director of the Serious Fraud Office and BAE Systems PLC, Approved Judgment, 10 April 2008, published at http://www.thecornerhouse. org.uk/pdf/document/JR-Judgment.pdf.

102 Ibid.

103 Ibid.

104 Leigh and Evans, 'BAE: secret papers reveal threats from Saudi prince' (see n. 74 above).

105 *Guardian*, 10 April 2008.

106 Ibid.

107 A. C. Grayling, 'The law triumphant', *Guardian*, 15 April 2008, http://www.guardian. co.uk/commentisfree/2008/apr/15/thelawtriumphant.

108 'Can we stop grovelling to the Saudis?', *Daily Mail*, 11 June 2007, http://www.dailymail. co.uk/debate/columnists/article-461108/Can-stop-grovelling-Saudis.html.

109 'Keeper of the Saudi secrets', *The New York Times*, 14 June 2007, http://www.nytimes. com/2007/06/14/opinion/14thu3.html?_r=2.

110 David Howarth, 'Mystery of the Saudi "threat"', *Guardian*, 1 August 2008, http://www. guardian.co.uk/commentisfree/2008/aug/01/bae.saudiarabia.

111 R. Cook, *Point of Departure* (London: Simon & Schuster, 2003).

112 David Leigh, 'Woolf commands fact-free zone with aplomb', *Guardian*, 6 May 2008, http://www.guardian.co.uk/world/2008/may/06/bae.baesystemsbusiness1.

113 Ibid.

114 http://ir.baesystems.com/investors/storage/woolf_report_2008.pdf; Eveline Lubbers and Wil van der Schans, 'The Threat Response Spy Files', November 2004, http://www.evcl. nl/spinwatch/TRFrontpage.htm; and CAAT, '2005 CAAT Steering Committee statement on spying', http://www.caat.org.uk/about/spying.php.

115 Leigh, 'Woolf commands fact-free zone with aplomb' (see n. 112 above).

116 Ibid.

117 David Leigh, 'The unanswered questions', *Guardian*, 7 May 2008, http://www.guardian. co.uk/world/2008/may/07/bae.armstrade.

118 My personal notes taken at the BAE AGM, Queen Elizabeth Conference Centre, 7 May 2008.

119 David Robertson and Matt Spence, 'BAE pleads guilty to US criminal charge', *The Times*, 1 March 2010, http://business.timesonline.co.uk/tol/business/industry_sectors/engineering/article7046011.ece.

120 'BAE announces surprise departure of former chief Sir Dick Evans', *The Times*, 30 March 2010.

121 'BAE goes big on "green" weapons', BBC News, 26 October 2006, http://news.bbc.co.uk/1/hi/technology/6081486.stm.

122 Ibid.

123 Ibid.

124 Mark Townsend, 'BAE drops plans to make "green bullets"', *Guardian*, 24 August 2008, http://www.guardian.co.uk/business/2008/aug/24/baesystems.military.

125 David Leigh and Terry Macalister, 'New BAE investigation doomed to failure, claims chairman', *Guardian*, 8 May 2008, http://www.guardian.co.uk/business/2008/may/08/BAesystemsbusiness; there was a similar reaction in 2009 to claims of its being an ethical company: Terry Macalister, 'Critics attack BAE Systems over attempt to become "ethical" arms firm', *Guardian*, 6 May 2009, http://www.guardian.co.uk/business/2009/may/06/baesystems-arms-trade.

126 David Leigh, 'New head of Serious Fraud Office defies talk of crisis', *Guardian*, 18 April 2008, http://www.guardian.co.uk/world/2008/apr/18/bae.foreignpolicy.

127 Simon Bowers, 'Senior SFO prosecutors quit as new director changes priorities', *Guardian*, 10 June 2008, http://www.guardian.co.uk/business/2008/jun/10/3.

128 David Leigh, 'Law lords: fraud office right to end bribery investigation in BAE case', *Guardian*, 31 July 2008, http://www.guardian.co.uk/world/2008/jul/31/bae.armstrade.

129 Ibid.

130 Ibid.

131 'Not the last word', *Guardian*, 31 July 2008, http://www.guardian.co.uk/commentisfree/2008/jul/31/baesystemsbusiness.saudiarabia.

132 Leigh, 'Law lords: fraud office right to end bribery investigation in BAE case' (see n. 128 above).

133 Ibid.

134 'Black Money', *Frontline*, PBS (see n. 53 above).

135 Drawn from conversations with a number of attendees at the event and also Trevor Maggs, 'Has staff morale collapsed at the SFO?', trevormaggs.com, 31 March 2010.

8. And Justice for None?

1 For an excellent discussion of the burden of evidence in relation to arms-dealing trials, see L. van den Herik, 'The Difficulties of Exercising Extraterritorial Criminal Jurisdiction: The Acquittal of a Dutch Businessman for Crimes Committed in Liberia', *International Criminal Law Review*, Vol. 9 (2009), pp. 211–26.

2 Doug Farah and Stephen Braun, *Merchant of Death* (London: John Wiley & Sons, 2007), pp. 192–203.

3 Ibid.

4 Ibid., pp. 202–3.

5 Ibid.

6 Ibid., p. 203.

7 D. Farah and S. Braun, 'The Merchant of Death', *Foreign Policy*, 1 November 2006.

8 'Viktor Bout's Last Deal', Mother Jones, 18 March 2008.

9 Farah and Braun, *Merchant of Death*, Chapter 14; 'Flying Anything to Anybody', *The Economist*, 18 December 2008; and 'Merchant of Death denies arming terror', *Guardian*, 15 March 2009.

10 'W Sieci Terroru', *Tygodnik Nasza Polska*, nr 42 (663), 2008.

11 'Monzer Al Kassar: The Prince of Marbella – Arms to All Sides', *Frontline* World, PBS, May 2002, www.pbs.org/frontlineworld/stories/sierraleone/alkassar.html; and DEA Public Affairs, 'DEA investigation nets international arms dealer with ties to terrorist organizations', press statement, 8 June 2007, www.justice.gov/dea/pubs/states/newsrel/nyc060807.html.

12 'Meet the "Prince of Marbella" – is he really supporting Iraq's insurgency?', *Observer*, 1 October 2006.

13 An excellent account of the sting operation that led to Al Kassar's arrest can be found in P. R. Keefe, 'The Trafficker', *The New Yorker*, 8 February 2010.

14 US Attorney's Office, 'International arms trafficker Monzer Al Kassar and associate sentenced on terrorism charges', press release, 24 February 2009.

15 Ibid.

16 'Taking Down Arms Dealer Viktor Bout', *Men's Journal*, 12 December 2008.

17 'Mystery Briton is key witness in "Merchant of Death" arms sting', *Sunday Times*, 8 February 2009.

18 Sealed Complaint: Violations of Title 18, United States Code, Sections 2339B and 3238, United States of America v. Viktor Bout (and aliases), Southern District of New York, 27 February 2008, para. 5.

19 Ibid.

20 Ibid.

21 Ibid., para. 7.

22 Ibid., para. 8.

23 'Missile System Designed to Destroy Aircraft', US Code Part I, Chapter 113B, § 2332g. Available from www.law.cornell.edu.

24 Sealed Complaint: United States of America v. Viktor Bout (see n. 18 above), paras. 12–13.

25 Ibid., para. 16.

26 Ibid., para. 19.

27 Ibid., paras. 22 and 24.

28 C. Hanley, Affidavit in Support of Request for Extradition in the Matter of United States of America v. Viktor Bout (and aliases), Case No. 08, Cr. 365, United States District Court Southern District of New York, 28 April 2008, para. 24.

29 Ibid., para. 28.

30 'Taking Down Arms Dealer Viktor Bout', *Men's Journal*, 12 December 2008.

31 'Smulian, accused partner of Viktor Bout, is held', Bloomberg, 11 March 2008.

32 'Mystery Briton is key witness in "Merchant of Death" arms sting', *Sunday Times*, 8 February 2009.

33 J. Milione, Rebuttal Affidavit Concerning Request for Extradition in the Matter of United States of America v. Viktor Bout (and aliases), Case No. 08, Cr. 365, United States District Court Southern District of New York, 17 February 2008.

34 Judgment: Offense against Act on Extradition in the Matter between the Public Prosecutor (Thailand) and Mr. Viktor Bout, Bangkok Criminal Court, 11 August 2009, Black Case No. 3/2551.

35 Ibid.

36 Quoted on *ABC World News*, 24 October 2009.

37 'Viktor Bout wonders why the US wants him so badly', *Bangkok Post*, 16 August 2009.

38 Judgment: Offense against Act on Extradition (see n. 34 above)

39 'The notorious Mr. Bout', *Washington Post*, 13 August 2009.

40 E. Royce, *et al.*, 'Letter to Attorney General [Eric] Holder and Secretary of State Clinton re: Viktor Bout', 11 February 2009.

41 'Alleged arms dealer protected by Russia', *Christian Science Monitor*, 24 October 2009.

42 'Why the "Merchant of Death" might not stand trial', *Foreign Policy*, 11 August 2009.

43 Ibid.

44 Ibid.

45 Judgment: Offense against Act on Extradition (see n. 34 above).

46 '"Merchant of Death" could face new charges', *Taipei Times*, 19 February 2010.

47 Sealed Complaint: United States of America v. Viktor Bout (and aliases) and Richard Chichakli (and aliases), Southern District of New York, S1 09 Cr. 1002, March 2010.

48 'Suspected Russian arms dealer Viktor Bout to be extradited to US', *Guardian*, 20 August 2010.

49 Ibid.

50 'Arms suspect vows to win case in U.S. after extradition order', *The New York Times*, 20 August 2010.

51 See 'Viktor Bout has a chance to be back to Russia', *The Voice of Russia*, 13 November 2010.

52 'Viktor Bout, suspected Russian arms dealer, extradited to New York', *Guardian*, 16 November 2010.

53 Based on confidential interviews with sources in the Department of Justice and the Department of State, conducted in November 2008 and February 2010.

54 'U.S., Russia face off over alleged arms trafficker', *Washington Post*, 23 August 2010.

55 'The inner circle of the Taylor regime', The Perspective, 1 January 2001.

56 For a full account of investigations into Kouwenhoven by Global Witness, The Perspective and the UN, see Amnesty International and TransArms, *Dead on Time – Arms Transportation, Brokering and the Threat to Human Rights*, ACT 30/007/2006, 9 May 2006.

57 Judgment in the Matter of Public Prosecutors Office (Holland) vs Gus Kouwenhoven, District Court of The Hague (Criminal Law Section), LJN: AY5160/09/750001-05, 7 June 2006.

58 Ibid., section 2.

59 Ibid.

60 Ibid., section 6.

61 Ibid., section 7.

62 Ibid.

63 Ibid.

64 Ibid., Section 8.

65 Judgment passed in Appeal Pronounced by the District Court in The Hague on 7 June 2006 in the Criminal Case against Gus Kouwenhoven, 10 March 2008, LJN: BC7373, 09-750001-05.

66 Van der Herik, 'The Difficulties of Exercising Extraterritorial Criminal Jurisdiction', *International Criminal Law Review*, pp. 218–19.

67 Ibid., pp. 219–20.

68 Campagne tegen Wapenhandel, 'Tussenhandel in wapens onvoldoende aangepakt', press release, 13 May 2009.

69 Judgment on Further Appeal of the Court of The Hague on 10 March 2008, Number 22/004337-06 in Criminal Proceedings against Gus Kouwenhoven, Supreme Court, S. No. 08/01322, 20 April 2010.

70 'Anatomy of two arms dealers', *Asia Times*, 19 June 2004.

71 W. Mapelli, 'Request for the Enforcement of an Order for Pre-Trial Detention – Article 272 et seq. of the Italian Criminal Procedure Code', Public Prosecutor: Tribunal of Monza, Criminal Records Bureau Number 8644/00/Form 21, 11 June 2011.

72 Ibid.

73 Ibid.

74 Email interview with Walter Mapelli, August 2010.

75 Ken Silverstein, 'Comrades in Arms', *Washington Monthly*, January/February 2002.

76 Email interview with Walter Mapelli, August 2010.

77 Amnesty International and TransArms, *Dead on Time*, pp. 60–63.

78 Ibid.

79 B. Wood, 'The Prevention of Illicit Brokering of Small Arms and Light Weapons: Framing the Issue', in *Developing a Mechanism to Prevent Illicit Brokering in Small Arms and Light Weapons* (Geneva: United Nations Institute for Disarmament Research (UNIDIR), 2007), pp. 4–6.

80 Interview with source close to the investigation interviewed in Italy, December 2009; and email interview with Walter Mapelli, August 2010.

81 M. Brunwasser, 'Leonid Efimovich Minin: From Ukraine, a New Kind of Arms Trafficker', PBS/*Frontline* World Investigative Series: 'Sierra Leone Gun Runners', May 2002, www.pbs.org/frontlineworld/stories/sierraleone/minin.html.

82 Email interview with Walter Mapelli, August 2010.

83 Interview with source close to the investigation interviewed in Italy, December 2009.

Section III: Business as Usual

9. Things Fall Apart – with Help from BAE

1 This figure, as calculated by the authors, is based on the stated rand cost of the deal until 2008 (which are the only figures given) plus the amount that had been budgeted for the remaining payments until 2011. Interest payments will continue to be made until 2018. To this figure was added an estimate of the 'hidden' costs as calculated from data in the South African Treasury's Affordability Report and from the South African Auditor General. (2008 Estimates of National Expenditure, Vote 19: Defence, p. 379. Available at: www. treasury.gov.za.)

2 The detail of this deal, and the claims made here, are contained in my books *After the Party: A Personal and Political Journey inside the ANC* (Jeppestown: Jonathan Ball, 2007) and *After the Party: Corruption, the ANC and South Africa's Uncertain Future* (London: Verso, 2009); Paul Holden's *The Arms Deal in your Pocket* (Jeppestown: Jonathan Ball, 2008) confirms and expands on these claims. Holden was the principal researcher on this book. For an academic account of the deal and its consequences see A. Feinstein, P. Holden and B. Pace, 'Corruption and the Arms Trade: Sins of Commission', in *SIPRI Yearbook 2011* (Oxford: OUP, 2011).

3 'Navy fires first salvo in push to keep afloat', *Sunday Times*, 8 May 1994.

4 'Guns vs. butter? Corvettes decision looms for new SA', *Weekend Argus*, 26 February 1995.

5 'BAE and the Arms Deal: Part 1', Moneyweb, 14 August 2007, www.moneyweb.co.za.

6 Ibid.

7 'Strategic Defence Packages: Draft Report of the Auditor-General', Chapter 5: 'Advanced Light Fighter Aircraft (ALFA) and Lead-In Fighter Trainer (LIFT)', undated, Richard Young/C²I² personal archive (PAIA requests). Used with kind permission of Richard Young.

8 Ibid.

9 'Strategic Defence Packages: Joint Report', Chapter 4, 2001, www.info.gov.za; and 'BAE and the Arms Deal: Part 1', Moneyweb, 14 August 2007, www.moneyweb.gov.za.

10 'Strategic Defence Packages: Joint Report', Chapter 4, paragraph 4.3.6.3, www.info. gov.za.

11 Ibid.
12 'BAE and the Arms Deal: Part 1', Moneyweb, 14 August 2007, www.moneyweb.co.za.
13 'Strategic Defence Packages: Joint Report, 2001', Chapter 4, para. 4.51.10, www.info.gov.za.
14 Ibid., paras 4.5.3.6 and 4.5.5.3.
15 For an eye-opening study of the role of the use of offsets in the defence trade see J. Brauer and J. P. Dunne (eds.), *Arms Trade and Economic Development: Theory, Policy and Cases in Arms Trade Offsets* (London: Routledge, 2004).
16 'DA wants review of arms deal offsets', *Pretoria News*, 14 September 2010.
17 'South African unions threaten to escalate strike', BBC News, 26 August 2010.
18 P. Holden, and H. Van Vuuren, *The Devil in the Detail* (Jeppestown: Jonathan Ball, forthcoming).
19 Hansard, 'National Assembly: Questions and Replies', Wednesday, 10 October 2001, Vol. 43A, p. 4103.
20 Draft of introductory chapter, 'Methodology Employed', undated, Dr Richard Young personal archive (PAIA requests). Used with kind permission of Dr Richard Young.
21 'PE set to become Viking Mecca', *Eastern Province Herald*, 2001; and 'Local firms line up for foreign gain in arms deal', *Business Report*, 6 November 2002.
22 Y. Jonson and N. Resare, 'Tourists pay for Jas/Gripen fighter jets', 6 February 2007. Kindly translated from the original Swedish by Fredrik Sperling.
23 Ibid.
24 'BAE and the Arms Deal', Moneyweb, 14 August 2007, www.moneyweb.co.za.
25 S. Sole and E. Groenink, 'Pierre Steyn speaks out about the arms deal', *Mail & Guardian*, 2 February 2007.
26 'MK boss was bought', *Noseweek*, No. 52 (December 2003); P. Kirk, 'Three foresightful architects', *Citizen*, 16 December 2003; and E. Groenink and S. Sole, 'The musketeers who bought the jets', *Mail & Guardian*, 2 February 2007.
27 South African Government Information Service, 'National Industrial Participation (NIP) – Defence Summary: Project Description', September 1999, http://www.info.gov.za/issues/procurement/background/nip.htm.
28 'MK boss was bought', *Noseweek*, No. 52 (December 2003); Kirk, 'Three foresightful architects'; and Groenink and Sole, 'The musketeers who bought the jets', *Citizen,* 16 December 2003, *Mail & Guardian*, 2 Febuary 2007.
29 'Soldiering ahead in business', *Saturday Star*, 6 November 1999; and 'How Modise wrangled SA's jet fighter deal', *Mail & Guardian*, 3 November 2001.
30 Feinstein, *After the Party* (2007), p. 176.
31 Ibid., p. 177.
32 G. Murphy, British Serious Fraud Office, Affidavit submitted as Annexure JDP-SW12 in the High Court of South Africa (Transvaal Provincial Division) in the matter of *Ex Parte* the National Director of Public Prosecutions (applicant) re: an application for issue of search warrants in terms of Section 29(5) and 29(6) of the National Prosecuting Authority Act, No. 32 of 1998, as amended (2008).
33 Ibid.
34 Ibid.
35 Ibid.
36 Ibid.
37 'The arms dealer who could bring down Zuma', *Independent*, 27 November 2008; 'Million-

aire accused of propping up Mugabe', *Guardian*, 27 November 2008; and 'Smoke, sex and the arms deal', *Mail & Guardian*, 28 October 2008.

38 'Treasury Designates Mugabe Regime Cronies', statement issued by the United States Department of the Treasury, 25 November 2008; and Council Decision 2011/101/CFSP of 15 February 2011 concerning restrictive measures against Zimbabwe, in the *Official Journal of the European Union*, 16 February 2011; and the Department of the Treasury, Office of Foreign Assets Control, 'Specially Designated Nationals and Blocked Persons', 21 June 2011, http://www.treasury.gov/ofac/downloads/t11sdn.pdf.

39 G. Murphy, British Serious Fraud Office, Affidavit (see n. 32 above).

40 Ibid.

41 Ibid.

42 Stefaans Brümmer and Sam Sole, 'The house the arms deal bought', *Mail & Guardian*, 3 December 2010.

43 Ibid.

44 Holden, *Arms Deal in Your Pocket*.

45 Feinstein, *After the Party*; and www.theshadowworld.com for 'Memorandum from ThyssenKrupp Executive Confirming Bribe to "Chippy" Shaik, Head of Procurement in the South African National Defence Force'.

46 Judgment in the Constitutional Court of South Africa, Case CCT 86/06 [2008] ZACC7, Schabir Shaik (and his companies) versus the State, decided on 29 May 2008.

47 'Ruling was not Mpshe's to make', *Cape Argus*, 8 May 2009.

48 'Action against Schabir Shaik welcomed', *Mail & Guardian*, 14 March 2011.

49 Pride Chigwedere, George Seage III, Sofia Gruskin, Tun-Hou Lee and Max Essex, 'Estimating the Lost Benefits of Antiretroviral Drug Use in South Africa', *JAIDS* Online, 16 October 2008.

50 Holden and Van Vuuren, *Devil in the Detail*; and 'R70 000 000 000', *City Press*, 10 April 2011.

51 Ibid.

52 Ibid.

53 Ibid.

54 Ibid.

55 'SA groaning under the weight of patronage and corruption', *Business Day*, 22 June 2009.

56 *Mail & Guardian* editorial, 12 January 2007.

57 'Funds pinch may ground SA's R10bn Gripen fleet', *Business Day*, 26 October 2010.

58 'Air force boss slams poor state of affairs', *The Times*, 4 April 2010.

59 Ibid.

60 Extrapolated from contracts LGS/S2010/4406 and ELGS/2006/193 (including yearly extensions). Available for download from www.armscor.co.za.

61 'The dud sub', *The Times*, 3 August 2008.

62 At the time of the deal Tanzania was 151st on the UN's Human Development Index, out of 173 countries.

63 'BAE in new corruption probe as Tanzanian minister resigns', *Daily Mail*, 21 April 2008, http://www.dailymail.co.uk/news/article-561000/bae-new-corruption-probe-Tanzanian-minister-resigns-500-000-bribery-claim.html.

64 'Military radar probe: The key suspects . . . And the case against them', This Day, 15 February 2010, http://www.thisday.co.tz/?l=10648.

65 'Tanzania', *Guardian*, 7 June 2007, http://www.guardian.co.uk/world/2007/jun/07/bae9.

66 The predecesor to the Department for International Development.

67 Clare Short, 'BAE's government-backed rip-off', *Guardian*, 'Comment is Free', 1 October 2009, http://www.guardian.co.uk/commentisfree/2009/oct/01/bae-deal-blair-sfo.

68 'BAE: the Tanzanian connection', *Today*, BBC Radio 4 , 1 October 2009, http://news.bbc.co.uk/today/hi/today/newsid_8284000/8284510.stm.

69 Rob Evans and Paul Lewis, 'BAE deal with Tanzania: military air traffic control – for country with no airforce', *Guardian*, 6 February 2010, http://www.guardian.co.uk/world/2010/feb/06/bae-tanzania-arms-deal.

70 'Tanzania', *Guardian* (see n. 65 above).

71 'Tanzania radar sale "waste of cash"', BBC News, 14 June 2002, http://news.bbc.co.uk/1/hi/uk_politics/2044206.stm.

72 'BAE: the Tanzanian connection', *Today* (see n. 68 above)

73 'Tanzania radar sale "waste of cash"', BBC News (see n. 71 above).

74 'Tanzania "needs costly radar system"', BBC News, 21 December 2001, http://news.bbc.co.uk/1/hi/uk_politics/1723728.stm.

75 'Tanzania radar sale "waste of cash"', BBC News (see n. 71 above).

76 'BAE: the Tanzanian connection', *Today* (see n. 68 above).

77 Ibid.

78 'Tanzania', *Guardian* (see n. 65 above).

79 'BAE: the Tanzanian connection', *Today* (see n. 68 above).

80 David Hencke, Charlotte Denny and Larry Elliot, 'Tanzania aviation deal "a waste of money"', *Guardian*, 14 June 2002, http://www.guardian.co.uk/uk/2002/jun/14/politics.tanzania.

81 Charlotte Denny, 'Backlash over costly hi-tech for Tanzania', *Guardian*, 21 December 2001, http://www.guardian.co.uk/world/2001/dec/21/tanzania.politics.

82 'Radar sale threatens aid to Tanzania', BBC News, 20 March 2002, http://news.bbc.co.uk/1/hi/uk_politics/1882651.stm.

83 'Tanzania "needs costly radar system"', BBC News (see n. 74 above).

84 Ibid.

85 Patrick Wintour and Charlotte Denny, 'Overruled: Short loses in aid row', *Guardian*, 20 December 2001, http://www.guardian.co.uk/politics/2001/dec/20/uk.Whitehall.

86 David Hencke, 'Ministers at odds over £28m deal', *Guardian*, 20 March 2002, http://www.guardian.co.uk/politics/2002/mar/20/armstrade.foreignpolicy.

87 'Tanzania responds to air traffic furore', BBC News, 29 January 2002, http://news.bbc.co.uk/1/hi/world/africa/1788922.stm; 'Backlash over costly hi-tech for Tanzania', *Guardian*, 21 December 2001, http://www.guardian.co.uk/world/2001/dec/21/tanzania.politics; and 'Overruled: Short loses in aid row', *Guardian*, 20 December 2001, http://www.guardian.co.uk/politics/2001/dec/20/uk.Whitehall.

88 'Overruled: Short loses in aid row', *Guardian*, 20 December 2001, http://www.guardian.co.uk/politics/2001/dec/20/uk.Whitehall.

89 'Tanzania radar sale "waste of cash"', BBC News (see n. 71 above).

90 Clare Short, 'BAE's government-backed rip-off' (see n. 67 above).

91 Ibid.

92 'Radar sale threatens aid to Tanzania', BBC News (see n. 82 above). As the scandal intensi-

fied the House of Lords attempted to amend a new Act before Parliament, by adding a test for whether an arms export deal is compatible with sustainable development, as contained in the EU Common Position. Patricia Hewitt and Geoff Hoon attempted to have the amendment excised, arguing again that British jobs should trump any other consideration. They also pointed out that the Tanzanian export licence would be revoked if the amendment was successful. The legislative outcome, as so often, was a fudge.

93 'Short to visit Tanzania as fraud claims fly', *Guardian*, 26 June 2002, http://www.guardian. co.uk/politics/2002/jun/26/tanzania.foreignpolicy.

94 David Leigh, 'The arms deal, the agent and the Swiss bank account', *Guardian*, 15 January 2007, http://www.guardian.co.uk/world/2007/jan/15/bae.freedomofinformation.

95 Ibid.

96 '10 questions that Tanil Somaiya should answer', This Day, http://www.jamiiforums. com/jukwaa-la-siasa/28304-tanil-somaiya-kukutana-na-waandishi-5.html.

97 Leigh, 'The arms deal, the agent and the Swiss bank account' (see n. 94 above).

98 '10 questions that Tanil Somaiya should answer', This Day (see n. 96 above).

99 'Military radar probe', This Day (see n. 64 above).

100 'Tories launch challenge over corruption claims in $40m radar sale to Tanzania', *Guardian*, 30 January 2007, http://www.guardian.co.uk/politics/2007/jan/30/conservatives. foreignpolicy.

101 'Military radar probe', This Day (see n. 64 above).

102 Ibid.

103 Leigh, 'The arms deal, the agent and the Swiss bank account' (see n. 94 above).

104 Ibid.

105 'Tories launch challenge over corruption claims in $40m radar sale to Tanzania', *Guardian* (see n. 100 above).

106 '10 questions that Tanil Somaiya should answer', This Day (see n. 96 above).

107 'Military radar probe', This Day (see n. 64 above).

108 '10 questions that Tanil Somaiya should answer', This Day (see n. 96 above).

109 '93bn military trucks deal', This Day, http://www.jamiiforums.com/jukwaa-la-siasa/2740-93bn-military-trucks-deal-2.html.

110 Ibid.

111 '10 questions that Tanil Somaiya should answer', This Day (see n. 96 above).

112 'Tanzania', *Guardian* (see n. 65 above).

113 'Military radar probe', This Day (see n. 64 above); and 'Tanzanian minister quits over BAE investigation', *Guardian*, 22 April 2008, http://www.guardian.co.uk/politics/2008/ apr/22/defence.bae.

114 'Military radar probe' (see n. 64 above).

115 Account Number: 59662999; Bank Code Number: 204505.

116 'Dr Edward Hosea corners SFO', *Guardian*, 14 February 2010, http://www.jamiiforums. com/habari-na-hoja-mchanganyiko/52982-dr-edward-hosea-corners-sfo.html.

117 'Military radar probe', This Day (see n. 64 above).

118 Ibid.

119 J. Lewis Madorsky of Cleveland, Ohio, in the US, and Goodman Derrick LLP of the UK.

120 'Military radar probe', This Day (see n. 64 above).

121 Ibid.

122 'Your office may have been bugged by BAE, investigators told MP', *Daily Mail*, 3 October 2009, http://www.dailymail.co.uk/news/article-1217919/Your-office-bugged-bae-investigators-told-MP.html.

123 'BAE Systems: "Liberal Democrat Norman Lamb's bugging claim is preposterous"', *Daily Telegraph*, 4 October 2009, http://www.telegraph.co.uk/finance/newsbysector/industry/6259700/BAE-Systems-Liberal-Democrat-Norman-Lambs-bugging-claim-is-preposterous. html. Retrieved 8 August 2010.

124 'Your office may have been bugged by BAE, investigators told MP', *Daily Mail* (see n. 122 above).

125 'Tories launch challenge over corruption claims in $40m radar sale to Tanzania', *Guardian* (see n. 100 above).

126 'BAE's Dick Olver rejects Government's UK trade post', *Daily Telegraph*, 16 July 2010, http://www.telegraph.co.uk/finance/newsbysector/epic/badot/7893149/BAEs-Dick-Olver-rejects-Governments-UK-trade-post.html.

127 'US embassy cables: BAE's "dirty deal" to sell radar to Tanzania revealed', *Guardian*, 19 December 2010, http://www.guardian.co.uk/world/us-embassy-cables-documents/116436.

10. After the Wall: Capitalism BAE-Style

1 Interview with Alfons Mensdorff-Pouilly, Vienna, 3 September 2010.

2 'Austrian count claims small underpants breached his human rights', *Daily Telegraph*, 12 February 2010, http://www.telegraph.co.uk/news/worldnews/europe/austria/7222007/Austrian-count-claims-small-underpants-breached-his-human-rights.html.

3 'BAE "bribery" lobbyist faces new investigations', *Austrian Times*, 24 March 2010, http://www.austriantimes.at/news/Business/2010-03-24/21888/BAE_%27bribery%27_lobbyist_faces_new_investigations.

4 Interview with the author John Besant on *Uppdrag Granskning* and *Dagens Eko*; 'Brigadier Timothy Landon: the extraordinary life of the white sultan', *Independent*, 12 July 2007, http://www.independent.co.uk/news/world/middle-east/brigadier-timothy-landon-the-extraordinary-life-of-the-white-sultan-456942.html; 'Brigadier Tim Landon', *Daily Telegraph*, 12 July 2007, http://www.telegraph.co.uk/news/obituaries/1557161/Brigadier-Tim-Landon. html; and 'Brigadier Tim Landon', *The Times*, 20 July 2007.

5 Interview with Alfons Mensdorff-Pouilly, Vienna, 3 September 2010.

6 BAE Sentencing Memorandum, CRIMINAL NO.: 1:10-cr-035 (JDB), US Department of Justice, http://www.justice.gov/criminal/pr/documents/03-01-10%20bae-sentencing-memo.pdf.

7 Sam Sole, 'BAE's global bribing campaign', *Mail & Guardian*, 12 February 2010, http://www.mg.co.za/article/2010-02-12-baes-global-bribing-campaign.

8 David Leigh and Rob Evans, 'BAE chiefs "linked to bribes conspiracy"', *Observer*, 7 February 2010, http://www.guardian.co.uk/world/2010/feb/07/bae-chiefs-linked-bribes-conspiracy.

9 Ibid.

10 Ibid.

11 Vaclav Havel, *The Art of the Impossible: Politics as Morality in Practice* (New York: Knopf, 1997).

12 Sven Bergman, Joachim Dyfvermark and Fredrik Laurin, 'Gripen – the secret agreements', *Uppdrag Granskning*, 20 February 2007, transcript at http://svt.se/content/1/c8/01/44/71/73/The%20Secret%20Agreement.pdf.

13 Rob Evans and Ian Traynor, 'US accuses British over arms deal bribery bid', *Guardian*, 12 June 2003, http://www.guardian.co.uk/uk/2003/jun/12/politics.military.

14 Mark Milner, 'BAE contract swept away by Czech floods', *Guardian*, 20 August 2002, http://www.guardian.co.uk/business/2002/aug/20/naturaldisasters.weather.

15 Magnus Bennett, 'UK may give air force free fighter planes', *Prague Post*, 15 May 2003, http://www.praguepost.com/archivescontent/37288-uk-may-give-air-force-free-fighter-planes.html.

16 David Leigh and Rob Evans, 'Czech Republic', *Guardian*, 7 June 2007, http://www.guardian.co.uk/world/2007/jun/07/bae23.

17 Magnus Bennett, 'Jet deal criticized for lack of tender', *Prague Post*, 24 April 2003, http://www.praguepost.com/archivescontent/37153-jet-deal-criticized-for-lack-of-tender.html.

18 United States Department of State, Briefing Memorandum, 'To: EB – E. Anthony Wayne, From: EB/IFD – Janice F. Bay, Subject: Your Meeting with UK MOD Permanent Under Secretary Kevin Tebbit, Friday July 19, 10 a.m. (15 minutes)', http://image.guardian.co.uk/sys-files/Guardian/documents/2010/04/23/BAETebbitWayne.pdf.

19 Ibid.

20 Ibid.

21 Ibid.

22 Ibid.

23 Nelson D. Schwartz and Lowell Bergman, 'Payload: taking aim at corporate bribery', *The New York Times*, 25 November 2007, http://www.nytimes.com/2007/11/25/business/25bae.html?pagewanted=3&_r=2.

24 Evans and Traynor, 'US accuses British over arms deal bribery bid' (see n. 13 above).

25 Bergman *et al.*, 'Gripen – the secret agreements' (see n. 12 above).

26 Ibid.

27 Ibid.

28 Ben Schiller, 'Agency investigates Senate Gripen vote', *Prague Post*, 20 November 2002, http://www.praguepost.com/archivescontent/36226-agency-investigates-senate-gripen-vote.html.

29 'Postview', *Prague Post*, 23 December 2003, http://www.praguepost.com/archivescontent/38465-postview.html.

30 František Bouc, 'Dark Clouds', *Prague Post*, 5 May 2005, http://www.praguepost.com/archivescontent/40980---dark-%3Cbr%3E%3Cbr%3Eclouds.html. In addition, some 20 per cent of indirect offset investments would go into environmental projects, 16 per cent to electronic firms, 11 per cent to the transport sector and 10 per cent to the iron and steel sector. The Industry and Trade Minister, Milan Urban, then said that around half of the projects would boost exports of Czech industrial products abroad, while 40 per cent of the projects featured investment in the country and 10 per cent would be invested in research and development.

31 Ibid.

32 Ibid.

33 Ibid.

34 Bergman *et al.*, 'Gripen – the secret agreements' (see n. 12 above).

35 Ibid.

36 Ibid.

37 Ibid.

38 Ibid.

39 This is a mock-up of the agreement based on the information provided to me by Fredrik Laurin.

40 Bergman *et al.*, 'Gripen – the secret agreements' (see n. 12 above).

41 Ibid.

42 Ibid.

43 David Leigh and Rob Evans, 'Count named in BAE corruption inquiry', *Guardian*, 21 February 2007, http://www.guardian.co.uk/business/2007/feb/21/arms.uknews.

44 Bergman *et al.*, 'Gripen – the secret agreements' (see n. 12 above).

45 Ben Schiller, 'BAE confirms Omnipol purchase', *Prague Post*, 8 May 2003, http://www.praguepost.com/archivescontent/37257-bae-confirms-omnipol-purchase.html.

46 This is a mock-up of the agreement based on the information provided to me by Fredrik Laurin.

47 Leigh and Evans, 'Czech Republic' (see n. 16 above).

48 Bergman *et al.*, 'Gripen – the secret agreements' (see n. 12 above).

49 Ibid.

50 Ibid.

51 This company was used in a fraud scheme unrelated to Jelinek. See Indictment United States against Frank Dolney, Nick Pirgousis, Quentin Quintana, Joseph Ferragamom, John Donadio, Rocco J. Donadio, William G. Brown, Gary Todd, Mario Casias, Vladimir Ziskind, Vlad Goldenberg, CR no. 04-159, http://www.justice.gov/usao/nye/vw/Pending Cases/CR-04-159_Indictment_US_v_FRANK_DOLNEY.pdf.

52 Bergman *et al.*, 'Gripen – the secret agreements' (see n. 12 above).

53 Leigh and Evans, 'Count named in BAE corruption inquiry' (see n. 43 above).

54 This is a mock-up of the lease agreement based on the information provided to me by Fredrik Laurin.

55 'Brigadier Timothy Landon', *Independent* (see n. 4 above); and Ulla Schmid and Martin Staudinger, 'Die einfachen Geschäftsverbindungen des kleinen Bauern Alfons M.', *Profil*, 15 February 2010.

56 Schmid and Staudinger, 'Die einfachen Geschäftsverbindungen'.

57 Ibid.

58 David Leigh and Rob Evans, 'Austria set to prosecute over BAE arms sales', *Guardian*, 19 June 2009, http://www.guardian.co.uk/world/2009/jun/19/austria-bae-arms-sales.

59 Schmid and Staudinger, 'Die einfachen Geschäftsverbindungen'.

60 Ulla Schmid, 'Der Fall Mensdorff-Pouilly: Neue Spuren führen nach Liechtenstein', *Profil*, 24 January 2011, http://www.profil.at/articles/1104/560/287153/der-fall-mensdorff-pouilly-neue-spuren-liechtenstein.

61 Ibid.

62 Schmid and Staudinger, 'Die einfachen Geschäftsverbindungen'; and 'Tote reden nicht', *Profil*, 9 March 2009. Hamsa died in his early forties of a heart attack in 2007.

63 Schmid and Staudinger, 'Die einfachen Geschäftsverbindungen'; 'Tote reden nicht', *Profil*, 9 March 2009; and G. Murphy, British Serious Fraud Office, Affidavit submitted as Annexure JDP-SW 12 in the High Court of South Africa (Transvaal Provincial Division)

in the matter of *Ex Parte* the National Director of Public Prosecutions (applicant) re: an application for issue of search warrants in terms of Section 29(5) and 29(6) of the National Prosecuting Authority Act, No. 32 of 1998, as amended (2008), Annexure B, p. 8.

64 Derived from Schmid and Staudinger, 'Die einfachen Geschäftsverbindungen'.

65 Sven Bergman, Joachim Dyfvermark and Fredrik Laurin, 'Gripen – under cover', *Uppdrag Granskning*, 27 February 2007, http://svt.se/content/1/c8/01/44/71/73/Transcript%20Jan%20Kavan.pdf.

66 Ibid.

67 Ibid.

68 'Case of Kavan's safe shelved – press', *CTK Daily News*, 11 February 2003; 'The trials and more trials of Jan Kavan', *Prague Post*, 22 July 1998, http://www.praguepost.com/archivescontent/28792-the-trials-trials-and-more-trials-of-jan-kavan.html; and 'Murky case of the hitman and her leaves Czechs shaken', *Scotsman*, 13 August 2002.

69 Bergman *et al.*, 'Gripen – under cover' (see n. 65 above).

70 Ibid.

71 Ibid.

72 Ibid.

73 Ibid.

74 Ibid.

75 Ibid.

76 Kavan in a letter and oral communication to SVT – Swedish Public Broadcasting – 19 February 2007.

77 Bergman *et al.*, 'Gripen – under cover' (see n. 65 above).

78 Ibid.

79 'Bribery rumours', letter, *Guardian*, 16 March 2007, http://www.guardian.co.uk/politics/2007/mar/16/freedomofinformation.uk; and František Bouc, 'Gripen corruption probe deepens', *Prague Post*, 7 March 2007, http://www.praguepost.com/archivescontent/3169-gripen-corruption-probe-deepens.html.

80 Bergman *et al.*, 'Gripen – the secret agreements' (see n. 12 above).

81 Ibid.

82 Ibid.

83 Ibid.

84 Ibid.

85 Sven Bergman, Joachim Dyfvermark and Fredrik Laurin, 'Gripen – the Hungarian deal', *Uppdrag Granskning*, 5 June 2007, http://svt.se/content/1/c8/01/44/71/73/Gripen%20Hungary.pdf.

86 Sven Bergman, Joachim Dyfvermark and Fredrik Laurin, 'The Gripen–Valurex International', script, *Uppdrag Granskning*, 27 February 2007, http://svt.se/content/1/c8/01/44/71/73/Valurex.pdf.

87 Ibid.

88 Ibid.

89 'Fraud complaint against Mensdorff-Pouilly in Eurofighter case', *Austrian Times*, 22 December 2008.

90 Ibid.; and William Green, 'Mensdorff-Pouilly family grave vandalised', *Austrian Times*, 3 September 2009, http://www.austriantimes.at/news/General_News/2009-09-03/16082/Mensdorff-Pouilly_family_grave_vandalised.

91 'Fraud complaint against Mensdorff-Pouilly in Eurofighter case', *Austrian Times*, 22 December 2008.

92 'BAE bribery Count's jail time extended', *Austrian Times*, 16 March 2009, http://www.austriantimes.at/news/Business/2009-03-16/11827/BAE_bribery_Count%B4s_jail_time_extended.

93 'New investigation calls as BAE lobbyist walks free', *Austrian Times*, 8 February 2010, http://www.austriantimes.at/news/Business/2010-02-08/20407/New_investigation_calls_as_BAE_lobbyist_walks_free.

94 Interview with Alfons Mensdorff-Pouilly, Vienna, 3 September 2010.

95 Response to question by Vince Cable MP, Hansard, 23 January 2007, Column 1666W.

96 Rob Evans, 'Fraud investigators raid BAE agent's Austria home', *Guardian*, 30 September 2008, http://www.guardian.co.uk/world/2008/sep/30/BAE.

97 'BAE Systems lobbyist held on bribery charges', Bloomberg, 28 February 2009, http://gulfnews.com/business/general/bae-systems-lobbyist-held-on-bribery-charges-1.55459.

98 'Former BAE agent charged with corruption', SFO press release, 29 January 2010, http://www.sfo.gov.uk/press-room/latest-press-releases/press-releases-2010/former-bae-agent-charged-with-corruption.aspx.

99 Rob Evans and David Leigh, 'Gummer backs count's plea for bail in BAE case', *Guardian*, 4 February 2010, http://www.guardian.co.uk/business/2010/feb/04/bae-austrian-bribes-gummer-mensdorff.

100 Leigh and Evans, 'Austria set to prosecute over BAE arms sales' (see n. 58 above); and interview with Austrian prosecutor, Vienna, 3 September 2010.

101 'FBI to probe Gripen scam', *Czech News*, 25 November 2009, http://aktualne.centrum.cz/czechnews/clanek.phtml?id=653955.

102 Klára Jiřičná, 'Gripen inquiry ordered reopened', *Prague Post*, 5 May 2010, http://www.praguepost.com/news/4332-gripen-inquiry-ordered-reopened.html.

103 David Leigh and Rob Evans, 'Meeting of prosecutors increases BAE pressure', *Guardian*, 3 May 2007, http://www.guardian.co.uk/world/2007/may/03/bae.armstrade.

104 'JAS Gripen – inquiry is dropped', *Uppdrag Granskning*, 17 June 2009, http://svt.se/2.101059/1.1597705/jas_gripen_–_inquiry_is_dropped.

105 Ibid.

106 Ibid.

107 Ibid.

108 Ibid.

109 Email communication with the office of Vaclav Havel, 17 September 2010.

110 Nelson D. Schwartz and Lowell Bergman, 'Payload: taking aim at corporate bribery', *The New York Times*, 25 November 2007, http://www.nytimes.com/2007/11/25/business/25bae.html?pagewanted=3&_r=2.

111 *Népszabadság*, 2 March 2009.

112 Ibid.

113 '*New York Times* alleges bribery in Hungarian Gripen purchases', Politics.Hu, 27 November 2007, http://www.politics.hu/20071127/new-york-times-alleges-bribery-in-hungarian-gripen-purchases.

114 'Hungary inks Gripen lease MoU', *Defence Daily*, 27 November 2001, http://findarticles.com/p/articles/mi_6712/is_38_212/ai_n28875765/.

115 Leigh and Evans, 'Austria set to prosecute over BAE arms sales' (see n. 58 above).

116 Bergman *et al.*, 'Gripen – the Hungarian deal' (see n. 85 above).

117 Ibid.

118 Ibid.

119 Ibid.

120 AFP, 'Hungary to probe Gripen deal', *The Local*, 18 June 2007, http://www.thelocal. se/7643/20070618/.

121 '*New York Times* alleges bribery', Politics.Hu (see n. 113 above); and http://www. budapesttimes.hu/index.php?option=com_content&task=view&id=2326&Itemid=134.

122 Interview with Alfons Mensdorff-Pouilly, Vienna, 3 September 2010.

123 Ibid.

124 Ibid.

125 Ibid.

126 Drawn from Anthony Sampson, *The Arms Bazaar* (London: Hodder and Stoughton, 1977).

127 SIPRI Military Expenditure Database, http://milexdata.sipri.org. Accessed 31 July 2011. In 2010, Sweden was the seventh-largest arms supplier in the world.

128 Quoted in *The New York Times*, 11 April 2008.

129 'India rejects Saab Gripen fighter bid', *The Local*, 28 April 2011.

130 Swedish Peace and Arbitration Society, *As the Carousel Spins Weapons: A Report on the Swedish Military-Industrial Complex and 10 of Its Most Powerful Players*, September 2010; and *The New York Times*, 17 May 1987.

131 This account is drawn from *Forbes* magazine, 30 July 1997, *Merinews*, 5 March 2007, *The Times of India*, various dates, *The New York Times*, 1 March 1997, and conversations with an investigative reporter involved in breaking the story.

132 Quoted in 'Bofors has risen again', *The Hindu*, 6 January 2011.

133 'Bofors: BJP wants PM to apologise', *The Hindu*, 5 January 2011.

134 Quoted in 'Bofors has risen again', *The Hindu*, 6 January 2011.

135 'Cong unfazed; BJP wants SIT probe into Bofors kickbacks', *Indian Express*, 4 January 2011.

136 'No political pressure on Bofors gun: army chief', Indo-Asian News Service, 26 September 2001.

137 Pranay Gupte and Rahul Singh, 'Money! Guns! Corruption!', *Forbes*, 7 July 1997, http:// www.forbes.com/forbes/1997/0707/6001112a.html.

138 Interview with Thomas Tjäder at ISP in Stockholm, 25 November 2010.

139 Celsius was owned by the state, before being bought by Saab.

140 Swedish Peace and Arbitration Society, *As the Carousel Spins Weapons*.

11. *The Ultimate Cop-Out*

1 'BAE Systems plc', SFO press release, 5 February 2010, http://www.sfo.gov.uk/press-room/latest-press-releases/press-releases-2010/bae-systems-plc.aspx.

2 Director of the Serious Fraud Office Summary Grounds for Contesting the Claim, para. 18, http://www.caat.org.uk/issues/BAe/jr/SFO_Grounds_2010-3-10.pdf.

3 Gleaned from sources close to the investigation.

4 BAE Sentencing Memo, CRIMINAL NO.: 1:10-cr-035 (JDB), http://www.justice. gov/criminal/pr/documents/03-01-10%20bae-sentencing-memo.pdf.

5 Quoted in 'BAE admits guilt over corrupt arms deals', *Guardian*, 6 February 2010.

6 Ibid.

7 Ibid.

8 'Attorney General's Guidelines on Plea Discussions in cases of Serious or Complex Fraud', 18 March 2009, http://www.attorneygeneral.gov.uk/Publications/Documents/AG%27s%20Guidelines%20on%20Plea%20Discussions%20in%20Cases%20of%20Serious%20or%20Complex%20Fraud.pdf. On p. 6: 'In deciding whether or not to accept an offer by the defendant to plead guilty, the prosecutor will follow sections 7 and 10 of the Code relating to the selection of charges and the acceptance of guilty pleas. The prosecutor should ensure that: The investigating officer is fully apprised of developments in the plea discussions and his or her views are taken into account.'

9 This comment is from a senior lawyer in the private sector who was close to the SFO investigation.

10 'Courts could tear up BAE plea bargain', *Daily Mail*, 8 May 2010; and Susan Hawley, 'Innospec ruling forces major change to SFO approach to dealing with overseas corruption', Corruption Watch, 19 April 2010, http://corruptionwatch-uk.org/2010/04/19/first-uk-executive-jailed-for-bribery/.

11 'Note for Opening', *Regina v. BAE Systems PLC*, Southwark Crown Court, 20 December 2010, http://www.sfo.gov.uk/media/133543/bae%20opening%20statement%2020.12.10.pdf; 'Judgement', *Regina v. BAE Systems PLC*, Southwark Crown Court, 21 December 2010, http://www.judiciary.gov.uk/media/judgments/2010/r-v-bae-systems-plc; and notes taken in court by Barnaby Pace.

12 Ibid.

13 Notes taken in court by Barnaby Pace.

14 'Judgement', *Regina v. BAE Systems PLC*, Southwark Crown Court, 21 December 2010 (see n. 11 above); and notes taken in court by Barnaby Pace.

15 'Note for Opening', *Regina v. BAE Systems PLC*, Southwark Crown Court, 20 December 2010 (see n. 11 above); 'Judgement', *Regina v. BAE Systems PLC*, Southwark Crown Court, 21 December 2010 (see n. 11 above); and notes taken in court by Barnaby Pace.

16 Ibid.

17 Quoted in 'Arms deal details consigned to dark', *Business Day*, 8 February 2010.

18 Ibid.

19 Andrew Feinstein, *After the Party: Corruption, the* ANC *and South Africa's Uncertain Future* (London: Verso, 2010), pp. 260–63.

20 Ibid., p. 282.

21 Ibid., p. 285.

22 Ibid., p. 284.

23 Ibid.; and 'Why I let Fana Hlongwane off the hook – Simelane', Politcsweb, 21 March 2010. Also see 'Hlongwane order dropped', News24, 19 March 2010.

24 This document can be viewed at www.theshadowworld.com.

25 'Result of Saab's ongoing internal investigation regarding South African consultant contract', press statement issued by Saab Group, 20 May 2011, www.saabgroup.com. Downloaded 20 May 2011.

26 'Saab completes internal investigation regarding consultant contract in South Africa', press statement issued by Saab Group, 16 June 2011, www.saabgroup.com. Downloaded 16 June 2011.

27 Ibid.

28 Ibid.

29 D. Maynier, 'The Fana Hlongwane documents – David Maynier', Politicsweb, 23 June 2011, www.politicsweb.co.za.

30 The document can be viewed at www.theshadowworld.com.

31 Abduel Elinanza, 'Dar to probe radar scandal despite $46m payout', AllAfrica, 15 February 2010, http://allafrica.com/stories/201002150075.html. Retrieved 8 August 2010.

32 'Dr Edward Hosea corners SFO', *Guardian on Sunday*, 14 February 2010, http://www.jamiiforums.com/habari-na-hoja-mchanganyiko/52982-dr-edward-hosea-corners-sfo.html. Retrieved 8 August 2010.

33 'Confirmed: Radar billions destined to local charities', *Guardian on Sunday*, 14 March 2010, http://www.ippmedia.com/frontend/index.php?l=14439. Retrieved 8 August 2010.

34 'Chenge gets clean bill on radar scam', *The Citizen*, 9 November 2010; Chenge was not elected Speaker.

35 'Chenge case not yet closed, says UK', *The Citizen*, 11 November 2010.

36 Thomas Hochwarter, 'MPs' anger over Mensdorff-Pouilly', *Wiener Zeitung*, 8 February 2010, http://www.wienerzeitung.at/DesktopDefault.aspx?TabID=4082&Alias=wzo&cob=470621; the Schengen area comprises the twenty-five European countries who have entered into the Schengen Agreement.

37 Michael Peel, 'BAE deal saw count's bribes case dropped', *Financial Times*, 21 April 2010.

38 Ibid.

39 Campaign against the Arms Trade, Corner House v. Director of the Serious Fraud Office, BAE Systems and Count Alfons Mensdorff Pouilly, 'Reply to defendants and first interested party's summary grounds', High Court, 17 March 2010, http://www.caat.org.uk/issues/BAe/jr/Reply_2010-03-17.pdf.

40 'Money! Guns! Corruption!', *Forbes*, 7 July 1997.

Section IV: The Arms Superpower

12. Legal Bribery

1 Quoted in Eugene Jarecki, *The American Way of War* (New York: Free Press, 2008), p. 52, from whom for this section is drawn.

2 Eugene Jarecki, *Why We Fight*, Sony Pictures Classics, 2005.

3 Quoted in Jarecki, *American Way of War*, p. 53.

4 Jarecki, *American Way of War*, pp. 53–5 and 57–61; and Garry Wills, *Bomb Power: The Modern Presidency and the National Security State* (New York: Penguin Books, 2010).

5 Jarecki, *American Way of War*, pp. 53–5 and 57–61.

6 Calculated in constant inflation-adjusted 2005 dollars from the Pentagon's National Defense Budget Estimates, http://comptroller.defense.gov/defbudget/fy2011/FY11_Green_Book.pdf.

7 Jarecki, *American Way of War*, pp. 77–8.

8 Ibid., pp. 85–9 and 96.

9 Ibid., p. 140.

10 Ibid., p. 145.

11 Ibid., pp. 144–6.

12 Ibid., pp. 149–51.

13 Ibid., pp. 151–4.

14 Ibid., pp. 154 and 159.

15 Calculated in constant inflation-adjusted 2005 dollars from the Pentagon's National Defense Budget Estimates, http://comptroller.defense.gov/defbudget/fy2011/FY 11_Green_Book.pdf.

16 Quoted in Jarecki, *American Way of War*, pp. 191–2.

17 Ibid.; and James Ledbetter, *Unwarranted Influence: Dwight D. Eisenhower and the Military-Industrial Complex*, Yale University Press, 2010.

18 'Unindicted and Misunderstood', *Slate*, 9 February 2010.

19 Murtha's earmarks keep airport aloft', *Washington Post*, 19 April 2009.

20 'John Murtha dies', *Washington Post*, 9 February 2010.

21 'Unindicted and Misunderstood', *Slate*, 9 February 2010.

22 'The Murtha Method', Center for Public Integrity, 8 September 2009.

23 'PMA lobbyist pleads guilty', Center for Public Integrity, 27 September 2010.

24 'Murtha's nephew got defense contracts', *Washington Post*, 5 May 2009.

25 Ibid.

26 'Nephew mentioned Rep. Murtha in dealings as contractor', *Washington Post*, 12 May 2009.

27 Ibid.

28 'Bribery plea in firm with Murtha ties', *Washington Post*, 8 July 2010.

29 'John Murtha dies', *Washington Post*, 9 February 2010.

30 'Murtha defends earmarks to his District', *Washington Post*, 30 May 2009.

31 'Critics claim John Murtha is capitalizing on a corrupt system, but he's not apologizing', *Pittsburgh Post-Gazette*, 29 September 2010.

32 Murtha's earmarks keep airport aloft', *Washington Post*, 19 April 2009.

33 'Rep. Murtha's earmarks lead to fewer jobs than promised', *Washington Post*, 31 December 2009.

34 Drawn from 'John Murtha: the Old Soldier who said "Bring the troops home"', *The Nation*, 8 February 2010.

35 http://tpmlivewire.talkingpointsmemo.com/2010/02/lockheed-martin-takes-out-full-page-ad-memorializing-murtha.php.

36 Silverstein, Ken, *Turkmeniscam: How Washington Lobbyists Fought to Flack for a Stalinist Dictatorship* (London: Random House, 2008), p. xviii.

37 George Crile, *Charlie Wilson's War* (London: Atlantic Books, 2007), p. 82.

38 Ibid.

39 'Murtha and the FBI: The Director's Cut', *The American Spectator*, 29 September 2006. The same article claims that Murtha was less than truthful about his involvement in the scam, that he was keen to enter into a long-term deal with the fake sheikh, whom he met subsequently, and that he helped the sheikhs enter the US rather than report them to the FBI or the ethics committee, of which he was a member.

40 Crile, *Charlie Wilson's War*, p. 22.

41 Ibid.; and 'Charlie Wilson', *The Economist*, 18 February 2010.

42 Quoted in Crile, *Charlie Wilson's War*, p. 20.

43 Crile, *Charlie Wilson's War*, p. 19.

44 Ibid., p. 10.

45 Ibid., pp. 165 and 238.

46 Ibid., p. 11.

47 'Charlie Wilson', *The Economist*, 18 February 2010.

48 Crile, *Charlie Wilson's War*, p. 5.

49 Ibid.

50 Quoted in ibid., p. 10.

51 Steve Coll, *Ghost Wars: The Secret History of the CIA, Afghanistan, and Bin Laden, from the Soviet Invasion to September 10, 2001* (London: Penguin Books, 2004), p. 91.

52 Chalmers Johnson, *Dismantling the Empire: America's Last Best Hope* (New York: Metropolitan Books, 2010), p. 85.

53 Crile, *Charlie Wilson's War*, Epilogue.

54 Ibid.

55 Ibid.

56 Ibid.

57 Johnson, *Dismantling the Empire*, p. 87.

58 Quoted in Crile, *Charlie Wilson's War*, p. 508.

59 Ibid., p. 521.

60 Ibid., p. 523.

61 Johnson, *Dismantling the Empire*, p. 89.

62 'Charlie Wilson and the political uses of being a "character"', Crosscut.com, 11 February 2010.

63 'John Murtha dies', *Washington Post*, 9 February 2010.

64 R. Grimmett, *Conventional Arms Transfers to Developing Nations 2002–2009*, Congressional Research Service, 10 September 2010, CRS-71, http://www.fas.org/sgp/crs/weapons/R41403.pdf.

65 Dr Sam Perlo-Freeman, Head of the SIPRI Military Expenditure Project, http://www.sipri.org/media/pressreleases/milex.

66 Interview with senior Capitol Hill aide who has worked on arms trade issues for many years, Washington DC, November 2008.

67 A. Bacevich, *The New American Militarism* (London: OUP, 2005), Introduction; and interview with the author, Boston, Mass., 14 November 2008.

68 President Dwight D. Eisenhower, in a televised farewell address to the nation, 17 January 1961.

69 Various examples presented in Anthony Sampson, *The Arms Bazaar* (London: Hodder and Stoughton, 1977), and Johnson, *Dismantling the Empire*.

70 Sampson, *Arms Bazaar*, Chapter 10.

71 William Hartung, *Prophets of War* (New York: Nation Books, 2011), Chapter 2, from which this section is drawn. See Hartung for more detail on Lockheed's early history.

72 Ibid., p. 40.

73 Ibid., p. 53.

74 The story of the C-5A Galaxy is drawn primarily from Hartung, *Prophets of War*, chapter 5.

75 Hartung, *Prophets of War*, p. 72.

76 Fitzgerald's consultant successor was a partner at Arthur Young and Company – Lockheed's chief accounting firm – who had participated in the cover-up of the cost overruns

on the C-5A. After a Congressional outcry, in which the appointment was likened to 'sending a bulldog to guard a hamburger', it was rescinded. (Ibid., pp. 79–80.)

77 Quoted in Hartung, *Prophets of War*, pp. 80–81.
78 Ibid., p. 87.
79 Ibid., p. 91.
80 Ibid., p. 93.
81 Ibid., p. 97.
82 Ibid., pp. 102–3.
83 Ibid., p. 103.
84 Ibid., p. 107.
85 Ibid., p. 110.
86 This idea is drawn from Jarecki, *American Way of War*, p. 193.
87 This account is drawn from a lengthy conversation with Spinney, Alexandria, 1 March 2010, and subsequent communication by email. It also draws on Jarecki, *American Way of War*, Chapter 5.
88 Interview with Chuck Spinney, Alexandria, 1 March 2010.
89 Drawn from Jarecki, *American Way of War*, Chapter 6.
90 Quoted in Jarecki, *American Way of War*, p. 206.
91 Interview with Chuck Spinney, Alexandria, 1 March 2010.

13. In the Name of Uncle Sam

1 Chalmers Johnson, 'Death Spiral at the Pentagon', TomDispatch.com, 2 February 2009.
2 Naomi Klein, *The Shock Doctrine* (London: Penguin Books, 2007), p. 157.
3 Ibid., p. 330.
4 This example is drawn from Anthony Sampson, *The Arms Bazaar* (London: Hodder and Stoughton, 1977), Chapter 13.
5 William Hartung, *Prophets of War* (New York: Nation Books, 2011), pp. 115–16.
6 Sampson, *Arms Bazaar*, p. 224.
7 Hartung, *Prophets of War*, p. 117.
8 Sampson, *Arms Bazaar*, Chapter 13 and pp. 275–6.
9 Quoting hearings before the Senate Committee on Banking, Housing, and Urban Affairs on 'Lockheed Bribery', 25 August 1975, pp. 29–30, in Hartung, *Prophets of War*, p. 118.
10 Hartung, *Prophets of War*, p. 120; and an anonymous source in Germany.
11 Sampson, *Arms Bazaar*, pp. 122–3 and 128–9.
12 Ibid., pp. 138–9.
13 Ibid., pp. 134–6.
14 Memo from marketing executive, DD Stone, quoted in Hartung, *Prophets of War*, pp. 123–5, from which this account is drawn.
15 Memos between Dobbins, Cleland and Mitchell, quoted in Hartung, *Prophets of War*, p. 125.
16 Drawn from Sampson, *Arms Bazaar*, p. 192.
17 Quoted in Hartung, *Prophets of War*, p. 126, from which this account is drawn.
18 Ibid.
19 Church Committee evidence quoted in ibid., p. 127.

20 Ibid.

21 Drawn from Sampson, *Arms Bazaar*, pp. 192–3.

22 David Leigh and Rob Evans, 'Adnan Khashoggi', *Guardian*, 7 June 2007, http://www.guardian.co.uk/world/2007/jun/08/bae52.

23 Quoted in Sampson, *Arms Bazaar*, p. 197.

24 Drawn from Sampson, *Arms Bazaar*, Chapter 16.

25 Ibid.

26 Quoted in Hartung, *Prophets of War*, pp. 129–30, from which this account is drawn.

27 Hartung, *Prophets of War*, p. 130.

28 Ibid.

29 Drawn from Hartung, *Prophets of War*, p. 131; and Sampson, *Arms Bazaar*, p. 274.

30 Hartung, *Prophets of War*, p. 131.

31 Claimed in Sampson, *Arms Bazaar*, p. 279.

32 Quoted in Hartung, *Prophets of War*, pp. 131–2, from which this account is drawn.

33 Ibid.

34 See for instance, SEC Release 34-15570, 15/2/1979, http://content.lawyerlinks.com/default.htm#http://content.lawyerlinks.com/library/sec/sec_releases/34-15570.htm; and 'Again, Political Slush Funds', *Time*, 24 March 1975, http://www.time.com/time/magazine/article/0,9171,946547,00.html.

35 Henry H. Rossbacher and Tracy W. Young, 'The Foreign Corrupt Practices Act within the American Response to Domestic Corruption', 15 *Dickinson Journal of International Law* (1997), pp. 509, 518.

36 House Report, 1977, Unlawful Corporate Payments Act, No. 114, 95th Congress, 1st Sess., http://www.justice.gov/criminal/fraud/fcpa/history/1977/houseprt-95-640.pdf. Retrieved 7 October 2010.

37 United States Department of Justice website, 'Lay-Person's Guide to FCPA', http://www.justice.gov/criminal/fraud/fcpa/docs/lay-persons-guide.pdf. Retrieved 2 September 2009.

38 Ben R. Rich and Leo Janos, *Skunk Works: A Personal Memoir of My Years at Lockheed* (New York: Little, Brown & Co., 1994).

39 Miriam F. Weismann, 'The Foreign Corrupt Practices Act: The Failure of the Self-Regulatory Model of Corporate Governance in the Global Business Environment', *Journal of Business Ethics*, 2009, pp. 615–61.

40 Ibid.

41 FCPA Blog, 'There are moral problems', 23 August 2007, http://fcpablog.squarespace.com/blog/2007/8/23/there-are-moral-problems.html. Retrieved 11 September 2010.

42 Alvaro Cuervo-Cazurra, 'The Effectiveness of Laws against Bribery Abroad', *Journal of International Business Studies*, Vol. 39 (2008), No. 4, pp. 634–51.

43 Mary Jacoby, '*Forbes*' Unbalanced Look at FCPA Enforcement', Main Justice, 10 May 2010, http://www.mainjustice.com/2010/05/10/commentary-forbess-unbalanced-look-at-fcpa-enforcement/; Nathan Vardi, 'How Federal Crackdown on Bribery Hurts Business and Enriches Insiders', *Forbes*, 24 May 2010, http://www.forbes.com/forbes/2010/0524/business-weatherford-kbr-corruption-bribery-racket_print.html. There is a revolving door in Washington, albeit much slower for FCPA prosecutors than many others. An extreme case was Billy Jacobson, a Criminal Fraud Division Prosecutor who, while enforcing the FCPA, had the oil services firm Weatherford International self-report itself to the Department of Justice (DOJ) over bribes paid in Europe. He left the DOJ to join Fulbright and

Jaworski LLP as a senior partner, the same law firm hired by Weatherford International. Jacobson worked on Weatherford's compliance plan for Fulbright before leaving to join the company itself, earning a reported $4m a year. (Jacoby, '*Forbes*' Unbalanced Look at FCPA Enforcement'.)

44 See 15 U.S.C. §§78dd-1 (b) and (f) (3) [section 30A of the Securities and Exchange Act of 1934]. The law lists a number of examples for this routine governmental action: (i) obtaining permits, licences, or other official documents to qualify a person to do business in a foreign country; (ii) processing governmental papers, such as visas and work orders; (iii) providing police protection, mail pick-up and delivery, or scheduling inspections associated with contract performance or inspections related to transit of goods across country; (iv) providing phone service, power and water supply, loading and unloading cargo, or protecting perishable products or commodities from deterioration; or (v) actions of a similar nature. Essential actions that should be done as part of normal governmental business. Actions that would require the subordination of an official's duty is not part of an action ordinarily or commonly performed by a governmental official and therefore illegal, not fitting into the exception. This translates as US companies being able to pay off border guards to stamp their documents as and when they should but it would be illegal to pay them to have them stamped before their turn or to reduce the customs fees.

45 See 15 U.S.C. §§78c(a)(8), 78dd-1(a).

46 See § 78dd-3(a), (f)(1).

47 OECD, *United States: Phase 2, Report on Application of the Convention on Combating Bribery of Foreign Public Officials in International Business Actions and the 1997 Recommendation on Combating Bribery in International Business Transactions*, 2002, www.oecd.org/dataoecd/52/19/1962084. pdf, retrieved 9 October 2010; and Weismann, 'The Foreign Corrupt Practices Act', *Journal of Business Ethics*.

48 House Report, 1977, Unlawful Corporate Payments Act, No. 114 (see n. 36 above).

49 Hearings before the Subcommittee on Telecommunications, Consumer Protection, and Finance of the Committee on Energy and Commerce, House of Representatives, 97th Cong., 1982, p. 256.

50 Ibid., p. 265.

14. Taking the Mickey, the Toilet Seat and the Hammer . . .

1 Drawn from William Hartung, *Prophets of War* (New York: Nation Books, 2011), pp. 133–5.

2 Figures quoted in ibid., p. 135.

3 Drawn from ibid., pp. 136–7.

4 Quoted in ibid., p. 137, from which this account is drawn.

5 Ibid.

6 Hartung, *Prophets of War*, pp. 138.

7 Ibid., pp. 138–40.

8 Ibid., p. 144.

9 Ibid., p. 145.

10 Ibid., p. 149.

11 Ibid., pp. 150–51.

12 Ibid., pp. 152–3.

13 Ibid., pp. 153.

14 Ibid., pp. 153–4.

15 Quoted in ibid., p. 154.

16 Hartung, *Prophets of War*, pp. 154–5.

17 Ibid., p. 155.

18 Quoted in Hartung, *Prophets of War*, pp. 155–7, from which this account is drawn.

19 Steven R. Salbu, 'Bribery in the Global Market: A Critical Analysis of the Foreign Corrupt Practices Act', *Washington and Lee Law Review*, Winter 1997, pp. 229–87.

20 Jack G. Kaikati *et al.*, 'The Price of International Business Morality: Twenty Years under the Foreign Corrupt Practices Act', *Journal of Business Ethics*, 26 (April 2000), pp. 213–22.

21 'Corruption: U.S. Firms Handicapped', *Intelligence Newsletter*, 21 March 1996, p. 7.

22 W. Cragg and W. Woof, 'The U.S. Foreign Corrupt Practices Act: A Study of Its Effectiveness', *Business and Society Review*, 107 (1) (2002), pp. 98–144.

23 Walsh, interview.

24 Drawn from interview with Chuck Spinney, Alexandria, 1 March 2010, and subsequent communication by email; and Eugene Jarecki, *The American Way of War* (New York: Free Press, 2008), pp. 199–200.

25 Interview with Chuck Spinney, Alexandria, 1 March 2010.

26 The work was published as *Defense Facts of Life: The Plans/Reality Mismatch* (Boulder, Colo., and London: Westview Press, 1985).

27 Chalmers Johnson, 'Death Spiral at the Pentagon', TomDispatch.com, 2 Febuary 2009, p. 56.

28 Kevin Phillips, *American Dynasty* (London: Allen Lane, 2004), pp. 151–2 and 179–84.

29 Ibid., pp. 182–99.

30 See Craig Unger, *House of Bush, House of Saud* (London: Gibson Square, 2007), Appendix C.

31 Ibid., p. 101.

32 Larry Gurwin and Adam Zagorin, 'All That Glitters', *Time*, 6 November 1995, http://www.time.com/time/magazine/article/0,9171,983662-7,00.html.

33 All these statistics sourced from Carlyle Group website, 'Firm Profile', http://www.carlyle.com/company/item1676.html.

34 Melanie Warner, 'What Do George Bush, Arthur Levitt, Jim Baker, Dick Darman, and John Major Have in Common? (They All Work for the Carlyle Group.) What exactly Does It Do? To Find Out, We Peeked down the Rabbit Hole', *Fortune*, 18 March 2002, http://money.cnn.com/magazines/fortune/fortune_archive/2002/03/18/319881/index.htm.

35 Tim Shorrock, 'The Carlyle Group – Crony Capitalism Goes Global', *The Nation*, 26 March 2002, http://www.rense.com/general21/gf.htm.

36 Oliver Burkeman and Julian Borger, 'The ex-presidents' club', *Guardian*, 31 October 2001, http://www.guardian.co.uk/world/2001/oct/31/september11.usa4.

37 Steve Lohr, 'Gerstner to be Chairman of Carlyle Group', *The New York Times*, 22 November 2002, http://www.nytimes.com/2002/11/22/business/gerstner-to-be-chairman-of-carlyle-group.html.

38 Carlyle Group website, 'Arthur Levitt, Senior Advisor', http://www.carlyle.com/team/item5771.html.

39 Dan Briody, *The Iron Triangle: Inside the Secret World of the Carlyle Group* (New York: John Wiley & Sons, 2003), p. xiii; Jason Lewis, 'REVEALED: How protection teams claim thousands of pounds of taxpayers' money to guard former Prime Ministers', *Daily Mail*, 4 July 2010, http://www.dailymail.co.uk/news/article-1291838/White-water-rafting-Sir-John-Major.html.

40 'Three former leaders leave posts at Carlyle Group', *The New York Times*, 6 August 2004, http://www.nytimes.com/2004/08/06/business/company-news-three-former-leaders-leave-posts-at-carlyle-group.html?ref=fidel_v_ramos.

41 Tim Shorrock, 'Carlyle's tentacles embrace Asia', *Asia Times*, 20 March 2002, http://www.atimes.com/china/DC20Ad02.html.

42 Carlyle Group website, 'Thomas F. (Mack) McLarty, Senior Advisor', http://www.carlyle.com/team/item5871.html.

43 Ibid., 'Randal K. Quarles, Managing Director', http://www.carlyle.com/team/item9821.html.

44 BAE Systems website, US Board of Directors, http://www.baesystems.com/WorldwideLocations/UnitedStates/AboutBAESystemsUnitedStates/USBoardofDirectors/index.htm.

45 Laura Peterson, 'United Defence Industries L.P.', Center for Public Integrity, http://projects.publicintegrity.org/wow/bio.aspx?act=pro&ddlC=60.

46 Briody, *Iron Triangle*, extract available online at http://www.fahrenheit911.com/library/book/carlyle/index.php.

47 Eric Leser, 'Carlyle empire', *Le Monde*, 29 April 2004, http://www.culturechange.org/CarlyleEmpire.html.

48 Shorrock, 'The Carlyle Group – Crony Capitalism Goes Global' (see n. 35 above).

49 National Audit Office, 'The Privatisation of QinetiQ', 23 November 2007.

50 Kenneth N. Gilpin, 'Military Contractor Sold to Buyout Firm', *The New York Times*, 27 August 1997, http://www.nytimes.com/1997/08/27/business/military-contractor-sold-to-buyout-firm.html.

51 'UNITED DEFENSE IN DEAL FOR BOFORS WEAPON SYSTEMS', *The New York Times*, 16 June 2000, http://www.nytimes.com/2000/06/16/business/company-news-united-defense-in-deal-for-bofors-weapon-systems.html.

52 Global Security website, 'United Defense Industries', http://www.globalsecurity.org/military/industry/udi.htm.

53 Andrea Rothman and Edmond Lococo, 'BAE buys United Defense to tap U.S. military sales (Update10)', Bloomberg, 7 March 2005, http://www.bloomberg.com/apps/news?pid=newsarchive&sid=aBEULP60GE.Y&refer=uk.

54 Bob Cox, 'Pennsylvania company buys Vought for $1.4 billion', *Star Telegram*, 23 March 2010.

55 Triumph Group Inc., 'Military Programs: Triumph Aerostructures – Vought Aircraft Division', http://www.triumphgroup.com/companies/triumph-aerostructures-vought-aircraft-division/about-us/military-programs.

56 Shorrock, 'The Carlyle Group – Crony Capitalism Goes Global' (see n. 35 above).

57 Tim Shorrock, 'US–Taiwan: the guiding hand of Frank Carlucci', *Asia Times*, 19 March 2002, http://www.atimes.com/china/DC19Ad02.html.

58 David Ottaway, *The King's Messenger: Prince Bandar Bin Sultan and America's Tangled Relationship with Saudi Arabia* (New York: Walker & Company, 2008), p. 164.

59 Robert G. Kaiser, 'Enormous wealth spilled into American coffers', *Washington Post*, 11 February 2002, http://www.library.cornell.edu/colldev/mideast/enormss.htm.

60 Laura Peterson, 'Privatizing Combat, the New World Order', Center for Public Integrity, 28 October 2002, http://projects.publicintegrity.org/bow/report.aspx?aid=148.

61 Global Security, 'Office of the Program Manager Saudi Arabian National Guard Modernization Program', http://www.globalsecurity.org/military/agency/dod/opm-sang.htm.

62 Leser, 'Carlyle empire' (see n. 47 above).

63 Center for Public Integrity, 'Windfalls of War: Campaign Contributions of Post-War Contractors', http://projects.publicintegrity.org/wow/resources.aspx?act=contrib.

64 Spelling varies; for example, Said Aburish spells his name Walid bin Tallal and Briody refers to him as Prince Alwaleed bin Talal.

65 Said Aburish, *The Rise, Corruption and Coming Fall of the House of Saud* (London: Bloomsbury, 2005), p. 82; and Briody, *Iron Triangle*, p. 51.

66 Time/CNN, '2001 Global Influentials: 18. Prince Al-Waleed'.

67 Shorrock, 'The Carlyle Group – Crony Capitalism Goes Global' (see n. 35 above).

68 Briody, *Iron Triangle*, pp. 51–9.

69 Ibid.

70 Kaiser, 'Enormous wealth spilled into American coffers' (see n. 59 above).

71 Ibid.

72 Briody, *Iron Triangle*, pp. 145–6; and Burkeman and Borger, 'The ex-presidents' club' (see n. 36 above).

73 Steve Coll, *The Bin Ladens: Oil, Money, Terrorism and the Secret Saudi World* (London: Penguin Books, 2008), pp. 424–6.

74 Ibid., p. 520.

75 Quoted in Hartung, *Prophets of War*, pp. 166–7, from which this section is drawn.

76 Hartung, *Prophets of War*, pp. 168 and 181–6.

77 Ibid., p. 168, from which this section is drawn.

78 Ibid., p. 169.

79 Ibid., p. 170.

80 Drawn from ibid.

81 Quoted in ibid.

82 After a Congressman branded the scheme 'payoffs for layoffs' Augustine agreed to donate the taxpayer portion of his windfall to charity.

83 Quoted in Hartung, *Prophets of War*, p. 173, from which this section is drawn.

84 Hartung, *Prophets of War*, p. 188.

85 Ibid., p. 191.

86 William D. Hartung, *How Much are You Making on the War, Daddy?* (New York: Nation Books, 2003), p. 40.

87 Hartung, *Prophets of War*, p. 193.

88 Figures quoted in ibid., p. 197.

89 Farmus was acquitted on charges of corruption but the court deemed he had revealed a confidential document to bidding companies, though not in return for money (Polen-Forum, 29 January 2007). Szeremietiew was subsequently dismissed from the government. After a series of trials he was eventually acquitted on all charges in November 2010 (wyborcza.pl, 9 November 2010).

90 Barre R. Seguin, 'Why did Poland Choose the F-16', George C. Marshall European Center

for Security Studies, No. 11, June 2007, http://www.marshallcenter.org/mcpublicweb/MCDocs/files/College/F_Publications/occPapers/occ-paper_11-en.pdf; Clare McManus-Czubinska, William L. Miller, Radoslaw Markowski and Jacek Wasilewski, 2004, 'Why is Corruption in Poland "a serious cause for concern"?', *Crime, Law and Social Change*, 41(2), pp. 107–32; *Newsline*, Radio Free Europe, 26 August 2002, http://www.rferl.org/content/article/1142745.html; Gregory Filipowicz, 'An Existentialist Shift: The F-16 Reaching into Iraq', Dedefensa.org, 11 June 2005; and Ahmedullah, 'Arms Sales: The U.S.–French Tug of War', *Bulletin of the Atomic Scientists*, Vol. 59, No. 5, September/October 2003.

91 'Emergency landing of Polish F-16s', *Polish News*, 2/10/2007.

92 Calculated from Johnson, 'Death Spiral at the Pentagon', and Nick Turse, *The Complex* (London: Faber and Faber, 2008).

93 C. Johnson, *The Sorrows of Empire* (London: Verso, 2006), pp. 62–3.

94 Quoted in Hartung, *Prophets of War*, pp. 192–3.

95 Hartung, *Prophets of War*, p. 193.

96 *The Economist*, 14 July 2011, http://www.economist.com/node/18958487?story_id=18958487&fsrc=rss.

97 Johnson, *Sorrows of Empire*, p. 63.

98 Conversation with Hartung, New York, December 2008. This had happened on a smaller scale after the Clinton administration, with the Defense Secretary, Bill Perry, and one of his Deputies, John Deutch, who also served as CIA Director, taking seats on a host of defence company boards.

99 Quoted from P. Wolfowitz, *Defense Planning Guidance for the 1994–1999 Fiscal Years* among others.

100 Jarecki, *American Way of War*, p. 12.

101 Ibid.

102 Project for the New American Century, *Rebuilding America's Defenses: Strategy, Forces and Resources for a New Century*, Washington DC, September 2000, http://www.newamericancentury.org/RebuildingAmericasDefenses.pdf.

103 As seen in the 2002 policy document entitled 'The National Security Strategy of the USA' and explicated in Bush's 'Axis of Evil' State of the Union speech, 2003.

104 Hartung, *Prophets of War*, p. 209.

105 Jarecki, *American Way of War*, pp. 25–8.

106 Project for the New American Century, *Rebuilding America's Defenses*, p. 51.

107 Jarecki, *American Way of War*.

108 Interview with Andrew Bacevich, Boston, Mass., 14 November 2008.

109 *The New York Times*, 4 February 2007.

110 Quoted in Naomi Klein, *The Shock Doctrine* (London: Penguin Books, 2004), p. 300, from whom some ideas in this section are drawn.

111 Klein, *Shock Doctrine*, pp. 300–301.

112 These figures and those in the following paragraphs are calculated from a variety of sources, including Naomi Klein, Eugene Jarecki, Travis Sharp and conversations the author has had with a range of sources in government and the defence industry.

113 Travis Sharp, 'Fiscal Year 2010 Pentagon Defense Spending Request: February "Topline"', Center for Arms Control and Non-proliferation, 26 February 2009.

114 Turse, *The Complex*.

115 Ibid.

116 William D. Hartung and Michelle Ciarrocca, *The Ties That Bind: Arms Industry Influence in the Bush Administration and Beyond*, World Policy Institute, October 2004.

117 Klein, *Shock Doctrine*.

118 KBR was a subsidiary of Halliburton until April 2007 when a series of adverse judicial findings caused Halliburton to sell its stake in KBR.

119 Pratap Chatterjee, *Halliburton's Army* (New York: Nation Books, 2009).

120 Klein, *Shock Doctrine*.

121 David Bromwich, 'The Co-President at Work', *New York Review of Books*, 20 November 2008.

122 L. Dubose and J. Bernstein, *Vice: Dick Cheney and the Hijacking of the American Presidency* (New York: Random House, 2006); and Turse, *The Complex*.

123 This is based on a conversation with Chuck Lewis, founder of the Center for Public Integrity.

124 Klein, *Shock Doctrine*.

125 Quoted in ibid.

126 Klein, *Shock Doctrine*, and conversations with sources.

127 Nixon referring to Rumsfeld, 1971.

128 Klein, *Shock Doctrine*.

129 See, for instance, William Hartung, 'Reagan Redux: The Enduring Myth of Star Wars', *World Policy Journal*, Vol. 15 (1998).

130 Figures from Hartung, *Prophets of War*.

131 Quoted in Jarecki, *American Way of War*.

132 Ibid.

133 Ibid.

134 Rachel Monahan and Elena Herrero Beaumont, 'Big Time Security', *Forbes*, 8 March 2006, http://www.forbes.com/2006/08/02/homeland-security-contracts-cx_rm_0803homeland.html.

135 Interview with Chuck Spinney, Alexandria, 1 March 2010.

136 Drawn from Jarecki, *American Way of War*.

137 Quoted in ibid.

138 For more on this notion see the writings of Bacevich, Engelhardt and Johnson, *Sorrows of Empire*.

139 See Garry Wills, *Bomb Power: The Modern Presidency and the National Security State* (New York: Penguin Books, 2010), for an excellent description of how executive power has been increased since the Second World War, to reach its zenith in the current era.

140 'U.S. stocks rise, erasing losses on London bombings; gap rises', Bloomberg, 7 July 2005.

141 Klein, *Shock Doctrine*, p. 302; and Monahan and Herrero Beaumont, 'Big Time Security' (see n. 134 above).

142 'TIMELINE: NBC, Universal through the 20th century and beyond', Reuters, 3 December 2009.

143 Klein, *Shock Doctrine*.

144 Hartung, *How Much are You Making on the War, Daddy?* Perle stated in his resignation letter that he 'did not want to distract from the urgent challenge . . . as I cannot quell criticism of me based on errors of fact' (Newsmax.com, 24 March 2003).

145 Hartung, *How Much are You Making on the War, Daddy?*

146 Quoted in Klein, *Shock Doctrine*.

15. Illegal Bribery

1 Project on Government Oversight, 'Fill 'Er Up: Back-Door Deal for Boeing Will Leave the Taxpayer on Empty', 7 May 2002, http://www.pogo.org/pogo-files/reports/national-security/back-door-deal-for-boeing/ns-btld-back-door-deal-for-boeing.html.

2 Leslie Wayne, 'Documents show extent of lobbying by Boeing', *The New York Times*, 3 September 2003, http://www.nytimes.com/2003/09/03/business/documents-show-extent-of-lobbying-by-boeing.html; and William D. Hartung, *How Much are You Making on the War, Daddy?* (New York: Nation Books, 2003), p. 126.

3 Known as the KC-135 'R'.

4 General Accounting Office, Briefing for Senate Armed Service Committee, 'Preliminary Information on Air Force Tanker Leasing Issues', May 2002, http://www.pogoarchives.org/m/cp/cp-boeing767c.pdf.

5 FY 2002 Air Force Unfunded Priority List, submitted by General John P. Jumper, Air Force Chief of Staff, 22 October 2001, http://www.pogoarchives.org/m/cp/cp-boeing767e.pdf.

6 Memo to Senator John McCain from Mitchell E. Daniels, Jr, Director of Office of Management and Budget, 3 May 2002, http://www.pogoarchives.org/m/cp/cp-boeing767b.pdf.

7 General Accounting Office, 'Preliminary Information on Air Force Tanker Leasing Issues' (see n. 4 above).

8 Memo to Senator John McCain from Mitchell E. Daniels, Jr, Director of Office of Management and Budget, 18 December 2001, http://www.pogoarchives.org/m/cp/cp-boeing767a.pdf.

9 Ibid.

10 Ibid.

11 Memo to Senator Kent Conrad from Mitchell E. Daniels, Jr, Director of Office of Management and Budget, 2 November 2001, http://www.pogoarchives.org/m/cp/cp-boeing767d.pdf.

12 Hartung, *How Much are You Making on the War, Daddy?*, p. 126.

13 Project on Government Oversight, 'Fill 'Er Up' (see n. 1 above).

14 Letter and report to Senator John McCain from Department of Defense Inspector General Joseph E. Schmitz, 3 May 2002, http://www.pogoarchives.org/m/cp/cp-boeing767f.pdf.

15 R. Jeffrey Smith and Renae Merle, 'Rules circumvented on huge Boeing defense contract', *Washington Post*, 27 October 2003, http://www.washingtonpost.com/ac2/wp-dyn/A21584-2003Oct26?language=printe.

16 Wayne, 'Documents show extent of lobbying by Boeing' (see n. 2 above); for McCain's own account of receiving the documents, see his press release at http://mccain.senate.gov/public/index.cfm?FuseAction=PressOffice.Articles&ContentRecord_id=dfd71eae-28c5-41ff-99b4-a362135d276f&Region_id=&Issue_id=1bd7f3a7-a52b-4ad0-a338-646c6a780d65.

17 Smith and Merle, 'Rules circumvented on huge Boeing defense contract' (see n. 15 above).

18 Center for Security Policy, *Precision-Guided Ideas: 2002 Annual Report*, http://web.archive.org/web/20030630032717/www.centerforsecuritypolicy.org/Center2002AR.pdf.

19 Smith and Merle, 'Rules circumvented on huge Boeing defense contract' (see n. 15 above).

20 Hartung, *How Much are You Making on the War, Daddy?*, p. 129.

21 Smith and Merle, 'Rules circumvented on huge Boeing defense contract' (see n. 15 above).

22 Ibid.

23 Caroline Daniel, James Harding, Joshua Chaffin and Marianne Brun-Rovet, 'A cosy relationship: Boeing's Pentagon deal bears testament to its skilful lobbying efforts', *Financial
Times*, 8 December 2003.

24 Dan Cook, 'Boeing Given Nod on Tanker Lease', *Military Aerospace Technology*, Vol. 1 (2),
1 May 2002, http://web.archive.org/web/20071114184441; http://www.military-aerospace-
technology.com/article.cfm?DocID=335.

25 John Tirpak, 'Tanker Twilight Zone', *Air Force Magazine*, February 2004, http://www.
airforce-magazine.com/MagazineArchive/Pages/2004/February%202004/0204tanker.aspx.

26 Kimberley Palmer, 'Former Air Force acquisition official released from jail', Government
Executive.com, 3 October 2005, http://www.govexec.com/dailyfed/1005/100305k2.htm.

27 Rebecca Leung, 'Cashing in for profit?', *60 Minutes*, CBS, 5 January 2005, http://www.
cbsnews.com/stories/2005/01/04/60II/main664652.shtml; and Wayne, 'Documents show
extent of lobbying by Boeing' (see n. 2 above).

28 Wayne, 'Documents show extent of lobbying by Boeing' (see n. 2 above).

29 Smith and Merle, 'Rules circumvented on huge Boeing defense contract' (see n. 15 above).

30 Ibid.

31 Wayne, 'Documents show extent of lobbying by Boeing' (see n. 2 above).

32 Ibid.

33 Ibid.

34 Smith and Merle, 'Rules circumvented on huge Boeing defense contract' (see n. 15 above).

35 Ibid.

36 Ibid.

37 Ibid.

38 Ibid.

39 Ibid.

40 Ibid.

41 Renae Merle, 'Lockheed adds Director fresh from the Pentagon', *Washington Post*, 27 June
2003.

42 National Corruption Index, 'Edward Aldridge', 19 May 2008, http://www.national
corruptionindex.org/pages/profile.php?category=cat&selectcats=52&catidorcorp=Individual
&checkview=1&profile_id=532.

43 Leung, 'Cashing in for profit?' (see n. 27 above).

44 Ibid.

45 Palmer, 'Former Air Force acquisition official released from jail' (see n. 26 above).

46 Leung, 'Cashing in for profit?' (see n. 27 above).

47 Ibid.

48 Renae Merle, 'Pentagon's Druyun thrust herself into role of power', *Washington Post*, 21
November 2004.

49 Alan Bjerga, 'Ex-Boeing CFO pleads guilty in tanker deal scandal', *Seattle Times*, 16
November 2004, http://seattletimes.nwsource.com/html/businesstechnology/2002091816_
webboeing16.html.

50 'An anxious time for Boeing as a fired worker starts to talk', *The New York Times*, 16 June
2004.

51 George Cahlink, 'Ex-Pentagon procurement executive gets jail time', Government
Executive.com, 1 October 2004, http://www.govexec.com/dailyfed/1004/100104g1.htm.

52 'Ex-official goes to prison', *The New York Times*, 5 January 2005, http://query.nytimes.com/gst/fullpage.html?res=9B04EEDB1339F936A35752C0A9639C8B63.

53 Cahlink, 'Ex-Pentagon procurement executive gets jail time' (see n. 51 above).

54 Palmer, 'Former Air Force acquisition official released from jail' (see n. 26 above).

55 Cahlink, 'Ex-Pentagon procurement executive gets jail time' (see n. 51 above).

56 Palmer, 'Former Air Force acquisition official released from jail' (see n. 26 above).

57 Ibid.

58 Leung, 'Cashing in for profit?' (see n. 27 above).

59 R. Jeffrey Smith, 'Roche cited for 2 ethics violations', *Washington Post*, 10 February 2005, http://www.washingtonpost.com/ac2/wp-dyn/A12344-2005Feb9?language=printer.

60 'Profile: James Roche', Right Web, 1 August 2009, http://www.rightweb.irc-online.org/profile/Roche_James#_edn10.

61 Office of Senator John McCain, 'McCain deplores Boeing tanker scheme', press release, 23 May 2003, http://www.globalsecurity.org/military/library/news/2003/05/mil-030523-dodo.htm.

62 'Profile: James Roche', Right Web (see n. 60 above).

63 Orbital, 'Orbital names Dr. James G. Roche to Board Of Directors', press release, 25 May 2005, http://www.orbital.com/NewsInfo/release.asp?prid=508.

64 'Dr. James G. Roche joins CompuDyne's Board of Directors', *Businesswire*, 9 September 2008, http://www.allbusiness.com/government/government-bodies-offices-government/11553368-1.html.

65 George Cahlink, 'Two top Air Force officials to resign', GovernmentExecutive.com, 17 November 2004, http://www.govexec.com/dailyfed/1104/111704g2.htm.

66 Peter Pae, 'US: Boeing to pay fine of $615 million', *Los Angeles Times*, 16 May 2006, http://www.corpwatch.org/article.php?id=13582.

67 Mike Allen, 'Details on Boeing deal sought: Senators raise questions about White House involvement', *Washington Post*, 8 June 2005, http://www.washingtonpost.com/wp-dyn/content/article/2005/06/07/AR2005060701751.html.

68 Project on Government Oversight, 25 May 2006, 'Defense Inspector General originally hid Boeing role in scandal report: White House and Congress' Roles in tanker lease deal still unclear', http://www.pogo.org/pogo-files/alerts/government-secrecy/gs-foia-20060525.htm.

69 'Holes in the tanker story', *Washington Post*, 20 June 2005, http://www.washingtonpost.com/wp-dyn/content/article/2005/06/19/AR2005061900705.html.

70 Allen, 'Details on Boeing deal sought' (see n. 67 above).

71 'Holes in the tanker story', *Washington Post* (see n. 69 above)

72 Project on Government Oversight, 'Defense Inspector General originally hid Boeing role in scandal report' (see n. 68 above).

73 Hearing of the Senate Armed Services Committee, 7 June 2005.

74 Jeremy Scahill, *Blackwater: The Rise of the World's Most Powerful Mercenary Army* (London: Serpent's Tail, 2008), p. 387.

75 Cam Simpson, 'Commander: Contractors violating U.S. trafficking laws', *Chicago Tribune*, 23 April 2006, http://www.corpwatch.org/article.php?id=13513; Scahill, *Blackwater*, p. 384.

76 Scahill, *Blackwater*, p. 388.

77 'Boeing protests U.S. Air Force tanker contract award', Boeing press release, 11 March 2008, http://boeing.com/news/releases/2008/q1/080311b_nr.html.

78 Government Accountability Office, 'Statement regarding the bid protest decision resolv-

ing the aerial refueling tanker protest by the Boeing Company', 18 June 2008, http://web. archive.org/web/20080625201918; http://www.king5.com/sharedcontent/northwest/pdf/ gao_boeing.pdf.

79 Dana Hedgpeth, 'Pentagon postpones tanker competition', *Washington Post*, 11 September 2008, http://www.washingtonpost.com/wp-dyn/content/article/2008/09/10/AR2008 091000986.html?hpid=sec-business.

80 Jon Ostrower, 'Northrop Grumman declines to bid on latest KC-X RFP', *Flight International*, 9 March 2010, http://www.flightglobal.com/articles/2010/03/09/339205/northrop-grumman-declines-to-bid-on-latest-kc-x-rfp.html.

81 A surprise third bidder, US Aerospace, coupled with the Ukrainian manufacturer Antonov, also entered the fray. However, its bid was excluded after it submitted its proposal five minutes after the deadline. US Aerospace protested at this exclusion but the GAO upheld it in October 2010.

82 Andrea Shalal-Esa, 'EADS backer charges politics in tanker', Reuters, 21 September 2010, http://www.reuters.com/article/idUSTRE68J54R20100921.

83 A fighter ace is defined as any pilot who has made five kills.

84 Marcus Stern, Jerry Kammer, Dean Calbreath and George Condon, *The Wrong Stuff* (New York: Public Affairs, 2007), pp. 25 and 289.

85 Jerry Ethell and Alfred Price, *One Day in a Long War* (New York: Random House, 1989), p. 110; and Stern *et al.*, *Wrong Stuff*, p. 33.

86 Stern *et al.*, *Wrong Stuff*, p. 50.

87 Ibid.

88 Ibid., p. 58.

89 Ibid., p. 6.

90 Ibid., p. 241.

91 Kitty Kelley, 'Ace in the Hole: Duke Cunningham's Wife Tells All', *New Republic* Online, 17 August 2006.

92 Bates was ultimately rebuked by the House Ethics Committee and warned as to his future conduct. ('Ethics panel gives Rep. Bates light penalty in sexual harassment case: Congress: woman who brought charges against San Diego lawmaker is "disgusted"', *Los Angeles Times*, 19 October 1989.)

93 Stern *et al.*, *Wrong Stuff*, p. 65.

94 Ibid., p. 68.

95 Ibid., p. 74.

96 Dana Wilkie, 'Cunningham version of weekend confrontation disputed', Copley News Service, 8 September 1998.

97 'Cunningham exchanges angry words with constituent', Associated Press, 6 August 1998.

98 Stern *et al.*, *Wrong Stuff*, p. 80.

99 Ibid., p. 215.

100 Ibid.

101 Ibid.

102 Ibid., pp. 213–23.

103 Marcus Stern and Joe Cantlupe, 'Ties between contractor, Congressman questioned', Copley News Service, 17 June 2005.

104 Stern *et al.*, *Wrong Stuff*, pp. 253–61; Kelley, 'Ace in the Hole', *New Republic* Online, 17 August 2006.

105 Associated Press, 'Cunningham moving to Arizona prison', *Washington Post*, 5 January 2007, http://www.washingtonpost.com/wp-dyn/content/article/2007/01/05/AR2007 010501858.html.

106 Seth Hettena, 'Mitch Wade's sentence', 15 December 2008.

107 Stern *et al.*, *Wrong Stuff*, p. 165.

108 Ibid., p. 44.

109 Ibid., p. 47.

110 Judy Bachrach, 'Washington Babylon', *Vanity Fair*, August 2006, http://www.vanityfair. com/politics/features/2006/08/washington200608?currentPage=all.

111 Stern *et al.*, pp. 101–27.

112 Ibid., pp. 129–42

113 Ibid., p. 166.

114 Ibid., p. 170.

115 Ibid., p. 177.

116 Ibid., p. 169.

117 Ibid., p. 181–95.

118 Ibid., p. 3.

119 Associated Press, 'Defense contractor pleads guilty to bribery', MSNBC, 24 February 2006, http://www.msnbc.msn.com/id/11535676/.

120 Teri Figueroa, 'Congressman's briber finally makes bail', *North County Times*, 6 January 2009, http://www.nctimes.com/news/local/sdcounty/article_8e6aefcc-0508-58d8-a455-2ed227c78143.html; Rachel Slajda, 'Duke Cunningham briber rakes in $10k at poker tourney', Talking Points Memo Muckraker, 28 July 2010, http://tpmmuckraker.talking pointsmemo.com/brent_wilkes/.

121 David Johnston, 'Ex-CIA official admits corruption', *The New York Times*, 29 September 2008, http://www.nytimes.com/2008/09/30/washington/30inquire.html?_r=2&adxnnl= 1&ref=randy_cunningham&adxnnlx=1287518428-T1GiMk3n9QiVUOhq/QwkmQ.

122 Bachrach, 'Washington Babylon' (see n. 110 above).

123 Zachary Roth, 'Foggo sentenced to over three years in prison', Talking Points Memo Muckraker, 26 February 2009, http://tpmmuckraker.talkingpointsmemo.com/2009/02/ foggo_sentenced_to_over_three_years_in_prison.php.

124 Zachary Roth, 'Cunningham crony charged in $92 million mortgage fraud', Talking Points Memo Muckraker, 4 June 2009, http://tpmmuckraker.talkingpointsmemo. com/2009/06/cunningham_crony_charged_in_92_million_mortgage_fr.php.

125 'Cash pours in for Murtha's top aide in Pa. race for seat', *Washington Post*, 26 April 2010; and 'Anti-government? Not in Rep Murtha's old district', *Washington Post*, 20 May 2010.

126 'Cash pours in for Murtha's top aide in Pa. race for seat', *Washington Post*, 26 April 2010. There is no suggestion that these contributions were illegal in terms of US law or that Representative Critz has engaged in any illegality.

127 'Murtha's earmarking not unusual among subcommittee members', *Washington Post*, 9 November 2009.

128 'Value of congressional earmarks increased in fiscal 2010', *Washington Post*, 18 February 2010.

129 Taxpayers for Common Sense, earmark database for HR 3, final version as signed by the President on 10 August 2005; and Stern *et al.*, *Wrong Stuff*, p. 85.

130 Office of Management and Budget, 'FY 2009 Earmarks by Appropriations Subcommittee',

http://earmarks.omb.gov/earmarks-public/2009-appropriations-by-spendcom/summary.html.

131 Stern *et al.*, *Wrong Stuff*, p. 87.

132 Govtrack.us, S. 3335: Earmark Transparency Act, 111th Congress, 2009–10, http://www.govtrack.us/congress/bill.xpd?bill=s111-3335.

16. Beyond Utopia, Hope?

1 On Pentagon spending, see Rebecca Williams, 'House Appropriations Releases FY 12 Spending Caps', The Will and the Wallet (website), Washington DC, Stimson Center, 12 May 2011, available at http://thewillandthewallet.squarespace.com/blog/2011/5/12/house-appropriations-releases-fy12-spending-caps.html; on war costs, see Amy Belasco, *The Cost of Iraq, Afghanistan, and Other Global War on Terror Operations since 9/11*, Congressional Research Service, 29 March 2011, Table 2, p. 8.

2 Frida Berrigan, 'How Shovel-Ready is the Pentagon?' TomDispatch.com 12 March 2009.

3 'FY 2012 Base Defense Budget Represents a Turning Point', Center for Strategic and Budgetary Assessments, 14 February 2011, http://www.csbaonline.org/publications/2011/02/fy-2012-base-defense-budget-represents-a-turning-point/.

4 Berrigan, 'How Shovel-Ready is the Pentagon?'

5 Chalmers Johnson, 'Death Spiral at the Pentagon', TomDispatch.com, 2 February 2009.

6 William Hartung, *Prophets of War* (New York: Nation Books, 2011), from which this section is derived.

7 Ibid., p. 3.

8 Berrigan, 'How Shovel-Ready is the Pentagon?'

9 Hartung, *Prophets of War*, p. 4.

10 Quoted in Sydney J. Freedberg, Jr, 'On the Sea and in the Air, Military Bills Come Due', GovernmentExecutive.com, 20 March 2008.

11 Hartung, *Prophets of War*, p. 1.

12 Ibid., p. 5.

13 Ibid., pp. 4–5.

14 Drawn from ibid., pp. 5–6.

15 Interview with Chuck Spinney.

16 Hartung, *Prophets of War*, p. 6.

17 Harry Stonechipher interviewed in the *Wall Street Journal*, quoted in ibid., p. 7.

18 Information gleaned from Reuters and AboveTopSecret.com, 2 June 2009.

19 *Defence Talk*, 22 June 2009.

20 Hartung, *Prophets of War*, p. 10.

21 Ibid., p. 11.

22 Ibid., p. 16.

23 Ibid., p. 17.

24 T. Capaccio, 'Lockheed F-35 program faces $1 billion cut in U.S. Senate spending measure', Bloomberg News, 16 December 2010.

25 Johnson, 'Death Spiral at the Pentagon'.

26 Quoted in Hartung, *Prophets of War*, pp. 18–19.

27 Bloomberg, 21 April 2011, http://www.bloomberg.com/news/2011-04-21/lockheed-martin-f-35-operating-costs-may-reach-1-trillion.html.

28 Ibid.

29 Interview with Pierre Sprey, Washington DC, May 2011.

30 The Congressional Research Service, quoted in Hartung, *Prophets of War*, p. 230, from which this section is drawn.

31 Federation of American Scientists, Arms Sales Monitoring Project.

32 Derived from 'US Weapons at War 2008', New America Foundation, December 2008, http://www.newamerica.net/publications/policy/u_s_weapons_war_2008_0.

33 Hartung, *Prophets of War*, p. 179.

34 Ibid., pp. 179–80.

35 Drawn from Johnson, 'Death Spiral at the Pentagon', p. 279.

36 Ibid., pp. 279–80.

37 Ibid.

38 Hartung, *Prophets of War*, pp. 230–31.

39 Ibid.

40 Ibid.

41 Ibid., p. 232.

42 Ibid., pp. 235–6.

43 Ibid., p. 239.

44 Ibid., p. 240.

45 Ibid., pp. 242–3.

46 'LCS Contracts Awarded to Lockheed Martin, Austal USA', *DefenseNews*, 29 December 2010, http://www.defensenews.com/story.php?i=5339223.

47 'Lockheed, Austal's littoral ships to cost at least $37 billion', Bloomberg, 19 April 2011, http://www.bloomberg.com/news/2011-04-19/lockheed-austal-s-littoral-ships-to-cost-at-least-37-billion.html.

48 Hartung, *Prophets of War*, pp. 243–6.

49 Ibid., pp. 248–9.

50 All figures are from ibid., pp. 29–30. The top three defence contractors combined received $75bn and the top ten $152bn in 2008.

51 Kelly Patricia O'Meara, 'Rumsfeld inherits financial mess', Insight on the News, 3 September 2001, http://findarticles.com/p/articles/mi_m1571/is_33_17/ai_78127727/.

52 'Building affordability', DefenseNews, 26 July 2010; 'Pentagon says it's moving toward being "audit-ready"', CNN, 25 February 2011.

53 'Senators call for an audit of the Pentagon', RT, 16 May 2011.

54 'GAO blasts weapons budget', *Washington Post*, 1 April 2008.

55 'U.S.–U.K.–Australian trade treaties finally pass committee', DefenseNews, 21 September 2010.

56 See 'Missing Iraq reconstruction billions', *Independent*, 16 February 2009.

57 Ibid.

58 Guy Lawson, 'Arms and the Dudes', *Rolling Stone*, 31 March 2011.

59 TPM, 'AEY Inc', July 2008.

60 A. Tilghman, 'Army awarded AEY contract after "recommendation" from firm's financial backer', Talking Points Memo (TPM) Muckraker, 24 June 2008, http://tpmmuckraker.

talkingpointsmemo.com/2008/06/aey_contract_after_recomendation_from_firms_financial_
backer.php.

61 'Supplier under scrutiny on arms for Afghans', *The New York Times*, 27 March 2008.

62 Ardian Klosi, *The Gerdec Disaster: Its Causes, Culprits and Victims* (Tirana: K&B, 2010).

63 Ibid.

64 Ibid.

65 Ibid.

66 Ibid.

67 Ibid.

68 Ibid.

69 Ibid.

70 Ibid.

71 'Supplier under scrutiny on arms for Afghans', *The New York Times*, 27 March 2008.

72 Klosi, *Gerdec Disaster*.

73 Interview with Hugh Griffiths, Stockholm, November 2010.

74 Lawson, 'Arms and the Dudes', *Rolling Stone*, 31 March 2011.

75 Interview with Hugh Griffiths, Stockholm, November 2010; and 'Supplier under scrutiny
on arms for Afghans', *The New York Times*, 27 March 2008.

76 'Supplier under scrutiny on arms for Afghans', *The New York Times*, 27 March 2008.

77 Klosi, *Gerdec Disaster*.

78 Ibid.; and 'American envoy is linked to arms deal cover-up', *The New York Times*, 24 June
2008.

79 'U.S. ambassador to Albania cleared in ammo cover-up', *Los Angeles Times*, 19 March 2009.

80 'Miami gun runner gets 4 years', Talking Points Memo (TPM) Muckraker, 4 January 2011,
http://tpmmuckraker.talkingpointsmemo.com/2011/01/miami_gun_runner_gets_4_
years_says_good_times_werent_worth_it.php#more.

81 This account is drawn from an interview with Feruzan Durdaj, Gerdec, 26 May 2010; and
Klosi, *Gerdec Disaster*.

82 This account is drawn from an interview with Feruzan Durdaj, Gerdec, 26 May 2010; and
Klosi, *Gerdec Disaster*.

83 Klosi, *Gerdec Disaster*.

84 Ibid.

85 Miriam F. Weismann, 'The Foreign Corrupt Practices Act: The Failure of the Self-Regulatory
Model of Corporate Governance in the Global Business Environment', *Journal of Business
Ethics*, 2009, pp. 615–61.

86 OECD, *United States: Phase 2, Report on Application of the Convention on Combating Bribery of
Foreign Public Officials in International Business Actions and the 1997 Recommendation on Combating Bribery in International Business Transactions*, www.oecd.org/dataoecd/52/19/1962084.
pdf.

87 Nelson D. Schwartz and Lowell Bergmann, 'Payload: taking aim at corporate bribery',
The New York Times, 25 November 2007, http://www.nytimes.com/2007/11/25/business/
25bae.html.

88 Jeffrey Cramer, 'The FCPA Game Has Changed: Trends in Enforcement', Main Justice,
23 April 2010, http://www.mainjustice.com/2010/04/23/commentary-the-fcpa-game-has-
changed-trends-in-enforcement/.

89 Shearer & Sterling LLP, FCPA Digest of Cases and Review Releases Relating to Bribes to Foreign Officials under the Foreign Corrupt Practices Act of 1977 (as of February 13, 2008), Danforth Newcomb & Philip Urofsky Partners, Shearman & Sterling LLP (New York, New York).

90 Brandon L. Garrett, Structural Reform Prosecution, 93 Va. L. Rev. 853, 860, 886, 890 (2007).

91 Richard L. Cassin, *Bribery Everywhere: Chronicles from the Foreign Corrupt Practices Act* (lulu. com, 2009), p. 10.

92 OECD, *United States: Phase 2, Report on Application of the Convention on Combating Bribery of Foreign Public Officials in International Business Actions and the 1997 Recommendation on Combating Bribery in International Business Transactions* (2002), p. 23, www.oecd.org/dataoecd/52/19/ 1962084.pdf.

93 Ibid., p. 16. Retrieved 9 October 2010.

94 OECD, *United States: Phase 2, Follow up report on the implementation of the Phase 2 Recommen- dations on the Application of the Convention on Combating Bribery of Foreign Public Officials in International Business Actions and the 1997 Recommendation on Combating Bribery in International Business Transactions* (2005), www.oecd.org/dataoecd/7/35/35109576.pdf.

95 Shearman & Sterling LLP, *US v. Lockheed Corporation*, http://fcpa.shearman.com/?s=matt er&mode=form&id=38.

96 Cassin, *Bribery Everywhere*, p. 10.

97 Tom Mcghie and Jenny Little, 'BAE pension windfall wipes out £285m fine', *Daily Mail*, 13 February 2010, http://www.dailymail.co.uk/money/article-1250840/BAE-pension- windfall-wipes-285m-fine.html.

98 Dan Margolies, 'Cocktails and wiretaps signal new anti-bribery era', Reuters, 5 April 2010, http://www.reuters.com/article/idUSTRE6342MO20100405?pageNumber=2.

99 'New rules on US airport laptop searches', Reuters, 28 August 2009, http://www.pcpro. co.uk/news/enterprise/351172/new-rules-on-us-airport-laptop-searches.

100 Cassin, *Bribery Everywhere*, p. 54.

101 McKenna Long & Aldridge, 'Financial reform bill includes FCPA whistleblower provision', Lexology, 26 July 2010, http://www.lexology.com/library/detail.aspx?g=b41be68e-996f- 499f-9d1e-392bbcaba3b6.

102 Cassin, *Bribery Everywhere*, p. 141.

103 Stefaans Brümmer and Sam Sole, 'How arms-deal "bribes" were paid', *Mail & Guardian*, 5 December 2008, http://www.mg.co.za/article/2008-12-05-how-arms-deal-bribes-were- paid.

104 KBR used its joint venture with Technip and Snamprogetti Netherlands BV (a subsidiary of Saipem SpA of Italy) and JGC of Japan to operate through three shell companies in Madeira, Portugal, which held consulting contracts with agents who passed bribes to Nigerian officials. Ownership was hidden by being held indirectly through KBR's UK company, M. W. Kellogg Ltd. The three companies were named Madeira Company 1, 2 and 3. The boards of 1 and 2 included US citizens, but the third, through which the con- sultancy contracts were held, did not have any US citizens in the company as 'a further part of KBR's intentional effort to insulate itself from FCPA liability'. (Cassin, *Bribery Everywhere*, p. 37.)

105 Steptoe & Johnson LLP, 'French companies prepare to pay hundreds of millions to U.S. authorities in foreign corruption matters', Lexology, 15 July 2010, http://www.lexology. com/library/detail.aspx?g=c81d5e07-c77d-413c-9147-4a82c59cfe56.

106   Tara Patel, 'Technip poised to win contracts as shares top CAC (Update2)', Bloomberg, 31 December 2009, http://www.businessweek.com/news/2009-12-31/technip-poised-to-win-contracts-as-shares-top-cac-update2-.html.

107   Fiona Phillip, '7-year prison term for engineering executive illustrates new reach of anti-bribery law', Main Justice, 30 April 2010, http://www.mainjustice.com/2010/04/30/commentary-7-year-prison-term-for-engineering-executive-illustrates-new-reach-of-anti-bribery-law/.

108   'Debarment for BAE', FCPA Blog, 4 March 2010, http://www.fcpablog.com/blog/2010/3/4/debarment-for-bae.html.

109   Cassin, *Bribery Everywhere*, p. 23.

110   Leah Nylen, 'FCPA debarment bill introduced in house', Main Justice, 25 May 2010, http://www.mainjustice.com/2010/05/25/fcpa-debarment-bill-introduced-in-house/.

111   For a detailed account of the sting on Ardebili see the eight-part report starting with John Shiffman, 'Shadow war: hunting Iranian arms brokers', *Philadelphia Enquirer*, 17 September 2010, http://www.philly.com/philly/news/20100917_YARDLEY__APRIL_2004_To_capture_a_global_arms_smuggler.html?viewAll=y.

112   This account is summarized from ibid., from which the quotations are taken.

113   Dan Margolies, 'Cocktails and wiretaps signal new anti-bribery era', Reuters, 5 April 2010, http://www.reuters.com/article/idUSTRE6342MO20100405.

114   'FBI's anti-corruption unit to expand', Main Justice, 24 June 2010, http://www.mainjustice.com/2010/06/24/fbis-anti-corruption-unit-to-expand/.

115   Bruce Carton, 'FCPA enforcement in 2010: prepare for blastoff', Securities Docket, 10 March 2010, http://www.securitiesdocket.com/2010/03/10/fcpa-enforcement-in-2010-prepare-for-blastoff/.

116   Dan Margolies and Jeremy Pelofsky, 'UPDATE 2 – U.S. charges 22 with bribery involving arms sales', Reuters, 19 January 2010, http://www.reuters.com/article/idUSN192000 7620100119?pageNumber=1.

117   Margolies, 'Cocktails and wiretaps signal new anti-bribery cra' (see n. 113 above).

118   Neal Keeling, 'Millionaire businessman held by FBI in arms "sting"', *Manchester Evening News*, 3 February 2010, http://menmedia.co.uk/manchestereveningnews/news/s/1191265_millionaire_businessman_held_by_fbi_in_arms_sting.

119   Margolies and Pelofsky, 'UPDATE 2' (see n. 116 above).

120   Dan Margolies, 'US request to detain arms sting defendant denied', Reuters, 22 January 2010, http://www.reuters.com/article/idUSN2214138020100122.

121   Ken Stier, 'U.S. cashes in on corporate corruption overseas', *Time*, 7 April 2010, http://www.time.com/time/business/article/0,8599,1977526,00.html.

122   Project on Government Oversight, 'The sting, part II: foreign bribery investigation claims another contractor scalp', 27 January 2010, http://pogoblog.typepad.com/pogo/2010/01/the-sting-part-ii-foreign-bribery-investigation-claims-another-contractor-scalp.html.

123   Stier, 'U.S. cashes in on corporate corruption overseas', (see n. 121 above).

124   Carton, 'FCPA enforcement in 2010' (see n. 115 above).

125   Ibid.

126   'Defense wants information on informant in dramatic FCPA white-collar sting case', Crime in the Suites, 16 July 2010, http://crimeinthesuites.com/defense-wants-information-on-informant-in-dramatic-fcpa-white-collar-sting-case/.

127 Peter J. Henning, 'Going undercover for a white-collar sting', *The New York Times*, 21
     January 2010, http://dealbook.blogs.nytimes.com/2010/01/21/going-undercover-for-a-
     white-collar-sting/.

128 Warren Richey, 'FBI sting nets 22 executives charged with paying bribes abroad', *Chris-
     tian Science Monitor*, 19 January 2010, http://www.csmonitor.com/USA/Justice/2010/0119/
     FBI-sting-nets-22-executives-charged-with-paying-bribes-abroad.

129 'Defense wants information on informant', Crime in the Suites (see n. 126 above).

130 'Africa sting updates', FCPA Professor Blog, 7 April 2010, http://fcpaprofessor.blogspot.
     com/search/label/Gabon.

131 Dan Margolies, 'Defendant to plead guilty in arms sting case', Reuters, 5 March 2010,
     http://www.reuters.com/article/idUSTRE62503D20100306.

132 Richey, 'FBI sting nets 22 executives' (see n. 128 above).

133 'Defendants attack cooperator's drug addiction in huge foreign bribery case', Main Justice,
     7 June 2011.

134 Africa sting updates', FCPA Professor Blog (see n. 130 above).

135 Margolies and Pelofsky, 'UPDATE 2' (see n. 116 above).

136 'FBI's anti-corruption unit to expand', Main Justice (see n. 114 above).

137 Stier, 'U.S. cashes in on corporate corruption overseas' (see n. 121 above).

138 Robert Reich, *Locked in the Cabinet* (New York: Vintage Books, 1997), pp. 30 and 41.

139 R. Pollin and H. Garrett-Peltier, *The US Employment Effects of Military and Domestic Spend-
     ing Priorities: An Updated Analysis*, Political Economy Research Institute, University of
     Massachusetts, Amherst, October 2009.

140 Ibid.

141 The ideas in this section are drawn from Frida Berrigan, 'How Shovel-Ready is the Penta-
     gon?', TomDispatch.com, 12 March 2009, and conversations with other leading analysts
     of the defence sector.

142 Ibid.

143 All figures from ibid.

144 Ibid.

145 *Barron's*, 2 March 2009.

146 Berrigan, 'How Shovel-Ready is the Pentagon?'

147 Cited in ibid.

148 'Remembering soldiers and defense lobbying, T-Paw's Mideast slipup and more in capital
     eye opener: May 30', Center for Reponsive Politics, Opensecrets.org, 30 May 2011, http://
     www.opensecrets.org/news/2011/05/ceo-5-30-2011.html.

149 Conversation with Chuck Lewis, December 2008; and investigations by Center for Public
     Integrity: 'Outsourcing the Pentagon', http://projects.publicintegrity.org/pns/report.
     aspx?aid=385.

150 Conversation with Andrew Cockburn, December 2008, Washington DC.

151 Conversation with Chuck Lewis, Washington DC, December 2008.

152 Interview with Chuck Spinney, 1 March 2010.

153 Ibid.

154 Interview with Bill Hartung, 28 July 2010.

155 Ibid.

156 See, for instance, 'Karzai issues decree disbanding private security firms', CNN, 17 Octo-
     ber 2010.

157 'Obama announces framework for cutting deficit by $4 trillion over 12 years', *Washington Post*, 13 April 2011.

158 Email communication from Winslow Wheeler, 14 April 2011.

159 See, for instance, 'Panetta comes armed with background in budget fights', *The New York Times*, 27 April 2011.

160 'Defense Buck Does Not Stop with This Debt Deal,' Straus Military Reform Project, 2 August 2011.

161 'Lowering America's war ceiling?' TomDispatch.com, 2 August 2011, www.tomdispatch.com/blog/175425/tomgram%3A_engelhardt%2C_two-faced_washington/.

162 Frank James, 'Obama lobbying ban hits DC reality', *Chicago Tribune*, 22 January 2009, http://www.swamppolitics.com/news/politics/blog/2009/01/obama_lobbying_ban_hits_realit.html.

163 *USA Today*, 16 April 2008.

164 Quoted in Hartung, *Prophets of War*, from which this paragraph is drawn.

165 Interview with Chuck Spinney, 2 December 2010.

166 Quoted in W. T. Wheeler (ed.), *The Pentagon Labyrinth* (Washington: Center for Defense Information, World Security Institute, 2011).

167 Ibid.

17. America's Shop Window

1 R. Bergman, 'The Secret War with Iran', OneWorld, 2008. The US Marine Corps expressed a similar view in 1990: Major Cozy E. Bailey, 'U.S. Policy towards Israel: The Special Relationship', CSC,1990, http://www.globalsecurity.org/military/library/report/1990/BCE.htm.

2 This excludes homeland security contracts, government-to-government/police-to-police training or military services contracts.

3 *SIPRI Yearbook 2010* (Oxford: OUP, 2010), pp. 286 and 320–21.

4 OECD, *OECD Reviews of Labour Market and Social Policies* (Paris: OECD Publishing, January 2010), p. 18.

5 From an interview with the economist and military analyst Shir Hever, Jerusalem, May 2010.

6 Ibid.

7 This historical survey is derived from ibid. and email conversations with and information from the defence analyst and activist Jimmy Johnson.

8 From an interview with Shir Hever, Jerusalem, May 2010.

9 Ibid.

10 Neve Gordon, 'Israel – Homeland Security Capital', in Lyo Zureik and Abu-Laban (eds.), *Surveillance and Control in Israel/Palestine: Population, Territory and Power* (London: Routledge, 2011), p. 163.

11 From an interview with Shir Hever, Jerusalem, May 2010.

12 Naomi Klein, *The Shock Doctrine* (London: Penguin Books, 2007), p. 435.

13 Ibid., pp. 436 and 439.

14 Ibid., p. 440.

15 Interview with Shir Hever, Jerusalem, May 2010.

16 Quoted by Shir Hever in interview.

17 Frida Berrigan, 'Made in the USA: American Military Aid to Israel', *Journal of Palestine Studies*, Vol. XXXVIII, No. 3 (Spring 2009), pp. 6–21.

18 'Arms unto the Nations', Globes Online, 29 April 2003.

19 'US and Israel in $30bn arms deal', BBC News, 16 August 2007, http://news.bbc.co.uk/1/hi/6948981.stm.

20 Amnesty International, *Israel/OPT: Fuelling Conflict: Foreign Arms Supplies to Israel/Gaza*, MDE 15/012/2009, 23 February 2009.

21 *New Statesman*, 26 January 2009.

22 Berrigan, 'Made in the USA'.

23 Although many of the AMCs are domestically procured and not with FMF funds.

24 Berrigan, 'Made in the USA'.

25 Bergman, 'The Secret War with Iran'

26 Ibid.

27 Ibid.

28 What follows is drawn from ibid. with additional information from my sources.

29 For documents on Israel's role in Iran–Contra see http://www.negedneshek.org/2011/03/operation-tipped-kettle/.

30 Drawn from Bergman, 'The Secret War with Iran', with additional information from my sources.

31 Quoted in ibid.

32 Drawn from Bergman, 'The Secret War with Iran', with additional information from my sources.

33 Ibid.

34 Ibid.

35 Interview with Ronen Bergman, Tel Aviv, May 2010.

36 Drawn from Bergman, 'The Secret War with Iran'.

37 Quoted in ibid.

38 Drawn from Bergman, 'The Secret War with Iran'.

39 Ibid.

40 Quoted in Bergman, 'The Secret War with Iran'.

41 Ibid.

42 Ibid.

43 Ibid.

44 'Fear of Russia ends Israeli support for Georgia', *Israel Today*, 11 August 2008.

45 See A. Egozi, 'War in Georgia: the Israeli connection', YNet News, 10 August 2008.

46 Quoted in ibid.

47 Ibid.; and 'Israel's military on display in Georgia', *Forward*, 11 September 2008. In mid-2011, Ziv's firm, Global CST, solicited business from the Georgian breakaway republic of Abkhazia. Should a contract emerge, Global CST will have trained both the Georgian forces and those of the Abkhazian breakaway republic in the next war. Israeli access to Abkhazia comes, not coincidentally, as military relations with Russia continue to warm. Abkhazia has Russian patronage and would have been inaccessible to Israelis previously. (See also n. 51 below.)

48 From an interview with Shir Hever, Jerusalem, May 2010.

49 Interview with an Israeli journalist, Yossi Melman, May 2010.

50 Ibid.

51 'Why does Israel have links to a breakaway state supported by Hamas?', *Haaretz*, 5 May 2011; and 'Israeli security firm executives in Abkhazia', *Georgian Daily*, 15 April 2011.

52 See brochure at www.theshadowworld.com.

53 Berrigan, 'Made in the USA'.

54 Ibid.

55 'Sources: Israeli businesswoman brokering E. Guinea arms sales', *Haaretz*, 12 November 2008.

56 'Arms unto the Nations' Globes Online, 29 April 2003.

57 J. Johnson, 'Israelis and Hezbollah haven't always been enemies', 11 September 2006, http://www.williambowles.info/syria_lebanon/israel_hezbollah.html.

58 Sasha Polakow-Suransky, *The Unspoken Alliance: Israel's Secret Relationship with Apartheid South Africa* (New York: Pantheon Books, 2010).

59 The right of return gives any Jew the right to live in Israel and acquire Israeli citizenship, which can be very useful in terms of access to travel and banking facilities in Europe.

60 'Olmert's corruption indictment latest in host of Israeli cases', Bloomberg, 30 August 2009.

61 See for, instance, the use of stolen UK identities in the assassination of a Hamas official in Dubai in January 2010.

62 As Jimmy Johnson points out, this is also because the Israeli economy has no place for many of them to pursue a civilian life.

63 From an interview with Shir Hever, Jerusalem, May 2010.

64 From an interview with Yossi Melman, Jerusalem, May 2010.

65 Ibid.

66 Interview with former arms salesman who wishes to remain anonymous, Jerusalem, May 2010.

67 J. Mearsheimer and S. Walt, *The Israel Lobby and US Foreign Policy* (New York: Farrar, Straus and Giroux, 2008).

68 This is drawn from William Hartung, *Prophets of War* (New York: Nation Books, 2011), p. 232.

69 Berrigan, 'Made in the USA'.

70 Quoted in ibid.

71 Figures from Hartung, *Prophets of War*, p. 233.

72 Berrigan, 'Made in the USA'.

73 Ibid.

74 Quoted in Hartung, *Prophets of War*, pp. 233–4.

75 Berrigan 'Made in the USA'.

76 Figures from Hartung, *Prophets of War*, p. 234.

77 Ibid.

78 Quoted in Berrigan, 'Made in the USA'.

79 Ibid.

80 Ibid.

81 The ban was in place from 2007 to 2010. See 'State Department lifts ban on exports of night-vision goggles', *Washington Times*, 24 February 2010.

82 The interview with this source was conducted in May 2010.

83 Ibid.

84 Berrigan, 'Made in the USA'.
85 'Despite row, U.S. and Israel sign massive arms deal', *Haaretz*, 25 March 2010.
86 'US–Saudi arms deal ripples from Iran to Israel', *Miami Herald*, 21 October 2010, http://www.miamiherald.com/2010/10/21/1883887/us-saudi-arms-deal-ripples-from.html#ixzz13gn2ZR1l; and 'Israel's Barak approves US F-35 fighters purchase', Reuters, 15 October 2010.
87 Interview with Shir Hever, Jerusalem, May 2010.

18. Making a Killing: Iraq and Afghanistan

1 Quoted in William Hartung, *Prophets of War* (New York: Nation Books, 2011), p. 197.
2 Ibid., p. 208.
3 Ibid., pp. 210–11.
4 Ibid., pp. 211–12.
5 Quoted in Eugene Jarecki, *The American Way of War* (New York: Free Press, 2008), p. 217.
6 Hartung, *Prophets of War*, p. 213; Naomi Klein, *The Shock Doctrine* (London: Penguin Books, 2007), p. 425.
7 Human Rights Watch, *Genocide in Iraq: The Anfal Campaign against the Kurds* (1993), http://www.hrw.org/legacy/reports/1993/iraqanfal/.
8 Roger Hardy, 'The Iran–Iraq war: 25 years on', BBC News, 22 September 2005, http://news.bbc.co.uk/1/hi/4260420.stm.
9 Derek Hopwood, 'British Relations with Iraq', BBC, 2 October 2003, http://www.bbc.co.uk/history/recent/iraq/britain_iraq_01.shtml.
10 'Iran–Iraq War', Twentieth Century Atlas, http://users.erols.com/mwhite28/warstat2.htm#Iran-Iraq. Number of lives lost seems to range between 377,000 and 1.2 million with most giving the figure as over 500,000 deaths.
11 'The Spider's Web: The Secret History of How the White House Illegally Armed Iraq', *Foreign Affairs*, March/April 1994.
12 'Gonzales's Iraq expose – Hill chairman details US prewar courtship', *Washington Post*, 22 March 1992.
13 William Hartung, *And Weapons for All* (New York: Harper Perennial, 1995), p. 224.
14 Ibid.
15 See A. Sampson, *The Arms Bazaar in the Nineties: From Krupp to Saddam* (Dunton Green: Coronet, 2008), Afterword.
16 Hartung, *And Weapons for All*, p. 240.
17 'The Arsenal: Who Armed Baghdad', *Time*, 11 February 1990.
18 'Rumsfeld's Account Book: Who Armed Saddam?', *Counterpunch*, 24 February 2003.
19 Ibid.
20 Sampson, *Arms Bazaar in the Nineties*, pp. 367–8.
21 'Sarkis Soghanalian', PBS/*Frontline* World, May 2002, as part of PBS/*Frontline* World Special: 'Gallery of International Arms Dealers', www.pbs.org.
22 Ibid.
23 Sampson, *Arms Bazaar in the Nineties*, pp. 363–4.
24 See R. Scott, *Report of the Inquiry into the Export of Dual-Use Goods to Iraq and Related Prosecutions*, Vol. 3 (1996).

25 Ibid. and 'Arms-to-Iraq pair welcome payout', BBC News, 9 November 2001.

26 Ibid.

27 'The Arsenal: Who Armed Baghdad', *Time*, 11 February 1990.

28 Ibid.

29 Sampson, *Arms Bazaar in the Nineties*, pp. 367–8.

30 Stockholm International Peace Research Institute, Database of Weapons Transfers, www.
    sipri.org/contents/armstrade/at_data.html.

31 Ibid., p. 369.

32 Project for the New American Century, 'Statement of Principles', 3 June 1997. Available
    for download from www.newamericancentury.org.

33 Ibid.

34 Project for the New American Century, *Rebuilding America's Defenses*, September 2000,
    p. i. Available for download from www.newamericancentury.org.

35 Open Letter from the Project for the New American Century to the Honourable
    William J. Clinton, 26 January 1998, available for download from www.newamerican
    century.org.

36 Klein, *Shock Doctrine*, Chapter 15.

37 'President Bush announces major combat operations in Iraq have ended', remarks by the
    President from the USS *Abraham Lincoln*, 1 May 2003. Available for download from
    http://georgewbush-whitehouse.archives.gov.

38 S. Bowen, *Hard Lessons: The Iraq Reconstruction Experience. A Report from the Special Inspector
    General for Iraq Reconstruction (SIGIR)*, Chapter 27, p. 8. Available for download from
    www.nytimes.com.

39 See D. Trautner, 'A Personal Account and Perspective of the US Army Logistics Civil
    Augmentation Programme (LOGCAP)', paper presented at Conference of Army Histor-
    ians, 15 July 2004; and T. Christian Miller, *Blood Money* (New York: Back Bay Books,
    2007), p. 75.

40 M. Schwartz, *Department of Defense Contractors in Iraq and Afghanistan: Background and Analysis*,
    Congressional Research Service, R40764, 2010, p. 5. Available for download from www.
    crs.gov.

41 Ibid., p. 8.

42 *Contractor's Support of US Operations in Iraq*, Congressional Budget Office, August 2008,
    pp. 1–3.

43 *Contingency Contracting: DoD, State and USAID Continues to Face Challenges Tracking
    Contractor Personnel and Contracts in Iraq and Afghanistan*, United States Government
    Accountability Office, GAo-10-1, October 2009, p. 19. Available for download from
    www.gao.gov.

44 *At What Cost? Contingency Contracting in Iraq and Afghanistan*, Interim Report by the
    Commission on Wartime Contracting, June 2009, p. 44.

45 See, for example, 'Kellogg, Brown and Root (KBR) to pay $8m to settle allegations of
    fraud', US Department of Justice press release, 29 November 2006, available for download
    from www.usdoj.gov; P. Chatterjee, *Halliburton's Army* (New York: Nation Books, 2009),
    pp. 63–5; and *Halliburton's Questioned and Unsupported Costs in Iraq Exceed $1.4 Billion*, Joint
    Report prepared for Rep. Henry A. Waxman and Sen. Byron L. Dorgan, United States
    House of Representatives: Committee on Government Reform (Minority Staff), 27 June
    2005, p. 15, available for download from http://dpc.senate.gov.

46 J. Mayer, 'Contract Sport', *The New Yorker*, 16 February 2004.

47 'Halliburton's Boss from Hell', *Salon*, 21 July 2004.

48 'Cheney is still paid by Pentagon contractor', *Guardian*, 12 March 2003.

49 Chatterjee, *Halliburton's Army*, p. 72.

50 J. Stiglitz and L. Bilmes, *The Three Trillion Dollar War* (London: Penguin Books, 2009), p. 15.

51 *Halliburton's Gasoline Overcharges*, Report prepared for Reps. Henry A. Waxman and John D. Dingell, United States House of Representatives: Committee on Government Reform (Minority Staff), 21 July 2004. Available for download from http://dpc.senate.gov.

52 Quoted in D. Rasor and R. Bauman, *Betraying Our Troops: The Destructive Results of Privatizing War* (New York: Palgrave Macmillan, 2008), pp. 59–67; and Miller, *Blood Money*, pp. 142–8.

53 *At What Cost?*, Interim Report by the Commission on Wartime Contracting, pp. 10–11.

54 Ibid., p. 13.

55 Testimony of April Stephenson, Director: Defense Contract Audit Agency before the Commission on Wartime Contracting, 4 May 2009. Available for download from www.wartimecontracting.gov.

56 Ibid.

57 Bowen, *Hard Lessons*, p. 17 (see n. 39 above).

58 See Jeremy Scahill, *Blackwater: The Rise of the World's Most Powerful Mercenary Army* (London: Serpent's Tail, 2007), pp. 145–66.

59 Ibid., p. 155.

60 'This year, contractor deaths exceed military ones in Iraq and Afghanistan', Propublica, 23 September 2010, www.propublica.org.

61 Miller, *Blood Money*, p. 76.

62 'Hired guns from SA are flooding Iraq', *Cape Times*, 4 February 2004.

63 'Balkans soldiers find fortune in Baghdad', IPSNews, 12 May 2004.

64 'The enforcer', *Guardian*, 20 May 2006.

65 D. Campbell, 'Marketing the new dogs of war', Center for Public Integrity, 30 October 2002. Available for download from www.publicintegrity.org.

66 Ibid.

67 Ibid.

68 'Tim Spicer's world', *The Nation*, 29 December 2004.

69 'The Rule of Order 17', *Newsweek*, 28 June 2006.

70 Coalition Provisional Authority Order Number 17, CPA/ORD/27 June 2004/17, Section 4, para. 3. Available for download from www.iraqcoalition.org/regulations.

71 'Lawyers, guns and money', United Press International, 4 April 2008.

72 'The Rule of Order 17', *Newsweek*, 28 June 2006.

73 'Red, White and Mercenary in Iraq', *Salon*, 4 October 2007.

74 Ibid.

75 See Scahill, *Blackwater*, pp. 145–66.

76 'The Bush Administration's Ties to Blackwater', *Salon*, 2 October 2007.

77 Ibid.

78 'POGO joins bi-partisan group of Senators in demanding Obama oust the SIGAR', 23 September 2010, http://www.pogo.org/pogo-files/alerts/government-oversight/go-igi-20100923.html.

79 'Blackwater "set up $1m hush fund after Iraq shootings"', *Sunday Times*, 12 November 2009.

80 Ibid.; '3 Blackwater guards called Baghdad shootings unjustified', *The New York Times*, 16 January 2010; and 'Blackwater in Baghdad: "It was a Horror Movie"', *Salon*, 14 December 2007.

81 Settlement Summary: Xe Services LLC (Xe) (Formerly Blackwater Worldwide), United States Department of State, Consent Agreement (CA), 18 August 2010 and Consent Order in the Matter of the United States Department of State Bureau of Political and Military Affairs and Xe Services LLC, 8/13 August 2010. Both available for download from www.pmddtc.state.gov.

82 Ibid.

83 Letter from Edolphus Towns, Chairman of US Congress Committee on Oversight and Government Reform, to the Hon. Hilary R. Clinton, Secretary of State, 26 August 2010. Available for download from www.oversight.house.gov.

84 *At What Cost?*, Interim Report by the Commission on Wartime Contracting.

85 *Replacing and Repairing Equipment Used in Iraq and Afghanistan: The Army's Reset Programme*, Report by the Congressional Budget Office, September 2007, p. x. Available for download from www.cbo.gov.

86 Ibid.

87 Ibid., pp. 18–22.

88 'Afghanistan withdrawal: Barack Obama says 33,000 troops will leave next year', *Guardian*, 23 June 2011.

89 Tom Engelhardt, 'Details of secret pact emerge', AlertNet, 23 August 2011.

90 *Replacing and Repairing Equipment Used in Iraq and Afghanistan* (see n. 86 above), p. xii.

91 Ibid., p. 14.

92 A. Belasco, *The Cost of Iraq, Afghanistan and Other Global War on Terror Operations since 9/11*, Paper for the Congressional Research Service, 2 September 2010, Table 7, p. 30. Available for download from www.crs.gov.

93 Ibid., p. 24.

94 Ibid.

95 C. Schumer and C. Maloney, *War at Any Price: The Total Economic Costs of the War beyond the Federal Budget*, Report by the Joint Economic Committee, 13 November 2007. Available for download from www.cfr.org.

96 Stiglitz and Bilmes, *Three Trillion Dollar War*, pp. 15–16.

97 *Replacing and Repairing Equipment Used in Iraq and Afghanistan*, p. ix (see n. 86 above). Available for download from www.cbo.gov. See also Belasco, *Cost of Iraq, Afghanistan and Other Global War on Terror Operations* (see n. 93 above).

98 Stiglitz and Bilmes, *Three Trillion Dollar War*, p. 16.

99 'Pentagon redefines "emergency"', *Wall Street Journal*, 3 January 2007.

100 Ibid.

101 'Estimated Costs of US Operations in Iraq and Afghanistan and Other Activities Related to the War on Terrorism', Statement of Robert A. Sunshine, Assistant Director for Budget Analysis: Congressional Budget Office before the Committee on the Budget, US House of Representatives, 31 July 2007. Available for download from www.budget.house.gov.

102 T. Sharp, 'Problems with Using Supplemental Budget Process to Fund Ongoing Military

Operations in Iraq and Afghanistan', Center for Arms Control and Non-Proliferation, March 2008. Available for download from http://armscontrolcenter.org.

103 *DoD Needs to Take Action to Encourage Fiscal Discipline and Optimize the Use of Tools Intended to Improve GWOT Cost Reporting,* Report to Congressional Committees, Government Accountability Office, GA0-08-68, November 2007, p. 33. Available for download from www.gao.gov.

104 Hartung, *Prophets of War*, p. 213.

105 Ibid.

106 Ibid.

107 P. Chatterjee, 'Meet the new interrogators: Lockheed Martin', CorpWatch, 4 November 2005, www.corpwatch.org.

108 Hartung, *Prophets of War*, pp. 214–19.

109 Tim Shorock, *Spies for Hire: The Secret World of Intelligence Outsourcing* (New York: Simon & Schuster, 2008), p. 12.

110 'BAE Systems benefits from Iraq, Afghanistan armoured vehicles', *Daily Telegraph*, 15 October 2008.

111 'BAE Systems completes acquisition of Armor Holdings, Inc.', press release ref. 204/2007, 31 July 2007, www.baesystems.com.

112 'Drone Wars', *Forbes*, 6 January 2009.

113 Share prices calculated using online tools available from the NYSE and FTSE websites.

114 Ibid.

115 Belasco, *Cost of Iraq, Afghanistan and Other Global War on Terror Operations*, p. 30 (see n. 93 above).

116 Share prices calculated using online tools available from the NYSE and FTSE websites.

117 Ibid.

118 Belasco, *Cost of Iraq, Afghanistan and Other Global War on Terror Operations*, p. 30 (see n. 93 above).

119 D. Farah and S. Braun, *Merchant of Death* (Hoboken, NJ: John Wiley & Sons, 2007), pp. 214–17.

120 Ibid., p. 225.

121 Ibid., p. 226.

122 Ibid., p. 221.

123 Ibid., p. 232.

124 Ibid., p. 249.

125 Amnesty International, *Blood at the Crossroads: Making the Case for a Global Arms Treaty*, ACT 30/011/2008, September 2008, p. 45.

126 Ibid.

127 Ibid.

128 See www.agilitylogistics.com.

129 'Taos industries team wins Logcap IV task order in Afghanistan', *Business Wire*, 13 July 2009.

130 See www.agilitylogistics.com.

131 Amnesty International, *Dead on Time – Arms Transportation, Brokering and the Threat to Human Right*, ACT 30/008/2006, p. 104.

132 Amnesty International, *Blood at the Crossroads*, p. 46; and B. Wood, 'International Initiatives to Prevent Illicit Brokering of Arms and Other Related Materials', in *Disarmament Forum*, No. 3 (2009), p. 10.

133 *Report of the Panel of Experts Appointed Pursuant to Paragraph 4 of Security Council Resolution 1458 (2003) Concerning Liberia*, S/2003/498, 24 April 2003, pp. 19–21.

134 'British businessman to testify against "Merchant of Death"', *Independent*, 27 July 2008; and Farah and Braun, *Merchant of Death*.

135 'Case Studies: Aerocom', Stockholm International Peace Research Institute, undated, www.sipri.org.

136 Amnesty International, *Blood at the Crossroads*, Chapter 7.

137 Ibid.; and 'UK guns in al-Qaeda hands', *Guardian*, 19 March 2006.

138 'UK guns in al-Qaeda hands', *Guardian*, 19 March 2006.

139 Ibid.

140 Ibid.

141 Ibid.

142 *Stabilizing Iraq: DoD Cannot Ensure That US-Funded Equipment Has Reached Iraqi Security Forces*, Report to Congressional Committees, Government Accountability Office, GAO-07-711, July 2007, p. 8. Available for download from www.gao.gov. The body responsible for the programme was the Multinational Security Transition Command-Iraq, or MSTC-I.

143 Ibid., p. 11.

144 'Missing US arms probe goes global', *Asia Times*, 17 August 2007.

145 'Chevron joins the US–Ukraine Business Council', press release, 5 August 2009, US–Ukraine Business Council. Available for download from www.usubc.org.

146 www.sasi-corp.com/forsales.html.

147 Ibid.

148 'US probes company's covert operations', *Washington Post*, 30 December 1998.

149 Ibid.

150 All contract information accessed via the Federal Procurement Data System, www.fdps.gov. The contract was made up of a number of separate, smaller orders, the largest order a touch under $28m, signed on 22 February 2007. See contract number/Referenced IDV: W91CRB04D0024.

151 Aram Roston, 'The Unquiet American', *Washington Monthly*, 5 June, 2005.

152 Ibid.

153 Miller, *Blood Money*, p. 230.

154 Dale Stoffel's CV, exhibit 1 from seized hard drive posted online on 26 April 2005 by the 'Political Committee *Mujahideen* Central Command', www.albasrah.net.

155 Human Rights Watch, *Bulgaria: Money Talks – Arms Dealing with Human Rights Abusers*, 1 April 1999, D1104, available from www.unhcr.org. Accessed 4 April 2010.

156 Ibid.

157 Ibid.; Roston, 'Unquiet American'; and Miller, *Blood Money*, p. 231.

158 Roston, 'Unquiet American'.

159 R. Perucci and E. Wysong, *The New Class Society: Goodbye American Dream?* (Lanham, Md: Rowman & Littlefield, 2003), p. 124.

160 'Iran used Chalabi to dupe US, says report', *Seattle Times*, 22 May 2004.

161 Aram Roston, *The Man Who Pushed America to War* (New York: Nation Books, 2008), p. 248.

162 Ibid.

163 Congressional Record: Proceedings and Debates of the 108 Congress, Second Session (Washington DC: US Government Printing Office, 2 June 2004), p. 11322.

164 Roston, 'Unquiet American'.

165 According to company registers filed with the Panamanian central company registrar.

166 *Wye Oak Technology Inc. v. Republic of Iraq*, in the United States District Court for the Eastern District of Virginia, Submission by John Quinn and David Stoffel, Filed 20 July 2009, Civil Case No. 1:09CV793, paras. 10–14.

167 'Iraq: corruption, missing millions and two dead contractors', Associated Press, 28 January 2006.

168 Complaint Exhibit 2 submitted as attachment to *Wye Oak Technology Inc. v. Republic of Iraq* (see n. 167 above).

169 'U.S. Army failed to investigate warnings of corruption', *Los Angeles Times*, 14 March 2005.

170 *Wye Oak Technology Inc. v. Republic of Iraq* (see n. 167 above), para. 18.

171 'Salameh: government cannot force return of Iraqi money', *Daily Star* (Lebanon), 6 February 2004.

172 'U.S. Army failed to investigate warnings of corruption', *Los Angeles Times*, 14 March 2005; and 'Contractor accused of fraud in Iraq', *Seattle Times*, 9 October 2004.

173 *Wye Oak Technology Inc. v. Republic of Iraq* (see n. 167 above), para. 27.

174 Roston, 'Unquiet American'.

175 Ibid.

176 'Memorandum of Understanding', 20 June 2004 (unsigned), from seized hard drive posted online on 26 April 2005 by the 'Political Committee *Mujahideen* Central Command', www.albasrah.net. Also available at www.theshadowworld.com.

177 Ibid.

178 It's assumed Newco was just a place-holder.

179 Memorandum of Understanding' (see n. 177 above).

180 Ibid.

181 msnbc, 12 November 2004.

182 *Wye Oak Technology Inc. v. Republic of Iraq* (see n. 167 above), para. 29.

183 'Inquiry on graft in Iraq focuses on US officers', *The New York Times*, 14 February 2009.

184 *Wye Oak Technology Inc. v. Republic of Iraq* (see n. 167 above), para. 29.

185 'Inquiry on Graft in Iraq Focuses on US Officers', *The New York Times*, 14 February 2009.

186 'Response to Motion for Order Pursuant to Customer Challenge Provisions of Right to Financial Privacy Act' in the Matter of Anthony B. Bell (Movant) v. Special Inspector General for Iraq Reconstruction (Respondent) in the United States District Court, Northern District of Georgia, Civil Action No. 3:09-mi-00003 and 3:09-mi-00002, 2 March 2009.

187 'Declaration of Special Agent James J. Crowley' submitted as supporting evidence in 'Response to Motion for Order Pursuant to Customer Challenge Provisions of Right to Financial Privacy Act' in the Matter of Anthony B. Bell (Movant) v. Special Inspector General for Iraq Reconstruction (Respondent) in the United States District Court, Northern District of Georgia, Civil Action No. 3:09-mi-00003 and 3:09-mi-00002, 2 March 2009.

188 'Afghanistan withdrawal: Barack Obama says 33,000 troops will leave next year', *Guardian*, 23 June 2011.

189 Ibid.

190 'US troops may stay in Afghanistan until 2024', *Daily Telegraph*, 19 August 2011.

191 Belasco, *Cost of Iraq, Afghanistan and Other Global War on Terror Operations* (see n. 93 above). The total cost for the three projects examined – wars in Iraq and Afghanistan and enhanced security at US bases in the region – was $1.121tn.

192 Ibid.

193 Ibid.

194 Ibid.

195 'Economic Cost Summary: Costs of War', www.costsofwar.org. Downloaded 2 July 2011.

196 'The true cost of the Iraq War: $3 trillion and beyond', *Washington Post*, 5 September 2010.

197 Ibid.

198 Ibid.

199 'Potential Jobs', www.costsofwar.org. Downloaded 2 July 2011.

200 'Costs of War Summary', www.costsofwar.org. Downloaded 2 July 2011.

201 Amnesty International, *Blood at the Crossroads*, Section 7; 'Afghanistan: Arms Proliferation Fuels Further Abuse', Amnesty International public briefing, 2008, www.amnesty.org; M. Bhatia, 'Small Arms Flows into and within Afghanistan', in M. Bhatia, and M. Sedra, *Afghanistan, Arms and Conflict* (Abingdon: Routledge & Small Arms Survey, 2008), p. 38.

202 P. Cockburn, *The Occupation: War and Resistance in Iraq* (London: Verso, 2007), p. xxii.

203 Ibid.

204 For an excellent account of corruption scandals facing the Al-Karzai government, see P. Chatterjee, 'Paying Off the Warlords: Anatomy of a Culture of Corruption', in N. Turse (ed.), *The Case for Withdrawal from Afghanistan* (London: Verso, 2010), pp. 81–6.

205 'Woman said to have been used as human shield for bin Laden', *Washington Post*, 2 May 2011.

206 Cockburn, *The Occupation*, p. xxii.

207 Stiglitz and Bilmes, *Three Trillion Dollar War*, p. 15.

Section V: The Killing Fields

19. Cry, the Beloved Continent

1 'President Bush Creates a Department of Defense Unified Command for Africa', White House statement, 6 February 2007, http://georgewbush-whitehouse.archives.gov. Africom was fully operational by late 2008.

2 Richard H. Robbins, *Global Problems and the Culture of Capitalism* (Boston, Mass.: Allyn and Bacon, 2002).

3 D. Fruchart, 'Case Study: Rwanda, 1994–Present', in *United Nations Arms Embargoes: Their Impact on Arms Flow and Target Behaviour*, Report by the Stockholm International Peace Research Institute (SIPRI), 2007, pp. 2–5.

4 Human Rights Watch, *Arming Rwanda – The Arms Trade and Human Rights Abuses in the Rwandan War*, 1 January 1994, A601, available at http://www.unhcr.org/refworld/docid/3ae6a7fc8.html.

5 Ibid.

6 For an excellent analysis of the relationship between the Rwandan genocide and the

economic crisis caused by declining coffee prices, see P. Verwimp, 'The Political Economy of Coffee, Dictatorship and Genocide', *European Journal of Political Economy*, Vol. 19, Issue 2, June 2003, pp. 161–81.

7   Fruchart, 'Case Study: Rwanda, 1994–Present', pp. 2–5.

8   Human Rights Watch, *Arming Rwanda* (see n. 4 above).

9   Ibid.

10 'Profile: Agatha Habyarimana, the power behind the Hutu presidency', *Guardian*, 2 March 2010.

11 L. Melvern, *Conspiracy to Murder: The Rwandan Genocide* (London: Verso, 2006), p. 50.

12 Ibid.

13 Ibid., pp. 55–6.

14 Ibid., pp. 21–32.

15 Ibid., p. 21.

16 P. Mangarella, 'Explaining Rwanda's 1994 Genocide', *Human Rights and Human Welfare*, Vol. 2, Issue 1, Winter 2002.

17 N. McNulty, 'French Arms, War and Genocide', *Crime, Law & Social Change*, Vol. 33 (2000), p. 107.

18 Fruchart, 'Case Study: Rwanda, 1994–Present', pp. 5–10.

19 N. Alusala, 'The Arming of Rwanda and the Genocide', *African Security Review*, Vol. 12 (2004), No. 2, p. 138.

20 Ibid.

21 Human Rights Watch, *Arming Rwanda* (see n. 4 above).

22 Ibid.

23 Ibid.

24 Fruchart, 'Case Study: Rwanda, 1994–Present', pp. 5–10.

25 Melvern, *Conspiracy to Murder*, pp. 57–8.

26 Ibid.

27 McNulty, 'French Arms, War and Genocide', p. 109.

28 'France's shame?', *Guardian*, 11 January 2007; and Stephen Ellis, email communication, 19 June 2011.

29 McNulty, 'French Arms, War and Genocide', p. 110.

30 Ibid.

31 Ibid., pp. 110–11.

32 Fruchart, 'Case Study: Rwanda, 1994–Present', pp. 6–7.

33 Ibid.

34 Ibid., p. 6.

35 'Rwanda's mystery that won't go away', BBC News, 29 November 2006. See also 'Habyarimana killed by his own forces', *The New York Times*, 12 January 2010; and 'Habyarimana killed by his own army – UK experts', *The East African*, 10 January 2010.

36 *Committee of Experts Investigation of the April 6, 1994 Crash of President Habyarimana's Dassault Falcon-50 Aircraft*, Media Guide, Republic of Rwanda, January 2010, pp. 5–6. Available for download from http://mutsinzireport.com.

37 Zach Dubinsky. 'The Lessons of Genocide', in *Essex Human Rights Review*, Vol. 2 (2005), No. 1, p. 112; and 'Rwanda leader defiant on killing claim', BBC News, 30 January 2007.

38 'Bloody trade that fuels Rwanda's war', *Independent*, 23 November 1996.

39 M. Phythian, 'The Illicit Arms Trade: Cold War and Post-Cold War', in M. Phythian

(ed.), *Under the Counter and over the Border: Aspects of the Contemporary Trade in Illicit Arms* (Dordrecht, Netherlands: Kluwer Academic Publishers, 2000), pp. 21–4.

40 'Arming Africa: who is the second largest supplier of weapons on the world? China? France? Russia? No, it's Britain', *Independent*, 19 November 1996.

41 Ibid.; and Fruchart, 'Case Study: Rwanda, 1994–Present', p. 17.

42 Fruchart, 'Case Study: Rwanda, 1994–Present', p. 17.

43 Phythian, 'The Illicit Arms Trade' pp. 21–4.

44 'Rwanda: how the genocide happened', BBC News, 18 December 2008; and 'OAU sets inquiry into Rwandan genocide', *Africa Recovery*, Vol. 12, No. 1, August 1998.

45 Ibid.

46 Estimate calculated from the figure of 800,000 killed.

47 'Sex Violence: A Tool of War', Lessons from Rwanda: The United Nations and the Prevention of Genocide, www.un.org/preventgenocide.

48 Ibid.

49 See P. Verwimp, 'Machetes and Firearms: The Organization of Massacres in Rwanda', *Journal of Peace Research*, Vol. 43 (2006), No. 1.

50 Ibid.

51 For a detailed and eviscerating account of colonial rule in the Congo, see Adam Hochschild, *King Leopold's Ghost* (London: Pan Macmillan, 2006).

52 For a detailed biography of Lumumba, see R. McKown, *Lumumba: A Biography* (London: Doubleday, 1969), L. De Witte, *The Assassination of Lumumba* (London: Verso, 2001), and L. Zeilig, *Lumumba: Africa's Lost Leader* (London: Haus, 2008).

53 R. Fredland, *Understanding Africa: A Political Economy Perspective* (Lanham, Md: Rowman & Littlefield, 2001), p. 128.

54 *Country Profile: The Democratic Republic of Congo*, Action for Southern Africa Report, www.actsa.org.

55 'Who killed Lumumba?', BBC News, 21 October 2000.

56 See De Witte, *Assassination of Lumumba*, and 'US Role in Lumumba Murder Revealed', *AllAfrica* and *Washington Post*, 22 July 2002. The latter article, by Dr Stephen Weissman, an African expert once employed by the US House of Representatives, suggests that the assassination of Lumumba took place at exactly the same time as the CIA was running Project Arrow, a campaign to fund opponents to Lumumba, which, tellingly, made payments to the generals who eventually murdered Lumumba. A one-page memo, released by the Agency in 2007 among a cache of documents, described a 'project involving the assassination of Patrice Lumumba, then premier of the Republic of Congo. ... Poison was said to have been the vehicle.' ('CIA releases files on past misdeeds', *Washington Post*, 27 June 2007.) In 2002, forty-one years after the murder, Belgium officially apologized for its role in Lumumba's death ('Lumumba apology: Congo's mixed feelings', BBC News, 6 February 2002).

57 N. McNulty, 'The Collapse of Zaire: Implosion, Revolution or External Sabotage?', *Journal of Modern African Studies*, Vol. 37 (1999), No. 1, p. 59

58 His new name in full was Mobutu Sese Seko Nkuku Ngbendu Wa Za Banga, which means 'The all-powerful warrior who, because of his endurance and inflexible will to win, will go from conquest to conquest, leaving fire in his wake.'

59 H. Weiss, 'War and Peace in the Democratic Republic of the Congo', *Current African Issues*, No. 22 (2000).

60 'Mobutu Sese Seko, 66, longtime dictator of Zaire', *The New York Times*, 8 September 1997.

61 See McNulty, 'Collapse of Zaire', p. 59.

62 Joe Bavier, 'Congo's New Mobutu', *Foreign Policy*, 29 June 2010.

63 M. Wrong, 'The Emperor Mobutu', *Transition*, No. 81/82 (2000), p. 99–102.

64 Weiss, 'War and Peace'.

65 See, for example, Howard French, 'Kagame's Hidden War in the Congo', *New York Review of Books*, 24 September 2009.

66 'Leaked UN report accuses Rwanda of possible genocide in the Congo', *Guardian*, 26 August 2010. See also 'UN discovers possible DRC genocide', News24, 26 August 2010.

67 'UN revises DRC "genocide" report', Al-Jazeera, 1 October 2010.

68 Weiss, 'War and Peace'.

69 Ibid.

70 Ibid.

71 D. Fruchart, 'Case Study: Democratic Republic of Congo, 2003–2006', in *United Nations Arms Embargoes: Their Impact on Arms Flows and Target Behaviour* (Stockholm: Stockholm International Peace Research Institute (SIPRI), 2007), pp. 2–3.

72 A. Hochschild, 'Heart of Sadness: Congo', *Amnesty Magazine*, www.amnestyusa.org.

73 Amnesty International, *Democratic Republic of Congo: Children at War*, September 2003, AFR 62/034/2003, p. 4, footnote 8.

74 J. Murison, 'The Politics of Refugees and Internally Displaced Persons in the Congo War', in J. Clark (ed.), *The African Stakes of the Congo War* (New York: Palgrave Macmillan, 2002), p. 228.

75 Amnesty International, *Democratic Republic of Congo: Children at War*, p. 1.

76 'DR Congo's women in the frontline', BBC News, 6 November 2002.

77 Ibid.

78 See Amnesty International, *Democratic Republic of Congo: Children at War*, p. 1.

79 Hochschild, 'Heart of Sadness: Congo'.

80 Fruchart, 'Case Study: Democratic Republic of Congo, 2003–2006', pp. 2–3.

81 Ibid., p. 3.

82 *Final Report of the Panel of Experts on the Illegal Exploitation of Natural Resources and Other Forms of Wealth in the Democratic Republic of Congo*, 16 October 2002, S/2002/1146, paras. 12–24.

83 Ibid., para. 39.

84 Ibid.

85 Ibid., para. 40.

86 Ibid.

87 Ibid.

88 'The arms dealer who could bring down Zuma', *Independent*, 27 November 2008; 'Millionaire accused of propping up Mugabe', *Guardian*, 27 November 2008.

89 'Smoke, sex and the arms deal', *Mail & Guardian*, 28 October 2008.

90 Ibid. See Chapter 9 for Bredenkamp's denial of a major role with BAE and his closeness to Mugabe.

91 *Final Report of the Panel of Experts on the Illegal Exploitation of Natural Resources and Other Forms of Wealth in the Democratic Republic of Congo*, 16 October 2002, S/2002/1146, para. 56.

92 Ibid.

93 Ibid.

94 Ibid., Annex II, Category II.

95 *Report of the Panel of Experts on the Illegal Exploitation of Natural Resources and Other Forms of Wealth of the Democratic Republic of Congo*, 23 October 2003, S/2003/1027, paras. 22–9.

96 Ibid., para. 23.

97 The Office of Foreign Assets Control (OFAC) of the US Department of the Treasury administers and enforces economic and trade sanctions based on US foreign policy and national security goals against targeted foreign countries and regimes, terrorists, international narcotics traffickers, those engaged in activities related to the proliferation of weapons of mass destruction, and other threats to the national security, foreign policy or economy of the United States: www.ustreas.gov/offices/enforcement/ofac.

98 'Treasury Designates Mugabe Regime Cronies', statement issued by the United States Department of the Treasury, 25 November 2008.

99 See Council Decision 2011/101/CFSP of 15 February 2011 concerning restrictive measures against Zimbabwe, in the *Official Journal of the European Union*, 16 February 2011, and Department of the Treasury, Office of Foreign Assets Control, 'Specially Designated Nationals and Blocked Persons', 21 June 2011, http://www.treasury.gov/ofac/downloads/t11sdn.pdf.

100 Amnesty International, *Democratic Republic of Congo: Arming the East*, AFR 62/006/2005, July 2005, pp.. 53–4.

101 *Final Report of the Panel of Experts on the Illegal Exploitation of Natural Resources and Other Forms of Wealth in the Democratic Republic of Congo*, 16 October 2002, S/2002/1146, para. 107.

102 Ibid., para. 72.

103 Amnesty International, *Democratic Republic of Congo: Arming the East*, pp. 53–4.

104 Ibid.

105 Ibid.

106 Fruchart, 'Case Study: Democratic Republic of Congo, 2003–2006', p. 5.

107 B. Johnson-Thomas and P. Danssaert, *Zimbabwe – Arms and Corruption: Fuelling Human Rights Abuses*, International Peace Information Service, July 2009, www.ipisresearch.be.

108 Ibid.

109 Tom Cooper and Pit Weinert, 'Zaire/DRC since 1980', ACIG.org, http://www.acig.org/artman/publish/printer_190.shtml; and Ryan Dilley, 'The "trainer" jet the UK loves to Hawk', BBC News, 29 May 2002, http://news.bbc.co.uk/1/hi/uk/2012743.stm.

110 'Zimbabwe–China relations: who benefits?', a speech by Wilf Mabanga delivered at the University of the Witwatersrand, 8 April 2011.

111 See 'Global and Inclusive Agreement on Transition in the Democratic Republic of the Congo: Inter-Congolese Dialogue', signed in Pretoria on 16 December 2002, available for download from www.reliefweb.int.

112 Ibid.

113 See Peter Danssaert and Brian Johnson-Thomas, *Greed and Guns: Uganda's Role in the Rape of the Congo*, International Peace Information Service, 2005. Available for download from www.ipisresearch.be.

114 *Conflict Minerals and the Democratic Republic of Congo*, Report by Business for Social Responsibility, 2010, p. 1. For a detailed history of mining in the DRC from the colonial era to the present, and its impact on conflict, see *The Role of the Exploitation of Natural Resources in Fuelling and Prolonging Crises in the Eastern DRC*, International Alert, 2009.

115 *Conflict Minerals and the Democratic Republic of Congo*, Report by Business for Social Responsibility, 2010, p. 1.

116 *Report of the Security Council Mission to the Democratic Republic of the Congo*, S/2010/288, 30 June 2010, paras. 3–6.

117 Ibid., para. 8.

118 'UN : DRC mass rapes defy belief', *Mail & Guardian*, 24 September 2010.

119 Resolution 1493 (2003) Adopted by the Security Council at Its 4797th Meeting, 28 July 2003, S/RES/1493 (2003).

120 Fruchart, 'Case Study: Democratic Republic of Congo, 2003–2006', pp. 9–11.

121 Resolution 1596 (2005) Adopted by the Security Council at Its 5163rd Meeting, 18 April 2005, S/RES/1596 (2005); and Resolution 1807 (2008) Adopted by the Security Council at Its 5861st Meeting, 31 March 2008, S/RES/1807 (2008).

122 Amnesty International, *Democratic Republic of Congo: Arming the East*, pp. 66–70.

123 Joe Bavier, 'Congo's New Mobutu', *Foreign Policy*, 29 June 2010.

124 Human Rights Watch, *Transparency and Accountability in Angola: An Update*, New York, 2010, p. 1.

125 Ibid.

126 Ibid., p. 2.

127 'Human Development Report 2009 – HDI Rankings', http://hdr.undp.org/en/statistics.

128 Human Development Indicators –Angola (Rank 143), 2009, http://hdr.undp.org .

129 For an excellent and brief summary of Angola's colonial heritage, see M. Newitt, 'Angola in Historical Context', in P. Chabal and N. Vidal (eds.), *Angola: The Weight of History* (New York: Columbia University Press, 2008). Pages 28–33 are particularly useful for a discussion of the slave trade. For a more detailed account of the slave trade in Angola, see Joseph C. Miller's mammoth *Way of Death* (Madison: University of Wisconsin Press, 1997).

130 'Angola Profile: Timeline', BBC News Africa, 19 July 2011.

131 T. Hodges, *Angola: From Afro-Stalinism to Petro-Diamond Capitalism* (Norway and Indiana: International African Institute and James Currey, 2001), pp. 6–8.

132 Ibid.

133 Human Rights Watch Arms Project and Human Rights Watch/Africa, *Angola: Arms Trade and Violations of the Laws of War since the 1992 Elections*, 1994, p. 8. See also see W. Minter, *Apartheid's Contras* (Johannesburg: Witwatersrand University Press, 1994).

134 'Jonas Savimbi – Obituary', *Independent*, 25 February 2002.

135 'Jonas Savimbi', *The Economist*, 28 February 2002.

136 A. Mazrui, *The Warrior Tradition in Modern Africa* (Leiden: Brill, 1977), p. 227.

137 Human Rights Watch Arms Project and Human Rights Watch/Africa, *Angola: Arms Trade and Violations of the Laws of War*, p. 9; and D. Herbstein and D. Evenson, *The Devils are among Us: The War for Namibia* (New York: Zed Books, 1989), p. 175.

138 C. Legum, *Africa Contemporary Record: Annual Survey and Documents, Vol. 18* (Teaneck, NJ : Holmes & Meier, 1987), p. A-33.

139 Christopher Andrew, *For the President's Eyes Only* (London: HarperCollins, 1995), p. 412; R. Immerman and A. Theoharis, *The Central Intelligence Agency: Security Under Scrutiny* (Westport, Conn.: Greenwood Press, 2006), p. 412.

140 A. Vines, *Angola Unravels: The Rise and Fall of the Lusaka Peace Process* (New York and London: Human Rights Watch, 1999), p. 7.

141 For a detailed study of US covert support in Angola, see J. Stockwell, *In Search of Enemies: A CIA Story* (New York: W. W. Norton & Company, 1997).

142 J. Potgieter, 'Taking Aid from the Devil Himself: Unita's Support Structures', in J. Cilliers

and C. Dietrich (eds.), *Angola's War Economy* (Pretoria and Cape Town: Institute for Security Studies, 2000), p. 260.

143 *Truth and Reconciliation Commission of South Africa Report, Vol. 2,* 1998, Chapter 2, paras. 50–73.

144 Ibid.

145 A. Vines, 'Angola: Forty Years of War', in P. Batchelor, K. Kingama and G. Lamb (eds.), *Demilitarisation and Peace-Building in Southern Africa* (Aldershot and Burlington: Ashgate Publishing, 2004) p. 78.

146 Ibid.

147 Resolution 864 (1993) Adopted by the Security Council at Its 3277th Meeting, 15 September 1993, S/RES/864 (1993).

148 Vines, 'Angola: Forty Years of War', p. 78.

149 Ibid., pp. 79–80.

150 Ibid.

151 Ibid.

152 S. Roberts and J. Williams, *After the Guns Fall Silent: The Enduring Legacy of Landmines* (Washington: Vietnam Veterans' Association of America and Oxfam, 1995), p. 109.

153 See *Report of the Panel of Experts on Violations of Security Council Sanctions against Unita,* 10 March 2000, S/2000/203.

154 Ibid., para 49.

155 C. Dietrich, 'UNITA's Diamond Mining and Exporting Capacity', in Cilliers and Dietrich (eds.), *Angola's War Economy*, p. 274.

156 Ibid., p. 278.

157 Ibid.

158 J. Sherman, 'Profit vs Peace: The Clandestine Diamond Economy of Angola', *Journal of International Affairs,* 1 April 2001, pp. 2–3.

159 Vines, *Angola Unravels,* Chapter IX.

160 See *Report of the Panel of Experts on Violations of Security Council Sanctions against Unita,* 10 March 2000, S/2000/203, paras. 16–17.

161 Ibid.

162 Global Witness, *All the Presidents' Men,* March 2002, p. 11.

163 Ibid.

164 Ibid.

165 K. Silverstein, 'The Arms Dealer Next Door', In These Times, 22 December 2001.

166 Global Witness, *All the Presidents' Men,* March 2002, p. 11.

167 Ibid., p. 12.

168 Ibid.

169 E. Allen and N. Intalan, 'Anatomy of a Scandal', *World Policy Journal,* Vol. 27 (2010), No. 1, pp. 14–15.

170 Ibid.

171 Ibid.; and Global Witness, *All the Presidents' Men,* March 2002, p. 11.

172 'Profile of Arcadi Gaydamak', BBC News, 13 July 2007.

173 Judgment, Tribunal de Grande Instance de Paris, 11ème Chambre: 3ème Section, République Française, Au Nom du Peuple Français, No. 0019292016, p. 206.

174 Silverstein, 'Arms Dealer Next Door'.

175 Judgment, Tribunal de Grande Instance de Paris, 11ème Chambre: 3ème Section, République Française, Au Nom du Peuple Français, No. 0019292016, pp. 170–71.

176 Resolution 864 (1993), United Nations Security Council, 15 September 1993, S/RES/864, para. 19.

177 Judgment, Tribunal de Grande Instance de Paris, 11ème Chambre: 3ème Section, République Française, Au Nom du Peuple Francais, No. 0019292016, pp. 170–71.

178 Global Witness, *All the Presidents' Men*, March 2002, p. 11.

179 Mitterrand: 'French establishment players convicted over arms to Angola scandal', *Sunday Times*, 28 October 2009. Pasqua: 'French power brokers convicted over arms to Angola', Reuters, 27 October 2009; 'France ex-minister Pasqua acquitted over Angola arms', BBC News, 24 April 2011.

180 Silverstein, 'The Arms Dealer Next Door'. The GOP returned the contributions following Falcone's detention.

181 Allen and Intalan, 'Anatomy of a Scandal', pp. 14–15.

182 Ibid.

183 Ibid.

184 Ibid.

185 Quoted in *Counterpunch*, 26 February 2008, and Dominique Manotti, *Affairs of State* (London: Arcadia Books, 2009), Epigraph.

186 Vines, *Angola Unravels* p. 7.

187 D. Farah and S. Braun, *Merchant of Death* (Hoboken, NJ: John Wiley & Sons, 2007), pp. 80–84.

188 Ibid.

189 Belarus, Brazil, Bulgaria, Canada, the Czech Republic, Hungary, Kazakhstan, Moldova, Peru, Poland, Russia, Slovakia, South Africa, Spain and Ukraine. (Information generated via the SIPRI customizable arms trade database: http://armstrade.sipri.org.)

190 Ibid.

191 *Report of the Panel of Experts on Violations of Security Council Sanctions against Unita*, 10 March 2000, S/2000/203, paras. 18–20.

192 Ibid.

193 Ibid.

194 Ibid.

195 Global Witness, *For a Few Dollars More*, April 2003, pp. 21–3.

196 'Revealed: ex-Soviet officer turns sanction buster', *Financial Times*, 10 July 2000.

197 *Report of the Panel of Experts on Violations of Security Council Sanctions against Unita*, 10 March 2000, S/2000/203, paras. 28–31.

198 Global Witness, *For a Few Dollars More*, April 2003, p. 23.

199 Ibid.

200 'Africa's gems: warfare's best friend', *The New York Times*, 6 April 2000.

201 *Report of the Panel of Experts on Violations of Security Council Sanctions against Unita*, 10 March 2000, S/2000/203, paras. 28–31.

202 Ibid.

203 *Report of the Panel of Experts on Violations of Security Council Sanctions against Unita*, April 2000, S/2002/486, paras. 17–18.

204 'Jonas Savimbi: Obituary', *Guardian*, 25 February 2002.

205 *Africa South of the Sahara 2004* (London: Europa Publications, 2004), p. 45.

206 Ibid.

207 'Angola rebel leader's death confirmed', BBC News, 24 February 2002.

208 *Angola's Wealth: Stories of War and Neglect*, September 2001, Oxfam Briefing Paper, p. 6; and 'Digging up Angola's deadly litter', *Christian Science Monitor*, 27 July 2001.

209 V. Britain, 'Angola: What Kind of Peace after Decades of War?', *Conflict, Security & Development*, Vol. 2 (2002), No. 2.

210 K. Menkhaus, 'Governance without Government in Somalia', *International Security*, Vol. 31, No. 3 (Winter 2006/2007), p. 74.

211 For a detailed examination of the role of clan-based networks in the politics of Somalia, see H. Adam, 'Militarism, Warlordism or Democracy?', *Review of African Political Economy*, No. 54, July 1992.

212 Ismail I. Ahmed and R. H. Green, 'The Heritage of War and State Collapse in Somalia and Somaliland: Local-Level Effects, External Interventions and Reconstruction', *Third World Quarterly*, Vol. 20 (1999), No. 1, pp. 115–16.

213 Ibid.

214 *Report of the Panel of Experts on Somalia Pursuant to Security Council Resolution 1425 (2002)*, S/2003/223, p. 13.

215 Ibid.

216 Ibid.

217 K. Medani, 'Financing Terrorism or Survival?: Informal Finance and State Collapse in Somalia and the US War on Terrorism', *Middle East Report*, No. 223, Summer 2002, p. 7.

218 Ahmed and Green, 'The Heritage of War and State Collapse in Somalia and Somaliland', pp. 116–17.

219 Ibid., pp. 116–20.

220 Medani, 'Financing Terrorism or Survival', pp. 6–10.

221 Ahmed and Green, 'The Heritage of War and State Collapse in Somali and Somaliland', p. 116.

222 Menkhaus, 'Governance without Government in Somalia', p. 80.

223 See *Report of the Panel of Experts on Somalia Pursuant to Security Council Resolution 1425 (2002)*, S/2003/223.

224 Ahmed and Green, 'The Heritage of War and State Collapse in Somalia and Somaliland', p. 119.

225 Ibid.

226 Ibid.

227 Ibid., pp. 119–120.

228 Ibid.

229 L. Cliffe, *Armed Violence and Poverty in Somalia*, Centre for International Cooperation and Security/University of Bradford: Department for Peace Studies, March 2005, p. 7.

230 'Somalia: in the market for war', *Guardian*, 7 June 2010.

231 'Arms dealers revel in Somali war business', Reuters, 9 June 2009.

232 Ibid.

233 Cliffe, *Armed Violence and Poverty in Somalia*, pp. 8–9.

234 *Report of the Panel of Experts on Somalia Pursuant to Security Council Resolution 1425 (2002)*, S/2003/223, paras. 118–37.

235 Cliffe, *Armed Violence and Poverty in Somalia*, pp. 8–9.

236 'Arms dealers revel in Somali war business', Reuters, 9 June 2009.

237 'Peacekeepers sell arms to Somalis', BBC News, 23 May 2000.

238 *Report of the Panel of Experts on Somalia Pursuant to Security Council Resolution 1425 (2002)*, S/2003/223, para. 21.

239 Ibid., para. 41.

240 Ibid., para. 42.

241 Ibid., para. 43.

242 Ibid.

243 Ibid., paras. 43–7.

244 Ibid.

245 *Somalia: Continuation of War by Other Means?*, Report No. 88, International Crisis Group/ Crisis Group Africa, 2004, p. 7.

246 *Report of the Panel of Experts on Somalia Pursuant to Security Council Resolution 1425 (2002)*, S/2003/223, para. 48; it should be noted that Munye denies any connection to arms dealing.

247 'Israeli, American indicted for gun running to Somalia', 28 June 2010, www.politico. com.

248 'Inside Intel: a man, a plan, a near kidnapping, Panama', *Haaretz*, 15 July 2010.

249 Indictment in the matter of United States of America v. Joseph O'Toole and Chanoch Miller, United States District Court, Southern District of Florida, Case No: CR-COHN, 17 June 2010.

250 Ibid.

251 Ibid.

252 Ibid.

253 Ibid.

254 Judgment in a Criminal Case, USA v. Joseph O'Toole, United States District Court: Fort Lauderdale, Case No. 0:10CR60177-COHN-1, 14 December 2010.

255 Judgment in a Criminal Case, USA v. Chanoch Miller, United States District Court: Fort Lauderdale, Case No. 0:10CR60177-COHN-1, 14 December 2010.

256 R. De Wijk, 'The New Piracy: The Global Context', *Survival*, Vol. 52, No. 1, February– March 2010, p. 40.

257 Ibid., pp. 40–42.

258 Ibid.

259 'Somali pirates living the high life', BBC News, 28 October 2008.

260 'Somali pirates capture Ukrainian cargo ship loaded with military hardware', *Guardian*, 27 September 2008.

261 'Somali pirates "free arms ship"', BBC News, 5 February 2009.

262 Ibid.

263 Anderson, 'The New Piracy: The Local Context'.

264 De Wijk, 'The New Piracy: The Global Context', p. 42.

265 Ibid.

266 'Somali pirates living the high life', BBC News, 28 October 2008.

267 See 'Al-Shabaab', US Counter-Terrorism Calendar 2010, www.nctc.gov/site/groups/al _shabaab.html, and 'Al-Shabaab: Backgrounder', Council on Foreign Relations, 28 July 2010, www.cfr.org.

268 Human Rights Watch, *Harsh War, Harsh Peace: Abuses by al-Shabaab, the Transitional Federal Government and ANISOM in Somalia*, 2010, p. 2.

269 'Somalia's Al Shabaab rebels push towards palace', Reuters, 25 August 2010.

270 'Letter from Somalia', *The New Yorker*, 14 December 2009.

271 'UN Report: Eritrea delivering arms to Al-Shabaab to overthrow government in Puntland', Associated Press, 19 August 2010.

272 Ibid.

273 'Who are Al-Shabaab?', *The New Vision* (Uganda), 17 July 2010.

274 See Human Rights Watch, *Harsh War, Harsh Peace*, pp. 27–32.

275 Ibid., p. 17.

276 Ibid., pp. 17–18.

277 Ibid.

278 'MI5 chief warns of terror threat from Britons trained in Somalia', *Guardian*, 17 September 2010.

279 Ibid.

280 'Somalia: famine, Al-Shabaab complicate U.S. food delivery in face of severe malnutrition', *Huffington Post*, 21 July 2011.

281 The official, who asked to remain anonymous, was interviewed in early 2010 in Washington DC.

282 For an excellent study of identity politics and the contests over resources in modern Sudan and Darfur, see A. De Waal and J. Flint, *Darfur: A New History of a Long War* (London: Zed Books, 2008).

283 Ibid.

284 J. Flint, *Beyond 'Janjaweed': Understanding the Militias of Darfur* (Geneva: Small Arms Survey, 2009), pp. 11–12.

285 A. Vines, 'Counter-Insurgency on the Cheap', *Review of African Political Economy*, Vol. 31 (2004), No. 2, p. 720.

286 I. Gambari, *Situation in Sudan*. Report presented at the United Nations Association of the United States of America Model United Nations Conference, New York, 2005. Available for download from www.un.org.

287 Human Rights Watch, *Sudan, Oil and Human Rights*, 2003..

288 'Aid groups warn of Sudan civil war risk', BBC News, 7 January 2010.

289 'Millions dead in Sudan civil war', BBC News, 11 December 1998; and 'Sudan: Nearly 2 Million Dead as a Result of the World's Longest Running Civil War', US Committee for Refugees, 2001.

290 'Background Note: Sudan', Bureau of African Affairs: US Department of State, 29 June 2010, www.state.gov.

291 Flint, *Beyond 'Janjaweed'*, p. 16.

292 Ibid.

293 Gambari, *Situation in Sudan*, pp. 3–4 (see n. 286 above). This is obviously a simplified account of complex ethnic and identity constructs.

294 Ibid.

295 Vines, 'Counter-Insurgency on the Cheap', pp. 720–21.

296 Ibid.

297 De Waal and Flint, *Darfur*, p. 47.

298 Ibid., p. 50.

299 Ibid., pp. 50–52.

300 T. Dagne and B. Everett, *Sudan: The Darfur Crisis and the Status of North–South Negotiations*,

Report prepared for the US Congress by the Congressional Research Service/Library of Congress, 2004, p. 2.

301 P. Wezeman, 'Case Study: Darfur, Sudan, 2004–2006', in *United Nations Arms Embargoes*, pp. 2–3.

302 Ibid., pp. 3–4.

303 Flint, *Beyond 'Janjaweed'*, pp. 18–19.

304 Dagne and Everett, *Sudan*, pp. 2–3. Note that *Janjaweed* is also variably spelt *Janjawid* and *Janjawiid*.

305 Gambari, *Situation in Sudan*, pp. 4–5 (see n. 286 above).

306 'Q & A: Sudan's Darfur conflict', BBC News, 23 February 2010.

307 Ibid.

308 Ibid.

309 Human Rights First, *Investing in Tragedy: China's Money, Arms and Politics in Sudan*, March 2008, pp. 3–5, www.humanrightsfirst.org.

310 Ibid.

311 Ibid.

312 Ibid., p. 13.

313 Ibid., pp. 3–13.

314 Human Rights First, *Investing in Tragedy*, p. ii (see n. 309 above).

315 'A Deadly Love Triangle', *Weekly Standard*, 6 August 2008, and 'The Islamic Republic of Sudan?', *Foreign Policy*, 10 June 2010.

316 'A Deadly Love Triangle', *Weekly Standard*, 6 August 2008.

317 Human Rights First, 'Arms Sales to Sudan', www.stoparmstosudan.org.

318 'Sudan, Iran sign military cooperation agreement', *Sudan Tribune*, 8 March 2008.

319 'The Islamic Republic of Sudan?', *Foreign Policy*, 10 June 2010.

320 Ibid.

321 'Iran President hails "strategic ties" with Sudan', *Sudan Tribune*, 16 September 2010.

322 Information generated via the SIPRI Customizable Arms Trade Database: http://arm strade.sipri.org.

323 Ibid.

324 Amnesty International, *Blood at the Crossroads: Making the Case for a Global Arms Trade Treaty*, ACT 30/011/2008, September 2008, pp. 88–9 . See also Wezeman, 'Case Study: Darfur, Sudan, 2004–2006'.

325 Amnesty International, *Blood at the Crossroads*, pp. 88–9.

326 Ibid.

327 Ibid., p. 94.

328 Ibid., pp. 94–5.

329 Ibid.

330 See, for example, *Report of the Panel of Experts Established Pursuant to Resolution 1591 (2005) Concerning Sudan*, UN Security Council, S/2009/562, 29 October 2009, p. 32–52.

331 Human Rights First, *Investing in Tragedy*, pp. 3–5.

332 Ibid.

333 *Report of the Panel of Experts Established Pursuant to Resolution 1591 (2005) Concerning Sudan*, UN Security Council, S/2009/562, 29 October 2009, p. 3.

334 'Genocide too', *The Economist*, 13 July 2010; 'African nations divided over Bashir genocide

charge', Reuters, 25 July 2010; and 'Sudanese President Bashir faces fresh genocide charges', AFP/France24, 13 July 2010.

335 'Court worry at Omar al-Bashir's Kenya trip', BBC News, 28 August 2010.

336 'Over 99 percent of South Sudan vote to separate', *Mail & Guardian*, 30 January 2011.

337 'Tunisia suicide protestor Mohammed Bouazizi dies', BBC News, 5 January 2011.

338 'Tunisia: President Zine al-Abidine Bel Ali forced out', BBC News, 15 January 2011.

339 'Egypt protests: three killed in day of revolt', BBC News, 26 January 2011.

340 'Egypt's Last Pharaoh? The Rise and Fall of Hosni Mubarak', *Time*, 12 February 2011.

341 Ibid.

342 A. Shatz, 'Mubarak's Last Breath', *London Review of Books*, Vol. 32, No. 10, 1 May 2010.

343 R. Bush, 'Politics, Power and Poverty: Twenty Years of Agricultural Reform and Market Liberalisation in Egypt', *Third World Quarterly*, Vol. 28 (2007), No. 8, p. 1601.

344 Shatz, 'Mubarak's Last Breath'.

345 Bush, 'Politics, Power and Poverty'.

346 Ibid.

347 Shatz, 'Mubarak's Last Breath'.

348 Ibid.

349 'Where's Hosni Mubarak's money? Ask front man Hussein Salem', ABC News Radio, 2 March 2011.

350 Ibid.

351 'Hussein Salem caught in Dubai with $500m', Globes, 31 January 2011.

352 'Hosni Mubarak detained over corruption allegations', *Guardian*, 13 April 2010.

353 'Egypt asks Interpol to arrest businessman Hussein Salem', Egypt News, 22 March 2010; 'Fate of the ousted president inches further along', Ahram Online, 24 May 2011, http://english.ahram.org.eg/NewsContent/1/64/12862/Egypt/Politics-/Fate-of-the-ousted-president-inches-further-along.aspx.

354 'Egypt's arms industry depends on U.S.', Aol News, 15 February 2011.

355 J. Sharp, *Egypt: The January 25 Revolution and Implications for U.S. Foreign Policy*, Congressional Research Service, RL33003, 2011, www.crs.gov.

356 Ibid.

357 Ibid.

358 Ibid., p. 24.

359 Ibid.

360 SIPRI Military Expenditure Database, www.sipri.org.

361 SIPRI Arms Transfer Database, www.sipri.org/contents/armstrad/output_types_tiv.html.

362 Ibid.

363 Ibid.

364 Ibid.

365 Ibid.

366 P. Chatterjee, 'Egypt's military-industrial complex', *Guardian*, 4 February 2011.

367 Ibid.

368 Ibid.

369 'Egyptian police using U.S.-made tear gas against demonstrators', ABC News, 28 January 2011.

370 Chatterjee, 'Egypt's military-industrial complex', *Guardian*, 4 February 2011.

371 'Egypt protest pictures highlight the arms trade's unintended consequences', 29 January 2011, www.warisbusiness.com.

372 'Controversial tear gas canisters made in the USA', CNN, 28 January 2011.

373 'Arms export deals: MPs criticise UK's stance', BBC News, 5 April 2011.

374 'David Cameron visits Egypt with arms industry group to help civilian "Transition"', *Scotsman*, 22 February 2011.

375 Ibid.

376 'Cameron attacked for Egypt visit with defence sales team in tow', *Independent*, 22 February 2011.

377 'Qaddafi forces fire cluster bombs into civilian areas' *The New York Times*, 15 April, 2011; and 'Nato must send in troops to save Misrata, say rebels', *Guardian*, 16 April 2011.

378 'Rebels overrun Gaddafi compound', BBC News Africa, 23 August 2011.

379 'Qaddafi's Great Arms Bazaar', *Foreign Policy*, 8 April 2011.

380 'McCain: The War isn't Over until We Secure Qaddafi's 10 Tons of Mustard Gas', *Business Insider*, 23 August 2011.

381 'After the fall, U.S. concerned about Libya weapons', Reuters, 22 August 2011.

382 M. Eljahmi, 'Libya and the US: Gaddafi unrepentant', *Middle East Quarterly*, 2006 (Winter), pp. 11–14.

383 Human Rights Watch, *Libya: Words to Deeds*, 24 January 2006, www.hrw.org/en/node/11480/section/11.

384 'Sudan's shadowy Arab militia', BBC News, 10 April 2004.

385 A. Cordesman, *A Tragedy of Arms: Military and Security Developments in the Mahgreb* (Westport: Praeger, 2002), p. 206.

386 According to the SIPRI Arms Trade Database, www.sipri.org.

387 Ibid.

388 Ibid.

389 Cordesman, *Tragedy of Arms*, p. 208.

390 Ibid.

391 A. Cordesman and A. Nerguizian, *The North African Military Balance: Force Developments and Regional Changes*, Center for Strategic & International Studies (CSIS), 2010, p. 34, www.csis.org.

392 Cordesman, *Tragedy of Arms*, pp. 185–6.

393 Ibid.

394 Ibid.

395 According to the SIPRI Arms Trade Database, www.sipri.org.

396 W. Kegö, A. Molcean and G. Nizhikau, 'Belarus Arms Trade', Policy Brief No. 60, Institute for Security & Development Policy, 14 March 2011.

397 'Belarus Defence Industry', Global Security, 2005, www.globalsecurity.org; 'Lukashenko: the dictator in the dock', *Independent*, 9 March 2011; and 'Libyan cash finds use in Belarusian arms', RT, 1 March 2011, http://rt.com/news/cash-arms-gaddafi-belarus/.

398 'The Tyrant of Belarus: Gaddafi's Friend Far, Far to the North?', *Time*, 2 March 2011.

399 R. Takeyh, 'The Rogue Who Came in from the Cold', *Foreign Affairs*, Vol. 80 (2001), No. 3, p. 64.

400 Ibid.

401 Ibid., p. 66.
402 SIPRI, Arms Embargo Database, 'EU arms embargo on Libya', www.sipri.org.
403 'EU lifts weapons embargo on Libya', BBC News, 11 October 2004.
404 'Lockerbie bomber Megrahi living in luxury villa six months after being at death's door', *Daily Telegraph*, 20 February 2010.
405 'Secret letters reveal Labour's Libyan deal', *Sunday Times*, 30 August 2009.
406 Transcript obtained by CAAT in FOI request.
407 'Political help behind Libya's arms trade, says official', *The Times*, 5 September 2009.
408 'Libya, Russia agree $1.8bn arms deal: Putin', Reuters, 30 January 2010.
409 Ibid.
410 'EU arms exports to Libya: who armed Libya?', dataset spreadsheet downloaded from www.guardian.co.uk. Author's own calculations.
411 Ibid.
412 'Libyan Arms Deals Come Back to Haunt Europe', *Der Spiegel* Online, 24 February 2011.
413 'EU arms exports to Libya' (see n. 410 above).
414 'BAE Systems to share £200 million arms deal with Libya', *Daily Mail*, 3 August 2007, http://www.dailymail.co.uk/news/article-472958/BAE-Systems-share-200-million-arms-deal-Libya.html#ixzz1JXPeQYEQ.
415 'Libyan rebels receiving anti-tank weapons from Qatar', *Guardian*, 14 April 2011, http://www.guardian.co.uk/world/2011/apr/14/libya-rebels-weapons-qatar.
416 'Libyan Arms Deals Come Back to Haunt Europe', *Der Spiegel* Online, 24 February 2011.
417 'EU arms exports to Libya' (see n. 410 above).
418 'SA sold R70m in arms to Libya', *The Times* (South Africa), 10 April 2011.
419 'Libya army transport deal frozen after US approval', *Daily Herald*, 12 March 2011, http://www.dailyherald.com/article/20110312/news/703129979/#ixzz1LDMvusfR; and 'Uprising puts an abrupt end to recent surge in U.S. military exports to Libya', WorldTribune.com, 8 March 2011, http://www.worldtribune.com/worldtribune/WTARC/2011/ss_military0247_03_08.asp.
420 'Ivory Coast: Laurent Gbagbo captured by French Special Forces, rival claims', *Daily Telegraph*, 11 April 2011.
421 B. Klaas, 'From Miracle to Nightmare: An Institutional Analysis of Development Failures in Côte d'Ivoire', *Africa Today*, Vol. 55 (2008), No. 1.
422 Ibid., p. 113.
423 Ibid.
424 Ibid., p. 114.
425 D. Balint-Kurti, 'Ready for Peace, Ready for War', *The World Today*, Vol. 63, No. 5, May 2007, p. 25.
426 Ibid.
427 Ibid.
428 'Robert Guéï: deposed ruler', BBC News, 20 October 2000; and A. Vines, 'Peace on a Precipice', *The World Today*, Vol. 61, No. 1, January 2005, p. 23.
429 Vines, 'Peace on a Precipice', *The World Today*, Vol. 61, No. 1, January 2005, p. 23.
430 'Ivory Coast: Gbagbo held after assault on residence', BBC News Africa, 11 April 2011.
431 Balint-Kurti, 'Ready for Peace, Ready for War', p. 25.
432 Ibid.

433 Vines, 'Peace on a Precipice', p. 23.

434 See Human Rights Watch, *Côte d'Ivoire: The Human Rights Cost of the Political Impasse*, 21 December 2005, www.hrw.org.

435 'Refugees fleeing Côte d'Ivoire tell their stories', UN World Food Programme News, 5 April 2011, www.wfp.org.

436 See Global Witness, *Hot Chocolate: How Cocoa Fuelled the Conflict in Côte d'Ivoire*, www.globalwitness.org.

437 See Global Witness, *Making It Work*, 2005, pp. 8–15, www.globalwitness.org.

438 UN Security Council Resolution 1572, November 2004, available from www.sipri.org.

439 *Report of the Chairman of the Security Council Committee Established Pursuant to Resolution 1572 (2004) Concerning Côte d'Ivoire on His Mission to Côte d'Ivoire*, S/2005/790, para. 68, www.un.org.

440 Amnesty International, *Blood at the Crossroads*, pp. 28–32.

441 *Report of the Group of Experts Submitted Pursuant to Paragraph 7 of the Security Council Resolution 1584 (2005) Concerning Côte d'Ivoire,* S/2005/699, 2005, para. 11.

442 Amnesty International, *Blood at the Crossroads*, pp. 28–32.

443 Ibid.

444 *Report of the Group of Experts Submitted Pursuant to Paragraph 7 of the Security Council Resolution 1584 (2005) Concerning Côte d'Ivoire,* S/2005/699, 2005, paras. 85–6.

445 'UN investigates Zimbabwe–Ivory Coast arms trade claims', *Guardian*, 4 March 2011.

446 Ibid.

447 'Belarus breaks Ivory Coast arms embargo – UN chief', BBC News, 28 February 2011.

Section VI: End Game

20. Bringing Peace to the World

1 A. Sampson, *The Arms Bazaar in the Nineties: From Krupp to Saddam* (Dunton Green: Coronet, 2008).

2 'Khashoggi's Fall: A Crash in the Limo Lane', *Vanity Fair*, September 1989.

3 Ibid.; and 'Swiss extradite Khashoggi to US', *The New York Times*, 20 July 1989.

4 Seymour Hersh, 'Lunch with the Chairman', *The New Yorker*, 17 March 2003.

5 Securities and Exchange Commission v. Ramy Y. El-Batrawi, GenesisIntermedia, Inc., Ultimate Holdings, Ltd., Adnan M. Khashoggi, Richard J. Evangelista, Wayne Breedon, and Douglas E. Jacobson, Civil Action No. CV-06-2247 (MRP) (C.D. Ca.), Targeted News Service, 2 April 2010; and 'Saudi financier Adnan Khashoggi settles SEC lawsuit', Bloomberg, 31 March 2010.

6 Quoted in 'Khashoggi's Fall', *Vanity Fair*, September 1989.

7 Hersh, 'Lunch with the Chairman', *The New Yorker*, 17 March 2003.

8 'An arms dealer returns, now selling an image', *The New York Times*, 14 November 2009.

9 Interview with Joe der Hovsepian, Amman, Jordan, 14 May 2010.

10 Patrick Radden Keefe, 'The Trafficker', *The New Yorker*, 8 February 2010.

11 This account of the operation is drawn from ibid., and other sources.

12 Ibid.

13 Quoted in ibid.

14 'Child sex abuse guilt', *Herald Sun*, 21 November 2006.

15 'Slovenia to ask Australia for extradition of Nicholas Oman', Slovenian Press Agency, 23 November 2006.

16 *Guardian*, 5 and 9 August 2010. It was established that Campbell had handed the diamonds over to the chief executive at the time of the Mandela Children's Foundation, who still had them in his possession at the time of the trial.

17 'The televangelist and the warlord', *The Nation*, 11 August 2010.

18 'Prosecutors hint Russian suspect sought arms deal in Libya as judge clears path for trial', *Washington Post*, 2 August 2011, http://www.washingtonpost.com/politics/courts-law/prosecutors-hint-russian-suspect-sought-arms-deal-in-libya-as-judge-clears-path-for-trial/2011/08/02/gIQAOxHypI_story.html.

19 Some of these ideas were developed in conversation with Peter Danssaert, but the final opinions expressed are mine alone.

20 'Mensdorff-Pouilly paid £372,000 compensation by UK for imprisonment', *Croatian Times*, 27 May 2011, http://www.croatiantimes.com/news/Around_the_World/2011-05-27/19592/Undie_Payments; 'Mensdorff wins £400,000 in damages from UK taxpayer', *Daily Telegraph*, 27 May 2011, http://www.telegraph.co.uk/news/uknews/law-and-order/8542570/Austrian-count-who-complained-over-prison-underpants-wins-damages-says lawyer.html.

21 Bill Lehane, 'U.S. help sought in Gripen probe', *Prague Post*, 18 August 2010, http://www.praguepost.com/news/5432-u-s-help-sought-in-gripen-probe.html.

22 'Czech corruption busting promise tested', *Wall Street Journal*, 12 November 2010.

23 Based on conversations with sources close to all these investigations.

24 'Proposed Charging Letter re: Investigation of BAE Systems plc Regarding Violations of the Arms Export Control Act and the International Traffic in Arms Regulations', May 2011, available from www.pmddtc.state.gov/compliance/consent_agreements/baes.html.

25 Ibid.

26 Ibid.

27 Ibid.

28 Ibid.

29 Ibid.

30 Ibid.

31 'Statement of Offence' in the matter of the United States of America v. BAE Systems plc, Violation: Title 18, United States Code, Section 371 (conspiracy), United States District Court for the District of Columbia, paras. 18–29.

32 Ibid.

33 US Department of State Bureau of Political-Military Affairs, 17 May 2011, 'Proposed Charging Letter', http://www.pmddtc.state.gov/compliance/consent_agreements/pdf/BAES_PCL.pdf.

34 'Chrimial [sic] charges filed against defense firm Saab', *The Swedish Wire*, 9 September 2010,. The book is N. Resare, *Bribery, Power and Aid – Jas and the South Africa Affair* (Stockholm: Natur & Kultur, 2010).

35 Numerous press articles following the publication of the information referred to the payments baldly as bribes. See, for example, 'Saab admits bribes paid in SA arms deal', News24/SAPA, 6 June 2011, www.news24.co.za. Downloaded 6 June 2011.

36 'Ferrostaal: Final Report, Compliance Investigation', Devoise & Plimpton LLP, 13 April 2011, pp. 58–67.

37 'Submarine cash revealed', *Kathimerini*, 12 April 2010, http://archive.ekathimerini. com/4dcgi/_w_articles_politics_0_12 April 2010_116293.

38 C. Rhodes, 'The submarine deals that helped sink Greece', *Wall Street Journal*, 10 July 2010; 'Probe into German–Greek arms deals reveals murky side of defence sales', 12 August 2010, http:www.defense-aerospace.com; and J. Schmitt, 'How German Companies Bribed Their Way to Greek Deals', *Der Spiegel*, 11 May 2010, http://www.spiegel.de/inter national/europe/0,1518,693973,00.html.

39 'Algarve businessman embroiled in international scandal', *Algarve Resident*, 9 April 2010, http://www.algarveresident.com/story.asp?XID=35767.

40 J. Schmitt, 'Germany's Ferrostaal Suspected of Organizing Bribes for Other Firms', *Der Spiegel*, 30 March 2010,http://www.spiegel.de/international/business/0,1518,686513,00. html.

41 Ibid.

42 'Submarine scandal continues', *Algarve Resident*, 29 April 2010, http://www.algarveresident. com/story.asp?ID=36752.

43 A. Khalip and A. Palment, 'Portugal accuses 10 of fraud in submarines case', Reuters, 2 October 2009, http://www.reuters.com/article/2009/10/02/portugal-submarines-id USL257190620091002.

44 'Taiwan wins arms suit', *Straits Times*, 5 May 2010. (DCNS was called DCN prior to 2007.)

45 'Defence scandals: Taiwan wins, Malaysia waits', *Malaysian Mirror*, 6 May 2010.

46 DCNS, 'Second Scorpene SSK arrives in Malaysia', *Defence Talk*, 13 July 2010, http:// www.defencetalk.com/second-scorpene-ssk-arrives-in-malaysia-27458/; and S. M. Kamal, 'Government says spent RM6.7bn on Scorpene submarines', *Malaysia Insider*, 22 June 2010, http://www.themalaysianinsider.com/malaysia/article/government-says-spent-rm6. 7b-on-scorpene-submarines/.

47 J Manthorpe, 'The prime minister, the private investigator, the murder of a Mongolian model, and 114 million euros', *Vancouver Sun*, 15 November 2010; J. Manthorpe, 'Ghost of Mongolian model continues to haunt Malaysian Government', *Vancouver Sun*, 5 July 2010; and A. Miller, 'Casualties of warfare', *Southeast Asia Globe*, 7 July 2010.

48 'Malaysia's submarine deal surfaces in France', *Asia Sentinel*, 16 April 2010, http://www. asiasentinel.com/index.php?option=com_content&task=view&id=2406&Itemid=178.

49 Manthorpe, 'The prime minister, the private investigator', *Vancouver Sun*, 15 November 2010; Manthorpe 'Ghost of Mongolian model', *Vancouver Sun*, 5 July 2010; and Miller, 'Casualties of warfare', *Southeast Asia Globe*, 7 July 2010.

50 'Saudi Prince Bandar, Standing and Role', Tactical Report, 29 September 2010.

51 'Bandar lawsuit dismissed, appealed', *Aspen Daily News*, 22 January 2009, http://www. aspendailynews.com/section/home/131860.

52 'UK training Saudi forces used to crush Arab spring', *Guardian*, 28 May 2011, www.guard ian.co.uk/world/2011/may/28/uk-training-saudi-troops.

53 'Bandar's Return', *Foreign Policy*, 22 April 2011, http://shadow.foreignpolicy.com/ posts/2011/04/22/bandars_return.

54 'Saudi Arabia uses UK-made armoured vehicles in Bahrain crackdown on democracy pro-testers', CAAT press release, 16 March 2011, http://www.caat.org.uk/press/archive.

php?url=20110316prs; 'UK government challenged over failure to revoke arms exports to Saudi Arabia', CAAT press release, 24 June 2011, http://www.caat.org.uk/press/archive. php?url=20110624prs.

55 'Freed mercenary calls for Mark Thatcher to "face justice"', *Independent*, 4 November 2009.

56 *SIPRI Yearbook 2010* (Oxford: OUP, 2010).

57 AADB Communication, http://www.frc.org.uk/aadb/press/pub2407.html.

58 'SFO probes EADS defence contract with Saudi Arabia', *Daily Telegraph*, 29 May 2011, http://www.telegraph.co.uk/finance/financial-crime/8545282/SFO-probes-EADS-defence-contract-with-Saudi-Arabia.html.

59 'Exports warning as bribery law is delayed', *Financial Times*, 31 January 2011.

60 'Kenneth Clarke denies weakening new anti-bribery law', *Guardian*, 30 March 2011, http://www.guardian.co.uk/law/2011/mar/30/clarke-denies-weakening-bribery-law?C MP=twt_gu.

61 'Corruption Perception Index 2010 Results', Transparency International, 26 October 2010, http://transparency.org/policy_research/surveys_indices/cpi/2010/results.

62 'Ex-BAE chairman is recruited by Kazakhstan', *Guardian*, 4 December 2006.

63 'Corruption Perception Index 2010 Results', Transparency International, 26 October 2010, http://transparency.org/policy_research/surveys_indices/cpi/2010/results.

64 *Daily Telegraph*, 10 June 2010.

65 BAE Systems news release, 1 September 2008, http://www.baesystems.com/Newsroom/ NewsReleases/autoGen_10881105125.html#Before.

66 Gleaned from a response to a question at the BAE AGM, May 2011.

67 Mike Koehler, 'Is BAE's monitor independent?', 'FCPA Professor', Corporate Compliance Insights, 2 September 2010.

68 www.carlyle.com, various.

69 Greenberg Quinlan Rosner Research, UK Post-Election Frequency Questionnaire, 7-9 May 2010, http://www.greenbergresearch.com/articles/2445/5674_uke11050910fq.uk.pdf.

70 'Tony Blair: "I'm basically a public service guy"', *Daily Telegraph*, 6 September 2010.

71 'Lectures see Tony Blair earnings jump over £12m', *The Times*, 29 October 2008.

72 'Tony Blair to boost earnings as paid speaker for Mayfair hedge fund', *Guardian*, 25 January 2010.

73 'Tony Blair: "I'm basically a public service guy"', *Daily Telegraph*, 6 September 2010.

74 'Tony Blair's new "bank" for super-rich', *The Australian*, 22 August 2010.

75 Ibid.

76 'BAE Systems hires Britain's former envoy to Saudi Arabia', *Guardian*, 8 February 2011.

77 *Washington Post*, 16 July 2004.

78 'DOJ notables crowd courtroom as FCPA sting trial begins', Main Justice, 18 May 2011, http://www.mainjustice.com/2011/05/18/doj-notables-crowd-courtroom-as-fcpa-sting-trial-begins/.

79 'The Chamber of Commerce, the FCPA and Rupert Murdoch', Main Justice, 14 July 2011, www.mainjustice.com/justanticorruption/2011/07/14/the-chamber-of-commerce-the-fcpa-and-rupert-murdoch/.

80 'Blackwater founder moves to Abu Dhabi, records say', *The New York Times*, 17 August 2010.

81 'Xe, formerly Blackwater, announces new chief', CNN, 1 June 2011, http://edition.cnn. com/2011/US/06/01/xe.blackwater.chief/.

82 'Blackwater's new ethics chief', Wired.com, 4 May 2011, www.wired.com/dangerroom/2011/05/blackwaters-new-ethics-chief-john-ashcroft/.

83 'Ashcroft finds private-sector niche', *Washington Post*, 12 August, 2006.

84 Loren Thompson, 'How Boeing Won the Tanker War', *Forbes*, 28 February 2011, http://blogs.forbes.com/beltway/2011/02/28/how-boeing-won-the-tanker-war/.

85 'US–Saudi arms plan grows to record size', *Wall Street Journal*, 14 August 2010; 'US confirms $60bn plan to sell Saudi Arabia arms', BBC News, 20 October 2010, http://www.bbc.co.uk/news/world-us-canada-11587348.

86 'US to sell $60bn in advanced arms to Saudi Arabia', *Daily Telegraph*, 20 October 2010.

87 This figure only includes DOD-brokered deals, so privately negotiated deals would be in addition to this figure. 'Proposed US arms sales reach new heights', *Arms Control Today*, March 2011, www.armscontrol.org/act/2011_03/US_Arms_Sales.

88 'Boeing may earn $24 billion from Saudi aircraft and helicopter orders', Defpro.daily, 21 October 2010, http://defpro.com/daily/details/676/; 'US signs $60bn Saudi arms deal as Iran's influence grows', *Belfast Telegraph*, 22 October 2010. See also news releases dated 20 October 2010 from http://www.dsca.mil/sc_news/archive-2010.htm#November.

89 '$60 billion arms sale to Saudi Arabia a needed boost for defence firms', *The Hill*, 24 October 2010.

90 Project on Government Oversight, 'Despite getting ripped off, army rallies to defense of Boeing', 7 July 2011, pogoblog.typepad.com/pogo/2011/07/despite-getting-ripped-off-army-rallies-to-defense-of-boeing.html.

91 Ibid.

92 'US signs $60bn Saudi arms deal as Iran's influence grows', *Belfast Telegraph*, 22 October 2010.

93 'US Congress notified over $60bn arms sale to Saudi Arabia', *Guardian*, 21 October 2010.

94 'Barack Obama throws full US support behind Middle East uprisings', *Guardian*, 20 May 2011.

95 'In Saudi Arabia royal funds buy peace for now', *The New York Times*, 8 June 2011.

96 'Why Mitch McConnell is worse than Charles Rangel', Salon.com, 16 November 2010.

97 'I'd definitely defend Mugabe at the Hague – Charles Taylor's lawyer', *Sunday Telegraph*, 26 September 2010.

98 See Chapters 9 and 19 for Bredenkamp's denial of the allegations made against him.

99 'The memo that sank the arms probe', *Mail & Guardian*, 3 June 2011.

100 'France ex-minister Pasqua acquitted over Angola arms', BBC News, 24 April 2011.

101 'Op-ed: Charles Pasqua, the politician no one dares to send to jail', *Digital Journal*, 24 July 2010.

102 'Angolagate: Pasqua acquitted on appeal', AFP, 24 April 2011.

103 Ibid.

104 'French ex-minister acquitted in "Angolagate" trial', SAPA/*Business Report*, 29 April 2011.

105 Ibid.

106 'Head of State, Pierre Falcone discusses Angolagate outcome', *Angola Press*, 18 May 2011.

107 This account is drawn from 'Sarkozy urged to testify to inquiry into Pakistan arms sale kickbacks', *Guardian*, 18 November 2010; 'Pakistan, Chirac a bien bloqué les com' des intermédiaires balladuriens', Bakchich, 19 June 2009; and French source.

108 Ibid.

109 Ibid.

110 Ibid.

111 'UK hails "new epoch" in relations with regime accused of war crimes', *Independent*, 1 October 2010.

112 Information provided by Tanzanian investigative journalist, Erick Kabendera, November 2010.

113 'BAE criticised by UK MPs over Tanzania corruption', BBC News, 19 July 2011, http://www.bbc.co.uk/news/world-africa-14204115; Uncorrected Transcript of Oral Evidence, 19 July 2011, International Development Committee, HC 847-i, http://www.publications.parliament.uk/pa/cm201012/cmselect/cmintdev/uc847-i/uc84701.htm.

114 'Experts fear looted Libyan arms may find way to terrorists', *The New York Times*, 3 March 2011; 'Antiaircraft missiles on the loose in Libya', *The New York Times*, 14 July 2011.

115 Jeffrey Sachs, 'The Horn of Africa crisis is a warning to the world', *Guardian*, 28 July 2011, www.guardian.co.uk/global-development/poverty-matters/2011/jul/28/horn-africa-drought-warning.

116 Ardian Klosi, *The Gerdec Disaster: Its Causes, Culprits and Victims* (Tirana: K&B, 2010).

117 Guy Lawson, 'Arms and the Dudes', *Rolling Stone*, 31 March 2011.

118 'Armed again', *Miami New Times*, 5 February 2009.

119 'Arms dealer faces new charges', *The New York Times*, 23 August 2010.

120 'Enfant terrible of arms dealing in prison after sting operation', *Independent*, 25 August 2010.

121 Project on Government Oversight, '"Stoner arms dealer" gets 14-year ban from federal contracting', 2 June 2011, http://pogoblog.typepad.com/pogo/2011/06/stoner-arms-dealer-gets-14-year-ban-from-federal-contracting.html.

122 Lawson, 'Arms and the Dudes'.

123 'Munitions supplier sentenced on defense procurement fraud and lying to Army on government munitions contract', press release, United States Attorney's Office, Southern District of Florida, 23 March 2011.

21. Future Imperfect

1 If one considers all spending related to defence and national security, the US alone spends over a trillion dollars a year, with the rest of the world spending about the same again. See N. Turse (ed.), *The Case for Withdrawal from Afghanistan* (London: Verso, 2010).

2 For the initial, minimal effects of the global crisis on defence spending, see 'Report: Global military spending so far unaffected by economic downturn but expected to slow', *San Francisco Examiner*, 30 March 2010, and the SIPRI *Yearbook 2010* (Oxford: OUP, 2010), especially the Introduction to Chapter 5. While general state spending in the US is anticipated to increase by a meagre 3 per cent in 2010/11, defence spending is expected to rise by 4.2 per cent according to 'Obama's 2011 Budget', *Guardian* Data Blog. In the UK spending will be cut by 14 per cent, while defence spending will be cut by 8 per cent: 'Spending Review 2010: Q&A', *Daily Telegraph*, 20 October 2010. France will cut overall public spending by 5 per cent in 2011 and 10 per cent in 2011–13, while defence spending will fall by less than 4 per cent: 'French premier outlines spending cuts', *Wall Street Journal*, 6 May 2010, and 'France to slash defense spending', *Defense News*, 1 July 2010. In Germany defence spending will be cut by 3 per cent while overall spending will be cut by 3.8 per cent: 'Changes coming as Bundeswehr faces budget cuts', *Defense News*, 27 May 2010.

3 See, for example, M. Glenny, *McMafia*, (London: The Bodley Head, 2008), and http://www.fbi.gov/about-us/investigate/organizedcrime.

4 Interview with Joe der Hovsepian, Amman, Jordan, 14 May 2010.

5 Ibid.

6 Statistics on Chinese defence activities are hard to come by, but the country reports that it spent $100bn on its military in 2009, which experts believe is a significant underestimate (Chinese Ministry of Finance, *Report on the Implementation of the Central and Local Budgets for 2008 and on the Draft Central and Local Budgets for 2009*, 5 March 2009). SIPRI estimates that China's military expenditure in 2010 was $119bn (SIPRI Military Expenditure Database, http://www.sipri.org/research/armaments/milex/resultoutput/milex_15). Its arms exports between 2005 and 2010 are calculated at $4.338bn (constant 1990 US dollars), making it the world's seventh-largest exporter, but again this is likely to be an underestimate (SIPRI Arms Transfers Database, 2010 figure, http://armstrade.sipri.org/armstrade/html/export_toplist.php).

7 Richard Bitzinger, 'The Return of the King: China's Re-emergence as an Arms Dealer', Jamestown China Brief, 7 September 2009.

8 'Sri Lanka forces committed war crimes, says UN', *Independent*, 17 April 2011.

9 Jon Lee Anderson, 'Death of the Tiger: Sri Lanka's Brutal Victory over Its Tamil Insurgents', *The New Yorker*, 17 January 2011. Russia and Pakistan supplied small arms and artillery shells.

10 M. Gurtov, 'Swords into Market-Shares: China's Conversion of Military Industry to Civilian Production', *The China Quarterly*, No. 134 (June 1993), p. 216.

11 See E. Medeiros, R. Cliff, K. Crane and J. Culverson, *A New Direction for China's Defence Industry*, RAND Report for Project Air Force, 2005. Available from www.rand.org.

12 'China stealth fighter a "masterpiece" of homegrown technology', *Daily Telegraph*, 25 January 2011; and 'China stealth fighter "copied from parts from downed US jet"', BBC News, 24 January 2011.

13 Ibid.

14 Gary K. Busch, 'The Chinese Military-Commercial Complex: The Globalisation of the Chinese Military Corporations', unpublished.

15 For more detail on the history and current status of the Chinese weapons trade see www.theshadowworld.com.

16 This summary has been compiled from a conversation with Adam Isaacson at the Washington Office on Latin America, July 2010, and the SIPRI *Yearbook 2010*.

17 Sarah Fort, 'Billions in Aid, with No Accountability', Center for Public Integrity, 31 May 2007, http://projects.publicintegrity.org/MilitaryAid//report.aspx?aid=877.

18 For more detail on the history and current status of the arms trade and Pakistan, see www.theshadowworld.com.

19 'India tops weapons purchase table', BBC News, 31 August 2005, http://news.bbc.co.uk/1/hi/world/south_asia/4200812.stm.

20 'Indian defence deals worth $42 billion up for grabs', *Times of India*, 27 February 2011, http://articles.timesofindia.indiatimes.com/2011-02-27/india/28638182_1_indian-defence -defence-deals-defence-ministry.

21 'India takes a NAM-style route on $11bn fighter contract', *Independent*, 28 April 2011.

22 Discussion with Professor James Stewart, former Appeals Counsel, Office of the Prosecu-

tor, International Criminal Tribunal for the former Yugoslavia, and leading academic in the area of corporate responsibility for international crimes.

23 See A. Feinstein, P. Holden and B. Pace, 'Corruption and the Arms Trade: Sins of Commission', in *SIPRI Yearbook 2011* (Oxford: Oxford, 2011).

24 Milton Leitenberg, *Deaths in Wars and Conflicts in the 20th Century*, Cornell University Peace Studies Program, Occasional Paper #29, 3rd edn, 2006, http://www.google.co.uk/ url?sa=t&source=web&cd=6&sqi=2&ved=0CEAQFjAF&url=http%3A%2F%2Fwww.clin gendael.nl%2Fpublications%2F2006%2F20060800_cdsp_occ_leitenberg.pdf&rct=j&q= Deaths%20in%20Wars%20and%20Conflicts%20in%20the%2020th%20Century&ei=YH-- TePrINKHhQfehMnaBQ&usg=AFQjCNEjijwFGsDhKLoztO2QtsKaRoJhKQ&cad =rja. The study of deaths due to armed violence or conflict is obviously difficult as there are numerous ways of estimating the casualties of war. Leitenberg's figure attempts to include not only the deaths of soldiers on the battlefield but the known 'indirect deaths' suffered largely by civilians due to conflict, though clear information on this number is scant and it is therefore almost always underestimated according to Keith Krause, Robert Muggah and Achim Wennmann, *Global Burden of Armed Violence*, Geneva Declaration Secretariat, September 2008, http://www.genevadeclaration.org/fileadmin/docs/Global-Burden-of-Armed-Violence-full-report.pdf. On average in recent conflicts the ratio of indirect deaths to direct deaths caused by conflict is conservatively estimated as four to one. The figure also takes into account the millions killed by 'human decision', which includes such non-wartime, politically caused deaths as those in the Soviet gulags or in the Chinese 'rectification campaigns'. It can be argued that the arms trade, in its modern form as described in this book, started in the late nineteenth and early twentieth centuries and has played a role in providing the tools of this destruction.

Index

In Arabic names the definite article (Al or al-), used as a prefix, is ignored in the ordering of entries.

AAC (Arms Acquisition Council) 177, 178
Abacha, Sani 127
ABB 298
Abbas, Mohammed (Abu Abbas) 157
Abbaspour, Majid 383
Abdul Aziz of Saudi Arabia 12, 13
Abdullah, Abdullah Ahmed 120
Abdullah of Saudi Arabia, Prince 36, 49
Abecassis, Cyril 86
Abidjan 494, 495, 496
Abidjan Freight 118, 124
Abkhazia 385
Abrams tanks 410, 486
Abscam bribery scandal 244
Abu Abbas 157
Abu Ghraib 365, 414
Achille Lauro 157
ACS (Affiliated Computer Services) 413
ACS (Aviation Consultancy Services) 449
ADCS Inc. 325
Adelphia 354
Adolff, Jurgen 509
AE Services 222, 223
AEDC (Aerospace Engineering Design
    Corporation) 76–7
Aegis 407, 408
AEI 14, 15, 16
Aerocom 418
Aeromacchi 177, 178
Aeronautics Defense Systems 384
Aerospace Engineering Design Corporation
    (AEDC) 76–7
Aerospace Industries Association (AIA)
    367–8
Aérospatiale 400

AEY Inc 343, 347, 521
Affiliated Computer Services (ACS) 414
Afghanistan 343, 346
    Afghan–Soviet war 54–55, 245–6
    and Badeeb 59
    and Bout 115–16, 156
    and global Islamic militancy 247–8
    Northern Alliance 115–16
    Taliban *see* Taliban
    and terrorism 247–8; 9/11 attacks 248
    and the US xxviii, 245–8, 341, 370,
        401–4, 406–7, 409–16, 421–2,
        427–30, 431, 456; timeline for
        withdrawal of US troops 410, 427
African National Congress (ANC) xx, 72,
    456, 516–17
    and BAE 175–87, 230, 231
Africom 436
AHI plc 91
AIA (Aerospace Industries Association)
    367–8
Aids 187, 442
AIPAC (American Israel Public Affairs
    Committee) 44, 45, 48, 94, 377
Air Cess 118, 464
Air Charter 462
Air Defence Variants (ADVs) 35
Air Pass 464
Airbus 307, 309, 317–18
    Bandar and an Airbus xiii, 53, 87, 96–7
Airwork 14, 15, 16
Aitken, Jonathan 77, 78–9, 91, 92
AK-47s 71, 123, 167, 245, 399, 400, 407, 417,
    418, 419, 439, 442, 447, 451, 468, 469,
    471, 472, 477, 496

AKAZU 437, 438
Albademil 345
Albania 343–52, 451, 520
   Gerdec 346, 347–8, 349–52, 520
Albaugh, Jim 311
Alderman, Mark 371
Alderman, Richard 151, 225, 226, 227–8, 511
Aldridge, Edward C. Jr 312, 317
Aldridge, Julia 86, 232
Alenia Aerospazio 139–41
Alexander, Jane 295
Alexandria, Virginia 421, 503
ALFA 22
Algernon, Carl-Fredrik 223–4
Allawi, Ayad 424
Allawi, Ghazi 424, 425, 426
Allawi family 424
Allen, Deborah 150
Allen, Robert 136
Allen & Overy 129
Allende, Salvador 28
Allied Maintenance 93
Alne, David 268
ALS Technologies Inc. 364, 393
Alvirez, Daniel 364
Alwaleed bin Talal bin Abdul Aziz al Saud, Prince 286
American Israel Public Affairs Committee (AIPAC) 44, 45, 48, 94, 377
ammunition 26, 28, 61–2, 68, 106, 110, 112, 116, 117, 118, 121, 123, 160, 246, 343–4, 345–8, 350, 380, 417–18, 438–9, 440, 441, 442, 451, 456, 460, 469–70, 472, 496, 520, 521
Amnesty International 13–14, 154, 343, 347, 390, 496, 528
ANC *see* African National Congress
Anderson, Glenn 275
Andersson, Per 213
Angola 53, 117, 120, 445, 447, 453–65, 517–18
   Angolagate 459–62, 518
   civil war 453–65
   FNLA 454, 455, 456
   MPLA 53, 454–5, 456, 457, 459
   oil 453–4, 460

UN arms embargo 461
UNITA 53, 117, 445, 454, 455–9, 461, 462–5
Annan, Kofi 125
Ansar al-Jihad 426
Antarctic Mariner 123, 166–8
anti-tank missiles 110, 441, 492
Antonovs 110, 112, 160, 478, 481, 496
Antwerp 121
Apache helicopter 337
Apple Corporation 296
Arab Gathering (Al-tajammu Al-Arabi) 477
Arab Socialist Baath Party 397
Arab Spring 483, 488, 493, 510, 516
Arabian American Oil Company (ARAMCO) 13
Arad, Ron 382–3
ARAMCO (Arabian American Oil Company) 13
Ardebili, Amir Hossein 359–61
Argentina 262, 399
Arktis Pioneer 72
Armenia 344
Armor Holdings 363, 414
Arms Acquisition Council (AAC) 177, 178
Arms Export Control Act (US) 269, 278, 409, 506
arms industry overview xxii–xxix, 522–30
Arms Moravia 451
Arms Trade Treaty (ATT) 528–9
Armscor 62, 63, 71–2, 176, 439
Armstrong 5, 8 *see also* Vickers-Armstrong
Arstow Commercial Corporation 183
Arusha Accords 437
Ashcroft, John 514
Aspin, Les 289
al-Assad, Bashar 92
El-Assir, Abdul Rahman 518
al-Athel, Sheikh Fahad 78
Attlee, Clement 9
Atwood, James 30, 31
Augustine, Norm 287–8, 289–90, 297, 336
Australia 342
Austria 197–9, 233
Aviation Consultancy Services (ACS) 449

AWACS 48–50, 51, 53
Ayas, Said 78, 92

B1 bomber 257–8
Babangida, Ibrahim 106
BAC (British Aircraft Corporation) 12, 14,
    17, 18, 40
  Lightning Fighters 15–16
Bacevich, Andrew 249, 295
Badeeb, Ahmed 58, 59
Badihi, Boaz 387
BAE xvii, xxvii, xxviii, xxx, 12, 35, 75, 79,
    149–50, 221, 336, 355, 357, 511, 512,
    513, 523
  and the Czech Republic 199–218
  Gripen aircraft *see* Gripen aircraft
  Hawks *see* Hawk aircraft
  and Hungary 218–20
  and Libya 492, 493
  and Mensdorff-Pouilly 197–9
  and Red Diamond Trading Ltd 85, 182,
    192, 205, 206, 219, 507
  and Saudi Arabia 35–8, 39, 355 *see also* Al
    Yamamah deal
  SFO investigations *see* Serious Fraud
    Office: investigations into BAE
  share prices 414–15
  and South Africa 175–88, 230–32, 517
  and Tanzania 188–96, 228–9, 232–3,
    519–20
  Tornado jets 35, 36–8, 39, 77, 87, 130
  and United Defense Industries 285
  and the US 200, 218, 226, 227, 358,
    414–15, 506–8, 516
  Warton 40
  and the Al Yamamah deal 77, 78–81,
    82–7, 127–53, 355 *see also* Al Yamamah
    deal
Baghdad 403, 425
  Airport 416
Bah, Ibrahim 103, 105, 120
Bahrain 223, 510
Bakavu Aviation Transport 450
Baker, Howard 275
Baker III, James 50, 282, 283, 286

Bakhsh, Abdullah Taha 283
Balkans 5, 116 *see also specific countries*
Balladur, Édouard 459, 518
Bamieh, Sam 53
Banca Nazionale del Lavoro (BNL) 397–8
Bandar bin Sultan bin Abdul Aziz Al-Saud,
    Prince xvii, 31, 35, 36, 39–55, 74, 75,
    77, 87, 88, 94–7, 137, 141, 147, 151,
    245, 286, 395, 510, 512
Bangladesh 526
Banyamulenge 445–6
Banyarwanda 437
Barak, Ehud 392
Barbie, Klaus 27
Barclays Bank 189–90, 191, 194, 514
Barre, Mohamed Siad 466–7
Bartak, Martin 506
Bartel, Margaret 'Peg' 424
Basescu, Traian 339
al-Bashir, Omar 478, 480–81, 482, 519
Bates, Jim 320
Bath, James 282–3
Bausch, Gerard 26, 28
al-Bayoumi, Omar 74
BDM Consulting 285
Beckett, Margaret 140
Bedie, Henri Konan 494–5
Begin, Menachem 49–50
Behery, Ahmed Ibrahim 93
Beirut 61, 62, 93, 527
Belarus 480, 490–91, 496, 497
Belgium 117, 119, 121, 122, 156, 436, 440
  and the Congo 444
Bell, Anthony 426
Bell, Timothy 138
Bell (Canadian firm) 94
Ben Ali, Zine El Abidine 483
Beretta weapons 418–19
Bergman, Ronen 373, 379, 380
Bergman, Sven 202
Berisha, Sali 346, 520
Berlau, Henrik 221
Berlin Wall, fall of 56, 422, 445, 459, 460
Berlusconi, Silvio 127
Bernecker, Josef 214–15

Bernhard of the Netherlands, Prince 264–5, 269
Bernhard, Operation 27
Bicesse Accords 459
Billetal 24
Bilmes, Linda 411, 413, 428, 431
bin Laden, Osama 59, 116, 247, 248, 430–31, 474, 527
bin Laden, Salem 283
bin Laden, Shafiq 286
bin Laden family 286
Bisset, Alastair 487
Bistrong, Richard 363, 364
BKSH 423–4
Black Hawks 37, 77, 285, 486
Black, J. Cofer 408
black market xxiii, 23, 420, 523
Black September group 157
blackmail 80, 146, 153
Blackwater/Xe xxix, 358, 407, 408–9, 514
Blackwell, Mickey 336
Blair, Cherie 513
Blair, Tony xiii, 130, 138, 141–2, 144, 145, 146, 147, 177, 188, 190, 200, 227, 395, 513
Bloodstone, Operation 156
blowback xxviii, 30, 246–8, 294, 400, 493
Blue Planet 207
Blumenthal, Sidney 408
Bluvstein, Leonid *see* Minin, Leonid
BMARC 77
BND (Bundesnachrichtendienst) 20, 30
BNL (Banca Nazionale del Lavoro) 106, 397–8
Bockarie, Sam (aka 'Mosquito') xix, 120
Boeing xxviii, 200, 250, 275, 290, 337, 339, 375, 515
    and Druyun 308, 309, 310–11, 312–14
    and Egypt 486
    F-15 *see* F-15 fighter jets
    GBU-39 bombs 389, 393
    GPS-guided bombs 393
    KC-767 tanker scandal 305–18
    V-22 290
    and the War on Terror 334, 366–7

Boeing and Douglass 240
Boer War 5
Bofors 221, 222–3, 223, 284, 528
Boker, John R. Jr 19, 20
Bolivia 5, 27, 527
Bolton-Lee, Anouska 82
Bosnia 68, 116, 151, 343, 418, 470–71
    UN arms embargo 157
Bouazizi, Mohammed 483
Bourne, Sir John 128–9
Bout, Alla 164
Bout, Viktor xxviii, 115–19, 124, 154, 155–7, 158–65, 416–18, 418, 443, 450–51, 462–3, 464, 505
Bowen, Stuart 426–7
Boyd, John R. 257, 258, 280–81, 282
Brackel, Karl von 29
Bradley Fighting Vehicles 284, 285, 410, 414
Branch Energy 117
Braun, Michael 158
Braun, Stephen 115
Brazil 337, 374, 454, 527
Bredenkamp, John 183–5, 443, 448–50, 517
Bremner III, Paul 406–7, 408
bribery xxv, 5–6, 9, 86, 224, 362–3 *see also* corruption; kickbacks
    Abscam scandal 244
    and BAE *see* corruption: and BAE
    Bribery Act, UK 512
    OECD Anti-Bribery Convention 86, 131, 136, 144, 152
    and political campaign contributions 368
    the US and illegal bribery 305–29
    the US and legal bribery xxv–xxvi, 237–61, 516; and foreign weapons sales 262–72
Britain *see* United Kingdom
British Aerospace 12, 189–90 *see also* BAE
British Aircraft Corporation *see* BAC
British Mediterranean Airways 93
British Petroleum 491
British Virgin Islands (BVI) 84–5, 86, 87
Brodman Business 205–6
Brogan, D. W. 237

Brown, Carl 194–5
Brown, Gordon 190, 513
Brown, Stephen 399
Buchanan 123, 165, 166–7
Bulgaria 106, 159, 442, 496
  Bulgarian arms 106, 117, 121
Bumpers, Dale 332
Bundesnachrichtendienst (BND) 20, 30
Bureau of Labour Statistics (BLS, US) 368
Burkina Faso 99–100, 101, 110–11
Burma xxvii, 526
Burns, Nicholas 377
Bush, George H. W. 31, 52, 273, 278, 282,
  283, 284, 286, 287, 381
  militarism under the Bush administra-
    tion 282–6
Bush, George W. xvii, xxvi, 243–4, 282,
  283, 292, 293, 299, 310, 311, 346, 365,
  366, 401, 403, 461, 514
  militarism under the Bush administra-
    tion 292–304, 401–2 *see also* War on
    Terror
Bush, Jeb 290, 401
Bush, Jonathan xviii, 74
Bush family 282–6
Buttler, Smedley Darlington 238–9
Byrd, Robert 396–7
Byron, Beverly 321

C-5A Galaxy 251–2, 253–6, 274
C-5B 275
CAAT (Campaign Against the Arms Trade)
  145, 146, 147, 149, 195, 233, 511
Cable, Vince 227
Caetano, Marcelo 454
Cairo 483
Calabar 125
Calcaterra, Kristina 107
Caldwell, Pat 363
Cameron, David 487
Campaign Against the Arms Trade (CAAT)
  145, 146, 147, 149, 195, 233, 510
Campbell, Kurt 371
Campbell, Naomi 504–5

Camus, Philippe 307
Card, Andy 310, 311
Carlucci, Frank C. 283, 285
Carlyle Group 282, 283–6, 486–7, 513
Carter, Ashton 368–9
Carter, Billy 104
Carter, Jimmy 44, 46, 47, 48, 104, 258
Casey, William 52–53, 54, 380
Cast Lead, Operation 390, 392, 393
Castro, Fidel 23
Cavalla Reforestation and Research
  Plantation, Liberia 109, 110
CBO (Congressional Budget Office) 305,
  410, 411
CEC 507
Celsius 224
CENREX 469
Center for a New American Security
  (CNAS) 371
Center for Public Integrity 304
Center for Security Policy 308
Centrafrican Airlines 118
Central African Republic 118, 120
Central Iraq Trading Company 424
Cepin, Jornej 66, 67
Chad 447, 475, 476, 477, 489
Chalabi, Ahmed 423
Chalabi, Mohammed 425
Chapman, General 257–8
Charter, Richard 183
Chartered Engineering and Technical
  Services 110
Cheney, Dick xxvi, 39, 243–4, 282, 290,
  293, 295–6, 297–8, 299, 301, 302, 401,
  402, 403, 404, 514
  and Halliburton xxvi, xxix, 290, 293,
    297–8, 355, 357, 397, 402, 404, 404–5
Cheney, Lynne 290
Chenge, Andrew 193–4, 232, 233, 519
Cheque to Cheque investigation 107
Cheyenne helicopter 255
Chichakli, Richard 163
Chidgey, David, Baron 144–5
Chile 27–8, 216, 262, 527

China xxvii–xxviii, 303, 337–8, 374, 386,
    421, 525–6
  Chinese air force 386
  Chinese arms xxviii, 32, 344, 390, 421,
    481, 520, 526–7; ammunition 346,
    348, 520
  and Merex 29, 31–2
  NORINCO 29, 31, 32, 526
  and Sudan 479, 481, 526
  and the US 337–8, 386, 529
  and Zimbabwe 451, 526
Chinook helicopter 486
Chirac, Jacques 461, 518, 519
Chodan, Wojciech 357
Church, Frank 44
CIA 15, 28, 30, 121, 218, 327, 360, 399, 408,
    417, 419, 421, 444, 503
  and Afghanistan 245, 246, 247–8
  and Cummings/Interarms 23, 25
  and D'Onofrio 103
  and Egypt 22
  and the FCPA exemption 278
  and Indonesia 265–6
  and the Iran–Contra affair 379–82
  and Iraq 381, 398
  and Israel 382, 383
  and Al-Kassar 504
  and Lockheed 250, 251
  and Riggs Bank xviii, 74
  and Taylor xix, 99
  and US covert operations 239, 245, 246
CIC (Commercial International Corpor-
    ation) 183
Cinisello Balsamo xviii, 113–14
Circle of Friends, Germany 28
Cirincione, Josef 300–301
Citicorp 286
Clark, Alan 218
Clark Amendment (1976) 455–6
Clemins, Archie 308–9
Cleveland, Robin 314
CLI (Committee for the Liberation of Iraq)
    395
Cliff, Mark 205
Clinton, Bill 288, 289, 336, 402

Clinton, Hilary 162
cluster bombs 377, 389–91, 413
CNAS (Center for a New American
    Security) 371
Coalition Provisional Authority (CPA)
    403, 408, 426–7
Cockburn, Andrew 368
Cockburn, Patrick 431
Cockcroft, Lawrence 153
Cohen, William 290
Coherent Systems International 242
Cold War 10–11, 30, 238, 251, 302, 444
  and Angola 454, 455, 458–9
  arsenal 69
  and Somalia 466
  and Sudan 475
Cole, USS 248
Coll, Steve 246
Colombia 159, 269, 337, 399, 527
  Revolutionary Armed Forces of
    (FARC) 157–60, 161, 163, 399, 527
Colonia Dignidad 28
Columbus, Christopher 84–5
Combined Systems Inc. (CSI) 486–7
Commercial Agricola 27
Commercial International Corporation
    (CIC) 183
Commission on Wartime Contracting
    405–6
Committee for the Liberation of Iraq (CLI)
    395
Commodity Credit Corporation 398
Compaore, Blaise 100
Compaq 286
Compudyne 315
Condit, Phil 314
Congo, Democratic Republic of 120, 156,
    344, 443–53
  UN arms embargo 452–3
Congressional Budget Office (CBO) 305,
    410, 411
Conlog 181
Conrad, Kent 306
Contras, Iran–Contra affair 30–31, 51–3,
    278, 379–81, 398

Cook, Robin 148, 189

Cooper Directive 17

Cordesman, Anthony 400, 490

Corner House 145, 146, 147, 152, 233

corruption xvii–xviii, xxii, xxiii, xxv, 24,
    55, 108, 118, 223, 357
    Angola, money and 453–65
    and BAE xxvii, 225–34, 357, 358; in the
        Czech Republic 199–218; and
        Mensdorff-Pouilly 198–9; in South
        Africa 176–88, 230–32, 517; in
        Tanzania 188–96, 519; Al Yamamah
        deal 55, 75–97, 127–53, 173, 355 *see also*
        Al Yamamah deal
    blackmail 80, 146, 153
    bribery *see* bribery
    and democracy xxv, 145, 147–8, 173, 234,
        276, 303, 372, 430–31, 524
    and difficulties with prosecutions 154–72
    DOJ investigations 272, 352–3, 355, 357,
        364, 512
    Foreign Corrupt Practices Act (FCPA,
        US) 270, 271–2, 277–8, 353–4, 355,
        356–8, 362, 363–5, 514
    and Gerdec 346, 347–8, 349–52, 521
    International Anti-Corruption and
        Good Governance Act (2000) 354
    in Iraq and the CPA 426–7
    in Japan 263–4, 268–9
    kickbacks *see* kickbacks
    in Lockheed's Polish deal 291–2
    and MICC deals *see* MICC
    in Saudi Arabia 75
    SEC investigations *see* Securities and
        Exchange Commission
    SFO investigations *see* Serious Fraud
        Office
    sting operations 157–61, 207–12, 244,
        358–65, 514
    in the Swedish arms industry 221–4
    and US defence contractors 343–53

Côte d'Ivoire *see* Ivory Coast

countertrade *see* offsets

Covenant of the League 7

Cowie, Matthew 131–3, 134, 135, 234

Cowper-Coles, Sir Sherard 137, 140–41,
    513–14

CPA (Coalition Provisional Authority)
    403, 408, 426–7

Cranston, Alan 256, 277

Craven, Sir Charles 10

Crile, George 246

Critz, Mark 328

Croatia 60, 61, 62–4, 65, 68, 469
    UN arms embargo 62, 63, 68, 157

Crowdy, Dame Rachel 9–10

Crowley, James J. 426

CSI (Combined Systems Inc.) 486–7

Cuanavale, Cuito 457

Cuba 23, 455, 459

Cummings, Sam 23–4, 25–6, 286

Cunene 456

Cunningham, Eddie 79–81, 127

Cunningham, Randy 'Duke' 318–28, 514

Curial, Jean-Bernard 459, 462

Czech Republic 198, 199–217, 339

Dafermas, Konstantin 68

al Dahab, Abdel Rahmen Suwar 476

Dahab Al E'amar Co. Ltd 420

Dallas Cowboys 42, 83

Darfur 475 83

'Darius' (CIA undercover agent) 360–61

Darkwood 496

Darling, Alistair 138

D'Armiento, Anthony 340

Darwish, Ali 120, 121

Darwish, Mohammed abu 425

Dasaad, Isaak 265–6

Dassault, Marcel 11–12, 14

Dassault 400

Davies, Denzil 76

DCAA (Defence Contract Audit Agency,
    US) 406

DCNS 509–10

De Beers 458

De Decker, Joe 458

De Decker, Ronnie 458

de Lille, Patricia 229–30

de Wijk, Rob 472

DEA (US Drug Enforcement Agency) 157–61, 164, 358

Deaver, Michael 52

Deepwater 339–40

Defense Contract Audit Agency (DCAA, US) 406

Defence Export Services Organisation (Deso) 75, 84, 87, 94, 140, 176

Defense Logistics Agency 416

Defense Policy Advisory Committee on Trade (DPACT) 287, 289

Defense Policy Board (DPB, US) 303, 304

Defense Solutions 396

DeLeon, Rudy 307

Delijorgji, Mihal 344, 345, 347

Deliu, Uran 352

Dembrowski, Jerry 469

democracy, corruption's undermining of xxv, 145, 147–8, 173, 234, 276, 303, 372, 430–31, 524

Democratic Republic of Congo (DRC) 120, 156, 344, 443–53
UN arms embargo 452–3

der Hovsepian, Joe 56–8, 60, 61, 62, 63–5, 70–73, 105, 116, 154, 420–21, 502, 503, 525

Deso (Defence Export Services Organisation) 75, 84, 87, 94, 140, 176

Deutch, John 287, 288–9

Deutsche Merex 58, 59–60, 65

Dhahran bombing 247

DHS (Department of Homeland Security, US) 293, 295, 296, 301, 340, 358, 361–2 *see also* ICE

diamonds 98, 102–3, 105, 106, 111, 113–14, 117, 119–21, 154, 171, 454, 458, 496, 504–5

Dibrancs, Janis 469

Dick, W., Jr 255

Dickinson, Hugh 85

Dicks, Norman 310, 311

Diendere, Gilbert 110

DINA (Chilean Secret Police) 28

Disney 286

Diveroli, Efraim 343, 344, 346, 347, 348, 514, 521

Djan Djajanti 123

Dodd–Frank Wall Street Reform and Consumer Protection Act 357

Doe, Samuel Kanyon 99, 100, 101

Doerfel, Gerhard 64

DOJ (Department of Justice, US) 272, 352–3, 355, 357, 364, 512

Donnelly, Thomas 294

D'Onofrio, Roger 103–4, 105, 107, 505

Donohue, Mark 309

Dooley, Thomas 77

dos Santos, José Eduardo 457, 459, 460, 517–18

DPACT (Defense Policy Advisory Committee on Trade) 287, 289

DPB (Defense Policy Board, US) 303, 304

DRC *see* Democratic Republic of Congo

drones xxiv, 301, 334, 374, 375, 376, 394, 414

Drug Enforcement Agency (DEA, US) 157–61, 164, 358

drug trafficking 106, 107–8, 157, 346, 525, 527
War on Drugs 157, 527

Druyun, Darleen 308, 309, 310–11, 312–14, 514

Druyun, Heather 312–13

Dubai 223, 361, 526–7

Dubovy Mlyn 205, 507

Duncan, Larry 371

Durdaj, Erida 349

Durdaj, Erison 349, 351, 520

Durdaj, Feruzan 349, 351, 352

Durdaj, Rajmonda 349, 351, 352

Durdaj, Roxhens 349, 351

Durham, Henry 253–4

Dutch Campaign Against the Arms Trade 169

Dutton, Frederick 44–5, 46, 47, 49

Dyfvermark, Joachim 202, 207–8

Dyncorp 418

EADS 139, 185, 307, 317–18 *see also* Airbus

Earmark Transparency Act 329

earmarking, congressional 241–2, 243, 249,
325, 328–9, 516
Economic Community of West African
States (ECOWAS) 101
monitoring group, ECOMOG 101, 106
Ecuador 399
Edwards, Geoffrey 14–15, 16
Edwards, Tony 38
Egeland, Jan 390
Egypt xxviii, 439, 483–8, 526
and Israel 483–4, 485
and Lockheed 354, 486
and Mertins 21–2, 26–7
and Saudi Arabia 47–8
and the Soviet Union 26–7
and the UK 487
and the US xxviii, 26–7, 485–8
Eisenhower, Dwight D. xxvi, 238, 239, 240
Eisenhower, Susan 240
El-Assir, Abdul Rahman 518
Elbit Systems Ltd 375, 376, 414
Electra aircraft 250
elipton bomb 69
Ellingford, Tony 508–9
Elmo, Francesco 105
Engel, Gerhard 26
Engelhardt, Tom 371
Enron 286, 354
Ensch, Jack 319
Enterprise 31
Envers Trading Corporation 192–3
Epps, Jack 320
Equatorial Guinea 386–7
Eritrea 473
Ersavci, Ahmet 425–6
Erste Bank 216
Ethiopia 466, 467, 468, 473
ETTE (Exotic Tropic Timber Enterprises)
109–10, 114
Eurocopter 94
Eurofighter Typhoon jets 130, 133, 135, 136,
139–41
European Investment Bank 191
European Union 154, 449, 490, 492, 493
Evans, Rob 79, 84, 85, 86, 93, 127, 207–8

Evans, Sir Richard (Dick) 40, 81, 84, 93,
127, 129, 137, 150, 232, 512
Evdin Ltd 346–7
Executive Outcomes 117
Exocets 400
Exotic Tropic Timber Enterprises (ETTE)
109–10, 114
Eyadema, Gnassingbe, of Togo 464

F-15 fighter jets 35, 36, 44–6, 48, 49, 515
F-16 fighter jets 44, 218, 219, 291, 292, 337,
338, 377, 389, 390, 413, 486
F-22 fighter jets 288, 290, 294, 331–5, 396
F-35 fighter jets 293, 306, 334, 335–6, 371,
393
F&C Asset Management 145–6
Fadlallah, Sheikh Mohammed 54
Fahd of Saudi Arabia 35, 36, 44, 46, 47, 48,
49, 50, 51, 53, 54
Fahrmbacher, Wilhelm 21
Faina, MV 472
Fairchild Weston 32
Faisal of Saudi Arabia 18, 59
Faisal, Prince, son of Turki bin Nasser 82–3
Falcone, Pierre 459–60, 461, 462, 518
FAR (Rwandan Government Army) 440,
441
Farah, Douglas 115, 121, 162
FARC (Revolutionary Armed Forces of
Colombia) 157–60, 161, 163, 399, 527
Farmus, Zbigniew 291
Farouk I of Egypt 21–2
Farrow, Mia 505
Fasth, Lars Göran 213–14
Faye Samantha 80
Al-Fayed, Dodi 267
Al-Fayed, Mohammed 267
FBI 25, 74, 120, 122, 216, 241, 244, 323,
362–4, 397–8, 399
FCPA *see* Foreign Corrupt Practices Act
Ferrostaal 186, 508–9
FIAT 104
Fidra Holdings 205
Field Activities Command (USAFAC) 29
Firestone Tyre company 102

First Saudi Investment Co. 92
First World War 6, 7, 8, 403–4
Fitzgerald, Ernie 252, 253, 254–5, 274, 275, 276, 522
Flournoy, Michèle 369, 371
FMF (Foreign Military Financing, US) 377
FNLA (Frente Nacional de Libertação de Angola) 454, 455, 456
Foggo, Kyle 'Dusty' 324, 327
Forces Novelles 495, 497
Ford, Gerald 269
Foreign Assets Control (OFAC, US) 184, 417, 450
Foreign Corrupt Practices Act (FCPA, US) 270, 271–2, 277–8, 353–4, 355, 356–8, 362, 363–5, 514
Foreign Military Financing (FMF, US) 377
Forster, Tom 198
Forum Filatelico 115
Forum Liberia 114–15
Foxbury 206
Foya 105, 120
France xxvii, xxviii, 11–12
    Angolagate 459–62, 517
    and Iraq 400
    and Libya 489, 492
    and Pakistan 518–19
    and Rwanda 437, 439–41
    and Saudi Arabia 35–6
Franco, Francisco 22
Frank, Barney 321, 365
Franton Investment Ltd 194
Freeh, Louis 95–7
Freeman, Chas 38–9
Freeman, Roger 76
Freetown xviii–xxi, 102, 126
Freikorps 27
Frente Nacional de Libertação de Angola (FNLA) 454, 455, 456
frigates 127–8, 175, 185, 230, 509
Frisén, Anders 214
Fur 475, 476

Gabon 362–3
Gabstar 204

Gaddafi, Muammar 100, 399, 477, 488–93, 497, 509, 520
Galaxy, C-5A 251–2, 253–6, 274
Galaxy group 108
Galloway, George 77
Gandhi, Rajiv 221–2, 223
GAO (General Accounting Office, US) 253, 276, 306, 318, 367, 398–9, 404, 413, 419
Gardiner, Peter 81, 127
Gardiner, Sam 298
Garlick, Helen 127, 131–3, 134, 136–7, 142–3, 153, 234
Gates, Robert 294, 330, 331, 334, 335, 340, 342, 369
Gaydamak, Arcadi 387, 460, 461, 462, 518
Gaza Strip 376, 390, 392, 484, 487
Gazelle helicopter 400, 440
Gbagbo, Laurent 494, 495, 496, 497
Gberie, Lansana 110
GBU-39 bombs 389, 393
GEC 138
Gecamines 448
Gehlen, Reinhard 19–20, 22–3, 26
Gehlen Org 20–23
Gelli, Licio 66
General Accounting Office (GAO, US) 253, 276, 306, 318, 367, 398–9, 404, 413, 419
General Dynamics 486
General Electric Company 273, 285, 303, 515
General Investment Group 425
Geneva disarmament conference 8
George, Barry 127, 128
George H. W. Presidential Library 282
Georgia 344, 384–5
Georgiades, Tony 508–9
Gerdec 346, 347–8, 349–52, 520–21
German Frigate Consortium 186
Germany xxvii, xxviii, 27
    Circle of Friends 28
    German Intelligence 19–20, 26, 30, 31, 57
    and Iraq 400

and Libya 489, 492
and Lockheed 264, 337
Luftwaffe planes 23–4
Nazi 10, 19, 250
and Pakistan 24–5, 30
remilitarization hopes 23
and Saudi Arabia 24
Gertler, Dan 107
Gesiecke & Devrient 64
Ghadry, Nihad 55
Ghailani, Ahmed Khalfan 120, 121
Ghorbanifar, Manucher 379, 380, 381
Gilmour, Ian, Baron 75–6
Gingrich, Newt 289, 320, 321
Giorgi, Franco 61, 62–3, 70, 105
Glenn, John 44, 50
Global Crossing 303
Global CST 385
global military expenditure xxii
Global Star Holdings 123
Global Witness 124, 154
GMT 379
Goebbels, Joseph 22
Gold, David 513
Goldsmith, Peter, Baron 129, 131, 132, 133,
    136, 137, 142–4
Gonzales, Henry B. 398
Gorbachev, Mikhail 54–5
Gordon, Bob 311
Gould Corporation 274
GPS-guided bombs 393
Grassley, Chuck 280, 281, 282, 316–17
Grayling, A. C. 147–8
Green Devils 21
grey market xxiii, 523
Griffiths, Hugh 347
Grindler, Larry 227
Gripen aircraft 175–6, 177–8, 180, 188,
    198, 199–217, 218–19, 221, 291,
    506–7
Gripen International 214, 215
Gross, Robert 250, 265
GRU 115
Grumman, Northrop 45
Guantanamo Bay 414

Guatemala 23, 238
Gueckedou 165–6
Guéï, Robert 170, 495–6
Gulfstream 298
    jets 192
Gummer, John 216

Habyarimana, Juvénal 436–7, 438, 441
Haifa bint Faisal bin Abdul Aziz Al-Saud,
    Princess 43, 74
Haig, Alexander 302
Haig, Alexander Jr 49
Hale, Brenda Marjorie, Baroness 152
Halliburton xxvi, xxix, 282, 290, 297–8,
    355, 357
    and Cheney xxvi, 293, 297–8, 402,
        404–5
    and the Iraq war 397, 404–5
    KBR subsidiary see KBR
    and the Republican party 405
Hamas 385, 392, 393
Hambrusch, Heinz 29
Hamsa, Wolfgang 207
Haqani, Jalaluddin 247, 248
Hargeisa 467
Hariri, Saad 93
Harith, Mohammad 423
Harken Energy 283
Harris Bank 205
Harrison II, Larry D. 348
Hartung, Bill 250, 252, 276, 287, 293, 300n,
    332, 334, 335, 341, 369, 371–2, 413–14
Hasek, Jan 507
Hashemi, Bari 382
Hastert, J. Dennis 310, 311
Al Hatteen 106
Haughton, Dan 255–6, 264, 268, 269
Hauser, Ernest 264
Hava, Richard 204–5
Havel, Vaclav 199, 217
hawala 119, 472
Hawk aircraft 35, 37, 175–6, 177–8, 180, 184,
    187–8, 449, 451, 506
Hawker Siddeley Aviation 12
Hawkins, Willis 255

Hawley, Susan 147, 152–3, 225, 232
Heath, Edward 263
Heckler and Koch 12, 85
Heinz, John 277
Hekmatyar, Gulbuddin 247, 248
Hel 68
helicopters 94–5, 118, 159, 160, 175–6,
    193, 399, 410, 440–41, 460, 481,
    492, 527
  Apache 337
  Black Hawk 37, 77, 285, 486
  Cheyenne 255
  Chinook 486
  Gazelle 400, 440
  Mi-24 245, 480, 481
  Puma 400
Hellfire missiles 337, 413
Henry III, Patrick 345
Herbert Smith 512
Hercules C-130J 393
Herik, Larissa van den 168
Hermes 145
Herring, Joanne 245
Heseltine, Michael 35, 36, 78
Hever, Shir 388, 394
Hewitt, Patricia 190
Hezbollah 93, 156, 359, 379, 381, 387, 388,
    390
Hirsch, Gal 384
Hlongwane, Fana 177, 183, 184, 185, 231–2,
    508
Holder, Eric 162
Holland *see* Netherlands
Honduras 324
Hoon, Geoff 190
Horn of Africa 520 *see also* Eritrea;
    Ethiopia; Somalia
Hoseah, Edward 196, 232, 234
Hotel Africa, Monrovia 122
Houphouët-Boigny, Félix 100, 494
Howarth, David 148
Hoxha, Enver 343–4
HQ Marketing Services 85
Huawei 526
Huderfield Enterprises Inc. 183

Hudson bombers 250
human rights 13, 48, 140, 145, 172, 175, 370,
    431, 435, 473, 476, 482, 487, 496, 526,
    530
Human Rights Watch 390, 423
Hungary 198, 217–20
Hussa, Princess 41
Hussein of Jordan 266
Hussein, Saddam xvii, 29, 31–2, 60, 247,
    397, 398, 400, 403
Hutu 436, 438, 441, 442, 445, 446

Ianieri, Richard 242
IANSA 528
IBC (International Business Consult) 103,
    105–6
Ibn Saud (Abdul Aziz) 12, 13
ICAO (International Civil Aviation
    Organization) 189
ICC (International Criminal Court) 482
ICE (Immigration and Customs
    Enforcement) 359, 360–62
ICU (Islamic Courts Union) 472–3
IDA (Institute for Defense Analyses) 311
IDF *see* Israeli Defence Force
Ignatenko, Oleksandr 119
Ilia, Shlomo 387
Ilyushins 116, 118, 160
Immigration and Customs Enforcement
    (ICE) 359, 360–62
INC (Iraqi National Congress) 423
INCAR Tanzania Limited 193
India 24, 222–3, 337, 526, 527, 527–8
    and Israel 374
Indonesia, and Lockheed 265–6, 269
Inouye, Daniel 335
Inslee, Jay 424
Institute for Defense Analyses (IDA) 311
Interahamwe 438, 440, 445, 447
Interarms (International Armament
    Corporation) 23, 25
International Anti-Corruption and Good
    Governance Act (2000) 354
International Business Consult (IBC) 103,
    105–6

International Civil Aviation Organization
(ICAO) 189
International Criminal Court (ICC) 482
internet, online purchase of arms and
technology 359, 525
Intersystems Beirut 62
Iran xxvii, 24, 338, 344, 526
Iran–Contra affair 30–31, 51–53, 278,
379–81, 398
Iran–Iraq war 48, 224, 397
and Israel 378–84
and Sudan 477–8
and Sweden 223
UN arms embargo 360
and the US 30–31, 238, 359–62; 1980
hostage crisis 279; and Israel
378–82
Iraq 106, 337, 338
dual-use exports to 398–400
and France 400
and Germany 400
Iran–Iraq war 48, 224, 397
Israeli bombing in 50
Al-Kassar's support of Sunnis 157
Kuwait invasion 39, 60, 247, 400–401
and Merex 420–21
Ministry of Defence 424–5, 426
and MZM 326
oil 404; Oil for Food scandal 29
and the Soviet Union 400
and Sweden 223
and the US 156, 243, 298, 300, 342–3,
381, 395–431
weapons of mass destruction xvii, 396,
402, 423
Iraqi National Congress (INC) 423
Irbis Air 416
iron triangle *see* MICC
Isenberg, David 420
Islamic Courts Union (ICU) 472–3
Islamic militancy *see also specific militiant
organizations*
and 9/11 *see* September 11 attacks
Afghanistan 247–8
Isle of Man 442

Israel 302, 337, 338, 344, 373–94
economy 375, 376
and Egypt 483–4, 485
and Georgia 384–5
and Hezbollah 381, 387, 390
and Iran 31, 378–84
and Israel 515
and Lebanon 50, 338, 376, 389–91, 392, 393
military budget 373
Mossad 26, 373, 382, 383, 384
oil installations 43
and the Palestinians 141, 373–4, 376, 392,
484
and Rwanda 442
and Saudi Arabia 15, 44, 49
and South Africa 387
and the UK 377
and the US 35, 38, 44, 49–50, 302,
373–94, 515; AIPAC 44, 45, 48, 94, 377
War on Terror industry 375–6
Israel Aerospace Industries 385
Israel Aircraft Industries International 514
Israel Military Industries Ltd 386–7
Israel Shipyards Ltd 386–7
Israeli Defence Force (IDF) 376, 377–8, 388,
390, 392, 393, 394
Italy xxvii, xxviii, 103–4, 171
fascist 250
and Libya 104, 492
and Lockheed 265, 269
Saudi Arabia and the Italian Christian
Democrats 53–4
and Somalia 466
ITT Aerospace 515
Ivory Coast 100, 101, 112, 493–7
and Liberia 100, 112, 495
UN arms embargo 496–7

J. P. Morgan Chase 513
Jack, Michael 138
Jackson, Bruce 289, 290–91, 296, 297, 395
Jackson, Henry 275
Jackson, Michael 293
James, Gerald 90
Janjaweed 476, 481, 489

Japan
  and Lockheed 262–4, 268–9, 337
  Russo-Japanese conflict 5
  sale of US Electras to 250
  and the US 268
Jarecki, Eugene 237, 294–5
Javits, Jacob 44
Jawharat Al Mahabba Co. Ltd 420
Jawhart Al-Eman Co. Ltd 420
Jelinek International 205
Jelinek, Otto 205
JEM (Justice and Equality Movement)
  478
Jet Line 418
John Murtha Johnstown–Cambria County
  Airport 242–3
Johnson, Alan 191
Johnson, Chalmers 248
Johnson, Joel 338
Johnson, Lyndon B. 251, 297
Johnson, Yormie, Prince 99–100, 101
Johnson-Sirleaf, Ellen 126
Jones, David 50
Jones, Thomas 45
Jones Consultants 93
Jordan, Hamilton 44, 47
Justice and Equality Movement (JEM) 478

Kababankola Mining Company 448, 449
Kabbah, Ahmed 407
Kabila, Joseph 451, 453
Kabila, Laurent 446–7, 451
Kabir, Imad 463–4
Kagan, Robert 294
Kangura 437–8
Karadzic, Radovan 69, 70, 107
Karzai, Hamid 370
Kasa-Vubu, Joseph 444
Al-Kassar, Ghassan 504
Al-Kassar, Monzer, 'Prince of Marbella' 31,
  157–8, 161, 469–70, 503–4
Katanga 444
'Kate' foundation 206–7
Katz, Dov 107

Kavan, Jan 208–13
Kayswell Services Ltd 184
Kazakhstan 512
KBR (Kellogg Brown & Root) xxix, 297,
  317, 343, 355, 357, 358, 404, 405–6,
  409, 420, 514
KC-767 air-refuelling tanker scandal
  305–18
Kellogg Brown & Root *see* KBR
Kennedy, Edward (Ted) 277
Kennedy, John F. 240
Kenya 472, 482
Kezerashvili, Davit 384
KGB 115
Khalid of Saudi Arabia 50
Khalid, Prince 87, 88
Khalilzad, Zalmay 401
Khartoum 116, 476, 478, 479, 481
Khashoggi, Adnan 15, 89, 266–8, 269, 303,
  379, 380, 501–3
Khiweli, Mohammed 89–90
Khomeini, Ayatollah Ruhollah 30, 378
kickbacks 192, 212, 223, 268, 323, 427, 509,
  518–19
Kigali 437, 441
Kilfoyle, Peter 227
King, Ian 487
Kinshasa 446, 447, 451, 463
Kintex 106
Kissinger, Henry 43, 262, 268, 376
Klein, Naomi 302, 303, 375–6
Klein, Yair 107, 387
Klinghoffer, Leon 157
KLM 265
Kodak 286
Kodama, Yoshio 263
Koehler, Mike 355
Komba, Gaby 190–91
Kontogiannis, Thomas 328
Korb, Lawrence 289
Korean War 251
Kotchian, Carl 265, 268, 269–70
Kotzer, Amos 382
Kouwenhoven, Gus 122–4, 165–9, 505

KPMG 511
Kraft, Herman 203–4
Krupp, Alfred 3, 10
Krupps 5
KSA 241–2
Kuburare, Jean 440
Kuchera Defense Systems 242
Kucinich, Dennis 391–2
Kukan, Milan 68
Kurdish Workers Party (PKK) 338
Kuss, Henry J. 25
Kuwait 513
    invasion by Iraq 39, 60, 247, 400–401
Kuzin, former General 69
Kwast, Christer van der 217

Labour Party, UK 9 *see also* New Labour
Lainovic, Branislav ('Dughi') 70
Lamb, Norman 189–90, 191, 194–5
Landmine Action 391
Landon, Tim 198, 206
Langdale, Timothy 142
Lansdowne Partners 513
Latin America 250, 527 *see also* South
    America *and specific countries*
Latvia 469–70
Laurin, Fredrik 202
Laurisch, Gunter 29
Lavi jet fighter 374
Lavrov, Sergey 163–4
Layman, John 281
Lebanon 61, 62, 71, 93, 156, 376, 380–81,
    389, 399
    Hezbollah *see* Hezbollah
    and Israel 50, 338, 376, 389–91, 392, 393
Lechleitner, Patrick 359, 360
Lefebvre, Olvidio 265
Leigh, David 78–9, 84, 85, 86, 93, 127, 149,
    192
Leonardi, Fulvio 69
Leopard tanks 58
Leopold, Ray 282
Léotard, François 459
Lesker, Klaus 509

Lester, Michael 129, 134
Levi, Edward 268
Levin, Carl 275
Levinson, Riva 423–4
Levitt, Arthur 283
Lewis, Charles 284, 405
Lewis, Chuck 368
Lewis, Jerry 331–2
Libby, I. Lewis 'Scooter' 401, 514
Liberia xviii, xix, 67, 98–9, 100–107,
    109–10, 111–12, 117–26, 169–70, 505
    Anti-Terrorism Unit 107
    Foya province 105, 120
    'Greater Liberia' 101–2, 106
    and the Ivory Coast 100, 112, 495
    Truth and Reconciliation Commission
        125
    UN arms embargo 67, 103, 107, 418
Liberians United for Reconciliation and
    Democracy (LURD) 121, 124
Libya xxviii, 38, 61, 100, 447, 451, 488–93,
    505, 519
    and Belarus 491
    and Darfur 477, 478
    and France 489, 492
    and Germany 489, 492
    and Italy 104, 492
    and the Lockerbie bombing 490, 491
    oil 104, 477, 489, 490, 491
    and Russia 489, 490, 492
    and South Africa 492–3
    and terrorism 490
    and the UK 491, 492
    UN arms embargo 490, 491, 492
    and the US 104, 489, 490, 493
Libya–Arab–Georgia Friendship Society 104
Liechtenstein 206
Lightning fighters 15–16
Limad 108
Lindström, Sten 234
Lipumba, Ibrahim 232–3
Littoral Combat Ship (LCS) 340
Lloyd George, David 5, 7, 9
Lloyds TSB 86, 514

Lockerbie bombing 490, 491
Lockheed Corporation/Lockheed Martin
    xxvi, xxviii, 10, 14, 16, 200, 218, 244,
    250–56, 262–70, 287–97, 298, 300,
    312, 337–41, 354, 514, 515, 523
    and the Air Force 251, 252, 253, 254, 274,
        275–6, 332, 334
    Boeing settlement with 315
    C-5A Galaxy 251–2, 253–6, 274
    C-5B 275
    Cheyenne helicopter 255
    and Deepwater 339–40
    and Egypt 354, 486
    F-16s *see* F-16 fighter jets
    F-22 fighter jets 288, 290, 294, 331–5, 396
    F-35 fighter jets 293, 306, 334, 335–6,
        371, 393
    and Germany 264, 337
    Hellfire missiles 337, 413
    Hercules C-130J 393
    and Indonesia 265–6, 269
    and the Iraq war 395–7
    and Israel 338
    and Italy 265, 269
    and Japan 262–4, 268–9, 337
    Littoral Combat Ship 340
    mergers and acquisitions 287
    missile defence 288, 338–9
    Multiple-Launch Rocket System
        389–90, 391, 413
    and the Netherlands 264–5, 269
    and the Pentagon 252, 253, 255, 259, 269,
        273, 274, 275, 288, 293, 371–2, 412
    and Poland 291–2, 339
    and Romania 290, 337, 338, 339
    and Saudi Arabia 266–8
    share prices 415
    spare parts scandal 274–5
    Starfighters 15, 263, 264
    Strategic Defense Inititiative 277
    and Turkey 337, 338
    and the War on Terror 366–7, 413–14,
        415
Logistics Civil Augmentation Programme
    (LOGCAP) 297, 404, 409, 418

Lombard Odier 86
Long, David 45, 47
Long, Russell 46
Loral Corporation 287
LORAP camera 32
Lord of War 154
Lotz, Wolfgang 26
Lukashenko, Alexander 490
Lumumba, Patrice 444
LURD (Liberians United for Reconciliation
    and Democracy) 121, 124
Lusaka Protocols 462
Lynn III, William J. 371

McArthur Baths 180
McCaffrey, Barry 395–6
McCain, John 305, 307, 309, 310, 315,
    317, 335
McConnell, Mitch 516
McDonald, Allan 184
McDonnell Douglas 45, 312, 399
Macedonia 60
McFarlane, Robert 51, 52, 53
machetes xx
McKee, Michael 312
McNulty, Paul 313
mafia 103–4, 108
Magliocchetti, Paul 241
Magna 91
Mai-Mai 447, 452, 453
Maiman, Yosef 485
Major, John 40, 176, 283–4, 513
Malaysia 138, 510
Manbar, Nahum 382–4
Mandela, Nelson 72, 175, 176, 508
Mandelson, Peter 92
Mann, Simon 90, 91, 511
Manor Holdings 205, 507
Mapelli, Walter 169–70, 171
Marconi Electronic Systems 12
Marcos, Ferdinand 501
Marcos, Imelda 501, 502
Markov, Sergei 161–2
Martin Marietta 287, 288, 289
Martinovic, Jozo 62–3, 64

Marxism 455

Massalit 476, 478

Massoud, Ahmad Shah 116

Matrix Churchill 400

Mauritania 399

Mayes, Donald 421

Maynier, David 230, 231

Mazzega, Lorenzo 61, 62, 63, 64, 69, 70

MBDA 492

Mbeki, Thabo 175, 176, 177, 182, 185, 186,
    508, 517

MD Helicopters 515

Mead, Steve 199, 202, 208, 209, 210–11, 213

Mearsheimer, J. 389

Mediu, Fatmir 345–6, 347, 348, 520

Megrahi, Abdelbaset Ali Mohammed Al-
    491–2

MEICO (Military Export–Import
    Company) 344, 345, 346

Melman, Yossi 386, 388–9

Mensdorff-Pouilly, Alfons ('Ali'), Count
    197–9, 203–4, 205–6, 207, 208, 214–16,
    218–20, 226, 228, 233, 505–6, 507

mercenaries/private security contractors 16,
    20, 90, 117, 285, 404, 406–9, 494–5,
    514

The Merchants of Death 8

Merex 19, 23–32, 56–73, 262, 420
    Deutsche Merex 58, 59–60, 65
    lack of successful prosecutions in the
        network 154–71
    Merex AG 58–9
    Merex Corporation (US branch) 25–6,
        58, 503
    Taylor and the Merex network 98–126

Merkt, Rene 86

Merlin International Ltd 192

Meroni, Rudolf 107

Merrill, Ralph 343

Mertins, Gerhard 20–28, 29–30, 31–2,
    57–58, 64–5, 105

Mertins, Helmut 31, 58, 60, 65, 422, 503

Mertins, Joerg Thomas ('JT') 58, 60, 65,
    503

Mertins family 420

Mesa/Envisioneering 422

Meuser, Fred 264, 265

Mexico 525, 527

Mi-8s 481

Mi-24s 245, 480, 481

MI5 474

MI6 383

MIC (military-industrial complex, US)
    250–52, 282, 300, 301

MICC (military-industrial-Congressional
    complex, the iron triangle) 240, 249,
    256–61, 273–7, 283–6, 301–2, 514–15,
    523, 530 *see also* bribery: the US and
    legal bribery
    and illegal bribery 305–29
    and the Obama administration 330–72,
        514–16
    and the 'reset' policy 410–13, 414–15

Michopulos, Petros 210–11, 212

Mifgai, General 41

MiG fighter jets 116, 319, 481

Mil-Tec 442

Milan anti-tank missiles 441, 492

military-industrial complex (MIC, US)
    250–52, 282, 300, 301

military-industrial-Congressional complex
    see MICC

Military Reform Movement (MRM, US)
    258

Miller, Chanoch 470–71

Miller, T. Christian 407

Mills, C. Wright xxvi

Milo, Roni 384

Milo, Shlomo 384

Miltex 423

minesweepers 37–8

Minin, Leonid xviii, xix, xxi, xxviii, 107–15,
    118, 119, 124, 169–71, 387, 496, 505

Minxolli, Dritan 347–8

Mirage jets 11, 35–6, 291, 400

Misha'al bint Fahd al Saud, Princess 48

Mishkin, Saul 362–3

Missiourine, Vladimir 108

Mitrasur Corporation 91

Mitterrand, François 36, 459, 462

Mitterrand, Jean-Christophe 440, 459, 461, 462

Mkapa, Benjamin 191–2, 193

MLRS (Multiple-Launch Rocket Systems) 389–90, 391, 413, 480

MNRD (National Republic Movement for Democracy and Development) 436

Mobutu Sese Seko (born Joseph Désiré) 120, 121, 399, 444–5, 463

MODEL (Movement for Democracy in Liberia) 124

Modise, Joe 176, 177, 178, 181, 182, 184, 509

Mogadishu 465, 466, 468, 472, 473

Mogford, Steven 83

Mohamed, Ali Mahdi 470

Mohammed, Fazul Abdullah 120–21

Mohammed, Prince 15

Mold Transavia 118

Moldova 464

Monrovia xix, 100, 101, 106, 109–10, 120–21, 124, 126, 418
    Hotel Africa 122

Montagu, Sir Nicolas 130

Montero, Sonia 459

Moorby, Dennis Anthony 105, 107

Moresco 223

Morocco 337

Morris, Willie 17

Mossad 26, 373, 382, 383, 384

Mossberg, Walt 281

Movement for Democracy in Liberia (MODEL) 124

Movement for Quality Government in Israel 388

Movimento Popular de Libertação de Angola (MPLA) 53, 454–5, 456, 457, 459

Moyo, Brigadier 449

MPA 197, 198, 204, 219

MPLA (Movimento Popular de Libertação de Angola) 53, 454–5, 456, 457, 459

MRM (Military Reform Movement, US) 258

Mubadala 513

Mubarak, Alaa 485

Mubarak, Gamal 484, 485

Mubarak, Hosni 47, 483–4, 485, 520

Mugabe, Robert 183–4, 448, 449, 497, 517

Mulhalal, Khalid 48

Al Mulk Holdings SA 91

Multinational Security Transition Command–Iraq ('Mitskey') 424

Multiple-Launch Rocket Systems (MLRS) 389–90, 391, 413, 480

Munye, Omar 470

Murray, Williamson 331

Murtech 242

Murtha, John 240–44, 248–9, 325, 328, 329, 331–2

Murtha, Robert C., Jr 242

Murtha, Robert C. 'Kit' 241–2

Museveni, Yoweri 437

Mutual Legal Assistance 127

MZM Inc. 322, 323, 325–7

Naaman, Nabil 91

Nadia, MV 469–70

Najran Co. Ltd 420

Namibia 447

Nassar, Suleiman 354

Nasser, Gamal Abdel 21–2, 484

Nassour, Aziz 120, 121–2, 122, 124

Nathan, Remy 515

National Audit Office (NAO) 128–9

National Defence Industries Council 138

National Patriotic Front of Liberia (NPFL) 100–103, 106, 123, 165, 166

National Republic Movement for Democracy and Development (MNRD) 436

NATO xxviii, 10
    and Albania 344–5
    Czech Republic's admission to 199
    and Kouwenhoven 122
    and Libya 488, 493
    and Pakistan 24
    stock 68

Nazis and neo-Nazis 10, 19–32, 59, 250

NBC 303

Netanyahu, Binyamin 385, 393, 460

Netherlands 165, 166, 167–8, 363
  and Lockheed 264–5, 269
Neto, Agostinho 454
New Horizons Consultants (NHC) 385
New Labour xxvii, 137, 140 *see also*
  individual ministers
  and Tanzania's deals with BAE 188, 189,
  190, 196
Newco 426
Ngwane Defence 185
NHC (New Horizons Consultants) 385
Nicaragua 399
  Nicaraguan Contras, Iran–Contra affair
  30–31, 51–53, 278, 379–81, 398
Nigeria 26, 101, 106, 353, 357, 363
  Taylor in 125–6
Nill, Taylor 67, 103
9/11 terrorist attacks *see* September 11
  attacks
Nir, Amiram 380–82
Nixon, Richard 240–41, 253, 263, 266, 299
No Living Thing, Operation xix, 110
Nobel, Alfred 3, 220–21
Nordenfelt 4, 5
NORINCO 29, 31, 32, 526
Norris, Stephen 286
North, Oliver 31, 52, 286, 380–81, 514
North Korea xxvii, 298, 299
Northrop Grumman xxviii, 14, 15, 16, 250,
  265, 267, 285, 296, 314–15, 317, 318,
  336, 339–40
  share prices 415 (fig.)
  and the War on Terror 366–7, 414
Norway 337
Novelmight 85
NPFL (National Patriotic Front of Liberia)
  100–103, 106, 123, 165, 166
Ntaryamira, Cyprien 441
nuclear weapons/technology 11, 69–70,
  106, 162, 273, 277, 298, 330, 387, 398,
  402, 490, 527
Nunn, Sam 279
Nura, Princess 83
Nurol 493
Nyanda, Siphiwe 185

Nye, Gerald P. 8
Nye Committee 8–9

Obama, Barack 162, 248–9, 302, 328, 330,
  335, 341, 365, 367, 368–9, 370, 372,
  393, 410, 427, 430, 515–16
  MICC under the Obama administration
  330–72, 514–16
Obasanjo, Olusegun 125, 126
Obiang, Teodoro 386–7
Odessa 108
O'Donnell, Sir Gus 129
OECD *see* Organisation for Economic
  Co-operation and Development
OFAC (Foreign Assets Control, US) 184,
  417, 450
Office of Management and Budget (OMB,
  US) 306, 308, 310–12, 314, 329
offsets 178–80, 181, 183, 201, 208, 218–19,
  291, 529
Ogade War 466
Ogden, David 162
oil
  Angola 453–4, 460
  Bosnia 69
  Iraq 404; Oil for Food scandal 29
  Israeli installations 43
  Libya 104, 477, 489, 490, 491
  mafia 108
  Russia 108, 162
  Saudi Arabia 13, 47, 285; Al Yamamah
  deal *see* Al Yamamah deal
  Sudan 477, 479, 482–3
  Ukraine 108
  and the US 247
Ojjeh, Abdulaziz 93
Ojjeh, Akram 88
Ojjeh, Mansour 88, 93
Okapi Air 450
Olmert, Ehud 383, 388, 392
Olver, Dick 149–50, 151, 196, 512
Oman, Mark 103
Oman, Nicholas 65–70, 103, 105, 107, 116,
  154, 504
Oman 198

OMB (Office of Management and Budget, US) 306, 308, 310–12, 314, 329
Omnipol 204, 507
O'Neill, Thomas 'Tip' 244, 275
Operation Bernhard 27
Operation Bloodstone 156
Operation Cast Lead 390, 392, 393
Operation No Living Thing xix, 110
Operation Protea 456
Operation Seashell 378–80
Operation Shakespeare 360–62
Orbal Marketing Services 68, 103
Orbán, Viktor 218
Orbital Sciences Corporation 315
Organisation for Economic Co-operation and Development (OECD) 136, 144–5, 217, 353
  Anti-Bribery Convention 86, 131, 136, 144, 152
  Working Group on Bribery 152
Oriental Timber Company (OTC) 123–4, 165–7
osmium 70
Ossaily, Samih 120, 121, 122
OTC (Oriental Timber Company) 123–4, 165–7
O'Toole, Joseph 470–71
Ouattara, Alassane 494, 495, 496, 497
Ovadia, Yardena 386–7
Owen, David 17
Oxfam 528

pacifism 8
Packouz, David 343
Pademba Road Prison xix
Pakistan 24–5, 29–30, 337, 338, 343, 430–31, 510, 526, 527
  and France 518–19
  and the US 24–5, 527
Palestine/Palestinians 49, 72, 141, 344, 373–4, 375, 376, 392, 484
  PLO 50
Palme, Olof 221–2, 223
Panavia Tornado jets 35, 36–8, 39, 77, 87, 130

Panetta, Leon 370
Paniguan, Richard 492
Papa, Michele 104–5
Paraguay 5
Paris Air Show (2009) 303, 318, 375
Park, Tongsun 29
Pasqua, Charles 460, 461, 462, 518
Patriot Act 431
PCCB (Prevention and Combating of Corruption Bureau) 232–3
Pelemann, Johan 170
Penfold, Peter 407
Pentagon xxv, xxvi, 32, 52, 165, 243, 256, 342, 427 *see also* United States of America: Department of Defense
  9/11 attacks *see* September 11 attacks
  and the B1 bomber 257–8
  and Blackwater 409
  budgets xxii, 330, 366, 367–72, 411, 412 *see also* United States of America: defence spending; and spending on the wars in Iraq and Afghanistan 409–16, 427
  and Halliburton 297–8
  and Khashoggi 267–8
  lack of auditing 342
  and Lockheed 252, 253, 255, 259, 269, 273, 274, 275, 288, 293, 371–2, 411
  Logistics Civil Augmentation Programme 297
  and MICC *see* MICC
  'restructuring costs' 288
  Spinney's views 256–8, 259, 278–82, 332–3, 368–9, 372, 396
People's Liberation Army xxvii
Peregrine 354
Peres, Shimon 381, 383
Pergau Dam controversy 138
Perle, Richard 277, 293, 303–4, 309
Perroots, Leonard 421
Perry, William 287, 288, 289, 368
Peru 27, 527
Peter, Lawrence 408
Petraeus, David 424
Pharaon, Gaith 14, 16

Philby, Jack 13
Phillips, Kevin 282
Piatti-Fünfkirchen, Michael 215
Pilatus aircraft 35
Pillay, Navi 452
Pinari, Ylli 344, 346, 347
Pinochet, Augusto 28, 74, 262
Pinole, George 378
piracy 471–2
PKK (Kurdish Workers Party) 338
Planet Air 450
PLO 50
PMA Group 241
PNAC (Project for the New American
    Century) 290, 293–4, 395, 396, 401–2
Polakow-Suransky, Sasha 387
Poland 31, 157, 291–2, 339, 382, 469
Portugal 31, 454, 509
Poseidon Trading Investments Ltd 75, 84,
    86, 128
Powell, Charles 91, 92, 93, 145
Powell, Colin 287, 302, 423
Powell, Jonathan 91, 141, 145, 513
PPA (Protective Products of America Inc.)
    363
Pratt & Whitney 274
Prefinor 206, 219
Prescott, John 190
Prevention and Combating of Corruption
    Bureau (PCCB) 232–3
Previte, Bill 243
Prince, Erik 408, 514
Private Security Company Association of
    Iraq 408
private security contractors *see* mercenaries/
    private security contractors
Project for the New American Century
    (PNAC) 290, 293–4, 395, 396, 401–2
Protea, Operation 456
Protective Products of America Inc. (PPA)
    363
Proxmire, William 252–3, 255

In-Q-Tel 290
Qaboos bin Said Al Said 198

Al Qaeda xxi, xxviii, 98, 248, 343, 387, 419,
    503, 519
  and Bout 119
  and the RUF 119–21
  and Al-Shabaab 474
  and Somalia 465, 474
  and Taylor 119–22
Qatar 216
QinetiQ 284
Qoreish diatribes 477–8
Quandt, Herbert 22
Quandt, Magda 22
Quattrocchi, Ottavio 222–3
Quiwonkpa, Thomas 99

Rabin, Yitzhak 383
Radio-Télévision Libre des Mille Collines
    (RTLMC) 438
Rafidan 425, 426
Rafsanjani, Ali Akbar Hashemi 379, 480
Rahman, Prince Abdul 14, 16
Ramos, Fidel V. 284
Rangel, Charles 516
Rashidi, Idrissa 194
Rasor, Dina 274, 275
Rauch-Kallat, Maria 198
Ravid, Barak 392
Raytheon 88, 371, 422, 515
RCD-Goma 452
Reagan, Nancy 52
Reagan, Ronald 38, 45–6, 49, 50–51, 54, 55,
    258, 273, 275, 277, 328, 365, 455–6
  military build-up under Reagan
    administration 273–82
Red Diamond Trading Ltd 84, 85, 128, 182,
    192, 205, 219, 507–8
Reema bint Bandar, Princess 83
Reich, Robert 365
Remer, Otto Ernst 21
Revolutionary United Front (RUF) xviii–
    xxi, 100, 102–3, 105, 106, 107, 117, 119
  and Al Qaeda 119–21
Rezeigat 476
Rice, Susan 474
Riggs Bank xviii, 74–5, 87, 262, 386, 514

Rivers, L. Mendel 251, 254, 255
Robert Lee International (RLI) 79, 80, 81
Roberto, Holden 455
Robertson, Pat 505
Robleda, Fernando 109, 110, 114–15, 170
Roche, James 307–8, 310, 311, 314–15, 316
rocket-propelled grenade launchers *see*
    RPG launchers
Rogers, William P. 268
Rolls-Royce 12, 76–7, 263
Romania 127–8, 159, 160, 216
    and Lockheed 290, 337, 338, 339
Roosevelt, Franklin D. 237, 298–9
Roosevelt, Kermit 267
Roosevelt, Kim 15
Rose, Sir John 138
Roston, Aram 423
Rouse, Michael 232
Royal Air Force (UK) 250
Royal Ordinance 12, 77, 85
Royal Timber Company 123
Royce, Edward Randall ('Ed') 162–3
RPF (Rwandan Patriotic Front) 437, 438,
    440, 441, 442–3, 445, 446
RPG launchers 110, 123, 167, 417, 439, 442,
    451, 469
RTLMC (Radio-Télévision Libre des
    Mille Collines) 438
Rudd, Nigel 356
Rudel, Hans 27
RUF *see* Revolutionary United Front
Rumsfeld Commission 299–300
Rumsfeld, Donald 269, 290, 293, 298–300,
    301, 302, 303–4, 308, 310, 312, 316,
    365, 401, 402, 403, 408, 425, 514
Ruprah, Sanjivan 112, 117, 118, 119, 124, 155
Russell, Richard 251
Russia xxvii–xxviii, 5, 69, 374, 528
    and Bolivia 527
    and Bout 156, 161–2, 163–4
    and Georgia 384–5
    and Libya 489, 490, 492
    oil 108, 162
    Russian weapons and Afghanistan/the
        Taliban 116

Russo-Japanese conflict 5
    and Sudan 480, 481
    and the US 529
Rwanda 116–17, 344, 436–43, 445, 450
    Civil Defence 438
    and the Congo 445–7, 448, 451–2, 453
    and France 437, 439–41
    genocide 436–43
    Habyarimana regime 437, 438–9, 445
    UN arms embargo 441–2
Rwandan Government Army (FAR) 440,
    441
Rwandan Patriotic Front (RPF) 437, 438,
    440, 441, 442–3, 445, 446

Saab 213–14, 217, 221–4, 231, 508, 517
    BAE partnership xxvii; in the Czech
        Republic 199–218; in South Africa
        175, 177–85, 231
    Gripen aircraft *see* Gripen aircraft
SAAF (South African Air Force) 177–8,
    180, 188
SAC (Southern Ammunition Company
    Inc.) 345
Sadat, Anwar 47, 48, 483–4
Saddam Hussein *see* Hussein, Saddam
Sadiq, General 26–7
al-Sadr, Muqtada 430
Safadi, Mohammad 87, 92–4, 137, 511
Safadi Group 93
Saferworld 528
SAIC 345
Said, Karim 88
Said, Rosemary 87
Said, Wafic 87–9, 90, 91–2, 93, 137, 511
Said Business School 91–2
Said Foundation 91
St John, Sylvia 80
Al Salam contract 138, 139–41
Salem, Hussein 484–5
Samar Airlines 163
Sambur, Marvin 310, 313, 315
Sampson, Anthony 4
Samruk 512
San Air 118, 451

SANDF (South African National Defence Force) 185
Sandline International 407
Sanip 183, 231
Sankara, Thomas 100
Sankoh, Foday xix, 100
Sanson, Alex 91–2
Santorum, Rick 425
Sarbanes Oxley Act (SOX) 355
Sarkozy, Nicolas 492, 518, 519
SASI (Sweet Analysis Services Inc.) 421–2
Saudi Arabia 12–18, 35–55, 269
    and Afghanistan 54–5
    and Angola 53
    and the Contras 51, 52–3
    and Egypt 47–8
    and France 35–6
    and Germany 24
    and Iraq 39, 60
    and Israel 15, 44, 49
    and the Italian Christian Democrats 53–4
    and Lockheed 266–8
    and Merex 58, 59–60
    National Guard 285, 510, 511
    oil 13, 47, 285 *see also* Al Yamamah deal
    and the Soviet Union 54–5
    and the UK xvii, 15–18, 35–8, 39–40, 48, 55, 75, 141–9; Al Salam contract 138, 139–41; Al Yamamah deal *see* Al Yamamah deal
    and the US xvii–xviii, 15, 35, 36, 38–9, 44, 48–50, 272, 378, 515–16; and Bandar xvii–xviii, 42–55; and the Bush family 282–6; and the Carlyle Group 283–6
    and Charlie Wilson 246
Saudi Arabian National Guard 285
Savimbi, Jonas 455, 457, 463, 464–5
Scarlett, Sir John 144
Schäfer, Paul 28
Schengen Agreement 233
Schmitz, Joseph 316–17, 408–9
Schmitz report 315–17
Schneider–Creusot 5
Schwartz, Charles 286

Schwend, Fritz 27
Scopes, Julian 199, 209, 216, 218, 512
Scorpion 68
Scorpions (South African anti-corruption unit) 182
Scotland, Patricia Janet, Baroness 151
Scottish Aviation 12
Seagroatt, Conrad 186–7
Seahawk MK jets 24
Seaman's Union in Copenhagen 221
Sears, Mike 312–13, 314
Seashell, Operation 378–80
Second World War 10, 237–8, 366, 404
Securities and Exchange Commission (SEC) 253, 268, 270–71, 272, 278, 352, 353–4, 357, 502
SEI (Shiraz Electronic Industries) 359–60
Semov, Vadim 109, 110
September 11 attacks 119, 248, 294–5, 300, 402
    highjackers xviii, 74
    military spending after 303, 325, 334, 367, 409–15
Serbia 5, 69, 418
Serious Fraud Office (SFO)
    and corruption in Saudi Arabian National Guard 511–12
    investigations into BAE 188, 216, 225–33; in Hungary 219; in South Africa 182–3, 184, 230–32, 517; in Tanzania 193, 194–6, 228; and the Al Yamamah deal 80–81, 84, 85, 87, 93, 127, 127–53
SFO *see* Serious Fraud Office
Al-Shabaab 468, 472–5
Shah of Iran, Mohammad Reza Pahlavi 24
Shaik, 'Chippy' 177, 180, 184, 185, 230, 509
Shaik, Mo 186, 230, 509
Shaik, Schabir 185, 186, 187, 509
Shakespeare, Operation 360–62
Al-Shalaan, Anwar Bin Fawaz Bin Nawaf, Prince 71
Shapiro, Andrew 515
Sharjah 116, 118
Sharon, Ariel 380, 385

Sharp, John 80, 84
Shaw, George Bernard 3
Shawcross exercise 133, 136, 139, 146–7
Shearer, William G. 8
Shibleh, Ramy 391
SHIFCO (Somali High Seas Fishery Corporation) 470
Shinawatra, Thaksin 284
Shiraz Electronic Industries (SEI) 359–60
Shivacom Group 192
Short, Clare 189, 190, 191
Shultz, George 277
Siemens Plessey Systems (SPS) 188–9
Sierra Leone xviii–xxi, 98, 102, 103, 106, 107, 117, 407, 496
  Special Court for 124, 125
Sietlova, Jitka 200
Sifcorp 88
SIGAR (Special Inspector General for Afghanistan Reconstruction) 409, 427
Sikorsky 77, 486, 515
Simelane, Menzi 231
Simpson, William 41, 53–4
Singapore 223, 269, 374
Skorzeny, Otto 22, 27
Sky Bird 63
SLM/A (Sudan Liberation Movement/ Army) 478, 479
Slovenia 60, 66–8, 70, 116, 504
Smith, Roger 265
Smulian, Andrew 158–9, 161, 505
Sobotka, Premysl 200–201
Socialist Reich Party (SRP) 21
Soderberg, Nancy 363
SOFREMI 460
Soghanalian, Sarkis 399
Somaiya, Tanil 192, 193, 232
Somali High Seas Fishery Corporation (SHIFCO) 470
Somalia 156, 465–75
  and piracy 471–2
  and Al-Shabaab 472–4
  UN arms embargo 157, 465, 468, 469, 470
Sommer, A. A., Jr 270–71

South Africa xxiv–xxv, 175, 216, 230–32, 439, 507
  Aids/HIV versus arms spending 187
  and Angola 456, 457
  and BAE 175–88, 230–32, 517
  Department of Trade and Industry 179–80
  and Ferrostaal 508–9
  and Israel 387
  and Libya 492–3
  Public Accounts Committee 175, 176, 180–82
  and the UK 176–7
  UN arms embargo 62, 439
South African Air Force (SAAF) 177–8, 180, 188
South African National Defence Force (SANDF) 185
South America 27–8, 374, 526, 527 *see also specific countries*
South Korea 337
South Pacific Islands Airlines 324
South-West African People's Organization (SWAPO) 456
South Yemen 43, 70–72
Southern Ammunition Company Inc. (SAC) 345
Soviet Union
  and Afghanistan 247; Afghan–Soviet war 54–55, 245–6
  and Angola 455, 457, 459
  Cold War *see* Cold War
  collapse of 108, 118
  and the Congo 444
  and Egypt 26–7
  and Gehlen 19–20
  and Iraq 400
  and Libya 489
  Military Institute of Foreign Languages 115
  and Saudi Arabia 54–55
  and Somalia 466
  and Sudan 475
  and the US 238, 239–40, 251; and the Afghan–Soviet war 245–6; bomber gap 239; missile gap 239–40; US military build-up 273–82

SOX (Sarbanes Oxley Act) 355
Spain 5, 157–8
Special Inspector General for Afghanistan
    Reconstruction (SIGAR) 409, 427
Spetsehnoexport 112
Spicer, Tim 407–8
Spiller, Jonathan 363
Spinney, Franklin 'Chuck' 256–8, 259,
    278–82, 300, 301, 332–3, 336, 368–9,
    372, 396
Sprey, Pierre 336
SPS (Siemens Plessey Systems) 188–9
Sri Lanka 526
SRP (Socialist Reich Party) 21
Stanley, Albert 'Jack' 357
'Star Wars' missile defence 277, 288, 300,
    339
Starfighters 15, 263, 264
Stark, USS 422
Steenberg, Michael 63, 71, 72, 73
Stennis, John 254
Stern, Marcus 321–2, 323
Stevens, Robert 334, 341
Stevens, Ted 308
Stiglitz, Joseph 411, 428, 431
sting operations 157–61, 207–12, 244,
    358–65, 514
Stockton, Peter 278
Stoffel, Dale 422–7
Stokes, Donald 79
Stokes Report 79
Stonehouse, John 14, 16
Stow Securities 93
Strategic Defense Inititiative (SDI) 277
Strauss, Franz Josef 58, 264
Straw, Jack 137, 190
Strikemaster fighter jets 16–17
Student, Kurt 21
submarines 4, 175, 186, 188, 508–9, 518
Sudan xxvii, 344, 447, 475–83
    and China 479, 481–2, 526
    and Iran 477–8
    and oil 477, 479, 482–3
    and the UK 519
    UN arms embargo 481, 482

Sudan Liberation Movement/Army
    (SLM/A) 478, 479
Suharto of Indonesia 265, 269
Sukhoi Corporation 69
Suleiman, Omar 483
Sultan bin Abdul-Aziz Al Saud, Prince 14,
    15, 17, 36, 38, 40–42, 48, 87, 88, 245,
    266, 286, 510, 513
Sumption, Jonathan 151
Super Vision International 418
surface-to-air missiles 157, 159, 160, 361,
    400, 441, 496
Svenska Inc. 222, 223
Svoboda, Ivo 202, 208, 215
SWAPO (South-West African People's
    Organization) 456
Swaziland 118
Sweden xxvii, 220–24
Sweet Analysis Services Inc. (SASI) 421–2
Sweet, Patrick 421
Swift International Services 105–6
Switzerland 65, 86, 192, 198–9
Symington, Stuart 25, 239
Syria xxvii, 157
Sytex 414
Szabó, János 218
Szeremietiew, Romuald 291

Tabatabai, Sadeq 379
TAG Aviation 93
TAG Construction 88
Taiwan 337–8, 510
Al-tajammu Al-Arabi 477
Takieddine, Ziad 518
Takla, Leila 354
Taliban xxviii, 248, 343, 359, 402–3
    and Bout 116
Tamils 526
Tammivuori, Erkki 111–12, 424, 505
Tammivuori, Olavi 111
Tanaka, Kakuei 263, 268–9
tanks 12, 27, 58, 377, 421, 458, 460, 463, 472,
    480, 488, 490, 491, 493, 527
    Abrams 410, 486
Tanzania 188–96, 216, 228–9, 232–3, 519–20

Tanzania People's Defence Forces (TPDF) 193

Taos Industries 418–19

Taylor, Bob 56, 98

Taylor, Charles Ghankay xix, xxi, 56, 74, 98–103, 105, 106–7, 109, 110, 111, 114, 115, 117, 119, 123, 124–6, 165–6, 167, 418, 495, 496, 504–5

Taylor, Chucky (Junior) 111–12, 115

TBA (Tony Blair Associates) 513

Tebbit, Sir Kevin 81, 127, 129, 130, 200

Technip 357

Technology Strategies Alliances (TSA) 288

Teets, Peter 292

Teicher, Howard 89–90

Temex Industries 418

terrorism
    9/11 *see* September 11 attacks
    and Afghanistan 247–8
    and business 302–3 *see also* War on Terror: and business
    Libyan 490
    War on Terror *see* War on Terror

Tesler, Jeffrey 357

Thailand 160, 161, 162–4

Thales 509–10 *see also* Thomson-CSF

Thatcher, Margaret 12, 35, 36, 39, 54, 55, 88, 90, 513

Thatcher, Mark 55, 75, 88, 89–91, 511

Third World Relief Agency 116

Thomasberg Hotel und Sportanlagen 59

Thomet, Heinrich 347

Thomson-CSF (now Thales) 186, 400

Thorn EMI 76

ThyssenKrupp 185, 230

Tirana 345, 346

Tishchenko, a Russian deputy 207

Tjäder, Thomas 224

toilet seats 274, 396

Tolbert, William 99, 101

Tolleson, Lee Allen 364

Tomlinson, Richard 383, 384

Tonga 66

Tony Blair Associates (TBA) 513

Top Gun 319, 320

Tornado jets 35, 36–8, 39, 77, 87, 130, 200

Tosenovsky, Evzen 201

Tower, John 281

Townley, Michael 28

TPDF (Tanzania People's Defence Forces) 193

Traini, Pierre 170

Transmaritima 27

Transparency International (TI) 512

Traveller's World Ltd 81

Trebicka, Kosta 346–7, 348, 352

Tremalt Ltd 448–9

Trigger, David 77–8

Trireme 303

Truman Doctrine 238, 293

Truman, Harry S. 237, 238

Trump, Donald 502

TSA (Technology Strategies Alliances) 288

Tunisia 483, 515

Turkey 5, 265, 269, 284, 337, 338, 374

Turki al-Faisal, Prince 43–4, 58, 59, 80

Turki bin Nasser, Prince 81–2, 93, 95

Turner, Mike 137–8, 140, 232, 356, 357

Turse, Nick 296

Tutsi 436, 437, 438, 441, 442, 445–6

Tyco International 354

Tyler, Rodney 90

Typhoon jets 130, 133, 135, 136, 139, 147

Uganda 437, 440, 445
    and the Congo 446–7, 450, 451–2, 453

Ukraine 108, 110, 112, 118–19, 421, 451, 496

Ukrspetsexport 110

UKTI DSO (UK Trade & Investment Defence & Security Organisation) 492

Unger, Craig 282

UNITA (União Nacional para a Independencia Total de Angola) 53, 117, 445, 454, 455–9, 461, 462–5
    UN arms embargo 457, 458, 461, 462

United Arab Emirates 116, 337, 338, 513, 514, 527

United Defense Industries 284–5

United Kingdom
    and BAE xvii, xxvii

Bribery Act 512

British arms industry before the Great War 6

British arms industry in the Cold War 10–11

Defence Export Services Organisation *see* Deso

Department of Trade and Industry 189–90

and Egypt xxviii, 487

Intelligence 383, 474

and Iraq 400

and Israel 377

and Libya 491, 492

MI5 474

MI6 383

Ministry of Defence 16, 17, 36–7, 39, 76, 81, 84, 127, 128, 139, 190

National Audit Office 128–9

New Labour *see* New Labour

and the Nye Committee 9

Overseas Development Administration 189

RAF 250

Royal Commission on the private manufacture of arms 9

and Saudi Arabia xvii, 15–18, 35–8, 39–40, 48, 55, 75, 141–9; Al Salam contract 138, 139–41; Al Yamamah deal *see* Al Yamamah deal

SFO *see* Serious Fraud Office

and Al-Shabaab 474

and South Africa 176–7

and Sudan 519

and the US 10, 342, 362

United Nations (UN)

and Albania 344–5

arms embargoes xxix, 63, 71, 157; Angola 461; Bosnia 157; Croatia 62, 63, 68, 157; Darfur 481; DRC 452–3; Iran 360; Ivory Coast 495, 496–7; Liberia 67, 103, 107, 418; Libya 490, 491, 492; Rwanda 441–2; Somalia 157, 465, 468, 469, 470; South Africa 62, 439; Sudan 481, 482; UNITA 457, 458, 461, 462

and Bout 118, 119, 124, 158

and Bredenkamp 449–50

and the Congo 446, 452

and Gbagbo 494

ICAO 189

investigations 119, 124, 165

and Kouwenhoven 165–6

Libya interventions 488

Panel of Experts on the Ivory Coast 497

pursuit of an International Arms Trade Treaty 528–9

Register of Conventional Arms 386

Security Council Panel of Experts on Sudan 482

and Taylor 124–5, 165

troops 468

United States Agency for International Development (USAID) 420, 503

United States of America

9/11 attacks *see* September 11 attacks

and Afghanistan xxviii, 245–8, 341, 370, 401–4, 406–7, 409–16, 421–2, 427–30, 431, 456

and Africa 435–6

Air Force 257, 274; and the Boeing KC-767 scandal 305–18; and Lockheed 251, 252, 253, 254, 274, 275–6, 332, 334

and Angola 455–6, 457

and Argentina 262

Arms Export Control Act 269, 278, 409, 506

Army 277, 333, 343, 404, 405, 410, 515, 521; Intelligence 21, 22, 25

and Australia 342

and BAE 200, 218, 226, 227, 358, 414–15, 506–8, 516

and Bandar xvii–xviii, 42–55

and Bout 157–65, 505

Bureau of Labour Statistics 368

and Castro 23

and Chile 28, 262

and China 337–8, 386, 529

Coast Guard 339–40

in the Cold War 10–11, 238, 251

United States of America – *contd*.
Commission on Wartime Contracting 405–6
Congressional Budget Office 305, 410, 411
congressional earmarking 241–2, 243, 249, 325, 328–9, 516
covert operations 238–9, 245
Defence Contract Audit Agency 406
defence spending xxii, 238, 240, 249, 273, 279–80, 286–7, 296, 299–300, 365–72, 402; budgets *see* Pentagon: budgets; and 'reset' policy 410–13, 415; on the Wars in Iraq and Afghanistan 409–15, 427–9
Defense Authorization Bill (2002) 306–7
Defense Policy Advisory Committee on Trade 287, 289
Defense Policy Board 303, 304
democracy 430–31
Department of Defense xxvi, 32, 238, 276, 296, 300, 337, 341–2, 366, 370–71, 406, 408, 411, 414, 420, 421–2, 423, 520; budgets *see* Pentagon: budgets; Pentagon *see* Pentagon; spending *see (above)* defence spending
Department of Homeland Security 293, 295, 296, 301, 340, 358, 361–2 *see also* ICE
Department of Justice 272, 352–3, 355, 357, 364, 512
Drug Enforcement Agency 157–61, 164, 358
and Egypt xxviii, 26–7, 485–8
embassy bombings 247
Field Activities Command (USAFAC) 29
Financial Reform Bill 357
Foreign Assets Control 184, 417, 450
Foreign Corrupt Practices Act 270, 271–2, 277–8
Foreign Military Financing 377
and Gehlen Org 20

General Accounting Office 253, 276, 306, 318, 367, 398–9, 404, 413, 419
and Gerdec 348–9, 520–21
and Guatemala 238
and the ICU 473
and illegal bribery 305–29
Immigration and Customs Enforcement 359, 360
Intelligence 296, 379, 421; Army Intelligence 21, 22, 25; and Bout 155–6; CIA *see* CIA; FBI *see* FBI; Intelligence Industrial Complex market 414; Nazi/neo-Nazi connections 20, 21, 26, 27, 29; and Taylor 99
and Iran 238, 359–62; 1980 hostage crisis 279; Iran–Contra affair 30–31, 51–53, 278, 379–81, 398; and Israel 378–82
and Iraq 156, 243, 298, 300, 342–3, 381, 395–431
and Israel 35, 38, 44, 49–50, 302, 373–94; AIPAC 44, 45, 48, 94, 377
and Japan 268
and Al-Kassar 157–8, 161, 503–4
Korean War 251
and legal bribery xxv–xxvi, 237–61, 516; and foreign weapons sales 262–72
and Libya 104, 489, 490, 493
militarism 237–8, 249 *see also (above)* defence spending; under G. H. W. Bush administration 282–6; under G. W. Bush administration 292–304, 401–2 *see also* War on Terror; military build-up under Reagan administration 273–82; military-industrial complex 250–52, 282, 300, 301; military-industrial-Congressional complex *see* MICC; 'reset' policy 410–13
Military Reform Movement (MRM) 258
missile defence programme 277, 288, 299, 300, 339
Munitions Control Board 9
national debt 428

National Security Act (1947) 238
Navy 274
and the Nye Committee 8–9
Office of Congressional Ethics 241
Office of Management and Budget 306,
    308, 310–12, 314, 329
and oil 247
and Pakistan 24–5, 527
Patriot Act 431
Pentagon *see* Pentagon
pre-war sales of aircraft to Europe 250
and Russia 529
and Saudi Arabia 15, 35, 36, 38–9, 44,
    48–50, 272, 378, 515–16; and Bandar
    xvii–xviii, 42–55; and the Bush family
    282–6; and the Carlyle Group 283–6
Securities and Exchange Commission
    253, 268, 270–71, 272, 278, 352, 353–4,
    357, 502
and Al-Shabaab 473, 474
and Somalia 466
and the Soviet Union 238, 239–40, 251;
    and the Afghan–Soviet war 245–6;
    bomber gap 239; and military
    build-up 273–82; missile gap 239–40
and Spain 5
and Sudan 476
and Taylor 125–6
Truman Doctrine 238, 293
and the UK 10, 342, 362
and Vietnam 240, 297, 404
War on Drugs 157, 527
War on Terror *see* War on Terror
and First World War 403–4
and Second World War 237–8, 366, 404
as world's largest arms player 249
Uranus project 30
Urban, Milan 201
USAID (United States Agency for
    International Development) 420, 503
USSR *see* Soviet Union

V-22 290
Vadai, Ágnes 219–20
vakuum bomb 69

Valurex 205–6, 209–10, 214, 507
van der Kwast, Christer 216
Vance, Cyrus 47
Vector Microwave Research Corp. 421
Venezuela 23–4, 527
Vermaak, Armscor official 72, 73
Vessey, John (Jack) 52
Vickers 5, 6, 8, 9–10
Vickers-Armstrong 8, 11, 12
Vidyarthi, Anoop 442
Vienna 197
Vietnam 240, 297, 404
Vinland Saga 71
Vinnell 285, 286
Virgin Islands 84–5, 86, 87
Vithlani, Sailesh 189, 192–3, 194, 228–9, 232
Vorster, B. J. 387
Vosper Thorneycroft 77
Vought 285

Wade, Mitch 322–4, 325, 326–7
Al-Waleed bin Talal bin Abdul Aziz al
    Saud, Prince 286
Walker, Chris 417
Walt, S. 389
Walters, Tome, Jr 217
War on Drugs 157, 527
War on Terror 248, 295–7, 301, 302, 355,
    356, 366–7, 375–6, 402–4
    and American democracy 430–31
    and business 325, 334, 366–7, 375–6, 402,
        413–15, 431; Lockheed 366–7, 413–14,
        415–16
    and Pakistan 430
Wardle, Robert 129, 131–3, 136, 137, 140,
    141, 142–3, 144, 153
Warner, John 317
Watchman air traffic control system 189, 191
Waterfall, John 42
Watson, Rob 487
Wazan, Eli 61–2, 71, 72
weapons of mass destruction xvii, 69–70,
    396, 402, 423, 490, 527 *see also* nuclear
    weapons/technology
    dual-use items 398–400

Weber, Vin 290

Webster, Clarence 8–9

Weinberger, Caspar 51, 52, 273, 274, 278

Wemple, Joseph 422

Werretal 24

Wessel, Gerhard 19

West Africa xviii, 4, 101, 494 *see also specific countries*

West Bank 376

West, John 45, 46, 47, 48

Westland Helicopters 37

Wheeler, Winslow 370, 371

White, David 218

Wilkerson, Lawrence 301

Wilkes, Brent 324–5, 326, 327

Williams, Earle 285

Wilson, Charlie 244–8, 323

Wilson, David 405

Wilson, William 53

Wilson, Woodrow 7

Winograd Commission 392

Winship, Tony 80, 82, 84

Withers II, John L. 348

Wolfowitz, Paul 273, 290, 293, 310, 316, 337, 396, 401

Wood, Nick 348

Woodward, Bob 54

Woolf, Harry Kenneth, Baron 149

Woolf report 149, 190

Worgitzky, Hans-Heinrich 26

World Bank 189, 484

World Finance Group Ltd 324, 325

World Trade Center, 9/11 attacks *see* September 11 attacks

World Trade Organization 179, 318

Worldcom 286, 354

Wright, Ted 514

Wye Oak Technologies 423

Xe Services *see* Blackwater/Xe

Al Yamamah deal xvii, 35, 36, 37–8, 39–40, 55, 75–97, 173, 355
  and the Salam deal 138, 139–41
  SFO investigation 80–81, 84, 85, 87, 93, 127–53
  and the Shawcross exercise 133, 136, 139, 146–7

Yapp, Mr (spokesman of Vickers) 9

Yelenik, Shimon 121, 387

Yemen 43, 70–72, 157, 469, 472, 474, 503

Young, Andrew 275

Yugoslav conflict 60–70

Yule, Tony 42

Zaghawa 476

Zaharoff, Basil 3–7

Zaire 437, 445–7, 463 *see also* Democratic Republic of Congo

Zantovsky, Michael 201

Zayna, Raymond 425

ZDI (Zimbabwe Defence Industries) 451

Zhao Fei 31–2

Zhirinovsky, Vladimir 69, 162

Zia-ul-Haq, Muhammad 59, 246

Zimbabwe xxvii, 347, 447, 448–9, 451, 526

Zimbabwe Defence Industries (ZDI) 451

Ziv, Yisrael 384

Zoller, Ori 121

ZTS-Osos 460

Zuma, Jacob 185, 186–7, 230–31, 492–3, 517

Zurich Financial Services 513

Zvinavashe, General 449